Planning Children's Play
and Learning in the
Foundation Stage

Planning Children's Play and Learning in the Foundation Stage

Second edition

Jane Drake

 David Fulton Publishers

To Katie and Joshua Drake

David Fulton Publishers Ltd
The Chiswick Centre, 414 Chiswick High Road, London W4 5TF

www.fultonpublishers.co.uk

First published in Great Britain by David Fulton Publishers 2001
This edition published in Great Britain by David Fulton Publishers 2005

10 9 8 7 6 5 4 3 2 1

David Fulton Publishers is a division of Granada Learning Limited, part of ITV plc.

Note: The right of Jane Drake to be identified as the author of this work has been asserted by her in accordance with the Copyright, Designs and Patents Act 1988.

Copyright © Jane Drake 2005

British Library Cataloguing in Publication Data
A catalogue record for this book is available from the British Library.

ISBN 1–84312–151–4

Typeset by FiSH Books, London
Printed and bound in Great Britain

Contents

Acknowledgements

Crown copyright is reproduced with the permission of the controller of Her Majesty's Stationery Office.

I wish to thank

Children, parents and practitioners across the city of Leeds, particularly those who have allowed me to use photographs and examples of their work in this book.

My colleagues within the Leeds Early Years Partnership advisory team who are an ongoing inspiration.

Leeds Early Years Development Team for their role in my professional development over a number of years.

The Elisabeth Svendsen Trust for Children and Donkeys for granting permission to use their name, and a photograph of their staff and one of their donkeys, in Chapter 4.

The following colleagues, family and friends for their professional and moral support during the writing of the first and second edition of this book: Jane Barnfield, Chris Barnfield, Mona Fairholme, Jo Kurasinski, Susan Buxey, Claire Clements, Fred Drake, Helen Sefton and Sarah Grossick.

Preface

It is now over four years since *Curriculum Guidance for the Foundation Stage* was published by the Qualifications and Curriculum Authority (QCA) and almost as long since the first edition of this book was completed. I'm sure that many of you working with very young children have welcomed the guidance and find it difficult to imagine life before the introduction of the 'pink file'! For others who are relatively new to the foundation stage, the training in using the guidance continues and evolves to meet the diverse needs of teams and individual practitioners. This edition of *Planning Children's Play and Learning in the Foundation Stage* offers easily accessible information and guidance linked closely to government expectations for the foundation stage. It aims to support all practitioners in implementing the curriculum in ways that will be meaningful and motivating to children.

Since writing the first edition of *Planning Children's Play and Learning in the Foundation Stage*, my own practice has moved on. I have been privileged to work as a Partnership Advisory teacher in Leeds with a wide range of settings in the city. Not only has this given me an insight into the variety of issues facing different settings but also the opportunity to work alongside a team of exemplary foundation stage teachers at the cutting-edge of developments in foundation stage practice. The last few years have been a very exciting journey for me professionally and it is the knowledge and understanding that I have gained through working closely with settings and the advisory team that have provided the impetus for producing this second edition.

Although neither the QCA guidance nor the principles on which the first edition of this book was based have changed, there has been scope to update material in terms of practical support and ideas. Additional material has been included in response to identified needs across all sectors, particularly in the areas of planning and assessment. A summary of content at the end of each chapter reinforces key points for good practice and offers a framework for self-evaluation.

Whoever we are and wherever we work, we must remain united in our common aim to bring quality to the early years. We must recognise the urgency to provide an exciting and appropriate curriculum for children *now*, children who will never have the chance to be three, four or five years old again. We must acknowledge the need for success at this early stage in order to develop the confidence and embedded learning necessary to embrace the next stage. Above all, we must never lose sight of the child's right to a playful childhood or lose touch with the child inside ourselves.

Jane Drake
January 2005

Introduction

Adults who criticise teachers for allowing children to play are unaware that play is the principal means of learning in early childhood. It is the way through which children reconcile their inner lives with external reality. In play, children gradually develop concepts of casual relationships, the power to discriminate, to make judgements, to analyse and synthesise, to imagine and to formulate. Children become absorbed in their play and the satisfaction of bringing it to a satisfactory conclusion fixes habits of concentration which can be transferred to other learning.

(Department of Education and Science 1967, para 523)

Since the introduction of the *Curriculum Guidance for the Foundation Stage* (QCA) issued in May 2000 by the Government, changes have been taking place in teams and settings nationally which have impacted on how and what children learn in the early years. All children, from the age of three to the end of the reception year, are now part of a continuous stage and the range of settings in which the foundation stage curriculum is delivered has widened to include local authority nurseries, nursery centres, playgroups, pre-schools, accredited child minders in approved networks, schools in the independent, private or voluntary sectors, and maintained schools. All settings in receipt of the nursery grant are supported by a qualified teacher and regionally work is being done to strengthen links between settings to improve continuity for children.

The QCA guidance offers practitioners a breakdown of the goals and broad expectations for children at different developmental stages. Activities and learning experiences that take place in the early years setting should enable children to make progress on the 'learning journey' through the bands of 'stepping-stones' towards and sometimes beyond the early learning goals.

In addition to being familiar with 'sequential patterns of development' (Department of Education and Science 1990), there needs to be a clear perception by practitioners of the characteristics of young children as learners. How children learn is a complex issue and precise definitions are elusive, but it is necessary to identify features of effective learning before discussing ways of planning content and mode. Fisher (1996) offers clarification of this matter, suggesting that young children learn by 'being active', 'organising their own learning experiences', 'using language' and 'interacting with others'.

These four significant aspects of learning are evident in the other reports and studies, for example, the Rumbold Committee (Department of Education and Science 1990) recognised that:

- Learning should be primarily first-hand, experiential and active. Young children need opportunities and space to explore and discover.
- Children's independence and autonomy needs to be promoted. Children should be encouraged to take responsibility for their learning.
- Talk is central to the learning process. It should be reciprocal and often initiated and led by the child.
- Young children are social beings and learning should take place in a social context.

It is over three decades since the Plowden Committee (Department of Education and Science 1967) acknowledged the importance of play, and defined its role, in the learning process. Although, during that time, initiatives in education have been many and debates over the content and delivery of the curriculum vociferous, play is still valued as a way in which young children learn and promoted as an appropriate context in which to embed the early years curriculum.

The Government's explanation of the benefits of play in *Curriculum Guidance for the Foundation Stage* clearly reiterates some of the points made in the Plowden report. When considered in the light of earlier definitions of the means by which learning takes place, this explanation proffers a very strong case for planning a curriculum rich in play opportunities.

Through play, in a secure environment with effective adult support, children can:

- Explore, develop and represent learning experiences that help them make sense of the world
- Practise, and build up ideas, concepts and skills
- Learn how to control impulses and understand the need for rules
- Be alone, be alongside others or co-operate as they talk or rehearse their feelings
- Take risks and make mistakes
- Think creatively and imaginatively
- Communicate with others as they investigate or solve problems
- Express fears or relive anxious experiences in controlled and safe situations

(QCA 2000)

The ability to 'think creatively and imaginatively' is a key phrase in understanding how young children begin to make sense of the world around them and links into their learning. As adults, we use our creative and imaginative skills every day to solve practical problems or to empathise with the feelings of others and these skills and attitudes are developed through playful experiences throughout life. In all our planning for young children we should be offering opportunities for open-ended learning and celebrating individuality. Learning is a process not a product, a journey of discovery with endless outcome possibilities. Summing up creativity and imagination is a difficult task but as Duffy says:

> *Creativity* is about connecting the previously unconnected in ways that are new and meaningful to the individual; *imagination* is about internalising perceptions and ascribing objects and events with new meanings. Creativity and imagination may be hard to define but they are part of what makes us uniquely human.
>
> (Duffy 1998)

Also emphasised in the *Curriculum Guidance* document is the notion that play and work are indistinguishable to the young child. This, again, is not a new concept. Isaacs, in the book *The Nursery Years*, stated that:

> Play is indeed the child's work, and the means whereby he grows and develops.
>
> (Isaacs 1929)

So, play should not be seen by the adult as a separate activity. For children, it is an integral and necessary part of their lives in the setting, and at home. Through play and first-hand experiences, children are motivated to learn and their learning needs can be identified and met.

However, it is not enough to simply subscribe to the 'learning through play' philosophy. Free play in an ill-equipped environment with little thought given to the opportunities and support offered is not guaranteed, or even likely, to lead to appropriately challenging learning experiences for all children. For experiences of the highest quality to take place, children's play and learning needs to be carefully planned. This does not necessarily mean that the practitioner will directly plan the content, or specific outcome, of play, although a more focused approach to activities is sometimes appropriate. Rather, he or she will create a fertile environment (including quality provision and adult support) that enables children to flourish as active learners through play. An inclusive approach will recognise and address the needs of all children within the provision, taking account of individual starting points for learning. Children should have opportunities for indoor and outdoor play and be able to make choices about where their learning takes place. They should be able to become deeply involved in their learning without unnecessary disruption and to return to ideas and experiences over time to ensure that knowledge and understanding becomes firmly embedded.

The early learning goals set expectations for children's achievements by the end of the reception year, 'but are not a curriculum in themselves' (QCA 2000). It is the responsibility of the practitioner to plan opportunities which will enable children to make progress in their learning.

It is worth determining at this stage what is understood by the term 'curriculum'. The word has, historically, been more usually associated with prescribed frameworks for education in schools but, for foundation stage children, is defined by QCA (2000) as 'everything children do, see, hear or feel in their setting, both planned and unplanned'.

In accepting this broad definition, practitioners should recognise the diversity of children's learning and acknowledge that their learning is not always confined to what has been directly planned, or intended, by the adult. Indeed, learning is by no means restricted to what children do in the setting. The knowledge that parents have about their children is crucial in understanding and planning for their learning. Practitioners should ensure that effective systems are in place for the sharing of information and must take into account the range of experiences and interests children bring to the setting. If a programme is to be effective in motivating children and in promoting meaningful, cross curricular learning, there must be flexibility and a 'built in' system of evaluation which feeds into the planning process enabling practitioners to identify, and respond to, individual interests.

Although it is important to appreciate that learning is a continuous and accumulative process and does not begin or end in 'key stages', it should also be pointed out that the curriculum provided for children in the foundation stage, whichever early years setting they attend, will certainly be different to that offered to older children. However, while a curricular framework in the foundation stage may be more 'concealed', and learning less discrete, it is nonetheless essential in order to provide a structure for planning and assessment of children's learning. The six areas of learning (as defined by QCA 2000) serve as a basic structure around which to plan experiences and activities, although the holistic nature of young children's learning should never be disregarded:

- Personal, social and emotional development
- Communication, language and literacy
- Mathematical development
- Knowledge and understanding of the world
- Physical development
- Creative development

In conclusion to this chapter, and as an introduction to the main content of the book, the following summary is offered:

The aim of the foundation stage educator is to provide a broad and balanced curriculum, and opportunities that will enable all children to develop knowledge, concepts, skills and attitudes. This learning will often take place in the context of purposeful play, and always in a meaningful situation. Children will access the curriculum through a well-planned and appropriately resourced learning environment that takes account of the characteristics of young children as learners, and the developmental course they take.

Remaining chapters focus on the challenging task facing practitioners in planning and supporting such a curriculum.

> Those adults who are sufficiently open-minded to let themselves be guided by children will be able to see children exercising control over their world through play.
>
> (Hurst 1991)

CHAPTER 1

Planning the learning environment and quality areas of provision

For children to have rich and stimulating experiences, the learning environment should be well planned and well organised. It provides the structure for teaching within which children explore, experiment, plan and make decisions for themselves, thus enabling them to learn, develop and make good progress.

(QCA 2000)

The content of this chapter is organised as follows:

Provision in the learning environment

The environment that is created in the early years setting should be exciting to children, inspiring in them an eagerness to explore and a zest for learning. Quality provision serves to support and challenge young children in their development across all areas of learning. Through the learning environment, and supported by the practitioner, all children can access a broad and balanced curriculum and make progress from their own starting point towards the early learning goals and beyond.

When planning the environment, the practitioner needs to give consideration to which 'areas' should be included in the basic provision. The physical characteristics of the setting will influence decisions in terms of facilities and equipment available, and it may be that restricted space does not allow practitioners to offer the range of provision on a daily basis that they would choose in an ideal world. In the case of limited space, practitioners will need to plan carefully to ensure that the permanent provision (i.e. the provision offered to children every day) covers the basic curriculum and that the learning environment is enhanced regularly through the addition of extra resources (perhaps on a rotational basis) and the planning of focus activities (see Chapter 2) in order to further develop and extend children's learning in certain areas.

The environment that is planned, and the curriculum that is offered, should be inclusive for all children. Of course every child is unique and it is the responsibility of the practitioner to identify and assess each individual's strengths and needs and to plan appropriately for these. However, within the group there may be children who require additional support in accessing the curriculum and the nature of their needs may have practical implications on the planning of the environment. For example, children with visual impairment need to be familiar with the layout of provision, they need to know that furniture and equipment will be in the same place every day and, if anything is changed, they should be involved in the rearrangements. All children need opportunities to learn through sensory exploration but for those with sensory impairment it is particularly important that they have access to appropriate equipment and experiences. For example, provision may include balls with different surfaces and containing bells or beads, books with large print or Braille, tactile clues such as using sandpaper 'labels' to identify a child's possessions, visual props such as puppets for use during story-telling in the book corner and scented water in the water tray.

Any information that is available before a child with special needs enters the setting should be used to support staff in preparing the environment appropriately (see also Chapters 4 and 6). Such preparation may include the provision of ramps or handrails for a child with physical or motor disabilities, white tape stuck on the edge of steps for a visually impaired child or the ordering of cotton gloves for a child with eczema to use in the sand tray.

The following areas of provision are recommended:

- Role-play area
- Construction area
- Mark-making/office area
- Maths area
- Water area
- Sand areas (wet and dry sand)
- Workshop area
- Malleable materials area (clay, dough, etc.)

- Music area (making and listening to music)
- Painting area
- Book corner
- IT area

There should also be regular opportunities planned and appropriate equipment available, for baking and various other food preparation activities.

Equipment for practising and developing physical skills such as climbing and balancing should be part of the permanent provision, and a list of suggested resources is included later in this chapter (under the heading 'The outside area').

The role of the adult in supporting learning

It is not enough merely to plan and set up good-quality areas of provision – the adult must actually value these areas as effective learning environments and spend time supporting children's learning in them.

The role of the adult is crucial in identifying children's needs, assessing their stage of development and intervening in play to support individuals in moving forward. The timing and nature of such interventions will greatly influence the quality of the learning experiences that take place within the environment. Practitioners need to plan adult time in areas of provision to observe and engage in play, either supporting a planned focus or responding spontaneously to children's learning interests.

In her book, *The Nursery Teacher in Action*, Margaret Edgington writes about 'enabling children to learn' – the following explanation of the role of the teacher in supporting children's learning can be applied to all practitioners working in early years settings:

> Teachers enable each child to learn and develop by helping them to sustain their current interests, and also by interesting them in new things. The role of the enabler involves her in using a number of teaching roles and strategies. Sometimes she initiates experiences with a view to stimulating, supporting or extending interest. Sometimes she acts as a role model for the children to encourage particular kinds of dispositions or skills. Sometimes she demonstrates skills or imparts knowledge. Often she uses a combination of these strategies. Whichever approach she uses, she keeps the needs of the children in mind to help her determine the optimum moment for learning – the moment when the child wants to, or needs to, learn.
>
> (Edgington 1998)

When working with young children, the following key points will be helpful in ensuring high-quality interactions:

- Be positive and respectful with children:
  a) Make sure that you are physically positioned at their level and maintain eye contact.
  b) Speak in a calm and interested manner making sure that your voice is clearly audible but not too loud.
  c) Praise children's attempts and achievements.
- Be aware of, and sensitive to, children's needs and interests:
  a) Find out about children's individual learning needs and interests by observing and listening to them in a range of contexts within the setting.
  b) Listen to, and share information with, parents and carers.
- Be prepared to support children's ideas and interests by adding resources to areas of provision or by planning an appropriate focus.
- Set high but realistic expectations. Be consistent in your expectations of children's behaviour. Make sure that your expectations are always appropriate to the child's stage of development and are rooted in observation-based assessments.
- Encourage children to be independent. Support them in making choices and decisions.
- Use questioning to challenge children's thinking and extend their learning. Ask open-ended questions, for example; 'What will happen if...?', 'Why did you...?', 'How can we...?'
- Recognise when not to intervene in children's play, although you may still want to observe.
- Remember that sometimes children need time to observe before they are ready to join in.

In order for the practitioner to fulfil all aspects of his or her role effectively, he or she must plan provision carefully, giving thought to all areas of learning and the full range of needs within the setting.

Planning the environment

In planning the environment, it may help practitioners to view provision as a structure which scaffolds children's learning but also allows them the freedom to experiment, investigate and pursue personal interests. Children should be encouraged to become active and independent learners and feel confident in 'trying out' ideas in a supportive and 'safe' setting.

Provision should be organised in a way that offers children opportunities for working individually, in pairs or groups, with an adult and for observation of other children at play. It should be constant enough for children to return to areas over a period of days or weeks to develop ideas and modify their work. Children should have daily opportunities to become deeply involved in their learning, often through self-initiated activities or experiences over an extended period of time, and this means teams looking carefully at the structure of their day or session. Every time children are required to stop and conform to a routine, their play and learning is interrupted. Questions should be asked as to the justification for these disruptions and it may be that practitioners can find alternative ways of planning for activities such as whole group snack time. A self-service snack system, supported as appropriate by an adult, will encourage independence and enable children to access a drink and snack during a natural break in their play. Similarly, if children only access the outdoor area as a whole group and for a limited period of time, opportunities for learning will be restricted. Over-long 'carpet time' sessions are inappropriate and also cut into children's time for being active. Of course, there will be occasions when group sessions are planned (although these should always meet the needs of all involved children) and expectations may change as children near the end of the reception year. However, throughout the foundation stage children must be supported as active learners, encouraged to make independent choices about their learning and allowed uninterrupted periods of involvement.

> Children need to know that some things will remain the same each day, for example, that the woodworking bench and necessary materials and tools will always be there for them to use; that there will always be some paint; that those favourite books, or a story read today, will be there again to enjoy tomorrow. They need to know that if they begin something today they will be able to complete or add to it tomorrow, thus developing their own continuity of thought and action.
>
> (Nutbrown 1999)

Displays have an important part to play in the creation of a stimulating environment and their role in promoting learning will be discussed in Chapter 5.

In developing long-term plans for areas of provision, practitioners will be able to ensure that sufficient, ongoing, opportunities are provided across the areas of learning and that the curriculum is balanced. An overview of all the plans will show clearly how each area of learning is developed throughout the setting (see example on page 47). The process of long-term planning will help practitioners to focus their own thoughts and ideas and will, if undertaken collaboratively, establish a clear, whole team approach and commitment to the curriculum. The plans should be regularly reviewed by the team and modified in response to assessments of children's use of, and observed learning in, each area of provision. (See Chapter 6, page 176 – 'Evaluating and improving the provision'.)

Long-term plans should be clearly written and follow a common format. They should be made readily available to any adult involved in supporting children in the learning process and also to adults visiting the setting in a monitoring or inspecting role. They offer a framework for teaching and learning and an explanation of curricular aims.

The depth of planning involved in creating a rich learning environment may not always be understood by visitors, and the 'free flow' system in operation in many settings is sometimes regarded rather dismissively as children 'just playing'.

However, as discussed in the Introduction, children learn to make sense of the world around them through play – it is their 'work' and as such should be afforded the high status and considered planning it deserves. It is as a result of thoughtful and informed resourcing and organisation of the environment in which children play that learning experiences of the highest quality consistently take place.

Planning an area of provision should start with the question: what opportunities for learning do we want to offer children? In all areas of provision, there should be planned opportunities for:

- Practising and refining skills
- Acquiring knowledge, developing concepts and consolidation
- Developing positive attitudes to learning

Such opportunities for learning should be identified in plans. Also included in a long-term planning structure for areas of provision will need to be:

- Key areas of learning and pertinent early learning goals
- Resources: permanent, rotated, additional (e.g. to support a particular topic or focus activity) organisation of resources and area
- Anticipated learning experiences and activities; suggested extension or focus activities (see also Chapters 2 and 3)
- The role of the adult in supporting learning

Teams of practitioners may decide to adopt a framework for long-term planning recommended by, for example, their LEA, or they may devise their own. If the latter decision is taken, practitioners should ensure that all the above points are addressed.

Practitioners may choose to display information, such as a brief explanation of learning intentions and a list of key early learning goals, in each area of provision. Such information can be a useful prompt to adults working with children in the area. It may also give parents and carers a deeper understanding of children's learning, enabling them to more effectively support their own child's learning. (Other ways of communicating information to parents and carers are explored in detail in Chapter 4.)

The inside area

Commercially produced resources are numerous and vary enormously in quality and usefulness. Equipment should be selected according to its effectiveness in supporting planned learning and there will probably be a number of alternatives which will be equally successful in facilitating learning.

The following example illustrates the variety of resources that could be used to support children on their journey towards a specific goal in a particular area of provision.

Area of provision

- Sand

Key area of learning

- Mathematical development

Working towards early learning goals

- Use language such as 'heavier' or 'lighter' to compare two quantities

Possible resources

- Bags of sand, empty bags (to be filled with sand and compared in weight)
- A range of stones and pebbles (to be compared with each other and against amounts of sand)
- A range of graded plastic cylinders (to be filled with sand and compared in weight)
- A selection of 'junk' containers, for example, yoghurt pots, margarine pots and plastic bottles (to be filled with sand and compared in weight)
- Four identical containers to be filled with, for example, sand, sawdust, cotton wool, water and then compared in weight
- Simple balance
- Plank balanced on a narrow wooden block (children attempt to keep the plank horizontal by placing sand bags of equal weight on each end)

In order to encourage independent learning, resources in areas of provision should be readily available and accessible to children, and should be stored in clearly labelled drawers, boxes or baskets, or on templated open shelving or unit tops (see page 17).

It is a characteristic of many early years practitioners that they are 'hoarders' and reluctant to throw anything away in case it 'comes in useful'. It is true that such resources often prove to be very valuable in supporting learning and as practical storage equipment and, of course, reduce the strain on limited budgets. The workshop area is usually a very popular area requiring a constant supply of 'junk' materials to feed children's enthusiasm for design and technology and it is a good idea to encourage parents to become hoarders of such materials too.

Other examples include the following:

- Large, transparent, plastic 'pop' bottles with the neck and top removed have a wealth of uses, for example, as containers for growing beans, as containers for exploring capacity and volume, as containers for holding water (children mark-making using water and brushes outside). The cut-off tops of bottles can be used as funnels in the sand and water areas.

- Plastic film canisters make useful individual PVA glue containers – their tight-fitting lids ensure that glue remains in good condition.

- Old kitchen equipment can be used for making marks, exploring shape and creating texture in clay (e.g. forks, potato mashers, spoons, biscuit cutters, rolling pins), for investigations into the properties of water and sand (e.g. slotted spoons, sieves, tea strainers, colanders) and for imaginative play in the home corner (e.g. baking tins, plastic bowls, wooden spoons).

- Lengths of plastic guttering can be used to build exciting 'water ways' or 'marble runs'.

- Old car tyres can be used by children outside, as numbered 'targets' (for throwing beanbags into), or as part of an obstacle course.

- Large cardboard boxes (e.g. packaging for furniture or large electrical equipment) make exciting 'den' structures.

- Old, disconnected, telephones can be used very effectively in the office, home corner and other areas of provision to encourage children to engage in interactive conversation with adults and other children and to express thoughts and ideas verbally.

- Wire frames from old lampshades serve as frameworks for mobiles, for example, to display children's model fish hanging above the water tray.

Practitioners may decide to make resources in order to ensure that they specifically fit their requirements, for example, props to support story-telling or -making, songs and rhymes such as laminated pictures of characters or parts of text and character puppets (very simple card cut-out characters attached to wooden lolly sticks are effective) or postboxes for the office displaying the name of the setting and session times.

Additional or rotated resources should be well organised and catalogued to ensure that all members of staff are aware of what is available and where it is stored. Practitioners may decide to catalogue under areas of learning, areas of provision or topic areas – there is no right or wrong way here, but the method of organisation should be a matter for discussion by the whole team. Systems should be easy to understand and use and storage arrangements should be practical within the setting.

Examples of additional or rotated resources include the following:

- Story boxes or bags, for example, *Dear Zoo* by Rod Campbell (the book, letter to the zoo, plastic zoo animals in boxes or containers and 'puppy' soft toy) and *Billy's Beetle* by Mick Inkpen (the book, story tape, plastic beetle in a small box, 'Billy' puppet and 'sniffy dog' soft toy).

- Role-play resource boxes containing equipment for, for example, a hospital, clinic, Post Office, travel agents and shop.

- Mathematical equipment[1] such as capacity jugs and cylinders, length measuring equipment, balancing or weighing equipment, (standard and non-standard), dice, 'spinners' (number, colour, shape, etc.) sorting, matching or counting toys and pattern-making equipment – to be introduced to areas of provision as appropriate.

- Boxes of resources which will promote imaginative play in different areas, for example, in the sand area – to create a desert or jungle environment – imitation plants (garden centres usually supply a wide range), rocks, pebbles, stones, plastic insects, and reptiles. (NB Pineapple tops make very effective 'palm trees'.)

- Games – lotto, board games, card games, dice games.

- Topic resource boxes, for example, 'Transport' – fiction and non-fiction books, photographs or models of different modes of transport, road maps, underground maps, train/boat/bus/aeroplane tickets, road signs and equipment for setting up road systems in the outside area.

Some practitioners may be faced with the problem of sharing a hall or room with other groups and this has implications for organisation of the setting. In such cases, much of the equipment will probably have to be stored away at the end of a session and set out again at the beginning of the next session. It is vital, then, that all involved adults are aware of what provision should be offered to children in order to meet curriculum requirements and that a plan is available of how the basic provision should be organised. In drawing up such a plan, it is important to remember that the arrangement of furniture greatly influences the child's learning. Open areas allow children to observe other children working but more enclosed areas can enable them to concentrate for longer periods, leading to extended explorations and investigations.

---

[1] Much of this equipment will probably be included in the basic provision in certain areas, but duplicates and alternatives should be available for children to use in other areas in order to develop particular skills and concepts.

Developing literacy and numeracy

In a well planned environment, the development of literacy and numeracy will take place in all areas of provision and will form an integral part of activities.

Nigel Hall, in his book *The Emergence of Literacy*, states that:

> Children should never need to ask if they can engage in purposeful literacy acts. If a classroom provides an environment where the status of literacy is high, where there are powerful demonstrations of literacy and where children can freely engage in literacy, then children will take every opportunity to use their knowledge and abilities to act in a literate way.
>
> (Hall 1987)

The attitudes towards, and commitment to, literacy established during the early years are crucial in the development of children as readers and writers.

Mark-making equipment should be available in all areas of provision,[2] consisting of a range of mark-making tools (pencils, crayons, ball point pens and fibre tip pens, etc.), paper (the use of recording 'frames', shopping lists and memo pads will encourage children to write for a purpose, but plain paper should also be available), folded cards or sticky labels (for children to mark with their name and use to identify work such as models) and clipboards. Practitioners may want to provide two or three extra writing resource boxes in a central area which children can transport to, and use in, any activity.

Young children should be encouraged to use the equipment purposefully and to make marks to convey meaning. Their achievements as emergent writers and readers should be celebrated and all developmental stages in literacy development recognised and valued by practitioners. The following examples of children's mark-making to communicate meaning show a range of purposes for writing within the early years setting.

Telephone message (Figure 1.1)

This message was written as the child (aged 3 years, 6 months) played in the office. Pretending to engage in a telephone conversation with her Mum, she made marks in response to imagined contributions from Mum. During this activity, the practitioner scribed the child's talk (* indicates points at which the child made marks on the paper):

Figure 1.1
Telephone message
(child's work)

> 'Yes... yes... I'm at nursery. Yes... Yes...* No... I'm going to the shop, what do you want? Fish and chips*... Milk*... Grandma is coming for me at nursery*... I'm having my milk now... Bye.'

---

[2] A wider range of writing equipment will be permanently available in the office area (see long-term plan for this area).

Shopping list (Figure 1.2)

This shopping list was written by a child (aged 3 years, 3 months) during role-play in the home corner. He used a circular mark to represent each word on his list and 'read back' the list pointing to a different mark, moving down the page, each time he said a word: '…eggs – bread – chips – carrots – beans – pizza – sausages – apples'. The different marks at the top represent his name. He shows an understanding of features of lists and attempts writing to communicate meaning.

Figure 1.2 Shopping list (child's work)

Lion's visit – building a den: recording frame (Figure 1.3)

This child (aged 3 years, 11 months) spent time building a den for 'Lion' in the construction area. She chose to make a record of her work and completed the 'frame' independently (having previously been shown how to use it). She then showed her work to the adult and gave the following verbal explanation:

Name _____

I built a den for The Lion and his family. This is what the den looks like:

To build the den I used:

cardboard boxes
wooden bricks
paper
material
tape

Figure 1.3 Lion's visit – building a den: recording frame (child's work)

'This picture [pointing to the drawing in the top box] is Lion – he is in his den. The leaves are on the top. That [marks to the left of the drawing] is Lion's name.'

When asked what she had used to build the den, she pointed to the marks in the bottom box and said 'boxes, bricks, paper, material, tape'. The child has identified her work by making marks at the top of the page to represent her own name. This example shows that the child knows the difference between writing and drawing and makes that distinction in her own mark-making. She has written to inform, understanding that writing can be read.

Bear warning! (Figure 1.4)

This message was written by a child (aged 4 years) to an absent member of staff due to return the next day. The child had been enthusiastically involved in an imaginary 'bear hunt' in the outside play area during the morning. He asked another adult to give his message to the person concerned and offered this explanation:

> 'We've seen the bear. It's hiding. It's waiting to get us! [Pointing to his mark-making] Dear teacher... there's a bear at nursery. Don't go outside... the bear will get you. If you want to go out, wait for me and Michael... we know where the bear's cave is.'

The child also drew a picture of the bear (with sharp teeth to show how fierce it was). A clear distinction is made between writing and drawing – marks (writing) are arranged in strings horizontally and display elements of letters (including a recognisable 's' and 'l').

Figure 1.4 Bear warning! (child's work)

Although it is essential to provide children with a good variety of high-quality fiction and non-fiction books (both in a designated book area and to support learning in other areas of provision), the environment must also offer children a much wider range of reasons and opportunities to read. The presence of bus timetables, recipe cards, magazines in racks and telephone directories in areas of provision will encourage children to incorporate reading into their play. Labels and signs which inform and instruct should be displayed in all areas of the setting, conveying meaning through the written word and through pictures and symbols.

Figure 1.5 Following a recipe to make pasta in the home corner

Cards displayed in areas of provision which invite children to engage in a particular activity serve a dual purpose – to attract interest in the activity and to engage children in reading for a purpose (e.g. 'Would you like to write a party invitation? Who will you invite to the Teddy Bears' Tea Party?' – illustrated with a written invitation and a picture of a bear). It is a good idea to build up a bank of such 'activity cards' which can be repeatedly used. Displaying the cards in moulded, perspex photograph frames will ensure that they are protected from glue, water and paint.

Examples of children's mark-making should be displayed around the setting and their work used, where possible, as a resource by other children, for example, plans made by children of their 'construction kit' models, and lists (words or pictures) of components used, can be laminated and displayed[3] in the construction area, or made into books, and used by others to reproduce an identical model. Practitioners may decide to scribe young children's verbal explanations or ideas and display them alongside drawings or photographs of models.

Children should have access to a card displaying their name which they can use in their play at any time, for example, to support them when naming a painting or model, or when signing a card or letter. Some children will need to have a picture (probably a duplicate of the picture displayed on their coat peg) displayed alongside their name as they develop skills of visual discrimination. Children can also use their name card to register that they are waiting to work in a certain area. By attaching their card to a carpet tile on the wall in the area, or by writing their name on a list, they become 'first in the queue' to work there. When a space becomes available, the practitioner, or other children, will notify the child.

Working towards early learning goals for communication, language and literacy

- Read a range of familiar and common words and simple sentences independently
- Write their own names such as labels and captions and begin to form simple sentences, sometimes using punctuation

---

3   Carpet tiles attached to the wall in each area serve as a good display board – children's work, labels, signs, pictures, posters, poems, rhymes, numbers, plans and instructions will readily 'stick' to the tiles if 'hoop and loop fastening tape' is applied to the back of each. Resources can be changed quickly and frequently and children are able to move them around on the board. This may not be practical in all settings, in which case portable 'carpet tile' boards (sandwich board style) can quite easily be made for use in all areas of provision.

Practitioners should be aware of the different goals for 'writing' and 'handwriting'. Again, the planned environment can provide appropriate experiences for children in developing the skills required to eventually produce recognisable letters in their writing. The early stepping-stones for 'handwriting' include achievements such as 'using one-handed tools and equipment' and 'drawing lines and circles using gross motor movement'. Threading beads, cutting with scissors, making marks with fingers in dry sand or making circular shapes by waving a ribbon in the outdoor area are all appropriate ways of supporting children's handwriting development in the early stages.

It is essential that children practise, in order to develop, speaking and listening skills, and these skills are not always given a high-profile in planning. It can help to increase adult awareness of the importance of learning areas such as 'language for communication' and 'language for thinking' and their place in the curriculum, by discussing and highlighting opportunities. The following example focuses on children's speaking and listening experiences and includes links to 'linking sounds and letters' and 'reading'.

Workshop area of provision

Opportunities for development of speaking and listening skills are highlighted in italics.

Activities and learning experiences

- Making imaginative and functional models using 'junk' materials. *Explaining how the model was made and what materials and equipment were used* (e.g. making beds for Goldilocks and the three bears – children could test the beds for strength and then *use them as a prop in their own story-telling*)

- Making musical instruments to produce a variety of sounds and *comparing children's musical instruments, discriminating between different sounds.*

- Building large-scale models with other children, *discussing plans* and working collaboratively

- Following written and pictorial plans and instructions and *following instructions from an audio tape*

- Exploring properties of materials and *talking about characteristics using descriptive language*

Working towards early learning goals for communication, language and literacy

- Enjoy listening to and using spoken and written language, and readily turn to it in their play and learning
- Explore and experiment with sounds, words and texts
- Use language to organise, sequence and clarify thinking, ideas, feelings and events
- Sustain attentive listening, responding to what they have heard by relevant comments, questions or actions
- Interact with others, negotiating plans and activities and taking turns in conversation

Adults working in the setting should take every opportunity to model literacy skills (e.g. writing shopping lists, passing on telephone messages – written and verbal, writing letters, cards, invitations, writing 'reminder' notes, giving and responding to verbal instructions, following written plans, reading stories and information books) and to work alongside the children, supporting them in the development of writing, reading, speaking and listening skills.

> Children's mathematical development arises out of daily experiences in a rich and interesting environment.
>
> (QCA 2000)

It is important that numbers are displayed throughout the setting and accessible to children. Vertical and horizontal 'number lines' should be in evidence and can be presented in a variety of ways.

For example:

- Number train – each carriage numbered 1–10 (the corresponding number of 'lolly stick' puppets can be placed in each carriage, e.g. one rabbit, two frogs)
- Number washing line – children peg numbered clothes onto the washing line in the correct order
- Number ladder attached to the wall – each rung is numbered and children help 'Monkey' (soft toy) to climb the ladder counting as he steps on the rungs
- Autumn leaves – cardboard or real leaves (these will be preserved if laminated) numbered and hanging from trees outside or hanging from mobiles inside

A 'bank' of numerals and number lines in each area of provision will encourage children to use numbers in their play.

Story boxes, as well as offering rich opportunities for development of language and literacy skills, can be planned with objectives for numeracy in mind.

Kipper's Toybox by Mick Inkpen is an ideal story through which to develop counting skills. The provision of a cardboard box containing Kipper's toys and a copy of the book in the book area will inspire children to retell the story counting the animals in and out of the toybox.

The way in which equipment is stored and presented to children can, as well as encouraging independent learning, support the development of mathematical concepts as illustrated in the following 'water area' example:

Resources

- Three measuring cylinders (a range of sizes)

Organisation

- Children select cylinders from, and return them to, templates of the bases of the cylinders applied to the open shelf in size order. This will encourage discussion of size and use of language such as 'bigger', 'smaller' and 'circle', and of positional language such 'as next to'. 'Upright' templates applied to the back of a shelving unit will also encourage comparison of height and the use of related language. Numbering of the cylinders, 1, 2, 3, and corresponding numbering of templates, will encourage counting with one-to-one correspondence, and matching, naming and ordering of numerals.

Working towards early learning goals for mathematical development

- Say and use number names in order in familiar contexts
- Count reliably up to ten everyday objects
- Recognise numerals 1–9
- Use language such as 'circle' or 'bigger' to describe the shape and size of solids and flat shapes

In areas such as the workshop, painting area, malleable materials area and water area where children are required to wear aprons as they work, the provision of, for example, four numbered aprons in each area serves a few purposes. Numbered aprons hung on numbered hooks will encourage children to match and order numerals 1–4, to use the number names, for example, 'I'll use number 1 apron and you have number 2'. The number of children working in an area will be restricted by the number of aprons available (e.g. four aprons: four children) and children will soon begin to use vocabulary involved in addition and subtraction, for example, 'There are only three children in here – there's one more apron – you can come in, then there will be four.'

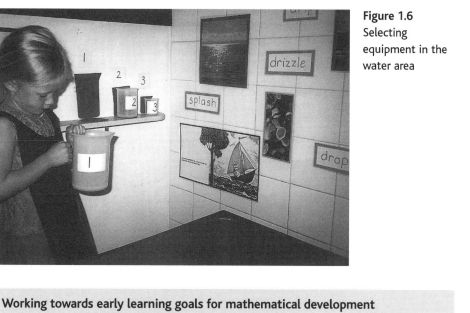

Figure 1.6
Selecting equipment in the water area

Working towards early learning goals for mathematical development

- Say and use number names in order in familiar contexts
- Count reliably up to ten everyday objects
- Recognise numerals 1–9
- In practical activities and discussion begin to use the vocabulary involved in adding and subtracting

Sorting resources can be part of the 'tidying up' routine and to engage children in purposeful activities of this nature, practitioners will, again, need to give careful consideration to the storage of resources in areas of provision. Storage containers should be 'sturdy' and clearly labelled with words, symbols and/or pictures. Children will need to be taught how to sort the resources and given an explanation of the criteria used. Practitioners may decide to change the sorting criteria for a particular resource from time-to-time in order to encourage the development of certain concepts, for example, interlocking bricks – these can be sorted according to colour, length, shape or purpose.

Long-term plans for areas of provision

This next section of Chapter 1 looks in detail at and gives specific guidance on long-term planning for children's learning in the following areas of provision:

- Construction
- Water

- Office/mark-making
- Role-play (home corner)
- Painting

Long-term plans are organised under the headings:

- Learning opportunities
- Key areas of learning
- Early learning goals in key areas of learning
- Resources
- Organisation
- Learning experiences and activities
- Adult role
- Key questions
- Vocabulary

These plans are offered as exemplars. It is hoped that practitioners will be able to adapt them for use in their own setting, and refer to the model when planning other areas of provision.

Where space is abundant and the setting well staffed, it will be possible to offer children a full range of equipment all the time, although staff will undoubtedly decide to plan additional resources to support topic work or focus activities. Other practitioners will need to carefully plan the rotation of resources to ensure that children have constant access to equipment that provides them with intended learning opportunities.

In every well planned area of provision, valuable learning is likely to take place across the curriculum. Practitioners should always be aware of the numerous and diverse learning experiences possible and take every opportunity to extend children's learning in all areas. However, each area of provision has its own particular strengths in terms of promoting learning in key areas, and these are identified on the exemplar plans. Practitioners may wish to focus on different key areas of learning and this is perfectly acceptable as long as the resources reflect and support the focus, and the curriculum is broad and balanced across the setting as a whole. The goals included in each plan are those on which learning is most clearly focused in the key areas.

There will be a certain amount of repetition from plan to plan and practitioners will note that some goals are evident in a number of different plans. This is inevitable when producing separate and complete plans for each area of provision and only serves to emphasise, once again, how entwined the curriculum is with the environment.

'Organisation' and 'adult role' are other examples of sections in which certain points will be common to a few areas of provision. For the purpose of this book, these 'common points' are listed below, and only points exclusive to the area are included in each plan. However, in practice, it is advisable to produce long-term plans inclusive of all aspects of these sections. This will ensure that every plan is useful in its own right as a support for those adults working with children in that particular area – cross-referencing can be frustrating to the busy practitioner and confusing to the visitor.

Aspects of organisation common to all areas of provision

- Resources easily accessed by children to encourage self-selection and independent learning
- Clear cataloguing of and storage arrangements for rotated or additional resources and a rota or plans for their inclusion in the provision
- Daily checking, and replenishing, of consumable resources (e.g. mark-making equipment)
- Regular focus activities and periods of observation planned
- Key early learning goals displayed in the area
- Children sign list, or engage in a similar activity, to register that they have worked in the area

Aspects of 'adult role' common to all areas of provision

The adult will:

- Provide good-quality resources and organise the area
- Be aware of the goals in the key areas of learning and the steps taken on the journey towards the goals
- Interact with children asking questions and making suggestions to support their learning
- Be familiar with key vocabulary – model, and support children in their use of, key words
- Work alongside children, modelling skills and attitudes
- Read with children from fiction and non-fiction books, plans, instruction cards, etc.
- Scribe children's ideas and thoughts and display their work
- Observe children's learning and use of the provision
- Assess children's development and progress

All long-term plans refer to examples of focus activities sited in that particular area of provision – detailed plans for these activities can be found in other chapters of this book and page references are given for each.

The wide range of children's learning needs within the foundation stage is reflected in the planned provision and suggested learning experiences or activities and resources should enable progress to be made from individual starting points, through the 'stepping-stones' towards the key early learning goals.

Construction area

Practitioners will need to provide as large a space as possible as work in the construction area often expands as it develops and frequently involves a number of children working on a 'project'. It may be that two or three children choose to work individually in the area in which case there will still need to be ample room to avoid frustrations and physical limitations on their work. The area will probably need to be carpeted or a rug provided as children tend to spend most of their time in this area sitting, kneeling or lying on their tummies.

'Small-world' equipment, although not construction equipment, is included in the 'resources' list. Its use by children in this area often results in the extension of an activity and in the development of language and creativity (for example – see 'Jungle Play' plans, Chapter 3).

Children should be taught to value other children's work and to celebrate achievements. An area for displaying children's models (e.g. a wall shelf, cupboard top, free-standing open shelving unit – see Chapter 5, Figure 5.6) should be made available and children encouraged to make a name card for display next to their work. Although the display area needs to be in a position where children can look at and talk about each other's work, they should be discouraged from touching or handling the work of others without their permission.

The following plan focuses on construction provision inside the setting – there will also be rich opportunities for construction on a larger scale in the outside play area and a list of appropriate resources can be found later in the chapter ('The outside play area').

Learning opportunities

Skills: Exploring, building, constructing, assembling, joining, planning, problem-solving, evaluating, modifying, adapting, recording, explaining, expressing ideas, observing, comparing, estimating, questioning, selecting and using equipment appropriately and writing or making marks to communicate meaning.

Attitudes: Valuing and showing respect for resources and other children's work, independence, co-operation, interest, enthusiasm, enjoyment, responsibility, concentration, perseverance and confidence.

Understanding and knowledge: Being familiar with the names, characteristics and uses of different construction kits and components, making comparisons (e.g. shape, size, length, colour), measuring length (non-standard), increasing spatial awareness, counting with one-to-one correspondence, developing understanding or use of mathematical language, finding out how to make a strong or balanced structure, using reference books or diagrams and plans to inform own planning and constructing, being aware of design purposes, making up or recreating stories, and recreating roles.

Key areas of learning

- Knowledge and understanding of the world (design and technology)
- Mathematical development
- Communication, language and literacy

Working towards early learning goals in key areas of learning (QCA 2000)

- Ask questions about why things happen and how things work
- Build and construct with a wide range of objects, selecting appropriate resources, and adapting their work where necessary
- Select the tools and techniques they need to shape, assemble and join the materials they are using

(Knowledge and understanding of the world)

- Count reliably up to ten everyday objects
- Use language such as 'circle' or 'bigger' to describe the shape and size of solids and flat shapes
- Use everyday words to describe position
- Use developing mathematical ideas and methods to solve practical problems

(Mathematical development)

- Enjoy listening to and using spoken and written language, and readily turn to it in their play and learning
- Use language to recreate roles and experiences
- Use talk to organise, sequence and clarify thinking, ideas, feelings and events
- Interact with others, negotiating plans and activities and taking turns in conversation
- Attempt writing for various purposes, using features of different forms such as lists, stories and instructions

(Communication, language and literacy)

Resources

- Open shelving, templated for, for example, wooden blocks
- Open shelf unit on which to display children's models
- Plastic storage baskets and boxes clearly labelled with equipment names and pictures – (e.g. cut out from catalogues)
- Carpet tiles on wall or free-standing board
- A range of appropriate fiction and non-fiction books
- Plans[4] (e.g. architects' plans, 'flat pack' furniture plans), diagrams, instructions, photographs of constructions (e.g. Eiffel Tower, fairground wheels and houses from different cultures) – displayed on wall or board
- Maps – roads and underground
- Examples of mechanical toys and clock workings
- Large set of wooden 'unit' blocks
- Construction kits (it is better to provide three to four well stocked sets which will enable children to develop a range of skills than lots of poorly stocked sets which will lead to frustration) – interlocking bricks, equipment with connectors, cogs and wheels, screws and bolts
- Train track and train
- Small-world people, farm animals, zoo animals, dinosaurs, cars
- Mark-making equipment – plastic carrying basket containing pens, pencils, rulers, small, blank, folded card labels (for children to name their own work), clipboards, plain paper, simple planning 'frames'
- Measuring 'sticks'
- An A4 file containing plastic pockets in which children can file their own work to create a central resource of children's plans for use by whole group

Organisation

- Aspects exclusive to the construction area (see page 19 for 'common aspects')
- Large, carpeted area to be available

Learning experiences or activities

- Handling and exploring equipment
- Making models with adult support
- Making own models independently

---

4 Include examples of children's work and photographs.

- Working collaboratively to produce a group model
- Designing and making for a purpose, for example, make a container for the straws on the milk table (such challenges can be repeated and children asked to use different construction sets)
- Talking about own and others' work, identifying successful areas and suggesting improvements
- Explaining to an adult or other children how a model has been made
- Following instructions (pictorial, written or from an audio tape)
- Giving verbal instructions to an adult or another child
- Looking at non-fiction books and plans and using information to support own work
- Recording own work (sequencing cards, drawings, lists)
- Naming work and signing the area 'register'
- Dismantling models, sorting and counting components and matching resources to templates using mathematical language and correct names
- Using stories or experiences as a stimulus for creative play and small-world equipment to build environments around their models

■ **Examples of focus activities in this area:** see 'Jungle Play' and 'Lion's visit' plans, Chapter 3

Adult role

Aspects exclusive to construction area (see page 19 for 'common aspects').

The adult will:

- Model skills involved in building and constructing
- Support children in making and reading plans
- Make diagrams and lists showing components used in a child's model

Key questions

What did you use to make your model? How did you make it? What did you do first? What do you need to make a car? What does the plan tell us? Can you find the component parts shown on the plan? What is the purpose of your model? Which part do you think works the best? How could we make the tractor move? Will it go faster if we use bigger or smaller or more wheels? Is the garage big enough for the car? How could we make it bigger? What will happen if a car knocks into it – can we make it stronger? Can you build a bridge tall enough for the bus to go under?

Vocabulary

Big(ger), small(er), long(er), short(er), tall(er), circle, square, rectangle, triangle, sphere, cube, cuboid, cone, cylinder, names of component parts, number names (1–10), positional language (e.g. next to, in front of, on, under, behind), directional language (e.g. forwards, backwards).

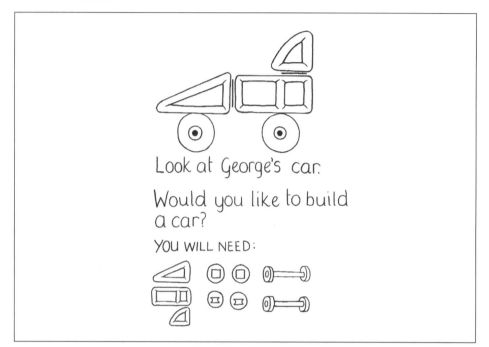

Figure 1.7 George's car – practitioner's drawings of the components used by George in his model will support other children in their attempts to produce an identical car

Water area

The water area needs to be carefully positioned to allow staff easy access to taps and a sink. Some puddles on the floor are inevitable during enthusiastic investigations and surfacing should be 'non-slip'. There should be enough room for children to move freely around the water tray and also for them to construct water ways, siphoning systems, etc. Practitioners may want to restrict the number of children working in the area and, as mentioned earlier in the chapter, provision of a specified number of waterproof aprons is an effective way of limiting the group size. Aprons should be easy for children to put on and take off and should cover as much of their clothing as possible.

A tiled wall area around the tray is a good idea but not practical in all settings. Storage containers should be waterproof and, ideally, have holes in the base and sides as resources are often put away wet and soon become mouldy if not allowed to dry out properly – plastic baskets are suitable and readily available in many supermarkets and hardware shops.

It is difficult to display books in the water area without risking damage to them, although there are some book stands on the market which do offer protection (e.g. perspex cookery-book stands). Laminated blank sheets of paper for use with markers enable children to record without the worry of soaking their paper – these can be displayed on carpet tiles[5] on the wall or on a board, or can be attached to clipboards.

Learning opportunities

Skills: Investigating, experimenting, estimating, comparing, using descriptive or key vocabulary, problem-solving, selecting and using equipment appropriately.

Attitudes: Sharing or turn taking, co-operation, collaboration, independence, enthusiasm, curiosity, motivation, concentration, confidence, respect for resources and the work or ideas of others.

Understanding and knowledge: Developing an understanding of: volume, capacity, size, shape, number, displacement, forces (e.g. floating or sinking, siphoning), absorption, dissolving and heating or cooling. Being familiar with or using mathematical language related to these concepts.

Key areas of learning

- Knowledge and understanding of the world (scientific development)
- Mathematical development
- Communication, language and literacy

Working towards early learning goals in key areas of learning (QCA 2000)

- Investigate objects and materials by using all of their senses as appropriate
- Find out about, and identify some features of, living things, objects and events that they observe
- Look closely at similarities, differences patterns and change
- Ask questions about why things happen and how things work

(Knowledge and understanding of the world)

---

[5] Markers can also be kept on the carpet tile if a strip of 'hoop and loop fastening tape' is attached to the shaft.

- Say and use number names in familiar contexts
- Use language such as 'more' or 'less', 'greater' or 'smaller', 'heavier' or 'lighter', to compare two numbers or quantities
- Use language such as 'circle' or 'bigger' to describe the shape and size of solids and flat shapes
- Use developing mathematical ideas and methods to solve mathematical problems

(Mathematical development)

- Use talk to organise, sequence and clarify thinking, ideas, feelings and events
- Interact with others negotiating plans and activities and taking turns in conversation

(Communication, language and literacy)

Resources

- Water tray (with differing base levels)
- Water – sometimes coloured (using food colouring)
- Mop and bucket
- Wooden board to fit across the tray (perhaps with an arrangement of pipes fitted through holes drilled in the board)
- Open shelving templated for jugs, cylinders
- Plastic storage baskets, labelled
- Four waterproof aprons
- Graded sets of jugs, measuring cylinders, beakers, buckets
- Funnels, sieves, slotted spoons, ladles, water wheels, watering cans, siphons, tubes, pumps
- Natural materials such as sponges, corks, pebbles, pumice stones, shells, drift wood, fir cones, bark
- Transparent plastic bottles (different sizes or same size but marked at different levels with waterproof tape)
- Tea set – cups, teapot, jug, spoons
- A range of small-world creatures, people, boats
- Clipboard, laminated paper, markers
- Posters, photographs, poems (preferably laminated) and fiction and non-fiction books

Organisation

Aspects exclusive to the water area (see page 19 for 'common aspects'):

- Four children only allowed in the area (to be controlled by the provision of four aprons)
- Resources easily accessed by children, and equipment allowed to drain until dry
- Water tray to be emptied at the end of every session
- Colour to be added to the water as planned (in short-term planning)

Learning experiences or activities

- Observing other children working in the area
- Observing or exploring properties of water
- Pouring from and filling containers, counting how many of one fit into another
- Comparing and ordering containers
- Matching equipment to templates
- Investigating and experimenting using appropriate equipment and materials, for example: displacement – transparent plastic containers, pebbles, coloured water; heating and cooling water – ice blocks (perhaps coloured, or containing objects such as buttons) added to warm water in the tray, snow in the tray
- Discussing ideas with adults and other children
- Making predictions and drawing simple conclusions
- Simple recording – checklists, charts
- Imaginative 'sea world' play
- Using stories as a stimulus for imaginative play

■ **Examples of focus activities in this area:** see 'Making boats', Chapter 2, page 70 and 'Investigating snow', Chapter 3, page 111.

Adult role

Aspects exclusive to the water area (see page 19 for 'common aspects').

The adult will:

- Ensure safety at all times (e.g. any excess water on the floor to be mopped up)
- Encourage children to experiment and 'find out'
- Work alongside children experimenting and modelling use of equipment

Key questions

What do you think will happen if: We pour the water from this container into that one? We tip the jug this way? We lift up this end of the tube whilst the water is inside? We put a stone into this jug (full of water)? We put the sponge into the water? We squeeze the sponge in the water? Do you think the shell will float? Can you find something that you think will sink? Were you right? Why do think it sinks? How many jugfuls of water do you think will fit into the bucket? Do you think the jug holds more or less water than the cylinder? How can we make water travel upwards? How can we make the boat move in the water without touching it?

Vocabulary

Full(er), empty, emptier, big(ger), small(er), tall(er), short(er), wide(r). long(er), thin(ner), heavy, heavier, light(er), wet, dry, warm, hot, cold, freeze, melt, pour, flow, float, sink, equipment names.

Office and mark-making area

The office area is the obvious place in which to focus on developing learning in the area of communication, language and literacy. Resources should be provided which enable and encourage children to engage in reading, writing and speaking and listening activities for a 'real' purpose.

The area does not require the same amount of floor space as, for example, the construction area, but should be large enough to allow for movement of individuals without disturbance to other children. Many practitioners find that 'enclosing' the office area on two or three sides (using tall shelving units or screens) encourages children to concentrate for longer periods by excluding unnecessary distractions. This structure also reduces the volume of noise in the area, enabling the children to more easily engage in interactive conversation (e.g. using telephones).

Practitioners will need to be permanently looking out for resources to enhance the provision in this area, for example, old catalogues, telephone directories, obsolete forms and used tickets. The rate at which children use consumable resources, such as paper, in the office is surprisingly fast – it can be quite a challenge to supply according to demand.

The provision of a variety of different papers and formats (e.g. lined, squared, headed writing paper and memo pads) will encourage children to engage in meaningful writing for a range of purposes. Practitioners can easily design these themselves and, if access to a photocopier is available, they should keep a file of master copies to enable them to quickly replenish stocks.

Learning opportunities

Skills: Recording; mark-making (to communicate meaning); using mark-making tools with control; reading (pictures, symbols, words); designing and making; decision-making; observing; forming relationships; listening; communicating through talk (explaining, expressing, discussing, negotiating, questioning and requesting).

Attitudes: Independence; enjoyment; motivation; confidence; concentration; co-operation; interest in and respect for the ideas and work of others.

Understanding and knowledge: Understanding that meaning can be communicated through writing, and that reading is a way of accessing information from the written word; knowing the basic conventions of written English; developing a knowledge of the sounds and letters used in English; understanding that spoken language can be used to communicate, negotiate and discuss; understanding the importance of listening in an interactive conversation.

Key areas of learning

● Communication, language and literacy
● Personal, social and emotional development

Working towards early learning goals in key areas of learning (QCA 2000)

● Enjoy listening to and using spoken and written language, and readily turn to it in their play and learning
● Use talk to organise, sequence and clarify thinking, ideas, feelings and events
● Interact with others, negotiating plans, activities and taking turns in conversation
● Hear and say initial and final sounds in words, and short vowel sounds within words
● Link sounds to letters, naming and sounding the letters of the alphabet
● Read a range of familiar and common words and simple sentences independently
● Know that print carries meaning and, in English, is read from left to right and top to bottom
● Attempt writing for various purposes, using features of different forms such as lists, stories and instructions
● Write their own names and other things such as labels and captions and begin to form simple sentences, sometimes using punctuation
● Use their phonic knowledge to write simple, regular words and make phonetically plausible attempts at more complex words
● Use a pencil and hold it effectively to form recognisable letters, most of which are correctly formed

(Communication, language and literacy)

- Continue to be interested, excited and motivated to learn
- Maintain attention, concentrate and sit quietly when appropriate
- Have a developing awareness of their own needs, views and feelings and be sensitive to the needs, views and feelings of others
- Form good relationships with adults and peers
- Select and use activities and resources independently

(Personal, social and emotional development)

Resources

- Round table and four chairs
- Wall space or large, permanent board (possibly covered in carpet tiles for use with 'hoop and loop fastening tape')[6] displaying, for example, greetings cards, invitations, signs, labels, alphabet, photographs of children writing for different purposes
- Large permanent board (or wall) displaying children's name cards (removable)
- Cork notice board
- Calendar
- Postbox
- Open shelving unit
- Two telephones
- Keyboard
- Bank of 'Can you ring this telephone number...?' cards
- Telephone directories, catalogues, brochures
- Laminated message board (A4) with marker pens
- Address books, diaries, memo pads
- Bank of word or phrase cards (e.g. 'Happy Birthday', 'with love from', 'to')
- Paper, various sizes: blank, lined, squared, headed
- Forms, tickets
- Folded card (for making greetings cards), postcards
- Envelopes, used stamps
- Sticky labels, card labels, tape, glue sticks
- Hole punches, staplers, scissors, sharpeners, rubbers
- Pencils, biros, felt pens, crayons
- Clipboards

---

[6] Children are more likely to use displayed labels and signs in their play if they can remove and transport them to where they are working.

Organisation

- Aspects exclusive to the office area (see page 19 for 'common aspects')
- Different order forms, letter headings, blank invitations, etc. to be introduced regularly
- Area to be situated in a quiet position away from 'thoroughfares'

Learning experiences or activities

- Mark-making using a variety of tools
- Writing for a range of purposes, for example, invitations, letters, orders, greetings cards, postcards, telephone messages, envelopes, memos, lists, forms, diary entries
- Posting or receiving written communications
- Writing own name, for example, signing letters
- Reading for a range of purposes, for example, letters/cards/notes/invitations from friends, own writing, catalogues, brochures, telephone numbers
- Discussing work and ideas with adults and other children
- Dialling telephone numbers and holding two-way telephone conversations with adults and other children
- Example of focus activity in this area: see 'Jasper's Birthday', Chapter 2, page 64

Adult role

Aspects exclusive to the office area (see page 19 for 'common aspects').

The adult will:

- Model reading and writing in a variety of situations and for a variety of reasons
- Hold telephone conversations with children in the area
- Ensure that all letters, etc. are collected from the postbox daily and distributed to the children concerned

Key questions

- Would you like to answer the telephone? Who is it? Why did they ring? Can you take a message? Can you read the message to me? Who would you like to ring up? What is their telephone number? What will you ask or tell them? Can you read your letter to a friend? How do you know who the letter is from? What will you write on the envelope? Which books would you like to order from the book club? Can you find your name card? Which is the first letter in your name? What sound is at the beginning of your name? Can you find the letter 'b'? Can you make a 'b' with your pencil? Would you like to send your friend a birthday card? Can you find her name card? What would you like to write? Can you find the label that says 'Happy Birthday?'

Role-play – the home corner

The home corner is an example of a role-play area. Through role-play, children learn about real life and relationships in a 'safe' situation, and can represent experiences and ideas creatively in their play. A well planned role-play area should also provide rich opportunities for developing language and literacy, offering purposes for writing, reading, speaking and listening.

The possibilities for role-play in early years settings are almost infinite but the range and quality of provision is largely dependent on the fertility of the practitioner's imagination. Areas for role-play are often constructed as part of a theme, or may be planned in response to a child's, or group of children's, interests.

Listed below are some examples:

- Hospital, doctor's surgery or clinic
- Post Office, bank
- Travel agents
- Supermarket
- Shoe shop
- Toy shop
- Hairdressers
- The 'Three Bears' House'
- Aeroplane, bus, train, boat
- Bear cave or lion's den
- Castle
- Hotel, café, restaurant
- Ice cream van
- DIY store
- Library

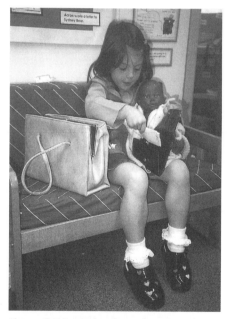

Figure 1.8 Preparing for a shopping trip

In many settings, if space allows, the home corner is part of the permanent provision and additional role-play areas are constructed temporarily in other sites, often in the outside area. Sometimes the home corner may consist of a kitchen with dining and sitting area, sometimes it will have a bedroom. Often a change, or rearrangement, of furniture will reawaken interest in the home corner, as will a focus activity such as a birthday party or the arrival of a new baby (doll). The home corner can also provide opportunities for discussing physical disability sensitively and positively through the use of persona dolls wearing, for example, hearing aids or glasses or using wheelchairs.

The following long-term plan relates to a home corner area comprising of kitchen and dining or sitting area:

Learning opportunities

Skills: Sharing, taking turns, observing, communicating, imagining, initiating and developing imaginative ideas, recreating roles and story-making.

Attitudes: Respect for self and others, independence, co-operation, caring, social awareness, sensitivity, self-assurance, resourcefulness and enjoyment.

Understanding and knowledge: Extending language; using skills for a real purpose; developing understanding of, and knowledge about, relationships or roles, cultures and needs of others or purposes of writing, reading and talking; 'real life' and home environment or social 'rules' and codes of behaviour and appropriate expression of feelings.

Key areas of learning

● Personal, social and emotional development

● Communication, language and literacy

Working towards early learning goals in key areas of learning (QCA 2000)

● Have a developing awareness of their own needs, views and feelings and be sensitive to the needs, views and feelings of others

● Have a developing respect for their own cultures and beliefs and those of other people

● Respond to significant experiences, showing a range of feelings when appropriate

● Work as part of a group or class, taking turns and sharing fairly, understanding that there need to be agreed values and codes of behaviour for groups of people, including adults and children, to work together harmoniously

● Understand what is right and wrong and why

● Consider the consequences of their words and actions for themselves and others

● Understand that people have different needs, views, cultures and beliefs which need to be treated with respect

● Understand that they can expect others to treat their needs, views, cultures and beliefs with respect

(Personal, social and emotional development)

By the end of the foundation stage, most children will be able to:

- Enjoy listening to and using spoken and written language, and readily turn to it in their play and learning
- Use language to imagine and recreate roles and experiences
- Use talk to organise, sequence and clarify thinking, ideas, feelings and events
- Interact with others, negotiating plans and activities and taking turns in conversation
- Attempt writing for various purposes, using features of different forms such as lists, stories and instructions

(Communication, language and literacy)

Resources

- Home corner furniture at child height: cupboards, sink, washing machine, table, four chairs, sofa, cooker
- Draining rack, kitchen utensils, trays, chopping boards, saucepans, wok, colander and imitation food
- Cups, saucers, bowls, plates, cutlery (in coloured sets)
- Tea towels, oven gloves, table cloth
- Recipe cards, books
- Pegs, washing line, iron, ironing board
- Brush, dustpan, vacuum cleaner
- Open 'wardrobe' storage unit (on castors), coat hangers
- 'Dressing-up' clothes (from a range of cultures)
- Dolls (male, female with different skin colours)
- Baby clothes, blankets, shawls, bath, pushchair
- Mark-making equipment, note pads, shopping lists, paper, notelets, envelopes, invitations, birthday cards
- Telephone, address book, telephone directory

Organisation

Aspects exclusive to the home corner (see page 19 for 'common aspects').

- Furniture arranged to create the feeling of a real room
- Enough space allowed for cupboard doors to open easily, and for children to be able to move freely around furniture

Learning experiences or activities

- 'Playing out' real life situations and personal experiences
- Fantasy play and story-making
- Dressing-up
- Discussing experiences and ideas, negotiating roles and delivering messages
- Making 'props' for play
- Writing for a purpose (e.g. shopping lists, telephone messages, invitations)
- Celebrating birthdays and festivals

- ■ **Example of role-play focus activity:** See 'Post Office role-play', Chapter 3, page 108

Adult role

Aspects exclusive to the home corner (see page 19 for 'common aspects').

The adult will:

- Engage in role-play with the children
- Plan additional resources for celebrations

Key questions

Who would you like to invite for tea? How will you invite him? (Telephone? Written invitation?) What will you make for tea? What does he like to eat? What do you need to make pizza? Can you find a recipe for pizza in the book? Why is your baby crying? How does she feel? What can you do to make her feel better? What are you going to buy at the shop? What do you need from the shop for your baby? What do you need to take with you to the shop?

Vocabulary

- 'Feelings' vocabulary, for example, happy, sad, cross, angry, worried or frightened
- Vocabulary related to resources, for example, cup, saucer and plate

The painting area

The painting area should, ideally, be situated near to a sink so that children can fill up their own water pots and wash up utensils without leaving too long a paint trail on the floor.

Although ready-mixed paints are appropriate in some circumstances (e.g. printing), children should be offered frequent, and regular, opportunities to mix their own powder paint, exploring colour blending and a range of consistencies.

If children are mixing their own colours, it is not necessary to provide them with a large range, but the primary colours (red, yellow and blue) should be available, as these can not be mixed using other colours. By mixing two primary colours together, children will be able to produce the secondary colours (purple, orange and green). Blue and red mixed together will make purple, red and yellow produce orange, and blue and yellow make green. The addition of white will produce lighter tints, and black (which should be used sparingly), darker shades.

Children need to be taught routines and use of resources, and will probably need regular reinforcement until they feel confident in the area. Some younger children are much more interested in the

Figure 1.9 Mixing colours in the painting area

process of mixing paint than in the application of paint to paper and should be allowed to pursue this interest.

Easels are very popular in early years settings and allow two children to work in a relatively small space. However, it can be frustrating for children, when using watery paint, if their marks are constantly distorted by 'trickles'. Some activities in this area are much more successful on a horizontal surface and, for obvious practical reasons, tables should be covered in a plastic-coated cloth or newspaper. It is not necessary to provide chairs in the painting area; children will be less restricted in their brush strokes if working from the standing position. Aprons should be provided in a place easily accessible to children.

Learning opportunities

Skills: Experimenting, recording, predicting, decision-making, describing, explaining, expressing ideas and opinions, mark-making, designing, imagining and creating.

Attitudes: Interest, motivation, independence, co-operation, perseverance, confidence.

Understanding and knowledge: Developing a knowledge about, and understanding of, the changes that occur when powder paint is mixed with water, and when colours are mixed together; understanding two- and three-dimensional representation and composition, organising colours and shapes to produce an image; increasing knowledge about line, tone, shape, space, pattern, texture and form (i.e. the elements of art); knowing purposes of tools and properties of materials and developing an appreciation of art and artefacts.

Key areas of learning

- Creative development
- Knowledge and understanding of the world

Working towards early learning goals in key areas of learning (QCA 2000)

- Explore colour, texture, shape, form and space in two and three dimensions
- Respond in a variety of ways to what they see, hear, smell, touch and feel
- Use their imagination in art and design, music, dance and imaginative role-play and stories
- Express and communicate their ideas, thoughts and feelings by using a widening range of materials, suitable tools, imaginative and role-play, movement, designing and making, and a variety of songs and musical instruments

(Creative development)

- Investigate objects and materials by using all of their senses as appropriate
- Find out about, and identify some features of, living things, objects and events they observe
- Look closely at similarities, differences, patterns and change

(Knowledge and understanding of the world)

Resources

- Large, square table (at a comfortable height for standing to work) covered with a waterproof, self-coloured, cloth ('busy' patterns can be distracting when creating an image)
- Two easels with trays attached
- Trolley: surface templated for water pots, palettes, paint containers; tray storage for brushes (varying thicknesses, round and flat), spatulas, rollers, wooden printing blocks, sponges, a range of 'found objects' for making marks with paint (e.g. cotton reels, washing up brushes, corks, plastic lids)
- Open shelved paper cupboard; rectangles of paper of varying size and proportions; textured paper (e.g. woodchip wallpaper cut into rectangles); white and coloured paper
- Drying rack (preferably holding work horizontally to avoid paint dripping)
- White, wooden cube (for displaying objects for observation)

- Reproductions of artists' work
- Powder paint (reds, blues, yellows, white, black) ready-mixed paint, water-based printing inks
- Instructions for paint mixing (see Chapter 3, page 89, 'Mixing textured paint')
- Pencils (for naming work)
- 'Gallery' displaying the work of children and famous artists

Organisation

Aspects exclusive to the painting area (see page 19 for 'common aspects')

- Limit of four children working in the area
- A range of techniques to be explored, and skills taught, through focus activities

Learning experiences and activities

- Mixing powder paint with water, mixing colours
- Applying paint to paper, drawing with paint using a range of tools
- Painting from observation and imagination
- Collaborative painting on large sheets of paper
- Printing, for example: with sponges, vegetables, leaves, hands, string, card; on fabric, paper, card, wood; taking mono prints (spread mixed paint on a perspex sheet, draw into the paint with finger, press paper onto the image); making bubble prints (mix washing up liquid with paint in a tray or bowl, blow with a straw until bubbles reach above the rim, place paper over the bubbles); press printing (draw an image onto a piece of specially produced polystyrene using a pencil or modelling tools, roll on ink or paint and press onto paper)
- Pattern-making (repeat and random)
- Painting own models made in the workshop
- Mixed media work
- Adding extra ingredients to paint to produce different textures
- Discussing children's work and the nursery gallery
- Looking at and discussing the work of artists

■ **Example of focus activity in this area:** See 'Mixing textured paint', Chapter 3, page 89

Adult role

Aspects exclusive to the painting area (see page 19 for 'common aspects')
The adult will:

- Teach and reinforce routines and colour names
- Model skills and demonstrate techniques

Key questions

What do you think will happen if you mix red with blue? Which colours did you mix together to make green? Which is your favourite colour? Is this blue lighter or darker than that blue? Which brush will make a thin or thick mark? What do you think will happen if you add more water to your paint? Have you used thick or thin paint? What is your painting about? What do you think this painting is about? What do you like best about this painting? What kind of line or shape have you made?

Vocabulary

Colour names: red, blue, yellow, orange, purple, green, white, black (other colours if children are ready), descriptive words related to the elements of art, for example, line: wiggly, straight, wavy, zig-zag; texture: rough, bobbly, lumpy, smooth.

The outside area

> Well planned play, both indoors and outdoors, is a key way in which young children learn with enjoyment and challenge.
>
> (*Curriculum Guidance for the Foundation Stage*, QCA 2000)

The outside play area is often described as an area of provision but should not be viewed merely as an additional area, more as a part of the whole setting in which all other areas of provision can be set up and all areas of the curriculum covered. The size and features of outside areas vary tremendously from setting to setting and it may be necessary to plan areas of provision in the outside area on a rotational basis. Many teams organise their outdoor area into zones, for example, wheeled toys, climbing and balancing, exploration and investigation (sand and water trays, digging plot, wild area), role-play and quiet area (books, seating). Equipment is then organised within each zone.

Staffing arrangements also have a bearing on the organisation of this area. All settings should aspire to the ideal of offering children free access to the outdoor area throughout the session, but where this is not possible, creative planning should ensure that children have as much access and choice as possible.

Activities taking place in areas of provision inside can often be extended very successfully outside by introducing different resources, for example, learning about how water travels and how it can be used to move objects:

- *Inside* – using tubes, marbles and 'pouring' containers in the water tray. Children pour coloured water into the tube and watch it travel along the tube as they lift up one end. They put a marble in one end of a tube and keeping the tube reasonably level, use water to 'push' the marble along inside the tube.

- *Outside* – using plastic drainage tubes, pipes and guttering (can be purchased from builders' merchants and are relatively inexpensive), two or three water trays, large buckets and bowls, marbles and balls of different sizes, 'pouring' containers. Children work together on a large-scale constructing complex waterways, investigating how water travels on inclines, moving water from a tray at one level to another tray at the same or a different level, and using water to 'push' balls along level guttering and transport them to another tray.

Figure 1.10 Water investigations in the outside area

Working towards early learning goals for knowledge and understanding of the world

- Investigate objects and materials by using all of their senses as appropriate
- Ask questions about why things happen and how things work

The outside area also offers opportunities for physical activity and development of gross motor skills which are largely impossible in the inside environment. It is important to ensure that children are allowed sufficient space in which to run, ride (e.g. bikes and scooters) and climb and that each of these activities is afforded its own designated area. Other activities should encourage the development of throwing and catching skills, balancing, jumping and hopping.

Working towards early learning goals in physical development

- Move with confidence, imagination and safety
- Move with control and co-ordination
- Show awareness of space, of themselves and of others
- Use a range of small and large equipment
- Travel around, under, over and through balancing and climbing equipment

Exciting investigations of the outside environment can lead to valuable learning taking place, particularly in the area of 'knowledge and understanding of the world'. Practitioners should anticipate such learning experiences and plan an outside area that will provide children with a wealth of opportunities to find out about the natural environment and a range of stimuli which will prompt them to ask questions about the world around them.

It is usually possible, even in the smallest of outside areas, to organise such activities as:

- A 'growth investigation' – a range of flowers and vegetables can be grown from seed in pots, troughs or tyres filled with compost

- Developing a 'wild area' in which children will be able to observe seasonal changes – a small piece of land planted with grass and wild flower seeds, evergreen shrubs, spring

Figure 1.11 Watering the plants

bulbs, plants or shrubs that encourage butterflies, for example, buddleia

- A 'mini-beast investigation' – introduce a few logs and large stones to the wild area – children will be fascinated by the insect life they discover daily underneath the logs and stones

Figure 1.12 Searching for centipedes

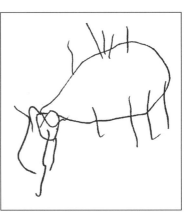

Figure 1.13 Beetle – drawn from observation in the outside area (child's drawing)

Working towards early learning goals in knowledge and understanding of the world

- Find out about, and identify some features of, living things, objects and events they observe
- Look closely at similarities, differences, patterns and change
- Ask questions about why things happen and how things work

Every effort should be made to promote literacy and numeracy in the outside area. Opportunities for children to practise and develop reading and writing skills are as numerous outside as they are inside but practitioners may decide to select some different resources for use outside, for example, on a dry day, children will welcome the opportunity to make marks, and perhaps write their name, on walls and paving slabs using a paintbrush dipped into a pot of water (see Figure 1.14). Mark-making on a large-scale allows children freedom of movement and expression – a roll of decorator's lining paper is inexpensive and, rolled out and

Figure 1.14 Mark-making with brushes and water in the outside area

secured to the ground with masking tape, provides a 'canvas' large enough for a group of children to work individually or collaboratively with a range of tools. Laminated sheets of A4 card and marker pens can be more practical than paper in wet areas and can also be cleaned and 'recycled'. Portable baskets containing mark-making equipment (including clipboards) are also a useful resource in the outdoor play area.

Roadways (drawn in chalk on the ground) are always popular with bike riders and the addition of road signs and arrows encourages purposeful reading. Children will very quickly learn to recognise 'stop' and 'go' on a hand-held sign and to respond appropriately. Other examples of signs that can be displayed outside include 'bus stop', 'taxi rank', 'building site – wear hard hats', maps of the outside play area, shop and garden centre signs, 'follow the trail' arrows, 'are you wearing your outdoor shoes?' Children will often offer their own suggestions and should be encouraged to make and use their own signs.

A bank of illustrated question cards made available to children in the outdoor area will also encourage the development of reading skills, for example, 'Can you find a ladybird?' or 'Have you watered the carrots today?' If the pictures are clear and simple, even the youngest of children will be able to 'read' the card and with support, respond to the questions.

> **Working towards early learning goals in communication, language and literacy**
>
> - Read a range of familiar and common words and simple sentences independently
> - Know that print carries meaning and in English, is read from left to right and top to bottom
> - Attempt writing for various purposes, using features of different forms such as lists, stories and instructions
> - Write their own names and other things such as labels and captions and begin to form simple sentences, sometimes using punctuation
> - Use their phonic knowledge to write simple regular words and make phonetically plausible attempts at more complex words

Number plates on wheeled toys which children match to numbers on 'garages' as they park their vehicles encourage number recognition, matching and counting. As they become familiar with the system, children will begin to refer to bikes by their number:

'It's my turn to play on number three bike now!'– 'Look, 'two' bike is still in the garage, you can go on that.'

Other ways of developing mathematical learning outside include:

- Hopscotch and grid games painted on the ground
- 'Chant' games such as 'What time is it Mr Wolf?'

- 'Giant' dice games (roll a three – walk three steps across the playground – who will reach the other side first?)
- Playing positional language games, for example, hide the teddy behind the tree or in front of the den or in the sand tray
- Throwing beanbags into numbered boxes in the correct order (this activity could be presented as, for example, throwing fish to the sea lions)
- Making tally charts or tick lists – how many butterflies/cars/people/birds have we seen from the playground during the session?
- Observing insects in 'bug boxes' and counting legs and wings
- Following the 'bear trail' – children step on numbered paw prints to reach the bear's cave
- Posting activities – matching, for example, shapes on envelopes to shapes on postboxes around the area
- Drawing around children's shadows on a sunny day – comparing length and shape
- Measuring children's height against a wall and making a chalk mark for each child
- Growing sunflowers against a wall – comparing height and recording growth by marking the top of the sunflower in chalk on the wall every week
- Potting plants or planting seeds – comparing different pots – how much compost does this one hold? Does it hold more than that one?
- Fishing for numbered fish in a water tray: using laminated card fish (numbered, and with a metal paper clip attached) and string fishing rods with a small magnet attached – can you catch number one fish? Which number is left in the water?
- Comparing weights or balancing weights – using a rope thrown over a tree branch with a bag full of sand attached to one end, children fill the bag attached to the other end of the rope with sand until the two bags are balanced
- Selecting boxes of suitable size and shape to use as containers for stock in their role-play shoe shop

All early learning goals for mathematical development are worked towards through this range of activities.

Dens are guaranteed to capture the imagination of young children and the outdoor area is an ideal place in which to set up a bear cave, lion's den, camping holiday tent, teddy bears' hideout or desert island retreat – the possibilities are endless. Wooden structures (e.g. a pyramid) provide a firm framework around which to build a den, but if these are not available large cardboard boxes, tables, etc. can be used effectively. Long lengths of fabric (old curtains or sheets are ideal) draped over the framework instantly create an exciting environment. Other resources can be introduced – the choice of these will depend on the nature of the children's play.

'Shadow play' on a sunny day also offers rich opportunities for creative development as illustrated in Figure 1.15. Following a story session during which the practitioner read *Where the Wild Things Are* by Maurice Sendak, children experimented with the shadows made by their own body shapes and created some very ferocious-looking 'wild things'.

Figure 1.15 Shadow play: creating 'wild things'

Working towards early learning goals in creative development

- Use their imagination in art and design, music, dance, imaginative and role-play and stories
- Express and communicate their ideas, thoughts and feelings by using a widening range of materials, suitable tools, imaginative role-play, movement, designing and making, a variety of songs and musical instruments

Opportunities for personal, social and emotional development are many in the outdoor area. Well planned and exciting activities taking place in this area often play a significant role in motivating children to learn and inspiring in them a desire to explore and investigate the world around them. Children learn to share, and take turns on, equipment and to follow clear codes of behaviour in order to work safely. They develop a responsibility for the care of living things and the environment and are offered opportunities to work independently, in pairs and as part of a group.

To list all the equipment used in the outdoor play area would be to duplicate much of the content of the long-term plans for areas of provision included in 'The inside area'. For this reason, only examples of resources that are exclusive to the outdoor area are listed next:

- Climbing equipment – frames, ladders, slides (positioned on soft surface)
- Fabric tunnels and plastic barrels

- Wheeled toys – bikes, scooters, go-carts
- Road signs
- Police/traffic warden/lollipop person uniforms
- Large wooden blocks, for example, hollow blocks, wooden planks
- Large plastic mats, carpet squares
- Old car/bus steering wheels
- Tyres
- Milk crates
- Cones
- Logs, tree stumps
- Bats, racquets, balls
- Beanbags
- Hoops and rubber quoits
- Skipping ropes
- 'Den' frameworks, lengths of fabric
- Lengths of guttering (can be stored on brackets attached to the wall)

Figure 1.16 Builders at work

- Large water trays, buckets
- Plastic sand tray or permanent, brick-built sand pit
- Shallow builders' tray, old wooden bricks (see Figure 1.16)
- Trowels, spades, rakes
- Hard, builders' hats
- Wheelbarrow
- Watering cans, plant pots, troughs
- Portable mark-making resource baskets
- Plastic water pots, paint brushes and decorators' brushes

■ **Examples of focus activity plan for the outside area:** 'Going on a "Bear Hunt" – obstacle course' (page 78).

When all long-term plans have been completed, provision as a whole should reflect curricular breadth and balance. A simple overview such as the next example will provide a record and also highlight any gaps.

OVERVIEW OF THE CURRICULUM THROUGH LONG-TERM PLANNING OF PROVISION

Cluster groups of goals	Personal, social and emotional development*						Communication, language and literacy						Mathematical development			Knowledge and understanding of the world						Physical development					Creative development			
	1	2	3	4	5	6	1	2	3	4	5	6	1	2	3	1	2	3	4	5	6	1	2	3	4	5	1	2	3	4
Sand area																														
Wet							X	X					X		X															
Dry							X	X				X	X		X															
Mark-making/											X	X														X	X			
Office									X	X	X	X														X			X	
Home corner		X	X				X					X																	X	X
Technology workshop																	X									X	X		X	X
Construction area								X					X	X	X		X													

*The area of personal, social and emotional development should underpin all learning. For example, the 'self-care' aspect will be promoted through the organisation of all areas of provision which will include independent access of resources for children. Only the key areas of learning identified on long-term plans are included in the overview. These are a decision for individual teams and may vary from setting to setting.

Figure 1.17 Overview of the curriculum through long-term planning of provision

Safety

The issue of safety is something that concerns many practitioners when planning for the outdoor area and of course it is crucial to protect children from serious harm. However, an environment with absolutely no risk is also an environment with no challenge. It is therefore important to create a balance allowing children to learn how to assess risk themselves and to operate safely within the environment. In order to decide what is an 'acceptable' risk and to eliminate 'unacceptable' risks, it is useful to meet as a team to discuss the issue and to draw up a risk assessment. There are many formats available for this purpose and these include sections identifying the hazard and those at risk, judging the level of risk, outlining steps to be taken in minimising or eliminating the risk. Such assessments should be regularly reviewed and modifications made with the knowledge of all team members. Any incidents recorded in the accident book should be used to inform these reviews.

Key Points for Good Practice

- Offer areas of provision on a continuous basis to enable children to develop ideas and understanding over time. Where physical limitations dictate that areas are rotated, make sure that each area is available for a long enough period of time to allow for revisiting.
- Encourage children as independent learners and thinkers within the environment, organising provision to promote self-selection and decision-making.
- Make sure that routines do not unnecessarily interrupt children's learning experiences.
- Be aware of your role in supporting children's learning needs and interests within provision.
- Draw up long-term plans as a whole staff team and link the planning to developments in provision.
- Identify key areas of learning in plans for each area of provision but reflect curricular breadth and balance through provision as a whole.
- Recognise the importance of outdoor learning and plan for all areas of the curriculum through outdoor provision.
- Ensure that the learning environment is inclusive and that the needs of all individuals within the group are met through provision.
- Reflect a variety of cultures through provision.
- Regularly evaluate provision and review long-term plans.

The environment is the mechanism by which the teacher brings the child and different areas of knowledge together.

(Bruce 1987)

CHAPTER 2

Planning for a focus

Children deepen their understanding by playing, talking, observing, planning questioning, experimenting, testing, repeating, reflecting and responding to adults and to each other. Practitioners need to plan learning experiences of the highest quality, considering both children's needs and achievements and the range of learning experiences which help them make progress. Well planned play is a key way children learn with enjoyment and challenge during the foundation stage.

(QCA 2000)

The content of this chapter is organised as follows:

- What is a 'focus activity'? (page 50)
- Why plan focus activities? (page 51)
- Deciding on a framework for planning focus activities – what should be included? (page 51)
- To what extent should focus activities be planned in advance? (page 52)
- Using a medium-term plan to support focus planning (page 53)
- Planning a focus activity (page 55)
- What should practitioners consider when evaluating the focus activity? (page 63)
- Examples of focus activity plans (page 63)
- Key points for good practice (page 80)

Chapters 1, 2 and 3 are primarily concerned with the long-term planning of provision and with the short-term planning of activities and experiences within that planned environment. It is, however, worth explaining and defining the whole planning process before making the leap from long- to short-term. This 'process' involves three stages, one feeding into the other, and is explained in Figure 2.1.

LONG-TERM PLANNING

The learning environment is defined in terms of resources, organisation, adult role and potential learning experiences. Planned provision across the setting offers a broad and balanced curriculum (over the six areas of learning) and learning opportunities for all children. This planning will form a permanent basis (although it should be reviewed regularly) for medium- and short-term planning.

MEDIUM-TERM PLANNING

A 'unit' of learning is planned for a period of time to take place within the learning environment and the curricular framework (duration will vary but is often between three and six weeks). Planning includes focus activities and anticipated experiences linked to, for example, predictable interests (festivals, seasons, outside visits), a curricular focus or a theme. Assessment opportunities, key areas of learning, early learning goals, enhancement to provision and intended outcomes for the end of the period are identified. Sometimes medium-term plans are organised into sub sections (such as a week-by-week breakdown) to aid the process of informing short-term planning.

SHORT-TERM PLANNING

This involves planning in response to individual needs and interests, and includes activities and experiences selected from the medium-term planning. Short-term planning is usually undertaken on a weekly or daily basis and details learning objectives, foci for observation and assessment, targets and support for individuals, resources, key vocabulary, staff responsibilities, practical information (e.g. speech therapy appointments, anticipated timings of story sessions).

Figure 2.1 The planning process

What is a 'focus activity'?

A focus activity is an activity or experience that is planned in order to achieve particular objectives. Provision is organised in a way that will enable children to develop certain skills, knowledge, concepts and attitudes and the role of the adult in supporting their learning is clearly defined.

Why plan focus activities?

Reasons for planning a focus activity include:

- To target, and address the specific needs of, individual children and a group of children
- To highlight a particular area of learning and work towards achieving goals in that area
- To extend play initiated by the children and develop individual and group interests (this area will be covered more fully in Chapter 3, 'Starting points for developing learning through a focus')

Practitioners may also decide to plan a focus in an area of provision in order:

- To monitor children's use of resources and the effectiveness of an area of provision in achieving aims stated in the long-term plans (see Chapter 1)
- To monitor children's progress, assess needs, and record achievements (see Chapter 6)

Deciding on a framework for planning focus activities – what should be included?

It is important to bear in mind the purpose of the plan in terms of its use to the educator when deciding on a structure or format. The main questions to ask when determining what to include should be:

- Who will be using the plan?
- How will the plan support practitioners in structuring high-quality learning experiences?
- What information does the practitioner need in order to be well prepared and provide a rich learning environment?
- How will the plan support the adult in challenging children's thinking and extending their learning?

The plan must 'work' for those using it and standard formats may need to be modified to meet the needs of individual practitioners and teams of practitioners. It may be that the plan will be used by parent helpers, students or temporary staff unfamiliar with the setting, as well as by the permanent members of the team. Content may vary according to the setting and the age of the children.

The team need to discuss what to include in their planning structure, and then select or design a 'workable' format which helps practitioners to organise information in a way which is useful to them. Listed below are suggested elements for consideration:

- Focus areas of learning – the objectives may be cross-curricular or linked to a particular area of learning
- Learning objectives – these should be included in a prominent place on the plan
- QCA early learning goals – which particular goals will children be working towards during the activity?
- Target group – the activity may be planned to meet individual or group needs, or may be an activity open to all children but with opportunities for differentiation
- Children's prior learning – what knowledge and understanding can they build on?
- Date, time and expected duration
- Introduction, main activity, finishing off – content for each part of the activity presented in a clear sequence
- The role of the adult
- Questions to ask in order to extend children's learning
- Extension activities
- Key vocabulary
- Resources – basic provision, equipment and materials needed to enhance areas of provision
- Opportunities for assessment – what will the adult observe? How will observations be recorded? How will the information be used?
- Evaluation of the activity
- Next steps – what does the practitioner need to do to support and challenge the child?

To what extent should focus activities be planned in advance?

When planning for children's learning for the next few weeks (see 'medium-term planning', Figure 2.1), practitioners will discuss, as a team, activity ideas linked to objectives and will probably include these on a medium-term plan. Opportunities for child-initiated learning may also be anticipated in advance. There will, however, be frequent occasions when the practitioner will want to respond to children's immediate interests, enthusiasms and needs and plan a focus activity accordingly. Decisions of this nature will obviously need to be taken 'in progress' and in response to staff evaluation. Weekly plans should be flexible enough to allow adults to plan a focus at short notice (see Chapter 3).

It is not a productive use of time to be re-writing large amounts of information and practitioners should guard against such practice. Medium-term (see next example) and long-term plans (see Chapter 1) should help to focus and support adults in their short-term planning, but are not concerned with activity details.

A medium-term plan can provide a useful bank of ideas for focus planning but should never be so rigid or dominant as to exclude spontaneous planning in response to observed needs and interests. Predictable interests such as seasons, community events, weather conditions or schematic interests (e.g. enveloping, containing, transporting, trajectories) can be prepared for in advance and plans kept on file. Ideas can then be drawn from these medium-term plans and fed into short-term planning to support interests as they arise. They can also be used to motivate children to explore new experiences. Plans should always be evaluated for future reference and adults should not worry that they have not covered *all* planned learning – this probably indicates that they have adopted a more responsive approach to planning and achieved a balanced of adult- and child-initiated activities.

Using a medium-term plan to support focus planning

Example medium-term plan:

AUTUMN

Date and duration

- October/November 2004. This plan will be implemented as seasonal changes are observed

Key areas of learning

- Knowledge and understanding of the world (exploration and investigation), mathematical development (numbers as labels and for counting and shape, space and measures)

Suggested focus activities and anticipated experiences

- Walk around the nursery garden or school grounds observing changes
- Walk to park involving parents and carers
- Using collection trays to gather natural items of interest
- Gathering fallen leaves using wheelbarrows, long handled brushes and rakes
- Putting small stickers on leaves on trees in the nursery garden and monitoring what happens to them, recording a mark on a sheet every time one of the leaves falls and is found on the ground
- Investigating what happens to leaves when they are wet and dry

- Handling and talking about autumn leaves, using language related to size, shape and colour
- Sorting (e.g. number of points) and ordering leaves
- Looking at skeleton leaves on black paper
- Constructing autumn collection display
- Making leaf prints, rubbings, collages
- Drawing from observation
- Colour-mixing explorations, for example, red plus yellow equals orange
- Discussing seasonal changes and features of the weather
- Photographing trees at various stages documenting the changes from summer through autumn to winter

Enhancements to provision

Outdoor area: Rakes, sweeping brushes, plastic shovels, wheelbarrows, buckets, leaf collection sacks, gardening gloves, trays, clipboards, pencils or crayons, digital camera, magnifying glasses, binoculars, Wellington boots and rain coats, coloured stickers, number line.

Paint: Colour-mixing equipment (spatulas, yellow and red powder paint, palettes, water pots, brushes), photographs of autumn scenes.

Sand: Leaves, conkers, conker 'shells', acorns, etc.

Water: Autumn leaves.

Interactive display: Autumn posters, pictures, photographs, poems and story books. Natural items collected by children.

Book corner: Fiction and non-fiction books about autumn.

Vocabulary and questions

Vocabulary: Autumn, summer, winter. Weather vocabulary, for example, rain, wet, dry, foggy, sunny, cloudy, frosty, windy. Tree, trunk, branch, leaf. Colour names: green, red, yellow, orange, brown. Shape and measure language, for example, triangle, long, short, small, big, smaller, bigger,

Questions: Have you noticed what is happening in the nursery garden? How many different colours can you find? What will happen to the leaves after they have changed colour on the tree? Can you find another leaf the same colour or shape as this one? Which leaf do you think will fall off the tree next? How many of our 'marked' leaves have fallen? How many are still on the tree? How is this wet leaf different from the dry one? What do you think will happen if we put the wet leaf on the radiator? Look at the pattern on this leaf – is it the same as that one?

An overview of key areas of learning addressed through medium-term plans can be drawn up to show curricular breadth and balance in a similar way to the charting of long-term plans described in Chapter 1 (page 17).

Planning a focus activity

What will the children learn?

This is probably the most important, and should be the first question asked when planning any activity. What we want the children to learn should be the starting point for planning, and the activity, a vehicle for the children's learning.

Objectives may target a particular area of learning or be cross-curricular, but should always be clearly defined. Too many objectives become unmanageable – fewer (two or three will often be enough) carefully considered objectives will enable the adult to focus observations and interventions to support the child on their journey towards the intended outcomes. Focus areas of learning should be highlighted on the plan, and pertinent early learning goals identified – this will help practitioners to assess children's achievements in terms of national expectations.

Identifying the reason for planning an activity is the first step towards defining objectives. The practitioner may want to target a particular group of children and relate objectives to their needs – a focus can be an effective way of addressing the special educational needs of individuals. In order to set objectives at an appropriate level for the targeted children, the practitioner should take into account prior learning and achievements, and consider where the children need to go next.

For example:

A group of children have spent time over a period of days investigating a range of containers in the water area. They have poured and filled and talked about their observations, for example, Adam, pouring water from a jug – 'Look! It's going – now it's gone! I'm going to put some more in – right up to the top!' Sarah, using a large container full of water to fill a smaller one – 'It won't fit in it's going over the top'. The practitioner decides to build on this experience and extend the children's mathematical learning through a focus activity. The learning objectives are:

- To make comparisons between containers in terms of capacity
- To use mathematical language[1] when talking about their observations

---

[1] Key vocabulary should be identified on the plan, in this case: 'full', 'empty', 'more', 'less'.

When the practitioner decides to focus on goals in a particular area of learning, and intends for many children to access the activities, learning objectives should reflect the range of needs, and opportunities for differentiation stated on the plan, for example, early learning goal for communication, language and literacy.

By the end of the foundation stage, most children will be able to:

- Retell narratives in the correct sequence, drawing on the language patterns of stories

Having made the decision to focus on this particular goal, the practitioner will need to look carefully at the learning that needs to take place before the goal is achieved, and at where individuals are on their journey towards achieving the goal. Learning objectives which take into account the range of needs should then be defined and included, for example:

- To listen with interest, and respond, to a story
- To talk, and respond to questions, about events in a story
- To sequence story illustrations and talk about each picture in turn
- To retell, from memory, key events from a story in sequence
- To retell a story showing an understanding of the elements, and using language such as 'once upon a time', 'then', 'next', 'in the end'

It is important to remember that, although objectives may target certain areas of the curriculum, other learning will take place during the course of the activity – this may or may not be anticipated but should be valued. The purpose of setting objectives is to focus, not restrict, learning.

Once learning objectives have been identified, the nature and content of the activity can be decided.

The activity – what will the children do?

The next step is to plan an activity that will help children to achieve objectives. The activity should capture their interest and should be embedded in a context that is meaningful to them.

> *Learning objectives:*
> - To select appropriate tools and materials to build and construct
> - To retell key events, in sequence, from a familiar story

Activity: Building houses for the 'Three Little Pigs'

To help the adult in structuring the activity, a sequence of elements will probably be identified in the plan. In the case of the 'Three Little Pigs' example used, these could include:

Introduction

The adult will read the story of *The Three Little Pigs* and encourage the children to discuss reasons why the wolf was able to blow down the first two houses but not the third.

Main activity

Children will construct three houses using straw, sticks and bricks (wooden, or plastic interlocking). They will talk about the story as they work, discussing characters and events.

Finishing off and follow-up

Children will test each construction for strength using bellows to emulate the wolf's 'blowing'. The made houses will be displayed, and resources made available, all week so that children can revisit, and other children engage in, the activity. Laminated illustrations from *The Three Little Pigs* book will be displayed alongside the made houses and children encouraged to sequence these and retell the story to a friend.

Opportunities for differentiation and extension work

These should also be identified on the plan:

- Recording materials used in the construction of the house (tick lists, written lists, pictorial lists)
- Discussing which materials were the most successful and why (in terms of their properties)
- Looking at materials used to build real houses and architects' designs
- Making a plan of the made house or designing a different house
- Recording (audio tape) instructions for making a house
- Using 'Little Pig' puppets and puppet theatre to reconstruct the story
- Recording (audio tape) children retelling the story

Where will the activity take place?

This is an important decision and there will often be a number of alternatives to consider. The nature and quality of the children's learning will be determined to a large extent by the environment in which it takes place. Practitioners may choose to site the activity in an existing area of provision (possibly enhanced with additional resources) or may decide to create a new 'area' which will serve as a particularly rich and appropriate setting for the intended learning.

The following example illustrates the diversity of children's writing experience and the influence of the immediate environment on their learning.

Learning objective: To use writing to convey meaning

Table 2.1 The potential for writing in different areas

Example area	Potential writing experiences
Office	Letters, birthday cards, telephone messages, order forms, memos
Home corner	Party invitations, shopping lists, recipes, menus, telephone messages, catalogue orders, recounts stories
Construction	Plans, lists, traffic signs, instructions
Water	Poems, lists, records of 'findings'
Book area	Stories, book reviews, information

The choice of area may be influenced by the interests of targeted children. Those children who prefer to spend their time building castles in the construction area may not be inspired to engage in a writing activity in the office – this would be good reason, then, to take the writing to the construction area and ensure that it had meaning for those children. Activities could include: listing the resources they had used to build their castle, writing a story about their castle, writing invitations to the 'Castle Ball' and addressing envelopes to their favourite toys, making signs which direct the guests to the ballroom.

Figure 2.2 Taking a telephone message in the home corner

Alternatively, the adult may want to encourage children to work in an area that they rarely choose to frequent in order to develop certain skills and knowledge. In this case, the nature of the activity needs to have appeal for those children. For example, a group of children who show little enthusiasm for working in the construction area, but who frequently choose to play in the home corner, could be encouraged to engage in a building and constructing activity in the construction area by being challenged to build a table for their teddy bears' picnic, or a bed for their dolls, which they could then transfer to, and use, in the home corner.

Resources – what should be added to basic provision?

The resources offered to the children will be very influential in shaping their learning and should always be of the highest quality.

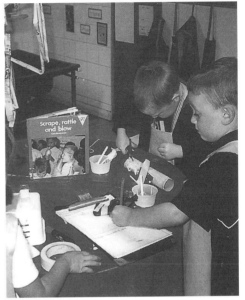

If an activity is sited in a permanent area of provision, it may be that the basic resources in this area are adequate in supporting the specific learning identified in the plan. It will almost certainly be the case that children use basic resources to some extent.

Practitioners may decide to 'enhance' provision in an area by adding extra resources in order to attract the children to the activity, stimulate imagination, help them to develop particular skills, knowledge and concepts, and as an extension of the basic provision.

Figure 2.3 Making musical instruments in the workshop area

Making musical instruments in the workshop

- *Basic workshop resources*: cardboard tubes, range of plastic tubs and pots, cardboard boxes, plastic bottles, treasury tags, paper clips, paper fasteners, rubber bands, glue (sticks and PVA), glue spreaders, sellotape, masking tape
- *Additional resources*: a range of musical instruments, tape recorder and a range of taped music; for use in 'shakers': sand, dried peas, beads, buttons, pebbles, dried leaves; for use on 'drums': pieces of fabric, thin plastic sheeting; recording 'frames'(for use by children – see Figure 2.4)

Figure 2.4 Making a musical instrument – recording frame

When a temporary area is set up, it will comprise mostly of resources additional to basic provision, although some will probably be duplicated in other areas of the setting.

Role-play: Builder's Office linked to a construction site

- Duplicated resources: pens, pencils, crayons, paper, clipboards, scissors, glue sticks, telephones
- New resources: builder's merchant's catalogues, invoice forms, order forms, architect's plans, walkie talkies/mobile phones

---

It is important to remind practitioners at this stage of their role as a valuable resource in the context of children's learning.

Adult role – what will the adult do?

The precise role of the adult will vary according to the activity but in general terms it is to support, directly or indirectly, the children's learning.

Direct support will involve:

- Stimulating children's interest in an activity

- Providing high-quality resources
- Listening and responding to children's talk
- Questioning children in order to extend learning (questions should be differentiated to address individual needs – see examples of activity plans)
- Working alongside children, modelling skills and use of key vocabulary
- Encouraging, reassuring and praising children
- Valuing and celebrating children's achievements

A period of observation before intervening in children's play will help the adult to decide on the timing and nature of the support.

> To make certain that positive intervention does not become futile interfering in a child's learning process, it must be preceded by sensitive observation and interaction with the child.
>
> (Nutbrown 1999)

Indirect support includes assessment, which starts with observation of children at work. In some circumstances, observation will be the main role of the adult, but there will be times when balancing interaction with observation seems an almost impossible task. This aspect of the educator's role will be explored in greater depth in Chapter 6, but, with regard to the focus activity, practitioners may find that referral to the learning objectives on the plan helps them to focus their observations, as in the following example.

Learning objectives

- To identify and talk about features of living things
- To use books as a source of information

Activity: observing tadpoles

Observation

- Kylie, watching the tadpoles, remarked: 'Look! Their legs are growing – I can see them wriggling when they swim. They haven't got any arms but their tails are very long – their tails are swimming too.' Kylie spent a few minutes studying the tadpoles and then asked 'When will they go on the rock – when will they jump?' Supported by Mrs Taylor, she found a book about frogs and pointed to a picture of a tadpole saying 'That's like ours – it's got legs and it's got a tail'. She was interested in looking at the 'frog development' pictures with Mrs Taylor – they discussed what would be the next stage of development for their tadpoles and agreed to watch out for any changes.

Assessment

- Kylie shows a keen interest in living things. She is able to recognise and talk about features of living things using everyday language. Kylie understands that information can be found in books. She is able, with support, to read pictures in information books to extend her own learning.

How long should a focus activity last?

The answer to this question is dependent on a number of factors and, although practitioners will need to allocate a 'time slot' on the weekly plan for pre-planned activities, it may be necessary to review timing as the week progresses. For example, children discover a snail in the outside play area on Monday and staff recognise the potential for developing a valuable learning experience. They decide to respond to the children's excitement and fascination by planning time on Tuesday and Wednesday to observe and find out about snails. They postpone the focus activity originally planned for Tuesday, to Thursday. In making this decision they are ensuring that both the snail investigation and the planned focus activity receive the adult input, and enthusiasm from the children, that they need to be successful in extending learning.

Practitioners may decide to review the length of time allocated to an activity as they gauge the children's response. It is difficult to anticipate duration and children's interest in the activity is often the deciding factor. Evaluation of the activity as a learning experience may lead staff to develop ideas and plan follow-up activities and extension work. It is often a good idea to make the additional resources used during the activity available for children to access (with or without adult input) for some time afterwards – this allows for exploration of ideas in a less structured context and consolidation of knowledge and concepts. Alternatively, the response of the children may have been disappointing and staff may decide to plan a different activity, but with the same learning objectives. In the latter case, the decision to 'cut short' the activity may be taken – there can be little purpose in pursuing an activity that holds no interest for the children.

How 'rigid' should the plan be?

The activity plan should be seen as a supportive framework within which the practitioner can work to challenge children's thinking and help them to make progress towards achieving intended outcomes. Objectives need to be 'tight' but the plan should be flexible enough to allow for professional judgement – it is the skill of the early years practitioner in recognising when and how to intervene in children's play as it progresses, and the quality of questioning in response to their play, which ensures that children benefit fully from the provision.

What should practitioners consider when evaluating the focus activity?

In order for an activity evaluation to be useful, it must provide practitioners with information that will enable them to improve their practice and focus future planning.

This will require consideration of a number of elements and it can be helpful to work within a framework or to use standard 'prompt' questions:

- How did the children respond to the activity? Did it capture their interest?
- Was the context appropriate or would another activity (or focus in another area of provision) have been more successful in achieving objectives?
- Look at the planned learning objectives – have these been achieved?
- How far are individuals or groups of children on their 'journey' towards the key early learning goals?
- What incidental learning took place and in which areas of the curriculum?
- What were the most effective strategies used by adults to support children's learning? How did this vary with different children and at different stages during the activity? Did the adult take on any unexpected roles?
- How will your observations feed into future planning? How could you extend learning further and support children's developing ideas and interests following the focus?
- What would you do differently next time if you planned this focus again?
- Are there any resource implications, for example, do you need to order new equipment or replace equipment?

Examples of focus activity plans

The following activities are planned in accordance with the guidelines given in this chapter. Learning objectives focus on a particular area of learning (personal, social and emotional development, language and literacy, mathematical development, knowledge and understanding of the world, physical development or creative development) and one example is given for each area of learning. Chapter 3 also includes examples of focus activity plans, some of which have cross-curricular learning objectives and others, objectives that focus on one area of learning. All activities have been 'tested' in an early years setting, have proved successful in achieving objectives and have been received with enthusiasm by children!

Examples of short-term planning for focus activities follow a common format and are organised under the following headings:

- Focus area of learning
- Learning objectives
- Early learning goals (QCA)
- Background and prior learning
- Introduction
- Main activity, key vocabulary and questions
- Finishing off and follow-up
- Adult role
- Key questions and vocabulary
- Resources

Communication, language and literacy: 'Jasper's Birthday'

This activity was planned during a topic on 'birthdays' and inspired many reluctant mark-makers to attempt writing. Jasper, a favourite puppet character, was used to motivate children and capture their imagination. The area of provision in which the invitation writing takes place is immaterial as long as adequate and appropriate resources are available to the child, although the most obvious choices are probably the office or the home corner. The initial activity will probably become the starting point for other imaginative and role-play activities which may offer additional opportunities for purposeful writing. It is a good idea to inform parents and carers of the focus of the activity so that they can support and extend their child's learning at home – children will probably want to invite their own soft toys to Jasper's birthday party!

FOCUS ACTIVITY: JASPER'S BIRTHDAY

Focus area of learning

- Communication, language and literacy

Learning objectives

- To understand that print conveys meaning
- To use own writing to communicate meaning
- To practise and develop writing skills in a real context

Working towards early learning goals for language and literacy (QCA 2000)

By the end of the foundation stage, most children will be able to:

- Know that print carries meaning and, in English, is read from left to right and top to bottom

- Attempt writing for various purposes, using features of different forms such as lists, stories and instructions

- Write their own names and other things such as labels and captions and begin to form simple sentences, sometimes using punctuation

(Writing)

- Use a pencil and hold it effectively to form recognisable letters, most of which are correctly formed

(Handwriting)

Background information and prior learning

All children will have experience of mark-making with a range of tools. They will be familiar with adults modelling purposeful writing and reading. They will be at different stages in their writing development and the adult will address individual needs in questions asked (adult role, key vocabulary and questions). All children will have met Jasper, the puppet, in other contexts on previous occasions. Most children will have first-hand experience of birthday parties.

Introduction

The adult will introduce Jasper and explain to the children that he is very excited because it is his birthday today. The children will be shown an envelope and parcel that have arrived in the post addressed to Jasper. They will be encouraged to guess what is inside and then a child will be invited to help Jasper to open his card and present. The group will sing 'Happy Birthday' to Jasper and be asked if they would like to join in his birthday celebrations.

Main activity

The children and the adult will discuss their own experiences of birthday parties. They will send birthday cards to Jasper, wrap up birthday gifts and plan a birthday party. Writing experiences will include signing names on cards and gift tags, writing envelopes, place names, menus and shopping lists for party food.

Finishing off and follow-up

The birthday party will be planned to take place in the home corner. Children will be encouraged to write party invitations to their own soft toys from home. Photographs will be taken of the party and displayed in an album in the home corner. Children may also help Jasper to write 'thank you' letters for his presents.

Adult role

The adult will:

- Provide resources
- Stimulate interest in the activity and engage in role-play
- Model writing skills
- Ask differentiated questions
- Be aware of each child's stage of writing development and support them at their own level
- Observe children (re: enthusiasm for mark-making, purposes for writing, pencil control and letter formation) and record observations

Key questions

What do you think is inside the envelope? Who has sent it? Why? What do you think the writing says? Where do we start to read the writing? What information do we need to include in the invitation? Can you see where Susie has written her name? What is your doll's name? Can you write her name on the envelope? Where will you write your name? Can you find your name card and copy your name or write your name without your name card? Can you read back your writing?

Resources

- Birthday card (written) in envelope addressed to Jasper
- Wrapped present with Jasper's name written on it
- Mark-making tools (pencils, pens)
- Paper, card, folded card (birthday cards, shopping lists, labels, etc.)
- Commercially produced, blank birthday cards
- Invitation writing frames
- Wrapping paper, tape

Mathematical development: 'make a game'

This activity was planned as part of a focus on mathematical development and, although key goals have been highlighted, it offers numerous learning opportunities in all three aspects of this curricular area. The activity was particularly successful when children worked together to agree rules and then engaged in playing the game they had devised.

FOCUS ACTIVITY: 'MAKING GAMES'

Focus area of learning:

- Mathematical development

Learning objectives

- To make up their own games
- To count, and to recognise and use numbers, up to six
- To explore pattern in their play using the language of position and orientation

---

Working towards early learning goals for mathematical development (QCA 2000)

- Count reliably up to ten everyday objects.
- Recognise numerals 1–9

(Numbers as labels and for counting)

- In practical activities and discussion begin to use the vocabulary involved in adding and subtracting

(Calculating)

- Talk about, recognise and recreate simple patterns

(Shape, space and measures)

Background information and prior learning

Long-term plans for areas of provision include opportunities for children to develop awareness and understanding of number and attributes such as colour, size and shape in a variety of contexts. Children will have had a number of opportunities to play simple board games with an adult in the setting and some will have had similar experiences at home.

Introduction

The adult will introduce the new resources to the children, allowing them time to handle and explore equipment and to talk about their observations. The group will discuss the contexts in which children have used dice or spinners before and discuss their experiences of board games. The adult will then encourage children to use equipment in a more focused way, for example, by rolling a die and then moving a button the same number of spaces (as the dots shown on the die) on a grid.

Main activity

Children will make up their own games, selecting from the equipment available and experimenting with rule structures. They will play games with each other and the adult. (See Figure 2.5 for examples of games made up by children).

Finishing off and follow-up

This activity will be available over a period of time to enable children to develop their ideas and modify games. Children will be encouraged to explain the rules of their games and their instructions will be scribed. Rules will be recorded on 'game cards' (see Figure 2.5). Parents will be invited to play children's made-up games in the setting and 'game sets' will be put together in boxes for children to borrow overnight. Adults will take opportunities to develop children's understanding of number and calculation within the context of their play primarily through modelling and questioning.

Adult role

The adult will:

- Gather resources and present in an organised and attractive way, for example, sorting equipment stored in segmented trays or labelled baskets
- Stimulate interest in the activity, modelling ideas and involving children in playing games
- Model use of key vocabulary
- Support children in making links and agreeing rules
- Challenge thinking through differentiated questioning
- Observe children and record evidence of their achievements towards the key goals

Key vocabulary and questions

Vocabulary: Number names (one–six), colour names, 'more', 'less', 'add', 'count', 'count on', 'next', 'first', 'last', 'same', 'different'.

Questions: The dice shows red, can you find a red reel to put on the grid? Whose turn is it now? How many more spaces does the blue button need to move before it reaches the end? How many spaces has your reel moved already? Your two dice show two and three – how many is that altogether? What colour do you need next to carry on your pattern?

Resources

- Laminated grids (some blank, some with a colour in each space and some with a number at the end of each column)
- Paper copies of blank grid
- Dice and spinners (spots, numerals and colours)
- Coloured pencils or felt pens
- Sorting equipment (e.g. buttons, plastic reels, transport sorting set)

Children's Games

Spotty Patterns

Rules:

- Roll the colour die.
- Choose a pen the same colour as the colour shown on the die.
- Make a coloured spot in a space on the grid.
- Carry on until all the spaces are filled and look at the pattern you have made!

Numbers and spots

Rules:

- Roll the number die.
- Draw the same number of spots in a space on the grid as the numeral shown on the die.
- Carry on until you have filled the spaces.
- Count how many spots are in each column – which is the 'winner'?

Bear race

Rules:

- Roll the colour die and, whatever colour shows, find a bear of the same colour and match it to a coloured spot on the board.
- When all the spots of one colour have been covered, the game in over and that colour has won!

Figure 2.5 Children's games

Figure 2.6 Making up games

Knowledge and understanding of the world: making boats

This activity was planned following an investigation of materials in the water tray. The practitioner wanted children to use their prior knowledge in responding to a challenge and solving a practical problem. The story *Where the Wild Things Are* by Maurice Sendak was a familiar tale and Max, a favourite character. The story was used to motivate the children, give purpose to their designing, and criteria for success when testing their boat 'structures'. The activity is a good example of using two areas of provision (water and workshop) in one activity, and could take place inside or outside.

FOCUS ACTIVITY: MAKING BOATS

Focus area of learning

- Knowledge and understanding of the world

Learning objectives

- To design and construct for a specific purpose
- To use prior knowledge in problem-solving
- To select tools and materials appropriately
- To evaluate the success of a design and make necessary modifications

Working towards early learning goals for knowledge and understanding of the world (QCA 2000)

- Build and construct with a wide range of objects, selecting appropriate resources, and adapting their work where necessary
- Select the tools and techniques they need to shape, assemble and join the materials they are using

(Designing and making)

Background information and prior learning

Children will have been given opportunities for exploration of materials. They will have talked about properties and investigated how different materials react when placed in water. Children will understand the concepts of 'floating' and 'sinking' and will be familiar with the key vocabulary. They will have experience of using a range of tools and materials in the workshop area. Children will be familiar with the story *Where the Wild Things Are*.

Introduction

The children will be reminded of the recently read story *Where the Wild Things Are*. The adult will explain to the children that Max's boat has a leak and cannot be used, but that he is desperate to visit the 'Wild Things' again. The adult will show the children models of Max and the Wild Things (Max placed at one end of the water tray and the Wild Things at the other) and ask for suggestions as to how Max could cross the 'ocean'. They will discuss suggestions (see key questions) and children will be challenged to build a boat that will carry Max to the 'Wild Things'.

Main activity

The children will build a boat for Max using tools and materials in the workshop (see 'resources'). They will look at information books about boats. They will talk about prior investigations and use their knowledge from these to inform their decisions. They will test their boat in the water tray to determine whether or not it floats and will make any necessary modifications.

Finishing off and follow-up

Children will put the 'Max' model in their boat and transport him to the other side of the 'ocean' and the 'Wild Things'. Some children will record their work (see resources).

Adult role

The adult will:

- Provide resources
- Stimulate children's imagination and interest in the activity
- Be aware of children's prior learning and build on their knowledge
- Ask questions in order to extend learning
- Support children in recording their work
- Observe the children re: appropriate use of tools and materials, ability to design for a purpose and evaluate success of their design or modify their design, ability to record work

Figure 2.7 Testing Max's boat in the water tray

Key vocabulary and questions

Vocabulary: Float, sink

Questions: How can we help Max to cross the 'ocean'? Examples of suggestions: Make a bridge – how could it stretch all the way across? What could we use to support it? Would it be too far for Max to walk? He could swim – is Max strong enough to swim all that way? How could he carry his suitcase? What would happen if there were sharks in the water? Make a boat – what would we use for the bottom of the boat, the cabin, the sail or the mast? What happens to this material if it gets wet? Do you think this plastic pot will float? Let's test it in the water tray – were you right? How could you stop your boat from sinking? Where will Max sit in your boat? Does your boat still float when it is carrying Max? What did you use to make your boat? Which materials were successful or unsuccessful?

Resources

- *Where the Wild Things Are* by Maurice Sendak
- Max and 'Wild Things' models
- Information books about boats
- Basic provision in workshop area and water area (see long-term plans for these areas of provision)
- Recording frames

Creative development: story-making and imaginative play

It seems that anything that is introduced to children out of a sealed box, bag or envelope can be exciting to them. Such an introduction, especially when children are encouraged to anticipate what might be inside, is usually very effective in stimulating imagination and inspiring enthusiasm for an activity. In this case, a key inside a decorated box is the stimulus but other resources could be just as successful in prompting creative ideas, for example:

- A tiara in a jewellery box
- A purse in a handbag
- An ornate silver spoon in a velvet pouch
- A photograph (e.g. a character or building) in an envelope
- A gem stone or piece of crystal in a small satin-lined box
- A large, exotic shell wrapped in tissue paper

Whatever the stimulus, during an activity of this nature the practitioner should provide children with the necessary resources for them to develop their imaginative ideas. The introduction of this particular activity took place in the book corner. This area was chosen because it was enclosed on three sides (and relatively free from distractions) and because there was ample provision for all involved children to sit comfortably. The story-making and imaginative play took place throughout the setting but, as play progressed and it was agreed that the key probably opened a box of treasure lost at sea, children and staff decided to build a ship in the outside area so that they could search for the treasure.

FOCUS ACTIVITY: STORY-MAKING AND IMAGINATIVE PLAY

Focus area of learning

- Creative development

Learning objectives

To respond imaginatively to a stimulus

To express thoughts and ideas through imaginative play

Working towards early learning goals for creative development (QCA 2000)

- Use their imagination in art and design, music, dance, imaginative and role-play and stories

(Imagination)

- Respond in a variety of ways to what they see, hear, smell, touch and feel
- Express and communicate their ideas, thoughts and feelings by using a widening range of materials, suitable tools, imaginative and role-play, designing and making, and a variety of songs and musical instruments

(Responding to experiences and expressing and communicating ideas)

Background information and prior learning

Children will have experience of listening to stories and of engaging in and observing imaginative play.

Introduction

The adult will show the children a 'very special box' and ask them to guess what is inside. The box will be opened to reveal a key (see resources). Children will be encouraged to handle the key in turn and describe how it looks and feels.

Main activity

The adult will lead the children, through questioning (see key questions), in creating a story around the key. They will express ideas which the adult will scribe. The children will then be encouraged to work as a group to develop their 'key story' ideas through imaginative play. Children will use the key, and other props (see resources), in their play.

Finishing off and follow-up

Children will be encouraged to share their stories and ideas with other children at a group gathering. Some children will record their story ideas pictorially and/or in a written form. A book will be compiled using photographs taken of resources and children's play, and children's story ideas (recorded by them or scribed by the adult). Children will be allowed continued access to resources, and time, to develop ideas.

Adult role

The adult will:

- Provide resources
- Stimulate interest in the activity and build up anticipation (re: opening the box)
- Ask questions, and make suggestions, in order to develop imaginative ideas
- Encourage children to express ideas, and value their contributions
- Scribe children's ideas
- Support children in recording their ideas at their own level

- Observe children's play re: response to activity, use of imagination, ability to express ideas.
- Record observations in individual profiles
- Photograph children at play
- Compile a book of their work

Key vocabulary and questions

Questions: Where do you think the box was found? Who left it there? What do you think is inside the box? Who does the key belong to? What has happened – has the person lost the key? – Has it been stolen? What will the key open – a secret door? – A box? – A cupboard? – A treasure chest? – A case? What will you do with the key? Where will you go – how will you use it? How will you find the owner of the key? Who will go with you? What happens on your journey to find the owner of the key?

Resources

- A 'special box' (e.g. painted gold and decorated with 'jewels') containing an elaborate key
- Additional resources such as large cardboard boxes, pieces of fabric, a variety of hats
- Mark-making tools, paper
- Camera

Personal, social and emotional development: showing and talking about special toys from home

The 'special toys' activity was planned during a 'Toys' topic but also to address the needs of some of the newer, or less sure children in the setting. Staff had recognised that group discussions were often dominated by the more confident children, and that some individuals were not participating at all. They planned an activity that would offer each child an opportunity to contribute without competition, and encourage all children to listen to, and value, the contributions of others.

Children are likely to feel more confident when talking about personal experiences, familiar situations and their own belongings, and some of the children's responses to the 'special toys' activity surprised even the staff. Supported by an adult, and with their own toy as a 'prop', children who usually took a passive role during group discussions were suddenly forthcoming, responding enthusiastically to questions and giving full demonstrations to the group of, for example, the capabilities of their remote-control cars or the musical ability of their singing teddy bears. The 'Special Toy Book' of photographs proved to be very popular and prompted much discussion between children.

FOCUS ACTIVITY:
SHOWING AND TALKING ABOUT SPECIAL TOYS FROM HOME

Focus area of learning

- Personal, social and emotional development

Learning objectives

- To share experiences and feelings in a familiar group
- To speak confidently when it is their turn
- To listen to, and value, the contributions of others

Working towards early learning goals for personal, social and emotional development (QCA 2000)

- Be confident to try new activities, initiate ideas and speak in a familiar group
- Maintain attention, concentrate, and sit quietly when appropriate

(Dispositions and attitudes)

- Have a developing awareness of their own needs, views and feelings and be sensitive to the needs, views and feelings of others

(Self-confidence and self-esteem)

- Work as part of a group or class, taking turns and sharing fairly, understanding that there need to be agreed values and codes of behaviour for groups of people, including adults and children, to work together harmoniously

(Making relationships)

Background information and prior learning

Attitudes of respect for the feelings of others and interest in the experiences and work of others are promoted through all areas of provision and learning. Children will be familiar with the following 'rule': sit quietly and listen when it is someone else's turn to speak. A letter of explanation about this activity will have been sent home and parents and carers encouraged to discuss with their child: choice of toy, reasons for choice, feelings about the toy, history of and experiences with the toy.

Introduction

The adult will invite the small group of children to bring their special toys and join her or him in a comfortable area of the setting. The children will be asked to sit in a circle.

Main activity

The adult will show the children a toy from her or his childhood and explain why the toy holds special memories. Individual children will be encouraged to talk about their own special toy and other children will be given opportunities to ask them questions. When all the children have had a turn, they will sing (to the tune of 'Here we go round the Mulberry Bush'):

> Jack showed us his car today, car today, car today,
> Jack showed us his car today – thank you Jack.

This song will be repeated for every child.

Finishing off and follow-up

Children's toys will be kept on the 'special toys display' until the end of the session. Photographs will be taken of each child with their toy and their comments about the toy scribed by the adult. These will be displayed in a 'Special Toy Book' to be kept in the book corner. (NB All children will be given the opportunity to take part in this activity over the course of two to three weeks.)

Adult role

The adult will:

- Help the children to feel relaxed in a comfortable and welcoming environment
- Encourage the children to talk about their toy, asking questions and showing interest in what they say
- Remind children of the 'rule' (see background information and prior learning) when necessary
- Take photographs of children and scribe their comments, compile book
- Observe children re: confidence in speaking in a group, ability to use language to express themselves, response to other children's contributions

Key vocabulary and questions

Questions: What have you brought to show us today? Why did you choose this toy to show us? What is special about the toy? What would you like to tell us about the toy? Who gave you the toy? Where and what do you like to play with the toy?

Resources

- Letter to parents and carers to be sent home prior to activity (see background information and prior learning)
- Adult's toy
- Children's toys
- Camera

Physical development: going on a 'Bear Hunt' – obstacle course

This is another example of a favourite story being used as the starting point for an activity (Chapter 3 offers further examples of stories as starting points). The 'Bear Hunt' took place in the outside area and this is the ideal site for the activity. A large hall could be used as a 'wet weather' alternative but, if the hall is not accessible on a permanent basis, use of the resources over the following few days (as recommended in the plan) may be difficult to organise. The activity allowed staff to observe a range of skills, enabling them to make clear assessments of children's physical development. Most children chose to participate in the activity and some continued to set up their own bear hunts long after the 'focus' had passed.

FOCUS ACTIVITY:
GOING ON A 'BEAR HUNT' – OBSTACLE COURSE

Focus area of learning

- Physical development

Learning objectives

- To develop jumping, balancing, climbing, hopping, running skills
- To move with imagination and confidence
- To develop spatial awareness

Working towards early learning goals for physical development (QCA 2000)

- Move with confidence, imagination and in safety
- Move with control and co-ordination

(Movement)

- Show awareness of space, of themselves and of others

(Sense of space)

Background information and prior learning

Children will have had daily opportunities to develop gross motor skills.

There will be children at different stages of physical development – the activity will be open to all children and the adult should be aware of the range and nature of needs in order to give effective support.

Introduction

The adult will read the story *We're Going on a Bear Hunt* by Michael Rosen, the children will join in with the words and actions. The adult will ask the children if they would like to go on a bear hunt. They will pack imaginary bags and begin their hunt.

Main activity

The children, with the adult, will follow the obstacle course to the bear cave. For example:

- Climbing over a mountain – climbing up a ladder and over the climbing frame
- Going through a dark tunnel – crawling through the barrel
- Walking over a bridge – balancing on a plank
- Wading through a muddy swamp – walking over tyres
- Crossing a river on stepping-stones – stepping on different-sized wooden hollow blocks
- Following a narrow path – walking on a wavy chalk line
- Walking through a thick forest – weaving in and out of cones
- Jumping over a stream – jumping over two parallel chalk lines

Children may want to chant the words from the 'Bear Hunt' story or make up their own chants. When they reach the bear cave, they will go inside, discover the imaginary bear and run to the other side of the play area.

Finishing off and follow-up

The 'Bear Hunt' obstacle course will be set up in the outside play area for a few days to allow children to revisit the activity and practise skills. The resources may be organised in a different way each day, or new resources introduced, in order to add interest or extend learning.

Adult role

The adult will:

- Set up obstacle course and bear cave in outside play area
- Read the story and stimulate interest in the activity
- Lead the 'Bear Hunt'
- Encourage children to join in
- Talk to them using suggested vocabulary
- Support children at their own stage of physical development
- Observe children re: physical skills, confidence, spatial awareness, and record their achievements

Key vocabulary and questions

Vocabulary: The adult will use, and encourage the children to use, words such as 'through', 'over', 'under', 'in', 'out', 'up', 'down'.

Questions: Can you go over or under the bridge? How will you get to the other side of the river? Is there enough room for you and Tom to be on the bridge at the same time? Can you step across the stream or do you need to jump? Can you walk in between the cones without touching them? Can you step from the middle of one tyre to the next without touching the rubber? Can you balance on the top of the tyre?

Resources

- *We're Going on a Bear Hunt* by Michael Rosen
- Tyres, wooden planks and blocks, barrel, ladders, climbing frame, cones, chalk

Key Points for Good Practice

- Remember that inspiration for focus planning can come from a variety of sources. Long- and medium-term plans will offer ideas but children's observed needs and interests should always be the paramount consideration.
- Guard against medium-term topic plans dominating children's experiences. Ideas should be offered but not imposed.
- Be aware that a focus should always have a purpose that is understood by the child and should take place in a meaningful context within the learning environment.
- Link plans to key early learning goals and differentiate them to address the needs of all children accessing the focus.
- Be prepared to abandon a pre-planned focus in favour of pursuing a spontaneous and more exciting interest. The original focus can always be introduced, if appropriate, at a later date.
- Value children's individual responses to a focus and support them in following up their own ideas.
- Recognise the importance of evaluating a focus and the positive impact that this can have on future practice. Make sure that there are systems in place so that practitioners can share such information.

The valuing and sharing of children's play by adults can only serve to increase the status of the activity and the self-esteem of the child.

(Abbot and Rodger 1994)

CHAPTER 3

Starting points for developing learning through a focus

By the end of the foundation stage, most children will:

● Continue to be interested, excited and motivated to learn.

(QCA 2000)

The content of this chapter is organised as follows:

Chapter 2 looked at why and how to plan a focus activity, this chapter aims to explore different stimuli for developing learning through focus activities in the early years environment. It consists mostly of ideas and plans which are offered as examples of starting points for activities and which are intended to be of practical use to the reader. The list is by no means exhaustive, merely a sample. Early years practitioners are on a constant quest for new and exciting ways of inspiring young children's learning and the sharing and pooling of ideas is to be encouraged. Practitioners may choose to use these plans in a variety of ways – they may follow the plans closely, decide to modify them according to setting and children's needs, or use them as a 'springboard' for their own ideas. Some plans focus learning objectives in one area of learning, others have broader intentions; all follow the same format as the focus activities in Chapter 2.

It is a privilege to work with young children, for whom learning is an exciting voyage of discovery, and also a great responsibility, since experiences in the early years play a vital part in shaping future attitudes to learning and in inspiring a continuing thirst for knowledge. It is the role of the early years practitioner to nurture and respond to children's natural curiosity and motivation and to engage them in the learning process.

An effective early years curriculum recognises the need for children to be 'active learners'. Through interacting with, and responding to, the world around them, children acquire skills and knowledge and develop concepts. Well planned provision in the early years environment will offer them a wealth of exciting opportunities for exploration and investigation (see Chapters 1 and 5).

Planning from children's interests and enthusiasms

The QCA *Curriculum Guidance for the Foundation Stage* (2000) acknowledges the 'provision for children to take part in activities that build on and extend their interests' as good early years practice. A young child's world is their 'classroom'. A great deal of their learning takes place outside the nursery or pre-school setting and this should be recognised by the practitioner. Interests and experiences that children bring from home should be valued, celebrated and, if appropriate, used as a starting point for developing learning in the early years setting. Children also develop interests within the setting and may even be inspired by another child's interests, becoming involved in related activities – this situation offers rich opportunities for the sharing of knowledge and ideas and can lead to valuable learning experiences across the curriculum.

For example:

Joe visited a safari park at the weekend and returned to nursery on Monday full of enthusiasm for the experience. He was given an opportunity to talk about his visit to a small group of children and to show the brochure and plastic elephant he had brought back. Other children were encouraged to ask him questions and a child was asked to bring the box of 'jungle animals' from the construction area. They looked at each animal in turn, naming them and discussing their features – Joe, and the other children, were encouraged to share knowledge and to use information books to further their knowledge.

A group of children (including Joe), inspired by the discussion, went to the construction area and spent the rest of the session building 'jungle environments' and story-making. The adult observed parts of their play and decided to plan a focus in the construction area the next day (see activity plan: 'Jungle Play').

FOCUS ACTIVITY:
'JUNGLE PLAY' (See Figure 6.7, Chapter 6)

Focus areas of learning

- Creative development
- Communication, language and literacy
- Personal, social and emotional development

Learning objectives

- To use resources imaginatively
- To take part as a speaker and a listener in a small group
- To express thoughts and story ideas
- To negotiate and work co-operatively

Working towards early learning goals for focus areas of learning (QCA 2000)

- Continue to be interested, excited and motivated to learn

  (Dispositions and attitudes)

- Interact with others, negotiating plans and activities and taking turns in conversation

  (Language for communication)

- Use language to imagine and recreate roles and experiences

  (Language for thinking)

- Use their imagination in art and design, music, dance, imaginative and role-play and stories

  (Imagination)

- Express and communicate their ideas, thoughts and feelings by using a widening range of materials, suitable tools, imaginative and role-play, movement, designing and making and a variety of songs and musical instruments

  (Responding to experiences and expressing and communicating ideas)

Background information and prior learning

Joe visited a safari park at the weekend. He enthusiastically shared his experiences with a small group of children and has inspired some imaginative 'jungle play' and story-making in the construction area. After observation of children's play, staff agreed that adding extra resources (see 'resources') to the area and planning some adult focus time would be likely to extend their learning in the focus areas. Targeted group: Joe, Lucy, Sameena, Jake and Andrew (this group will not be exclusive if other children choose to participate in the activity).

Introduction

The adult will show the children the extra resources and explain the purpose of these (i.e. for use by children in their 'jungle play').

Main activity (construction area)

Children will continue their 'jungle play' and story-making using basic provision in the construction area and additional resources (see Figure 6.7, Chapter 6).

Finishing off and follow-up

Additional resources and the children's constructions will remain in the area to allow for re-visiting of the activity and continuation of imaginative play and story-making. The precise nature of any follow-up work will be determined by the direction taken by the children in their play. There may be possibilities for making information or story books using photographs of the children's play, their ideas scribed by the adult and examples of their drawings and writing.

Adult role

The adult will:

- Value children's experiences outside the setting
- Provide resources
- Recognise when to intervene in children's play and when to 'stand back'
- Scribe children's imaginative and story ideas
- Question children about their play
- Observe children re: response to activity, ability to work co-operatively and express ideas, use of imagination in play
- Make a book or display (e.g. children's ideas, photographs of their play)

Key vocabulary and questions

Vocabulary: Animal names, for example, elephant, lion, giraffe, gorilla, crocodile.

Questions: How may different animals live in your jungle? Can you name the animals? Why has this lion climbed to the top of the mountain? Would you like to explain to Lisa why the snake is hiding under the leaves? Are there any people in the jungle? Why are they there? How did they get there? Would you like to go to this jungle? What can you feel, see and hear in the jungle?

Resources

- Basic resources in the construction area including box of 'jungle animals'
- Additional resources: fiction and non-fiction books about jungles and animals, pieces of fabric (different textures, natural colours), crepe and tissue paper, cellophane, cardboard tubes and boxes

The children's interest in the 'jungle theme' deepened. They revisited the construction area over the course of a few days, modifying their 'jungles' and creating more elaborate and imaginative stories. By this time other children were showing an interest in their work, some attempting to join in and others choosing to observe.

At this point the practitioner decided to plan another focus activity in order to develop particular skills using the jungle interest as a starting point. This time the whole group was involved as a letter from 'Lion' was read out:

FOCUS ACTIVITY: 'LION'S VISIT' (BUILDING A DEN)

Focus area of learning

- Knowledge and understanding of the world

Learning objectives

- Explore properties of materials
- To select and use tools and materials appropriately
- To design and construct for a specific purpose
- To make plans and lists of the materials they have used

Figure 3.1 Lion arrives in his box

Working towards early learning goals for focus areas of learning (QCA)

- Build and construct with a wide range of objects, selecting appropriate resources, and adapting their work where necessary
- Select the tools and techniques they need to shape, assemble and join the materials they are using

(Designing and making)

Background information and prior learning

A group of children have been pursuing a 'jungle interest' in the construction area. The focus activity planned in response to this interest has been successful in achieving its objectives and children are still very enthusiastic about the jungle theme. Staff have therefore decided to use the theme again, this time as a starting point for developing technology skills. This activity will be open to all children.

Introduction

The children will be shown a large, 'camouflaged' cardboard box and invited to guess who is inside. 'Lion' will then appear from inside his box and 'tell' the children that he has come to spend some time with them. He will present them with a letter (see 'resources') asking them to build a den for him and his family. Lion will explain to the children that he has brought a box of additional resources with him to help them in this task.

Main activity (workshop, construction area and outside play area)

Children will handle and talk about the resources in Lion's box. They will then use basic resources and Lion's additional resources to build a den to Lion's specifications. This activity can take place in any suitable area (see previous suggestions). They will be encouraged to make plans and lists as they work.

Finishing off and follow-up

Children will talk about the dens they have built, explaining what they did and used. They will test the dens according to the criteria in Lion's letter, for example, size, safety and warmth.

Adult role

The adult will:

- Make Lion's box and provide all other resources
- Stimulate interest in activity, building up excitement and anticipation during the introduction
- Work alongside children asking questions, modelling (building, drawing plans, writing lists) scribing children's ideas (lists, plans)
- Observe children re: appropriate selection and use of tools and materials, ideas, enthusiasm for and ability to record ideas

Key vocabulary and questions

Questions: Who do you think is inside the box? Where has he come from? How did he get here? What will you use to build the walls of the den? How can we make the walls stronger? How can we make and support the roof? Is the den wide and tall enough for Lion and his family? How can we make it wider or taller? How can we make the den warmer? What shall we use to cover the floor? What did we use to build our den?

Resources

- Lion (soft toy) inside a box camouflaged with, for example, brown and green paper, paint or material
- Lion's letter (see Figure 3.2)
- Lion's box of additional resources, for example, cardboard boxes, lengths of fabric, paper (crepe, tissue, etc.), balsa wood, scissors, string, masking tape
- Photographs of lions and jungle environments, maps of Africa, safari travel brochures
- Paper, pens, pencils
- Recording frame (see Figure 1.3, page 11)
- Outside resources: Milk crates, large cardboard boxes, tyres, wooden hollow blocks, planks, lengths of fabric, 'den' frame
- Outside equipment tick list (see Figure 3.3)

Dear Children,

Thank you for welcoming me to your nursery. Your teachers have told me about the exciting jungles you have created in your construction area and I was wondering if you would build a den for my family and me to stay in during our visit.

The den would need to be big enough for 3 cubs, their mother and me. It would also need to be warm and safe.

Can you help?

Yours hopefully,
The Lion.

Figure 3.2 Lion's letter

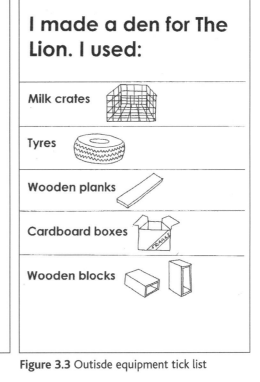

I made a den for The Lion. I used:

Milk crates

Tyres

Wooden planks

Cardboard boxes

Wooden blocks

Figure 3.3 Outisde equipment tick list

Figure 3.4 Lion's den in the construction area   **Figure 3.5** Lion's den in the outside area

The following example illustrates again how an experience that excites and engages a child can be used as a motivational 'springboard' for follow-up learning. In this particular nursery, children had been busy preparing for the arrival of two goldfish. When the fish were actually introduced, a number of children chose to spend a large part of the morning watching and talking about them. The practitioner took advantage of this opportunity for extending children's ideas and language and also scribed their comments. These words and phrases were crafted by the practitioner and children into a simple poem. The poem was then shared with other children, adults in the setting, parents and carers.

> Our Goldfish
> Fishes flying and dancing in the water,
> Their tails wobbling from side to side.
> Fishes laughing and talking – pop, pop,
> Their mouths sucking and blowing in and out.
> Fishes looking for food, playing hide and seek,
> Their eyes moving like a wheel – black and gold and shiny.
> Fishes sleeping quietly in their home,
> Bubbles going up and up – bump, bump, bump.

Sometimes children's interests are of a more tactile, investigative nature. The following activity was planned in response to a child's fascination with the consistency and texture of substances such as wet and dry glue, paint and cornflour 'gloop' (a mixture of cornflour and water which changes consistency as it dries out, and which provides compelling tactile experiences). It is one of many activities that could have been planned to allow the child further scope for exploration.

FOCUS ACTIVITY:
MIXING TEXTURED PAINT

Focus areas of learning

- Creative development
- Knowledge and understanding of the world

Learning objectives

- To explore texture and consistency in paint
- To investigate a range of materials

Working towards early learning goals for focus areas of learning (QCA 2000)

- Investigate objects and materials by using all of their senses as appropriate
- Look closely at similarities, differences, patterns and change

(Exploration and investigation)

- Explore colour, texture, shape, form and space in two and three dimensions

(Exploring media and materials)

- Respond in a variety of ways to what they see, hear, smell, touch and feel

(Responding to experiences and expressing and communicating ideas)

Background information and prior learning

Staff have noticed Simon showing a keen interest in texture and consistency. All children have experience of paint mixing.

Introduction

The adult will arrange resources on the 'paint table' and encourage children to touch and talk about the dry materials (e.g. sand, sawdust). She or he will then explain that they are going to mix some paint, add different materials to it and then use the paint as a medium to create an image on paper.

Main activity

Children will mix powder paint with water and then choose 'ingredients' to add. They will observe and talk about the changes that occur and compare 'mixtures'. They will then apply the paint to paper and discuss effects.

Finishing off and follow-up

Children's work will be allowed to dry and any changes during the drying process discussed. Their paintings will be displayed in the 'Gallery' alongside original paintings by artists (examples will be selected to show the use of texture, for example, thick oil paint).

Adult role

The adult will:

Provide resources

- Ask questions and encourage use of descriptive vocabulary
- Model use of descriptive vocabulary
- Observe children re: response to activity, expression of ideas and observations, use of descriptive language
- Construct 'Gallery' display

Key vocabulary and questions

Vocabulary: Children will be encouraged to use descriptive vocabulary related to texture and consistency, for example, runny, thick, lumpy, smooth, sticky.

Questions: What does it feel and look like? Is it difficult to stir? What do you think will happen if we add some more sand? What has happened to the sawdust now you have put it in the paint? How has it changed? Does it pour, drip or fall off your brush? Does it look and feel any different now that it has dried?

Resources

- Powder paint, water, plastic pots, brushes (a range of thicknesses)
- Paper: smooth and textured (e.g. 'woodchip' wallpaper)
- A range of 'ingredients', for example, sand, sawdust, PVA glue, rice, soil, flour, cold water paste (check that it is safe for use by children)
- Original oil paintings

Although an individual child's interest inspired this activity, it was popular with many. Staff were interested to observe that, while most children were keen to apply the paint to paper with brushes, the targeted child was more interested in mixing and stirring and only used the paper as a surface on which to 'drip' the paint mixture.

At this point it is worth including an example of a planning format that supports practitioners in documenting how observations are used to inform planning (see also Chapter 6). Using a simple sheet such as the one shown (see Figure 3.6) enables the whole team to be aware of children's interests and all practitioners to be involved in 'responsive' planning. A new blank sheet would be available each week and made accessible to all staff. It may be that the response is merely to add an appropriate item of equipment to an area of provision or the practitioner may decide to plan in more detail for a focus. The information collected on this sheet should then feed into evaluations and may impact on future planning. The completed sheets can be kept in the planning file as evidence of responsive practice. Introducing this type of documentation can help to raise the profile and status of supporting child-initiated learning where there has tended to be an overemphasis on adult-led activities.

Festivals and special occasions

The experiences that children bring from home will influence the nature of self-initiated learning and will also impact on how they access planned activities in the setting. In many settings there will be a range of cultural and racial backgrounds but in others the spectrum will be narrower.

Where the community reflects diversity, there will be a wealth of natural opportunities to celebrate festivals and special occasions within the context of children's real lives. Of course it is important to share these significant times with children and cultural experiences can provide exciting starting points for planning a focus. Families and friends of children will usually welcome an invitation to become involved with celebrations. They can also help practitioners to build up a knowledge and understanding of cultures that vary from their own. However, where this 'real' context for celebrating certain festivals does not exist, difficulties related to authenticity and meaning for the children may arise.

It is important that such celebrations do not become a 'token gesture', simplistic activities planned merely to satisfy perceived requirements of the curriculum. When festival celebrations are planned, they should be genuine and meaningful. They should not be seen as the definitive 'multi-cultural curriculum' but as enriching experiences planned within the context of a setting that embraces and celebrates diversity.

Ongoing opportunities for exploring and beginning to understand their own and other cultures must be woven into the fabric of the whole curriculum. Imaginative and creative play can offer a meaningful context in which to explore cultures and lifestyles that are outside their real life experience. It can also highlight for children the variety of ways in which a particular occasion can be celebrated, for example, birthdays will be associated with certain traditions for one family but these will differ between families. Exploration of, and discussion about, such differences at this stage will help children to learn acceptance and

Day of the week	MONDAY 17 May	TUESDAY 18 May	WEDNESDAY 19 May	THURSDAY 20 May	FRIDAY 21 May
Observation	Dry sand very shallow at one end of tray – Ryan discovered that he could make circular marks with his finger but was frustrated by other children disturbing his sand.	Water tray: Group of children deeply involved in filling/emptying containers and interested in water levels.	On arrival, lots of children reported on new road works next to the school building	Torrential downpour! Children excited by the sound of the rain on the corrugated roof and watching rain bouncing in puddles through windows.	Still raining!
Response (e.g. enhancements to provision, adult support, planned focus)	Provide smaller, shallow trays containing dry sand so that Ryan and other children can explore mark-making. Also provide chopsticks/ twigs/clay modelling tools as mark-making tools.	Add food colouring to water to make levels more visible through transparent containers. Mark half-full levels on containers with waterproof tape. Model use of key vocabulary: 'Full', 'empty', 'more', 'less'.	Outdoor area: Provided cones, hard hats, etc. Take digital photographs of road works to display and discuss with children.	Abandoned planned focus today. Took children out in small groups wearing splash suits and wellies. Covered umbrellas with foil and listened to sounds. Splashed in puddles.	Rain collection focus – key area of learning: knowledge and understanding of the world (exploration and investigation). See focus plan.
Evaluation comments	21/5 Trays popular with a large number of children. Next week a focus will be planned to support development towards handwriting goals using large shallow tray and salt. Look at stepping-stones in this area.	21/5 Offered lots of opportunities for assessing learning in area of shape, space and measures (mathematical development). Display key vocabulary in area. Include ideas in long-term plan for water area.		20/5 Children fascinated by rain pouring down drainpipes into drains. Plan for a focus on rain collection if weather conditions continue tomorrow. Gather resources: lengths of guttering, water trays, buckets, funnels.	21/5 Need to order two more splash suits. Include rain collection plan in the rain resource box.

Figure 3.6 Planning in response to observed needs and interests

respect. It is therefore crucial that opportunities for creative experiences of this nature are planned and starting points for furthering children's understanding recognised.

Training and sharing of knowledge between settings can help to deepen the understanding of practitioners and to increase their confidence in approaching other cultures. Reflection about their own culture can also lead practitioners to a deeper understanding of others.

Stories and nursery rhymes as starting points

Stories are a frequently used starting point for developing learning across all areas of the curriculum. Sometimes practitioners will choose a familiar and favourite story, or a well-known story character, as the stimulus but in other circumstances may decide that a new story would be more successful in exciting the children. Of course, even though key learning objectives may be focused on an area of learning other than communication, language and literacy, using a story book in this context will help to foster a love of books and to develop skills involved in learning to read. There is a wealth of beautifully illustrated children's literature on the market that provides practitioners with an almost infinite source of inspiration. Here are a few ideas:

The following 'bridge-building' activity was planned after staff had noticed that, although the large construction equipment was available to children outside on a daily basis, they were not using it with much intention. The aim was to give children a purpose for design and construction, and *The Billy Goats Gruff* story, as well as being a group favourite, offered a real purpose.

The activity should take place in the outside area if possible. Children will need plenty of space to manipulate equipment and time to test and modify structures. If a large group of children is keen to engage in the activity, it is a good idea to provide a long 'river' so that a number of bridges can be constructed.

FOCUS ACTIVITY:
BUILDING A BRIDGE FOR THE BILLY GOATS GRUFF

Focus areas of learning
- Mathematical development
- Knowledge and understanding of the world

Learning objectives
- To solve problems and to build for a specific purpose
- To use key mathematical language (see key vocabulary and questions)

STORY	POSSIBLE ACTIVITIES	MOST APPLICABLE EARLY LEARNING GOALS
Handa's Surprise by Eileen Browne	<ul><li>Circle time: being kind to friends</li><li>Making a 'carrier' for fruit</li><li>Tasting exotic fruits</li><li>Writing letters to Handa</li><li>Looking at features of our environment and comparing it with Handa's environment</li></ul>	<ul><li>Have a developing awareness of their own needs, views and feelings and be sensitive to the needs, views and feelings of others</li><li>Build and construct with a wide range of objects, selecting appropriate resources and adapting their work where necessary</li><li>Investigate objects and materials using all of their senses as appropriate</li><li>Attempt writing for various purposes, using features of different forms such as lists, stories and instructions</li><li>Observe, find out about and identify features in the place they live and the natural world</li></ul>
Titch by Pat Hutchins	<ul><li>Talk about own growth and development from babyhood, remember significant experiences</li><li>Measuring height (see page 98 for activity plan)</li></ul>	<ul><li>Find out about past and present events in their own lives, and in those of their families and other people they know</li><li>Use language such as 'more' or 'less', 'greater' or 'smaller', 'heavier' or 'lighter', to compare two numbers or quantities</li></ul>
Brown Bear, Brown Bear, What Do You See? by Bill Martin Jnr	<ul><li>Playing with rhyme: anticipating the next animal</li></ul>	<ul><li>Listen with enjoyment and respond to stories, songs and other music, rhymes and poems and make up their own stories, songs, rhymes and poems</li></ul>
Owl Babies by Martin Waddell	<ul><li>Talking about nocturnal animals and features of night and day</li><li>Exploring a dark den with torches</li><li>Circle time: 'settling-in' – helping new children to feel secure and happy in the setting</li></ul>	<ul><li>Find out about, and identify some features of, living things, objects and events they observe</li><li>Ask questions about why things happen and how things work</li><li>Have a developing awareness of their own needs, views and feelings and be sensitive to the needs, views and feelings of others</li></ul>
Rosie's Walk by Pat Hutchins	<ul><li>Setting up a Rosie's Walk obstacle course around the outside area</li><li>Looking at how flour is made, and using flour in baking</li><li>Making maps and plans: route to the park, plans of the outside area</li></ul>	<ul><li>Move with control and co-ordination</li><li>Look closely at similarities, differences, patterns and change</li><li>Find out about their environment, and talk about those features they like and dislike</li></ul>

Figure 3.7 Starting from a story: activities and goals

STORY	POSSIBLE ACTIVITIES	MOST APPLICABLE EARLY LEARNING GOALS
Where the Wild Things Are by Maurice Sendak	• Role-play – sailing to see the 'Wild Things' • Drawing/painting/making collages of Wild Things • Making up monster poems/chants • Floating/sinking investigations • Making boats (see page 70 for activity plan)	• Use their imagination in art and design, music, dance, imaginative and role-play and stories • Explore and experiment with sounds, words and texts • Investigate objects and materials using all of their senses as appropriate • Build and construct with a wide range of objects, selecting appropriate resources, and adapting their work where necessary
The Billy Goats Gruff (traditional)	• Sorting and ordering toy goats according to size • Building bridges (see page 93 for activity plan) • Making goat and troll puppets • Puppet show/role-play	• Use language such as 'circle' or 'bigger' to describe the shape and size of solids and flat shapes • Build and construct with a wide range of objects, selecting appropriate resources, and adapting their work where necessary • Use their imagination in art and design, music, dance, imaginative and role-play and stories
Kipper's Toybox by Mick Inkpen	• Counting toys in and out of the toy box • Making 'Sock Thing' puppets • Looking at toys from other times	• Count reliably up to ten everyday objects • Select tools and techniques they need to shape, assemble and join the materials they are using • Find out about past and present events in their own lives, and in those of their families and other people they know
The Very Hungry Caterpillar by Eric Carle	• Looking at the life cycle of a butterfly • Looking at colours and patterns on a butterfly's wings and make 'butterfly' prints or collages • Counting the pieces of fruit eaten by the caterpillar	• Find out about, and identify some features of, living things, objects and events they observe • Explore colour, texture, shape, form and space in two and three dimensions • Count reliably up to ten everyday objects

Figure 3.7 Starting from a story: activities and goals (continued)

Working towards early learning goals for focus areas of learning (QCA 2000)

● To use language such as 'more' or 'less', 'greater' or 'smaller', 'heavier' or 'lighter', to compare two numbers or quantities

● To use developing mathematical ideas and methods to solve practical problems

(Shape, space and measures)

● Build and construct with a wide range of objects, selecting appropriate resources, and adapting their work where necessary

(Designing and making)

Background information and prior learning

Most children will understand the concept of big and small. Some children will have been introduced to the concept of heavy and light. All children will have experience of working with the resources used in this activity. All children will be familiar with the story *The Billy Goats Gruff*.

Introduction

The adult will read the story of *The Billy Goats Gruff* to the children, encouraging them to join in, for example, 'Who's that trip-trapping over my bridge?'

Main activity

The adult, with the help of the children, will create a 'river' and 'fields' using lengths of fabric. Using wooden blocks, planks, etc. (see 'resources'), the children will then work together to construct a bridge(s) over the river.

Finishing off and follow-up

The children will, with adult support, talk about their bridges, for example, successful features, resources used, modifications made (see also 'key questions'). They will use the river, fields and bridges in their play, recreating *The Billy Goats Gruff* story and making up stories of their own.

Adult role

The adult will:

● Provide resources

● Read the story and stimulate interest in the main activity

● Model use of key vocabulary

- Be aware of children's prior learning
- Intervene in children's play as appropriate, asking questions in order to extend learning
- Observe children re: response to activity, use of key vocabulary, understanding of concepts, ability to problem solve, use of resources

Key questions and vocabulary

Vocabulary[1]: Big/bigger, small/smaller, middle-sized, heavy/heavier, light/lighter, under, on, over.

Questions: Who do you think is under the bridge? Where does the troll live? Who will go over the bridge next? Why does the goat want to go over the bridge? Who is on the bridge now? Which goat is bigger or smaller than the middle-sized Billy Goat Gruff? Which do you think is heavier than the small Billy Goat Gruff? Is your bridge strong enough to support the goats? How could you make it stronger? Is your bridge tall enough for the troll to live underneath? What have you used to build your bridge? Have you used the same resources as William?

Resources

- Story book – *The Billy Goats Gruff*
- Long lengths of fabric (e.g. blue/silver/grey/white for the river, green/yellow for the fields)
- Construction resources: wooden hollow blocks, wooden planks, milk crates, tyres

Involving a popular story character, such as Titch, in activities is a sure way to interest children and to enthuse them for learning. This 'Titch' activity was a variation on the height chart frequently used in early years classrooms to introduce the idea of height measurement. In this case, although all children did record their own height, the main focus was to compare their height with that of Titch using the vocabulary 'tall/taller' and 'short/shorter'. The activity was planned at 'medium-term' stage, as part of focus on 'mathematical development'.

---

[1] Some children will be ready to use comparative vocabulary. Other children will need more experience of using, for example, big and small but will benefit from adults and peers modelling the use of comparative vocabulary.

FOCUS ACTIVITY:
'ARE YOU TALLER THAN TITCH?'

Focus areas of learning

- Communication, language and literacy
- Mathematical development

Learning objectives

- To listen and respond to a story
- To understand the concept of height
- To use key 'height' vocabulary
- To make simple records and compare findings

> **Working towards early learning goals for focus areas of learning** (QCA 2000)
>
> - Listen with enjoyment and respond to stories, songs and other music, rhymes and poems and make up their own stories, songs, rhymes and poems
>
>   *(Language for communication)*
>
> - Use language such as 'more' or 'less', 'greater' or 'smaller', 'heavier' or 'lighter', to compare two numbers or quantities
>
>   *(Shape, space and measures)*

Introduction

The adult will read the story of *Titch* to the children using the key 'height' vocabulary.

Main activity

The adult will choose a child of 'average' height to draw around on a large piece of paper. Children will draw clothes and a face on the outline and name it 'Titch'. The adult will attach the drawing to the wall and children will measure themselves against Titch. They each mark their own height on the paper and write their name. They will 'read' their mark and say whether they were taller or shorter than Titch.

Finishing off and follow-up

The children will look at the height chart as a group and count how many children were taller, shorter or the same height as Titch. The Titch height chart will be displayed in an accessible place for children to revisit and discuss. Children will be encouraged to measure themselves against their friends and objects around, for example, the cupboard, the slide, and to use the words 'taller' and 'shorter' in comparison. A selection of rectangular wooden bricks will be templated vertically against the wall in height order to encourage measurement and comparison.

Adult role

The adult will:

● Provide resources

● Read the story and explain activity

● Support children in measuring and marking height

● Question children and model use of key vocabulary

● Observe children re: response to activity, understanding of height concept, use of key vocabulary

Key vocabulary and questions

Vocabulary: Tall/taller, short/shorter

Questions: Is Titch's brother taller than Titch? Is your brother taller than you? Are you taller than your friend? Can you find anyone who is the same height as you? Do you think you will be taller or shorter than our Titch on the wall? Were you right? Is Titch taller or shorter than you? Look at our chart – how many people are taller or shorter than Titch?

Resources

● *Titch* by Pat Hutchins

● Large sheet of paper

● Pens, pencils

Rhymes can also provide varied starting points for learning across the curriculum and some examples are listed in Figure 3.8.

The awareness of rhythm and rhyme is essential to the process of becoming a competent reader and repetition of familiar rhymes during an activity will increase children's awareness. The humour found in many of the traditional and modern nursery rhymes is very appealing to most children – making up new rhymes can be a hilarious experience for them and can become quite compulsive!

NURSERY RHYME	POSSIBLE ACTIVITIES	MOST APPLICABLE EARLY LEARNING GOALS
Humpty Dumpty	• Building a strong wall for Humpty Dumpty • Looking at brick patterns	• Build and construct using a wide range of objects, selecting appropriate resources, and adapting their work where necessary • Talk about, recognise and recreate simple patterns
Jack and Jill	• Finding ways of pulling/pushing objects up a 'hill', rolling objects down a 'hill'	• Ask questions about why things happen and how things work
London Bridge is Falling Down	• Looking at different bridge structures • Building bridges for different purposes	• Ask questions about why things happen and how things work • Build and construct with a wide range of objects, selecting appropriate resources, and adapting their work where necessary
Baa Baa Black Sheep	• Counting 1-2-3 • Looking at properties of wool, use wool for collage, weaving, sewing, threading, etc. • Weighing/balancing bags	• Count reliably up to ten everyday objects • Investigate objects and materials using all of their senses as appropriate • Use language such as 'more' or 'less', 'greater' or 'smaller', 'heavier' or 'lighter', to compare two numbers or quantities
Incy Wincy Spider	• Looking at, and drawing, spiders and their webs using magnifying glasses • Counting spiders legs	• Find out about, and identify some features of, living things, objects and events they observe • Count reliably up to ten everyday objects

Figure 3.8 Starting from a nursery rhyme: activities and goals

FOCUS ACTIVITY:
PLAYING WITH RHYME

Focus area of learning

● Communication, language and literacy

Learning objectives

● To listen attentively
● To enjoy and respond to nursery and other rhymes, and rhyming songs
● To show an awareness of rhyme and offer contributions of rhyming words

---

Working towards early learning goals for focus area of learning (QCA 2000)

● Listen with enjoyment and respond to stories, songs and other music, rhymes and poems and make up their own stories, songs, rhymes and poems

(Language for communication)

● Hear and say initial and final sounds in words, and short vowel sounds within words

(Linking sounds and letters)

Introduction

The children and adult will say some of their favourite nursery rhymes, and sing rhyming songs, together. The adult will invite children to play percussion instruments in accompaniment. They will listen for, and identify, the rhyming words.

Main activity

The adult will introduce some new, humorous versions of traditional nursery rhymes, For example:

> Twinkle, twinkle, chocolate bar
> Your Dad drives a rusty car
> Press the starter
> Pull the choke
> Off he goes in a cloud of smoke

(Taken from: Foster, J. (1991) *Twinkle Twinkle Chocolate Bar*. Oxford: Oxford University Press.)

> Humpty Dumpty sat on a chair
> While the barber cut his hair
> Cut it long
> Cut it short
> Cut it with a knife and fork

(Taken from: Rosen, M., Steele, S. (1993) *Inky Pinky Ponky*. London: Picture Lions.)

The children and adult will try to think of some versions of their own – the adult will encourage children by making suggestions and asking children for contributions of words to complete the rhyme. For example:

> Humpty Dumpty sat on a log
> Humpty Dumpty saw a _____

Children and adult will make up other rhymes, for example, (using the children's names).

> Josh is sitting on a chair
> Kate is eating a juicy _____
> Tom is standing on his head
> Liam is sleeping in his _____

The adult will scribe the children's ideas.

Finishing off and follow-up

The children's rhymes will be displayed on the wall and a book of children's rhymes will be compiled. Involved children will be encouraged to share their rhymes with other children. A note of explanation will be sent home with examples of the children's rhymes and parents and carers encouraged to make up rhymes with their children at home. Other poems, rhymes and stories with rhyming words in the text will be read to the children during the course of the week (see 'resources').

In other aspects of children's play, adults will capitalise on opportunities for developing awareness of alliteration, rhythm and rhyme, for example, in the sand area 'squishy and soft in the sand, cold and wet in my hand', in the outdoor area, 'we're splishing, splashing in the puddles', naming soft toys in the home corner 'Happy Harry' and 'Bobby Bear', singing or chanting whilst tidying up in the book area 'pick up the books and put them away, tidy and safe for another day'.

Adult role

The adult will:

- Provide resources including a range of rhymes
- Read new rhymes to the children
- Encourage children to make rhyming connections by giving examples and through repetition and emphasis of rhyming words
- Reassure and praise the children
- Display children's rhymes and make rhyme book
- Observe children re: enjoyment of and interest in activity, awareness of rhyme, contributions to new versions of nursery rhymes

Key vocabulary and questions

Vocabulary: The word 'rhyme' will be used by the adult

Questions: Can you hear the word that rhymes with wall? Can you think of another word that rhymes with wall and fall? Listen to these words, can you add any more? – dog, bog, jog, fog, _____ . Can you read our new rhyme?

Resources

- Books (rhymes, stories, poems) for example, *Round and Round the Garden* by Sarah Williams, *Each Peach Pear Plum* by Janet and Allan Ahlberg, *Hairy Maclary* by Lynley Dodd, *There's a Wocket in my Pocket* by Dr. Seuss, *All Join In* by Quentin Blake, *Dragon Poems* by John Foster and Korky Paul, *Machine Poems* collected by Jill Bennett
- Large sheets of paper, pens

Starting from works of art and music

Reproductions of artists' work, original works of art and artefacts from the present and other times, and from different cultures, can provide a stimulating starting point for learning across all areas. In using such stimuli, practitioners are giving children opportunities to become familiar with a selected work of art, or the work of a particular artist, and encouraging them as 'consumers' of art. Visits to art galleries can be very enriching and exciting experiences for young children but if these are not practical, galleries and museums often offer a 'loan service'.

'Belvedere' by M.C. Escher is a particularly good starting point for 'story-making' by children of all ages.

FOCUS ACTIVITY:
STORY-MAKING AND IMAGINATIVE PLAY

Focus areas of learning

- Creative development
- Communication, language and literacy

Learning objectives

- To respond to an artist's work
- To talk about observations
- To use language and imaginative role-play to express ideas
- To show an understanding of the elements of stories

Working towards early learning goals for focus areas of learning (QCA 2000)

- Use language to imagine and recreate roles and experiences

  (Language for thinking)

- Show an understanding of the elements of stories, such as main character, sequence of events and openings, and how information can be found in non-fiction texts to answer questions about where, who, why and how

  (Reading)

- Use their imagination in art and design, music, dance, imaginative and role-play and stories

  (Imagination)

- Respond in a variety of ways to what they see, hear, smell, touch and feel
- Express and communicate their ideas, thoughts and feelings by using a widening range of materials, suitable tools, imaginative and role-play, movement, designing and making, and a variety of songs and musical instruments

  (Responding to experiences, and expressing and communicating ideas)

Background information and prior learning

Children will have experience of expressing ideas through role-play and circle time activities. They will be familiar with looking at, and talking about, works of art (see long-term plans for areas of provision: painting, Chapter 1).

Introduction

The adult will explain to the children that he or she has brought a very special and exciting picture to show them (the reproduction will be displayed on a board but initially covered by a curtain). The adult will invite suggestions from the children as to what the picture might be about. The picture will then be revealed – 'Belvedere' by M.C. Escher.

Main activity (small group of children)

The adult will ask questions about the picture (see 'key questions') and encourage the children to share their observations. On a large piece of paper, the adult will scribe the children's ideas and together they will make up a story[2] about the characters and the building depicted.

Finishing off and follow-up

Children will be encouraged to use 'Belvedere' ideas in their play (additional resources will be provided as required to support play). The children involved in the story-making activity will share their ideas with the rest of the group. The picture and stories will be displayed for all children to look at and talk about. A 'Belvedere' story book using children's ideas will be compiled by the adult.

Adult role:

The adult will:

- Provide all resources
- Question children and encourage them to express their ideas
- Scribe children's ideas
- Join in children's imaginative play as appropriate
- Observe children re: use of imagination, ability to express ideas, understanding of elements of stories
- Display picture and children's work and make 'Belvedere' book

Figure 3.9 Revealing the work of art

---

[2]   Children could make up their own stories and use pictures or writing to record their stories.

Key vocabulary and questions

Questions: Where do you think the building is? What are these people doing in the building? Who are they? Where do you think the door at the bottom of the building leads to? Where is the key to the door? Find the man behind the barred window – why is he there? What is he saying? What is the woman at the top of the building looking at? What can she see? Who is the man on the bench? What is he making? What will he use it for? Look at the man and the woman climbing the stairs – what are they talking about? Would you like to go to the building? Who would you go with? How would you get there?

Resources

- A reproduction of 'Belvedere' by M.C. Escher (included in 'Taschen' poster pack: M.C. Escher)
- Large board and 'curtain'
- Large piece of paper, pens
- Additional resources (role-play props) as required

Similarly, listening to music can be a powerful stimulus particularly in terms of creative and language work. There are many commercially produced tapes and CDs which are suitable for use with children (e.g. instrumental 'mood' music, classical collections) but it is often a good idea to produce a compilation tape with which practitioners feel comfortable, and which will be tailored to fit intentions.

For example, after talking about *The Snowman* story (by Raymond Briggs) with children, the adult may decide to plan an activity with a creative focus. She or he would then select appropriate pieces of music for each part of the story and encourage children to respond to the music through dance and movement. The music chosen to relate to James and the Snowman flying through the air would be a calm and serene piece, whereas the party music would be lively, loud and with a 'dance beat'.

Working towards early learning goal for creative development

By the end of the foundation stage, children will be able to:

- Use their imagination in art and design, music, dance, imaginative and role-play and stories

Looking at musical instruments, and making their own music, can also inspire children's learning across a range of curricular areas as illustrated in Figure 3.10.

STIMULUS	POSSIBLE ACTIVITIES	MOST APPLICABLE EARLY LEARNING GOALS
Listening and responding to music	• Movement and dance using e.g. ribbons, scarves • Expressing feelings: how does this music make you feel? Is it happy/sad/angry music? Listen to the sad music, look in the mirror – can you make a sad face? • 'Painting to music': making marks to match the mood of the music (e.g. large swirling patterns, stamping footprints, splatter painting, angular zig-zag patterns)	• Use their imagination in art and design, music, dance, imaginative and role-play and stories • Respond in a variety of ways to what they see, hear, smell, touch and feel • Express and communicate their ideas, thoughts and feelings by using a widening range of materials, suitable tools, imaginative and role-play, movement, designing and making, and a variety of songs and musical instruments
Looking at/ listening to musical instruments	• Discriminating between instruments/matching sounds to instruments • Looking at/handling/playing/drawing instruments from own and other cultures • Looking at how musical instruments are made/making own instruments • 'Sound' word poems (listening to different instruments) e.g. 'Tinkling, ringing triangles, Booming, banging drums'	• Recognise and explore how sounds can be changed, sing simple songs from memory, recognise repeated sounds and sound patterns and match movements to music • Begin to know about their own cultures and beliefs and those of other people • Ask questions about why things happen and how things work • Explore and experiment with sounds, words and texts
Making music	• Using musical instruments (own and commercially produced) to accompany own singing/dancing • Exploring rhythm: counting beats, clapping names, playing simple rhythms on an instrument, marching to music/songs • Composing own tunes/sound strings and using a simple system of notation (e.g. based on colour or shape) to record own music • Perform own music to an audience • Record own music on audio tape	• Recognise and explore how sounds can be changed, sing simple songs from memory, recognise repeated sounds and sound patterns and match movements to music • Express and communicate their thoughts and feelings by using a widening range of materials, suitable tools, imaginative and role-play, movement, designing and making, and a variety of songs and musical instruments

Figure 3.10 Music as a stimulus: activities and goals

Visitors and outside visits

Outside visits, and visitors to the setting, offer a host of opportunities for planning exciting learning experiences. Practitioners may choose to link visits to a topic, or plan them with a particular area of learning in mind – whatever the original intentions, adults should be prepared for unplanned 'spin off' activities as enthused children notice.

Outside visits do not have to be sophisticated, or involve weeks of organisation. A simple walk around the local area can provide the starting point for a range of learning experiences and activities.

A WALK AROUND THE LOCAL AREA:	
POSSIBLE ACTIVITIES	MOST APPLICABLE EARLY LEARNING GOALS
• Looking at different buildings/shops, using knowledge in role-play in the setting • Looking at numbers/words in the environment (door numbers, street signs), making signs for the setting • Discussing and drawing 'landmarks' and features of the area, making plans of an area/route maps • Counting how many buses go past the park, making tally charts • Observing seasonal changes, bringing back, for example, autumn leaves for observational drawing/further investigation	• Use language to imagine and recreate roles and experiences • Recognise numerals 1–9 • Read a range of familiar and common words and simple sentences independently • Observe, find out about, and identify features in the place they live and the natural world • Count reliably up to ten everyday objects • Find out about, and identify some features of, living things, objects and events they observe

Figure 3.11 A walk around the local area: activities and goals

The following role-play activity was inspired by the visit of a Post Office worker known to many of the children as their local postman.

FOCUS ACTIVITY: POST OFFICE ROLE-PLAY

Focus area of learning

• Communication, language and literacy

Learning objectives

- To develop an understanding of the role of the Post Office
- To use knowledge of the Post Office in role-play
- To use writing as a means of communication

Working towards early learning goals for focus areas of learning (QCA 2000)

- Use language to recreate roles and experiences

(Language for thinking)

- Know that print carries meaning and, in English, is read from left to right and top to bottom

(Reading)

- Attempt writing for various purposes, using features of different forms such as lists, stories and instructions

(Writing)

Background information and prior learning

Children will have experience of writing for a variety of purposes. Children will be at different stages in their writing development – the adult will be aware of each child's prior achievements.

Introduction

The Post Office worker will visit the setting and explain to the children how the Post Office works – the service it offers the community, the different roles of the people who work there, the journey of a letter, etc. They will show the children the uniform worn and equipment used when delivering post. Children will be encouraged to ask questions.

Main activity

Children will:

- Work in the Post Office role-play area, for example, filling in forms, selling stamps and stationery, stamping passbooks and handling money
- Write letters to friends, family, etc., address envelopes and post letters
- Collect letters from postboxes
- Read labels and signs (see 'resources')

Finishing off and follow-up

Before the children go home, a child will be invited to deliver the post (with adult support). Children will take home letters written to them and to their family members.

The Post Office role-play area will be available for children for as long as they show an enthusiasm for working in the area.

Adult role

The adult will:

- Arrange the Post Office worker's visit and prepare the children for the visit
- Support children in asking questions during the introduction
- Provide role-play resources and ensure that the area is well stocked at all times
- Intervene in children's play as and when appropriate
- Ask questions in order to be aware of the extent of children's knowledge and to extend their learning
- Observe children re: purposes for writing, progress in writing development, use of language in role-play

Key vocabulary and questions

Vocabulary: Children will be familiar with 'Post Office' vocabulary, for example, stamp, letter, envelope, address, postbox.

Questions to visitor: What is the role of people who work behind the counter? Where do you deliver post? How many houses do you deliver to? Which streets do you deliver to? What happens to a letter after we put it in the postbox? Where does it go before it reaches its destination? Why do people go to the Post Office? How do you help them?

Questions to children: Who are you writing to? Why are you writing to them – what would you like to tell or ask them? Would you like to send a birthday card to Simon? Where do they live? Can you write their name on the envelope? Do you need to go and buy a stamp? Look at the Post Office signs – where can you buy a stamp? How much does it cost? Do you need some money from your Post Office account? Can you fill in a form? Where do you write your name?

Resources

- Post Office worker
- Post Office role-play area: an area of the setting with furniture arranged to provide a counter, a writing surface and a sitting area (where children can look at leaflets, read letters, etc.)

- Tills, money, stamps, forms (for different purposes), leaflets
- Writing paper, notelets, postcards, greetings cards, envelopes, pens, pencils
- Signs (words/pictures/words and pictures), for example, 'Buy your stamps here', 'Money bank', 'Postbox – times of collection: 11.00 am and 3.00 pm', 'Open' or 'Closed', children's name cards.
- Fiction and non-fiction books about the Post Office or letters (e.g. *The Jolly Postman* by Janet and Allan Ahlberg)

(See also 'Eeyore's visit to nursery', Figure 4.1)

Responding to the weather

The weather in Britain is characteristically unreliable and most practitioners will know the frustration of planning a paddling pool activity during a heat wave, only to wake up on the morning of the planned activity to torrential rain! This makes the task of 'timetabling' focus activities related to weather, or seasonal changes, almost impossible. Practitioners should be prepared to respond to weather conditions as they occur, although possible learning experiences and activities can be anticipated in advance. The arrival of snow is invariably greeted with great glee by children but is not always predicted and rarely lasts for more than a day or two. In the event of a snowfall, the practitioner will probably want to put other plans on hold and take full advantage of the opportunities offered by the 'snow experience'. It is a good idea then, to be prepared with ideas for developing learning and the following plan suggests ways in which children can learn about 'freezing' and 'melting' using snow as a starting point.

FOCUS ACTIVITY: INVESTIGATING SNOW

Focus areas of learning

- Communication, language and literacy
- Knowledge and understanding of the world

Learning objectives

- To investigate the characteristics and properties of snow
- To understand that water freezes and ice melts in response to changes in temperature
- To talk about their observations using key vocabulary

<table>
<tr><td>

Working towards early learning goals for focus areas of learning (QCA 2000)

● Extend their vocabulary, exploring the meanings and sounds of new words

(Language for communication)

● Use talk to organise, sequence and clarify thinking, ideas, feelings and events

(Language for thinking)

● Investigate objects and materials by using all of their senses as appropriate

● Look closely at similarities, differences, patterns and change

(Exploration and investigation)

</td></tr>
</table>

Background information and prior learning

Children have made ice lollies and been introduced to the words 'freeze' and 'melt'.

Introduction

Children will enjoy the snow outside, handling it and building and modelling with it, etc. They will look closely at snowflakes as they fall, 'catching' them on black paper.

Main activity

Children will collect snow in buckets and transfer it to the water tray. They will dig, build, mould and imprint and, as they play, will observe the snow melting. More snow will be introduced to the tray and the adult will offer children a jug of warm water to 'mix' with the snow. The adult will also introduce some large blocks of ice[3] (e.g. water frozen in margarine tubs) and encourage children to watch what happens to the snow when it is placed on an ice block.

Finishing off and follow-up

Snow will be introduced into the indoor water tray. During the few days following the activity, small ice cubes containing objects such as pebbles, shells, buttons, beads, wedges of citrus fruit, will be placed in the water tray. Children will collect the 'hidden' objects in a special container as the ice cubes melt. A balloon full of water (with a length of string inserted) will be frozen. The balloon 'skin' will then be removed and the 'ice balloon', on a string, made available to children.

Adult role

The adult will:

● Be prepared to respond immediately to the arrival of snow

---

[3] Take care that children do not 'burn' themselves on the ice.

- Prepare ice blocks and cubes in advance and store in readiness in the freezer
- Work alongside children, asking questions and introducing warm water or ice blocks at an appropriate time
- Model, and encourage use of, key vocabulary
- Observe children re: their observations, understanding of freezing and melting, use of key vocabulary

Key questions and vocabulary

Vocabulary: Warm, cold, freeze, frozen, melt.

Questions: What does the snow feel like? How do your hands feel after holding the snow? What could you use to make a 'snow castle'? How long do you think a snowflake will stay on your hand? What do you think will happen to the snowball if we pour warm water onto it? What will happen to the warm water when it is mixed with the snow?

Resources

- Snow!
- Water tray, spades, buckets, plastic pots, shells, brushes, tubes, black paper.
- Jugs of warm water (not too hot – safety is the paramount consideration. Tepid water will serve the purpose)
- Ice blocks
- Ice cubes (containing 'hidden' objects)

Key Points for Good Practice

- Be aware of the holistic nature of children's learning.
- Be flexible in your use of plans – if children's 'agenda' is different from what you have planned for them, abandon or postpone your plans in order to support their interest.
- Remember that identifying and understanding children's needs and interests starts with a period of observation. Sometimes observations in a number of contexts reveals an interest in a schema.
- Share information with parents and carers and find out more about children's current enthusiasms at home. Also share observations of children with other members of the team.
- Recognise and respect children's varied cultural experiences. Reflect and share these in the setting.

- Recognise the importance of the adult in supporting interests and extending learning.
- Remember that a child's interest can be used as a starting point for learning across a number of curricular areas.
- Value the learning process, fostering children's creativity and guarding against an overemphasis on concrete results.
- Never underestimate the power of a child's imagination as motivation for learning.

We need to feed the child's natural curiosity, the urge to explore, to try things out, to look more closely, to see what happens. We need to build on the child's disposition to explore and investigate, to satisfy the 'rage to know'.

(Fisher 1990)

CHAPTER 4

Establishing and developing positive links with home

Parents are children's first and most enduring educators. When parents and practitioners work together in early years settings, the results have a positive impact on the child's development and learning. Therefore, each setting should seek to develop an effective partnership with parents.

(QCA 2000)

The content of this chapter is organised as follows:

First contact

Prior to entering the setting, and during their early years, parents and the home environment will be central to a child's world and, in particular, to their emotional well-being. Many children will also have secured close bonds with professional carers, or carers within their family or circle of friends. Whatever the circumstances, for many children, starting nursery, pre-school, playgroup, or beginning a new relationship with a childminder can be a big milestone in their life. For both parents[1] and children, the prospect of entering this next stage,

---

[1] From this point the word 'parents' will be used to refer to all main carers, whatever their relationship to the child.

although exciting in many ways, is often tinged with apprehension. The role of the practitioner is crucial in allaying anxieties and in building up trust between home and the setting. Experiences in the early days form the foundation for future attitudes and relationships.

> A happy and open relationship with parents, based on confidence and trust, is crucial to the building of a successful relationship with their children.
>
> (Whitebread 1996)

It is important, then, that practitioners consider carefully how to ensure that the child's and parents' initial contact with staff and the setting is an enjoyable experience. Many settings organise induction or open days, or arrange visits to the setting, prior to the child's starting date. Parents and children will often be sent individual invitations and will be offered the opportunity to 'sample' activities whilst becoming familiar with staff and the physical surroundings. There may also be an explanation of the aims of the setting in the form of a talk by staff, perhaps illustrated by a slide show or displays.

Other practitioners visit children and parents in their own home at a time and date mutually agreed beforehand. This system has the advantage of allowing both parties freedom from distractions and is also a more intimate atmosphere in which parents may feel able to talk about concerns or personal circumstances which could affect the child. Young children will usually feel more relaxed and confident in familiar surroundings and visiting practitioners will find, in many cases, that the child sets the agenda, enthusiastically showing off their toys and pets! However, practitioners should be aware that some parents may feel uneasy at the prospect of a home visit at this early stage in the relationship – this could be due to a number of factors including negative experiences of education in their own childhood resulting in a lack of self-confidence or a mistrust of professionals. It is important to remember that the aim is to make the first contact between home and setting a positive experience, and the parent should always feel comfortable about the venue and nature of that first meeting – for this reason, any approach that is adopted by the practitioner, or team of practitioners, should be flexible.

The first meeting marks the beginning of a shared journey. The child's developing self-confidence and self-esteem is much more likely to flourish in a climate of respect and understanding between his or her parent and teacher. The child will already be part of a culture within the family and within the wider community and it is important that the practitioner understands this culture. At home and in the setting they must be supported in building up confidence in their own cultural identity. Families should feel confident that their experiences and traditions are valued and that they will be treated with dignity and sensitivity at all times.

If 'home visiting' is chosen as the preferred first contact, follow-up opportunities should also be planned for the child and parent to visit the setting before the official starting time; young children will feel more assured if they are able to visualise the provision and are familiar with some of the routines.

Planning, and carrying out, home visits

As any adult who works in an early years setting will appreciate, time is at a premium – there never seem to be enough hours in the day to fit all the jobs in! However, in the case of home visits, although there will be a limited amount of time available, it is important to allocate time-slots long enough to enable relaxed conversations between adults, and interaction with the child, to take place. Many settings plan time during working hours for visits – some school nurseries close for two or three days at the beginning of each intake term to enable staff to make home visits, although this is not always possible. Whatever the arrangements, practitioners need to be well organised and prepared in order to ensure maximum benefit to all involved. It is advisable for practitioners to visit in pairs both from the safety aspect and also because this allows more flexibility during the visit, for example, a parent may want to talk about a serious issue concerning the child's health or safety – in the event of two adults being present, one could talk with the parent, recording any necessary information, whilst the other engages with the child. It is important to discuss and define roles prior to visiting and each adult needs to be clear about their responsibilities – it is too late, once out of the house, to discover that neither has established whether or not the child is 'toilet trained'. Before embarking on visits, practitioners should always remember to inform an adult of their schedule, i.e. times of visits and addresses.

The following plan outlines some of the reasons for home visiting and offers suggestions for organisation, resources and the sharing of information. It is an example specific to one setting (arranging to carry out a number of visits over a period of a few days) – practitioners will need to tailor it to their own needs, may decide to adopt the framework for planning their visits, or may just choose to try out some of the ideas.

ORGANISING AND CARRYING OUT HOME VISITS

Dates: 5–8 September
Duration of each visit: 30 minutes

Aims of each visit

- To establish positive links between home and the setting
- To begin to develop a relationship between the child and staff

117

- To familiarise the parent with the aims of the setting – policies, routines, etc.
- To enable staff to become aware of child's home circumstances and relevant prior experiences
- To informally assess child's stage of development and readiness for the setting

Resources needed

- List of names, telephone numbers and addresses; timetable of visits
- Street map of local area
- Home visit record forms and questionnaires[2]
- Photograph album – a collection of annotated photographs showing children at play in the setting
- Soft toy character – Oscar the clown (see Figure 4.2, page 123)
- Small present for the child, for example, drawing book and crayons
- Booklet containing information about the setting
- 'About Me' leaflet[2]

Organisation and adult role

Arranging visits:

- Contact families to confirm that a visit is required and to arrange a suitable time
- Ensure that all information in booklets is correct and up-to-date
- Check that there are sufficient forms, booklets, etc. for every visit
- Gather all resources together, compiling individual packs of leaflets, forms, booklets, etc. in labelled bags

Carrying out the visits:

- Introduce staff by name to the parent and child
- Talk with, and listen to, the child putting her or him at ease (use props such as the photograph album, the drawing equipment and Oscar the clown to encourage conversation)
- Observe, in particular, the child's social, physical and language skills
- Explain to the parent, for example, how the setting and staffing is organised, strategies for settling children in to the setting, routines, systems of assessment, how information is communicated between staff and parents, rotas for parent help in the setting. Show the parent the photograph album and talk about activities

---

[2] See Chapter 6: 'Observing children's play, assessing learning and keeping useful records' for details of contents and purpose of forms, questionnaires and leaflets.

- Ask parent if there are any questions they would like to ask, information they need to share (if this has not already been recorded on a form or questionnaire) or any issues or concerns they would like to discuss

- Inform parent of any equipment the child will need, for example, a spare set of clothes, inside shoes

- Ask standard questions (if these have not already been answered during the course of conversation) and complete records

- Remind parent that they are welcome to visit the setting, with their child, prior to the official starting date

Following up visits:

- Plan starting dates for children, staggered if necessary
- Inform parent of the official starting date for their child
- Prepare individual equipment such as name cards, milk tags, coat peg labels
- Begin child's profile (see Chapter 6, page 181) by making a 'home visit' entry

The settling-in process

Children's responses to starting their new setting will vary enormously. Some will enter on the first day full of enthusiasm and confidence and eager to explore. Others will be much more reticent, preferring to observe from a 'safe' distance. Many may cope with a full session or day whilst some will benefit from shorter sessions in the beginning. Every child is different and practitioners must take their lead from the individual when devising programmes for 'settling-in'.

Settings also vary as to what is an appropriate or practical approach. In a situation where all 'foundation stage' children are together in a unit, transition into 'reception' should not cause any problems. But if children are arriving from other settings, reception class staff will find that children usually settle more easily if links are made with settings attended prior to starting school. The transition period should be carefully planned to allow children opportunities to experience activities in the class (e.g. an invitation to story session, or to lunch) and, where possible, should include visits by reception staff to children and their own setting or home (see home visits page 117). Similar transition arrangements should also be planned for children who are transferring from one setting to another at an earlier point during the foundation stage.

As a general rule, for three year olds starting in a new setting, parents should be encouraged to stay with their child for at least the first session, and for parts of, or complete, subsequent sessions until the child is settled. It may be that the child is happy to venture away from the parent immediately in which case the parent may decide to keep their distance, within the setting, on the first day. After observing the child's behaviour the parent may feel confident in leaving the child for a short period the next day. Invariably the child will soon be entering the setting confidently and be happy to wave 'goodbye' to the parent as soon as the routines have been completed. However, it does sometimes happen that a seemingly very confident child becomes 'clingy' after a few days in the setting, as if the novelty of the experience has worn rather thin. In such a case the practitioner and parent will need to review the situation and may decide that the child needs more support than originally anticipated.

Occasionally, a child will be happy to play with other children and explore the setting with a parent present but, even after a period of time, will be extremely reluctant for the parent to leave. It may be that the child is anxious about the possibility of the parent not returning. The child should not feel under pressure to 'make the break' before feeling ready and, in order to build up the child's confidence, the separation process will need to progress in small steps. The 'break' can also prove to be emotionally difficult for the parent, who may need support and understanding from the practitioner. The length of time could be built up gradually over a period of a few days until both parent and child feel comfortable about the parent leaving the building for part of the session. As the child realises that the parent always comes back, he or she will become less anxious about the separation until eventually he or she is happy to attend the whole session without the presence of the parent.

Many settings operate a system of 'key workers' – each child will have a member of staff 'assigned' to them and that adult will be responsible for greeting the child at the beginning of the each session, spending time working with, and observing, the child during the session and will liaise with parents. This can help the child to feel secure in the setting and often accelerates the process of settling in. Key workers may also be responsible for recording and reporting the achievements and progress of the children in their group.

The crucial word in the process is 'trust'. When a child is let down by an adult, the bond of trust will be damaged, and the child will feel insecure. Adults must be consistent, reliable and truthful – a child should always be told when a parent is about to leave the setting and when he or she will return. Slipping out of the door whilst the child is temporarily preoccupied, or distorting the truth about where they are going, are not actions conducive to building up a relationship of trust with a child. Practitioners should make time to talk with the parent about the child's progress, listening and responding to any concerns – the trust that develops between practitioner and parent during these early days is sure to impact positively on the development of the child.

Welcoming parents into the setting

It is the policy of most settings to encourage parents to spend time in the setting throughout their child's time there, and some parents are able and happy to come in on a regular basis. There is often an abundance of strengths and enthusiasms to be 'tapped' amongst the parents and carers – some may be able to play a musical instrument, others will have a particular interest in woodwork, sewing or gardening – whatever skills they have to offer, the practitioner should encourage them to share with the children in the setting. There are numerous other activities, many of them ongoing, with which parents can become involved on a day-to-day basis, for example, reading stories with the children, making models, building dens, baking, teaching routines in the painting area, joining in imaginative and role-play in the home corner.

Beginning of session routines, such as the self-registration systems and the 'question table' (see Chapter 5), provide a focus for children and parents on entry to the setting as well as offering sound learning opportunities for the child.

Self-registration usually involves the child, supported by the parent, taking a label or tag (displaying their own personal motif or photograph of self and/or name) and placing it in a designated place in order to register their presence in the setting. The labels may be hanging on coat pegs when the children arrive, or may be arranged on a table requiring children to select their own cards. The label may then, for example, be hung over a milk bottle or a named photograph attached with 'hoop and loop fastening tape' to a train or house displayed on the wall. A glance at the labels will inform the practitioner which children are present. Details of the 'question table' are included in Chapter 5, page 151.

Practitioners may also decide to organise social events and these are often run alongside planned activities involving the children, for example, a Christmas concert or 'sing-along' may be accompanied by coffee and mince pies. Such occasions offer parents opportunities to meet other parents and to chat informally with staff. It is advisable to give plenty of notice when planning events of this nature to allow parents with other commitments to make the necessary arrangements in order to attend. In many settings parents organise fund raising or social events themselves and this kind of involvement can be beneficial in helping to bind the partnership between practitioner and parent, as well as in providing very worthwhile experiences for all.

Parents are often invited to share experiences with their children and Figure 4.1 illustrates an example of such an occasion. Parents were invited to the nursery to meet 'Eeyore', a visiting donkey. Eeyore was accompanied by staff from the local donkey centre who talked to children and parents about caring for donkeys and the work of the Elisabeth Svendsen Trust for Children and Donkeys. The children were enthralled and eager to talk about their experiences. Because of the parents' involvement, they were able to discuss the visit with their children in detail, and with enthusiasm. The nursery decided to 'adopt' a donkey (on a sponsorship basis) from the centre and parents were very supportive. Parents, children and staff now had a shared commitment to the charity which not only benefited the Trust, but also served to strengthen links between home and setting.

Figure 4.1 Eeyore's visit to nursery

The setting itself should feel welcoming to the parent. Provision (a safe distance from the children's play area) of tea- and coffee-making facilities and an area where parents can sit comfortably and talk will be an attraction. Not all parents want to spend time working with children in the setting and some find it difficult because of caring for younger siblings, but they may be happy to offer their support by making or cataloguing resources – a 'working party' could be set up to, for example, make up story boxes or catalogue posters. Although the practitioner would be involved in the content of the work, parents could organise the rota and decide responsibilities for tasks. This can be a very successful way of involving parents in the curriculum and can also have positive social repercussions for many. The provision of a box of toys suitable for younger children and babies is also a good idea – parents will often be happy to contribute to this collection. Parents can be involved in the organisation of a book and toy lending library within the setting, sharing responsibility for the smooth running of the system, and for the maintenance of the resources, with the practitioner.

A 'parents' notice board' is an effective way of communicating information to parents such as forthcoming events in the setting, new staff appointed to work in the setting and holiday dates. Useful leaflets about local clinics, support groups, toy libraries, etc. can also be displayed and the board can be used by parents to inform each other about happenings in the community, for example, school fairs, jumble sales, aerobics classes. The provision of such a board will help to give parents a feeling of inclusion in the setting, will encourage social interaction between parents and will also convey the message that the setting does not work in isolation – that it is an integral part of the community.

Practitioners may also decide to take information (such as a summary of aims, session times, dates of open days and social events) about the setting into the wider community, displaying posters or leaflets in libraries, doctors' surgeries and clinics. This will serve to raise awareness of the setting in the community and encourage prospective parents to visit.

Planning home and setting 'link activities': introducing Oscar the clown

Working parents, and parents with other demanding commitments, are not always able to enjoy the frequent contact with the setting that they would like, but it is possible to plan activities involving parents and children which take place in the home. The visit of a soft toy character to the setting is a reliable way of engaging children and stimulating their imagination. This approach has already been suggested in the focus activity 'Lion's visit' (Chapter 3 page 85) during which a friendly lion spends time in the setting and challenges children to build him a den. The example used in this chapter is of Oscar, a brightly coloured, well-travelled clown who has, up to press, visited approximately a hundred and fifty homes in Leeds and been well cared for in all!

The aim of the 'Oscar project' is to develop children's learning in the areas of personal, social and emotional development and communication, language and literacy, and also to help develop positive links between home and the setting. If introduced at a time when new children are joining the setting, Oscar can also help to ease the settling-in process for children, for example, he could 'befriend' children who are feeling a little unsure; children could take responsibility for looking after Oscar whilst he is 'new' in the

Figure 4.2 Oscar with his suitcase

setting; they could explain a new activity to him, show him around the setting or merely invite him to watch as they play. The project is an idea which can easily be used in any setting, with little or no adaptation, and which is popular with both children and parents.

The following plan is presented in the same format as focus activities cited in other chapters but includes a wider range of possible objectives.

FOCUS ACTIVITY:
OSCAR THE CLOWN VISITS CHILDREN IN THEIR OWN HOMES

Focus areas of learning

- Personal, social and emotional development
- Communication, language and literacy

Learning objectives

- To develop a sense of responsibility
- To be aware of the needs of others
- To take turns
- To gain confidence in sharing experiences and expressing feelings in a group situation
- To listen and respond to other children's accounts of their experiences
- To understand that writing carries meaning
- To attempt writing to convey meaning
- To reinforce and develop links with home
- For parents and children to share in an experience initiated in the setting

---

Working towards early learning goals (QCA 2000)

- Continue to be interested, excited and motivated to learn
- Be confident to try new activities, initiate ideas and speak in a familiar group

(Dispositions and attitudes)

- Have a developing awareness of their own needs, views and feelings and be sensitive to the needs, views and feelings of others

(Self-confidence and self-esteem)

- Work as part of a group or class, taking turns and sharing fairly, understanding that there need to be agreed codes of behaviour for groups of people, including adults and children, to work together harmoniously

(Making relationships)

- Dress and undress independently and manage their own personal hygiene

(Self-care)

- Sustain attentive listening, responding to what they have heard by relevant comments, questions or actions

(Language for communication)

- Use talk to organise, sequence and clarify thinking, ideas, feelings and events

  (Language for thinking)

- Know that print carries meaning and, in English, is read from left to right and top to bottom

  (Reading)

- Attempt writing for various purposes, using features of different forms such as lists, stories and instructions

  (Writing)

Background information and prior learning

Children may have been introduced to Oscar during a home visit (See 'Home Visit Plan', page 117). Children and staff will have talked about personal hygiene, and in particular the need for washing, brushing teeth and combing hair.

Introduction

The adult will gather together a group of children on the first day of the 'Oscar project'. Oscar will be introduced to the children and they will be shown his suitcase and its contents (see 'resources'). The leading adult will explain that Oscar has come to spend time in the setting and needs somewhere to sleep at night. Some time for discussion and suggestions will be allowed. The adult will then tell the children that Oscar would like to stay for a night at each of their homes and will read an entry in his diary describing his visit to the home of a member of staff. They will discuss care of Oscar with a focus on personal hygiene and safety.

Main activity

Every day Oscar will go home with a different child. The child will be encouraged to care for Oscar, to share toys and experiences with him and to talk about photographs in his album. Parents will receive a letter of explanation and be asked to participate and, with the child, make an entry in Oscar's diary.

Finishing off and follow-up

In the weekly planning, time will be allocated for daily discussion of Oscar's visits to children's homes. Following each of Oscar's 'home visits', the child concerned will show the group the diary and talk about his or her experiences with the clown. Other children will be encouraged to ask the child questions about Oscar's visit. Photographs, letters to Oscar, diary entries, etc. will be displayed in the setting (on boards or made into books).

Adult role

The adult will:

- Provide resources – check contents of the suitcase after every visit
- Stimulate interest in the activity during the introduction
- Write a letter explaining the activity. Give a copy of the letter, and talk about the activity, to parents when it is their child's turn to take Oscar
- Support and encourage children as they talk about Oscar's visit to their house
- Read entries in Oscar's diary
- Ensure that all children are given the opportunity to take Oscar home

Key vocabulary and questions

Why do you think Oscar has come to the setting? What do you think he would like to play with? Where will he sleep tonight? Do you think he will be lonely in the setting by himself? Do you think Oscar would like to sleep at your house? How would you look after him? Which of your toys would you show him? What did you and Oscar do yesterday evening? Which other members of your family did Oscar meet? Did he remember to brush his teeth before he went to bed? Did you show him how to comb his hair? What did you and Oscar eat for your tea? Shall we read your entry in Oscar's diary? Would you like to read what you have written? Which part of Oscar's visit did you enjoy the most?

Resources

- Oscar (soft toy clown)
- Oscar's suitcase containing: his diary, photograph album, favourite toy, toothbrush, comb, a pencil and a letter from Oscar[3] addressed to the child
- Letter to parents – a brief explanation of the aims of the project and the required involvement from the parent

Figure 4.3 Snap from Oscar's photograph album

---

3 Content will include, for example, a 'thank you' for inviting him to stay, information about his favourite food, activities and toys, a list of items packed in his suitcase and a reminder to take care of him and to return him (with all belongings!) the following day.

> Monday
>
> Today Oscar came home with Natalia and she was very excited. He sat at the table at lunch time and ate cheese sandwiches with her. After lunch we all went to the post office and Natalia carried Oscar all the way. Oscar helped Natalia to post some letters and then we all came home. Oscar and Natalia played with toys for the rest of the afternoon. We went to Auntie Di's for tea – pasta, Natalia's favourite.
> At bed time, Natalia helped Oscar to clean his teeth and wash his face. Then they both brushed their hair and went to bed.

Figure 4.4 Natalia's entry in Oscar's diary: Mum and Natalia's writing – Natalia's writing reads 'Oscar came to play at my house'

Figure 4.5 Natalia's drawing – 'Me and Oscar and Mummy'

Children will often take Oscar with them to the supermarket, café, park, Grandma's house, the fair – some have even taken him on holiday for the weekend (see Figure 4.6) and come back with very exciting tales to tell about his adventures!

Figure 4.6 Oscar enjoys a family holiday with Laura and George

Working with parents to support and extend children's learning

In acknowledging parents as the child's 'first, and most enduring, educators' (QCA 2000), practitioners must recognise that their own role is inextricably linked to that of the parents. The learning process does not take place exclusively in the setting, nor does it only happen at home – experiences in all aspects of children's lives combine to broaden and deepen their learning. It is the role of the practitioner and parent to support the child in that process.

Parent and practitioners have much to learn from each other and an efficient system of communication should be in operation to facilitate the sharing of information. This will involve both parties in making time to talk and listen. Experience and training will equip the practitioner with the professional expertise needed to plan an appropriate and broad curriculum within the setting. But their expertise can have a wider impact when their approach includes involvement of parents in the planned curriculum. For children with special educational needs, it is crucial (and a legal requirement) that parents are involved in the planning process. In these circumstances, an Individual Education Plan (IEP) will be drawn up to identify and address those needs that are additional to the setting's usual curriculum. Parents know their child better than anyone and have a vital contribution to make, as equal partners in the team, to discussions about the plan.

This section of Chapter 4 focuses on building an effective partnership between parents and practitioners as educators.

It is worth mentioning at this point the many commercially produced resources on the market which claim to be aids to 'home learning', some of which can be useful if carefully selected. Some others, however, are at best a 'gimmick', and at worst, inappropriate for the child's stage of development and likely to lead to bad practice or confusion. Parents eager to give their child the best educational start in life are vulnerable to marketing ploys and are frequently persuaded to spend large amounts of money on so-called educational toys, videos and 'work books' of dubious quality. The reality is that very often, equally, or more, valuable learning experiences can take place at little or no expense in the home or local environment. Practitioners have an important role to play here in sharing their expertise and knowledge of how young children learn, in helping parents to interpret their children's play in terms of learning, and in offering suggestions of how learning can be supported at home. It may be appropriate to point out that children's learning should be contextual and purposeful, and to emphasise the value of conversation between adult and child.

Many parents will be keen to learn more about the early years curriculum and the activities planned for their children. An effective way of sharing ideas and curricular aims in a relaxed atmosphere is to hold an open day or evening and to invite parents to have 'hands on experience' of activities (some settings may organise a similar event prior to children starting the setting). Practitioners would be available to talk about children's play and learning, and to answer questions. A brief explanation of learning objectives, and photographs of children engaging in a range of activities, displayed in each area of provision can also provide some helpful information.

> Parents are particularly predisposed to understand play and its learning potential if invited to curriculum or topic sessions in school and allowed to experience for themselves some of the materials and resources children use.
>
> (Moyles 1989)

Some practitioners produce guidance leaflets for parents.[4] These can help to explain the learning that takes place in the setting, and can also be a very welcome support to those helping in the setting. However, practitioners should guard against overwhelming the parent with too much 'paperwork' – information should be useful, concise, easy to read and attractively presented. The content may be of a general nature (e.g. explanation of routines, areas limited to four children at a time, encouraging independence) but can also be specific to an area of provision, including information such as suggested activities, and ways in which the adult can support children's learning across the curriculum in, for example, the sand area. Reference to long-term plans may help practitioners in writing 'area of provision' leaflets.

Leaflets may also be produced which focus on the six areas of learning. These will offer information on how learning in a particular curricular area can be developed in different areas of provision (see example Figure 4.7). Figure 4.8 aims to help parents to support their children's learning in one particular aspect within the area of communication, language and literacy – linking sounds and letters.

Many practitioners plan focus activities and learning experiences within the setting around a particular interest or theme (e.g. ourselves, festivals) and the duration of such 'units' will vary. Other settings may choose to look at a particular area of learning (e.g. creative development) and focus on how children's learning can be developed in that area over a period of, for example, three weeks. Whatever the starting point for the medium-term planning, if practitioners inform parents of the content, and suggest home activities which will support the planned learning, the curriculum can be significantly enriched for the child.

---

4 These leaflets can also be useful to other adults working in the setting, for example, students, new staff.

MATHEMATICAL DEVELOPMENT IN THE NURSERY

You can support children's mathematical development in all areas of the setting. Listed below are some suggested activities:

- *Construction area*: looking at and comparing shapes of bricks; matching shapes to templates; sorting components (by colour, shape or size); counting the amount of component parts used to make a model, counting how many wheels altogether in two sets.

- *Painting area*: printing flat shapes; creating or recreating patterns and sequences looking at colour, size and shape.

- *Malleable materials*: making solid shapes; comparing length (who has made the longest snake?); sharing the dough (three children: three amounts of dough).

- *Home corner*: matching 1:1, for example, laying the table – spoon, cup, saucer for each child; shopping – dealing with money; counting and matching numbered clothes on a washing line; knock four times on the door before entering; counting candles on a birthday cake, calculating how many candles there will be if we add two more.

- *Office*: reading and dialling telephone numbers; writing numbers (e.g. house numbers on envelopes); matching numbered stamps to numbered postboxes.

- *Water area*: comparing containers (shape and size); filling and emptying containers; counting the number of jugs of water needed to fill a bowl.

- *Music area*: using instruments to explore rhythm – counting beats; clapping names (e.g. Sam – an – tha, 1 – 2 – 3); singing number songs, for example, 'Five Little Speckled Frogs'.

- *Sand area*: looking at solid shapes – using cuboids as moulds (wet sand); filling and emptying containers with sand; feeling sandpaper numbers on the wall; ordering size graded containers; weighing bags of sand.

- *Workshop area*: comparing and measuring lengths of wood; solving problems (e.g. how long does the piece of string need to be to go around the box? How many more boxes do we need?)

- *Book area*: looking at fiction and non-fiction books which involve, for example, counting, size, shape, height and length comparison; listening to number rhyme audio tapes.

Talking with the children as they play helps to develop their mathematical understanding as well as their language. They should be encouraged to use the following vocabulary and will learn the meaning of words through hearing you use them:

Numbers and counting: 1, 2, 3, 4, 5, 6, 7, 8, 9, 10 (higher number names if children are ready).

Calculation: add, one more/less, count on, altogether.

Shape: circle, square, triangle, rectangle, cylinder, sphere, cuboid, cone.

Size: big, bigger, small, smaller.

Length and height: long, longer, short, shorter, tall, taller.

Weight: heavy, heavier, light, lighter.

Capacity: full, fuller, empty, emptier.

Pattern: same, different, next to.

There are also a number of computer programs available which support children's mathematical learning. A member of staff will be happy to talk about these with you.

Figure 4.7 Mathematical development in the nursery: guidance leaflet

Preparing for 'phonics'

Early phonics develop through a wide range of experiences. Before they are able to identify sounds in words, children need plenty of opportunities to really listen to, and discriminate between, sounds. You can support your child's learning in this area by:

- Playing games such as making a sound (e.g. rustling paper, shaking a cereal box) behind a screen and asking your child to guess what has made the sound.

- Encouraging your child to listen to, and recognise, sounds in the environment (e.g. car engines, taps dripping, birds singing).

- Encouraging experimentation with voices, making sounds such as 'wheee!' when riding a scooter or 'whoosh' when pretending to be a rocket and different animal sounds.

- Sometimes varying your own voice when speaking, for example, whispering, growling, squeaking.

- Playing musical instruments with your child and talking about the sounds that different instruments make.

- Making up pairs or strings of words, choosing words that begin with the same sound, for example, happy Harry, delicious doughnuts, big blue ball.

- Singing or chanting rhymes. Clapping, tapping and stamping to rhymes.

- Talking about rhyming words and making up strings, for example, sun, bun, run, fun.

A strong indicator of success as a reader in later life is the child's ability to discriminate between sounds at this early stage.

Figure 4.8 Preparing for phonics

Once aware of the practitioner's plans, many parents will have exciting ideas of their own for developing their children's learning and should be encouraged to share these. Information can be displayed on a board in the setting or can be communicated through a letter from the staff as illustrated in Figure 4.9.

Practitioners may decide to include other information in the letter such as notification of a planned coffee morning, or they may choose to produce separate 'news' letters. Often children will go home at the end of the session proudly clutching a pile of paintings, drawings, models, etc. This sense of pride is to be fostered and such works of art are usually received with enthusiasm by parents. However, not all learning has a tangible 'end product' and it is important that the value of the learning process, and the conceptual achievements, is also understood by parents.

First Steps Nursery
'GROWTH AND LIVING THINGS'

Dear Parents and Carers,

Now that spring is with us, we will be looking particularly at 'growth and living things' with the children. We have planned some exciting activities including:

- Observing the life cycle of a butterfly and a frog (caterpillars and frogspawn are due to arrive next week – look out for the 'Living Things' display!)

- A visit to a local farm (parents and carers will be invited to join us – details to follow).

- A search for 'mini-beasts' in the outside play area.

- Growing a range of vegetables and flowers, observing and measuring their growth.

- A visit from a health visitor, talking about keeping healthy.

There are many ways in which you can help to develop your child's learning about 'growth and living things' at home. Here are a few suggestions from us – please let us know about your good ideas so that we can share them with other parents!

- A visit to the park looking at, and talking about, leaves, buds, flowers, insects.

- Making a scrapbook of things found in the park.

- A visit to the local garden centre to look at plants, seedlings, trees, shrubs.

- Digging and planting – there are many plants which will happily grow in pots on a window sill if access to a garden or allotment is difficult. (Cut-off carrot tops in a saucer of water quickly grow shoots and require little attention!)

- Talking about pets – how they have changed as they have grown, and the care they need.

- Talking about their own growth and the food/care they need to be healthy.

- Looking at photographs of themselves (from babyhood to present day).

Thank you for your co-operation – have fun investigating with your child!

The nursery staff

Figure 4.9 Letter to parents: 'Growth and living things'

Although practitioners aim to verbally share information about children's experiences on a daily basis, it can be helpful (particularly to parents who are unable to have daily contact with the setting) sometimes to send a brief written explanation of an activity enjoyed by a child home at the end of the day. This will be especially useful in the absence of an 'end product' to the activity. The production of a photocopiable pro forma (to which individual observations can be added) for use during focus activities reduces the length of time taken to record the information (see Figure 4.10). Where practitioners have access to a photocopier in the setting, written observations of spontaneous activities (intended for inclusion in profiles) could occasionally be photocopied and a copy sent to the parent with a standard explanation note attached. Such information may prove to be a useful prompt for children who, when asked about the day's activities, invariably respond with the easiest answer – 'Nothing', or perhaps, 'I don't know'! Although persistent questioning is unlikely to be the right course of action in such a situation, having some information about a particular activity will enable the parent to more effectively engage in conversation with the child about that activity, asking informed, and focused, questions. It will also help to raise the status of activities with no concrete 'end product' as valuable learning experiences. (See also Chapter 2, page 67, 'Making games' and Chapter 3, page 88, 'Our Goldfish'.)

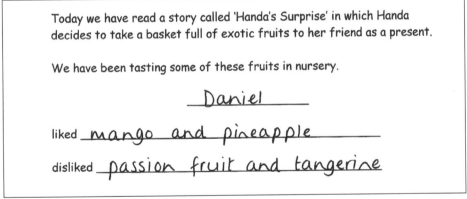

Figure 4.10 Explanation of 'tasting exotic fruits' activity

For parents who are unable to attend the setting on a daily basis, and indeed all other parents, video compilations or a series of digital photographs can be useful aids in discussion meetings. These can be used to highlight current interests in the setting and to talk about how these interests are reflected both in the setting and at home. Discussions can then include ideas of how to support those interests. They can also be used to document a learning journey or 'story' showing how a child's play and learning has evolved over a period of time. Photographic evidence is always helpful when sharing with parents the significance of particular experiences and in interpreting the learning in terms of the curriculum. Of course, such information sharing meetings can also serve as useful training sessions for less experienced staff.

Figure 4.11 shows how children's learning in the home and the setting is inseparable. This very long message was written by a child at home just as her younger sister was about to start attending the nursery. She was concerned that staff would not know how to look after her sister and, as a prolific emergent writer, recorded the necessary details on paper. She, with her mum and sister, brought in the written instructions the next morning, presented them to the nursery manager and read back her marks. She was then happy to leave her work with the manager, relieved that the important information had been imparted!

Figure 4.11 Looking after my sister

Children's 'profiles' should include photographic evidence of learning and are another way in which practitioner and parent can combine information to give a more complete picture of the child's learning achievements. Purposes of, and methods of compiling, profiles will be looked at in Chapter 6.

Story sacks containing a book, related props and a list of suggestions as to how parents can extend learning are a useful 'link' resource. Commercially produced story sacks are available from catalogues but teams often prefer to prepare their own, building up a bank over time. Children will be invited to take a sack home for a few nights and share story experiences with their family. Figure 4.12 shows an example of a supporting leaflet included in a story sack focusing on *The Very Hungry Caterpillar* by Eric Carle.

The provision of information such as play-dough recipes, instructions for how to make a sock puppet and lists of useful resources to include in a 'junk modelling box' at home will be appreciated by many parents. Children may also be asked to bring resources from home to support learning in the setting such as recycled materials (e.g. cereal boxes, cardboard tubes, yoghurt pots) for model-making in the workshop, items for an 'interest' table (e.g. natural forms, objects of a particular colour), photographs of themselves as babies for a display on 'growing up'. Children's achievements are often summarised more formally at intervals during and/or at the end of their time in the setting in the form of written 'records of achievement' for parents. These will be looked at in more detail in Chapter 6, but it is worth mentioning here the importance of giving parents opportunities to respond to, and discuss, the information included in such reports. Time should be planned for practitioners to talk, undisturbed (as far as possible), with parents about their child's progress.

> Conversations with parents can benefit all parties concerned. It benefits teachers because of their increased knowledge of the child, it benefits parents by making them genuine partners in their child's learning and it benefits children, who see home and school as mutually interested in their education.
>
> (Fisher 1996)

The two-way flow of information between practitioner and parent about the child is a vital aspect of the partnership. Children's achievements at home and in the setting should be celebrated as well as concerns voiced, and parents should feel comfortable in approaching staff. If the content of the discussion is of a sensitive nature, it will need to be conducted in privacy and confidentiality respected. It should be the aim of all key adults in a child's life to build an effective network system through which they can communicate information to support the child in making progress in all areas of learning. Sharing the knowledge that each of those adults has about the child is essential in addressing the needs of the 'whole child'.

STARTING WITH A STORY

The Very Hungry Caterpillar

By Eric Carle

Sharing stories can be a very enjoyable experience for both the adult and the child as well as being crucial to the child's development as a 'reader'. Try and find a slot in the day when you have plenty of time to spend with your child and settle down in a comfortable and quiet place. Here are a few general points to discuss that will help your child to understand how books 'work':

- Ask your child to look at the front of the book cover and to suggest what the book might be about.
- Talk about the author and the illustrator. Think about other books you may have read by the same author. Look for books by the same author in the library or bookshops.
- Encourage your child to find the first page and to turn the pages as you read.
- Talk about the difference between the illustrations and the text. Use words such as 'word', 'letter', 'picture'.
- Encourage your child to look carefully at the illustrations and to talk about what is happening in them, they may be able to tell the story, or make up their own, by 'reading' the pictures.
- Encourage your child to predict what might happen next in the story, or to guess how it might end. Use words such as 'start', 'beginning', 'next', 'after', 'then', 'end'.
- Talk about characters in the story.
- Retell the story together afterwards, sequencing key events in order. Use the illustrations and props as prompts.
- Make up your own stories using the same characters.

Stories can also help to develop children's learning in other areas

Here are a few activity ideas related to the story of *The Very Hungry Caterpillar*. You may want to try some of them with your child.

- Talking about the life cycle of a butterfly. Looking for caterpillars and butterflies in the garden or park.
- Looking in information books to find out the names of different butterflies, what they eat and where they live.
- Counting pieces of fruit in your fruit bowl. Counting out, for example, four grapes for each person.
- Talking about a healthy diet and the things that help us to grow.
- Looking closely at real apples, pears, plums, strawberries and oranges. Cutting the fruit up and looking at pips and stones.
- Drawing the fruit.
- Discussing the days of the week and talking about regular weekly activities, for example, 'On Monday we go swimming', 'On Tuesday we go to Grandma's house for tea'. Talking about what you had to eat yesterday and what you would like for tea tomorrow.
- Making butterfly wing pictures by painting a pattern on one side of a piece of paper, folding it over and pressing to produce a mirror image on the other side. Use a safety mirror to create symmetrical images of other objects.

Figure 4.12 *The Very Hungry Caterpillar*

Key Points for Good Practice

- Celebrate diversity and embrace the cultural experiences of children and families. Increase knowledge and understanding within the team of a range of cultures. Support the development of the child's own cultural identity.
- Value information from parents and other settings about a child's experiences prior to entering your setting.
- Listen with respect to parents' concerns and respond appropriately, for example, giving relevant information, reassurance with reasons, observing the child.
- Remember that much of children's learning takes place in the home or community. Throughout the foundation stage, take time to find out about children's individual interests and achievements outside the setting.
- Encourage parents to contribute to their child's profile. Emphasise that the profile is a celebration of the child's achievements.
- Involve parents in the planning and reviewing of their child's IEP and in the planning of the next phase (remember the parent's right to be involved in this process).
- Share your observations and assessments of children's learning with their parents on an ongoing basis and in summary reports.
- Be aware of those parents for whom English is an additional language. Where possible offer bilingual support for them during discussions.
- Make sure that systems are in place for communicating with those parents who do not have daily contact with the setting.
- Keep parents fully informed about the foundation stage curriculum.
- Involve parents in their child's learning in the setting and offer suggestions as to how they can appropriately support learning at home.

Nursery education should throughout be an affair of co-operation between the nursery and home and it will only succeed to the full if it carries the parents into partnership.

(Department of Education and Science 1967 para. 32)

CHAPTER 5

Planning display as part of the curriculum

Displays are focal points for learning.

(Lancaster 1987)

The content of this chapter is organised as follows:

The aim of the chapter is to define the purpose of display and to offer guidance in providing high-quality display which will be an integral part of the learning environment, and which will make a positive contribution to the children's development in all areas.

Why construct a display?

There are a number of reasons why a practitioner may decide to construct a display in the setting, including:

- To celebrate children's achievements
- To stimulate children's interest and/or imagination
- To engage children in an activity
- To extend children's knowledge in a particular area
- To provide information for adults

Planning a display

It is not necessary, in most cases, to write a full plan for a display, although this can be helpful in some circumstances and these will be discussed later in the chapter. It is, however, essential for all adults in the setting to be aware of the aims of the display and its proposed uses. It is a good idea to discuss display plans as a team, and asking questions in order to clarify purpose can be a useful exercise. For example:

- What is the learning focus of the display?
- Who will benefit from the display?
- What will they learn?

Having determined the reasons for constructing the display, the practitioner can then decide on the most appropriate methods of organisation and presentation. There will be a multitude of alternatives and decisions will, again, be influenced to a large extent by practicalities and physical features of the setting. Practitioners may not have access to permanent wall boards, shelving or suitable surfaces and will need to think about how to provide portable displays which can be stored away between sessions. Folding screens can be very useful pieces of equipment in such circumstances, as can wheeled storage units (with a surface at child level), portable frameworks (from which to hang children's work, objects of interest, etc.), free-standing open shelving and sandwich-style boards.

Throughout this chapter, examples of displays will be categorised as:

- *Wall*: this will refer to all displays fixed to a vertical surface, for example, wall-mounted boards, free-standing boards, screens
- *Table top*: including all horizontal surfaces (e.g. tops of cupboards, large trays or boards)
- *Shelf*: open shelving, fixed or free-standing
- *Suspended*: pieces of work or objects displayed by hanging them from a framework or permanent fixture in the setting

Whatever the type of display, it should be easily accessible to the child visually and (if appropriate) physically. This means making sure that displays are at a comfortable height for children and also that there is ample space around each for children to look at, or work with, displayed items. When the intended audience comprises solely of adults, wall displays should be at adult eye level. Ideally, both computer-generated and handwritten labels should be present in the setting. Where families with English as an additional language attend, labels in the appropriate language or script should be included. It may also be appropriate to provide labels in a large type or with tactile clues for visually impaired children.

The length of time a display stays in the setting is dependent on its purpose. Some displays will be constructed spontaneously, perhaps in response to children's immediate interests, and these may only be applicable for a brief period of time. Others are set up to complement work planned around a theme. Such displays may need to remain in the setting long enough for children to observe changes (e.g. tadpoles into frogs, seeds into plants during a 'growth and living things' topic) or may be altered by the practitioner at intervals during the 'topic' (e.g. if the planned learning is focused on 'books', the 'Looking at Books' display could be changed weekly to cover fiction, poetry, non-fiction or to celebrate the work of different authors). If a display is intended to engage children in an activity, ample time should be allowed for them to return to the activity, perhaps a number of times, to review or modify work and for reinforcement of concepts.

It may be that the display informs children about, for example, the different resources permanently on offer in an area of provision, in which case there would be justification for an extended period of display, as the relevance of that information is 'ongoing'. The practitioner should, however, be aware that display which becomes a 'permanent fixture' in the setting will probably cease to attract children's attention, or hold their interest, and its effectiveness may be significantly reduced after a certain period of time. (This may not be the case if adult time is regularly given to using long-term displays with children.) In any event, displays which are faded, 'tatty' or no longer complete are not going to inspire children to learn and should be dismantled.

In order to look in more depth at the different purposes and aspects of display the next part of the chapter is divided into three sections and explores ways in which display can be interactive, can celebrate work and can be informative. In practice many displays will, and should, include elements from two or all of these categories but examples have been selected according to their dominant purpose.

Display can be interactive

Interactive display can engage children physically and intellectually. It can actively involve children in first-hand learning experiences and challenge them, through questions and provision of appropriate and stimulating resources, to:

- Solve problems
- Design and build or make for a specific purpose (functional or fantasy)
- Find out (specific information or open ended)
- Follow instructions
- Have, and share, opinions

- Develop imaginative ideas
- Record information, observations, findings and imaginative ideas

The display may target a key area of learning or combine learning in two or three areas through a common theme. There may be a very specific intended outcome, or learning may be more open ended, the emphasis being on experimentation, exploration and investigation through the senses. Interactive display can also encourage collaborative and co-operative work.

Whatever the intended learning, for valuable experiences to be assured, practitioners must give high priority to planning the display.

Interactive display is one type of display where a more structured approach to planning will probably benefit both the practitioner and the child. Display of this nature should be regarded rather like a focus activity in that learning goals should be clearly defined and resources carefully selected. The adult role is also an important issue to be discussed by the team. During the period of time that the display is available, children will probably have free access to it and adults will need to intervene and support as appropriate. For this reason, all adults involved in the setting need to be aware of how to effectively support children working at the display from the time of its introduction. The nature of the support will vary from display to display, and child to child. The practitioner may need to focus on supporting the child in using the display independently, or may need to offer more direct learning support. Intervention will often be spontaneous, but there will probably be occasions when practitioners will want to plan time slots in the weekly planning for adult input, particularly to introduce the display (see 'leaf investigation', page 147) and to develop learning potential.

The main reason for producing a full, written plan for an interactive display is to inform, and remind, adults of its focus and objectives as and when they consider it appropriate to offer their support to children using the display. Plans will need to be easily accessible to adults and preferably displayed alongside the interactive display. They can also be a useful practical prompt for practitioners when repeating a display and gathering resources.

The following two plans are offered as examples. The reader will note that, although both displays fall into the category of 'interactive display', each sets different expectations in terms of children's use of resources. The 'shape and colour decision tree' is quite specific in its guidance, offering a series of instructions which will focus children's learning on some specific objectives. In the second example of the 'exploring sound' display, activities are of a more investigative nature and learning intentions more open ended.

INTERACTIVE DISPLAY:
SHAPE AND COLOUR DECISION TREE

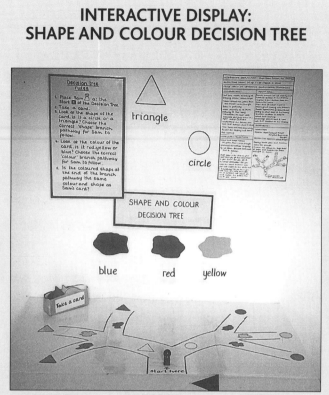

Figure 5.1 Shape and colour decision tree interactive display

Date of introduction and expected duration

- 6 January for 2 weeks

Type of display

- Table top or wall

Key area of learning

- Mathematical development

Learning objectives

- To match, recognise and name key colours and shapes
- To make decisions according to given criteria
- To develop logical thinking and to follow pathways

> **Working towards early learning goals in key areas** (QCA 2000)
>
> - Use language such as 'circle' or 'bigger' to describe the shape and size of solids and flat shapes
> - Use everyday words to describe position
> - Use developing mathematical ideas and methods to solve practical problems
>
> *(Shape, space and measures)*

Resources

- Horizontal surface and wall space or vertical board
- Decision cards (coloured shapes – red, yellow, blue – circle, triangle) in a box
- Colour and shape labels
- 'Sam' doll
- Decision tree drawn on large sheet of card[1]
- Decision tree instructions for use with or by children
- Copy of display plan (for adult)

Activities

Children will:

- Select a card and look at its shape
- Decide which shape 'branch' to take, circle or triangle?
- Follow the branch (with the card or 'Sam' doll) until it divides
- Look at the colour of the card
- Decide which colour 'branch' to take, blue, red or yellow?
- Follow the branch to its limit
- Compare the coloured shape at the end of the branch with the one on the card selected – is it the same?

Adult role

Adult will:

- Set up the display and check resources daily
- Introduce the display to children, explaining objectives
- Plan time for adult input (observing, and working with, children)
- Spontaneously support children as appropriate modelling use of key vocabulary and asking questions

---

[1] It is helpful to include a diagram of the layout of the decision tree at this point – see Figure 5.2.

Key vocabulary and questions

Vocabulary: Colour and shape names: red, blue, yellow, circle, triangle. Positional and directional language: up, down, forwards, backwards, next to, between

Questions: What colour is the circle? What shape is your card? Can you tell me two things about your card? (colour and shape) Have you got the same shape as your friend? Look at the shape of your card – which branch should you choose? Does your card match the coloured shape at the end of your chosen 'route'? Did you make the correct decisions? Did you reach the correct destination? Where do you think you made a mistake? Do you think you would reach the same destination with a different card? Where do you think this card would lead you? Can you explain the 'decision tree' rules to your friend?

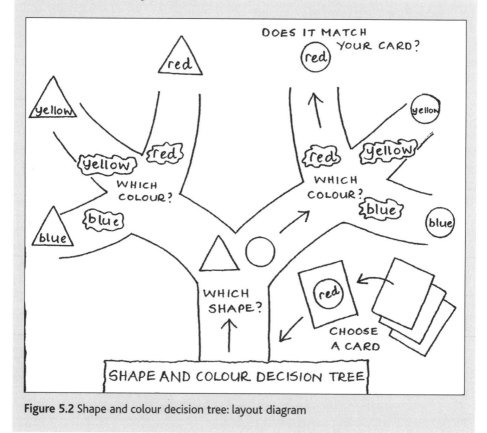

Figure 5.2 Shape and colour decision tree: layout diagram

INTERACTIVE DISPLAY:
EXPLORING SOUND

Date of introduction and expected duration

- 10 June for 3 weeks

Type of display

- Table top or suspended

Key areas of learning

- Communication, language and literacy
- Creative development

Learning objectives

- To listen to, and discriminate between, a variety of sounds
- To experiment with materials to produce different sounds
- To represent one sound with another

Working towards early learning goals in key areas (QCA 2000)

- Hear and say initial and final sounds in words, and short vowel sounds within words

  (Linking sounds and letters)

- Recognise and explore how sounds can be changed, sing simple songs from memory, recognise repeated sounds and sound patterns and match movements to music

  (Music)

- Express and communicate their ideas, thoughts and feelings by using a widening range of materials, suitable tools, imaginative and role-play, movement, designing and making, and a variety of songs and musical instruments

  (Responding to experiences and expressing and communicating ideas)

Resources

- A range of musical instruments including commercially produced instruments, instruments made by adults and children in the setting, instruments from other cultures

- Copper piping (cut to different lengths) suspended (to hang at different levels) from a large wire lampshade frame hung from the ceiling. Additional lengths of metal and plastic piping, wooden sticks and fabric-covered sticks provided for use by children to 'play' the hanging pipes
- A range of materials with which children can make their own instruments, for example, cardboard boxes, rubber bands, yoghurt pots, margarine pots, cardboard tubes, pieces of fabric, sand, dried peas
- A box of 'animal cards' – photographs of animals to be used as prompts for children when relating sounds to animals, for example, lion, mouse, elephant, crocodile, sparrow
- Fiction and non-fiction books about musical instruments
- A board (to be used as a screen)

Activities

Children will:

- Handle commercially produced, and other, instruments
- Listen to and compare sounds made by different instruments
- Talk about their observations using key vocabulary and descriptive language
- With an adult or friend, play sound matching games (play the instrument behind a screen and ask your friend to guess what is making the sound)
- Experiment with sound using one instrument – looking at the range of sounds that can be produced and how sounds can be changed
- Try different ways of making sounds using the materials provided
- Make an instrument and use it to accompany singing
- Think about the characteristics of an animal and find a sound that expresses the characteristics

Adult role

Adult will:

- Set up and introduce the display
- Replenish stocks of consumable resources daily
- Plan time to work alongside, and observe, children
- Intervene spontaneously as appropriate, asking questions and modelling use of key vocabulary

Key vocabulary and questions

Vocabulary: Loud, quiet. Children should also be encouraged to use descriptive language, and make up their own words, related to sounds, for example, rattling, banging, twanging, tinkling, pinging, swishing.

Questions: What kind of sound does the instrument make? Does it sound the same as this one? What kind of sound do you think this instrument will make? Can you find an instrument that makes a loud sound? Can you make an instrument that makes a rattling sound? What could you use to make a 'pinging' sound? Which instrument makes a sound like an elephant? What animal does this sound remind you of? Can you guess which instrument is making this sound?

When writing a plan, it is the content that is the important issue and, as long as the necessary information is included, the way in which it is organised and presented is a matter of preference. It is, however, helpful, once the team has made a decision regarding format, if all plans follow the chosen format.

The early years practitioner aims to encourage an independent approach to learning in young children and interactive display has an important role to play in encouraging both independent thought and independent use of resources. Young children's thinking can be challenged, and ideas developed, through stimulation of the imagination, exploration and investigation, and examples of displays included in this chapter illustrate a variety of 'starting points'. The way in which a display is arranged, labelled and used by adults will affect the way in which the child responds to, and interacts with, it. For example, clear instructions, signs and labels which are accompanied by pictures, photographs or symbols will more easily enable a child to complete a task independently. An introduction to the display including a verbal explanation, and questions, focused on the learning objectives can also support the child in using the display independently – this introductory session could be planned as an adult focus in the weekly planning.

Leaf investigation

Type of display
- Wall or table top

Key areas of learning
- Knowledge and understanding of the world
- Communication, language and literacy

Learning objectives

- To observe and compare leaves, looking at shape, pattern and size
- To talk about observations
- To understand that non-fiction books can inform and to use non-fiction books as a source of information

Resources

- Photographs, posters, non-fiction picture books, children's drawings and paintings with a leaf, tree, autumn theme
- A range of autumn leaves
- Magnifying glasses
- Question cards, labels and key vocabulary cards

Suggested content of practitioner's introduction

- Look what we have on our book display today – what do you think the books are about? How do you know?
- Here are some of the leaves we collected in the park yesterday
- Tell us what you already know about these leaves
- Let's see what else we can find out about the leaves
- Look closely at the leaves, what do you notice about them? Are they all the same colour and size? Can you see the patterns that the leaf 'veins' make?
- Look in the books. Look at the pictures, can you match any of our leaves to the pictures? What kind of tree does this leaf come from? What happens to leaves in the autumn?

Following a brief introduction such as this, children are equipped with a purpose and appropriate resources for learning and should (although further adult input at a later stage will be helpful) be encouraged to carry out an independent 'leaf investigation'. Resources should also be made available for them to record their findings (e.g. mark-making equipment, bookmarks).

Of course, as with any learning activity, the practitioner must plan for differentiation and displays should be of interest and use to children at various developmental stages. In the example of the 'leaf investigation', the resources provided will enable learning to take place at all levels from, for example, tactile explorations with no verbal observations, to the accessing of information about specific leaves through reading pictures and key words.

Figure 5.3 shows a display constructed in a setting attended by children throughout the foundation stage. It is a good example of a 'differentiated' display.

The examples given of 'possible activities' indicate the wide range of learning experiences that could take place on the 'journey' towards early learning goals, particularly in the areas of knowledge and understanding of the world, and communication, language and literacy. The display enables children to begin the journey at their own starting point – it can challenge all children, but will exclude none.

Come and make a rocket

Type of display

- Wall or table top

Key area of learning

- Knowledge and understanding of the world

Resources

- Signs (writing and diagrams): 'Come and make a rocket', 'You will need', 'Can you open the top to let the astronaut in?', 'Sign here when you have made your rocket'

- Components, 'astronaut' dolls, 'launching pad', pen

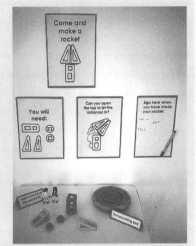

Figure 5.3 Come and make a rocket

Possible activities

- Handling, looking at, comparing and talking about the components
- Experimenting with the components, finding ways of fixing them together
- Looking at the joined components and deciding what the 'model' could be, for example, 'It looks like a tower!'
- Matching components to those on the 'You will need' sign
- Following the plan to build a rocket using the components[2]
- Exploring different ways of 'hinging' the top of the rocket
- Using the rocket in imaginative play or story-making activities
- Designing and making own rocket, talking about and recording plans or instructions (the child would need access to a range of components)
- Signing name (at own developmental stage of writing) to register engagement in the activity

---

[2] The display photographed offered a limited range of components (i.e. only those needed to build the rocket). Practitioners may decide to offer a wider range of components, requiring children to make the necessary selection when following the plan.

Children may be required to move around the setting in order to achieve objectives and displays could 'send' children on searches for objects or quests for information, perhaps following arrows or other signs. The following display is an example of this approach:

Billy's Beetle

Although this display offers good opportunities for retelling a favourite story (communication, language and literacy) and also for using everyday language to describe position (mathematical development), the practitioners chose ICT (knowledge and understanding of world) as the key area of learning. They had recently purchased some remote-control vehicles but in order for children to be able to control these effectively, they would need to be able to read the arrow symbols on the handset. They used the children's interest in the story *Billy's Beetle* (by Mick Inkpen) to introduce these symbols and to give physically active experiences of responding to them on a larger scale.

Billy's Beetle

Type of display

- Table top (also requires children to move around the setting)

Key area of learning

- Knowledge and understanding of the world

Resources

- A copy of the book *Billy's Beetle*
- An enlarged picture of Billy
- A sign: 'Where is Billy's Beetle?' and 'Follow the arrows', arrow signs (forwards, backwards, left, right – arranged around the setting and leading to the beetles)
- Small boxes
- Information books about beetles
- Plastic beetles will be hidden under a log or in amongst the grass in an area of the outdoor space

Activity

Children look at the story book, talking about characters and events in the story with their friends. They take a box and go to look for the beetle, following the signs until they reach the beetles. They then return the beetle to Billy. At the end of the session or day, the equipment will be replaced and one of the practitioners will move the signs to alter the route for the next day.

Looking at homes

Type of display

- Table top or wall

Key area of learning

- Knowledge and understanding of the world

Resources

- Close up photographs of brick and stone walls
- Photographs of builders at work
- Pictures of semi-detached, terraced, detached houses, caravans, flats, bungalows, homes from other countries
- Copies of architects' plans
- Books about animals' homes, etc.
- 'Challenge card': 'Can you build a house for Robina (small doll)?'
- Large selection of interlocking bricks

Activity

Children look at, and talk about, photographs and plans and build a house for a small doll using interlocking bricks. Individuals contribute to the building of the house over a period of time to produce a finished piece of work. The display will have, as well as offering information to children, engaged them in the practical application of their knowledge about building, given them an opportunity to practise a skill (joining bricks) and given them a purpose for building. Working with others on the construction will encourage evaluative discussion. Parents can be involved in learning experiences with their child through interactive display and the 'question table' is a popular, and effective, example of such a display.

The question table

The question table is often offered on a daily basis and can become part of the permanent provision. Children, supported by parents, are required, as part of the beginning of session routine, to register their response to a daily question with by placing their name card in a 'yes' or 'no'[3] container. The questions may refer

---

[3] This does not always have to be the case – children could be offered a number of alternative answers, for example, 'What is your favourite colour?' Children are required to put their name card in the red, blue or yellow bowl (labelled with colour names). Practitioners should take care not to confuse children by frequently changing the 'answering system'.

to, for example, interests in the setting, seasonal changes, or may aim to develop concepts.

Children may be asked to:

● Observe

● Reason

● Recall

● Compare

● Predict

● Express opinions and preferences

Figure 5.4 The question table

Although the name 'question table' implies a 'table top' type of display, this activity could be just as successfully presented on a wall, for example, name cards in the shape of apples, and with hoop and loop fastening tape attached to the back, could be removed from a wall-mounted carpet tile and displayed on either the 'yes' or the 'no' apple tree.

Listed below are some examples of questions:

● Did you pass a shop on your way to nursery today?

● Have the leaves started to fall off the trees yet?

● Are you wearing anything red today?

● Did you enjoy our 'dragon dance' yesterday?

● Is the ball in the box? (provide real objects)

● In our story yesterday, did the fox catch Rosie?

● Do you like to eat apples?

● Do you think it will rain today?

● Have you looked at our 'book of the week'?

● Have you got blue eyes? (provide a mirror)

A variation on the question table idea is the 'question book'. This is usually a large scrapbook covered in 'special' paper. The question is written at the top of the page, and children respond by signing their name in the 'yes' column or the 'no' column. It can be interesting for children to look back at previous pages with an adult, and compare responses to questions.

Other examples of interactive display

'Owl Babies' behaviour chart

Type of display

- Wall or suspended

Key area of learning

- Personal, social and emotional development

Working towards key early learning goal (QCA 2000)

- Work as part of a group or class, taking turns and sharing fairly, understanding that there need to be agreed values and codes of behaviour for groups of people, including adults and children, to work together harmoniously

---

Resources

- Setting's 'rules' sign (e.g. 'Be kind to other children and look after our toys')
- Large picture of an owl, tree pictures and a picture of three baby owls – pictures to be cut out, laminated and arranged vertically or horizontally large owl, trees, baby owls
- Sign: 'I want my Mummy!'
- Book: *Owl Babies* by Martin Waddell

Activity

Children will be familiar with the *Owl Babies* story. They, as a group, move the 'mummy' owl towards her babies (one tree at a time) in response to evidence that the rules are being adhered to. When mummy owl reaches her babies, the whole group receives a 'reward', for example, another visit from Oscar the clown (see Chapter 4, page 123).

Weaving a Christmas Tree

Type of display

- Table top

Key area of learning

- Creative development

> **Working towards key early learning goal (QCA 2000)**
> - Explore colour, texture, shape, form and space in two and three dimensions

Resources

- A willow twig 'wigwam' or large, triangular piece of plastic webbing (both available from garden centres – intended for training climbing plants)
- Box containing strips of green (a range of shades) fabric, ribbon and cord
- Key vocabulary labels, for example, weave, over, under, in, out

Activity

Children, and parents, select pieces of fabric, etc. to weave into the framework to create a 'woven Christmas tree' over a period of two to three weeks prior to Christmas. The tree can then be adorned with children's made decorations tied onto the framework.

Whose shoes?

Type of display

- Table top

Key area of learning

- Mathematical development

> **Working towards key early learning goal (QCA 2000)**
> - Use language such as 'circle' or 'bigger' to describe the shape and size of solids and flat shapes

Resources

- Five pairs of shoes (soles of various shapes and sizes)
- Templates of the shoes arranged in pairs on the table top
- Key vocabulary labels, for example, big, small

Activity

Children match the shoes to the correct templates looking carefully at size and shape.

Look how we have changed!

Type of display

- Wall

Key area of learning

- Knowledge and understanding of the world

Working towards key early learning goal (QCA 2000)

- Find out about past and present events in their own lives, and in those of their families and other people they know

---

Resources

- Folded cards attached to the wall – one for each child, showing a picture of the child as a baby on the front, and as they are now, inside
- Posters and pictures of 'babyhood'

Activity

Children guess who the baby photographs are, and then lift the flap to find out if they were correct. They talk about how they have changed (e.g. appearance, food, independence).

Where's Spot?

Type of display

- Table top

Key area of learning

- Mathematical development

Working towards key early learning goal (QCA 2000)

- Use everyday words to describe position

Resources

- Book: *Where's Spot?* by Eric Hill

- 'Spot' soft toy
- Photographs of Spot in different positions around the setting
- Question labels (e.g. Can you hide or find Spot under the table? On the cupboard? In the box? Under the chair?)

Activity

Children work with a friend, hiding and finding Spot, and using key 'positional' vocabulary to describe his location

Five Little Speckled Frogs

Type of display

- Table top or wall

Key area of learning

- Mathematical development

Working towards key early learning goal (QCA 2000)

- Count reliably up to ten everyday objects

Resources

- Rhyme: *Five Little Speckled Frogs*
- Numerals 1–5
- Real log
- Five frog models
- A pond (e.g. small silver foil tray, tissue paper 'pond weed', small stones – children could make this)

Activity

Children sing the rhyme, counting, and putting the frogs into the pool in turn.

Story characters

Type of display

- Table top or suspended

Key area of learning

- Communication, language and literacy

Working towards key early learning goal (QCA 2000)

- Show an understanding of the elements of stories, such as main character, sequence of events and openings, and how information can be found in non-fiction texts to answer questions about where, who, why and how

Resources

Silhouettes of familiar story book characters (e.g. Kipper, the monster from *Not Now Bernard*, Big Bear and Little Bear from *Let's Go Home Little Bear*) cut out of black sugar paper, laminated for durability and hung at different levels from a length of dowel suspended above the table top. All corresponding books displayed on the table top.

Activity

Children recognise and talk about the characters and match silhouettes to pictures in books.

Display can celebrate

Display can be used to celebrate:

- Children's achievements
- Adults' work (e.g. artists)
- Different cultures, languages, beliefs, interests and experiences

Using display for the purpose of celebration can promote learning in the area of personal, social and emotional development by helping to:

- Raise self-esteem
- Develop in children a respect for their own work and the work of others
- Develop in children respect for, and understanding of, different cultures and beliefs

Celebration of children's work is a reason for display with which most practitioners feel comfortable. Traditionally the display of children's artwork has become a characteristic feature of the early years setting. Of course it is important to value and celebrate work of this nature, but in doing so practitioners should not exclude work in other areas of the curriculum. Children's achievements in all areas of learning should be in evidence in the setting, and unique qualities and individuality recognised.

In selecting work for display, the practitioner should consider the achievements of the individual, and not judge all work against an inflexible standard in order to display the 'best' items. Although work of a high standard should indeed be displayed, and those children applauded for their achievements, it should not exclude, or undermine, the achievements of those at an earlier stage on the 'learning journey'.

When displaying children's work, the practitioner may choose to exhibit only the finished piece of work or may decide to show the process, or contributory work. A series of photographs of work in progress (e.g. models made in the workshop) is an effective way of showing how the child has arrived at the 'end product'. This type of display will not only serve as a teaching aid to other children, but will also communicate the message to children and adults that the learning process is as important as the end result. The photographic display is also a good way of celebrating learning achievements that produce no concrete, or permanent, evidence, for example, investigating snow in the water tray, mark-making with water and brushes in the outside area (see Figure 1.14) and shadow play (see Figure 1.15).

In the case of observational drawing or painting, it is a good idea, where possible, to display the stimulus alongside children's work. This will encourage further observation and discussion.

Activities planned around a theme will often generate some exciting work for display, for example, during a focus on 'hats', activities may be as diverse as trying on different hats and looking at themselves in a mirror, drawing themselves in hats from observation, making up stories about a bejewelled crown, decorating straw hats, and making hats in the workshop to support role-play. A display of children's work showing one aspect of this project could be constructed, or the 'one aspect' could be displayed in the context of all the other related learning.

Following the 'Jungle Play' and 'The Lion's Visit' focus activities described in Chapter 3, a display was constructed which incorporated the following:

- Photographs of 'jungle environments' built by children in the construction area
- Children's paintings of Lion
- Photographs of children constructing dens for Lion in the outside play area and the construction area
- Photographs of the finished den constructions with the lion 'in residence'
- Children's records of materials used to build the dens (picture tick lists, drawings, attempts at written lists)

- Children's letters to Lion
- Photographs of musical instruments made (spontaneously by children in the workshop) for Lion to play in his den
- Children's records of whether their musical instrument produced a 'loud' or 'quiet' sound

This display also included:

- Lion in his 'jungle box' and letters from Lion (see Figure 3.1 and Figure 3.2) to the children (the stimulus for 'Lion's Visit')
- A list of pertinent early learning goals

More general celebrations showing the range of activities in which children engage across all areas of provision will generate interest from parents and children, and can be quite enlightening to visitors. Figure 5.5 is an example of such a display. Content includes paintings, writing for different purposes, drawings, three-dimensional work, photographs of children working in areas of provision and brief explanations written by the practitioner.

Figure 5.5 Look what we do in nursery

Children's achievements can also be celebrated on audio tape, and a suitable tape recorder included on a table top display. 'Sound' poems (e.g. water sounds), word poems, singing, children making music and children talking about holiday experiences or favourite toys can easily be taped and children will enjoy listening.

Areas of provision such as the workshop and construction area should offer permanent display provision for the celebration of children's work and often the most practical type of display is the open shelf. The content of such display may be of a transient nature but it is important that children have a 'safe' place to put their work either as it is in progress or when it is finished. Children will learn to value their own work and that of others, and will enjoy looking at and talking about 'exhibits'. Folded cards and pencils should be supplied in order for children to make a name label to display next to their work.

Figure 5.6 Displaying children's work in the construction area

Part of the practitioner's role as an educator is to model skills and it is sometimes appropriate to include the work of adults in a display, preferably alongside the work of the children thereby giving equal status to both. This could be a model made in the setting by a parent, a carving by a local craftsperson, a letter written to the children by a member of staff, a photograph of a parent playing football for the local team or a reproduction of a painting by a famous artist.

An awareness of, and respect for, the beliefs and cultures of others should be part of the very fabric of the curriculum. Display should both reflect the attitude of respect and celebrate cultural diversity. Artefacts used should always be of good quality and authentic, and information accurate. Parents and other members of the community will often be happy to share traditions and help with the writing of dual language signs.

Acquaint children with cross-cultural symbols by collecting and displaying images of the sun, trees, birds and so on from various cultures and by talking about the moods the different images evoke. Does this bird look strong? Gentle? Helpful?

(Chapman 1978)

Other examples of display for celebration

Meet the authors

Type of display

- Table top or wall

Key area of learning

- Communication, language and literacy

Content

- Books by familiar authors (e.g. Eric Carle, Mick Inkpen, Pat Hutchins)
- Photographs and brief biographical sketch of each
- Book reviews by children and their parents
- Examples of books of children's work compiled by the practitioner
- Examples of children's story-making and writing attempts with photographs and brief biographical sketches of them

Celebrating

- Children as authors

The magic tree

Type of display

- Table top (workshop)

Key area of learning

- Knowledge and understanding of the world

Content

- A branch secured in a pot of sand to look like a tree
- Children's work (e.g. magic jewels, made jewellery, Christmas tree decorations) displayed hanging on the branch

Celebrating

- Children's skills (design and technology) and imaginative ideas

The Gallery[4]

Type of display

- Wall

Key area of learning

- Creative development

Content

- Children's paintings, prints, drawings and collages displayed alongside the work of established artists from different times and cultures

Celebrating

- Children as artists

The 'action' mobile

Type of display

- Suspended

Key area of learning

- Physical development

Content

- Photographs (pairs stuck together, back to back) of children (climbing, balancing, running, hopping, throwing, catching, kicking balls, crawling through tubes, riding bikes and scooters, sliding down the slide) hanging on thread (at different levels) and suspended from a wire frame, or from branches of a tree in the outside area

Celebrating

- Children's physical achievements (gross motor skills)

---

[4] The 'gallery' idea can also be used to display three-dimensional work.

The window hanging

Type of display

- Suspended

Key area of learning

- Creative development

Content

- Children's tissue paper collages on acetate sheet, joined together (by treasury tags threaded through holes at the top and bottom of each collage) and hung in front of a window

Celebrating

- Children's creative expression

Display can be informative

Most aspects of displays have now been covered in this chapter but guidance would not be complete without highlighting the purpose of display to communicate information. This reason for display has already been included as an aspect of other types of display, but there are cases when the main purpose of a display is to inform.

Display can be used to inform:

- Children
- Adults working in the setting
- Parents

The type of information displayed will vary but, in general terms, can be divided into the following areas:

- Information which directly supports the child in the learning process, either through factual content or instruction
- Information which helps the adult to support the child's learning
- Information which helps the adult to understand curricular aims and the nature of children's learning
- Practical information related to the organisation of the setting

Direct support can include the provision of books, posters, pictures and photographs to support a learning focus. For example, during a topic on water, the practitioner may construct a wall display in the water area which informs the child about various uses of water. This could include photographs of children using water in the setting for a variety of purposes, for example, drinking, bathing dolls, washing paint brushes, mixing paints, pouring from tea pots during tea parties, washing hands, watering plants. Posters and photographs of water being used outside the setting could also be displayed, for example, swimming pools, car washes, agricultural watering systems, narrow boats transporting people on canals, window cleaners. Topic work can also be supported by table top displays offering information in the form of artefacts such as bowls, plates, cups and cutlery made from different materials, and originating from different cultures, during a focus on 'food'. Many local authorities have a central stock of artefacts from which practitioners are able to select and borrow. Of course, it is best, where possible, to allow children to handle artefacts but it may be that some of the 'exhibits' are quite fragile and unlikely to stand up to constant handling. In this case they will have to be protected (perhaps in a plastic case) and children taught to look carefully. If practitioners wish the display to be 'interactive', children could be offered the necessary resources and encouraged to draw objects from observation.

Displays can also inform children about, and instruct them how to use, equipment in an area of provision. In, for example, the painting area a display could be constructed to show children the routines, and use of tools and materials, involved in mixing powder paint.

Mixing paint

In order for children to access the information independently, instructions should be illustrated with clear drawings or photographs.

- Put on a red apron
- Collect a palette, paint pots, water pot, spatula
- Take your water pot to the tap and fill it with water
- Choose a piece of paper and a brush
- Use the spatula to put some powder paint in the palette
- Use the brush to mix the paint with water
- Now you are ready to paint

This sort of information displayed in the setting is also very useful to adults in supporting children. When all adults encourage children to follow the same routines, these routines will become established quickly, and children will soon feel confident in using equipment independently.

Displaying information about curricular aims helps parents and other adults in the setting to understand how and why learning takes place. Such information can be displayed alongside other displays in explanation of activities or learning experiences, or can be sited in an area of provision giving examples, and aims, of cross-curricular learning. It will probably include reference to the key area of learning and early learning goals.

The following hints are of a practical nature and may be useful to practitioners when constructing displays.

Constructing displays: some practical hints

Wall display

- A simple, 'uncluttered' display is usually effective and easy to 'read'. The temptation to cram too much onto the board should be resisted – the result will probably be visual chaos and confusion for the children.

- Coloured work should be mounted carefully. Unless all the work has a common colour theme and can be unified by one colour (e.g. autumn leaves: orange), brightly coloured mounts and backing paper should be avoided as they will detract from, or conflict with, the displayed work. Black-and-white work such as pencil or charcoal drawings can more effectively be mounted on a bright colour.

- The mount should be kept fairly narrow, it is rarely necessary to exceed 1 cm. A slightly wider mount at the bottom will prevent the illusion of the work 'slipping' down.

- All lines should be straight. The composition of a display can be helped by the lining up of verticals and horizontals.

- Arranging items selected for display on the floor before attaching them to the wall is often a useful exercise. It will be easy to move them around until a final decision has been made.

- The composition of a child's work should not be altered by cutting away large amounts.

- To add another dimension to the wall board, a shelf can be attached. This can be used to display items such as books, toys and natural forms. Shelves can easily be made from strong cardboard boxes (see Figure 5.7). They can then

Figure 5.7 Making a shelf for a wall display

be painted or covered with paper or fabric. Once stapled to the wall, the 'box shelves' should provide a firm surface, although it is not advisable to display anything too heavy on them. (Shelves must be visually accessible to children.)

Table top display

- Wooden blocks or upturned boxes under draped fabric are effective in creating surfaces for display at different levels.
- Plywood cuboids (a range of sizes) painted in white emulsion can be used to display natural forms in a simple but eye-catching way.
- Free-standing labels can be made from folded card or signs and labels can be displayed in moulded perspex photograph frames.
- A covering of hessian can be an effective surface on which to display natural forms.

Shelf display

- Open 'grid' shelving units attached to the wall, mounted on unbreakable mirror sheets, make an interesting display. Items will be reflected in the mirror, giving the impression of another dimension, and children will be offered an alternative view of the items.
- Grid shelving units painted with matt black paint to show off white objects effectively and create a striking display.
- Shelves attached to adjustable brackets slotted into aluminium strips (all widely available in DIY stores) on the wall make a versatile structure for display. The height of the spaces between shelves can be altered, and shelves removed if necessary.
- Wide shelves (at least 30 cm) are necessary in the workshop area to avoid the frustration of larger models falling off.
- When space is limited, shelves can be hinged and folded flat to the wall when not in use.

Suspended display

- If a number of items are being displayed, they should hang at different levels and not obscure other items or displays from children's vision.
- Hanging items are constantly twisting and turning and may be more effective if double sided. This point is particularly applicable to hanging word labels.

- Practitioners should check that the display is not going to obstruct adults or children (or interfere with 'beamed' security systems!), and should guard against an 'oppressive' feeling in the setting resulting from too much material hanging from low ceilings.
- The effect of transparent or 'sparkly' displays will probably be enhanced if they are situated close to a light source.

Through trial and error, and through the sharing of practice between colleagues, the practitioner will build up a bank of ideas for display which can be adapted and combined to suit the needs of the children and characteristics of the setting. The examples given in this chapter are a small sample but show how display can, with a little imagination and planning, make an exciting contribution to the environment, inspiring children to want to learn and equipping them with the necessary tools and information to support them in their learning.

Key Points for Good Practice

- Remember that displays are part of the learning environment and should reflect the principles of the foundation stage curriculum.
- Think about the purpose of any display that you plan and make sure that it is successful in achieving objectives.
- When displaying children's work, remember that you are celebrating individuality and creativity. Present work with respect and value all stages of development.
- Use photographs to share experiences with no concrete outcome and to celebrate a process.
- Think about how you use display to motivate children. Talk with them about displays around the setting.
- Use display as a way to share information about the curriculum and how children learn with parents.
- Be creative in your use of equipment and space in producing displays.

Curiosity and intrinsic motivation are closely linked and there is no doubt they play an important part in helping children to develop positive attitudes towards learning. One of the main functions of the nursery is to provide a stimulating, enriching environment where children are encouraged to 'learn how to learn'.

(Curtis 1998)

CHAPTER 6

Observing children's play, assessing learning and keeping useful records

Assessment gives insight into children's interests, and possible difficulties in their learning from which next steps in learning and teaching can be planned.

(QCA 2000)

The content of this chapter is organised as follows:

- The assessment and planning cycle (page 168)
- Collecting information during the 'first contact' period (page 168)
- Observation and assessment in the setting (page 171)
- Recording and reporting (page 177)
- The Foundation Stage Profile (page 192)
- Key Points for Good Practice (page 192)

The assessment and planning cycle

Observation, assessment and planning are all vital aspects of the educator's role and part of an ongoing cycle of identifying and providing for children's learning needs. Figure 6.1 explains this cycle and shows clearly how one stage informs the next.

Collecting information during the 'first contact' period

Neither the learning process nor the 'assessment cycle' begin as the child enters the setting – parents have already spent three years with their child, observing and supporting her or his diverse learning, and will have assimilated a wealth of useful information. A child's learning will be continued, and built upon, in the setting. Prior experiences and achievements will influence the way in which a child approaches a new learning situation, and will impact on the learning that takes place. Practitioners should encourage parents to share information about their child on entry, and throughout their time at the setting.

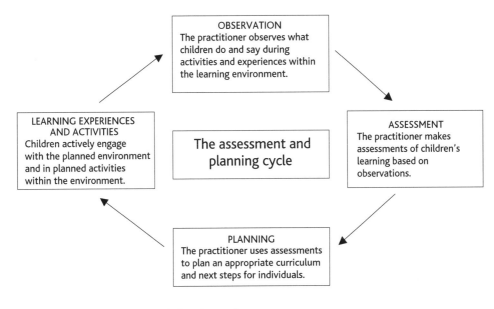

Figure 6.1 The assessment and planning cycle

In Chapter 4 ways in which useful information can be communicated between practitioner and parent are suggested. Ideas include the use of forms and questionnaires (during the 'first contact' period) on which to record personal details and also information about the child's previous experiences. The practitioner may complete the form during discussion with the parent or, alternatively, parents may be asked to complete it at their own convenience. Recorded information could include:

● Full name, date of birth, address and telephone number

● Names of main carers and siblings

● Home language

● Religion

● Contact names, addresses and telephone numbers

● Health – details of any contact with specialists or other agencies

● Previous pre-school experience (response re: settling-in, relationships with other children, activities enjoyed)

● Significant experiences such as a new baby in the family, loss of a family member, house move

● Particular interests

● Skill development, for example, using the toilet, dressing self, riding a tricycle, using tools (e.g. cutlery, a pencil)

- Any anxieties or behaviour issues

Many practitioners also produce an 'About Me' booklet which parent and child are encouraged to complete together at home. The child is often asked to bring the booklet back to the setting in order for the practitioner to talk with him or her about the content. It can then be included in the child's records. The 'About Me' booklet will probably require the adult and child to respond to statements such as the following:

- This is me. My name is _____
- I am _____ years old
- I live with
- My pets are
- My friends are
- My favourite book is
- My favourite toy is
- My favourite food is
- I am happy when
- When I come to pre-school, I will play with

Ample space should be available in each section for child's mark-making.

Some of the information collected at this early stage will be mainly of practical use to staff and some will be more directly useful in planning the curriculum for the child. A composite of all the information will help to give practitioners an understanding of where the child is on the 'learning journey', and provide a bank of knowledge which will enable the adult to interact more productively with the child.

During the period of first contact, information about the child can be acquired through observation of his responses during, for example, the home visit, as this practitioner's account illustrates:

As we arrived at the house for the home visit, Alistair flung open the door and shouted excitedly to his Gran – 'My teachers are here!' He was eager to look at the nursery photograph album and asked questions about the activities, particularly those taking place in the outside area. When asked if he liked to play outside, he responded 'Yes – I like to ride my bike – I want to go on that bike (pointing to the nursery tandem bike in the photograph). Alistair showed us his train track with pride and explained how he had fixed it together – Gran says that he spends a lot of time playing with his train, looking in his train books and watching his train video. As I talked with Gran, Stella [other member of staff] joined in the 'train play'. After a short while, Alistair's cousin [present during the whole visit] approached and asked to play. The two children became quite engrossed for about ten minutes, taking turns in pushing the train around the track to the shops, park, etc. At the end of the visit, I explained to Alistair that I had to go back to nursery and would see him again when he next came to nursery, and he replied 'Can I come back with you now?'

The account tells staff the following information, which can then be used, in conjunction with other information, when planning Alistair's 'settling-in' programme:

- He uses spoken language readily
- He is interested in what happens in nursery
- He is eager to come to nursery
- He is keen to play outside
- He likes to ride bikes
- He is interested in trains
- He is able to maintain concentration at a self-chosen activity
- He is able to share and take turns with another child
- He approaches adults with confidence in familiar surroundings

Observation and assessment in the setting

Victoria Hurst and Margaret Lally comment that:

> Children tell us about themselves through their behaviour, and there are clues to how we can best teach them to be found in their play and social interactions, in their conversations and the things they bring to school, in the way they use opportunities to explore new areas of learning and in the way they create stories, pictures, models and music.

> (Hurst and Lally 1992)

Observing children's play is the key to understanding their interests and learning needs and is a salient feature of the 'teaching' role. Practitioners will need to allow time for observation of children at play in the setting. Such 'observation time' may be pre-planned, with a definite focus, or may be incidental. Observations can be written down, or noted verbally, but however they are reported, practitioners should have an effective system for sharing observations. A brief, daily meeting when staff talk about their observations of children can be a successful way of 'pooling' information, as can regular entries in, and discussion of, children's profiles (see page 181).

The broad aim of observation is:

- To gather information that will enable the practitioner to assess children's learning and consequently plan an appropriate curriculum, providing for the full range of needs within the setting

More particularly, practitioners may decide to make focused observations with the ultimate aim of:

- Assessing the learning of individuals, identifying needs and planning 'next steps' for individuals and groups of children (such observations may focus on an area of learning, or one aspect of an area)

- Evaluating and improving areas provision in terms of learning opportunities for all children

- Raising the profile of an area of learning and ensuring that learning in this area is taking place for all children and throughout the setting

Observing and assessing individuals

Practitioners observe children in order to find out:

- What they are able to do (skills)
- What they know and understand (knowledge and concepts)
- How they approach learning (attitudes)

When observing individuals, the practitioner may 'track' a child over a period of time perhaps looking specifically at an area of development – this can be a particularly useful approach when there are concerns about a child's development. Alternatively, the child may be observed in a particular area of provision or during a focus activity. Sometimes a child is 'targeted' by the team, and all practitioners make observations as they come into contact with her or him over the course of a session, or a few sessions. Although it is essential to plan observations such as those just described, the necessity for practitioners to be constantly 'tuned in' to children's learning should be stressed. Opportunities to observe, and assess, should be taken as they arise. Quite often unplanned observations are made in response to a significant behaviour or activity, and these can provide just as useful information as the 'scheduled' observations.

Young children should not be put in a 'test' situation. Assessment should always take place in an appropriate context and when a practitioner decides to plan an activity in order to assess certain aspects of a child's learning, that activity must be purposeful and interesting to the child.

When making structured observations, it can be useful to refer to lists of statements or questions; these prompts will help the practitioner to focus observations and to make clear assessments. In the following example, the practitioner had planned, in the weekly planning, to observe new children during the settling-in period, and started with the questions:

- *Who* do I want to observe?

- What do I want to find out about the child?
- How will I find out that information?
- How will I use the information?

Observation of Natasha

I want to assess Natasha's social development (particularly relationships with other children and participation in group play), and to know where she is on her journey towards the following early learning goals:

- Form good relationships with adults and peers
- Work as part of a group or class, taking turns and sharing fairly, understanding that there need to be agreed values and codes of behaviour for groups of people, including adults and children, to work together harmoniously

(Personal, social and emotional development)

I will track her throughout the setting for a period of ten minutes observation on Monday, Wednesday and Friday. I will use the assessment to inform future planning of Natasha's learning in the area of social development.

The practitioner then observed Natasha bearing in mind the following questions:

Does she:

- Observe other children's play from a 'safe' distance?
- Work alone in an area of provision?
- Work alongside other children, but with no interaction?
- Attempt contact with other children in close proximity? (e.g. making eye contact or offering toys)
- Interact with other children during play, for example, through conversation about the activity, giving and receiving objects?
- Take turns and share?
- Work co-operatively with other children, negotiating and problem-solving?

At the end of the week, the practitioner had collected the following information:

Monday: Natasha spent ten minutes in the home corner. At first she 'hovered' in the doorway watching as Tom and Lindsey set the table and pretended to eat tea. The other two children then left the area and Natasha sat at the table, rearranged the plates and cups and pretended to drink. As others entered and left the area she continued her play at the table.

Wednesday: Natasha played (briefly) alone in the sand area filling containers left by other children. She then moved to the office (again, no children in the area) and began mark-making. Andrew entered and sat down at the table with her. She looked up and watched as he selected a pencil and some paper. Andrew asked Natasha if she would like a pencil, she shook her head, looked down and continued with her mark-making. After five minutes in the office, Natasha observed (for two or three minutes) two children playing in the water area and then wandered outside.

Friday: Natasha approached the workshop where three children were already working. She watched from a distance of half a metre until Mrs Dent encouraged her to put on an apron, select some materials and make a model. After a little more support from Mrs Dent re: appropriate use of tools, Natasha worked happily alongside the other children pausing occasionally to observe what they were doing. When Sally explained to her that she had made a model of a dinosaur, Natasha looked at her face, and although there was no verbal response, eye contact was made.

The practitioner analysed the information collected during the observations to make an assessment of her learning.

Assessment

Natasha does spend time observing other children's play and quite often engages in solitary play in an area. She can be reluctant to enter an area of provision if others are already working in the area. However, she is happy to work alongside other children if they enter the area after her, or if an adult supports her in entering the group and engaging in play. She is beginning to communicate with other children by non-verbal means, and to respond to their approaches.

The assessment of Natasha's social development was then used to plan her next steps in that area of learning.

Next steps

- To choose to work alongside other children more frequently and to gain confidence in entering an area in which other children are already working
- To develop non-verbal contact with other children (e.g. passing objects, smiling) and to begin to respond verbally

Planned experiences and activities

Adult input: Support Natasha in entering an area of provision already being used by other children. Teach and reinforce routines and appropriate use of equipment in each area. Spend time playing in areas of provision with groups of children (including Natasha), encouraging interaction between children.

Focus activities

- Teddy bears' tea party in the home corner – setting the table for children and bears, passing food to each guest, pouring tea for everyone

- Circle games: rolling the ball to a friend (saying the friend's name before rolling), passing the teddy around the circle, passing the smile around the circle (each child, in turn, smiles at the child sitting next to them)
- Making presents and writing letters and giving them to a friend

Of course, what the practitioner learnt about Natasha during the periods of observation will not have been restricted to the area of social development targeted. Other useful information will have been gleaned, for example, the practitioner will probably have been enlightened about Natalie's mathematical development from watching her filling containers with sand on Wednesday. Such information can be valuable to the practitioner in planning for other areas of learning, and its contribution to the whole picture of a child's learning development should not be disregarded. When making focused observations, the skill is in registering the 'additional' information, without being distracted from the focus of the observation.

Making assessments of individuals from a number of observations (focused or incidental) over a period of time, rather than from one isolated observation, will give a more accurate picture of a child's stage of development, revealing strands and patterns across a range of situations. Sometimes interests, or repeated behaviours (often referred to as 'schemas') become apparent and form the basis of planning for individuals. For example, a child might be observed joining paper clips together with treasury tags, playing with interlocking jigsaws, connecting components from a construction set, and taping together cardboard tubes. Such observations would indicate to the practitioner that the child is fascinated by 'connection' and may prompt her or him to offer the child a range of materials and equipment through which to explore this perception further.

The importance of matching the curriculum to the child has already been highlighted a number of times in previous chapters on planning but can not be overemphasised. It is as a result of observing and assessing individuals that the practitioner is able to define and address their needs. With sound assessment procedures in place, staff will be able to identify any special educational needs at an early stage, and produce effective Individual Education Plans (IEPs) to support children in making progress. Careful record keeping is crucial in providing information to facilitate planning for current needs but also in providing evidence of difficulties in the early stages which may impact on the provision of support later on.[1] (See also Chapters 1 and 4.)

In order to plan appropriately for the child's next steps, the practitioner needs to be aware of the stages that a child passes through on the journey towards, and

---

[1]   See SEN Code of Practice (DfES 2001) for categories of special educational needs.

beyond, the early learning goals. Some practitioners will have studied children's development in areas of learning during their initial training and perhaps through subsequent training, others may feel less confident in this area. The DfES guidance material (*Curriculum Guidance for the Foundation Stage*, QCA 2000) for practitioners in early years settings offers examples of children working at different stages and breaks down learning (in each curricular area) into 'stepping-stones'. Practitioners will find the guidance a helpful tool in understanding children's learning and in planning 'next steps'. The section 'What does the practitioner need to do?' within each aspect of learning offers suggestions as to how to support and extend children's learning appropriately for their stage of development.

As the practitioner observes children, it may become apparent that a few have reached a similar stage in their development and are ready for certain next steps at the same time, or that two or three children have a shared interest. It may then be appropriate to plan an activity (or series of activities) for this group.

Evaluating and improving the provision

In aiming to offer all children rich learning opportunities in areas of provision, practitioners will have produced long-term plans detailing key areas of learning, resources, organisation, anticipated learning experiences and activities, adult role and key questions and vocabulary (see Chapter 1). Regular observation of children's play in each area will provide teams with the necessary information to evaluate the success of the area in terms of children's learning, to review long-term plans and to make the necessary changes to improve provision.

Before spending time observing in an area of provision, it will probably be a good idea to read through the long-term plan for that area. Asking the following questions whilst observing in an area is also likely to be helpful:

- Which children are choosing to work in the area?
- Are all needs being met? (Taking into consideration: gender, special educational needs, disabilities, more able children, ethnic groups and religious, social and cultural backgrounds)
- Which resources are being used? (Frequently? Regularly? Occasionally? Never?)
- How are children using the resources?
- How are all areas of learning developed through the provision? Which are the dominant areas?
- What kind of activities and learning experiences are taking place?
- What have the children learnt?

Figure 6.2 illustrates how observations of children in the water area have been used by the practitioner, or team of practitioners, to:

- Plan possible follow-up activities and next steps for individuals
- Assess provision in the water area[2]

In order to check that there is breadth and balance in the curriculum, practitioners will need to study assessments of provision and this is one of the reasons for keeping clear records (see below, 'Recording and reporting'). As identified in the long-term plans, each area of provision will promote 'key' areas of learning (although learning will not be exclusive to these areas). An overview of assessment records for each area of provision will inform the practitioner as to how successfully the long-term aims are being met in practice. Discussion of these records by the team should then lead to any necessary changes being made.

Assessing how areas of learning are being developed in the setting

Practitioners can assess how a particular area of learning, or aspect of an area, is being developed throughout the setting using a similar procedure to that used in evaluating provision. Children will be observed in all areas of provision and with a focus on, for example, writing. The practitioner will look at the purposes for, and opportunities to, write that children are offered, and also at the provision of mark-making equipment and how this is used. The data collected from observations will then be collated and used to inform long-term planning.

Recording and reporting

Careful assessment and record keeping underpin all good educational practice. They are essential elements in securing effective continuity and progression.

(Department of Education and Science 1990)

Before making any decisions about record keeping systems, practitioners should first consider the following questions:

- *Why* are we keeping records?
- *How* will the records be used?
- *Who* will contribute to and use the records?
- *What* will be included?
- *Which* is the most useful way of presenting and storing recorded information?

---

[2] Other observations of children's use of water provision (made over a period of four weeks) were also considered as the team discussed implications for the future – it is advisable to make a series of observations when assessing provision in order to be sure that the full picture is reflected.

DATE: 10, 14 June		TIME AND DURATION: 9.30am for 15 minutes each day
CHILD	ACTIVITY	POSSIBLE NEXT STEPS FOR THE CHILD/FOLLOW-UP ACTIVITIES
Tamara	Lining up plastic bottles on the side of the tray, randomly selected from the shelf. Picking up bottles, one at a time, putting them down again. Pointing to each bottle in turn.	Counting experience and familiarity with number language, particularly number names one–five. Plan opportunities for counting in a 'real' context.
	Filling plastic bottles with water (using jugs) and then emptying them.	More 'filling and emptying' activities using various containers, perhaps in dry sand or home corner (tea parties). Understanding and using vocabulary: full and empty.
Shelley and Patrick	Playing with boats. Filling boats with water and watching them sink.	Finding out how many plastic pots full of water can be poured into the boat before it sinks. Further investigation: floating and sinking using a range of materials and objects. Making own boats. Understanding and using key vocabulary: float, sink
	'Story-making' about boats in a shark-infested sea.	Opportunities for developing story ideas and sharing them with other children.
Sean	Using water poured from plastic bottles to make the water wheel work.	Making water wheels using, for example, plastic spoons. Looking at other ways of moving objects using water
Kelly-Marie, Holly, Jordan	Using plastic containers, first child fills up a container, passes it to the next child who passes it to the third child who empties it into a transparent plastic bottle. Holly asked 'Is it full – put some more in?' and when it was full, said 'Now make it empty'. The other children responded appropriately	Counting how many containers full of water it takes to fill a jug, bowl, bucket, etc. Comparing containers re: capacity. Vocabulary: Kelly-Marie, Jordan: Confident use of full and empty, understand and begin to use comparative vocabulary, for example, more, less, fuller Holly – use increased range of comparative vocabulary with confidence. Develop 'chain gang' co-operative work, for example, can you pass the cup of water along a chain of five children without spilling any? – negotiation of roles.
	Making ice creams using yoghurt pots. 'Selling' ice creams.	Hot and cold, freezing and melting investigations in the water tray. Ice cream van role-play
Tim	Watching Kelly-Marie, Holly and Jordan's play.	Encouragement to join in play with other children and to become physically involved with resources in exploration and investigation.

GENERAL OBSERVATIONS:
- Children tend to leave equipment in the water tray when they move away from the area. This is inhibiting other children's play and discouraging some from entering the area.
- Most verbal interaction took place during imaginative play.
- Little attention was paid to pictures and photographs displayed in the area.

Figure 6.2 Observation and assessment: the water area

OBSERVED LEARNING IN THE SIX AREAS OF LEARNING:

COMMUNICATION, LANGUAGE AND LITERACY	MATHEMATICAL DEVELOPMENT
Giving verbal instructions to another child. Asking questions. Listening and taking turns in conversation. Use of descriptive language ('It's making a clapping noise like a waterfall'). Use of mathematical language, for example, full, empty, more. Some reference to resources by name. 'Story-making' – discussion of characters and events. Signing name on 'register' on leaving the area.	Investigating capacity – filling and emptying Early counting, and one-to-one counting of four children to four aprons. Use of mathematical language such as more, full, number names. Matching resources to templates looking at shape and height. Matching numbers on resources to numbers on templates.
PERSONAL, SOCIAL AND EMOTIONAL DEVELOPMENT	KNOWLEDGE AND UNDERSTANDING OF THE WORLD
Working together – one child holding a container whilst another pours water into it; 'chain gang' approach to passing resources. Child showing interest whilst observing others. Involvement in an activity. Concentration during an investigation. Independent selection and use of resources.	Investigating 'water power' (water wheels), floating and sinking Discussion of hot and cold in relation to ice creams Understanding that the water can make materials wet, and can 'spread' on a flat, non-absorbent surface (water spilt on clothing and floor)
CREATIVE DEVELOPMENT	PHYSICAL DEVELOPMENT
Story-making – using imagination and expressing ideas (boat and sharks story) Role-play – making and selling ice creams	Co-ordination – Pouring from one container to another, holding a container in one hand and pouring water into it from a container in the other hand, passing containers to the next child in the line.

TEAM DISCUSSION: IMPLICATIONS FOR THE FUTURE AND ACTION TO BE TAKEN:

- All staff to encourage children to replace resources before leaving the area. To ensure that provision is also supporting children in doing this, CP. will renew templates, replace storage boxes for tubes, shells, stones, yoghurt pots, etc. with shallow baskets and label these clearly with pictures and words.
- Plan 'link' activities between areas, for example, making water wheels in the workshop for use in the water tray; set up role-play area around the outside water tray (e.g. café – pouring cups of tea, ice cream van – selling lollies and ice cream made from crushed, coloured ice).
- Use coloured water to enable children to see water levels in containers more easily.
- Plan regular adult input with a focus on encouraging talk and use of key vocabulary during investigations, and supporting individuals and groups of children in moving forward in identified areas.
- Make display more interactive encouraging children to read picture and signs, answer questions and respond to challenges. Change display more frequently. Link displays to children's current interests and investigations.
- Order the following resources: set of graded (tall narrow) measuring cylinders, small-world people and sea creatures, plastic lolly moulds, shallow storage baskets for permanent and additional resources. Organise and catalogue additional resources according to concept development.

Further points for discussion by foundation stage staff:

- What can children learn from observing other children's play?
- How can resources encourage problem-solving?

Figure 6.2 Observation and assessment: the water area (continued)

In answer to the first question, there are usually a number of reasons why practitioners keep records and these will probably include:

- To make sure that information is available to, and easily shared with, all concerned parties
- To enable practitioners to monitor, or plot, the progress of individuals or groups of children
- To ensure continuity for the child
- To enable practitioners to check that breadth and balance in the curriculum is being maintained
- In order to be accountable to, for example, the LEA, school management, Ofsted

Records are used:

- As a 'central point' for the ongoing collection of information and/or evidence
- As a source of reference when planning for individuals or the curriculum
- As evidence to support assessments or referrals
- To communicate information to parents
- To communicate information to other professionals
- To inform summative reporting

Some records will be in daily use and need to be readily available at all times. Others will be accessed less frequently but all concerned parties should know where they are kept. There will be times when the content of records is of a sensitive nature, or is strictly confidential, and such information must be stored carefully to ensure that it is only available to its intended audience.

The obvious contributors to the records are the staff themselves, but practitioners should also consider how to include information from:

- Parents and carers
- Outside agencies (e.g. health visitors, speech therapists, GPs)

The suitability of record keeping systems for use in early years settings will depend on the purpose of the record, and its audience and contributors. Systems should be efficient and support, not hinder, the practitioner in their role as an educator. Time is a limited resource and a balance must be sought between recording observations and interacting with the children. Practitioners should set themselves realistic goals and only record what is useful. The next part of the chapter looks at some methods of recording and reporting information.

Individual profiles of children's work

The profiling system is in operation in many settings and can be a very successful way of combining observations and assessments made in the setting and in the home. The profile is started on the child's entry to the setting (often with a 'home visit' entry) and is an ongoing and formative record of a child's achievements. The profile will be used by the practitioner in assessing and addressing individual learning needs and, as well as being informative and attractive to the child and parent, should be effective in supporting the planning and reporting process. Information should be presented in a logical way, and should be easily accessible and useful.

Compiling a profile

There are a variety of ways in which information can be organised in a profile. Some practitioners favour the diary format, making entries in chronological order regardless of the curricular content of the learning. Others prefer to organise information according to curricular focus. In the latter type of profile, there will be a section for each of the six areas of learning and possibly a page for each aspect within the six areas. Entries will be made in chronological order within each section – this system has the advantage of showing clearly a child's progress in a particular area of learning and of immediately highlighting gaps in assessments. When producing a profile such as this, observations will be short and very focused. It is probable that watching a child involved in one activity or experience will generate a number of observations to be filed under different areas. It may also be necessary to cross-reference some evidence, for example, the observation shown in Figure 6.4 focuses on 'knowledge and understanding of the world' but could also provide useful information about the child's physical development (using tools and materials) and personal, social and emotional development.

In practical terms, the profile should be durable enough to withstand frequent handling over a considerable period of time. Entries can be made on sheets of paper which are then inserted into transparent plastic pockets and filed in a plastic-covered ring binder. Alternatively, a scrapbook could be used for entries and kept in an envelope file for protection. Practitioners will probably want to peruse the numerous stationery catalogues on the market before making a decision!

Again, effective systems need to be in place to ensure that members of staff do not become overloaded with paperwork and administration. For example, key workers responsible for entering observations (written by all staff) into children's profiles within their key group could request that observations are collected in plastic pockets on the wall in the office. These pockets would display the name of the key worker and the names of all children within the group. At the end of the session, staff would file their observations in the appropriate pocket. Key workers would then remove their pocket from the wall when planning to update profiles.

The content of the profile will include:

- Written observations
- Pieces of the child's work (e.g. mark-making, paintings)
- Photographs of children's work (perhaps work in progress, a three-dimensional model, a physical activity such as riding a bike)
- Contributions from parents or their comments scribed by the practitioner

(For examples of contents, see Figures 6.4, 6.5, 6.6, 6.7.)

When making entries in the profiles, practitioners should adhere to the following guidance:

- The emphasis should be on what the child *can* do – the profile is a record of the child's *achievements*
- Entries should be written objectively
- All entries must be dated
- Children's work and photographs should be annotated (e.g. notes made on area of provision in which the learning took place, analysis of learning, time span, adult or peer support received)
- When photographs or pieces of work relate to other written observations, there should be clear referencing
- In the event of an extended period of absence, this should be recorded in the child's profile
- Where possible, children should be involved in making entries (particularly own work and photographs)
- Practitioners should keep abreast of entries from home and add their own notes to these as appropriate

Recording observations and assessments for profiles

Written observations can be recorded straight away in the profile, or can be written on large, white adhesive labels to be added to the profile later. It can be helpful to keep a stock of labels or pieces of paper, and a pen, in each area of provision – it is very frustrating, having anticipated a milestone achievement, to miss the 'magic moment' whilst in search of tools and equipment with which to record it! Some practitioners prefer to write in a personal notebook and transfer information to the profile – these written observations are sometimes cut out of the book and glued into the profile.

There are also times when observations will be recorded on a standard format. There are three clear purposes for using a framework within which to record observations and assessments:

- To support the practitioner in focusing observations and assessments
- To support the practitioner in organising the written content
- To enable the reader to more easily understand and use information

When observing children in the setting, it can be physically difficult, and probably not necessary, to write down everything that is witnessed. Having access to a few carefully chosen headings on a sheet of paper will support the practitioner in selecting information to record. Information recorded on standard formats is easily accessed by colleagues who are also familiar with the format, and this shared understanding of the system will impact positively on the efficiency of team assessment and planning discussions.

Sometimes teams produce a simple pro forma on which to record observations during a planned activity. These can help practitioners to adhere to a specific observation focus and can, when completed, be stuck straight into the profile (see Figure 6.9). Practitioners will almost certainly find a standard annotation format useful, as illustrated in Figure 6.5. In the process of transferring jottings to such a framework, information will be organised in a more readable and logical form.

It will not, however, always be appropriate to use a pro forma for the recording of observations and sometimes a separate list of 'prompts' (as illustrated in the example 'Observation of Natasha', page 173), or a clear focus in the practitioner's mind, can be just as capable of effecting a coherent and useful record.

Although the reorganisation of some written material will be necessary (perhaps onto an annotation form), copying out long observations into profiles is an unproductive use of time and should be avoided where possible. Although children's work should always be presented in a respectful fashion, and entries neat and orderly, the profile is a working document and presentation should not take priority over content.

As mentioned earlier in this chapter, young children should not be placed in a 'test' situation which is likely to result in distorted assessments. It is possible to observe and assess children's learning in a range of curricular areas through a single experience or activity in an area of provision (see the example: Figure 6.3). Practitioners must take opportunities to watch children as they become deeply involved in a challenging, self-initiated activity – they can then be sure that they are seeing a true picture of what children know and can do. In the interest of making assessments against the stepping-stones, it is useful if practitioners use similar language to that used in the curriculum guidance document. Sometimes

Observations across the curriculum

Observing a child working in an area of provision can provide us with information about their learning across many areas of the curriculum as the following example shows:

NAME: Michael (aged 3 years, 11months)

DATE: 21 October 2004

TIME: 10.05–10.20am

CONTEXT:
Playing in the water area alone at first and then joined by two other children. Adult observing in the area giving occasional support as appropriate (e.g. asking questions, discussion, playing alongside). Equipment available: jugs, beakers, funnels, tea set, water wheels, buckets.

Area of learning	Observation
Mathematical development *(shape, space and measures)*	Playing in the water tray, using a plastic beaker to fill a jug with water, Michael said 'It's getting full now'. When he tipped the water out, he said 'Empty'.
Personal, social and emotional development *(dispositions and attitudes)*	Michael approached the water area with enthusiasm and explored the equipment with interest. He was delighted to see the water wheel go round as he poured water through the funnel and laughed as the water splashed onto his hand.
Creative development *(imagination)*	Playing in the water tray with another child, Michael filled up the teapot with water and poured some into a jug which he offered to his friend saying 'Want a drink? It's dinner time!'
Communication, language and literacy *(language for thinking)*	In the water tray – pouring water into the spout of a teapot through a funnel, Michael said 'Water's going in... then it [the lid] pops up... now it's full... It's going up to the top... press down the top [lid]... Now it's coming through the hole! [steam hole in the lid] Put more water in and make the top pop off!'
Personal, social and emotional development *(making relationships)*	Playing in the water tray with Liam, Michael rolled up his own sleeves and then helped Liam to roll up his. Later he included Liam in his investigation saying 'You hold this down and I'll pour the water in'. He also reminded Liam 'Don't throw water or the floor will get wet.
Physical development *(using tools and equipment)*	Playing in the water area, Michael showed good control and co-ordination as he carefully directed the end of the funnel with one hand and poured water into it from a jug with his other hand.
Knowledge and understanding of the world *(exploration and investigation)*	Michael selected a water wheel from the shelf whilst working in the water area. He made the wheel go round with his hand and then lifted up the wheel on its frame, looking from underneath to find out more about how it moved. He turned the wheel around again with his hand, but very slowly this time and looking closely. He was excited when he made it go very fast by pouring a whole jug full of water through its funnel!

Figure 6.3 Observations across the curriculum

a direct link with a stepping-stone or goal can be made and the appropriate phrase tagged onto the observation (see example: Figure 6.5). Reference to the section 'What does the practitioner need to do?' will support staff in planning for children's next steps.

Knowledge and understanding of the world (exploration and investigation and designing and making)

<u>12th February</u>

Today Sarah chose to work in the workshop and told Sandeep that she was going to make a kite. She selected the following materials: tissue paper, two lolly sticks, string, glue, sellotape and scissors. Sarah cut the paper with the scissors and fastened it to the stick with sellotape (having tried and rejected the glue because it was 'too wet'). As Sandeep held the kite, she fastened the string to it with sellotape. They took the finished kite outside and, pulling it behind her as she ran, Sarah shouted 'Look! It's flying! The wind's blowing it!'

Figure 6.4 Adhesive label entry: 'Kite observation'

Profiles as 'shared records'

Young children's profiles are an ongoing record of their achievements (from entering to leaving the setting) in all areas of learning and are often referred to as their 'special books'. Children should be encouraged to look at, and talk about, the contents and the learning it represents with friends, practitioners, parents and carers. For this reason, profiles should be made accessible (perhaps in book racks on the wall or open boxes), and should be easy to handle. They should be clearly named and ideally display a photograph of the child on the front so as to be instantly recognisable. When children feel 'ownership' of their profile, and a pride in their achievements, they will probably ask to make their own entries sharing experiences from home as well as in the setting.

Although practitioners will have talked with parents about profiles (purpose and content) during the first contact period, it is a good idea to display a notice of explanation and encouragement, similar to the following example, close to where the profiles are kept (see Children's profiles, page 188).

NAME Elizabeth	DATE 4 May 2004

OTHER CONTEXTUAL INFORMATION

Talking with an adult in a one-to-one situation. Selecting mark-making equipment independently.

AREA OF PROVISION

Accessing equipment from the office area to use on the table where the gerbils are kept.

OBSERVATION

After caring for the nursery gerbils at home for the weekend, Elizabeth was keen to share her experiences with adults and other children. She suggested that a member of staff should look after the gerbils for a night and wrote a list of care instructions for her. She divided the paper in half with a line and used 'bullet points' every time she started a new line of marks. She said each word carefully as she made marks to represent her speech. When her list was completed, she gave it to the practitioner and said 'This is how you look after the gerbils – now you can take them to your house'.

KEY AREA AND ASPECT OF LEARNING

Communication, language, literacy and writing.

ASSESSMENT

There is firm evidence towards the following stepping-stones and early learning goals:

● Ascribe meaning to marks (blue)
● Begin to break the flow of speech into words (green)

Elizabeth knows that information can be communicated through writing and is beginning to make marks in an attempt to record thoughts and ideas. She shows an understanding of some features of lists and is exploring these in her emergent writing.

NEXT STEPS

What does the practitioner need to do?

● Encourage Elizabeth to use different forms of writing.
● Act as a scribe for Elizabeth. Say each word as you write.

Figure 6.5 Care instructions for the gerbil and observation format

Figure 6.6 Writing care instructions for the gerbil

<u>17 September (construction area)</u>

Isaac spent 20 minutes building a jungle with a group of children. He contributed lots of ideas during discussions about plans and use of materials. He suggested making a waterfall using blue cellophane and white crepe paper and when it was finished he commented 'It looks splashy'.

Isaac continued to play with the jungle for 10 minutes after the other children had left the area – he built a 'sand mountain' (using a toy lorry and orange tissue paper) and a bridge so that the animals could 'go and have their babies there'. Isaac was keen to talk to Mrs R. about the jungle and introduced the animal characters to her before explaining where they all lived. He then went on to tell her about the small elephant's adventure (using the toy elephant to demonstrate actions):

'He was running, he lost his mummy. He went up the rocks and he fell down the waterfall. It was like a slide. Then he saw his mummy and he was happy.'

<u>Creative development (imagination and expressing and communicating ideas):</u>
Isaac used one object to represent another (e.g. tissue as sand). He introduced a story line into his play and entered into dialogue about his creation.

Figure 6.7 Jungle play in the construction area: observation (see Chapter 3, page 83 for 'Jungle Play' activity plan)

Figure 6.8 Jungle play in the construction area

Name Lewis	Date 19 October 2004	Stepping-stone Green
Key area of learning Mathematical development: Calculating		
Observation Playing with the coloured bears, Lewis picked up three red ones in one hand and two blue in the other. He then put them all on the grid, lined them up in the spaces and counted them, and told me that he had five altogether. Every time he rolled the die, he added one more bear (the same colour as shown on the die) and said the number that was one more than the previous total.		

Figure 6.9 Making Games: using a pro forma for recording observations during a planned focus activity (see Chapter 2, page 67 for 'Making Games' activity plan)

Children's profiles

The children's profiles are a celebration of their achievements and contain examples and photographs of work, and observations by nursery staff. They are intended to show learning in all areas (see Profiles as 'shared records', page 185):

- Personal, social and emotional development
- Communication, language and literacy
- Mathematical development
- Knowledge and understanding of the world
- Physical development
- Creative development

Children learn in many different situations and places, and much of their learning takes place at home. Please use the profile to record significant home learning experiences, and 'landmark' achievements. This will help to give a fuller picture of your child's learning, and will enable staff to share achievements. The profiles are always available and you are welcome to look through them at any time – your children will probably be only too happy to share theirs with you! The nursery staff regularly spend time looking at, and talking about, children's own profiles with them and are happy to discuss these records with you.

A brief explanation of each area of learning can also be included in the profiles. Practitioners often use short paragraphs quoted from the *Curriculum Guidance for the Foundation Stage* for this purpose.

See also Chapter 4 (page 133) for sharing information through discussions about a video compilation or a series of photographs.

Class and group files

There will be some information which will need to be accessible to staff but which should not be readily available to all adults in the setting. A ring binder divided into sections, one for each child, will be useful for the storage of information such as personal details collected during first contact period, and will be less cumbersome than individual files. Record card index boxes are compact and can provide a practical and convenient storage system for home addresses, telephone numbers and contact names.

Tick lists

Tick lists as a method of recording information should be used with caution. A tick in a box against a statement or question is of limited value in communicating information about a child – children's learning rarely progresses in 'boxed' stages. If this method is used, it should be supported by observations which offer an explanation of context and a more accurate assessment of learning.

Sometimes it can be useful to transfer certain information from a number of observations onto one 'checklist' record sheet to give an overview of, for example, how many children observed playing in the home corner used the mark-making equipment in that area. This could help practitioners in assessing how provision is being used. It can be useful to keep a tick list record of profile entries so that practitioners can see at a glance whether or not a child has been observed recently in a particular area of provision or learning. It may also be necessary to provide summary information for whole groups or classes for another setting and this may be presented on an overview grid (see 'summative reporting').

Another circumstance in which the use of a tick list might be justified is when children are required to register their presence in an area – this is often done by making a mark, or tick, next to their name. This type of record will only tell the practitioner that the child has been in the area, not what she or he has done or learnt.

Summative reporting

Teams should meet periodically to summarise children's achievements and to consider next steps (in some settings, this may be the responsibility of an individual practitioner). During such reviews, practitioners will make written records, although it would be a daunting task to commit to paper all that they know about the child! Information and evidence collected in profiles and through other assessments should be used to inform practitioners and support them in producing an accurate summary.

Many settings implement a policy of summarising what they know about children after the first few weeks following entry. This then provides a baseline from which practitioners are able to plan for children's learning, plot their progress and identify areas for concern. It is important, considering the variation in starting points for children, that these are carefully assessed and documented so that summaries at the end of a stage give the whole picture of their achievements rather than the limited information offered by some raw data.

In reporting upon children's progress to parents, the emphasis should be on informal discussion at regular intervals throughout the child's time in the setting. Written, summative reports to parents are not appropriate in all settings and where they are required, should be in addition to the before-mentioned discussions. Reports should be written in a positive way, stressing the child's achievements and interests. The way in which content is organised in the report will vary between settings, although quite often practitioners categorise information in the six areas of learning. There may also be space allowed for an example of the child's work, comments from the child and parents, and for identifying 'next steps'. It will be necessary, as pointed out in Chapter 4, to make time for discussion of the content of the report between parent and practitioner.

It is good practice, in the interests of continuity, to make communication links between settings, and practitioners should give careful consideration to what, and how, information is passed between professionals. Often, the written summative report will be sent on to the next setting. This system of reporting will be strengthened and supported if a more interactive approach to the 'passing on' of information is also in operation. Discussions between practitioners prior to the child's transition, and the sharing of profiles, can be very productive and illuminating.

Guidelines for writing summative reports

Consider these points when summarising a child's achievements and reporting on their progress in the six areas of learning:

- Remember the audiences you are writing for – information should be accessible and useful to both parents and practitioners.
- Summarise what you know about children in positive terms following discussions with key workers and other members of the team.
- Summaries should relate to the foundation stage curriculum but should also be individual to the child. Use the language of the early learning goals and stepping-stones to make links with the curriculum and illustrate some points with examples of what the child has actually done or said (probably quoted from profiles).
- To differentiate your statements further, tag on words and phrases such as 'occasionally', 'often', 'confidently', 'with support'.
- When you have completed a report, ask a colleague who knows the child well to read it through and make any suggestions as to how the statements could give a more accurate or individual summary.

When passing on information between settings within the foundation stage, particularly when children transfer from a nursery setting to the reception class, it is also useful to provide a group summary overview of where you assess individuals in terms of the stepping-stones colour bands. This will probably take the form of a grid which identifies areas of learning across the horizontal axis and children's names down the vertical margin. Assessments can then be recorded simply by marking each 'box' with the appropriate colour. Obviously such summaries should be backed by observation-based evidence and provides a limited 'best-fit' picture of children's learning.

Children frequently respond differently in new situations and unfamiliar surroundings. Their achievements will be affected by circumstances and environment and because of this, practitioners will find it useful to refer to records and reports from settings previously attended by the child when making assessments within the first few weeks.

The Foundation Stage Profile

> Throughout the foundation stage, as part of the learning and teaching process, practitioners need to assess each child's development in relation to the stepping-stones and early learning goals that form part of the *Curriculum Guidance for the Foundation Stage*. These assessments are made on the basis of the practitioner's accumulating observations and knowledge of the whole child.
>
> (QCA 2003)

The Foundation Stage Profile, introduced by the Government in 2003, is now in operation in reception classes. Teachers are required to assess against a given set of criteria, although the use of the booklet itself is not statutory.

There are thirteen assessment scales within the Foundation Stage Profile and each of these has nine points. Some of the early learning goals within the six areas of learning are separated out whilst others are grouped together. The first three points of the nine are based on stepping-stones, points four to eight relate to the early learning goals (but are not necessarily hierarchical) and the ninth point describes a level beyond the early learning goals. Also included in the Profile is a section on 'English as an additional language' which can be used to record and monitor children's development in their home language. The Foundation Stage Profile is designed to be inclusive and the handbook offers guidance in helping children with special educational needs to access the curriculum and in assessing their progress. Attainment of those children for whom the first three points of the scales are not descriptive of their learning can be recorded in another appropriate way at the end of the foundation stage.

Observation continues to be the key to successful assessment for learning throughout the foundation stage and the whole process should support practitioners in planning for children's next steps. Judgements are made on the basis of ongoing, observation-based evidence and LEAs should be working with schools to support the moderation process. The Profile is a framework for summing up knowledge about the children and can be completed at points throughout the year using evidence from ongoing assessments. Summary information using the Foundation Stage Profile scales will be shared with parents, passed on to Year One teachers and will also be forwarded by LEAs to the DfES.

Key Points for Good Practice

- Recognise the importance of observation as part of the teaching role and plan time to observe children.
- Assess children's learning based on observations made in a meaningful and purposeful context for the child. It is when children are deeply involved in their learning that you will find out what they really know and understand.

- Observe children in a number of different contexts before making final assessments to be sure that learning is firmly embedded.
- When recording observations of children's learning, be concise but include relevant information about context. To link observations to the stepping-stones and early learning goals and to make assessments easier, use language from the appropriate area of learning in the curriculum guidance document.
- Use assessments to inform your planning of children's next steps. Sometimes, 'next steps' will mean moving forward perhaps into the next stepping-stone band. However, children often need more learning experiences with a similar objective in a range of different contexts to ensure that their understanding is embedded. They may also need to revisit the same activity or experience to consolidate what they have learnt and to develop ideas.
- Make time for moderation to ensure consistency and accuracy. Compile a portfolio of evidence using observations of children in the setting.
- Make sure you are aware of children's 'starting points' before being in a position to comment on their progress.
- Remember that children's learning takes place wherever they are – at home, school, in the supermarket, on a walk to the park. Never underestimate the importance of listening and talking to children, parents and carers in order to build up a whole picture of children's achievements and needs.
- Value the contribution of the child's parents and the child her or himself in the planning and reviewing of IEPs. Remember the parent's right to be involved in this process.
- Set up effective systems for collecting and collating evidence that work for the whole team.
- Share summary information about your assessments of children's achievements and progress with parents and next settings.

In concluding this chapter, the following extract from Mary Jane Drummond's book *Assessing Children's Learning*, is offered as a summary of the purpose and role of assessment in the foundation stage:

> In assessment, we can appreciate and understand what children learn; we can recognise their achievements, and their individuality, the differences between them. We can use our assessments to shape and enrich our curriculum, our interactions, our provision as a whole; we can use our assessments as a way of identifying what children will be able to learn next, so that we can support and extend that learning. Assessment is part of our daily practice in striving for quality.
>
> (Drummond 1993)

CHAPTER 7

Looking forward

Having looked at planning for children's current learning interests and needs, and discussed long-term, curricular planning in detail, it now remains for the reader to look to the future and consider how best to plan the way forward for the setting and the team.

The content of this chapter is organised as follows:

Moving forward with colleagues

Good teamwork is essential if a setting is to provide a rich and secure environment for young children, and to make positive steps forward. All staff should be purposefully involved in discussions and decision-making about curricular and organisational issues, and about long-term developments. Such involvement will encourage attitudes of commitment and self-confidence, and will ensure a firm understanding of the aims of the setting by all staff, irrespective of background or current responsibilities.

There is much to be gained from the sharing of knowledge and ideas between colleagues. The strengths, skills, training and experience of all individuals should be valued and used to enrich and fortify the team as a whole. Roles should be complementary, not conflicting, and teams built on a foundation of:

- Communication
- Co-operation
- Respect
- Support

Communication between practitioners need not be restricted to the immediate team within which individuals work on a day-to-day basis. Indeed there are many childminders who spend much of their working time as the only adult with a group of children. The wider 'network' of practitioners offers a rich source of professional support. Inter-setting meetings, or visits to other settings during the working day, can prove to be both informative and stimulating. Meetings may be used as a forum for the sharing of good practice or the discussion of new initiatives, legislation and policies; practitioners can decide their own agenda, addressing issues of interest or concern to them in their situation.

In order to build a 'balanced' team with expertise and knowledge across a range of areas, a programme of professional development for staff will need to be planned. This programme should allow scope for individual professional interests to be developed as well as addressing the needs of the whole team and setting. This is an area which should be considered in the long-term so that all needs are co-ordinated and met over a period of time. Professional development can take a number of forms and practitioners will make judgements regarding suitability according to the content of the learning, the prior training and experience of the individual or individuals involved, the convenience of the timings (e.g. organisation of staff release time or cover) and cost. However, it should be said that, if a team has a serious commitment to staff development, and a clear view of the way forward, every effort will be made to find appropriate routes for development. It is a good idea to 'appoint' a member of the team as the person responsible for collating and presenting information about professional development opportunities. It may be that the local education authority offers courses or workshops tailored to the identified needs of the team, or arranged visits to, for example, other agencies to learn about services offered may be more useful.

Development planning

Practitioners should be constantly evaluating the service that is offered to children and parents, looking for ways to develop the setting. It is never possible to sit back and think that the job of planning for young children's learning is complete; a 'static' setting is inevitably a stale environment, unlikely to inspire children or adults.

Development is about:

- Evolving
- Growing
- Advancing

Some decisions regarding improvements will be made from day to day, and others as immediate needs arise, but, in order to organise and integrate the needs and successfully effect improvements, practitioners will need to agree a longer term plan for development. This plan will identify where the setting is at the starting point, and where practitioners intend it to be at the end of, for example, three years. It will broadly outline steps to be taken, and changes to be made, during that period. Development planning can be used to address issues such as curriculum development, staff development, organisation of staffing, building maintenance and alteration, and is about having a 'vision' for the future of the setting.

There will probably be many potential areas for development and prioritising can be difficult. Some will be obviously urgent and take priority, others will have to be 'put on hold' or scheduled for a later date. Sometimes a weakness will have been identified and the relevant area targeted for improvement, in other cases, practitioners will plan to build on successes. It is important to be realistic and guard against trying to tackle too much in a short space of time, targets should be manageable and organised in a time sequence.

When making decisions, practitioners should take into account factors such as the following:

- Financial constraints
- Expertise available
- Introduction of, for example, new government requirements
- Communication systems
- Time constraints
- Other responsibilities and commitments

Although plans will span a period of up to five years, they should be viewed as working documents and reviewed and amended in progress. For example, at the end of year one in a three-year plan, practitioners should evaluate success, revising the plan as necessary for years two and three, and perhaps adding targets for an additional year.

Action planning

Through the process of development planning, practitioners make decisions about *what* needs to be done in order to move the setting forward. Action planning is the process by which they clarify *how* improvements will be realised in practice. For example, practitioners may take an area targeted for development and draw up a programme for the forthcoming year. In their plan they will define:

- Key issue
- Objectives
- Action to be taken
- Roles and responsibilities
- Resource implications
- Criteria for success
- Monitoring success: responsibilities and methods
- Timescales

If a plan is to be implemented smoothly, all involved adults will need to be part of the planning process throughout and should fully understand their responsibilities. A commitment from all parties is necessary in order to effect a successful outcome within the allotted period of time.

Post-inspection action plans

Post-inspection action plans are about making improvements in areas where weaknesses have been identified during an Ofsted inspection. It may be that some of the issues for concern have already been recognised by the practitioner, or team of practitioners, and steps taken to address them. However, settings are required to draw up a 'post-inspection action plan' within 40 working days of receipt of the report. This is a statement of how the practitioner intends to address the key issues identified during the inspection. It will probably include short-, medium- and long-term intentions and should aim to have successfully achieved all targets within a year. Teams are obliged to provide the LEA with a copy of the plan if requested.

Foundation stage practitioners find themselves in a period of significant change and it is to their credit that they embrace initiatives with commitment and an open mind. However, in striving to keep abreast of developments in local and national policy and to be practicing in accordance with current thinking, it is easy to lose direction or cohesion as a team. Practitioners should give priority to developing a shared ethos and moving forward together. Above all they need to invest in time for talking and listening to each other.

> Working as a team is a process not a technique. It is rooted in an ideology of empowerment, encouraging adults (whether parents or staff) to take control of their own lives and giving children permission to do the same.
>
> (Whalley, M. in Pugh, G. 1996)

Bibliography

Abbot, L. and Nutbrown, C. (eds) (2001) *Experiencing Reggio Emilia,* Buckingham: Open University Press.

Abbot, L. and Rodger, R. (eds) (1994) *Quality Education in the Early Years,* Buckingham: Open University Press.

Anning, A. (1999) *Promoting Children's Learning from Birth to Five: Developing the New Early Years Professional,* Buckingham: Open University Press.

Anning, A. (ed.) (1994) *The First Years at School,* Buckingham: Open University Press.

Athey, C. (1990) *Extending Thought in Young Children: A Parent Teacher Partnership,* London: Paul Chapman Publishing.

Bennet, N., Wood, L. and Rogers, S. (1997) *Teaching Through Play: Teachers' Thinking and Classroom Practice,* Buckingham: Open University Press.

Blenkin, G. M. and Kelly, A. V. (eds) (1992) *Assessment in Early Childhood Education,* London: Paul Chapman Publishing.

Blenkin, G. M. and Kelly, A. V. (eds) (1996) *Early Childhood Education: A Developmental Curriculum,* 2nd edn. London: Paul Chapman Publishing.

Bruce, T. (1987) *Early Childhood Education,* Kent: Hodder and Stoughton.

Bruce, T. (1997) *Early Childhood Education,* 2nd edn. London: Hodder and Stoughton.

Bruce, T. (2001) *Learning Through Play,* Kent: Hodder and Stoughton.

Chapman, L. (1978) *Approaches to Art in Education,* New York: Harcourt Brace Jovanovich.

Cullingford, C. (1997) *Assessment Versus Evaluation,* London: Cassell.

Curtis, A. (1998) *A Curriculum for the Pre-School Child,* 2nd edn. London: Routledge.

David, T. (1990) *Under Five – Under Educated?,* Buckingham: Open University Press.

Department of Education and Science (1967) *Children and their Primary Schools: A Report of the Central Advisory Council for Education (England),* London: HMSO (The Plowden Report).

Department of Education and Science (1990) *Starting with Quality: The Report of the Committee of Inquiry into the Quality of Educational Experience offered to 3 and 4 year olds,* London: HMSO (The Rumbold Report).

DfES (1999) *Early Learning Goals,* London: Qualifications and Curriculum Authority.

DfES (2000) *Curriculum Guidance for the Foundation Stage,* London: Qualifications and Curriculum Authority.

DfES (2003) *Foundation Stage Profile Handbook,* London: Qualifications and Curriculum Authority.

Drake, J. (2003) *Organising Play in the Early Years,* London: David Fulton Publishers.

Drifte, C. (2002) *Early Learning Goals for Children with Special Needs,* London: David Fulton Publishers.

Drummond, M. J. (1993) *Assessing Children's Learning,* London: David Fulton Publishers.

Duffy, B. (1998) *Supporting Creativity and Imagination in the Early Years,* Buckingham: Open University Press.

Edgington, M. (1998) *The Nursery Teacher in Action,* London: Paul Chapman Publishing.

Fisher, J. (1996) *Starting from the Child?,* Buckingham: Open University Press.

Fisher, R. (1990) *Teaching Children to Think,* first published by Basil Blackwell, reprinted (1995) Cheltenham: Stanley Thornes.

Hall, N. (1987) *The Emergence of Literacy,* London: Hodder and Stoughton.

Hurst, V. (1991) *Planning for Early Learning: Education in the First Five Years,* London: Paul Chapman Publishing.

Hurst, V. and Lally, M. (1992) 'Assessment and the nursery curriculum' in Blenkin, G. M. and Kelly, A. V. (eds) *Assessment in Early Childhood Education* ch. 3 London: Paul Chapman Publishing.

Isaacs, S. (1929) *The Nursery Years: The Mind of the Child from Birth to 6 Years,* London: Routledge and Kegan Paul.

Kress, G. (1997) *Before Writing – Rethinking the Paths to Literacy,* London: Routledge.

Leeds Early Years Partnership Advisory Team (2004) *Exploring Outdoor Learning,* Leeds: Leeds City Council.

Lindon, J. (1997) *Working with Young Children,* 3rd edn. London: Hodder and Stoughton.

Lindsay, G. and Desforges, M. (1998) *Baseline Assessment: Practice, Problems and Possibilities,* London: David Fulton Publishers.

Macintyre, C. (2002) *Play for Children with Special Needs,* London: David Fulton Publishers.

Miller, L., Drury, R. and Campbell, R. (2002) *Exploring Early Years Education and Care,* London: David Fulton Publishers.

Moyles, J. R. (1989) *Just Playing,* Buckingham: Open University Press.

Moyles, J. R. (1994) *The Excellence of Play,* Buckingham: Open University Press.

National Society for Education in Art and Design (NSEAD) Lancaster, J. (ed.) (1987) *Art, Craft and Design in the Primary School,* 2nd edn. Corsham: NSEAD.

Nutbrown, C. (1999) *Threads of Thinking,* 2nd edn. London: Paul Chapman Publishing.

Office for Standards in Education (1999) *Handbook for Inspecting Primary and Nursery Schools with guidance on self-evaluation,* London: HMSO.

Office for Standards in Education (2000a) *Are You Ready for Inspection?: A Guide for Nursery Education Providers in the Private, Voluntary and Independent Sectors,* London: Ofsted, HMSO.

Office for Standards in Education (2000b) *Handbook for Inspecting Nursery Education in the Private, Voluntary and Independent Sectors including the Inspection Framework,* London: Ofsted, HMSO.

Ouvry, M. (2000) *Exercising Muscles and Minds,* London: The National Early Years Network, reprinted by National Children's Bureau in 2003.

Perry, R. (1997) *Teaching Practice – A Guide for Early Childhood Students,* London: Routledge.

Piaget, J. (1962) *Play Dreams and Imitation in Childhood,* London: Routledge and Kegan Paul.

Pugh, G. (ed.) (1996) *Contemporary Issues in the Early Years: Working Collaboratively for Children,* London: Paul Chapman Publishing.

QCA (website) (2000) www.qca.org.uk/early-years/Baseline-assessment-stage.htm.

QCA (2003) Foundation Stage Profile (Handbook). London: Qualifications and Curriculum Authority.

Whitebread, D. (ed.) (1996) *Teaching and Learning in the Early Years,* London: Routledge.

Index

Human Resource Management in a Business Context

2nd edition

John Kew and John Stredwick

Chartered Institute of Personnel and Development

Published by the Chartered Institute of Personnel and Development
151 The Broadway, London SW19 1JQ

This edition first published 2013
First published 2010
Reprinted 2012

Designed and typeset by Exeter Premedia Services, India
Printed in Great Britain by Bell & Bain, Glasgow

British Library Cataloguing in Publication Data
A catalogue of this publication is available from the British Library

ISBN 978 1 84398 317 0

Chartered Institute of Personnel and Development
151 The Broadway, London SW19 1JQ
Tel: 020 8612 6200
E-mail: cipd@cipd.co.uk
Website: www.cipd.co.uk
Incorporated by Royal Charter.
Registered Charity No. 1079797

Contents

List of figures and tables

Preface

It has been accepted for many years that human resource management does not operate in a vacuum. To be effective, it needs to be deeply embedded in the business environment of the organisation. It is essential that human resources contribute to the organisation's business strategy that both reacts to changes in the environment and identifies future changes that provides opportunities for operational success in a harshly competitive world.

The worldwide interest in business continues to grow at an extraordinary pace, fuelled by the burgeoning power and influence of Far Eastern economies and especially by the growth of China. An understanding of the business environment continues to be vital for all business and human resource students who wish to gain a fuller understanding of both the context in which business decisions are taken and the major influences in those decisions. As the context becomes more turbulent and unpredictable, it becomes more important to grasp the complexity of the many issues presented and the strategic options that can be followed.

Human Resource Management in a Business Context includes:

- first, updates on crucial political, economic and legal areas, including the European Union, international institutions and regulatory developments; wide coverage is given to the causes and implications of the recent world financial crisis and the swiftly changing demographic patterns
- second, a discussion of the internal business environment which identifies a variety of management issues and evaluates the forces shaping the HRM agenda in response to these issues, including a debate on the best practice/best fit debate
- third, the title has been changed and a number of chapters have been re-ordered, chiefly in response to the revised CIPD standards introduced in 2010.

This publication follows closely the CIPD module HRM in Context, but is suitable for students at all levels whose syllabus includes a module in Business Environment, as it covers all the standard subjects normally included in such modules. The emphasis is very much on developing the knowledge and understanding of students, while the main aim has been to make the text accessible and encourage students to follow up key issues by linking the text with up-to-date cases, activities and associated reading.

The distinctive feature of this book is the large number of practical activities and case studies which apply the theory to real-life situations. A large number of new case studies have been written for this edition and there is a seminar activity for each chapter, as well as a number of self-assessment questions. Feedback for all of the activities is provided in the companion website at **www.cipd.co.uk/olr** which supports the book, along with a large number of additional activities.

The information contained on this site is available free of charge to tutors, but tutors will need to register to gain access to the material. Visit **www.cipd.co.uk/tss-registration** to complete the online registration form. The site contains links to general business sites and advice to lecturers who adopt the text on how to use the book as part of a planned series of lectures. PowerPoint presentations will be available to accompany each chapter and there will be suggested feedback for activities, as well as additional activities.

A summary of the book's contents is as follows:

Chapter 1 sets the scene for the whole book – the interaction between the environment, the organisation, HR and strategy. We explore models of environmental analysis and models of organisational design.

Chapter 2 begins by summarising the development of management theory and examining the issues involved in management power, authority and legitimacy. This is followed by an examination of the contemporary analysis of human resource models and roles and the key issues facing human resource practitioners. Specific consideration is given to the role of human resources in areas such as quality assurance and customer care.

Chapter 3 begins with an analysis of supply and demand, followed by a consideration of market structures, including Michael Porter's Five Forces model. We then move on to the application of microeconomic theory to the working of the labour market and a consideration of changes in the industrial and employment structure of the UK.

Chapter 4 analyses the evolution of government policy in social, economic and industrial fields, and the impact of government policy on organisations. As developments in the UK are heavily influenced by the actions of the EU, we are concerned with both UK and EU policy. We start with formal legislative procedures in the UK and the EU, and then go on to consider informal influences on the evolution of policy. We then consider recent developments in policy in the UK.

Chapter 5 examines a wide range of legal and regulatory aspects, starting with an essential summary of the UK legal system and the way that regulation has developed in the fields of employment, health and safety, consumer and commercial law. The impact of regulation on particular sectors is discussed and the direction of regulation is debated, especially in relation to regulation of the financial sector.

Chapter 6 Since the end of the Second World War, the world economy has become more and more integrated. Partly this has been a deliberate, planned development. The International Monetary Fund, the World Bank and the General Agreement on Tariffs and Trade were set up to regulate the world economy and to ensure that the world did not suffer from a recurrence of the Great Depression of the 1930s. The European Economic Community, the predecessor of the European Union, was set up partly to ensure that France and Germany could never again go to war with each other. Other developments were only made possible as a result of technological developments in communication and transport, which enabled the growth of globalisation. We examine the impact of the EU and globalisation on HR practice in the UK.

Chapter 7 summarises the startling changes in demography in recent years, both in the UK and worldwide, discussing the major implications of an ageing population in the advanced economies and a still rapidly rising population growth in the developing countries. There is a debate about the natural flow of migrants from one grouping to the other. The influence on markets for goods and services and the challenges and opportunities in the employment field are considered in detail, together with government initiatives in key areas such as pensions and migration. This is followed by a focus on the major social trends and attitudes alongside the changing social structure. The causes of major social problems, such as the increase in criminal behaviour, are debated and the implications for employment and labour markets are examined. How organisations can react to the changes and the options available are considered.

Chapter 8 presents an analysis on technological change and its substantial influence on the business environment, especially in the fields of information and communication technology. The opportunities in the labour markets that technology offers, such as teleworking and online recruitment, are discussed together with the benefits and difficulties associated with such techniques. The reasons why there is considerable resistance to technology in certain quarters are examined.

Chapter 9 examines the nature of ethics and different approaches which can be taken to ethical problems. It discusses professional and business ethics, stakeholder theory, values and codes of ethics. The second half of the chapter analyses corporate governance, corporate social responsibility (CSR) and sustainability, the role of businesses, HR and the Government in promoting CSR, and the extent of compatibility between CSR and profit.

Chapter 10 analyses the nature of strategic management and identifies different models of strategy. It will analyse the stages of strategic decision-making – analysis, choice and implementation. The last part of the chapter will concentrate on the nature and practice of change management.

Chapter 11, the final chapter, explores the links between HR, strategy and performance, and examines the best practice, best fit and resource-based models of HR strategy.

We would like to acknowledge the help and encouragement we have received from colleagues and friends in writing this new text. A special word of thanks goes to Rod Smith, a long-standing colleague at Bedfordshire University, for his contribution to Chapter 2 and to the staff at the CIPD Library.

Continuing thanks are extended to our families for their encouragement, support and forbearance over an extended period.

CIPD qualifications map

Human Resource Management in Context

The content of this CIPD module is covered as follows:

Number	Learning outcome	*Human Resource Management in a Business Context* chapters
Understand, analyse and critically evaluate:		
1	Contemporary organisations and their principal environments	Chapter 1 – Human Resource Management in Context Chapter 9 – Ethics, Social Responsibility and Sustainability
2	The managerial and business environment within which HR professionals work	Chapter 2 – The Managerial Context of Human Resources
3	How organisational and HR strategies are shaped by and developed in response to internal and external environmental factors	Chapter 10 – Strategic Management Chapter 11 – HR, Strategy and Performance
4	The market and competitive environments of organisations and how organisational leaders and the HR function respond to them	Chapter 3 – The Competitive Environment Chapter 4 – Government Policy
5	Globalisation and international forces and how they shape and impact on organisational and HR strategies and HR practices	Chapter 6 – The World Economy
6	Demographic, social and technological trends and how they shape and impact on organisational and HR strategies and HR practices	Chapter 7 – Demographic and Social Trends Chapter 8 – Technology
7	Government policy and legal regulation and how these shape and impact on organisational and HR strategies and HR practices	Chapter 4 – Government Policy Chapter 5 – Regulation

Links to the CIPD HR Profession Map

CHAPTER 1

Building a picture

- 1.1.4   Use a range of analytical tools, personal experience and management information to develop a deep understanding of what's happening in the organisation and externally.
- 1.3.4   Spot opportunities and patterns within the total organisation, business and context and use these to develop new insights.

Business knowledge

- 1.20.4   Relevant internal and external business commentary – relating to the organisation and its competitors.
- 1.22.4   The sector in which the organisation operates and the other market factors that impact sustainable organisation performance.
- 1.23.4   The immediate and prospective political, economic, social, technological, legal and environmental (PESTLE) issues that may impact your organisation and its competitors.
- 1.24.4   The key sources of relevant external information that may impact the current and future health of the business.
- 1.25.4   The rationale for current organisational structures and espoused values and behaviour frameworks.

PROFESSIONAL AREA: ORGANISATION DESIGN

Assess current organisational design

- 3.5.4   Identify misalignment between current organisation and operations today, and the way it will need to operate in future to deliver organisation's strategy and goals.
- 3.11.4   Test the feasibility of operating models and the extent to which they meet the design criteria.

CHAPTER 2

CORE PROFESSIONAL AREA: INSIGHTS, STRATEGY AND SOLUTIONS

Building a picture

- 1.1.3   Use a range of analytical tools, personal experience and management information to build a rich picture of what's happening in the organisation.
- 1.3.4   Spot opportunities and patterns within the total organisation, business and context and use these to develop new insights.

Developing actionable insight

- 1.6.2 Raise risks with managers that may affect the long-term reputation of the organisation.

Developing situational HR solutions that stick

- 1.7.2 Develop and implement HR solutions that address actions emanating from insights, either to mitigate critical risk or capitalise on opportunity.
- 1.8.2 Support the implementation of change by working with managers to ensure they fully understand the rationale behind the change, the vision for the future, what needs to be done, and to surface the impact that the changes will have on the organisation and the people.
- 1.9.2 Support the timely and efficient delivery and evaluation of planned 'one-off' HR programmes and projects within the organisation.

Building capacity and capability

- 1.12.3 Implement appropriate processes to ensure that the organisation has the right people in sufficient numbers, in the right places and with the right experience and capabilities to deliver the goals of the organisation.

Organisational knowledge

- 1.25.2 Organisational structure and processes, decision-making processes, governance and any espoused values or behaviours.
- 1.27.2 A sense of how things really work in the organisation and the barriers to change.
- 1.34.2 How to deliver successful change programmes and the importance of engaging managers and employees in the change.

Set the context for design

- 3.3.2 Analyse data on organisation structure, accountabilities and spans of control to support business case development. Support in identification of criteria for change and critical success factors.
- 3.4.2 Ensure that managers clearly understand the likely impact/investment that will be required to make change happen.

Culture assessment and development

- 4.8.2 Support the design and implementation of a cultural change plan.
- 4.15.3 How to conduct a cultural audit and manage a cultural change programme.
- 4.16.2 The key stages in change management and the importance of identifying supporters, blockers and fence-sitters.

Employee engagement

- 8.14.3 The key drivers of employee engagement such as career growth and development opportunities, nature and challenge of the job, perceptions of organisational trust and integrity, relationship with line manager and pride in the organisation and product.
- 8.15.3 Approaches to communicating successfully with a diverse mix of people.

Service delivery and management

- 10.4.2   Strive to maintain continued service excellence during times of change, using existing processes and infrastructure. Lead the parallel-test of new approaches during implementation phase.
- 10.7.2   Adopt a customer-centric approach by focusing on the life cycle model and diverse employee needs during the joining employment phase, the in-service phase and during delivery.

CHAPTER 3

CORE PROFESSIONAL AREA: INSIGHTS, STRATEGY AND SOLUTIONS

Business knowledge

- 1.21.4   The total organisation, commercial and value drivers and how they impact on HR solutions for the business.
- 1.23.4   The immediate and prospective political, economic, social, technological, legal and environmental (PESTLE) issues that may impact your organisation and its competitors.
- 1.24.4   The key sources of relevant external information that may impact the current and future health of the business.

PROFESSIONAL AREA: RESOURCE AND TALENT PLANNING

Workforce planning

- 5.2.4   Lead the analysis of current resource and talent levels, taking into account factors such as current and future demand, demographics, attrition, capability by discipline, geography, critical and scarce skills.
- 5.7.4   Build resource planning around analysis of availability of HR talent (locally, regionally and internationally as appropriate).

Resourcing

- 5.19.4   Organisational needs for resourcing, organisational models to support resourcing, for example permanent, contractors, outsource, and the evolving global situation within the market for skills.
- 5.21.4   How to create talent and succession strategies to meet current and future organisational requirements.

PROFESSIONAL AREA: EMPLOYEE ENGAGEMENT

Employer brand

- 8.9.4   Lead the development and implementation of a clear employer brand proposition to attract and retain new and existing talent.

Diversity of needs

- 8.14.4   The key drivers of employee engagement such as career growth and development opportunities, nature and challenge of the job, perceptions of organisational trust and integrity, relationship with line manager and pride in the organisation and product.

CHAPTER 4

CORE PROFESSIONAL AREA: INSIGHTS, STRATEGY AND SOLUTIONS

Business knowledge

- 1.23.4   The immediate and prospective political, economic, social, technological, legal and environmental (PESTLE) issues that may impact your organisation and its competitors.
- 1.24.4   The key sources of relevant external information that may impact the current and future health of the business.

CHAPTER 5

CORE PROFESSIONAL AREA: INSIGHTS, STRATEGY AND SOLUTIONS

- 1.10.3   Develop action plans to mitigate risk emanating from the implementation of situational HR solutions.
- 1.14.2   Work with managers and employees to provide human resource and legal direction, advice, challenge and support.

HR professional knowledge

- 1.30.3   Knows or can access relevant law, in relevant local and international jurisdictions and what the organisation needs to do to mitigate relevant risk.

Resourcing

- 5.8.2   Ensure recruitment policies and approaches are regularly refreshed to remove bias and prevent discrimination.

Exit

- 5.16.3   Manage organisation redundancy programmes in line with organisation need and employment law within local jurisdiction.

Legal framework

- 5.18.2   Jurisdictional law, regulation and agreed policy in relation to resourcing, talent and exit.

Deliver learning and development solutions

- 6.15.3   Keep abreast of local and international legislative changes that may impact learning and talent development, eg HSE, food hygiene training and legal training.

Performance and reward policy

- 7.7.2   Keep abreast of legislative changes that impact performance and reward. Train and coach managers to ensure policies are followed and risks identified. Conduct equal pay reviews to ensure compliance with legislation.

Employee relations policy advice and guidance and complex casework

- 9.3.2   Develop relevant ER documentation, ensuring all contractual/legal documents and templates, including contracts of employment, compromise agreements, employee handbooks and standard discipline and grievance letters are kept up to date and in line with current legislation.

- 9.9.2   Work closely with managers, instructing them on their role and required actions. Keep appropriate records. Represent the organisation at external tribunals or equivalent.

Health and well-being

- 9.13.2   Advise and coach managers in aspects of employee health and well-being, ensuring internal policies and legislative requirements are followed appropriately.

Employment law

- 9.14.2   Strong understanding of or can access relevant current employment and discrimination law if appropriate in local and international jurisdictions, plus proposed changes. Knows what the organisation needs to do to mitigate risk.

CHAPTER 6

CORE PROFESSIONAL AREA: INSIGHTS, STRATEGY AND SOLUTIONS

Business knowledge

- 1.23.4   The immediate and prospective political, economic, social, technological, legal and environmental (PESTLE) issues that may impact your organisation and its competitors.
- 1.24.4   The key sources of relevant external information that may impact the current and future health of the business.

CORE PROFESSIONAL AREA: LEADING HR

Personal leadership

- 2.5.4   Build global mindset. Bring understanding and insight into HR management across any given country's society: its social structures, institutions and demographics, legal, regulatory and economic structure.

PROFESSIONAL AREA: PERFORMANCE AND REWARD

International, expatriate and executive reward

- 7.20.4   Consider constituent parts and levels of the international reward package for expatriates across the organisation, ensuring that there is coherence in the overall offer and that they are aligned with the organisation's strategy and plans.

Benchmarking

- 7.23.4   Understand the local and competitor landscape in terms of reward and understand the factors that determine their overall reward packages, eg critical and scarce skills, talent mobility.

PROFESSIONAL AREA: EMPLOYEE ENGAGEMENT

Internal communications

- 8.15.4   Approaches to communicating successfully with global communities of people.

CHAPTER 7

CORE PROFESSIONAL AREA: INSIGHT, STRATEGY AND SOLUTIONS

- 1.3.2 Consider the bigger picture at all times, observing connections, and draw conclusions about the impact of events and activities on each other.

Contextual knowledge

- 1.23.3 The immediate and prospective political, economic, social, technological, legal and environmental (PESTLE) issues that may impact your organisation and its competitors.

Diversity

- 6.28.2 How to design programmes and processes that provide equality of opportunity and avoid unintended bias.

Policy advice and guidance

- 7.7.2 Keep abreast of legislative changes that impact performance and reward. Train and coach managers to ensure policies are followed and risks identified. Conduct equal pay reviews to ensure compliance with legislation.
- 9.6.2 Give accurate and appropriate advice, training and support to managers who are managing difference and fair access to opportunities.
- 9.6.3 Design policies and practices and lead implementation to promote diversity and ensure fair access of opportunities.

CHAPTER 8

HR service delivery model

- 2.24.3 Options for HR technology models, how to design and commission new technology solutions for HR and how to monitor effectiveness once in place.

Technology

- 10.14.2 Thoroughly pilot the implementation of new technology across end-to-end processes and with multiple users to mitigate risk to service delivery.

CHAPTER 9

CORE PROFESSIONAL AREA: INSIGHTS, STRATEGY AND SOLUTIONS

Delivering situational HR solutions which stick

- 1.10.4 Lead in risk mitigation, governance and ethics strategies.

CHAPTER 10

CORE PROFESSIONAL AREA: INSIGHTS, STRATEGY AND SOLUTIONS

Building a picture

- 1.3.4   Spot opportunities and patterns within the total organisation, business and context and use these to develop new insights.

Developing actionable insight

- 1.4.4   Use your insights to challenge and shape executive thinking around the risks and benefits of decisions or planned strategy.
- 1.5.4   Align key influencers around purpose and strategies and ensure accountability for delivery.
- 1.8.4   Lead and champion the implementation of the most significant organisation change activities, such as reorganisations, mergers and acquisitions.

Delivering situational HR solutions which stick

- 1.11.4   Assess and review the impact of solutions, stay alert to changes in context and make appropriate corrections to strategy and solutions.

Building capacity and capability

- 1.16.4   Assess the organisation's culture and its ability to deliver competitive advantage in the short and long term.
- 1.17.4   Shape the evolving culture of the whole organisation in anticipation of future challenges as well as in response to current challenges.

Business knowledge

- 1.18.4   The vision and purpose of the organisation and how to build functional alignment (organisation design, strategy and plans) to this vision and purpose.

Organisation knowledge

- 1.27.4   Deep understanding of how things really work in the organisation and the barriers to change.

HR professional knowledge

- 1.32.4   How to lead and shape organisation transformational programmes.

PROFESSIONAL AREA: ORGANISATION DESIGN

Assess current organisation design

- 3.6.4   Work with senior leaders to assess the impact of the overall organisation design on factors such as behaviour, attitudes, culture, systems and communication.

OD strategy, planning and business case development

- 4.2.4 Ensure the consideration and integration of organisational values and behaviours in all organisational strategies, plans and programmes.

Culture assessment and development

- 4.7.4 Look ahead and lead the development and ongoing management of a culture that supports the need to change, learn, let things go and improve in order to position the organisation appropriately to deliver the long-term goals.
- 4.8.4 Lead and monitor the organisational cultural change programme to ensure that it leads to a sustained improvement in performance aligned to the organisation strategy and priorities.

Change communications

- 4.11.4 Ensure senior stakeholders understand the rationale for change, are engaged, aligned and fully supportive of the solution.

Culture change

- 4.15.4 How to manage a cultural change programme, integrating it into all organisational priorities.

PROFESSIONAL AREA: EMPLOYEE ENGAGEMENT

Employer brand

- 8.11.4 Lead processes to identify, articulate and reinforce the organisation's core values and behavioural expectations. Influence leadership at all levels to behave in a manner that is consistent with the values and behavioural expectations.

CHAPTER 11

CORE PROFESSIONAL AREA: INSIGHTS, STRATEGY AND SOLUTIONS

Delivering situational HR solutions which stick

- 1.7.4 Lead design of HR solutions that address actions emanating from insights, either to mitigate critical risk or capitalise on opportunity.
- 1.9.4 Sponsor and evaluate delivery of major, planned, new, high-impact HR programmes and projects across the organisation.

HR professional knowledge

- 1.32.4 What external HR (business and academic) thought leaders and benchmark organisations are doing in a variety of areas and considers how lessons may apply to own organisation.
- 1.33.4 How to develop organisation and HR strategies and operating plans.
- 1.34.4 How to lead and shape organisation culture. Can access and respond to the need for organisation agility.

Professional leadership

● 2.4.4   Articulate and communicate the HR value proposition to the organisation and externally.

Leading others

● 2.7.4   Maintain a long-term view of the organisation's direction, shaping and aligning the HR strategy in light of this.
● 2.9.4   Lead a cohesive and influential HR function/practice, building HR capability in business, context and organisation knowledge to drive sustainable business performance.

Leading issues: HR function design and service delivery

● 2.10.4   Design a fit-for-purpose HR function based on a long-term view on where the organisation is headed.
● 2.11.4   Design an adaptable HR function that can quickly shift/adopt different situational HR strategies.

HR service delivery models

● 2.24.4   Models and options for running the HR function (eg centralised, decentralised, account management, shared services, outsourced, integrated service delivery) and the risks and opportunities associated with these.

Walkthrough of textbook features and online resources

LEARNING OUTCOMES

LEARNING OUTCOMES

By the end of this chapter, readers should be able to understand, explain and critically evaluate:

- the role and functions of the European Union and its major institutions
- debates about the evolution of the European Union (integration and enlargement)
- the eurozone crisis of 2010 onwards
- major international bodies which impact on the business environment of organisations (IMF, World Bank, WTO)
- the causes and extent of globalisation processes

LEARNING OUTCOMES

At the beginning of each chapter a bulleted set of learning outcomes summarises what you can expect to learn from the chapter, helping you to track your learning.

CASE STUDY 1.7

OXFORD BUS

The Oxford Bus Company, a subsidiary of the transport group Go-Ahead, has a 'stakeholder board'. This consists of representatives of customers, a local pressure group representative, nominated by the National Federation of Bus Users, and the transport strategy officer of a local NHS trust, representing large employers, as well as company employees and managers. The board meets quarterly to discuss company performance and other matters of concern. Although purely advisory, it has been involved in vehicle design, ticketing and customer care issues. In future the company intends that one meeting a year will be held as an open meeting, to which members of the public will be invited.

Source: Weldon (2003)

CASE STUDIES

A number of case studies from different sectors and countries will help you to place the concepts discussed into a real-life context.

REFLECTIVE ACTIVITY 1.3

The hospital

How would you classify the following factors on a probability/seriousness matrix for a hospital trust? What contingency planning should the trust make?

- a serious accident on the local railway line, causing scores of deaths and injuries
- an ageing local population
- a leakage of radioactive material at a nuclear power station 200 miles downwind away.

REFLECTIVE ACTIVITIES

Questions and activities throughout the text encourage you to reflect on what you have learned and to apply your knowledge and skills in practice.

KEY LEARNING POINTS

- The general environment consists of factors which impact at an industry-wide level, while the task environment is primarily concerned with the immediate environment which impacts on an individual organisation within an industry.
- Organisations can be seen as open systems which interact with their environments.
- The STEEPLE model lists and classifies the major general environmental factors which impact on organisations.
- The main point of STEEPLE analysis is to identify key environmental drivers.
- Opportunities and threats to the organisation can be classified according to probability of success and attractiveness and probability of occurrence and impact, respectively.
- There are a wide range of different organisational structures, including bureaucracy, divisionalisation, matrix, network and virtual.
- Strategic alliances are of growing importance.
- Stakeholder theory states that organisations have responsibilities to a wide

KEY LEARNING POINTS

At the end of each chapter, key learning points consolidate your learning.

QUESTIONS

These review questions are aimed at reinforcing what you have learned in the chapter.

QUESTIONS

1   What do you think are the main differences between the general and the task environments?

2   What do you understand by the best fit model of HR?

3   Why did Weihrich suggest that SWOT analysis should be renamed TOWS analysis? What criticisms have been made of the SWOT/TOWS approach?

4   Give examples where structure follows strategy.

5   What do you think are the main strengths and weaknesses of the bureaucratic form of organisation?

6   Can you see any disadvantages of the network form of organisation?

EXPLORE FURTHER

Explore further boxes contain suggestions for further reading and useful websites, encouraging you to delve further into areas of particular interest.

EXPLORE FURTHER

This chapter covers a very wide range of subjects, so the list of additional reading can be extensive. You will find a long list in the reference section for this chapter, but here is an additional short selection:

THEORIES OF MANAGEMENT

Cole, G. (2010) *Management theory and practice*. 6th edition. London: Cengage Learning.

Mintzberg, H. (2009) *Managing*. Harlow: FT Prentice Hall.

POWER IN ORGANISATIONS

Jermier, J., Knights, D. and Nord, W. (1994) *Resistance and power in organisations*. London: Routledge.

SEMINARS

Each chapter ends with a longer activity, suitable for use in seminars, with questions.

SEMINAR ACTIVITY

ACTIVITY HOLIDAYS

The holiday industry

The holiday industry is in a state of flux. The mainstay of the industry, the foreign package holiday – two weeks in the sun, with everything – flight, accommodation, food, transfers and so on – provided by the tour operator – is in slow decline. In the 1980s, package holidays had 60 per cent of the market, but in 2005 this had fallen to 45 per

The trend is even more stark when we look at all holidays, rather than just package holidays. In 2004, travel agents and the Internet each had a one-third share of bookings, with the other third shared between family and friends and direct booking with a tour operator (*Marketing* 2004).

Until 2007, there were four major players in the UK overseas travel

ONLINE RESOURCES FOR STUDENTS

- Annotated web links – click through to a wealth of up-to-date information online.

- Activity feedback – track your learning with guidance on all in-text activities.

ONLINE RESOURCES FOR TUTORS

- Lecturer's guide – practical advice on teaching the HRM in Context module using this text.

- PowerPoint slides – build and deliver your course around these ready-made lectures, ensuring complete coverage of the module.

- Additional activities – for you to use with students in seminars or lectures.

- Additional case studies – for you to use with students in seminars or lectures.

To access the online resources for this textbook, visit www.cipd.co.uk/orl

CHAPTER 1

Human Resource Management in Context

LEARNING OUTCOMES

By the end of this chapter, readers should be able to understand, explain and critically evaluate:

- the distinction between the general and the task environment
- the relationships between the environment, organisations and strategy
- the STEEPLE model of environmental analysis
- the difference between placid, dynamic and turbulent environments, and their impact on organisations
- the identification of key environmental factors
- the use of SWOT analysis
- models of organisational structure – bureaucracy, divisionalisation, matrix organisations, networks and virtual organisations
- the use and limitations of strategic alliances
- the advantages and disadvantages of HR outsourcing and shared service centres
- stakeholder analysis
- E-V-R analysis.

CASE STUDY 1.1

VIETNAM, IRAQ AND AFGHANISTAN

In the early 1960s, the US intervened in the civil war in Vietnam. The North Vietnamese, under the political leadership of Ho Chi Minh, and the military leadership of Vo Nguyen Giap, had driven the French colonial government out of Vietnam in the 1950s, and the country had been divided in two – North Vietnam, under communist control, and South Vietnam, with a pro-Western government. The Northerners and their South Vietnamese communist allies, the Vietcong, had started a guerrilla civil war in the south against the South Vietnamese Government.

The Americans had overwhelming military superiority and won every pitched battle between the two sides, including the North's biggest attack, the Tet Offensive in 1968, when Vietcong soldiers infiltrated into the South Vietnamese capital, Saigon, and even penetrated the US embassy.

Even so, in the end it was the North Vietnamese and the Vietcong who won the war. The Americans lost over 50,000 dead (compared with more than a million Vietnamese dead) and in 1975 they finally pulled out of Saigon. The next day, 30 April 1975, the North Vietnamese army took the presidential palace in Saigon and the unified communist republic of Vietnam was born.

Why did the Americans lose? First, the North Vietnamese understood that ultimately the war was political, not military. If they could pin down the Americans for long enough, public opinion in the US would turn against the war and the loss of American life, and political pressure at home would force the Americans to pull out. Ho also had a clear aim: to unify Vietnam under the communist banner. The Americans did not. Were they supporting the South Vietnamese Government, fighting the Vietcong, seeking to defeat North Vietnam, or to stop the advance of world communism? An example of their ambivalence was the decision not to invade North Vietnam with a ground force, but to bomb the country, including its capital, Hanoi.

Second, the Americans had no clear strategy for fighting a guerrilla war. Their strategy was based on their overwhelming advantage in firepower, but this was of little use when every Vietnamese could be a potential guerrilla fighter. Typical was the way the Americans could do nothing to prevent the infiltration of fighters and equipment into Saigon in 1968. The 'overkill' approach used by the Americans also caused hundreds of thousands of civilian casualties, which helped to turn public opinion in the US, and throughout the West, against the war.

In 2001, after the Al-Qaeda attacks on New York and Washington on 11 September, a US-led coalition invaded Afghanistan, ostensibly to capture the Al-Qaeda leader Osama bin Laden, who was based there. Afghanistan looms over nineteenth-century British military history. In 1842, in the First Anglo-Afghan War, a British army was wiped out almost to a man, after conquering the country with little difficulty. In the Second Anglo-Afghan war of 1878–80, the British learned the lesson that it was very easy to intervene militarily in Afghanistan, but very difficult to withdraw. The British army went in with overwhelming military force, won the war, imposed political terms, and then quickly withdrew without attempting an occupation. The Russian intervention in the 1980s followed much the pattern of the 1840s. After suffering heavy losses from guerrilla action, they were forced into a humiliating withdrawal.

The American-led invasion followed much the same pattern again. The Taliban Government was quickly overthrown, although Osama bin Laden evaded capture. However, the Taliban then led a long and very effective guerrilla war, which tied down thousands of US and British troops. The war became increasingly intelligence-led, as the guerrillas merged into the civilian population. The Americans also developed the tactic of using pilotless drone aircraft to attack Taliban bases, both in Afghanistan and Pakistan. Failures of intelligence led to many cases of innocent civilians being killed in drone raids.

In 2003, a US-led coalition invaded Iraq. Again, there was a backdrop to the action. In 1990, Iraq, under Saddam Hussein, had invaded and occupied its neighbour Kuwait. A massive widely based but US-led coalition had expelled him from Kuwait in a brilliant military campaign. This operation had clear limited objectives – to liberate Kuwait – and commanded a high level of world support. The 2003 war was different. This time, the Americans had much less world support, did not have the clear endorsement of the UN, and were unable to make it clear to the world exactly why the invasion was happening. Was it to depose Saddam Hussein (regime change)? Was it because Saddam was alleged (incorrectly) to possess chemical and biological weapons (the so-called 'weapons of mass destruction')? Was it to protect ethnic and religious elements in the Iraqi population who had been persecuted by Saddam – the Kurds in the north and the Shi'ites in the south? Was it to fight world terrorism and, in particular, Al-Qaeda? Was it a desire on the part of the US president, George W. Bush, to complete the job which his father, George Bush Sr, had started as president in 1991? Or, as many observers cynically suggested, was it to seize control of Iraq's huge reserves of oil?

The Americans believed that they would be welcomed as liberators, and for a brief period there was relief among many Iraqis at the overthrow of Saddam, particularly among the Kurds, but also to some extent among the Shia in the British-occupied southern part of the country. However, the Americans had underestimated the underlying religious and political divisions in the country. Iraq was an artificial country, invented after the First World War from the wreckage of the Turkish empire. The Shia had close links with their co-religionists in Iran, while the Kurds had much more in common with the Kurdish minority in eastern Turkey than with the rest of Iraq.

Although the Shia were the majority in the country, the Saddam Government had been dominated by the minority Sunni, who were strong in Baghdad and central Iraq. The Sunni population was generally hostile to the Americans because they had overthrown Saddam, and they quickly started a guerrilla campaign against the Americans. The Shia sought revenge on the Sunni, while Al-Qaeda, which had previously had no influence in Iraq, took advantage of the chaos to move into the country.

The Americans were again involved in a guerrilla war, just as in Vietnam, and again they reacted in a heavy-handed fashion, launching punitive operations against guerrilla-controlled towns and making little effort to reconstruct the country or to win hearts and minds. American casualties rose into the thousands and Iraqi casualties into the hundreds of thousands.

Again, just as in Vietnam, the war was increasingly unpopular in the US and the guerrillas realised that in order to win, all they had to do was to outlast the Americans. In 2009, the US announced that its troops would cease to play a combat role, although 150,000 US troops remained in the country.

What has an account of wars in Vietnam and Iraq got to do with business? What lessons can we learn from the wars that are relevant to business environment and strategy? A surprising amount.

- *The need for clear objectives* – if a business does not know what it wants to achieve, any amount of strategic planning is irrelevant. There is a clear contrast between the totally clear objectives of Ho and Giap, and the confused objectives of the Americans in both Vietnam and Iraq.
- *An understanding of the environment* – the guerrillas in both Iraq and Vietnam were totally at ease in their local environments. The Americans, on the other hand, did not understand the motivation of their enemies in Vietnam, or the complex political environment in Iraq. The Vietnamese also understood and exploited the political environment in the US.

- *Understand the competition* – the Americans did not understand the strengths and motivations of their enemies in either Vietnam or Iraq.
- *An understanding of one's own resources* – the Vietnamese made the most of their limited military resources, while the Americans were hamstrung when the enemy in both Vietnam and Iraq neutralised their key resource, their overwhelming firepower.
- *The importance of organisational structure* – the difference in structure is epitomised by Robert McNamara, the US Secretary of Defense in the mid-1960s and one of the main architects of US strategy in Vietnam (Jackson 2009). As a young man, McNamara was involved in planning the US bombing offensive on Germany, an example of detailed logistical planning. After 1945 he rose to be president of the Ford Motor Company. Ford was a classic huge, bureaucratic, hierarchical US corporation which had given its name to a scientific approach to organisational structure ('Fordism'). The US Army under McNamara in Vietnam was equally rigid and bureaucratic. In contrast, the Vietcong was organised on a highly flexible cell basis and thus able to react much more quickly to changing tactical situations.
- *The importance of HR* – the North Vietnamese and Vietcong were highly motivated. The US Army, on the other hand, was largely a conscript army, most of whom did not want to be in Vietnam. To make matters worse, there were extensive exemptions from conscription (the draft), which made those who could not avoid the draft even more bitter about their fate. The alienation of the rank and file US soldier expressed itself in a contempt for the Vietnamese and also in occasional atrocities against civilians.
- *The importance of values and culture* – the communist beliefs of the Vietnamese gave them a motivation and a will to win that the Americans could not match. At a tactical level, the gung-ho, macho culture of the US Marine Corps made them ideal for spearheading the invasion of Iraq, but totally unsuitable for any campaign to win hearts and minds.
- *The importance of stakeholders* – businesses, like countries, have external stakeholders – third parties who can affect their actions. In Iraq, the key external stakeholders are Iran, with considerable influence over the Iraqi Shi'ites, and Turkey, the sworn enemy of the Kurds. In addition, a key stakeholder was US public opinion, which eventually turned strongly against both wars. The views of stakeholders must be taken into account in strategic management.
- *The importance of intelligence* – this is particularly crucial in a guerrilla war, where it is hard to identify who is the enemy and who is an innocent civilian. In business, intelligence-gathering involves general techniques such as environmental scanning as well as function-specific techniques such as wage surveys.
- *The importance of competences* – the key competence of the US Marine Corps was to be a killing machine, whereas totally different competences were needed for an army of occupation. Similarly, very different competences are needed to operate a drone over Afghanistan from a base in the US. War becomes a computer game.
- *The importance of an exit strategy* – businesses, like armies, need to know how to abandon a strategy at minimum cost. The Americans in Vietnam were forced to make a humiliating exit, while they have been heavily criticised over Afghanistan and Iraq for their seeming failure to have a clear exit strategy.

All of these themes will be explored later in this book.

HRM IN CONTEXT

The theme of this chapter, and indeed of the book as a whole, is the interaction between human resource management, the environment and the organisation. The theoretical underpinning for this approach is the best fit or contingency model of human resource strategy, particularly associated in the UK with John Purcell (Boxall and Purcell 2008).

This model argues that there is no one model of human resource strategy which suits all circumstances. Instead, different strategies are appropriate in different environmental and organisational settings.

You should bear in mind that the best fit model is not the only model of HR strategy. Other models include the best practice model, which argues that there is one approach to HR strategy, the high performance workplace model, which is suitable in nearly all organisational and environmental settings, and the resource-based model, which argues that resources, particularly human capital and core competencies, are much more important for HR strategy than the environment. All of these models will be explored in much more depth in Chapter 11.

The next sections will explore in more detail the relationships between the environment, the organisation and HR strategy. This will also be explored at greater length in Chapter 11.

WHAT IS THE ENVIRONMENT?

At its simplest, the environment is anything outside an organisation which may affect an organisation's present or future activities. Thus the environment is situational – it is unique to each organisation. As a result, we must always bear in mind the interaction between a particular organisation and its particular environment.

It is useful to think of the environment on two levels. One is the general environment (also known as the societal environment, the far environment or the macro environment). The other is the task environment (or the specific environment, the near environment or the micro environment).

Forces in the general environment have a major impact at the level of the industry. These forces include national culture, including historical background, ideologies and values; scientific and technological developments; the level of education; legal and political processes; demographic factors; available resources; the international environment; and the general economic, social and industrial structure of the country.

The task environment covers the forces relevant to an individual organisation within an industry. These include customers, suppliers, competitors, regulators, the local labour market and specific technologies.

The distinction between general and task environments is not a static one. Elements in the general environment are continually breaking through to the task environment and impacting on individual organisations.

A different but complementary approach is to see the organisation as an open system, which interacts in two main ways with its task environment. It takes in resources from the environment, converts them into goods and/or services and returns outputs to the environment in order to satisfy some need (Figure 1.1).

Figure 1.1 A systems model of the organisation and its environment

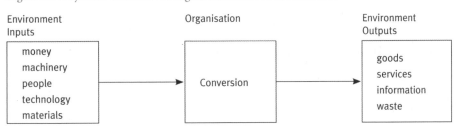

In order to function effectively in such a system, the organisation must fully understand both its input and its output environments.

A more complex variation is to add a third element – that of regulations which control the conversion process. The three elements (inputs, outputs and regulations) provide the organisation with both opportunities and constraints. All three elements are also subject to the influences of the general environment.

REFLECTIVE ACTIVITY 1.1

The systems approach

Identify inputs, outputs, regulators and the conversion process in:

- a manufacturer of baked beans
- a trade union
- your own organisation.

ORGANISATIONS AND STRATEGY

The simple systems model used above takes us only so far. It treats the organisation as a 'black box' and does not analyse what goes on inside the organisation. We now have to build further elements into our model – HR, strategy and organisational structure.

In the Case Study 1.1 we identified that the environment had an impact on HR. The political environment in the US, where the country was only 20 years away from the Second World War, led the US to rely on a conscript rather than a volunteer army to fight the Vietnam War. At the same time, HR had an impact on the environment – the alienation created by the draft affected the way in which the rank and file soldiers fought the war.

This gives us a two-way model of the relationship between the environment and HR (Figure 1.2).

Figure 1.2 The environment and HR

The next stage is to distinguish between HR strategy and HR practice. Here we assume that HR practice flows from HR strategy (Figure 1.3).

Figure 1.3 HR strategy and HR practice

The next stage is to put HR strategy in the context of the organisation's overall strategy. Here we see HR strategy as an integral part of overall strategy (Figure 1.4).

Figure 1.4 HR strategy and overall strategy

Finally, we need to add the organisation.

The great organisational theorist of the 1960s, Alfred Chandler, argued that 'structure follows strategy' (Chandler 1962). A more nuanced approach would suggest that there is a two-way flow between strategy and organisational structure, and similarly, that there is a two-way relationship between the environment and both structure and strategy, although the stronger flow would go from environment to structure and strategy, rather than the other way.

An example of strategy following structure was discussed in the *Harvard Business Review* (Slywotsky and Nadler 2004). The French producer of industrial gases, Air Liquide, was producing gases in small plants at customers' factories. An unrelated company reorganisation suddenly gave the on-site teams involved greater autonomy. They seized the new opportunities, developing new lines of business, which now make up 25 per cent of Air Liquide's revenue, compared with 7 per cent previously.

Figure 1.5 The environment, strategy and structure

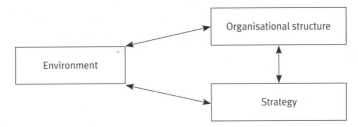

Putting everything together, we arrive at the following comprehensive model (Figure 1.6).

Figure 1.6 The comprehensive model

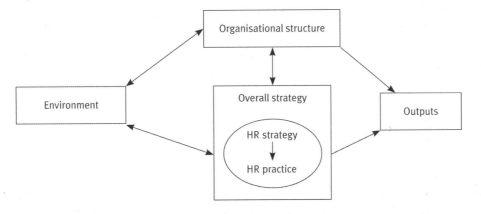

ANALYSING THE ENVIRONMENT

Most organisations will not have a great deal of problems in analysing their task environment. They know who their customers, suppliers, competitors, etc, are. Analysing the general environment is rather more complex. The first step will probably be to brainstorm a list of various environmental factors which seem to impact on the organisation. This is a start, but to progress further it will be necessary to classify these influences.

One widely used tool for classification is PEST analysis and its derivatives. PEST analysis breaks down environmental influences into four categories:

Political/Legal	taxation policy, European Union directives, trade regulations, geopolitical factors such as the 'war on terror', government stability, employment law, contract law, competition law, etc.
Economic	business cycles, economic growth, interest rates, supply and demand factors, competition factors, public spending, money supply, inflation, unemployment, disposable income.
Socio-cultural	demographic trends, income distribution, social mobility, lifestyle, attitudes to work and leisure, levels of education.
Technological	research and development, new inventions or innovations, speed of technology transfer, rates of obsolescence, development of systems.

PEST analysis was widely used during the 1980s and early 1990s. By the mid-1990s, it was becoming more common to talk of PESTLE analysis. Political and Legal were split from each other, and an extra factor, Environment, was added. This reflected a growing awareness of environmental factors and the first concerns about global warming.

By the early 2000s, PESTLE had evolved into STEEPLE, with the addition of Ethics, reflecting the development of concern for corporate social responsibility and business ethics.

The classification currently used is thus:

S	Social
T	Technological
E	Economic
E	Environmental
P	Political
L	Legal
E	Ethical

The STEEPLE model forms the structure of this book. We will be examining each of the STEEPLE elements in turn (although not in this order) and we will conclude by bringing everything together in an analysis of strategy formation.

The next stage in a STEEPLE analysis would be to identify what impact each identified factor would have on the organisation.

WHY DO WE NEED TO UNDERSTAND AND MANAGE THE ENVIRONMENT?

Organisations have a choice in how they manage their relationships with their environment. They can sit back and wait for the environment to change, without attempting to predict its behaviour, and then react to changes as they happen. Here they are being reactive – constantly fire-fighting immediate problems. Or they can identify and foresee changes in the environment and plan their responses before these changes happen. They are being proactive – planning for the future. A few organisations are in the fortunate position of being able to go even further and manage the environment in their own interests – at different times since 1900, Ford, IBM, Sony, McDonald's and Microsoft have done this.

The nature of the environment is also significant. Some organisations have static or placid environments, where it is reasonable to suppose that the future will be a continuation of the past. For example, this was true of many UK nationalised industries before privatisation. An organisation in this happy situation can afford to limit its analysis of its environment to past history. However, such an organisation is likely to be caught totally unawares if the nature of its environment does change rapidly. For example, many airlines in continental Europe were either owned by, or heavily protected by, their home governments. This cosy relationship was totally disrupted by the events of 11 September

2001, with the resultant rapid collapse of two national airlines, Swissair and Sabena, while, to add insult to injury, American Airlines received massive subsidies from the US Government.

Other organisations face turbulent environments, either because the environment is dynamic or in a state of rapid change, for example the pharmaceutical industry or the defence industry; or because the environment is complex, and thus difficult to analyse, for example a multinational company with interests in many countries or industries. Turbulent environments are uncertain.

Igor Ansoff (1987) argued that the extent to which an environment is turbulent depends on:

- changeability of the market environment
- speed of change
- intensity of competition
- fertility of technology
- discrimination by customers
- pressure from government and influence groups.

In order to cope with a turbulent environment, the organisation must be aggressively ready to change.

CASE STUDY 1.2

VIDEO BLUES – A TURBULENT ENVIRONMENT

On 18 June 2007 the BBC2 business programme, *Working Lunch*, highlighted the plight of Peter Citrine, owner of a video rental store on the Wirral. His turnover has fallen by 70 per cent in the last five years, even though several rival stores in his area have gone out of business. He is not alone. In June 2007, the rental chain Global DVD, with 47 stores, went into liquidation, following the third largest retail group, Apollo Video Film Hire, which failed in April, with the closure of 100 stores. In five years, the number of stores nationally has halved to less than a thousand.

The retail video rental market has been the victim of a whole series of hammer blows from changes in its turbulent environment.

Nobody rents or buys videos any more. The VHS format has been totally superseded by DVD, which means that store owners have had to replace a lot of worthless VHS stock.

DVDs are one of many markets in which supermarkets fight their price wars. The typical price of a DVD in a supermarket is £11, while some DVDs are imported from Jersey and sold for as little as £3.93, virtually the same as a rental fee. Since 2000, DVD sales have grown from 16 million to 227 million a year, while rentals have fallen from 200 million to 116 million.

Small stores like Peter Citrine's are hit by the dual pricing policy of the major film studios. DVDs for rental are charged at a much higher price – £25 rather than the £11 in a supermarket. This is permitted under the EU's Rental Rights Directive of 1992.

Until 2002, video stores benefited from a rental window of up to a year, during which the only sales allowed were to rental stores. This gave the rental stores the opportunity to recoup the higher price that they were charged before they faced competition from supermarkets. In 2002, Warner Home Video abolished the rental window, but still kept its dual pricing, followed by other suppliers.

The structure of the industry has changed. The Amazon model of orders placed through the Internet being met centrally from an enormous backlist of titles has been applied to the DVD market, by Amazon itself, by Blockbuster and, most successfully, by Lovefilm. Lovefilm has 400,000 subscribers, who in 2006 rented 2 million DVDs each month, 20 per cent of the UK market. The company owns 1.5 million DVDs, covering 75,000 titles, far more than a local store could stock. Through analysis of orders and customer feedback, it has a huge database of customers' hirings and preferences.

The online rental sector also has a different pricing structure. Customers pay a monthly fee, typically £9.99 a month, for which they can rent one DVD at a time, up to £14.99 for three DVDs at a time. Orders are placed by Internet and delivered by post. There are no limits on the total number that can be rented each month and no late fees. The online suppliers also have the opportunity to earn more revenue by including junk mail in the post with the DVDs.

As broadband speeds improve, it becomes easier to download films over the Internet. In May 2007, Tiscali started to offer legal downloads, charging between 99p and £3.49.

DVD rentals are also being hit by social changes. With the proliferation of TV channels available via satellite or Freeview, many showing films, competition for the DVD rental industry is constantly increasing and the market is also being hit by the increasing range and sophistication of games consoles.

In April 2007, Choices, the second biggest rental chain, issued a profits warning and its CEO, Anthony Skitt, said that it was unlikely that any retail video/DVD rental stores would survive the next five years. He was not far wrong. By January 2013, the market leader, Lovefilm, was wholly owned by Amazon and concentrated on online downloads, while Blockbuster was in administration (Halliday 2011; Garside 2013).

CASE STUDY 1.3

A CATASTROPHIC ENVIRONMENT – ARMENIA IN THE EARLY 1990s

Sometimes an individual, an organisation or a country faces an environment which can only be described as catastrophic. This was true of Armenia in the early 1990s. Modern Armenia, in the Caucasus, has only existed as an independent state since 1991, but both the causes of its crisis in the early 1990s, and some of the solutions, date back to the early twentieth century. At the outbreak of the First World War, Armenia was in two parts, Eastern Armenia, which was part of the Russian Empire, and Western Armenia, which was part of the Turkish Empire. During the War, from 1915 onwards, Turkey carried out extensive pogroms against the Western Armenian population, resulting in 1.5 million dead and the effective extinction of Armenian culture in Western Armenia. The remnants of the population emigrated to Eastern Armenia, Russia or, most importantly, the US, forming the worldwide Armenian diaspora, which is much bigger than the population of Armenia itself.

In 1921, Armenia became a republic within the USSR, and another of the defining events took place. On the borders of Armenia and Azerbaijan is an area known as Nagorno-Karabakh, mainly inhabited by Armenians. However, the area was awarded by Stalin to Azerbaijan.

By the late 1980s, events in the Caucasus were moving towards catastrophe for Armenia. In 1988, guerrilla warfare broke out in Nagorno-Karabakh between Armenian Karabakh nationalists and the Azerbaijan SSR. Also in 1988, there was a devastating earthquake in Northern Armenia, killing 25,000 and leaving hundreds of thousands homeless. This was a devastating blow for a country with a population of only 4 million. The earthquake also forced the closure of Armenia's only nuclear power station, which supplied 40 per cent of the country's energy, for checks and strengthening.

In 1991, with the break-up of the Soviet Union, Armenia became independent, but its troubles continued to mount. The USSR did not only break up politically, it also broke up as an integrated planned economy. This had two major effects for Armenia. Its heavy industry lost its markets elsewhere in the USSR and was unable to compete on a world scale. This led to massive unemployment. At the same time, supplies of gas to Armenia from Kazakhstan were disrupted and contacts had to be renegotiated. With the loss of nuclear power, this now meant that 70 per cent of Armenia's energy supplies had vanished. The country was subject to power cuts for 22 hours a day and had to deplete its already small supplies of woodland for heating fuel. At the same time, the war in Nagorno-Karabakh escalated into an all-out war between Armenia and Azerbaijan in 1992.

The potential was there for Armenia to become a failed state as desperate as Somalia or Haiti. However, this did not happen. Armenians are proud of their heritage and culture, and rallied round to cope with the shortages. By 1994, the nuclear power station was back in operation and the gas contracts renegotiated. A ceasefire was agreed in the Karabakh war in 1994, although a Cold War stand-off between Armenia and Azerbaijan has continued until the present. Economic production was redirected towards agriculture and a start was made on reforestation. Russia and the Armenian diaspora provided massive aid for the earthquake victims, while the diaspora invested heavily in rebuilding Armenia's infrastructure – the Armenian-American hedge fund billionaire Kerk Kerkorian, for example, has paid for much of the modernisation of Armenia's road system. Finally, a quarter of Armenia's population emigrated in the 1990s, reducing short-term pressure on resources but building up longer-term social problems, as those who emigrated were predominantly young men with skills which could be utilised in the US or Russia.

Source: The author's own experiences in Armenia in June 2011.

ENVIRONMENTAL SCANNING

Environmental scanning is defined by Choo (2001) as 'the acquisition and use of information about events, trends and relationships in an organisation's external environment, the knowledge of which would assist management in planning the organisation's future course of action'. Scanning can be as simple as reading the business press or as complex as a market research survey. The more uncertain the environment, the more likely an organisation is to scan. Choo quotes a number of studies which suggest that scanning tends to improve organisational performance.

Choo puts forward a two-dimensional model of environmental scanning based on the two dimensions of environmental analysability (can we analyse what is happening in the environment) and organisational intrusiveness (do we intrude actively into the environment to collect information). His model is illustrated in Figure 1.7.

Figure 1.7 Models of environmental scanning

| | | Organisational intrusiveness | |
		Passive	Active
Assumption about environment	Unanalysable	Undirected viewing	Enacting
	Analysable	Conditioned viewing	Searching

Source: adapted from Choo (2001)

Undirected viewing depends on casual information often obtained informally from personal contacts. Information builds up in an unstructured way and may or may not reach a critical mass where it triggers a reaction from the organisation. It is cheap, but runs the risk that the organisation may be taken by surprise by events which could have been predicted.

Conditioned viewing organisations believe that the environment can be analysed, but put little effort into doing so. Sources of information which are used are those generally available in the industry. This runs the risk that disruptive new changes in the environment (new technologies for example) will not be spotted.

Enacting organisations actively seek information which they can use for experimentation and testing the environment. For example, an organisation might introduce a new product based on its own gut feelings rather than market research and watch to see what happens. This is consistent with the view put forward by Schlesinger et al in a *Harvard Business Review* article in 2012, which advocates the use of small-scale, loss-limited experiments as the best way to cope with an unpredictable environment (Schlesinger et al 2012), and with James Quinn's logical incrementalism approach to strategic management, again based on small experimental steps (Quinn 1980), which is discussed further in Chapter 10.

In the searching mode, information-seeking is broad, open and based on a willingness to revise or update existing knowledge. The emphasis is on rigorous, systematic analysis. An example quoted by Choo is the US technology company Motorola, which is one of the few US companies which systematically monitors technology developments in Japan.

However good an organisation's environmental scanning, three issues must constantly be borne in mind. First, it is easy to be overwhelmed by an excess amount of information about the environment, leading to 'paralysis by analysis'. Second, the most serious threats are those which are 'over the horizon' and so most difficult to spot. Similarly, the best opportunities are those which nobody else has spotted and which are difficult to pick up with environmental scanning – what Kim and Mauborgne call 'Blue Ocean Strategy' opportunities (Kim and Mauborgne 2004). If all firms in an industry use the same environmental scanning approaches, they are likely to concentrate on the same obvious opportunities. The result will be intense competition for these overcrowded 'mountain-tops' (Gavetti 2011).

Finally, if the environment facing an organisation is dynamic, the organisation will need to have procedures for sensing future environmental changes, and contingency plans for dealing with a range of possible changes. This involves the technique known as scenario-building. This increases managerial awareness by examining what-if situations – if x happens, what will its impact be on us and what can we do about it? The technique was first developed by Shell in the early 1970s, when it correctly forecast the 1973 oil crisis and so was ready to deal with it. Schwartz (2003) argues that although most scenarios will be wrong, the mere fact of having been through the scenario-building process will make managers more able to cope with change.

CASE STUDY 1.4

WILD GARDENS

In the mid-1990s, British Airways carried out a scenario-planning exercise for 2005. Two scenarios were developed. One (called Wild Gardens) predicted:

1 rapid growth in Asia

2 a US recession

3 EU enlargement into eastern Europe

4 no single currency

5 a Tory election win in 1997

6 an EU-US open skies agreement, which partially opened up European routes to US competition, and vice versa.

They were right on three of the six – numbers 1, 3 and 6 – partially right on one (number 2), and wrong on the other two. However, what is more important is what they didn't foresee – the two most traumatic events to hit world aviation for many years, namely 9/11 and the Iraq war.

An organisation with a complex environment may need to break down the complexity, so that environmental analysis is decentralised to product groups or countries within the organisation.

The most difficult situation of all, of course, is where the environment is both dynamic and complex. Here the organisation may have to recognise that it cannot predict its environment and what is important is to foster a culture in the organisation that welcomes and is able to cope with radical change. The organisation must learn to live with chaos. One definition of a learning organisation is an organisation which has developed systematic procedures to ensure that it can learn from its environment.

REFLECTIVE ACTIVITY 1.2

Turbulent environments

In what ways have the environments of local authorities become more turbulent in recent years?

HOW TO ANALYSE THE ENVIRONMENT

Johnson et al (2011) propose a five-stage model in analysing the environment, as follows:

Stage 1   Audit of environmental influences
Stage 2   Assessment of nature of the environment
Stage 3   Identification of key environmental factors
Stage 4   Identification of the competitive position
Stage 5   Identification of the principal opportunities and threats.

Stage 1 involves the preparation of a STEEPLE analysis. Stage 2 builds on the placid/dynamic/turbulent classification of environments discussed above. Stage 3 involves a more sophisticated analysis, which may include:

- identifying a smaller number of key environmental influences – for example, for the NHS these might be demographic trends (ageing population), technological developments in healthcare, and implementation of government policy (public–private partnerships)
- identifying long-term drivers of change – for example, the increasing globalisation of markets for some products, eg consumer electronics, cars and pharmaceuticals.

The key principle here is that not all environmental influences are equally important. The analysis in Stage 3 involves identifying those that are most important.

Stage 4 (identifying the organisation's competitive position) will be tackled in the next chapter, using techniques such as Porter's Five Forces (Porter 1980).

Stage 5 (identifying principal opportunities and threats), involves another well-known technique, SWOT analysis.

SWOT stands for:
Strengths
Weaknesses
Opportunities
Threats

Strengths and weaknesses are inward-looking and particularly concerned with the resources of the organisation. Opportunities and threats are outward-looking and involve the analysis of environmental factors. The organisation should ensure that its strengths (or core competencies) are appropriate ones to exploit opportunities or to counter threats.

The CIPD suggests that opportunities and threats (the external environment) will emerge through a STEEPLE analysis, while strengths and weaknesses (the internal environment) can be analysed through a PRIMO-F framework:

- People – what do they do, do they have the appropriate skills?
- Resources – does the organisation have the right and adequate resources?
- Innovation – what new ideas are important to us?
- Marketing – how do they know what the organisation does?
- Operations – how is all this managed?
- Finance – prices, costs and investments (CIPD 2010).

However, the use of such a framework could encourage 'smokestack' thinking. Analysis of strengths and weaknesses requires that a holistic view is taken of the organisation as a whole.

Both opportunities and threats can be analysed using matrices. Opportunities can be assessed according to their attractiveness and the organisation's probability of success (Figure 1.8).

Figure 1.8 An attractiveness/probability of success matrix

| | | Probability of success | |
		High	Low
Attractiveness	High	1	2
	Low	3	4

Opportunities in cell 1 offer the greatest scope and organisations should concentrate on these. Cell 4 represents opportunities which in practice can be ignored. Cells 2 and 3 may be worth investigating further.

Threats can be assessed on the basis of their seriousness and their probability of occurrence (Figure 1.9).

Figure 1.9 An impact/probability of success matrix

Impact

		High	Low
Probability of occurrence	High	1	2
	Low	3	4

A threat which has a high probability of happening, and the likelihood of a considerable impact on the organisation (cell 1), will be a key factor which must be a driver of the organisation's strategy and for which detailed contingency plans must be prepared. At the other extreme (cell 4), a threat which has little likelihood of happening and little impact if it does happen, can be largely ignored. The threats in cells 2 and 3 should be carefully monitored in case they become critical.

It should be remembered that opportunities and threats are rarely mutually exclusive. Many factors can be both – indeed, the Chinese characters for 'threat' and 'opportunity' are identical (Nathan 2000). For example, the technological development of EFTPOS (Electronic Funds Transfer at Point of Sale) money transfer systems (using debit and credit cards) can be a threat to small retailers, as their use by competitors may give the latter a competitive edge, but can also be an opportunity, because they lessen the amount of cash likely to be in tills and so make the shop less attractive to thieves.

REFLECTIVE ACTIVITY 1.3

The hospital

How would you classify the following factors on a probability/seriousness matrix for a hospital trust? What contingency planning should the trust make?

- a serious accident on the local railway line, causing scores of deaths and injuries
- an ageing local population
- a leakage of radioactive material at a nuclear power station 200 miles downwind away.

SWOT AND STRATEGY

Weihrich (1982) argues that SWOT is misnamed. He suggests renaming it TOWS. His argument is that SWOT implies that strengths and weaknesses come first, but that this is mistaken. The only logical starting point for analysis is with opportunities and threats. They are outside the organisation, largely beyond its control and must be managed using the organisation's strengths and weaknesses. He thus argues that SWOT should be used as a contingency model.

Four combinations of opportunities, threats, strengths and weaknesses are possible, and each suggests a possible strategy:

- Strengths–opportunities (maxi–maxi) – the organisation should pursue strategies which make most use of its strengths to capitalise on opportunities.
- Strengths–threats (maxi–mini) – the organisation should use its strengths to minimise or neutralise threats.
- Weaknesses–opportunities (mini–maxi) – make the most of any new opportunities to overcome weaknesses.
- Weaknesses–threats (mini–mini) – this combination calls for a defensive strategy, to minimise internal weaknesses and avoid external threats.

CRITICISMS OF SWOT

As an analytical technique, SWOT has many strengths. It is simple, easy to understand and (at least at a superficial level) easy to use, and it does encourage managers to think about both the internal and external aspects of their business.

However, both Hill and Westbrook (1997) and Koch (2000) are very critical about how SWOT is used. Hill and Westbrook surveyed 50 companies and found that 20 carried out SWOT analysis. What they had in common was the generation of long lists, general descriptions, failure to prioritise, and no attempt to verify the points which were made. Most damning of all, no company actually used the results in later strategic analysis.

Koch takes a more analytical approach. He argues that the main weaknesses are:

- It generates strategies based on the past or present, not on the future.
- It cannot ensure the necessary rigour.
- In practice it is rarely deployed below corporate level, although the strategic positions of strategic business units (SBUs) will vary.
- The company needs to know (but will not know) the relevant performance levels of all of its competitors.
- It also needs to know (but does not know) future performance levels for competitors. It requires 'benchtracking' rather than benchmarking of competitors.
- The SWOT is rarely modified for different strategies. Something that may be a strength for one strategy will be a weakness for another.
- It is too broad.
- It is too vague.

All this suggests that SWOT is well past its sell-by date. However, Koch does suggest ways in which the technique can be made more effective:

- The boundaries and structure of the market, and anticipated changes, should be clearly defined.
- All changes in the environment capable of influencing future performance should be included.
- The corporate environment, structure, form, scope and intensity of competition should be properly examined and presented.
- There should be clear reference to anticipated changes in the environment.
- There should be clear reference to future objectives and strategies.
- There should be a SWOT for each SBU.
- There should be a SWOT for each proposed strategy.
- The SWOT should be constantly updated.

To summarise, SWOT must be made a forward-looking technique in order to be effective. A good analogy is with the due diligence process carried out when a company is contemplating a takeover. At its best, this is rigorous and ruthless subjecting all elements of the potential target to forensic analysis.

Bridgepoint, a European private equity company, assembles a team of six managers to carry out a due diligence, each of whom represents one of four viewpoints. One is the prosecutor, who plays the role of devil's advocate. The second is the less-experienced manager, whose involvement is a key part of his or her training. The third is a senior managing director, who no longer has any hierarchical function at the company and who therefore cannot be undermined by corporate politics. The final members of the panel are managing directors who still have operational roles. The team's goal is to provide a thorough, balanced and unbiased examination of the acquisition candidate (Cullinan et al 2004). A similar approach should be taken to SWOT.

In essence, SWOT is a simple framework and a potentially valuable tool which is often badly used by managers as an alternative to undertaking the grind of detailed internal and external analysis.

MODELS OF ORGANISATIONAL STRUCTURE

In this section we concentrate on the organisation and examine different models of organisational structure and their attendant strengths and weaknesses.

BUREAUCRACY

Formalisation of the bureaucratic form of organisation dates back to the sociologist Max Weber's work on government departments in the 1890s (Weber 1964) and the form reached its peak in the US of the 1950s and 1960s.

Weber identified three central principles of bureaucratic organisation:

- specialisation
- hierarchy
- impersonal rationality.

Specialisation

Labour tasks are highly divided and workers are recruited with specific skills to carry out specific roles. Tasks are functionally separated and organised into rigid departments ('smokestack management'). Movement from department to department would be unusual. Some departments, such as production, would carry out the core tasks of the organisation, while others, such as finance or HR, would provide technical or physical support for the core activities. This was identified by Fayol as the distinction between line and staff activities (Fayol 1916/1949). Parallels with Frederick Taylor's minute definition of tasks and Henry Ford's Model T production line should be obvious (Taylor 1947).

Hierarchy

Along with a rigid definition of tasks came a rigid definition of power and authority. The result was a hierarchical structure, with only those higher in the organisational hierarchy able to give instructions to those lower down. Promotion up the hierarchy was possible on the basis of either merit or seniority.

Impersonal rationality

In a bureaucracy, power belongs to the office, not to the office-holder. Power was based on rules, which provided precedents for action. Behaviour was rational, based on logical principles, not on individual whim or prejudice. Remember that it was not long before Weber that reforms were enacted in the UK to eliminate corruption and nepotism in the civil service and the army. Impersonal rationality at least in theory made corruption and nepotism impossible. Impersonal rules also form the basis for our present-day anti-discrimination legislation – the right to be judged on your own merit, not on your sex, gender, skin colour, nationality, religion, disability or sexual orientation.

As a form of organisation, bureaucracy had many strengths:

- It provided predictable and secure career paths for those who worked in them – the civil service 'job for life'.
- Rules provided a number of protections. They guaranteed fair treatment within the rules and avoided the arbitrary exercise of power, and they protected civil liberties, because everyone was subject to the rules.

However, there were also weaknesses:

- The rules could become so complex that the worker or the client of the organisation could feel helpless, confused and trapped. See, for example, Franz Kafka's *The Trial* (Kafka 1964) or the labyrinthine regulations surrounding present-day tax credits.
- Minute definition and sub-division of tasks could produce an alienated workforce, particularly as the hierarchical structure did not easily permit worker empowerment.
- Rigid adherence to rules could produce a 'jobsworth' mentality – 'no you can't do X, it's not in the rules' (Clegg et al 2008). Perhaps most crucially, its very rigidity, which is in some ways its greatest strength, is also its greatest weakness. A pure bureaucracy can only operate successfully in a placid environment and it becomes progressively less able to cope effectively as the environment becomes more turbulent.

Despite the weaknesses of the model, there are still strong bureaucratic elements in virtually all organisational forms today.

DIVISIONALISATION, OR M-FORM

This is a development of the bureaucratic organisation. As the organisation becomes larger, it becomes more difficult to manage everything from the centre. As a result, some decision-making is decentralised. The divisionalised organisation sets up a number of separate product, market or geographic divisions, each responsible for operational decisions, which will usually include production, marketing and some elements of HR (although US companies are more reluctant to delegate HR to divisions). Each division will thus be a mini-bureaucracy, competing against the other divisions. Strategic decisions will be taken at headquarters, including, crucially, investment decisions and allocation of capital, and setting and monitoring of targets (Boxall and Purcell 2008).

Divisionalisation was effectively invented by Alfred Sloan at General Motors in the 1920s. Here the motive was not so much to give more autonomy to operating divisions – Chevrolet, Buick or Cadillac – but to centralise authority over subsidiaries which had previously been independent businesses (Hales 2001). The divisional structure is particularly common among multinational corporations, with divisions usually organised on a country or regional basis.

The divisional form is more flexible than the pure bureaucracy, but as noted above, there is a tendency for the divisions themselves to become highly bureaucratised, which then limits their flexibility. There is also a tendency for US or UK divisional organisations to impose mainly short-term targets on their operating divisions – in contrast to the longer-term goals favoured by the Japanese.

A more extreme form of divisionalisation operates through strategic business units (SBUs). The typical SBU is smaller than the classic division and is based on a niche product, service or unit. Specialist services, such as IT or training, will often themselves be supplied by SBUs, which are profit centres in their own right. These may not just provide services within the organisation, but compete for outside business. An extreme example of this was the internal market in the BBC under John Birt in the 1990s. Here, under a programme called Producer Choice, programme makers were given budgets which they could spend either on in-house facilities or on external contractors. If the in-house facilities could not attract enough work, they were closed (Hales 2001). The intention was to increase efficiency, but the internal market process was so expensive that any benefits were more than cancelled out. Producer Choice was abandoned by the next director-general of the BBC, Greg Dyke.

GENERAL MOTORS, DIVISIONALISATION AND CHAPTER 11

On 1 June 2009, General Motors filed for Chapter 11 bankruptcy, the third biggest bankruptcy ever, after Lehman Brothers and WorldCom, and the biggest industrial bankruptcy. A month before, the third-biggest US carmaker, Chrysler, had also gone into bankruptcy (Clark 2009a). Was GM's failure, which followed losses of $81 billion over the previous four years, purely the result of the credit crunch, or were more deep-seated factors at play, and did they have anything to do with the way the company was structured?

In the 1950s, Charles Wilson, the then head of GM, declared: 'For years I thought that what was good for our country was good for General Motors, and vice versa' (Noyes 2009), while the management guru Peter Drucker said that it was General Motors who 'won the war for America' (Chakrabortty 2009). At its peak in 1955, GM's share of the US market was 54 per cent – now it is 19 per cent and falling, and GM has been overtaken by Toyota as the world's biggest carmaker.

General Motors was founded in 1908 in Flint, Michigan, when William Durant acquired the Buick Motor Company, still one of the core GM brands. By 1909, he had also bought Oldsmobile and Cadillac, as well as four other brands. The pattern for GM's strategy had already been set – growth through acquisition, a stark contrast to Henry Ford's strategy of organic growth. In the 1920s, the company moved into Europe, acquiring Vauxhall in 1923 and Opel in 1929 (Wearden 2009).

By the late 1920s, GM was under the control of the legendary management pioneer Alfred Sloan, much admired by Peter Drucker, who pulled together the sprawling GM empire and divisionalised its organisational structure. Each division targeted a social market niche – Chevrolet the entry-level blue-collar worker, Pontiac the sporty market, Buick established professionals and Cadillac top professionals. Each division introduced a new model every year, with the emphasis on styling rather than engineering (DesJardins 2007).

The strategy was successful. Ford, which stuck with its organic growth and its centralised bureaucratic organisational structure, was soon overtaken, and by 1954 GM had made its 50 millionth car. However, life became more difficult in the 1960s, as competition from Europe increased, while after 1973, GM, and the whole American car industry, was hit by the aftermath of the oil crisis. Suddenly, big, over-styled US gas guzzlers were yesterday's cars and the future lay with smaller, more economical and better-quality Japanese models. GM tried hard to introduce Japanese production methods and culture, but the fit with the traditional GM culture was too hard to achieve.

By the 1980s GM was making losses. Market share shrank and the CEO at the time, Roger Smith, made tens of thousands of redundancies. Smith was recently ranked 13th in a list of worst American CEOs of all time. Redundancies and loss of market share continued through the 1990s and 2000s. GM did try to escape from the spiral of decline. It formed a joint venture with Toyota in the 1980s, called NUMMI, in order to learn more about

Japanese techniques, and it simplified its organisational structure, concentrating its car models into two divisions, Midsize and Luxury Car Group, and Small Car Group (Grant 2008, p188) but it was already too late. By 2005, GM was making US losses of $1 billion and was crippled by falling market share, an unpopular product mix, rising raw material prices and the deadweight cost of US health insurance, which amounted to $1,500 per car (Worthington and Britton 2006). The collapse in 2009 had become inevitable. The last symbolic touch came in August 2009, when Toyota announced that the NUMMI plant was to close, the first plant closure in Toyota's history, and the end of its 25-year partnership with GM (McCurry 2009).

So what went wrong? Why did GM go bust, while its nearest rivals, Ford and Toyota, survived relatively unscathed?

Ford's bureaucratic and centralised organisational culture ensured that it could share parts between models, and Ford was also famous, or notorious, for its savage cost controls. Toyota was probably the most efficient of the Japanese car companies, brilliant at both lean production and quality management, and was famous for its flexibility and its innovation. GM had the advantages of neither. The duplication of facilities through its divisional structure cost money, and it did not exploit cost-saving opportunities to the same extent as its rivals. Chrysler suffered from the same disadvantages and was also crippled by its failed merger with Daimler.

Compared with its main rivals, GM was too US-centric. The UN agency UNCTAD produces a Trasnationality Index. This

measures the extent of globalisation of a company through three ratios – foreign sales as a percentage of total sales, foreign assets as a percentage of total assets, and foreign employment as a percentage of total employment. Aggregating these three figures gives the firm's Transnationality Index. In 2002, for Ford this was 47.7 per cent, for Toyota 45.7 per cent, but for GM only 27.9 per cent (Worthington and Britton 2006, p396). GM was thus much more dependent on the US market, while its rivals could spread their risks worldwide.

GM's period in bankruptcy was short. Unlike UK or European bankruptcy, US Chapter 11 bankruptcy is more of a technical device. It gives a corporation time to recover while shielding it from its creditors. A deal was quickly reached and GM's bankruptcy lasted only 40 days. The new GM was radically different from the old one. In future it would focus on only four brands – Chevrolet, Cadillac, Buick and GMC. Its blue-collar workforce would fall from 113,000 in 2006 to 38,000 in 2011. The number of US plants would fall from 47 to 31 and top management would be cut by 35 per cent. More radical still, the US Government now owns 60.8 per cent of GM, the Canadian Government 11.7 per cent, and a union-controlled pension fund 17.5 per cent. Creditors of the old company get 10 per cent and the old shareholders get nothing (Clark 2009b).

The rescue was successful. In 2010 the US Treasury sold 28 per cent of the company at a profit and, by May 2012, the company had posted nine consecutive quarters of profit (Higgins 2012).

THE MATRIX ORGANISATION

The matrix model of organisation was first developed in the US aerospace industry in the 1960s. Here the organisation is involved in a series of short- or medium-term projects, each of which has a finite life. Each project will require the services of a number of functional specialists, drawn from functional departments. Who is going to control these functional specialists – their departmental manager or the project manager? The solution offered in a matrix organisation is that he or she will be answerable to both the departmental and the project manager (Figure 1.10).

Figure 1.10 A matrix organisational structure

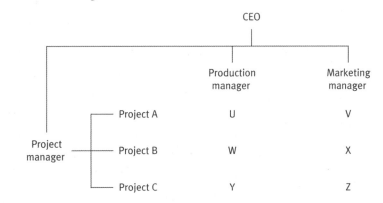

Production specialist U will report to his functional manager, the production manager, but while he is working on project A, he will be answerable to the project manager in charge of project A. He will also be working on project A alongside his colleague from marketing V.

The matrix structure has a number of advantages:

- Communication within the organisation is improved and as a result decisions can be made more speedily and effectively.
- Use of human and capital resources becomes more flexible.
- The use of project teams increases motivation, job satisfaction and personal development.

However, there can also be disadvantages:

- As each individual is answerable to at least two bosses, there can be problems of loyalty and feelings of insecurity.
- Power struggles are likely over decision-making and the allocation of resources between the functional and project managers.
- Although communication and decision-making should be improved, decisions may be more difficult to make as decision-making authority is diffused.
- The structure is particularly threatening to functional managers, who can see their power base eroded.

THE NETWORK ORGANISATION, OR N-FORM

The network organisation is a less formal version of the matrix organisation. The aim is to build up networks and connections between different parts of the organisation in order to break down rigid departmental smokestacks and to ensure the faster diffusion of ideas throughout the organisation.

This can be done in several ways. Unilever, for example, works hard to build up lateral relationships between managers in different divisions. Career development is carefully planned on a multiple spiral, with managers progressing between functions, divisions and countries (Boxall and Purcell 2008, p264).

Another approach is to use network managers, with several roles:

- boundary-spanners between levels and functions
- initiators of networks
- co-ordinators of information transfer
- conveyors of corporate vision downwards and advocates of decentralised initiatives upwards (Child 2005, p255).

A third approach is to use communities of practice. These are informal networks of people with common interests within an organisation (and often pulling in people from outside the organisation). Often run on the Internet or a company intranet, they enable quick informal communication of information and knowledge. All students know that you learn at least as much from your fellow students as from formal tuition, and communities of practice operate on the same principle of social learning (Clegg et al 2008). CIPD professional communities (a form of community of practice) had 88,480 participants on 20 August 2009, taking part in 12,310 discussions (www.cipd.co.uk/communities, accessed on 20 August 2009).

One key element in ensuring the success of any N-form organisation is culture. As Whittington and Mayer (2000) said, 'N-form works best with Eastern appreciation of the tacit, the embedded and the ambiguous, rather than the explicit, tightly specified knowledge systems of the West.'

Networks can operate outside as well as inside the organisation. Hansen and von Oetinger (2001) identified the concept of the T-shaped manager, with the vertical part of the T representing the manager's role within the organisation and the horizontal part of the T the role of networking outside the organisation.

The key resource in an N-form organisation is knowledge. Bettis (1991) argues that with the development of N-form, the M-form organisation is now an 'organisational fossil'. In the M-form, Chandler argued that 'structure follows strategy'. In the N-form, structure *is* strategy (Purcell 2005).

VIRTUAL ORGANISATIONS

In a virtual organisation, physical assets – buildings, machinery, etc – are replaced by computer networks. Warner and Witzel (2003, ch1) identify six characteristics of virtual organisations:

- *Lack of physical structure* – they have fewer physical assets and ultimately might exist solely in cyberspace.
- *Reliance on communications technology* – virtual organisations use communication networks supported by the Internet.
- *Mobile work* – members of teams no longer have to be in physical contact. They can work anywhere and communicate through ICT.
- *Hybrid forms* – some virtual organisations are brought together for short-term projects, such as producing a film or a book. Others are longer term, such as a virtual supply chain.
- *Boundaryless and inclusive* – virtual organisations often closely involve suppliers (through partnership sourcing) or customers (through customer relationship management). The fashion accessories company Topsy Tail, for example, had revenues of $80 million in 1998, but only three employees. It outsources everything and never touches its product (Child 2005).
- *Flexible and responsive.*

Perhaps the best example of a virtual organisation is Dell Computer Corporation. The key to Dell's business model is its direct sales strategy, which relies on demand pull. A computer is only produced against a firm customer order. The company therefore has no finished goods inventory or warehouses. It operates with half the staff and one-tenth the inventory of its competitors. On average it carries six days' work in progress stock, all held against firm orders. In 2000, 50 per cent of orders were received online (Gillespie 2000). The ordering system permits the customer to write their own specification (mass customisation). In theory, each computer sold is unique. When it receives an order, it sends electronic orders for components to its suppliers worldwide. These components are then assembled in a Dell factory and despatched direct to the customer. In some cases the process is totally virtual – for example, when Dell receives an order for a computer monitor, it is despatched direct to the customer from a supplier such as Sony (Child 2005).

STRATEGIC ALLIANCES

Strategic alliances are any medium- to long-term co-operative relationships between firms which involve joint working. They can variously be called alliances, partnerships or joint ventures. They have become increasingly common. Between 1996 and 2001, US companies formed 57,000 alliances (Dyer et al 2004). The average US corporation manages more than 30 alliances, while many have several hundred. By 2001, they already accounted for up to 15 per cent of the market value of the typical US company. However, it has been estimated that 60 per cent have been outright failures (Parkhe 2001).

Alliances can take many legal and contractual forms. These are illustrated and discussed in Child (2005, pp223–5). Contractor and Lorange (1998) identify six main objectives for alliances:

- reduction of risk
- achievement of economies of scale
- technology exchange
- countering competition
- overcoming government trade or investment barriers
- vertical quasi-integration advantages – linking the complementary contributions of partners in a value chain.

Dussauge and Garrette (1999) identified six different types, three between non-competing firms and three between competing firms.

Non-competing

- International expansion joint ventures – until the late 1990s, Western firms seeking to invest in China could only do so through a joint venture with a local firm.
- Vertical partnerships, between firms at different stages in the same value chain – for example Intel and Hewlett-Packard set up a joint venture to develop a new microprocessor.
- Cross-industry agreements – American Airlines and SNCF (French Railways) set up a joint venture to develop a computerised ticketing system.

Competing

- Shared supply alliances – these are common in the car industry.
- Quasi-concentration alliances, designed to counter competition – an example is Airbus Industrie, formed between competing European aircraft manufacturers to counter the threat from Boeing.
- Complementary alliances, designed to reduce risk and achieve synergy – these are common in the pharmaceutical industry. For example, in 1996, Pfizer used its superior marketing expertise to collaborate in the marketing of Lipitor, a cholesterol-reducing drug developed by a rival company, Warner-Lambert. By 1999, Lipitor had achieved sales of $3 billion a year (Dyer et al 2004).

Why do so many alliances fail? Many reasons have been put forward:

- *Communication problems* – a US–UK joint venture had to appear before a crucial British government hearing. The US firm asked the UK firm to 'table' several key points at the meeting. To the horror of the Americans, the British firm brought up these very issues at the hearing, leading to disaster. The Americans had forgotten that 'to table' in UK English means to 'place on the table', whereas in US English it means 'hide under the table'.

- *Culture clashes* – in the 1990s, Siemens, Toshiba and IBM were working together to develop a new memory chip. Siemens representatives were horrified when the Toshiba scientists appeared to go to sleep in meetings – a common practice among Japanese when the discussion does not directly concern them. The Japanese found it difficult to work in mixed-nationality groups speaking English. The Americans felt the Germans planned too much and the Japanese would not take decisions (Parkhe 2001).

- *Diverging strategic directions* – alliances which might have made perfect strategic sense at the time may diverge over time.

- *Failure to protect strategic knowledge* – in the early 1980s, Macintosh used Microsoft to develop software applications for the Apple Mac. As a result, Microsoft acquired crucial knowledge about Apple's mouse-based graphical user interface, which it then used to develop the Windows operating system. Eventually Apple brought an unsuccessful lawsuit against Microsoft to try to protect its intellectual property (Norman 2001).

- *Uneven benefits* – in 2001, Coca-Cola and Procter & Gamble formed a $4 billion joint venture that would control more than 40 brands contributed by the parent companies. However, the markets felt that P&G would get more out of the alliance than Coke. P&G's share price immediately rose 2 per cent, while Coca-Cola's fell 6 per cent. Predictably, the alliance lasted only six months (Dyer et al 2004). The same thing may well happen with the Internet search technology joint venture announced by Microsoft and Yahoo in July 2009, intended as a defensive alliance against the market leader, Google. Here the share price disparity has been even more marked. Microsoft shares rose 2 per cent, while Yahoo's fell 15 per cent. Both sides moved fast to defend the alliance. Steve Ballmer, CEO of Microsoft, described the Yahoo share price fall as 'sort of unbelievable', while Tim Morse, Yahoo's chief finance officer, said, 'It's a perfect fit for our strategy' (Waters and Menn 2009). The market's scepticism seems to have been justified. In the third quarter of 2011, Yahoo reported a fall in revenue of 5 per cent and attributed this to the search alliance with Microsoft (Crum 2011).

- *Exit problems* – Daimler Benz had a long-standing alliance with ABB called Adtranz. The alliance had been losing money and after Daimler-Benz merged with Chrysler, an ex-Chrysler executive suggested putting it into liquidation. The Daimler reaction was horror – 'You don't understand. This is Europe. Bankruptcy is not good over here.' Eventually ABB was bought out. In another example, Suzuki wanted to make redundancies at a joint venture in Spain. The result was riots outside the Japanese embassy in Madrid (Inkpen and Ross 2001).

REFLECTIVE ACTIVITY 1.4

Successful and unsuccessful partnerships – Galanz and Swissair

Galanz

Guangdong Galanz is the global leader in microwave manufacture, producing over 18 million units in 2004, 40 per cent of the global market. It is one of the largest home appliance manufacturers in China, employing 20,000 people and with 2004 revenues exceeding $1 billion.

This is a far cry from the first incarnation of the company, as the GuizhouDown Product Factory, a township enterprise set up by Quingde Leung in 1978, when the Chinese Government set up its first Special Enterprise Zones in Guangdong in southern China. The company washed and processed goose feathers for clothing companies such as Yves St Laurent. By 1992, the company had sales of $19 million and ranked in the top 100 village and township enterprises in China.

However, Leung was worried that intense competition would kill the textiles business and he took the momentous decision to diversify into microwaves, at that time a luxury item in China. He changed the name of the company to the Galanz Group of Guangdong, recruited experts from a radio factory in Shanghai and licensed microwave technology from Toshiba. In 1993, the company produced a trial run of 10,000 microwaves and persuaded the Shanghai No 1 Department Store to stock them.

In 1994 Chinese government policy changed and township enterprises were required to sell two-thirds of each enterprise to management. The result was a broad base of middle managers with a stake in the company's success.

Galanz was faced with fierce competition from the market leader SMC. However, ironically, SMC was crippled by its partnership agreement with the huge American white goods manufacturer Whirlpool. Whirlpool put in its own management team and required that all major decisions were cleared first through regional headquarters in Hong Kong and ultimately through corporate headquarters in Michigan. By 1995 Galanz had a 25 per cent share of the Chinese market, passing SMC, and by 1998 this had grown to half the market. Clearly further growth in the domestic market would be difficult.

In 1997, one result of the Asian financial crisis was that South Korean microwave manufacturers, including Samsung and LG, were accused of dumping microwaves on the European market. European manufacturers felt that they were unable to compete.

In a novel deal, Galanz offered to make their microwaves in China for half the European cost. European manufacturers shipped their whole production lines to Guangdong, where they could take advantage of Galanz's lower labour costs and efficient supply chain. The microwaves would then be exported back to Europe to be sold under the European companies' brand names. Galanz also secured permission from its partners to use their production facilities to produce Galanz-branded goods in China. Galanz signed up 200 European partners and its microwave production grew from 1 million in 1996 to 12 million in 2001.

The deal was a win–win. The European partners obtained product at a much lower cost than they could have produced themselves, while Galanz was able to expand and become a global presence without having to make heavy capital investments itself.

Source: Sull (2005)

Swissair

In the 1990s, Swissair was one of the most successful and respected airlines in the world, noted for its high quality, which permitted it to charge high prices. In 1998 it made a profit of SFr400million (around £200 million). Yet by 2000, the company was losing SFr 2.9 billion, and in October 2001 it went into receivership.

What went wrong? The immediate cause of the collapse was the world crisis in the airline industry following the terrorist attacks on 11 September 2001, but a more fundamental cause was Swissair's failed alliance strategy.

Until the late 1980s, the European airline industry was dominated by national carriers with effective monopolies in their home markets. This kept competition low and prices and profits high. However, the first steps towards liberalisation of the world airline industry came in 1988. This represented a threat to Swissair, with its small home market. In 1993, talks (codenamed Alcazar) were opened between Swissair, SAS (Scandinavian Airlines), KLM (the Netherlands) and Austrian Airlines. A new company was proposed, with Swissair, SAS and KLM each holding 30 per cent, and Austrian 10 per cent. However, Swiss public opinion was hostile to the idea of

Swissair losing its name and the talks broke down.

In 1994, Swissair hired McKinsey to develop a new strategy. Three options were put forward:

- Go it alone. Given the small size of the Swiss home market, this was not seen as viable.
- Develop a new business alliance (in effect a repeat of the Alcazar strategy). This was seen as high risk, but the most politically acceptable.
- Ally with one of the large European airlines (BA, Lufthansa or Air France). This was seen as the safest option, but politically unacceptable, as Swissair would inevitably be a very junior partner.

As a first step, in 1994 Swissair acquired a 49.5 per cent stake in the Belgian airline Sabena, which had only made a profit once in its 75-year history. Meanwhile, the world aviation industry was changing rapidly. In 1996, BA, American Airlines, Cathay Pacific and Qantas formed a new global alliance called Oneworld. Two other alliances followed – Skyteam, led by Air France, and Star, including United Airlines, Lufthansa and SAS.

Swissair decided to go for a strategy of forming a fourth alliance. It acquired minority stakes in the Polish airline LOT, the French company Air Littoral, the Italian airlines Air Europe and

Volare, and South African Airways (SAA), in addition to its existing holding in Sabena and Austrian Airlines. None of the partners, with the possible exception of SAA, was known as a strong airline.

Swissair already had long-standing alliance relationships with Delta and Singapore Airlines, both strong companies. However, Delta decided to join Skyteam in 1999, while Singapore Airlines joined Star. In 2000, an aggressive attempt to increase Swissair's stake in Austria led to that airline also defecting to Star. Meanwhile, the European market was increasingly being penetrated by the low-cost airlines Ryanair and easyJet. The latter set up a hub in Geneva, directly threatening Swissair on its home ground.

By mid-July 2001, Swissair had debts of SFr7.8 billion, six times the value of its equity, and its share price was a fifth of its peak in 1998. Given this weakness, 9/11 was merely the last straw. Both Swissair and its partner Sabena were doomed.

Source: Ruigrok (2004)

Question

1   Why do you think that Galanz was successful in its alliances and Swissair unsuccessful?

CASE STUDY 1.6

PARTNERSHIP FAILURE – THE HATFIELD TRAIN CRASH

In the mid-1990s, Britain's rail system was privatised. A single company, British Rail, was replaced with a network of partnerships, as the rail system was fragmented. Railtrack was made responsible for operating, developing and maintaining the physical track network, but did not operate trains. This was done by train operating companies (TOCs), which obtained medium-term contracts from the Government to operate particular lines. They then paid access charges to Railtrack for use of the track. Tensions inevitably built up between Railtrack and the operating companies. Railtrack

needed access to the track to carry out maintenance, but this prevented the operating companies from running trains. There were several high-profile rows over the West Coast Main Line, when Christmas maintenance over-ran, causing vociferous complaints from the TOC, Richard Branson's Virgin.

In addition Railtrack took the decision not to carry out its own maintenance, as British Rail had. Instead, maintenance was outsourced to seven main contractors, who in turn outsourced particular aspects to 2,000 sub-contractors. This meant that

Railtrack was dependent on sub-contractors over whom they had no control. Maintenance policy was also changed from planned replacement to replacement when required.

On 17 October 2000, a serious accident happened on the East Coast Main Line at Hatfield, when a rail broke under the wheels of a GNER express from London to Leeds. Four people died and 70 were injured.

Any fatal rail crash is a tragedy, but subsequent investigations proved that the accident was a disaster waiting to happen and that it was directly attributable to the breakdown in the relationships between the various players involved in the post-privatisation railway system.

In the winter of 1999, a routine inspection by Balfour Beatty, the main contractor, spotted cracks in a rail near Hatfield and recommended that the rail should be ground to get rid of the cracks. This would be carried out by a sub-contractor, Serco. Before this could be done, Balfour Beatty recommended that the rail should be replaced – by another sub-contractor, Jarvis. In March 2000, Railtrack agreed that the rail should be replaced as a 'priority #1', which meant that the work should be completed within a month.

The replacement was booked to be done on 19 March, but before this could be done, replacement rails had to be delivered to the site. However, the train delivering the new rails – owned by Railtrack and manned by Jarvis – was late, and the rails could not be delivered. The replacement slot was lost. After three more attempts, the rails were finally delivered at the end of April 2000.

Four months then passed while Railtrack attempted to negotiate a rail replacement date with Jarvis (which also had to be acceptable to the TOC, GNER). Eventually a date was set for the last week of November – a year after the original problem was spotted. Meanwhile, Railtrack was still worried about the deteriorating state of the rail and ordered it to be reground by Serco. This was done in September, though some experts think that the rail was already so damaged that regrinding may have made the problem worse.

Before the rails could be replaced, the Hatfield accident happened. As a result of the accident, crippling speed restrictions were placed on the whole railway network – a classic example of the stable door being shut after the horse has bolted. As an indirect result of the crash, Railtrack was taken into administration by the Government in October 2001 and replaced by the not-for-profit organisation Network Rail, which speedily brought its major engineering maintenance contracts back in-house.

The lessons for partnerships – the key need to agree on priorities (in this case, that passenger safety is paramount) and the crucial role of communication. It may also be significant that the partnerships in the rail industry were in effect imposed by the Government as part of rail privatisation, rather than being voluntary.

Sources: Child (2005), Jowit (2001)

STRUCTURAL CHOICE

Goold and Campbell (2002) propose nine design tests against which choice of structure can be evaluated:

1 The market-advantage test – if co-ordination between two steps in a production process is important to market advantage, they should be placed in the same structural unit.

2   The parenting-advantage test – if the centre aims to promote synergy, integration specialisms should be placed at the centre.

3   The people test – the structure must fit the skills of the people available.

4   The feasibility test – the structure must fit legal, stakeholder and other constraints.

5   The specialised culture test – a structure scores poorly if it breaks up important specialist cultures.

6   The difficult links test – does the structure set up links between parts of the organisation that are important but bound to be strained?

7   The redundant hierarchy test – too many layers of management cause undue blockages and expense.

8   The accountability test – there should be clear lines of accountability, often a problem with matrix organisations.

9   The flexibility test – is the structure flexible enough to cope with future change?

DOES STRUCTURE FOLLOW STRATEGY?

Alfred Chandler, one of the pioneers of strategic management, argued strongly that structure follows strategy. He quotes the example of Du Pont, which at the end of the First World War undertook a diversification strategy that initially was unsuccessful, mainly because the company kept its old functional structure, which was unable to cope with increased diversity. Once Du Pont switched to a divisional structure, its strategy thrived.

Hall and Saias (1980) argue that the causality can go the other way – strategy can follow structure. A decentralised multidivisional structure can quickly take up new diversification strategies, but finds it much more difficult to follow a strategy which is dependent on knowledge-sharing.

Amburgey and Dacin (1994) found that structure followed strategy, but only most of the time. Finally, Mintzberg (1998) concluded that 'structure follows strategy as the left foot follows the right', ie, that the two are linked and neither consistently leads the other.

REFLECTIVE ACTIVITY 1.5

Henry Mintzberg and organisational structure

Henry Mintzberg has put forward a number of hypotheses about how situational factors affect the structure and functioning of organisations:

- The older the organisation, the more formalised its behaviour.
- The larger the organisation, the more formalised its behaviour.
- The larger the organisation, the more elaborate its structure.
- The more dynamic an organisation's environment, the more organic its structure.
- The more complex an organisation's environment, the more centralised its structure.
- The more diversified an organisation's markets, the greater the propensity to split into market-based units or divisions.
- Extreme hostility in the environment drives any organisation to centralise its structure temporarily.

Question

1   From your knowledge of your own organisation, or any other organisations with which you are familiar, how far do you think these hypotheses are valid?

Source: Mintzberg (1998)

HR OUTSOURCING

Case Study 1.7 illustrates how outsourcing can be a key element of a partnership strategy. One popular candidate for outsourcing is HR. HR outsourcing can cover a wide spectrum of activities, from a small business using a local personnel freelancer to handle its HR on a part-time basis to a joint venture formed between a multinational company and an HR services company to handle all of the former's HR function. Here we are more concerned with the latter end of the spectrum, where control over significant elements of the outsourcer's HR function is outsourced to a partner organisation.

A 2009 CIPD survey found that 29 per cent of organisations sampled were using HR outsourcing, with 64 per cent increasing their use of outsourcing in the previous five years, and only 11 per cent reducing it (CIPD 2009). The top drivers for HR outsourcing were access to skills and knowledge not available within the organisation (71 per cent), improving quality (64 per cent) and cost reduction (61 per cent). Outsourcers seem to have achieved these objectives. Ninety-one per cent claimed to have accessed knowledge and skills, 83 per cent to have improved quality and 90 per cent to have reduced costs.

The most common functions to have been outsourced were legal, payroll, pensions, training and recruitment. Least likely to have been outsourced were resource planning, appraisal, strategy and policy. There seems to be a clear trend to outsource operational parts of the HR function and to keep more strategic elements in-house.

Also interesting are reasons given for not using HR outsourcing, even when the organisation involved outsources other significant functions. The three most commonly given reasons for not outsourcing HR were:

- effective, well-resourced HR team within the organisation (52 per cent)
- remain unconvinced of the benefits of HR outsourcing (35 per cent)
- already use effective shared service model (24 per cent).

Shared service centres are a common alternative to HR outsourcing, which will be discussed below.

In practice, HR outsourcing does not always go smoothly. BP, for example, was the first major company to sign a large HR outsourcing deal, with Exult in 1998. Exult was taken over by Hewitt in 2004, and the deal started to run into trouble. By 2006, Hewitt was losing $166 million, citing problems in HR outsourcing, while BP took back expatriate administration in-house and also gave two years' notice that it intended to end the contract with Hewitt. However, in February 2009, it signed a new contract, extending the scope of the contract worldwide (rather than just the UK and US), but taking most aspects of recruitment back in-house (Pickard 2009).

Another of the major HR outsourcing deals was BT's with Accenture. Initially, in 2000, the two companies set up a joint venture to run BP's HR function, but Accenture then bought out BT's share. Again, there were problems with the contract, mainly put down to a lack of effective communication. Some BT line managers were not even aware that HR had been outsourced and were surprised to receive bills from Accenture when they requested extra services. After extensive negotiations, the outsourcing contract was renewed for ten years in 2005, at a cost of £ 306 million (Pickard 2004; hrmguide 2005).

In 2006, Cable & Wireless, another of Accenture's clients, announced that it was not renewing its five-year contract, originally placed with the BT–Accenture joint venture. The main reason given was that Cable & Wireless had drastically downsized following the dot-com crash in 2001, from 57,000 staff to 14,000, and as a result could more easily do its own HR in-house. However, Ian Muir, the international HR director, admitted that some valuable tacit knowledge had been lost through outsourcing (Pickard 2006).

An alternative to HR outsourcing is a shared service centre. This involves the use of a call centre to give HR advice to line managers and, often, individual employees (Marchington and Wilkinson 2008). Three models are common:

- an in-house function
- an in-house function which also offers services on the open market to other organisations seeking to outsource their HR
- a specialist unit offering HR services for a number of employers in a network – this model is common among schools and in the NHS; an NHS example is discussed by Marchington and Wilkinson (2008, pp197–8).

REFLECTIVE ACTIVITY 1.6

Managing an HR outsourcing contract

You are responsible for managing an HR outsourcing contract in your organisation. What steps do you need to take to ensure that this contract is managed effectively?

REFLECTIVE ACTIVITY 1.7

Semco

Semco is a Brazilian manufacturing company, based in Sao Paulo and owned by Ricardo Semler. It is run like no other company. Its basic rule is that there are no rules:

- Workers make decisions.
- Management sets its own salaries and bonuses.
- Everyone has access to the company books.
- Shop floor workers set their own productivity targets and work flexi-time.
- Workers negotiate with management the level of profit-sharing and then decide among themselves who gets it.
- Before anyone is hired or promoted to a management position, they are interviewed, evaluated and approved by all the people who will work for them.
- Every six months, Semco managers are appraised by all their subordinates and the results are published for all to see.
- Workers have the option of taking 75 per cent of their basic pay and receiving a supplement taking it up to 125 per cent, but only if the company has a good year.
- Workers are encouraged to set up their own satellite companies to supply Semco.

- When a job opening occurs, a Semco employee who meets 70 per cent of its requirements is given preference over an outsider.
- Semco doesn't have an organisation chart. Only the respect of the led creates a leader.
- Ricardo Semler takes two months' holiday a year, leaves no contact number and does not himself contact the company. When he had a serious car accident in 2005, spending months in intensive care with a broken neck, the company maintained its 25 per cent-plus growth rate and ran seamlessly without him.
- The guiding rule on everything is common sense.

Semco is one of Latin America's fastest-growing companies, acknowledged to be the best in Brazil to work for and has a waiting list of thousands of applicants waiting to join it.

Question

1   Would you feel comfortable working for Semco?

Sources: Semler (1993), Fisher (2005).

STAKEHOLDERS

Stakeholders are 'those individuals or groups who depend on the organisation to fulfil their own goals and on whom, in turn, the organisation depends' (Johnson et al 2011). Stakeholders can be inside the organisation, such as shareholders or employees, or outside, such as customers or suppliers. In some cases, the relationship is legal, as with statutory regulatory bodies or lenders, or moral, as with the local community, or a mixture of the two, as with employees (to meet the requirements of the contract of employment and to respect legal employment rights (legal), and to fulfil the expectations of the psychological contract (moral)). In the case of the public sector, there are no shareholders, but a wide range of client stakeholders.

Note that the CIPD has a narrower definition of stakeholder. It includes only those parties who have a legal or financial relationship with the organisation. All others are defined as 'other interested parties' – the CIPD specifically mentions the media and the local community (CIPD 2003, pp6, 30). However, this narrow definition ignores the moral and ethical dimensions of stakeholder theory. For example, a local community may have no legal claim on a company that routinely but legally pollutes its environment, but few would deny its moral claim on the company.

Stakeholder theory states that organisations have responsibilities to a wide range of stakeholders. This can be contrasted with the stockholder theory of corporate governance, which states that the organisation's only responsibility is to its shareholders (stockholders in America). Stockholder theory has been defended from several different angles. One is the agency approach associated with Milton Friedman. He argues that managers are legally the agents of the organisation's owners (its shareholders), and under agency law are thus legally obliged to serve only their interests, as long as they keep within the law. Another is the logical argument put forward by John Argenti, who argues that it is logically impossible for an organisation to pursue multiple objectives – that is, it cannot simultaneously serve the interests of a range of stakeholders. In times of prosperity, the organisation might be able to deal out rewards in such a way as to keep all the stakeholders quiet, but in hard times, shareholders will take priority, if only because in the last resort, shareholders can sack the board of directors (Argenti 1993).

CASE STUDY 1.7

👁 OXFORD BUS

The Oxford Bus Company, a subsidiary of the transport group Go-Ahead, has a 'stakeholder board'. This consists of representatives of customers, a local pressure group representative, nominated by the National Federation of Bus Users, and the transport strategy officer of a local NHS trust, representing large employers, as well as company employees and managers. The board meets quarterly to discuss company performance and other matters of concern. Although purely advisory, it has been involved in vehicle design, ticketing and customer care issues. In future the company intends that one meeting a year will be held as an open meeting, to which members of the public will be invited.

Source: Weldon (2003)

Not all stakeholders are equal. Some are much more important to the organisation than others. The relative importance of stakeholders can be analysed using stakeholder mapping (Johnson and Scholes 1997, pp197–203). Stakeholder mapping classifies stakeholders by the power which they have over the organisation and the degree of interest which they have in it. These can be plotted on a two-by-two matrix (Figure 1.11).

Figure 1.11 Stakeholder matrix

Level of interest

		Low	High
Low	Power	A Don't bother	B Inform
High		C Satisfy	D Crucial

Source: adapted from Johnson and Scholes (1997)

Stakeholders of type A can effectively be ignored. They are not interested in the organisation and have little power to affect it anyway. Conversely, type D are critical and their interests must be taken into account at all times. Type B are interested in the organisation, but do not have the power to affect it significantly. They need to be kept informed, particularly as they may in turn be able to influence other stakeholders. Type C are passive stakeholders. They have great potential to influence the organisation, but at present little interest in doing so. They need to be kept quiet, so that they do not suddenly take an adverse interest in the organisation and shift into type D.

The implication is that stakeholders have to be actively managed. They can be crucial in mobilising support for the organisation or, if things go badly, they can cripple it.

CONNECTIONS BETWEEN THE ENVIRONMENT, STRATEGY AND ORGANISATIONAL DESIGN

In this section, we will examine Thompson's model of E-V-R congruence.

E-V-R CONGRUENCE

Thompson (2005) developed the concept of E-V-R congruence as a measure of how well an organisation is attuned to its environment. He develops the idea of SWOT analysis to incorporate values. In his model E represents the environment (the opportunities and threats part of a SWOT analysis), while R represents resources and V values, both of which are traditionally subsumed within the strengths and weaknesses sections of a SWOT. To Thompson, resources would be physical, while values represent the human strengths and weaknesses of the organisation, specifically its leadership and culture, as well as the underlying values which it holds.

More important than the mere idea of E-V-R is the concept of congruence. An organisation will achieve congruence when its environment, resources and values are mutually reinforcing. Its strategic position will be strong. A congruent organisation is illustrated in Figure 1.12.

Figure 1.12 The congruent organisation

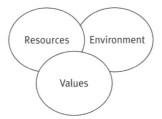

Thompson then identifies types of organisation where the three elements are not congruent (Figure 1.13).

Figure 1.13 The unconsciously competent organisation

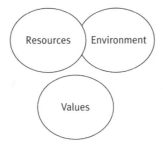

Here the values of the organisation are out of line with its environment and resources, but because environment and resources are still aligned, the organisation still works, at least on a superficial level. This type of organisation is likely to be complacent and runs the risk of serious trouble if its environment and resources start to drift out of line. The strategic imperative here is for a change in leadership style and a redefinition of values and culture.

Figure 1.14 The consciously incompetent organisation

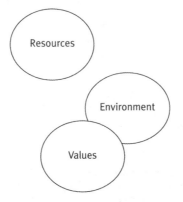

In the consciously incompetent organisation (Figure 1.14), the organisation is aware that there is a resource mismatch but tends to see it as a series of short-term problems. The organisation will tend to be reactive and to fight fires while being unable to take a long-term strategic view of resources.

Figure 1.15 Strategic drift

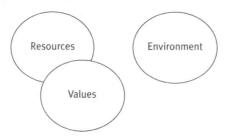

With strategic drift (Figure 1.15), the organisation has lost touch with its environment, perhaps because of complacency, perhaps because of failure to scan the environment effectively. It must either find a way to change its environment or to bring its resources and values back in line with changes in the environment.

Figure 1.16 The lost organisation

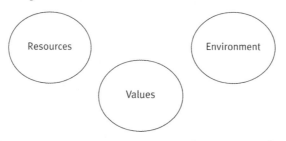

Unless the lost organisation (Figure 1.16) takes swift and drastic action to re-achieve congruence, in the long run it is doomed.

 REFLECTIVE ACTIVITY 1.8

The National Trust and E-V-R

The National Trust has as its core aim to 'look after special places, for ever, for everyone'. It is the largest private landowner in Britain, owning 640,000 acres, mostly rented out to tenants on commercial terms. It also owns 600 miles of Britain's coastlines, guaranteeing free public access to the coast, and around 300 houses and gardens, which are open free to members, and at a small charge to others. In 2005–06, there were 13.7 million visits to NT properties, of which 2.9 million, or around 20 per cent, were paying visits, while the rest were visits by members (National Trust 2006).

Clearly the National Trust estate is a hugely valuable asset, which on an open market valuation would be worth billions of pounds.

However, remember the words 'for ever' in the core purpose. The Trust is legally prohibited from selling property and the result is that in many ways the estate must be seen as a liability rather than an asset, which must be maintained at ever-growing expense (Legg 2005).

More conventional physical resources include National Trust gift shops at most sites and also extensive catering facilities (which earned £25 million in 2005–06, twice as much as admissions).

A key resource of the Trust is its membership. This has increased from 152,000 in 1971 to 3.4 million in 2006. Over the same period income has risen from £2.4 million to £337 million (Clover 2003). The Trust makes a healthy surplus of around £20 million a year, or about 6 per cent of turnover. In addition, the National Trust has 6,000 staff, many of them highly qualified in conservation, property management or gardening, and tens of thousands of active volunteers.

However, the membership is overwhelmingly white, middle aged and middle class, with little penetration in the inner cities, and it is thought that most members join solely to get free access to Trust properties. The activists, the volunteers, who to visitors are the public face of the NT, are older and more middle class than the membership – seen by many as representatives of the 'green welly' county set.

By the 1990s, the National Trust, though growing rapidly, was seen as increasingly out of touch – reactionary, elitist and part of the establishment, not interested in promoting social inclusion. Operation Neptune, a populist campaign begun in the 1960s to improve access to the coastline, has run out of steam.

Just as it was out of touch with modern urban society, it also antagonised many of its county-based members by getting involved in the hunting dispute. In 1997 it banned stag hunting on its property and was split over fox hunting, with each side accusing the other of dirty tricks. Part of the problem was the Trust's system of governance. It was controlled by a 52-member council, mostly nominated by interest groups like the RSPB and the Open Space Society, which met only four times a year. The council was widely seen as a self-perpetuating old boy network (Houlder 2003). The system also gave great power to the chairman, who controlled proxy votes which he could use at his discretion. The pro-hunting lobby complained that the proxy voting system was frequently used against them.

A turning point came with the appointment of a new director-general, Fiona Reynolds, in 2001. She had previously headed the Cabinet Office's women's unit, was close to New Labour, and talked of shedding the Trust's 'remote and elitist' image. She appointed Lord Blakenham, sometime chairman of the *Financial Times* and the RSPB, to review the National Trust's system of governance.

Blakenham reported in April 2003. He recommended that in future the governing body should be a 12-member board of trustees (effectively a board of directors). The council would remain and would in effect become a supervisory board on the German model. The proxy voting system should be replaced by postal voting. The board of trustees formally took control in 2005. The Blakenham report seems to have turned the tide. The national ban on foxhunting has also helped, defusing the main internal bone of contention. Reynolds has increased the educational role of the Trust, expanded family memberships, bringing younger people into membership, and has spearheaded a move into the inner cities, preserving back-to-back working-class houses in Birmingham and John Lennon and Paul McCartney's boyhood homes in Liverpool (Proby 2005).

In 2007, the National Trust published a new strategy document, covering the period to 2012 and beyond. This demonstrates an extension of the new thinking in the Trust. The key future role of the Trust was to be an environmental education group, engaging with government and society in a quest to find ways of tackling climate change. Fiona Reynolds stressed that this represented a return to the original aims of the Trust's founders, which emphasised social philanthropy and mutual benefit. As Reynolds said, 'This is going back to our roots. We are a cause. It's a profound moment of recognition' (Vidal 2007). Whether she can carry the more diehard and reactionary elements among the Trust's volunteers is another issue.

By 2012, the National Trust seemed to have taken on a more campaigning stance. In February, along with the Council for the Preservation of Rural England and the Royal Society for the Protection of Birds, it criticised government proposals for reform of the planning system, saying that the proposals were likely to have little or no positive impact on economic growth and could undermine public well-being (National Trust 2012a). In August it was announced that Dame Helen Ghosh, formerly permanent secretary at the Home Office, would replace

Fiona Reynolds as director-general (National Trust 2012b). It will be interesting to see whether this will lead to a change in Reynolds' populist policies.

Question

1   How do you think that the National Trust rates in terms of E-V-R convergence?

SUMMARY

This chapter has analysed the nature of environments and ways in which they can be analysed, the different types of organisational structure and the circumstances in which each is appropriate.

KEY LEARNING POINTS

- The general environment consists of factors which impact at an industry-wide level, while the task environment is primarily concerned with the immediate environment which impacts on an individual organisation within an industry.
- Organisations can be seen as open systems which interact with their environments.
- The STEEPLE model lists and classifies the major general environmental factors which impact on organisations.
- The main point of STEEPLE analysis is to identify key environmental drivers.
- Opportunities and threats to the organisation can be classified according to probability of success and attractiveness and probability of occurrence and impact, respectively.
- There are a wide range of different organisational structures, including bureaucracy, divisionalisation, matrix, network and virtual.
- Strategic alliances are of growing importance.
- Stakeholder theory states that organisations have responsibilities to a wide range of stakeholders.

QUESTIONS

1   What do you think are the main differences between the general and the task environments?

2   What do you understand by the best fit model of HR?

3   Why did Weihrich suggest that SWOT analysis should be renamed TOWS analysis? What criticisms have been made of the SWOT/TOWS approach?

4   Give examples where structure follows strategy.

5   What do you think are the main strengths and weaknesses of the bureaucratic form of organisation?

6   Can you see any disadvantages of the network form of organisation?

7   Why can strategic alliances fail?

8   Do you agree with the proposition that HR outsourcing is most suitable for very small or very large organisations?

9   Why do stakeholders require active management?

EXPLORE FURTHER

FURTHER READING

Mick Marchington and Adrian Wilkinson's book, *Human Resource Management at Work* 4th edition (2008), covers much of the material discussed in this chapter, particularly in Part 1 in general and Chapter 4 in particular.

USEFUL WEBSITES

A key website to assist your study is the CIPD site (www.cipd.co.uk). If you are not a member of the CIPD, you will be able to access only part of the site, but you will have access to the latest HR news and to factsheets on a range of HR topics. If you are a member, you will have access to a much wider range of materials, including the library, company profiles, Employment Law at Work and, most usefully, online journals. The CIPD provides direct access to about 350 journals, including *The Economist*, the *Harvard Business Review* and *HR Magazine*, and also gives you entry to the EBSCO database, which provides access to 3,000 journals, including all the leading HRM and HRD journals, as well as the American equivalent of *The Economist*, *BusinessWeek*. The CIPD members' site also gives you access to the archive of *People Management*.

AUDIO AND VIDEO MATERIAL

The CIPD produces monthly podcasts on a range of HR-related issues, where experts discuss or debate key issues. Many of these are relevant to the subject matter of this book (although not of this chapter).

A wealth of video material is available on the Internet, much of it on YouTube. A lot of this is poor quality, but high-quality material is produced by the *Harvard Business Review* and also by the Chartered Institute of Management Accountants. Videos relevant to this chapter include:

How to perform a SWOT analysis: a whiteboard video (5 minutes): www.mystrategicplan.com/resources/how-to-perform-a-swot-analysis-a-whiteboardvideo

Environmental scanning (4 minutes): www.youtube.com/watch?v=LN03WRRHlwc

CIMA E3 Lecture 3 – Environmental Analysis (6 minutes): www.youtube.com/watch?v=7uA3Z7i69bO&feature=bf_next&list=UUdMKlWhxld2ffqbQUb6ozg

CIMA E3 Lecture 4 – External Environment (9 minutes): www.youtube.com/watch?v=XUhmoWk9yLA&list=VVdbMKlWhxld2ffqbQUbGOzg&index=7&feature=plcp

CIMA E3 Lecture 11 – Organisational Structure (7 minutes): www.youtube.com/watch?v=KfAR9vTaZiE&feature=related

ACTIVITY HOLIDAYS

The holiday industry

The holiday industry is in a state of flux. The mainstay of the industry, the foreign package holiday – two weeks in the sun, with everything – flight, accommodation, food, transfers and so on – provided by the tour operator – is in slow decline. In the 1980s, package holidays had 60 per cent of the market, but in 2005 this had fallen to 45 per cent (*Daily Telegraph* 2006). In 2001, 20.6 million package holidays were sold and this had fallen to 19 million in 2006.

Looking more closely at market segments, the bottom of the package holiday market is relatively stable, although not very profitable. The top end is growing rapidly and has better profit margins. The segment which is really coming under pressure is the mainstream mid-market sector, which is in the most rapid decline and where the competition is fiercest, with wafer-thin margins.

The package holiday market as a whole is coming under increasing threat from the short break market, built around the budget airlines, particularly Ryanair and easyJet. Increasingly people take a number of short, often city-based, breaks, booking both their flight and their accommodation through the Internet. The other major growth area is the specialist package holiday segment, loosely described as activity holidays, about which more later.

At the same time as the traditional package holiday was declining, the method of selling them has been changing. In 1999, 61 per cent of package holidays were booked through a high street travel agent, but by 2003 this had fallen to 49 per cent. At the same time, the number of bookings made direct with a tour operator, or through the Internet, both rose.

The trend is even more stark when we look at all holidays, rather than just package holidays. In 2004, travel agents and the Internet each had a one-third share of bookings, with the other third shared between family and friends and direct booking with a tour operator (*Marketing* 2004).

Until 2007, there were four major players in the UK overseas travel industry. All are vertically integrated, operating retail travel agents as well as tour operations and an airline. The market leader, Thomson, is owned by the German company TUI, while Thomas Cook is also German owned. First Choice and the weakest company, My Travel, are UK plcs.

Different companies have adopted different strategies to cope with changes in the market. Thomson has concentrated on marketing different segments of its packages, rather than the complete traditional package holiday. If the customer wants to buy just a flight, or just accommodation, that is fine with Thomson. First Choice has gone for market segmentation. It is concentrating on two major segments, the bottom of the package market and the much more upmarket specialist (particularly activity) segment. In early 2007, it put its mainstream package operations up for sale, with both My Travel and Thomas Cook interested. However, these two companies decided to merge instead, leaving My Travel out in the cold. In response, in the spring of 2007, First Choice and Thomson/TUI agreed to merge.

The activity holiday market

An activity holiday is broadly defined as a holiday in which some form of physical exertion is the main reason for the holiday. It covers a wide range of activities, including skiing, boating, golf, walking, cycling, fishing and birdwatching, as well as multi-activity, which combines two or more activities.

Unlike mainstream package holidays, activity holidays are growing rapidly. Twenty-four per cent of the population claim to have taken an overseas activity holiday in the past five years, and a further 20 per cent say they are likely to in the future. Numbers of holidays sold (including UK holidays) are expected to almost double between 2001 and 2010, from around 5 million a year to around 10 million, with the value of holidays sold also doubling from around £4.5 billion to around £9 billion, or around 17 per cent of all holidays (*Keynote* 2006). At an average cost of nearly £1,000, activity holidays are also significantly more expensive than other packages, and much more profitable. In 2006 the operating profit of First Choice's activity holiday division made up half of all group profits (First Choice 2007).

This seminar activity will concentrate on two types of activity holiday, walking/trekking and multi-activity. Walking holidays are the most popular activity holiday, with 10 per cent of the population claiming to have taken a walking holiday in the past five years, while 9.5 per cent claim to have taken a multi-activity holiday.

However, the consumer profiles for the two types of holiday are different. Walking holidays are almost exactly split between male and female, and are more popular with the ABC1 social groups (broadly the middle class), people who live in the South, the Midlands and Wales, and single people. People are more likely to take a walking holiday as they get older, with penetration among the 45–54 age group (11.4 per cent) and 55–64 (10.8 per cent) higher than the penetration for the population as a whole (10 per cent). Multi-activity holidays are favoured by men (70 per cent) and the under-35s, but again have a bias towards ABC1s, the South and the single. Perhaps people who enjoy

activity holidays when they are young switch towards walking holidays as they get older.

Companies

This activity will look at five companies in the walking/multi-activity segments of the market. Two (Exodus and Waymark) are owned by First Choice, one (Explore) is owned by the holiday group Holidaybreak plc, and two by member organisations (HF Holidays by the Holiday Fellowship and Ramblers Holidays by the Ramblers Association).

Exodus

Exodus is one of two leading companies in the 'soft adventure' sector. It provides walking-trekking holidays combined with sightseeing, white-water rafting, sailing and other activities. Founded in 1973, it was taken over by First Choice in 2002. The number of bookings is unknown, but is believed to be in the region of 30,000 a year. Most holidays are outside Europe, including many in exotic locations, operated in liaison with indigenous specialist companies/guides.

Waymark

Waymark is a specialist walking company. The company is small, with around 4,500 bookings a year, but a loyal clientele. Like Exodus, it was taken over by First Choice in 2002, with the remit to grow volumes and margins. In 2004, its managing director, Stuart Montgomery, admitted that clients 'have a problem' with being part of First Choice (although First Choice ownership is very much played down in the Waymark advertising material) (*Travel Weekly* 2004). Most holidays are in Europe, often using local agents. In 2006–07 Exodus and Waymark started to cross-promote each other, and by 2012 Waymark was totally subsumed within the Exodus brand.

Explore Worldwide

Founded in 1981, Explore uses a similar business model to Exodus. The average price of holidays is around £1,000, often including a local payment paid at the start of the holiday. Holidays are usually offered on a bed and breakfast basis, with extensive use of local agents to guide tours. Explore was taken over by Holidaybreak in 2000 and forms about half of Holidaybreak's Adventure Travel division. The division had a turnover of £76 million in 2006 and operating profit of £5.6 million (Holidaybreak 2007). The average age of Explore clients is early 40s. About 30,000 holidays are sold each year and 45 per cent are repeat bookings. Like Exodus, most bookings are made direct, but the company also sells through local travel agents in Australia, Canada and the US.

HF Holidays

This is the oldest of the companies surveyed and also the biggest. Founded in 1913 and owned by the Holiday Fellowship, it has over 50,000 guests, over half in the UK. The company runs 17 country house hotels. It is noted for its 'English House party style of warm hospitality' (HF Holidays 2007) and has a very high degree of client loyalty. It claims that at least 80 per cent of customers come back again the next year. It explicitly aims at the 'grey' market and has the oldest client base of the companies surveyed.

Ramblers Holidays

Ramblers Holidays was founded by the Ramblers Association in 1946 and covenants its net profits to a charitable trust which supports environmental projects. Originally purely a walking company, in recent years it has expanded the proportion of sightseeing on many of its holidays and also runs a range of holidays concentrating on birds or flowers. More than half of the holidays are in Europe, but the proportion of long-haul (and more expensive) holidays has been increasing. In 2006 it introduced 'cruise and walk' holidays. It recently acquired

Countrywide Holidays to increase its UK holiday coverage and also offers a range of holidays aimed at the under-40s. Holidays are led by a volunteer leader from the UK, but on long-haul holidays, a local agency/guide is also used. In 2001, 17,000 holidays were sold, and in 2004 turnover was £14 million, giving a pre-tax profit of £1.1 million. Details are not available of the average age of clients, but from personal experience this seems to be mid-50s.

The recession appears to be accelerating the trend towards activity holidays, appealing as they do to an older and more affluent sector of the community. In particular, the 'active retired', many of whom retired early, seem to be largely unaffected by the recession.

Questions

1   Compile a STEEPLE analysis for the activity holiday industry.

2   Compile a SWOT analysis for Ramblers Holidays.

3   On long-haul holidays, Ramblers Holidays always uses a UK-based leader, directly employed by Ramblers, as well as a local guide, employed by their local partner organisation. Explore usually only uses a local guide. What do you think are the HR implications of this difference in policy?

4   How far do you feel that a tour operator like Ramblers or Explore is a virtual organisation?

5   What do you think has been the impact on Ramblers of the implementation of legislation against age discrimination? What about the impact on Club 18–30?

REFERENCES

Amburgey, T. and Dacin, T. (1994) As the left foot follows the right? The dynamics of strategic and structural change. *Academy of Management Journal.* Vol 37, No 6.

Ansoff, I. (1987) *Corporate Strategy.* London: Penguin.

Argenti, J. (1993) *Your organisation, what is it for? Challenging traditional organisational aims.* Maidenhead: McGraw-Hill.

BBC2. (2007) Independent cost. *Working Lunch.* 18 June.

Bettis, R. (1991) Strategic management and the strait-jacket: an editorial essay. *Organization Science.* Vol 2, No 3.

Boxall, P. and Purcell, J. (2008) *Strategy and Human Resource Management.* 2nd edition. Basingstoke: Palgrave-Macmillan.

Chakrabortty, A. (2009) What's bad for General Motors is good for the world. *Guardian.* 2 June.

Chandler, A.E. (1962) *Strategy and structure: chapters in the history of the American enterprise.* Cambridge, MA: MIT Press.

Chernack, T.J. and Kasshanna, B.K. (2007) The use and misuse of SWOT analysis and implications for HRD professionals. *Human Resource Development International.* Vol 10, No 4, December.

Child, J. (2005) *Organization: contemporary principles and practice.* Oxford: Blackwell.

Choo, C.W. (2001) Environmental scanning as information seeking and organizational learning. *Information Research.* Vol 7, No 1 (available at InformationR.net/ir/7-1/paper112.html).

CIPD. (2003) *Corporate responsibility and HR's role.* London: Chartered Institute of Personnel and Development.

CIPD. (2009) *HR outsourcing and the HR function: threat or opportunity?* Survey report. London: Chartered Institute of Personnel and Development.

CIPD. (2010) *SWOT analysis [online].* Factsheet. London: Chartered Institute of Personnel and Development. Available at: www.cipd.co.uk/hr-resources/factsheets/swot-analysis.aspx [Accessed 26 March 2013].

Clark, A. (2009a) General Motors declares bankruptcy – the biggest manufacturing collapse in US history. *Guardian.* 2 June.

Clark, A. (2009b) General Motors emerges from bankruptcy after 40 days. *Guardian.* 10 July.

Clegg, S., Kornberger, M. and Pitsis, T. (2008) *Managing and organizations.* 2nd edition. London: Sage.

Clover, C. (2003) Members 'suspect voting system in National Trust'. *Daily Telegraph.* 24 April.

Contractor, F. and Lorange, P. (1998) Why should firms cooperate? The strategy and economics basis for cooperative ventures. In: F. Contractor and P. Lorange (eds) *Cooperative strategies in international business.* New York: Lexington Books.

Crum, C. (2011) Yahoo revenue drop attributed to Microsoft deal. *WebProNews.* 19 October. Available at: www.webpronews.com/yahoo-earnings-2011-10 [Accessed 28 June 2012].

Cullinan, G., Le Roux, T. and Weddigen, R. (2004) When to walk away from the deal. *Harvard Business Review.* Vol 82, No 4.

Daily Mail. (2007) Internet kills the video store. 4 May.

Daily Telegraph. (2006) 2600 travel jobs axed as consumers book flights on Internet. 16 December.

DesJardins, J. (2007) *Business, ethics and the environment.* New Jersey: Pearson/Prentice Hall.

Dussauge, P. and Garrette, B. (1999) *Cooperative strategy: competing successfully through strategic alliances.* Chichester: John Wiley.

Dyer, J., Kale, P. and Singh, H. (2004) When to ally and when to acquire. *Harvard Business Review.* Vol 82, No 7/8, July/August.

Edgecliffe-Johnson, A. (2006) How upstarts continue to upset. *Financial Times.* 15 August.

Fayol, H. (1916/1949) *General and industrial management.* London: Pitman.

Financial Times. (2007) Video rentals. 8 January.

First Choice. (2007) www.firstchoiceholidaysplc.com [Accessed 3 August 2007].

Fisher, L. (2005) Ricardo Semler won't take control. *strategy + business.* Winter.

Garside, J. (2013) Blockbuster calls in administrators and joins high street casualty list. *Guardian.* 17 January.

Gavetti, G. (2011) The new psychology of strategic leadership. *Harvard Business Review.* Vol 89, No 7/8, July/August.

Gillespie, A. (2000) Dell Computers. *Business Review.* September.

Goold, M. and Campbell, A. (2002) *Designing effective organizations.* New York: Jossey-Bass.

Grant, R. (2008) *Contemporary strategy analysis.* 6th edition. Oxford: Blackwell.

Hales, C. (2001) *Managing through organization.* 2nd edition. London: Business Press/Thomson Learning.

Hall, D. and Saias, M. (1980) Strategy follows structure! *Strategic Management Journal.* Vol 1.

Halliday, J. (2011) Amazon finally reels in Lovefilm rental service. *Guardian.* 21 January.

Hansen, M. and von Oetinger, B. (2001) Introducing T-shaped managers. *Harvard Business Review*. Vol 79, No 3, March.

Hatch, M.J. (1997) *Organisation theory: modern symbolic and postmodern perspectives.* Oxford: Oxford University Press.

HF Holidays. www.hfholidays.co.uk [Accessed 14 July 2007].

Higgins, T. (2012) GM first quarter profits fall as losses in Europe widen. *Bloomberg.* 3 May. Available at: www.bloomberg.com/news/2012/05/03/gm-profit-falls-less-than-estimates-on-increased-sales [Accessed 28 June 2012].

Hill, T. and Westbrook, R. (1997) SWOT analysis: it's time for a product recall. *Long Range Planning.* Vol 30, No 1.

Holidaybreak. (2007) www.holidaybreak.co.uk [Accessed 14 July 2007].

Houlder, V. (2003) Dark cloud of suspicion hangs over National Trust. *Financial Times.* 26 April.

hrmguide. (2005) BT-Accenture contract renewed. Available at: www.hrmguide.co.uk/general/bt-accenture [Accessed 2 July 2012].

Inkpen, A. and Ross, J. (2001) Why do some strategic alliances persist beyond their useful life? *California Management Review.* Fall.

Jackson, H. (2009) Obituary: Robert McNamara. *Guardian.* 6 July.

Johnson, G. and Scholes, K. (1997) *Exploring corporate strategy.* 4th edition. Hemel Hempstead: Prentice-Hall.

Johnson, G., Whittington, R. and Scholes, K. (2011) *Exploring strategy.* 9th edition. Harlow: The Financial Times/Prentice Hall.

Jowit, J. (2001) Why an accident like Hatfield was waiting to happen. *Financial Times.* 22 February.

Joyce, P. and Woods, A. (1996) *Essential strategic management: from modernism to pragmatism.* Oxford: Butterworth-Heinemann.

Kafka, F. (1964) *The Trial.* New York: Secker.

Keynote. (2006) Activity holidays. February.

Kim, C. and Mauborgne, R. (2004) Blue ocean strategy. *Harvard Business Review.* Vol 82, No 10, October.

Koch, A.J. (2000) SWOT does not need to be recalled, it needs to be enhanced. Available at: www.westga.edu/~bquest/2001/swot2.htm [Accessed 4 October 2012].

Legg, R. (2005) Breach of trust. *Guardian.* 14 September.

Marchington, M. and Wilkinson, A. (2008) *Human resource management at work.* 4th edition. London: Chartered Institute of Personnel and Development.

Marketing. (2004) Trouble strikes the travel agent. 23 June.

McCurry, J. (2009) Deflation stalks Japan as jobless figure hits peak. *Guardian*. 29 August.

Mintzberg, H. (1998) The structuring of organisations. In: H. Mintzberg, J.B. Quinn and S. Ghoshal (eds) *The strategy process*. Hemel Hempstead: Prentice Hall Europe.

Nathan, M. (2000) The paradoxical nature of crisis. *Review of Business*. Vol 21, No 3.4.

National Trust. (2006) *Annual report and financial statements 2005–6*.

National Trust. (2012a) Economic case for planning reforms debunked. February. Available at: www.nationaltrust.org.uk/article-13563986 [Accessed 27 September 2012].

National Trust.(2012b) Dame Helen Ghosh new Director-General. August. Available at: www.nationaltrust.org.uk/article-13563983 [Accessed 27 September 2012].

Norman, P. (2001) Are your secrets safe: knowledge protection in strategic alliances. *Business Horizons*. Vol 44, No 6, November–December.

Noyes, T. (2009) Building a new General Motors. *Guardian*. 1 June.

Parkhe, A. (2001) Interfirm diversity in global alliances. *Business Horizons*. Vol 44, No 6, November–December.

Pickard, J. (2004) Should I stay or should I go? *People Management*. 25 March.

Pickard, J. (2006) Cable & Wireless calls time on outsourced HR. *People Management*. 26 October.

Pickard, J. (2009) BP and Hewittt renew HR outsourcing deal. *People Management*. 12 February.

Porter, M.E. (1980) *Competitive strategy*. New York: Free Press.

Porter, M.E. (1985) *Competitive advantage: creating and sustaining superior performance*. New York: Free Press.

Proby, W. (2005) Out of the country house and into the back to back. *Guardian*. 15 September.

Purcell, J. (2005) *Business strategies and human resource management: uneasy bedfellows or strategic partners?* University of Bath Working Papers 2005:16. Available at: www.bath.ac.uk/management/research/pdf/2005-16.pdf [Accessed 5 September 2012].

Quinn, J. (1980) *Strategies for change: logical incrementalism*. Homewood, IL: Irwin.

Ramblers Holidays. (2007) www.ramblersholidays.co.uk [Accessed 14 July 2007].

Ruigrok, W. (2004) A tale of strategic and governance errors. *European Business Forum*. No 17, Spring.

Schlesinger, L., Kiefer, C. and Brown, P. (2012) Newproject: don't analyse – act. *Harvard Business Review*. Vol 90, No 3, March.

Schwartz, P. (2003) *Inevitable surprises: think ahead in times of turbulence*. New York: Gotham Books.

Semler, R. (1993) *Maverick!* London: Arrow.

Slywotsky, A. and Nadler, D. (2004) The strategy is the structure. *Harvard Business Review*. Vol 82, No 2, February.

Sull, D. (2005) Dynamic partners. *Business Strategy Review*. Summer.

Taylor, F.W. (1947) *Scientific Management*. New York: Harper and Row.

Thompson, J., with Martin, F. (2005) *Strategic management: awareness and change*. London: Thomson.

Travel Weekly. (2004) Waymark still clients' choice. 3 January.

Vidal, J. (2007) Broader horizons. *Guardian*. 25 July.

Wallop, H. (2007) Retail video rental chain in liquidation. *Daily Telegraph*. 7 April.

Warner, M. and Witzel, M. (2003) *Managing in virtual organizations*. London: Routledge.

Waters, R. and Menn, J. (2009) Microsoft and Yahoo on defensive. *Financial Times*. 31 July.

Wearden, G. (2009) General Motors – countdown to collapse. *Guardian*. 1 June.

Weber, M. (1964) *The theory of economic and social organization*. New York: Free Press.

Weihrich, H. (1982) The TOWS matrix: a tool for situational analysis. *Journal of Long Range Planning*. Vol 15, No 2.

Weldon, S. (2003) The Go-Ahead Group plc. Article 13. CSR Best Practice Case Studies. Available at: www.article13.com [Accessed 6 July 2004].

Whittington, R. and Mayer, M. (2000) *The European corporation: strategy, structure and social science*. Oxford: Oxford University Press.

Worthington, I. and Britton, C. (2006) *The Business Environment*. 5th edition. Harlow: FT/Prentice Hall.

CHAPTER 2

The Managerial Context of Human Resources

LEARNING OUTCOMES

When you have completed this chapter, you should be able to:

- summarise the main theories of management, both traditional and contemporary

- explain the difference between power and influence and assess their suitability to a variety of management situations

- use and integrate conflict-handling styles in the process of managing conflict, including methods of operating repair situations

- identify the determinants of an effective customer care regime

- explain the difference between the group dynamics and the open systems approach to managing change and integrate this knowledge into your 'toolbox' of skills for effective change management

- contrast the four stages of quality management and put forward proposals to implement each stage successfully

- reflect on the ability of human resources to improve organisational performance

- explore the various models of human resources, identifying which is appropriate for differing employment contexts

- evaluate and interpret the various approaches to change management

- in all the above areas, identify the role of human resources to contribute towards successful prevention and resolution of identified problems.

INTRODUCTION

The majority of the context of this book concerns the effect and influences of the *external* environment on the role and function of human resources. This chapter deals with the effects *internal* to the organisation together with a brief résumé of the roles that human resources can play in meeting organisational needs. It starts by providing a summary of the theoretical approach to management, both classical and contemporary. The nature of power and conflict in organisations is then analysed. This is followed by an analysis of how different roles and structures of human resources can adjust to and provide effective service to managerial requirements. Finally, an examination is made of the specific human resource contribution to organisational change, quality assurance and customer care.

THEORIES OF MANAGEMENT

RATIONAL GOAL MODELS

These were the earliest models set out by three principal theorists in the early twentieth century. **Frederick Taylor** (1947) carried out his research at the Ford Motor Company on manufacturing management, while **Max Weber's** (1925) models of bureaucracy emerged from 30 years' studying large complex organisations, especially those under government control.

Their key findings relating to operating organisations efficiently overlapped to a large degree, for example:

- Rationality and scientific methods should be used to study work and experiment with human activity. Staff, for example, should be selected on merit, judged by a rational selection process.
- Jobs should be fractionised with extensive division of labour to allow individual employees to become highly specialised in jobs which were easy to learn.
- Systems and procedures of management (both in the factory and in the office) should clearly be written down with instructions as to how they should be followed.
- There should be separation of those that plan the work (set out in a clearly ranked managerial hierarchy) and those that actually carry the work out.
- It must be recognised that employees will tend towards economic self-interest in the way that they approach the work situation.

The third theorist, **Henri Fayol** (1947), concentrated on the art of management, identifying core management tasks (such as planning, organisation of work, control and co-ordination) and setting out principles of effective management that can apply in all organisations. These included:

- unity of command, with orders coming from one source only and clarity of organisation structure
- consistency of purpose, usually associated with centralised control (although he did recognise there were some circumstances where decentralisation could be appropriate)
- a widespread sense of order with a place for everything (supplies, plant and machinery, clean working conditions) and a place for everything, including fixed times for breaks and a well-understood organisation chart
- the operation of 'equity', where management operated not just within the law but within the spirit of the law, treating employees both fairly and kindly
- long-term employment at all levels leading to a sense of order and stability, rather than a constant change of personnel.

In their day, these three models represented a great step forward and often proved highly successful in practice, such as Taylor's changes in work practices at Bethlehem Steel, where, in one example, he reduced the number of workers needed in physical labour from 500 to 140, and the huge increase in productivity his ideas brought at Ford through the implementation of piece-work and other motivational schemes. Aspects of all three writers have some resonance today for human resource practitioners who support equitable and rational selection processes, and clear communication of management procedures from mission statements to fair sick pay schemes.

However, the overall approaches of so-called 'rational goal models' have major defects in the light of changes in society in the late twentieth and early twenty-first century:

- The main context of the studies on which these models were based has been very large organisations with dominant positions in their sectors who wish to enhance their dominance and eliminate potential competitors. The growth of regulatory environments, which began in the early part of the twentieth century in America but which became much more developed from the 1970s, aimed to prevent monopoly and create healthy competition. There have been many examples of governments legislating to break up organisations with dominant positions, through privatisation of monopolist utilities or through industrial reorganisation. There are therefore fewer organisations to whom the theories immediately apply.
- Establishing a prescribed system of work makes it much more difficult to react to changes in the marketplace. For example, the rapid technological changes in ICT and telecommunications have condemned companies who lack nimbleness in a quick-changing competitive environment to decline and often complete disappearance. Examples here are GEC-Marconi in the UK and Nortel in Canada.
- The lack of employee empowerment and the discouragement of flexibility had negative effects on employee commitment, innovation and engagement.

HUMAN RELATIONS MODELS

Although the needs of the employee at work had been considered by early psychologists, the field of human relations study grew through the disquiet felt by some researchers of the work organisation in large industrial organisations in the 1920s and its effect upon employees. The leading exponent here was Elton Mayo (1933), who carried out a series of experiments at the Hawthorne works consisting of measuring productivity and employee satisfaction when changing the physical environment and work systems of the employees.

The results indicated that productivity rose every time changes were made, even if these appeared to be negative, such as reducing the light sources and cutting down on rest breaks. The experiments demonstrated that favourable social relations and situations were a much greater influence on performance than physical conditions. Taylorism's claim of overriding employee economic self-interest was rejected. Expressions on encouragement worked better than management coercion and the influence of the peer group was high, emphasising the importance of informal groups within the workplace. It was recognised, therefore, that the group dynamics and social make-up of an organisation were an extremely important force in determining a successful organisation. From this stemmed growing awareness of the concepts of participation, greater trust, teamworking and openness – concepts that were supported by the growing personnel profession.

The practical implications of these two schools of thought (rational goals and human relations) were radically different and, for much of the latter half of the twentieth century, caused confusion among management as to which should be implemented in practice. Towards the end of the century, a number of theories were put forward to synthesise existing theories and to produce more practical advice regarding the conflict.

CONTEMPORARY MANAGEMENT THEORIES

Contingency theory

In simple terms, this theory states that there is no best practice in management and that using rational goal concepts can work in one environment and human relations concepts in another (Fielder 1967). What came to be regarded as much more influential was a two-prong process. First, the organisation's design and its subsystems (including its working processes and employee relations) must fit with its environment. So the Weber-style bureaucratic design matched with the Tayloristic style of management control may work in a prison or a nuclear-power station, where systems of control are absolutely vital, but a human relations style is much more appropriate in an advertising agency, where creativity and new ideas are paramount. Second, the quality and style of leadership are key to the successful implementation of the systems of management in place.

The contingency theory allows for predicting the characteristics of the appropriate situations for effectiveness. Three situational components determine the favourableness or situational control:

1   Group atmosphere – referring to the degree of mutual trust, respect and confidence between the leader and the subordinates.

2   Task structure – referring to the extent to which group tasks are clear and structured.

3   Leader position power – referring to the power inherent in the leader's position itself.

When there is a good leader–member relation, a highly structured task and high leader position power, the situation is considered a favourable situation.

Chaos and complexity theories

For many years, mathematicians and scientists had been finding that not all of nature's phenomena can be explained simply. For example, Edward Lorenz, a meteorologist from the Massachusetts Institute of Technology (MIT), was experimenting with computational models of the atmosphere and, in the process of his experimentation, he discovered one of chaos theory's fundamental principles – the Butterfly Effect. The Butterfly Effect is named for its assertion that a butterfly flapping its wings in Tokyo can impact weather patterns in Chicago. More scientifically, the Butterfly Effect proves that forces governing weather formation are unstable.

Chaos theory was adapted to management theory by Peters (1987) to identify that events can be rarely controlled, especially in a global economy. Chaos theory posits that systems naturally become more complex and, as they do so, they become more volatile and must expend more energy to maintain that complexity and therefore need a bigger structure to maintain stability. This trend continues until the system breaks down completely. It takes an effective management system to identify what is happening and try to prevent it. This theory has received additional credence from the recent credit crunch, where the complexity of financial instruments created by hedge funds and merchant banks arising principally from collateralisation of the US mortgage market created a bubble effect which eventually collapsed. The lack of a competent management system which allowed this to happen existed both in the banks, where top management did not understand the financial instruments, and in the regulatory system, which was both slow to act and badly structured (see Chapter 5).

Complexity is an interdisciplinary field which has emerged from the work of scientists associated with the Santa Fe Institute in the United States, such as Murray Gell-Mann, Stuart Kauffman and John Holland, and also scientists based in Europe, such as Ilya Prigogine and Brian Goodwin. Complexity theories lead us to view organisations as complex evolving systems which exist on the edge of order and chaos. It challenges the notion of striving for equilibrium and suggests instead that systems survive and thrive when they are pushed away from equilibrium.

A number of managing innovations is commonly associated with working effectively within a complex environment. This is shown in Case Study 2.1.

INTEGRATING COMPLEXITY THEORY AT HUMBERSIDE TRAINING AND EDUCATION COUNCIL (TEC)

Training and Enterprise Councils were established by the Government to promote local economic development. Within its region, a TEC would seek to ensure a programme of appropriate training for business and encourage organisations to take advantage of training opportunities made available. In 1998, Humberside TEC had 150 staff and a budget of £30 million.

For some time, its chief executive, Peter Fryer, had been studying complex adaptive systems and their implications for employing organisations and he made a conscious decision to explore how the principles of complexity theory could be integrated into the running of the TEC. Using this perspective, he took out of the organisation many of the traditional approaches to management, such as rules, hierarchy charts, budgets, appraisals, job descriptions and, importantly, those posts relating to checking and supervising.

In their place, he introduced a culture which treated all its staff as responsible adults and who were trusted to act in the best interests of the business. Within these parameters, staff were free to take whatever decisions they felt were appropriate. The purpose of this approach was to recognise that the real business of the organisation took place at the interface between the staff member and the client or stakeholder. Therefore, the more staff who were available at this interface and were able to take decisions on behalf of the TEC, the better the standards of service would become. As employees developed a sense of ownership of their contribution to the TEC, it became more effective and efficient, as was demonstrated by various independent benchmarking studies. The approach also encouraged employees to be more

creative, to feel a valued part of the organisation and consequently to work smarter.

The effect of this was to disperse the leadership throughout the organisation, with the chief executive taking up a 'holding' style of leadership. This style entailed:

- helping determine the broad framework of the organisation and communicating it so that employees knew the parameters within which they were free to take decisions
- identifying and feeding back both the internal and external emergent patterns in the environment.

This created the space within which possibilities could be explored by all employees, risks taken and mistakes made and built on by recognising the new opportunities which were not previously apparent. It also nurtured the culture of responsibility and accountability.

Examples of the practical implications are as follows:

- *Learn continuously* – the TEC as a system needed to respond to and form its environment. Learning was seen as integral to the job and mistakes are valued as learning opportunities. The only form which is completed by everybody each month to be passed to the managing director was one which asks what people have learned. This communicates the message that learning is highly valued.
- *Make processes ongoing* – the TEC was a self-organising system where learning, planning and evaluating are an ongoing process. Structures should follow, not lead and systems and processes should be based on the best people in the organisation

rather than the one or two people who might abuse the system. Many TEC policies were changed to trust people to use their judgement and take responsibility. For example, the expenses policy that any reasonable expenses incurred on TEC business will be reimbursed.

- One of the TEC's most powerful interventions was the formation of a steering group comprising people from the HR team and people from the IT team. The aim of this group was to implement IT in a way that encourages and increases learning. There was the realisation in the TEC that IT can be implemented in a number of ways on a continuum from controlling to empowering and it therefore seemed important to challenge assumptions about IT. These two groups of people differ quite markedly in their language and assumptions and priorities. The steering group gives them a common agenda and frequent opportunities to work together.

- Another example of creating space for *collaborative learning* was the process of developing and introducing 360-degree appraisal. This was undertaken by a group of volunteers who approached the task as an action research project. Every member of the group both contributed to the development and also piloted the system on themselves. The resulting system was a paperless appraisal system in which the appraisee was responsible for their own appraisal. Appraisal was now moving away from being a tool to 'know' or 'measure' employees and thus to better govern them and towards being a vehicle for learning, which was in the hands of the job-holder.

To help staff cope with this new freedom and responsibility, a substantial self-development support programme was introduced which emphasised the development of thinking and learning skills and developing self-confidence.

An important part of this approach was the annual stakeholder study, which was conducted independently through face-to-face interviews with a representative group of over 70 stakeholders. The study looked at both the progress towards meeting the aims of the TEC and also how well it was living its stated values. The report was published each year in an unabridged version, however critical it was, and formed the basis of the following year's TEC plans in an open and responsive fashion.

Some years later, the TECs were replaced by Learning and Skills Councils and Peter Fryer, before his departure, said:

> This approach to running the TEC has been incredibly successful in terms of levels of customer service and staff satisfaction. We have started to extend this style of leadership to all those in the community that interact with the TEC, through approaches such as contracting for outcomes. However, a word of caution: no matter how many times I tell this story and no matter how many caveats I put on it, it always sounds as though we knew where we were going and that we had some grand plan for becoming a learning organisation. But we didn't, and for those of you who have experienced complexity you will know that we couldn't have, because complexity just doesn't work that way.

Sources: University of Hull Business School (2007); Storr (2009)

POWER, POLITICS AND THE SEARCH FOR MANAGERIAL LEGITIMACY

INTRODUCTION

Power is the ability to do something, the capacity for producing an effect. The possession and exercise of power is, clearly, an essential aspect of management. Managers usually have to achieve results in situations where there are a number of forces both for and against the aims they are pursuing and/or the manner in which they are being pursued. Consequently, an understanding of the nature of power, and skill in its acquisition and use, are important attributes of effective managers.

The political nature of organisations is increasingly recognised by managers and the need for such recognition is well expressed by Burns (quoted in Pugh et al 1971, pp46–7):

> For a proper understanding of organisational functioning, it is necessary to conceive of organisations as the simultaneous working of at least three social systems. The first of these is the formal authority system derived from the aims of the organisation, its technology and its attempt to cope with its environment. This is the overt system in terms of which all discussion about decision-making normally takes place. But organisations are also cooperative systems of people who have career aspirations and a career structure, and who compete for advancement. Thus decisions taken within the overt structure inevitably affect the differential career prospects of the members, who will therefore evaluate them in terms of the career structure as well as the formal system, and will react accordingly. This leads to a third system of relationships which is part of an organisation – its political system. Every organisation is the scene of political activity in which individuals and departments compete and cooperate for power. Again all decisions in the overt system are evaluated for their relative impact on the power structure as well as for their contribution to the achievements of the organisation.

Political activity within organisations is often regarded as inappropriate behaviour. On the other hand, organisations of all kinds actively promote the development of leadership that is regarded as a key quality in managers. And yet, leadership has to do with the exercise of power and influence; it is the process of influencing others, and the use of power is one means by which leaders gain the support of those they lead.

POWER AND INFLUENCE

Macmillan (1978) draws a useful distinction between power and influence. He defines influence as the capacity to control and modify the perceptions of others, whereas power is defined as the capacity to restructure actual situations. Power and influence, in combination, determine political capability. Macmillan defines politics as the process that takes place when one or more 'actors' attempt to structure a situation so that their individual goals are promoted. An actor can be an individual, a group, an organisation or a nation.

In relation to their own staff, with whom, in the main, they would not be in competition, effective managers will normally use their influencing skills, rather than overt power, to persuade staff of the merits of proposed courses of action. The exercise of influence and power can be considered in terms of a continuum in which a manager may move from, for example, a neutral style to a more overt use of power. The following illustrates, in very simple terms, such a progression:

- 'This is something for your unit, Bill.' – neutral drawing of attention.
- 'This is the situation and I suggest you do so and so...' – reference to the needs of the situation.

- 'As your superior I am telling you to do this.' – influence sought by reference to formal authority.
- 'I'm moving you on to another section.' – the manager has demonstrated their power to restructure the actual situation.

Effective managers seldom need to move to the 'power' end of this continuum with their own staff and colleagues.

In other circumstances, however, overt use of power may be the more important factor in achieving desired results. For example, if several competing developers are bidding for the same plot of building land, the successful bidder will be the one who has the necessary purchasing power to outbid the rivals. In such circumstances power rather than influence is the dominant element in determining the political capabilities of the parties involved.

Thus, the exercise of power and influence has an internal and an external dimension.

BUSINESS AS A POLITICAL INSTITUTION

In discussing business as a political institution, Drucker (1981) points to the development, in a pluralist society, of all institutions as political institutions defined by their 'constituencies'. This makes it essential, in Drucker's view, for managers to think politically. He elaborates on this as follows:

> In a political system there are far too many constituencies to optimise. One must try to determine the one area in which optimisation is required but in all other areas – their number in a political system is always large – one tries to satisfice, that is, to find a solution in which enough of the constituencies can acquiesce. One tries to find a solution that will not create opposition, rather than one that would generate support. Satisficing is what politicians mean when they talk of an 'acceptable compromise'. Not for nothing is politics known as 'the art of the possible', rather than the art of the desirable. (Drucker 1981)

It is through the exercise of power and influence, then, that individuals and groups seek to persuade, induce or coerce others into following certain courses of action.

Power does not function in isolation. It provides a base, a springboard from which to act, but there are a number of preconditions that need to be satisfied before its potential can be realised. Fundamentally, power involves the ownership or control of resources, and the influence of such resources is governed by the degree of dependence that others have on them and the extent to which alternative resources are available.

Changes in the organisation, such as new technology, mergers and redundancies, can reduce the power of some parts of the organisation and reduce the power of others. So, power relationships can change, and these changes are dependent upon changes in the environment in which the organisation operates. The parallels with evolutionary psychology are unmistakeable. In summary, organisations are collections of linked coalitions whose relative power determines the decisions taken in the organisation relative to the environment facing the organisation.

INDICATORS OF POWER

Johnson and Scholes (1988), drawing on Pfeffer (1981), suggest that power may be assessed by looking for indications of it. They identify the following four factors as useful power indicators:

1   *Status of individual or group.* This may be indicated by position within the organisation, salary levels and reputation within and/or outside the organisation.

2   *Claim on resources.* The proportion of the organisation's resources claimed by a group can be a useful indicator of the group's power. If, in addition, the increase or decrease

of this proportion is known, this will indicate a parallel increase or decrease in the group's power. A comparison with the claim on resources of similar groups in other organisations can give a further indication of the relative power base of the individual or group concerned.

3   *Representation in powerful positions.* The functional areas of an organisation that are represented or not represented at board level provide a useful indicator of the influence of different functions on the major decisions of the organisation. The relative power of accounting, engineering or marketing, for example, may be the result of the functional origins of the organisation's founders or key decision-makers, and will inevitably affect the strategic orientation of the organisation.

4   *Symbols of power.* These are very varied and will be displayed both by those with formal power and by those whose power is derived from more informal sources. The demonstration of easy access to senior people, for example, can be an indicator of power.

(Johnson and Scholes 1988)

REFLECTIVE ACTIVITY 2.1

What indicators of power do you notice in your department or division of your organisation? Is it a high-status department/division? Is this confirmed by the indicators? Record your analysis and reflections in your self-development diary.

SOURCES OF MANAGEMENT LEGITIMACY

Morgan (1986) has identified the following power bases within the organisation which are among the most important sources of management power:

- The formal authority exercised by the owner/manager.
- Authority set out under legislation. This covers a very wide area including duty of care to employees, where employers can enforce health and safety rules, obligations under old master–servant common law which still apply (such as manager's right to enforce confidentiality of critical details – production methods, list of customers, etc) and duties to shareholders under public limited companies legislation.
- Authority as established by the formal organisation chart.
- Delegated authority, such as authority to spend under delegated budgets or instigate capital expenditure within prescribed limits.
- Authority through possessing vital knowledge or skills. For example, human resource practitioners may possess authority because of their skills in negotiating or their ability to win tribunals. IT staff may be the only employees able to fully understand aspects of the company's networking system. Research and development staff may have crucial knowledge of patented inventions. Certain production/maintenance staff may be the only employees who know how to carry out major alterations on vital production equipment.
- Political power (or connection power) can be exercised through the development of networks, both inside the organisation (inter-divisional networks) or external (customers, suppliers, lobbying, legal).
- Charismatic power, usually exercised at the top, is the simple but rare ability to convince all they meet that they know the correct answers and should be listened to.

- Reward power is that power exercised by managers who have the authority to give rewards that are valued by employees – bonuses, salary increases, benefits or other forms of recognition.
- Crisis power is the ability to manage under considerable uncertainty, such as prevails constantly in money markets or which occurs occasionally in other businesses, where instant decisions by those confident enough to grasp the opportunity are unquestioned.
- Countervailing power can be operated by specialists who can step in to oppose policies because of their special knowledge or authority. For example, the regulators, such as OFT, can step in to halt a merger or the tax authority to question dubious financial transactions. Internally, the auditors can do the same (but rarely do) but accountants can attempt to prevent excess spending or the HR manager to prevent an instant unfair dismissal. In the 1970s in the UK, the greatest countervailing power was exercised by the trade unions and this still applies today in isolated areas, such as London Underground.

REFLECTIVE ACTIVITY 2.2

What are the sources of power in your department or division of your organisation? How has this changed over time? Are the sources becoming more important? Or less? Record your analysis and reflections in your self-development diary.

POWER ACTIVITIES

We saw earlier that there is always competition for limited resources and that individuals have to create political strategies in order to pursue personal goals. This pursuit will inevitably involve political action with others, which will itself involve some assessment of their power bases.

Hunt (1979) recommends acquiring the expertise likely to be required by the organisation ahead of others, rather than joining a department whose status and influence appear to be in decline, and assessing and adopting the values, attitudes and behaviour of those with power. He suggests that managers should get results that are regarded as important by those who hold power and establish social contacts with powerful individuals.

In a similar vein, Schein (quoted by Dixon 1978) identifies a range of tactics typically used by managers in pursuing their objectives. The following are examples of these behaviours:

1   *Presenting a conservative image.* According to Schein, enthusiasm can be interpreted as threatening behaviour in some organisations. He suggests that important proposals should be phrased as nothing more than modest adjustments to the status quo. He argues that many controversial projects have started in a small way – perhaps as pilot schemes – and then linking them to some existing non-controversial programme. Radical changes can then be viewed as a normal development of current activities.

2   *Strike while the iron is hot.* Schein suggests that a manager should capitalise immediately on any success by bringing forward another project the manager wishes to progress.

3   *Instituting research.* Some projects are likely to face stiff opposition. Emotional subjects such as equal opportunities fall into this category. Research can provide hard data which conservative colleagues will find much more difficult to argue against.

Schein quotes the way in which such data are typically presented: 'Well here's the evidence. I don't necessarily believe all of it but we can't just ignore it, can we?'

Schein claims that these are all legitimate activities if they help the manager achieve their objectives. However, this sounds suspiciously like the ends justifying the means, and we each have our own views about that. It is difficult to generalise about what is acceptable behaviour in any particular situation, and we each have to reconcile conflicting pressures in coming to terms with the situation.

HANDLING CONFLICT

INTRODUCTION

Handling conflict is concerned with managing the differences between individuals and groups of individuals. In business, as in all activities, conflict is inevitable as the needs and objectives of business stakeholders vary. Examples of conflict are:

- conflict between the organisation and employees (and their unions) over the size of the pay increase or allowances
- conflict between the organisation and its suppliers over terms and conditions of the suppliers' contracts on price, quality and delivery schedules
- conflict between the organisation and its shareholders over the amount of profit to be distributed as dividends
- conflict between line management and human resources over the control and operation of the performance management system
- conflict between the production department and quality assurance (QA) over the interpretation of the operation of the QA system.

Other examples can involve conflicts with customers, with banks and the tax office.

Conflict can come about because of the need to change the way the organisation operates. It also has to be recognised that much of the conflict arises from a competitive environment. In both of these cases, it can be the general viewpoint that one side has to win and the other to lose. For example, the current conflict between Google and the newspaper industry is seen by the newspaper industry as one that will only be resolved with one of them gaining so much power over the other that one side will be fatally wounded (probably the newspaper industry).

One of the signs of a well-managed organisation is the ability to resolve conflicts peacefully and amicably while ensuring that participants do not badly lose face.

CONFLICT-HANDLING STYLE

A number of conflict style inventories have been in active use since the 1960s. Most of them are based on the managerial grid developed by Robert R. Blake and Jane Mouton (1964) in their Managerial Grid Model. The Blake and Mouton model uses two axes. 'Concern for people' is plotted using the vertical axis and 'Concern for task' along the horizontal axis. Each axis has a numerical scale of 1 to 9. These axes interact so as to diagram five different styles of management. This grid posits the interaction of task versus relationship and shows that according to how people value these, there are five basic ways of interacting with others.

Figure 2.1 Conflict-handling style (based on Blake and Mouton)

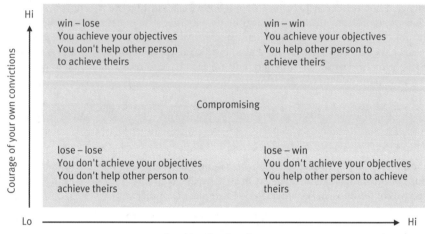

(Adapted from Thomas 1976)

In the model shown in Figure 2.1, the two axes are:

- courage of one's convictions
- consideration for others.

So, to be assertive, you need high courage of your convictions and high consideration of others.

Courage of your convictions

This refers to your ability to set an objective and pursue it. It implies single-mindedness – sometimes bloody-mindedness and ruthlessness. We can usefully think of the idea of having a *bottom line* to help us understand this concept. A bottom line is the line we will not retreat beyond, even under pressure. We will walk away rather than retreat. For example, imagine that you are a union negotiator dealing with the human resources (HR) director of a company for the annual pay review. This director offers you his sixth final offer. What do you do? You reject it, of course, and wait for his seventh final offer. Clearly he doesn't have a bottom line and so he will continue to retreat.

Consideration for others

This means trying to understand the objectives of the other person. By considering the other person's objectives, it may be possible to satisfy one's own objectives – meet your bottom line – and meet theirs at the same time. This is the cherished win–win position.

Combinations of these two dimensions give us the following five styles:

1   *A confrontational (aggressive) style* of conflict-handling, involving, for example, demanding apologies from others and redress of perceived 'wrongs', tends to be adopted by people who are high in concern for their own needs and low in concern for others' needs.

2   *An avoidance style*, which means refusing to acknowledge that a problem exists, while reducing interaction with the other person(s) as far as possible, results from low concern with both one's own and other people's needs. It does give the opportunity to gain time, however, and can be utilised in a situation where neutrality is important.

3   *An accommodation style*, apologising and conceding the issue to the other person regardless of the 'rights and wrongs' of the matter, goes with a low concern with one's own needs and a high concern with others' needs. It does ensure that peace is kept for the time being.

These three conflict-handling styles are all, in their different ways, undesirable, tending to reinforce the conflict and create more ill-feeling, to prolong it below the surface or to encourage further aggression in others. The remaining two styles are both more effective than these:

4   *A compromising style* is next best; this approach means bargaining, explicitly or implicitly, with the other person until a compromise is reached; though this is often a reasonable approach, there is the well-known danger that the actual compromise agreed on will be 'the worst of all worlds' and only be a temporary solution.

5   *A collaborative (assertive) style*, then, is the optimal. It involves an approach that treats the need to repair the relationship as a problem which the parties need to solve together. More guidance on how to implement this style is given below.

COLLABORATIVE STYLE

- Aggressiveness and submissiveness (avoiding and accommodating) get you nowhere. Don't use them.
- Ensure that you jointly identify what differences exist and analyse the cause of those differences.
- Be honest and relevant; stick to facts, not personalities.
- Consider the alternative solutions and work through the implications together, seeing which alternative is closest to each side.
- Each side should know its bottom line and stick to it, which is the point that each side will not cross. That bottom line should be honestly expressed so there is no misunderstanding.
- It is usually wiser to have an adjournment when a sticking point is reached to allow reflection from both sides and allow the points made to sink in. In most circumstances, a return to the meeting brings new ideas for a solution.
- When a solution is agreed, make sure there is no misunderstanding by going over it again and making sure it is correctly recorded.
- Ensure agreement is reached on how the preferred solution is implemented (although a certain vagueness in places is allowable – without this, no European Union agreement would ever be made).

This type of collaborative bargaining is often called *'integrated bargaining'*, where a solution is often win–win. The opposite approach, confrontational bargaining, is called *'distributive bargaining'*, where a win–lose result emerges.

REPAIR TECHNIQUES

Edgar Schein (1980) is one authority on organisational behaviour who has looked at the question of how to repair relationships after breakdown. It is clear from his discussion that the main requirement, as so often in face-to-face work, is to come to terms with your own psychological blockages. Being afraid that unpleasant events will be repeated often prevents people from starting to build bridges. For instance, you may be afraid that when you make an overture – a friendly or helpful remark – to someone else, they will snub you. Alternatively, you may find it easier to blame others than to work out how to renegotiate your relationship with them. These are some suggestions for overcoming one's own psychological barriers to bridge-building:

- Look for new elements in the situation that you may not have noticed before: for one thing, the other people in the situation may have changed in significant ways. Other people tend to be more flexible and adaptive than our assumptions about them allow; our impressions become straitjackets or self-fulfilling prophecies. The confrontation itself is likely to have affected them in some way: often, it is true, people become more rigid after such an experience, but some may wish to change even if they lack the skill to do so.
- Look to superordinate goals around which a new set of relationships can be built. If you needed to keep in touch with this person before, you still need to even though you have quarrelled.
- Force yourself to see what happened from the other person's point of view. A friend or sympathetic colleague can often help to make this process less painful than it would otherwise be.
- A colleague who is a good listener can also be very helpful if your blockage is emotional – hurt or anger. Talking it through, if necessary over and over, blunts the edges of emotions which otherwise may prevent you from being skilled in handling the repair interaction. Allowing some time to pass also helps in this because emotions tend to recede over time.

When you have handled yourself, you are ready to handle the situation, using, as recommended above, a collaborative approach. To succeed you should:

- Set up a meeting that is explicitly for the purpose of making the repair. This approach, which can be thought of as confronting the problem, is more likely to succeed than either evading it or attempting to build bridges in the course of other business. The best way to set up the meeting is to telephone the person with whom your relationship has broken down – or intercept them in the corridor – and say something along the lines of, 'Look, Andrew, do you think we should get together to sort out why we are at loggerheads like this? I do, because it's affecting my work, and making me miserable – I very much dislike being on bad terms with colleagues.' You may need to persist to get agreement to the meeting, but usually you can get it in the end, because the other party is aware that it is unreasonable to refuse. It is important not to be dragged into discussing the cause of the dispute itself at this stage, because your objective is to get agreement to the meeting, this agreement itself being the first stage in the bridge-building process. An intermediary may be used to set up the meeting if someone really suitable is available but this is less satisfactory because it reduces the amount of repair achieved by this first overture.
- In the meeting, allow the other person to express their negative emotions about what has happened, while keeping close control of your own. If you detect that they are in the grip of emotion that is not being expressed at the start, encourage them to bring it into the open. This may be painful for you, but is an essential first step in the bridge-building process. Make it clear that you are listening to and understanding what they say, though you do not necessarily accept that they are right.
- Make it clear that you do not intend the repair process to lead to further loss of face for either party.
- Treat the repair as a problem to solve jointly rather than a self-abasement: your objective is to reach agreement on a new basis for the relationship but your offer is not unconditional. You are trying to explore differences creatively and locate some common ground but you do need to protect yourself from any attempt by the other person to exploit your overture, perhaps to gain, unfairly, the point on which you differed before. If their position was unjustified before, it remains so now, even if you do want to apologise for having lost your temper. You will need to be articulate and assertive to clarify what you are and are not conceding.

REFLECTIVE ACTIVITY 2.3

Think of a situation that needs repair. Using the techniques described in this section, start this process. Record your reflections over time as you try to make this repair in your self-development diary.

Feedback on Reflective Activity 2.3

Actively reflecting on how to improve situations involving conflict is an excellent way of planning how to retrieve the situation. You should find that doing this exercise will make you more effective and confident.

FORCES SHAPING HUMAN RESOURCE MANAGEMENT AT WORK

In the course of this book we are examining the way that external effects influence the role and practices of human resources in practical terms. You will see many examples in each of the forthcoming chapters, but here are some brief extracts:

- *Social* – how demographic changes influence the need for human resources to engage in initiatives in flexible working and to widen the pool of recruitment.
- *Technological* – how technological developments have provided scope for new ways of working – in call centres and distance/teleworking.
- *Economic* – how economic cycles influence both the internal and external labour market and how human resources need to move swiftly to anticipate and utilise such changes.
- *Environmental* – how the growing international emphasis on environmental issues provides opportunities for human resources to lead in areas such as engagement with the community and secondment.
- *Political* – how developments in Europe have influenced the migratory pattern and employment regulation with the associated need for human resources to ensure advantages are gained from such changes.
- *Legal* – human resources need to respond to changes in the UK regulatory climate through ensuring organisations understand fully the implications of such changes and implement appropriate policies and procedures.
- *Ecological* – the growing support for socially responsible organisations provides the opportunity for human resources to take the lead in areas such as ethical behaviour codes towards employees, customers, the community and in business transactions.

We have already seen earlier the responses that human resources make to the some of the internal effects, such as internal structure, power, conflict and change. The remainder of the chapter deals with the way that human resources can be structured and the effect it can have.

MODELS AND ROLES OF THE HUMAN RESOURCE FUNCTION

Given that human resources can make a contribution to organisational performance – and there is a healthy debate how this can be affected – the next question relates to the models and roles of the human resource function that can effectively and cost-efficiently organise this contribution.

This next section, therefore, briefly examines the changing employment relationships before setting out the various models and roles of the human resource function as revealed by the last 30 years of research.

THE HUMAN RESOURCE EQUATION – MODELS OF THE EMPLOYMENT CONTRACT

The *traditional employment contract* was simple. In return for a wage or salary, the employee carried out the work indicated to the required standards. However, a subsidiary, unwritten contract has also been present in most employment contracts that is more difficult to pin down and often deals with unexpected and unforeseeable changes in the nature of the work concerned. This is often referred to as the *psychological contract*, first explained by Schein (1980) and discussed by many writers since (Herriot 1998; Conway and Briner 2005). This form of contract deals with the expectations that employees and employers have of their relationship, especially how each expects to be treated by the other.

In the *traditional* form, the format was for the employer to offer a secure and dependable income, a degree of job security, a safe environment and a possible opportunity for advancement, while the employee carried out the work indicated in the contract, followed the prescribed rules and standards and showed long-term loyalty. Although this contract never applied to large numbers of employees (temporary, low-paid and unskilled) and varied considerably by sector of employment, for the good majority to whom it applied, it reflected a dependable, foreseeable environment.

Since around the early 1980s, however, there has been a recognisable change in the nature of this contract which reflects the rapidly changing employment market and the unpredictability and volatility of the organisational context. This has led to a restating of the psychological contract. Employment for life is not the expected norm (police, prison and fire services excepted). There has developed a growing intensification of work in many sectors where employees are expected to work much longer hours and take on much more varied and flexible responsibilities beyond their apparent contractual duties, called 'going beyond contract'. In return, employers offer the opportunity to gain experience, learn extra skills and competencies and, in many cases, additional variable pay and bonuses. This has been identified as a change from a *relational* contract to a *transactional* contract, moving from an emotional commitment to one that can be regarded as a simple economic exchange (Taylor 2008).

In theory, this change in the psychological contract should have led to much lower levels of job satisfaction and equally low degrees of satisfaction with the state of the psychological contract. However, research by Guest and Conway (2002) in the late 1990s and early 2000s has found evidence to the contrary. In general, employees have expressed a reasonable (if varied) degree of satisfaction, both with their jobs and with their psychological contract. This may have been because, over the period 1995–2008, the UK enjoyed a steady period of economic growth with a healthy labour market, which meant that most employees unhappy with their employment could move on if they chose to do so, rather than remaining dissatisfied.

With a tight labour market and a shortage of key skills, employers have reacted by attempting to be much more attractive to key employees by setting out to develop an employer brand and becoming an 'employer of choice'. This has been achieved not just by increasing the salary rates but also by improving the employees' work–life balance, entering into extensive recognition initiatives which regularly support special employee achievements in the workplace and by introducing attractive benefits, such as flexible hours, the ability to work at home and systems of flexible benefits.

MODELS OF THE HUMAN RESOURCE FUNCTION

There are a number of examples of models illustrating the varying roles and styles for the operation of HR departments and practitioners, and here are three of them.

Karen Legge (1978) identified three HR practitioners ('personnel' in those days) who were seeking to develop their power within the organisation. The first of these is the *conformist innovator*, the person who works with the conventional organisational objectives and identifies with them, and comes up with initiatives that help the organisation towards achieving those objectives through cost saving, productivity increases and reducing conflict. The *deviant innovator*, on the other hand, stands somewhat aside from the conventional organisation aims and adopts an independent professional stance. The initiatives they recommend tend to be unconventional and their adoption will depend on their individual status and conviction, with the results somewhat unpredictable. Subject areas here could, today, involve proposals on work–life balance, empowerment or knowledge management. Their innovative ideas, which may face considerable opposition, can provide results which lead to the organisation obtaining clear competitive advantages. The third role is that of *problem-solver*, a more conventional role, one that looks to provide day-to-day assistance to the line management.

Storey's (1992) analysis set up a grid which contrasts on one axis how far the work undertaken is strategic or merely tactical and, on the other axis, the degree to which the human resource manager intervenes in the management process. This is shown in Figure 2.2.

Figure 2.2 HR interventions

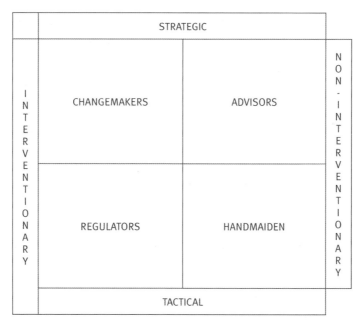

(Adapted from Storey 1992)

Working clockwise, human resource specialists who fall into the *advisor* category are those who focus on strategic issues but are not themselves responsible for carrying out the actions they recommend. *Handmaidens* are those who also have little part in implementing policy but they only operate at a tactical level, dealing with administration and the provision of welfare, training and basic recruitment. *Regulators* are, again, involved only in tactical issues but they are more interventionary, trying to ensure that the human resources policy is carried out properly in co-operation with line managers. The *changemakers*, on the other hand, are both strategic and interventionary, concerned less with administration and more with the broader view of people management in their organisations. A changemaker is expected to assess the organisation's needs, reach appropriate conclusions and then drive the required changes to completion. This is regarded, Storey indicates, as the proper role for an effective and senior human resource specialist.

Ulrich (1998) followed a similar tack but developed the model so that the x-axis measures the degree to which the HR practitioner manages the process and, on the other hand, manages the people involved, as shown in Figure 2.3.

Figure 2.3 Role of HR

	STRATEGIC		
M A N A G E M E N T O F P R O C E S S E S	CHANGE AGENT	BUSINESS PARTNER	**M A N A G E M E N T O F P E O P L E**
	ADMINISTRATIVE/ FUNCTIONAL EXPERT	EMPLOYEE ADVOCATE OR CHAMPION	
	TACTICAL		

(Adapted from Ulrich 1998, Ulrich and Brockbank 2005)

The *administrative/functional expert* manages the processes on a day-to-day basis, ensuring that policies on, for example, grievances, discipline, equal opportunities and incentive arrangements work effectively. This is not a role to be derided because it is generally vital to the organisation's smooth running. Recognition, however, does not come easily from this role as it is only really noticed when things go wrong. These activities have, in recent years, been prime candidates for outsourcing or some form of shared services system, which was detailed in Chapter 1.

The *employee advocate/champion* acts as a voice for employees on a day-to-day basis, working for an improvement in their position, their contribution and their engagement with the organisation. This role is intended, by improving their engagement, to improve their overall performance. In Ulrich's revised (2005) version, the role has been strengthened with an additional dimension of *human capital developer*, who works to develop employees as assets through extending their skills and developing their career.

The *change agent* works from a strategic viewpoint, attempting to ensure that employees go along with business changes, making sure that visions and values are translated into action and reality.

The *business partner* works with line management to ensure board strategy is developed and put into effect, identifying areas where action is required and instituting remedial initiatives. Line managers use them as consultants to debate issues in their area, such as salary and incentive issues and difficult disciplinary cases.

The concept of the business partner has found substantial support in recent years, adopted by a huge range of companies. It is interpreted in different ways but the central precept is the close relationships with business units, helping to solve practical problems and delivering real value to the organisation. Three examples are shown in Case Study 2.2.

CASE STUDY 2.2

BUSINESS PARTNERS AT ELIOR GROUP, GENERAL MOTORS AND PRUDENTIAL INSURANCE

Elior, a 5,400-employee European contract catering group, introduced business partnering in 2008 which provided benefits for both HR and business managers. HR professionals gained insights into business concerns while business managers appreciated the importance of a more scientific approach to people issues. Senior HR specialists could spend more time on strategic issues, such as succession planning and performance management, while line management have much greater control over performance management. A key difficulty involved in setting up the scheme was a lack of formal meetings for exchanging views and understanding between business partners where good practice could be exchanged.

In 2003, Vauxhall Motors at Ellesmere Port (part of General Motors) reorganised the HR departments, with HR staff either outsourced to specialist or routine roles or assigned to a business-focused role. The latter staff were trained to understand all aspects of the business and given a desk in the unit's open-plan offices next to the car production lines. They engage in day-to-day operations, such as assisting managers in performance

management, identifying training needs, coaching and discussing the facts and figures about people in their unit, their promotions, potential, disabilities and concerns. The main purpose is to develop close relationships with line managers and help to solve business issues through their knowledge of people management.

At Prudential Insurance, the HR business partner works in a business unit as a consultant, drawing down help from centres of excellence while a service centre deals with HR administration issues. As an example, one partner works in the marketing and innovation function running the people management side of a major change initiative to improve how to deal with customer complaints. Having worked out with the unit manager what needs to be achieved, the partner pulls together an HR team for the project, uses the recommendations of the specialist HR group and co-ordinates the delivery of the project. This needs skills in relationship-building and a good understanding of the business.

Sources: Hennessy (2009); Pickard (2004)

A survey by Roffey Park in 2009 found that 58 per cent of respondents judged the change to a business partner system to be successful, while only 10 per cent found it unsuccessful. It was most likely to become successful where the organisational culture had a higher level of sociability with high scores for focusing on people, building relationships and a concern for colleagues and where there was also a good degree of 'solidarity' (a strong focus on working together to deliver shared objectives) (Griffin et al 2009).

Purcell and Ahlstrand (1994) have taken a different approach, setting out the nine core activities that HRM departments should engage in to become fully influential in an organisation. They believe these to be applicable to most, but not all, medium to large organisations, but it will depend on the nature of the business and the way the organisation is directed. Some are indisputable, such as human resource planning and developing essential human resource policies; others are more debatable:

- *Corporate culture and communications* – organisations are bound together internally, not just by common ownership or by everything being included on the balance sheet. Culture, 'the ways we do things around here', is difficult to define but easy to identify, especially when it is articulated well and often. It is normally up to the chief executive to set out or redefine the principal aspects, the philosophy, the set of values and the essential style of management, but it is human resources that must be responsible for championing and disseminating these cultural aspects around the organisation in an effective fashion.
- *Human resource planning in strategic management* – developing a human resource plan which emerges from the strategic plan is the second core activity. This is clearly a core activity but one where the link is not always made as tightly as it should be.
- *Essential policy formulation and monitoring* – established policies and procedures remain an essential feature of an effective organisation and policies regarding the way people should act and be treated are no exception. Standards need to be set and monitored for compliance. The recognised difficulty here is striking the happy medium between a rigid bureaucratic set of procedures that deal with every eventuality but restrict innovation and empowerment and a set of vague guidelines that have many interpretations and are largely ignored.
- *'Cabinet Office' services* – this is a more unusual observation and based on the need for the chief executive to have advice from a trusted senior subordinate, one that is not linked to a major department, such as finance or sales, which would be liable to defend their own territory and not be regarded as independent. The advice would be principally concerning the implications for staff in general, succession planning for senior executives, but would also include the cultural development issues and some specific investigations set in place through issues raised by non-executive directors. This is a considerable source of power and influence for human resources and emerged from their personal relationship, not from their specific position.
- *Senior management development and career planning* – this is another undisputed, important role, even when longer-term planning is more difficult to undertake. It is linked with the succession planning process and with the need to develop managers with wide experience, so there is flexibility in place for strategic moves into new or existing marketplaces.
- *External advocacy – internal advice* – as human resources develop a close relationship with the chief executive, their 'cabinet' responsibilities may stretch to representing the organisation in the corridors of power. This is not just on local matters, such as trade association committees, but some political lobbying on crucial issues such as government legislation or interpretation of European directives. The internal advice is feeding matters such as this back to the executives in the organisation.
- *Information co-ordination* – this involves helping large organisations to co-ordinate necessary information across the group on pay, bargaining and general personnel statistics, such as headcount, turnover and absenteeism.
- *Internal consultancy and mediation services* – included in this role are aspects of organisational design and learning. The introduction of competencies would be an example here.

- *Human resources for small units* – an extension of the internal consultancy to part of the larger group that have little or no human resource presence.

Purcell and Ahlstrand recognise that this list does not indicate a comprehensive attention to all human resource matters. Training, health and safety, recruitment and pay issues do not come to the fore on their own. In fact:

> Our research shows that the role and authority of corporate HR departments is becoming more ambiguous and uncertain. ... Much of the activity identified ... places a premium on political and interpersonal skills and 'corridor power'. In this situation, the authority of corporate human resources staff comes more from their own expertise and style than from a clearly defined role and function. It has often been noted that human resource managers need to be adept at handling ambiguity. (Purcell and Ahlstrand 1994, p113)

In Chapter 10, the role of human resources in improving organisational performance is examined further.

RESOURCE-BASED VIEW OF THE ORGANISATION

Alongside these investigations, theories have been developed regarding the nature of human resources whereby they can be regarded as uniquely valuable to the organisation because they are a collection of assets (skills, competencies, experience) that are much more difficult to imitate or replicate, unlike other conventional assets such as land or capital. This is associated with the 'resource-based view' (RBV) of the organisation, where competitive advantage is associated with four key attributes – value, rarity, a lack of substitutes and difficult to imitate:

- Human resources are seen to be *valuable*; looking at employees of football teams, for example, the very skilled ones are certainly seen to be extremely valuable and some senior executives transfer to new organisations with an upfront payment. The cost of replacing employees who leave organisations is often high, especially if they are experienced and are seen by customers as important. As explained by Boxall and Purcell (2003):

> [Organisations]... can never entirely capture what individual... [employees]... know. Some of what we know – including many of our best skills – cannot be reduced to writing or to formulas. When we leave the firm, we take this knowledge with us. When whole teams leave... the effects can be devastating. (p83)

- *Rarity* is associated with value as there will always be a labour group which is in short supply: IT staff in the 1980s and 1990s, nurses and teachers in the early 2000s, plumbers most of the time. Organisations that have a steady supply of skills in short supply will have a competitive advantage.
- It is possible to *substitute for labour*, through automated call centres and production lines, but those organisations that possess skilled employees where such substitution is impossible (most service organisations, consultancies, etc) should be able to gain an advantage. It has been argued that the UK's competitive advantage has been maintained because of our very large service sector, whereas Germany's large manufacturing sector has been constantly chipped away by international competition and automation.
- Similarly, it is difficult to *imitate* the skilled work of employees. Cheaper versions of services can be available (self-service in restaurants) but the market for high-quality service by skilled employees is normally in a state of constant growth.

Having recognised the importance of people as a resource, it provides encouragement to employers to identify and then improve the quality of their 'human capital'. In terms of identification, the CIPD (Brown 2003) put forward a proposal in the form of a framework so organisations could report on the way they:

- acquire and retain staff, explaining how the firm sources its supply, the composition of the workforce in terms of diversity and employment relationships and its retention policies
- develop staff, including details of skill levels and development strategies
- motivate, involve and communicate with employees
- account for the value created by employees, including how they manage the bank of employee knowledge and the methods of determining team and individual performance.

HUMAN RESOURCES AND LEADERSHIP STYLES

The role of developing leadership skills is sometimes downplayed in UK writing, but it is very strong in American versions of successful HRM ambitions. Rucci (1997) has set out six key requirements for HR departments to add value to the organisation and ensure its own survival:

1   *Create change* – HR should move away from the control, standardisation and compliance model and encourage the development of an organisational capability of flexibility, speed and risk-taking. This will mean eliminating unnecessary rules and giving greater emphasis to individual judgement and accountability for line managers.

2   *Develop principled leaders* – top executives who ground themselves in a base of moral or ethical principles are few and far between, but it is they who lead organisations to sustained long-term success. HR needs to set in motion systems to develop such talent, especially leaders who have the courage of their convictions and an unwillingness to compromise on ethical issues.

3   *Promote economic literacy* – too much specialisation has led to many managers not having the breadth of outlook to understand the 'big picture' within the organisation. HR should give more emphasis to ensuring managers learn all the skills and knowledge so they can contribute advice on big policy decisions.

4   *Centre on the customer* – HR should help to create boundaryless organisations where the customers' viewpoint seriously influences policy decisions and ensure that customer-directed activity is central in performance reviews, promotion criteria and reward decisions.

5   *Maximise services/minimise staff* – HR needs to focus on its internal customers, identifying where it adds value and driving down its costs.

6   *Steward the values* – HR's role should not just be the organisation's conscience or the 'values police'. It should ensure that the values are understood and ensure that the progress is monitored and measured by embedding them in all HR activities – selection, training, performance management and reward.

The CIPD (2012) has identified an HR leadership approach which contains four key activities:

1   *Understanding the business model at depth* by knowing where value is created and destroyed across the complete value chain, revealing the improvement points around people and performance which drive value and identifying the opportunities to drive revenue and reduce costs through more effective use of employees.

2   *Generating insight and impact through evidence and data* to support initiatives – data that has been mined for insight, inspiration and impact, especially data in key areas such as employee engagement.

3   *Actively seeking opportunities for HR to connect and collaborate* with stakeholders, using curiosity, purpose and impact, often by stepping outside the HR boundary but always putting HR at the heart of business strategy.

4   *Leading with integrity, consideration and challenge*, including facing the emotional and ethical consequences of business decisions. This often involves serving all stakeholders rather than power structures, especially in the public sector.

These prescriptions reflect the nature of HR programmes entered into by progressive and successful companies. An example in practice is set out in Case Study 2.3.

CASE STUDY 2.3

HUMAN RESOURCE STRATEGIES AND ACTIONS AT AEHN

In the late 1990s, AEHN, an American acute care hospital, was faced by what it regarded as a tumultuous and unpredictable period in its history. The new CEO undertook to transform it from one that was largely stable and complacent to one that was 'nimble, agile and change-hardy' or it may not have survived. Alongside a number of strategic changes in direction, five key HR initiatives were set in motion:

1   *Achieving contextual clarity* – AEHN went to great lengths to be quite sure that employees at all levels understood the CEO's new vision for the organisation, the progress towards achieving that vision and the links between their individual and collective actions to raise organisational performance. Although using conventional methods, the messages were delivered in a fairly intense way, with bulletin boards refurbished with a constant flow of relevant stories and reports, banners saying 'Are you ready for change? Are your skills ahead of the game?' and a steady flow of short courses and meetings to illuminate the organisation's progress for all to understand. Workshops included subjects such as 'survival tactics in times of change'.

2   *Embedding core values* – central to the culture change process, embedding and sustaining the set

of core values became the fundamental driving force for the HR initiatives. Taken up by the top team after a year's debate, they were cascaded through the organisation with references woven into all forms of communication and into HR practices. For example, the selection process was revised to add an assessment of applicants' core values by means of situational interviewing and the performance management scheme was heavily revamped to focus on behavioural manifestations of the values.

3   *Enriching work* – a number of work redesign experiments were started to encourage much greater flexibility and empowerment. A position called Patient Care Associate was created to administer tests, take blood and do other duties that previously had been carried out by specialists; staff moved much more around units to fill gaps and to broaden perspectives and encourage social networks; self-managed teams were created to provide 'seamless, patient-focused care'.

4   *Promoting personal growth* – employees were encouraged to take responsibility for their personal growth to help them perform better and be prepared for promotions. This was helped by the introduction of 360-degree

feedback, which generated more convincing reasons for personal development and change. Alongside this, there was an agreed policy of zero tolerance of employees who failed to pursue any required self-development.

5   *Providing commensurate returns –* not a great deal could be done on substantially improving salaries so the programme concentrated on non-financial benefits. The work enrichment was one important step and the 'Recognise, Appreciate, Celebrate' initiative

was another. Staff received 'pat on the back notices' and a 'celebration of a risk taken award' (given for a good effort irrespective of result).

These initiatives were business-based and fit together well, so employees were able to understand both why the changes were necessary and also to see them as a coherent set which would benefit the patients, the staff and the organisation.

Source: Shafer et al (2001)

HR AND EMPLOYEE ENGAGEMENT

The concept of engagement centres on the degree to which employees 'buy into' the company culture, strategy and values. Few people would argue that engaged employees are far more likely to be productive and to employ the correct competencies to help achieve organisational success. The clearest example we have all seen is when we, as a customer, have faced employees who could not care much about our needs or expectations and provide us with appalling service. They are therefore not engaged in their jobs. Measuring the level of employee engagement and then taking initiatives to maintain and improve this level are therefore seen as key HR strategies.

The subject was considered so important by the Government that a substantial report on the subject was commissioned in 2009 (the Macleod Report). This confirmed the association of engagement with performance and the fact that:

> Engagement, going to the heart of the workplace relationship between employer and employee, can be a key to unlocking productivity and transforming the working lives of many people for whom Monday morning is an especially low part of the week. (Macleod and Clarke 2009, p2)

Measuring engagement

Engagement is usually measured by forms of staff surveys which ask detailed questions concerning employee attitudes to areas such as:

- understanding of organisational purpose
- commitment to key competencies, such as customer satisfaction, quality improvement, etc
- satisfaction in the job they carry out
- satisfaction with the rewards
- plans on staying or leaving the organisation
- willingness to go the extra mile
- willingness to put forward new ideas and to accept changes in their job and the organisation
- pride in working for the organisation
- agreeing to promote their organisation to their friends and recommend people to work for the organisation
- views on 'fairness' within the organisation
- degree of trust in senior management and their own manager

- belief that the organisation is a 'happy' or 'fun' place to work
- belief that the organisation cares about its employees
- belief that the organisation is serious about equal opportunities and diversity.

For some organisations, these surveys are complex and detailed because management believe the results to be critical to the success of the organisation. Nationwide Building Society, for example, describes the survey as 'their genome project, mapping the DNA of the organisation'. Two data modellers, the 'insight team', are dedicated to the outcomes, searching for correlations. Their research has found that, if employees are 2 per cent more satisfied, that translates into customers being more satisfied and buying more – and vice versa with dissatisfied employees. Nationwide customers like staff with longevity, so it is important for the organisation to find out what it is that makes staff stay and why they leave. One of the key outcomes of the surveys is that staff that strongly share the values are more likely to stay (Syedain 2009). At Marks & Spencer, survey results show that stores with high engagement scores have high mystery shopper and sales against target scores and lower absence (Arkin 2011).

Most research into retaining staff demonstrates that the employee's relationship with their immediate manager is one of the most important predictors of their length of service. The features of 'engaging' managers has been set out by the Institute for Employment Studies, summarised in Case Study 2.4.

CASE STUDY 2.4

👁 MANAGERS AND ENGAGEMENT

The Institute for Employment Studies has studied aspects of engagement for some years and their 2009 report examined how managers who inspire and engage their teams to perform well behave in their dealings with staff. Twenty-five managers, found to rate highly on engagement, were chosen from seven organisations and these managers were interviewed, together with their teams. They had varied responsibilities, from 4 to 5,000 staff.

The research discovered that the engaging managers had a lot of characteristics in common, but personality was not one of them. Some were energetic extroverts, others were quiet, even shy – some were intensely practical, while others were creative and innovative, or liked intellectual challenge. Most had been with their organisations for some time, but others were more recent recruits. Their behaviour towards their teams, however, was very consistent. The interest they took in people as individuals, and in developing and nurturing their teams, did not prevent them from tackling difficult issues such as breaking bad news and managing poor performance. The consensus was that honesty and openness was important, along with empathy and a demonstration that the manager had an understanding of their possible impact on staff.

Something else they shared was a focus on performance and an expectation that their teams would deliver to a high standard. The recession was biting when they carried out our research, and some of the private sector companies they visited were suffering, but the engaging managers recognised the need to maintain their engaging behaviours in bad times as well as good. The general feeling among engaged teams was that they were happy and enjoyed their work and there was a good atmosphere compared with other teams.

Source: Robinson and Hayday (2009)

The level of engagement is usually measured by way of staff surveys, but these do not always show the whole picture, as research by Gourlay et al (2012) has shown, because engagement may be transactional or emotional:

- Emotionally engaged employees are employees who enjoy the work they are doing, have high levels of well-being and enjoy working with their manager and co-workers. They also tend to have high levels of performance. They are truly 'engaged' to the organisation.
- Transactional engagement, on the other hand, is shaped by employees' concern to earn a living, to meet minimal expectations of the employer and their co-workers. They tend to respond positively to surveys but may not be high-performers. In other words, their responses to surveys can be misleading and, because they often display lower levels of organisational identification, they are more likely to display deviant behaviours and to leave the organisation when their personal or economic circumstances change.

Further, evidence was found that work intensification (ie greater pressure on employees to get results) may drive up transactional engagement at the expense of emotional engagement. So it is in the interests of organisations to take initiatives to improve emotional engagement rather than relying on statistical results from staff surveys which may disguise the true picture.

CUSTOMER CARE

Customers are the lifeblood of any organisation. If they do not receive satisfactory and even pleasurable experiences, they will go elsewhere. The purpose of customer care, therefore, is to ensure that customers' needs and expectations are met or exceeded so that they remain committed to that organisation. An American survey by Infoquest (2002) found that a totally satisfied customer contributes 17 times as much revenue to a company as a dissatisfied customer, but a totally dissatisfied customer decreases revenue by a factor of 30. So with twice as many satisfied customers as dissatisfied, a business will still be doing little better than standing still. Other surveys have shown that a 1 per cent increase in customer satisfaction translates into 3 per cent market value increase and that companies with higher regarded customer care systems increase their sales per annum twice as fast as organisations where customer care is poorly regarded (Fraterman 2009).

STRATEGIC APPROACH TO CUSTOMER CARE

Driving an effective customer care approach through the organisation requires a strategy that incorporates all aspects of the company's operations. Marketing must find out what products and services will meet customer needs and design and development departments must produce them in ways that provide sufficient choice and at acceptable prices. Production must produce goods that have very high quality levels backed up by guarantees that will satisfy customers. Distribution must ensure they are available for customers within acceptable deadlines. Even more important, employees throughout the organisation must buy in to the concept that customers must be treated fairly, speedily and with consideration to detail. Without the thorough commitment by staff and the built-in desire to 'go the extra mile', gaps will develop in the process through which customers will fall. So any strategic plan will have the employees at its centre.

The strategic plan will need to establish a set of *standards* and *measures* which will identify critical success factors in customer service. These will include:

- *measures of immediate customer dissatisfaction*, such as volume and value of goods returned within seven days or a month, number of service contracts cancelled within seven days, number of time-limited contracts which are not renewed

- *number and type of customer complaints*, identified by product and sales area
- *metrics associated with surveys of customer satisfaction* – many organisations, for example, ask customers to respond immediately after buying goods or services. For example, the national double glazing companies usually provide customers with a short questionnaire to fill in when the products are installed relating to their sales and installation experience. Other companies will circulate questionnaires to a selection of customers on service contracts on a periodic basis
- *measures of on-time production and delivery* compared with contracted times
- *quality and speed of response* to customer contact in terms of sales achieved, problem-solving and returning customers
- *for call-centres, specific metrics on call-handling*
- *metrics from mystery shoppers* – although the implementation of mystery shopping schemes was first regarded with suspicion by employees, there has been remarkable acceptance of the process, especially as most reporting systems do not identify specific employees but measure the general ambience of customer relations.

CUSTOMER CARE – THE EMPLOYEE DIMENSION

To thoroughly involve employees, the following areas need to be included in any customer care training programme:

- *Training employees in products and services*, so that all employees, not just sales, can be in a position to deal with customers' needs.
- *Specific training for sales staff*, especially retail staff, to ensure that sales made benefit both the organisation and the customer. Customers need to leave the sales environment feeling confident that they have not been persuaded to purchase by clever sales techniques. This may lead to short-term sales increase but ultimately will lead to poor customer relations and, in the worst cases, litigation. An important issue here is the danger of mis-selling. The Office of Fair Trading (OFT) has carried out two major investigations in this area. The first, in the 1990s, was into pensions mis-selling, and the second, in 2003, into the selling of extended warranties. In the first case, heavy fines were imposed on a number of companies involved and, in the second, the OFT imposed a number of conditions under which the financial service could be sold, both to ensure customers received better protection in the future.
- *A clear understanding of the standards established* in customer care and the processes operated. This is not always straightforward. Although guidelines are usually established in, say, when and how contracts can be changed or cancelled, it may be necessary to go outside of these guidelines as a means to solve difficult problems. The authority for such action used to be restricted to senior management, but some companies with sophisticated customer care systems have delegated authority to low levels to allow problems to be solved swiftly. They have found that this often wins back customers who do not have to wait to talk to a manager and whose anxiety or anger over the issue is quickly assuaged.
- *Specific training for service staff* in areas where the quality of service is the essential feature of the sale, such as in hotel and catering operations and in-flight service. The switch to call centre handling of sales and service operation since the mid-1990s has meant that specialised staff training is required in dealing with customers over the phone, although anecdotal experience leads most people to doubt that such training has taken place in many cases. In recent years, the specialised customer care in the health service has been the subject of comprehensive training, although results, again, still appear to be mixed.
- *Training in communication and problem-solving* – the development of the competency frameworks in organisations, where emphasis is placed on the necessary enhancement

of skills in communication and problem-solving, is closely related to customer care and not just restricted to immediate customer-facing staff. The ability to identify where contracts have gone wrong (problem-solving) and for staff to effectively communicate with each other to ensure problems are immediately solved and to prevent them happening again is crucial to the process of improving customer care.

● *Providing incentives for efficient customer care* – there is a growing trend for incentive schemes to contain a strong element of measuring and rewarding customer care performance, rather than simply using output or quantity measures. Often this change has been made because, under previous schemes, employees have acted to raise output at all costs without considering the consequences of poor quality, delivery times or unacceptable service quality. Examples here include the Sainsbury's store-based team incentive, which is wholly based on the CSI (customer satisfaction index) (IRS 2003), the DaimlerChrysler Aftersales Managers scheme,* where CSI scores represent 20 per cent of the managers' bonus, and AOS Heating, a small plumbing firm based in Cheshunt, where the bonus for the plumbers is entirely based on the customer ratings.*

● *Recognition of employee action* – as an additional reward for demonstrating the required employee behaviours, many organisations have instituted a formal system of recognition for excellent customer care. For example, Claridge's Hotel in London has a 'Pot of Gold' recognition scheme where an employee who has demonstrated 'service perfection' in the course of a day's work (a core value in the organisation) can be nominated by a fellow employee to take part in a 'lucky dip' from a pot of gold envelopes in the HR director's office. The reward can vary from an extra day of holiday or a facial treatment in the hotel's spa to an all-expenses paid night in the hotel's top suite, which would normally cost over £4,000 (IRS 2004).

*author's research

The aim of an integrated policy is to develop a customer care culture within the organisation where employees put the requirements of the customer first and behave in line with this belief.

Although customer care has developed primarily in the private sector as an essential way of improving the brand and enhancing profits, there have been a number of initiatives in the public sector, as shown in Case Study 2.5 concerning the MoD outsourced housing contract.

CASE STUDY 2.5

👁 CUSTOMER CARE AT THE MOD HOUSING CONTRACT

MODern Housing Solutions (MHS) is a dedicated venture company between Enterprise plc and Carillion plc constructed specifically to deliver the Housing Prime Contract, valued at £700 million over seven years, which maintains 43,000 units for service families' accommodation in England and Wales.

Re-enlistment rates have been found to be highly correlated to satisfaction with living accommodation of service families, so ensuring families have decent, habitable and stress-free

accommodation, regardless of rank, is vital to the future human resource plans for the defence forces. In previous years, the reputation for quality maintenance has not always been high, both in terms of work carried out and, in particular, the level of response. A key initiative in this contract has been the development of a dedicated customer care centre incorporating a 24-hour freephone helpdesk.

The customer care centre, which needed the highest level of security accreditation, was established in Liverpool with state-of-the-art telephony equipment which received, on average, 7,000 calls per week. According to Enterprise, after two years of operation, the service level has been running consistently above KPI requirements (such as 95 per cent of calls answered within two minutes), with customer satisfaction rates showing substantial improvements.

However, the National Audit Office showed a mixed view of customer satisfaction. When the new contract began in 2006, there was a higher than expected level of demand for repairs, which the helpdesk and other systems could not cope with. Many families

remain dissatisfied with the service, in particular with the understanding shown by helpdesk operators of the nature of the maintenance problems. Survey respondents reported that only 42 per cent of problems were rectified at the first visit and, in cases where the respondent felt the helpdesk had not understood their problem, it fell to 13 per cent. Having said this, however, families were generally satisfied with the manner in which the work was carried out and confirmed that there had been an upward trend in the contractor's performance against KPIs.

Sources: Enterprise (2009); National Audit Office (2009)

QUALITY MANAGEMENT

THE IMPORTANCE OF QUALITY MANAGEMENT

Quality management has moved on a long way from the traditional view that a quality product just meets the technical specification and that customers have to accept and pay for the product or the service if the company can show it has met that specification. Today, the successful companies are those that aim to produce products and services that exceed customers' expectations and reach success in that aim. Meeting the specification is just one step on the road to high quality.

In many industries, quality failures can be catastrophic. The failure in preventing fire spreading was one (among other) quality faults that caused the deaths of 189 people in the Piper AlphaNorth Sea oil rig disaster in 1989; the failure in signalling quality was a major cause of the Paddington rail crash in 1999, killing 30 people and, worldwide, other, larger disasters at Bhopal in India (Union Carbide) and Chernobyl caused multiple deaths and untold misery for thousands.

Quality remains a subjective subject. Organisations, such as Ferrari, the Ritz Hotel and Cartier, whose entire business is geared to producing products and services at the highest possible level, will not be so concerned with cutting costs, only with ensuring nothing ever goes wrong. Other organisations, such as McDonald's or Tesco, will seek to provide good-value (generally meaning cheap) products and services associated with a pleasant experience, with the costs being firmly under control. Both examples concern organisations that are totally focused on quality. Slack et al (2007) call the first example the *transcendent* approach and the second the *value-based* approach.

HIERARCHY OF QUALITY MANAGEMENT

It is possible to identify five developments in quality systems, as shown in Figure 2.4.

Figure 2.4 Quality management analysis

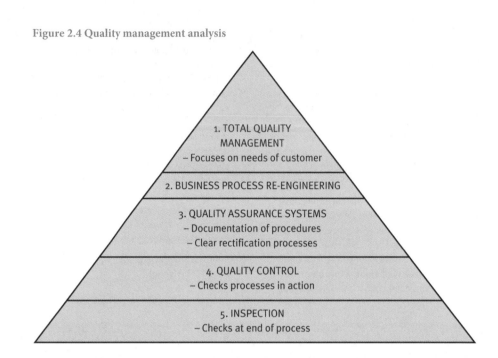

1. TOTAL QUALITY MANAGEMENT
– Focuses on needs of customer

2. BUSINESS PROCESS RE-ENGINEERING

3. QUALITY ASSURANCE SYSTEMS
– Documentation of procedures
– Clear rectification processes

4. QUALITY CONTROL
– Checks processes in action

5. INSPECTION
– Checks at end of process

Level 5 – Inspection

Inspection systems have been in place for centuries, with records available of the inspection that took place during the building of the Egyptian Pyramids more than 4,000 years ago. Inspection is generally an after-the-event activity concerned with identifying faults, removing defective items from the process and either reworking or scrapping them. Without inspection, faulty goods would proceed to the retailer and eventually the customer, where rejection would take place. Solving the problem at that stage would be much more costly and damages the company's reputation.

Inspection systems, however, have their difficulties:

- Having an inspector at the end of each process is expensive in labour cost and the work can be extremely tedious (although it is possible to replace human inspection with automated processes).
- Inspection may remove the immediate problem but it does not always attack the symptom of the problems.
- Operatives may not be too concerned with the quality of their work knowing that an inspector will pick up any faults in the process. Inspection is linked closely with Tayloristic principles of fractionalising work, which presents the inherent difficulties of reducing the value of the work and, hence, the operative's regard for it.

Level 4 – Quality control (QC)

QC is a step up from inspection in that it makes use of more scientific and statistical data in examining quality issues. This makes use of sampling techniques, relating both to the inputs (supplies, materials) and the outputs at different stages in the manufacturing process. Statistical results are compared with predictive charts and control limits. An obvious example of its use is in the water industry, where water is sampled and tested for numerous hazards before it is released into the water supply. The operations are normally controlled by a quality department which consists of training and qualified personnel. The benefit of quality control is that the problems are identified at an early stage in a thorough, scientific way. For example, the sampling of braking components before they are released on the assembly line will save the quality problems later of rejecting full braking units, in terms of both cost and time.

Difficulties still remain, however, especially the separation of quality management from the manufacturing process and the difficulties of ensuring that samples are representative.

Level 3 – Quality assurance (QA) systems

QA systems are quality systems that are subject to external verification. The most comprehensive and well known are the ISO 9000 series (International standards, launched in 1987) and European Foundation for Quality Management standards (EFQM), launched in 1999, which have both built on less complex systems introduced from the 1960s. They were initially introduced in industries where failure of the products would cause severe problems, including loss of life, such as guided weapons and the aircraft industry as a response to customers (especially governments) demanding complete assurance on the quality of the product.

At the heart of these standards is the initiating by the organisation of a comprehensive system of quality management throughout the organisation. This includes comprehensive identification of the correct manufacturing methods (no shortcuts allowed by employees!), methods of identifying customer satisfaction, full recording of all data and training of all employees concerned. The QA systems can apply to all organisations (manufacturing, service, government and not-for profit). Systems need to be agreed with the external agencies, who will make periodic unscheduled visits to ensure the quality processes are being followed. If there are gaps found by the external agencies, the accreditation can be withdrawn.

There is no doubt that quality assurance accreditation has improved the overall quality in organisations that have adopted the accreditation process. This has occurred both because of the comprehensive approach required and the discipline imposed throughout the organisation and also because all employees do become aware of the catastrophic effect that the removal of the accreditation would have on the organisation's reputation and act accordingly. The system encourages a regular rethink of processes and acting to meet feedback from customers. The accreditation can be used in marketing. Increasingly, large government and private contracts are offered only to organisations that have the appropriate accreditation.

Criticism of the QA systems essentially concerns the bureaucratic approach required. For example, every time a new process or material is introduced, this has to be reported to the accrediting body. The external verification procedures are also seen as draconian at times. The processes are costly. Too much emphasis is placed on following the quality manual, rather than using a sensible and flexible approach. As the manual constantly changes, some employees find it difficult to keep up with the changes. Finally, from an employee viewpoint, QA accreditation can be seen as a management imposition and employees may do no more than they have to, to follow the rules (Hill 1991).

Level 2 – Business process re-engineering (BPR)

BPR is the process of systematically examining every stage of production/service to ensure that value is added for the benefit of the customer at each stage of the value chain. It has arisen chiefly from the work of Porter (1985) and Hammer and Champy (1993), whose emphasis on getting ahead of the competition laid a strong emphasis on building quality into the product or service through a radical rethink of every process. In practice, this has meant speeding up decision-making, becoming much more responsive to the customer, allowing new ideas to shape internal processes and empowering employees.

This process incorporates many of the facets of QA accreditation (in fact, they can operate side by side) but there is a much greater emphasis on employees taking hold of quality issues themselves. In a number of radical solutions, such as at Vauxhall in Luton, employees agreed to the elimination of all inspection jobs because the attention they now gave to quality made inspection redundant (Stredwick 1997).

However, in the process of reducing bureaucracy and becoming more flexible, it has also led to de-layering management, reducing the number of employees (except in customer-facing areas) and, evidence indicates, placing more stress on employees at all levels. Although shown to be effective in many cases in improving quality, it is much criticised for its top–down and secretive approach, which leads to cost saving at the expense of employees.

Level 1 – Total quality management (TQM)

TQM is a strategic approach to quality that incorporates most, if not all, of the facets described at the lower levels. It attempts to take the best of the QA systems and BPR and incorporate them into a model of 'best practice'. It therefore expresses itself as culturally based and has a big emphasis on employee involvement. The key ideas were introduced to Japan by the Americans as the occupying force immediately after the Second World War as part of the process of resuscitating their manufacturing industry (Needle 2004). The main initiators of the concept were Deming (1986) and Juran (1988).

In organisational terms, it integrates the company systems with those of suppliers and, in a business-to-business environment, major customers as well. For example, the 'just in time' system operating with suppliers will be integrated with supply sample testing and production schedules. Strong attempts are made to eliminate all costs associated with control and failure and an emphasis is put on 'right first time' and 'right every time'.

There are the following associations with employee involvement:

- Key values, such as 'customer awareness', 'teamworking' and 'continuous improvement' are cascaded down the organisation through training, performance management and regular communication.
- TQM statements regularly emphasise teamworking, creative thinking and empowerment.
- Initiatives on improving quality are encouraged through concepts such as 'quality circles' and 'recognition schemes'. All of these initiatives support teams to work together to achieve improved quality. These are especially focused on preventing problems, rather than solving them.
- An important aspect of training includes multi-skilling, so employees understand the quality requirements on a number of jobs so they can cover for absence, vacancies and where sections have any additional pressures. This is in response to research which has indicated that, to nobody's surprise, poor quality is associated with lack of employee expertise.
- Another training aspect is better understanding of statistical and recording methods so employees understand what is actually happening in their department.
- Communication is enhanced with regular feedback on quality performance and employee recognition awards.

An effectively run TQM system will produce better benefits than the other systems set out in Figure 2.4 on their own. Despite this, not all TQM systems have been an unqualified success. Difficulties faced have included:

- Employees still regard TQM as a form of management control, which can work to stultify individual initiative and increase the stress faced by employees, especially where quality standards are not met.

- TQM is associated with a high-trust environment, especially where serious attempts at empowerment are made. Therefore, when employees made suggestions that are not taken up, or where employees are blamed for not implementing initiatives effectively, it can reduce that degree of trust and lead to cynicism.
- At times, the whole TQM approach is seen as a marketing device, unrelated to the reality of the situation.
- It can also remain a high-cost bureaucratic process, by its very nature.

HUMAN RESOURCE MANAGEMENT AND THE CHANGE AGENDA

THEORIES OF CHANGE MANAGEMENT

There are essentially two main groups of theories that underpin models of change management. They all have their respective benefits and they focus in principle on individuals, group and organisation-wide issues.

These two groups represent the major schools of thought concerning change management theory. They are:

1   the individual perspective school

2   the group dynamics school.

The individual perspective school

This, as its name suggests, focuses on the individual as the principal unit of change. It also has two major camps within the school: the 'behaviourists' and the 'gestalt-field' psychologists. The behaviourists believe behaviour is the result of an individual's interaction with their environment. The gestalt-field psychologists believe that an individual's behaviour is the product of their environment and their own reason. The behaviourists advocate that behaviour is learned and that the individual is a passive recipient of external and objective data. In addition, they hold that individuals respond to the manipulation of reward-enforcing stimuli. Behaviour that is rewarded will tend to be repeated. The behaviourist approach is very close to that of the classical school of management, which presented humans as cogs in a machine responding to the external stimuli being provided.

The gestalt-field psychologists claim that learning is a process of gaining or changing insights, outlooks, expectations or thought patterns. The group takes into account not only the behaviours or actions, but also the responses that these elicit.

In applying these theories to change, the behaviourists seek to achieve change by modifying the external stimuli acting upon the individual, as opposed to the proponents of the gestalt-field, who seek to help individuals or organisations change their understanding of themselves. In turn this leads to changes in behaviour. In simple terms, behaviourism is a 'carrot and stick' approach to achieving change. For example, systems of rewards and sanctions are very visible in sales environments, such as call centres and recruitment agencies.

Both of these approaches have had some influence in management of change. This approach, not surprisingly, has many characteristics of the human relations school of management, largely brought about through the work of Maslow (1943), which stresses the need for both internal and external stimuli in order to influence human behaviour. The human relations school, in understanding the role of the individual, also draws attention to the roles of social groups in organisations, as does the group dynamics school.

Pavlov and his dogs – Pavlov, a Russian psychologist, is possibly the most well-known behaviourist. In a famous experiment, Pavlov used a group of dogs. He rang a bell and then immediately produced food for the dogs. After a time, the dogs began to associate the ringing of the bell with the provision of food and began to salivate when they heard it. Once this stage had been reached, Pavlov rang the bell but did not provide food. The dogs still salivated on hearing the bell. Their behaviour had been changed.

Kurt Lewin and field theory – Kurt Lewin (1958) is a major figure in change management. He made major contributions in the areas of force-field analysis (a method of identifying and measuring resistance to change), group dynamics, organisational development, action research and field-gestalt psychology.

Hall and Lindzey (1978, p386) summarised the central features of Kurt Lewin's force-field theory as follows:

> Behaviour is a function of the field that exists at the time the behaviour occurs. Analysis begins with the situation as a whole from which are differentiated the component parts, and the concrete person in a concrete situation can be represented mathematically.

It is not only in the area of organisations that you see the application of these theories. Until the end of the 1980s, the therapy regime in mental hospitals used the 'carrot and stick' approach of the behaviourists. Since then, mental health therapy has adopted a development approach, more representative of the gestalt-field approach.

A detailed critique of Lewin's force-field theory is set out in Chapter 10.

The group dynamics school

Group dynamics is the field of study within the social sciences that focuses on the nature of groups. In management, we call them teams, but the terms are interchangeable. The main theme of the school is that the influence of the group or team may become very strong indeed and overwhelm the individual's actions and tendencies. So the group may well change the behaviour of the individual. This, effectively, also forms the basis of group therapy. There is particular interest in group dynamics at the moment because of the rise of online interaction made possible by the Internet.

Since the late 1970s in the UK, there has been great interest in 'teambuilding', which can involve a variety of activities from departmental 'away days' (days spent away from the workplace) to full-blown outward bound activity sessions run by ex-military types. The Leadership Trust in the UK is an excellent example of this.

Kurt Lewin is commonly identified as the founder of the movement to study groups scientifically. He coined the term group dynamics to describe the way groups and individuals act and react to changing circumstances.

William Schutz (1966) looked at interpersonal relations from the perspective of three dimensions: inclusion, control and affection (now called openness). This became the basis for a theory of group behaviour that sees groups as resolving issues in each of these stages in order to be able to develop to the next stage. Conversely, a group may also devolve to an earlier stage if unable to resolve outstanding issues in a particular stage. Schutz developed a psychometric instrument – fundamental interpersonal relations organisation (FIRO) – to incorporate these ideas.

Wilfred Bion (1961) studied group dynamics from a psychoanalytic perspective. Many of his findings were reported in his published books, especially *Experiences in Groups*. The Tavistock Institute has further developed and applied the theory and practices developed by Bion.

Bruce Tuckman (1965) proposed the four-stage model called Tuckman's stages for a group. Tuckman's model states that the ideal group decision-making process should occur in four stages:

1   *forming* (being polite to others and pretending to get on with them)

2   *storming* (dropping the pretence of politeness and focusing on the issues, even if emotions rise)

3   *norming* (getting used to each other and developing trust and productivity)

4   *performing* (working in a group to a common goal on a highly efficient and co-operative basis).

Later, Tuckman added an *ending* stage, recognising that the work of a group may come to an end and the group disbanded.

It should be noted that this model refers to the overall pattern of the group, but of course individuals within a group work in different ways. If distrust persists, a group may never even get to the norming stage.

The school's primary emphasis is on bringing organisational change about through teams and work groups rather than individuals. Lewin suggested that the rationale behind this is that because people in organisations work in groups, individual behaviours must be modified or changed in the light of the prevailing group practice and norms.

He went on to suggest that group behaviour is an intricate set of symbolic interactions and facets which not only affect group structure, but also modify individual behaviour. He argued that individual behaviour is a function of the group environment.

To enable change, according to the group dynamics school, the focus must be at group level and should concentrate on influencing and changing the group's norms, roles and values. Therefore, it is useless to concentrate on the behaviour of individuals (French and Bell 1984). In this context, norms are the rules or standards that define what people should do, roles are patterns of behaviour that individuals are expected to conform to, and values are the ideas and beliefs that individuals hold about what is right and wrong.

The group dynamics school has proved to be very influential in developing the theory and practice of change management. Mullins (2007) remarked 'that this can be seen by the very fact it is now usual for organisations to view themselves as comprising groups and teams, rather than merely a collection of individuals'.

French and Bell (1984) pointed out:

> The most important single group of interventions in OD are team building activities, the goals of which are the improved and increased effectiveness of various teams within the organisation. The team building meeting has the goal of improving team effectiveness through better management of task demands, relationship demands and group processes. The team analyses its way of doing things and attempts to develop strategies to improve its operation.

Here, norms, roles and values are examined, challenged and changed. Despite the emphasis many place on groups within organisations, others argue that the correct change management approach should be one that focuses on the organisation as a whole.

MANAGING INDIVIDUAL CHANGE

The DREC model – how individuals cope with change

Elisabeth Kübler-Ross (1969) was a psychiatrist and the author of the ground-breaking book *On Death and Dying*, where she first discussed what is now known as the Kübler-Ross model.

She proposed the now famous 'Five Stages of Grief' as a pattern of phases, most or all of which people tend to go through, in sequence, after being faced with the tragedy of their own impending death. The five stages of grief, in sequential order, are denial, anger, bargaining, depression and acceptance. The five stages have since been adopted by many as applying to the survivors of bereavement and, subsequently, to survivors of all change situations.

The 'Five Stages of Grief' model has become known in management circles as the 'Coping Cycle'. In this section, we use an adapted version of this model, known as DREC (denial, resistance, exploration and commitment). The model is shown in Figure 2.5

Figure 2.5 The DREC model

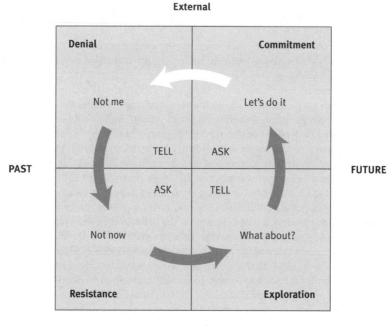

The stages of the cycle are as follows:

- **Denial** – initially, the individual concerned will refuse to accept that the change affects them. The immediate response is to say 'Not me!' At this stage of the cycle, the individual is still firmly attached to the past and the change is seen as something external. The best response is to give specific instructions to the individual, to tell them what to do next.
- **Resistance** – after a period of time, the individual will accept that the change will take place, but not now. The individual is still attached to the past, but not as strongly as before, and is beginning to internalise the need for change. The correct response to this is to ask the individual what they are going to do next.
- **Exploration** – by this stage, the individual has accepted the need for change and is beginning to explore options. They are now looking to the future and everything seems possible. But there are dangers. The individual will wish to experiment with everything, become overloaded and achieve nothing. Focus is needed and this is provided by telling the individual to choose their focus.
- **Commitment** – at this stage, the individual is fully committed to the change, has internalised it, has a clear focus and gets on with it. Individuals clearly face towards the future. They have internalised the change, need no telling, just asking to learn what they will do next.

There is one more danger: it takes time for individuals to work through the cycle. They cannot be hurried. Any attempts to rush them through the cycle may result in a cosmetic change from denial to commitment, but when individuals experience pressure or failure, they revert back to denial. When this happens, it is known as the Tarzan swing, because it represents Tarzan making two giant swings in quick succession.

HUMAN RESOURCES: THE CHANGE AGENT

Earlier in this chapter, the various models of human resources were identified and most of them emphasised that human resources has a key role as a change agent, especially the Ulrich model. There are numerous areas when this role can be played, such as:

- helping the organisation to adjust to changes in the external environment, both in the immediate term with legislative changes and with the longer term, such as changes in ethical behaviour and in advancing corporate social responsibility (see Chapter 9)
- leading negotiating teams in persuading unions to change working practices and become more flexible and efficient to meet the changing competitive environment
- involvement with mergers and acquisitions where, in this most sensitive area, changes may need to be taken quickly and, perhaps painfully, in the employee area; survivors need to be quickly turned round to ensure they contribute to the long-term benefit of the merged organisation
- initiating changes in the organisation's culture, such as introducing a new behavioural environment or an enhanced competency framework
- introducing innovations in reward, such as greater emphasis on performance-oriented rewards, moving away from job- or service-related payments – here, the creation of a robust and fair performance management system becomes crucial and this involves a substantial change programme for management and employees to ensure it works appropriately
- organising research into the degree of employee engagement through employee surveys and producing proposals aiming to increase the engagement metrics
- working with the board and consultants to create and develop an employee brand, using the defined organisational culture and building up an integrated system of recruitment and selection, learning and development, employee relations and reward and recognition which enhances that brand.

A further review of the role of human resources in change is found in Chapter 10.

SUMMARY

Throughout this chapter, the implications for human resource practitioners have been emphasised. In short, HR practitioners need to:

- understand the management systems and identity the power structure so they are able to use their influence selectively and effectively to improve organisational performance
- be regarded as an expert in handling conflict so people issues can be addressed fully and appropriately and resolved in the interests of the great majority of stakeholders
- be aware of the options available for the structure of the human resources function and be able to recommend the best option which is appropriate to the organisational context
- use their influence to improve employee understanding of the importance of systems of customer care and quality assurance and ensure that employees respond accordingly
- act in the best interests of the organisation in facilitating organisational change, ensuring that employees willingly support the required changes.

1   What did Fayol consider to be the main principles of effective management?

2   What is the Butterfly Effect?

3   According to Macmillan, what is the distinction between power and influence?

4   What is 'satisficing', according to Drucker?

5   What are the benefits of operating a 'business partner' HR system?

6   Identify the main important sources of management power, according to Morgan.

7   What are the crucial differences between a collaborative management style and an avoidance style?

8   What is the difference between emotional and transactional engagement?

9   What are the four key attributes of human resources that are associated with the resource-based view of the organisation, according to Boxall and Purcell?

10   Identify the main stages in the DREC model relating to change.

EXPLORE FURTHER

This chapter covers a very wide range of subjects, so the list of additional reading can be extensive. You will find a long list in the reference section for this chapter, but here is an additional short selection:

THEORIES OF MANAGEMENT

Cole, G. (2010) *Management theory and practice*. 6th edition. London: Cengage Learning.

Mintzberg, H. (2009) *Managing*. Harlow: FT Prentice Hall.

POWER IN ORGANISATIONS

Jermier, J., Knights, D. and Nord, W. (1994) *Resistance and power in organisations*. London: Routledge.

Pfeffer, J. (1992) *Managing with power*. Boston, MA: Harvard Business School Press.

HANDLING CONFLICT

Nicotera, A. (1995) *Conflict and organisations*. New York: State University of New York.

Rahim, A. (2001) *Managing conflict in organisations*. New York: Quorum Books.

MODELS OF THE HUMAN RESOURCE FUNCTION

Daniels, K. (ed.) (2008) *Strategic human resource management*. London: Chartered Institute of Personnel and Development.

Marchington, M. and Wilkinson, A. (2008) *Human resource management at work*. London: Chartered Institute of Personnel and Development.

ENGAGEMENT

Holbeche, L. and Matthews, G. (2012) *Engaged: unleashing your organisation's potential through employee engagement*. New York: Wiley and Sons.

CUSTOMER CARE

Cook, S. (2008) *Customer care excellence*. 5th edition. London: Kogan Page.

Johns, T. (1994) *Perfect customer care*. New York: Arrow Books.

QUALITY MANAGEMENT

Besterfield, D. et al (2003) *Total quality management*. New York: Prentice Hall.

Mauch, P. (2009) *Quality management: theory and practice*. London: CRC Press.

MANAGEMENT OF CHANGE

Hughes, M. (2006) *Change management*. 9th edition. London: Chartered Institute of Personnel and Development.

SEMINAR ACTIVITY

FIELD-GESTALT EXERCISES

Introduction

These are a series of exercises that you, as a student, can use to manage your own change. They are based on exercises used by life coaches, but they employ standard techniques such as critical incident techniques and gestalt. Students can work on these individually and then compare their results in small groups to aid the learning process. The group's most interesting examples can be shared with the whole class.

Rules for winning

This is an essential system to enable you to build on what you already do well, so that you can do even better. It uses the critical incident technique:

1   Recall a time when you succeeded in achieving something.

2   How did you manage to achieve the successful result? Use the following questions:

- What worked for you? – list the answers and write them down.

- What can you learn about yourself from these results? – write it down.
- What got in the way? – write it down.
- What can you learn from that? – write it down, in positive form.
- How will you overcome that difficulty next time? – write it down.

3   Rules for winning are personal to each individual and help you to identify positively how you as an individual overcome a given situation and achieve required objectives.

Golden moments

This uses ideas from gestalt psychology. Fundamentally, it asks you what you are feeling, seeing, sensing – but **not** thinking – in given situations.

1   Identify your bottom line, that is, the line you will not retreat beyond. It could be such things as trying to right injustice where you see it, not being treated as a doormat, standing up to

unreasonable fellow students you share a flat with, and so on.

2   Think of times when you exemplified your bottom line.

3   List times in your life when you achieved your objective – what did it feel like? (These last two experiences are the golden moments.)

These moments are personal to you and help you to affirm positively that you can achieve your objectives and stick to your bottom line.

The lifeline

1   Graph the highs and lows of your life on the following chart.

2   Label the highs and lows with life events, such as changing schools, a new job, father dying, and so on. For the purposes of the exercise, we are interested in the business-related highs and lows of the lifeline, and the messages these send to us.

3   Code the business-related highs and lows of the lifeline in this way:

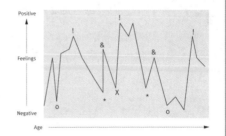

! I took a great risk

* I played it safe.

o Someone else made a major decision I thought should be mine.

+ I made one of my best decisions.

x I felt I had no control.

& I was in control.

What does this now tell you about yourself?

REFERENCES

Allison, G. (1971) *Essence of decisions: explaining the Cuban Missile Crisis.* New York: Little Brown and Company.

Arkin, A. (2011) Is engagement working? *People Management.* November. pp22–7.

Beach, S.D. (1980) *Personnel.* London: Macmillan.

Bion, W.R. (1961) *Experiences in groups: and other papers.* London: Tavistock (reprinted 1989, Routledge).

Blake, R. and Mouton, J. (1964) *The managerial grid: the key to leadership excellence.* Houston: Gulf Publishing Co.

Bosalie, P. and Dietz, G. (2003) *Commonalities and contradictions in research on human resource management and performance.* Paper presented at the Academy of Management, Seattle.

Boxall, P. and Purcell, J. (2003) *Strategy and human resource management.* Basingstoke: Palgrave.

Brown, D. (2003) A capital idea. *People Management.* 26 June. pp42–6.

Burke, W. (1980) *Organisation development.* Toronto: Little, Brown and Co.

Butler, V.G. (1985) *Organisation and management*. London: Prentice Hall.

CIPD. (2012) *Business savvy: giving HR the edge [online]*. London: Chartered Institute of Personnel and Development. Available at: www.cipd.co.uk/hr-resources/research/business-savvy-giving-hr-edge.aspx [Accessed 27 March 2013].

Conway, N. and Briner, R. (2005) *Understanding the psychological contract at work*. Oxford: Oxford University Press.

Danford, A., Richardson, M., Stewart, P., Tailby, S. and Upchurch, M. (2004) High performance work systems and workplace partnership: a case study of aerospace workers. *New Technology, Work and Employment*. Vol 19, No 1. pp14–29.

Deming, W. (1986) *Out of crisis: quality, productivity and competitive position*. Cambridge: Cambridge University Press.

Dixon, M. (1978) *Financial Times*. 2 November. p38.

Drucker, P. (1981) *Managing in turbulent times*. London: Pan Books.

Edwards, C. (2004) Five-star strategy. *People Management*. 8 April. pp34–5.

Enterprise. (2009) *Case study: customer contact centre with the MoD housing contract*. Available at: www.enterprise.plc.uk/_common/download/brochures/MoD%20%28MHS%29%20-%20Customer%20Contact%20Centre.pdf [Accessed 27 March 2013].

Fayol, H. (1947) *General and industrial management*. London: Pitman.

Fielder, F. (1967) *A theory of leadership effectiveness*. New York: McGraw Hill.

Fraterman, E. (2009) The case for customer satisfaction. Customerfocusconsult.com

French, W.L. and Bell, C.H. (1984) *Organization development*. Englewood Cliffs, NJ: Prentice Hall.

Geary, J. and Dobbins, A. (2001) Teamworking: a new dynamic in the pursuit of management control. *Human Resource Management Journal*. Vol 11, No 1. pp2–23.

Gourlay, S., Alfes, K., Bull, E., Baron, A., Petrov, G. and Georgellis, Y. (2012) *Emotional or transactional engagement – does it matter?* CIPD/Kingston University Research Report. London: Chartered Institute of Personnel and Development.

Griffin, E., Finney, L., Hennessy, J. and Boury, D. (2009) *Maximising the value of HR business partnering*. Horsham: Roffey Park Institute.

Guest, D. (1998) Combine harvest. *People Management*. 29 October. pp64–6.

Guest, D. and Conway, N. (2002) *Pressure at work and the psychological contract*. London: Chartered Institute of Personnel and Development.

Hall, C. and Lindzey, G. (1978) *Theories of personality*. New York: Wiley.

Hammer, M. and Champy, J. (1993) *Re-engineering the corporation*. London: Nicholas Brealey.

Hennessy, J. (2009) Take your partners and advance. *People Management*. 29 January. p26.

Herriot, P. (1998) The role of the HR function in building a new proposition for staff. In P. Sparrow and M. Marchington (eds) *Human resource management: the new agenda*. London: Financial Times/Pitman.

Hersey, P. and Blanchard, K.H. (1977) *Management of organizational behavior: utilizing human resources*. 3rd edition. Englewood Cliffs, NJ: Prentice Hall.

Hill, T. (1991) *Production and operations management: text and cases*. London: Prentice Hall.

Hunt, J. (1979) *Managing people at work*. London: Pan Books.

Huselid, M. (1995) The impact of human resource management practices on turnover, productivity and corporate financial performance. *Academy of Management Journal*. Vol 38. pp400–22.

IDS. (2004) The Royal Bank of Scotland group. *HR Studies Update*. Vol 769. March. pp14–17.

Infoquest. (2002) *Annual business survey*. Los Angeles: Infoquest.

IRS. (2003) Rewarding performance: Sainsbury's new bonus scheme. Employment Review 784. *Pay and Benefits*. 19 September. pp33–6.

IRS. (2004) Employment Review 792. *Pay and Benefits*. 23 January. pp33–4.

Johnson, G. and Scholes, K. (1988) *Exploring corporate strategy*. London: Prentice Hall.

Juran, J. (1988) *Quality control handbook*. New York: McGraw Hill.

Kübler-Ross, E. (1969) *On death and dying*. New York: Macmillan.

Legge, K. (1978) *Power, innovation and problem-solving in personnel management*. London: McGraw-Hill.

Legge, K. (2001) Silver bullet or spent round? Assessing the meaning of the 'high commitment management/performance relationship. In J. Storey (ed.) *Human resource management: a critical text*. London: Thomson Learning.

Lewin, K. (1958) Group decisions and social changes. In G.E. Swanson, T.M. Newcomb and E.L. Hartley (eds) *Readings in social psychology*. New York: Holt, Rinehart and Winston.

Macleod, D. and Clarke, N. (2009) *Engaging for success*. London: Department for Business, Innovation and Skills. Available at: www.bis.gov.uk/macleod-review [Accessed 27 March 2013].

Macmillan, I. (1978) *Strategy formulation: political concepts*. St Paul, MN: West Publishing Company.

Marchington, M. (2001) Employee involvement at work. In J. Storey (ed.) *Human resource management: a critical text*. London: Thomson Learning.

Marchington, M. and Grugulis, I. (2000) 'Best practice' human resource management: perfect opportunity or dangerous illusion? *International Journal of Human Resource Management*. Vol 11, No 6. pp1104–24.

Marchington, M. and Wilkinson, A. (2008) *Human resource management at work*. London: Chartered Institute of Personnel and Development.

Martin, N. and Sims, J. (1956) Power tactics. *Harvard Business Review*. Nov–Dec. p25.

Maslow, A.H. (1943) A theory of human motivation. *Psychology Review*. Vol 50. pp370–96.

Mayo, E. (1933) *Human problems of an industrialised society*. New York: Harpers.

Millward, N., Bryson, A. and Forth, J. (2000) *All change at work: British industrial relations, 1980 to 1998 as portrayed by the Workplace Industrial Relations Survey series*. London: Routledge.

Morgan, G. (1986) *Images of organisations*. Beverly Hills, CA: Sage Publications.

Mullins, L. (2007) *Management and organizational behaviour*. London: Pitman.

National Audit Office. (2009) Ministry of Defence service families accommodation. Available at: www.nao.org.uk/report/ministry-of-defence-service-families-accommodation/ [Accessed 27 March 2013].

Needle, D. (2004) *Business in context*. London: Thomson.

Peters, T. (1987) *Thriving on chaos*. New York: Knopf.

Pfeffer, J. (1981) *Power and organisations*. Boston, MA: Pitman.

Pickard, J. (2004) One step beyond. *People Management*. 30 June. pp27–31.

Pickard, J. (2009) Employee branding. *People Management*. 5 Nov. pp18–22.

Porter, M. (1985) *Competitive advantage: creating and sustaining superior performance*. New York: Free Press.

Pugh, D.S. (1978) Understanding and managing organizational change. *London Business School Journal*. Vol 3, No 2. pp29–34.

Pugh, D., Hickson, D. and Hinings, C. (1971) *Writers on organisations*. London: Penguin.

Purcell, J. (1999) Best practice and best fit: chimera or cul-de-sac? *Human Resource Management Journal*. Vol 9, No 3. pp26–41.

Purcell, J. and Ahlstrand, B. (1994) *Human resource management in the multi-divisional company*. Oxford: Oxford University Press.

Purcell, J., Kinnie, N. and Hutchinson, S. (2003) Open minded. *People Management*. 15 May. pp30–3.

Ramsey, H., Scholarios, D. and Harley, B. (2000) Employees and high performance work systems: testing inside the black box. *British Journal of Industrial Relations*. Vol 38, No 4. pp501–31.

Robinson, D. and Hayday, S. (2009) *The engaging manager*. Report 470. Brighton: Institute for Employment Studies. November.

Rucci, A. (1997) Should HR survive? A profession at the crossroads. *Human Resource Management*. Vol 36, No 1. pp169–73.

Sands, S. (2004) Don't let them send you to Nebraska. *Daily Telegraph*. 14 August.

Schein, E. (1980) *Organisational psychology*. Englewoods Cliffs, NJ: Prentice Hall.

Schutz, W. (1966) *The interpersonal underworld: FIRO – a three dimensional theory of interpersonal behavior*. Palo Alto, CA: Science and Behavior Books.

Scott, W.R. (1987) *Organizations: rational, natural and open systems*. Englewood Cliffs, NJ: Prentice Hall.

Shafer, R., Dyer, L., Kilty, J., Amos, J. and Ericksen, J. (2001) Crafting a human resource strategy to foster organisational agility. *Human Resource Management*. Vol 40, No 3. pp197–211.

Slack, N., Chambers, L. and Johnston, R. (2007) *Operations management*. 5th edition. London: FT Prentice Hall.

Storey, J. (1992) *Developments in the management of human resources*. London: Blackwell.

Storr, F. (2009) Humberside TEC, a learning company. Available at: www.trojanmice.com/articles/becoming/htm

Stredwick, J. (1997) *Cases in reward management*. London: Kogan Page.

Swart, J., Kinnie, N. and Purcell, J. (2003) *People and performance in knowledge-intensive firms*. London: Chartered Institute of Personnel and Development.

Syedain, H. (2009) Mutual benefit. *People Management*. 5 November. pp30–3.

Taylor, F. (1947) *Scientific management*. New York: Harper and Row.

Taylor, S. (2008) *People resourcing*. 4th edition. London: Chartered Institute of Personnel and Development.

Thomas, K. (1976) Conflict and conflict management. In M.D. Dunette (ed.) *Handbook of industrial and organisational psychology*. New York: Rand McNally.

Thompson, M. (2000) *The competitive challenge: final report: the bottom line benefits of strategic human resource management*. London: Society of British Aerospace Companies.

Tuckman, B. (1965) Developmental sequence in small groups. *Psychological Bulletin*. Vol 63. pp384–99.

Ulrich, D. (1998) *Human resource champions: the next agenda for adding value and delivering results*. Boston, MA: Harvard Business School Press.

Ulrich, D. and Brockbank, W. (2005) *The HR value proposition*. Boston, MA: Harvard Business School Press.

University of Hull Business School. (2007) *Case study: Humberside Training and Enterprise Council*. Available at Itsy.co.uk/sisn/orange/humber.doc [Accessed 27 March 2013].

Weber, M. (1925) *Economy and society*. Oxford: Oxford University Press.

West, M. and Patterson, M. (1998) Profitable personnel. *People Management.* 8 January. pp28–31.

Wickens, P. (1987) *The road to Nissan: flexibility, quality, teamwork.* Basingstoke: MacMillan.

Wood, P. (1995) The four pillars of human resource management; are they connected? *Human Resource Management Journal.* Vol 5, No 5. pp49–59.

CHAPTER 3

The Competitive Environment

LEARNING OUTCOMES

By the end of this chapter, readers should be able to understand, explain and critically evaluate:

- the fundamental economic problem of scarcity and choice, and the ways in which this problem is tackled by market and mixed economies
- determinants of supply and demand
- the main types of market structure, including perfect and monopolistic competition, monopoly and oligopoly, and their implications for price and output
- pricing strategy
- Michael Porter's Five Forces model of competitive structure
- portfolio approaches to SBU analysis, including the Boston Matrix and the Shell Directional Policy Matrix
- the working of the labour market – wage determination and employment levels; perfect competition and monopsony models of the labour market
- changes in the industrial and employment structure in the UK
- the feminisation of the workforce
- the growth of flexible forms of organisation
- the nature and importance of the psychological contract
- work–life balance
- the changing nature and role of trade unions
- HR responses to changes in the competitive environment.

ECONOMIC SYSTEMS

Different types of societies have organised their economies in different ways, but all have to produce answers to the same questions, whatever their economic system.

REFLECTIVE ACTIVITY 3.1

Scarcity and choice

Economists often say that economics is about scarcity and choice. What do you think they mean by this? What problems are caused by the conflict of scarcity and choice?

Three main models have emerged:

- the command economy
- the market economy
- the mixed economy.

Of these we will consider the market and mixed economies in some depth. The pure command economy we can dismiss quite quickly, as it no longer exists in any real sense, except perhaps in North Korea. Here all economic decisions are made by the state, or rather by a central planning authority acting on the state's behalf, which decides what will be produced, by whom and who gets it. However, a command mentality was powerful in Western economies at least until the 1970s. In the UK, large sectors of the economy were controlled by the state through nationalised industries. For example, the Labour Government of the 1960s decided that the way to meet the country's future energy requirements was through nuclear power, and in particular the development of untested advanced gas-cooled reactors (AGRs). The decision was disastrous. Each reactor took up to 20 years to build and they did not reach their planned output until the 1990s. In 1996 prices they cost over £50 billion to build (Kay 2003, pp91–3). When British Energy was privatised in 1996, the AGRs were sold for £1.9 billion, but only after the state agreed to underwrite liabilities for future decommissioning costs.

Nor was the private sector much different. The 1960s and 1970s were the heyday of detailed quantitative corporate planning, which in many companies bore a close resemblance to the Soviet Union's Five-Year Plans. A classic example, also discussed by Kay, was General Electric. When Jack Welch took over as CEO in 1981, he inherited what the US Defense Department described as 'the world's most effective strategic planning system'. Welch promptly dismantled the whole elaborate planning system and in its place brought in systematic decentralisation of decision-making (Kay 2003, pp96–7).

THE MARKET ECONOMY

Here economic decisions are taken on the basis of prices. There are no central planners and decisions are taken by millions of individual consumers and producers. Producers produce only what they can sell to consumers, workers sell their services to producers and receive income, which they use to buy goods and services from the producers. In the last resort it is thus the consumers who decide what is produced (consumer sovereignty) and the economy is a closed two-player system.

Figure 3.1 Flows in the market economy

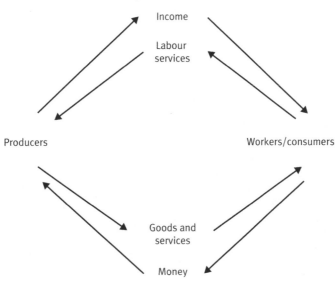

Our core economic problems are thus answered as follows:

- what is going to be produced – anything which consumers are prepared to buy (demand in the jargon)
- how is it going to be produced – in the most efficient way; if a producer is not efficient, he will be driven out of business by an efficient one
- who is going to get it – anyone who is prepared to pay for it.

MIXED ECONOMIES

In practice all economies are mixed to a greater or lesser extent. Command elements commonly include:

- a framework of law – the law of contract, company law
- publicly provided social goods such as defence, police, education, welfare and health
- publicly owned industries – the BBC in the UK, Amtrak in the US, Électricité de France in France
- state regulation of the level of economic activity
- control of economic behaviour – employment law, anti-trust law, anti-discrimination law, etc
- often the use of taxation to redistribute income as well as to raise revenue for public services.

Indeed, the state is essential to the efficient working of a capitalist economy. As President Obama said in a campaign speech in July 2012, 'Look, if you've been successful, you did not get there on your own. ... If you were successful, somebody along the line gave you some help.' He cited great teachers, government research, and roads and bridges as examples, echoing the work of the liberal sociologist Leonard Hobhouse (1864–1929), who argued that government investment, funded by taxation, was a fundamental requirement for effective capitalism, and that capitalism required the interaction of society, social capital and the entrepreneur. It is perhaps significant that Obama's argument was immediately condemned by Fox News as 'socialism' (Hutton 2012).

Throughout the rest of this chapter, we will be analysing the working of the mixed economy, with particular reference to the UK.

CASE STUDY 3.1

MARKETS IN THE NHS

In an article in the *Guardian*, a Sheffield GP, Paul Hodgkin, discusses the different types of market operating in the NHS:

- *The market economy* – this is the model which underpins the concept of patient choice, where informed consumers choose between different providers, thus driving up quality. Unfortunately, there are at least two snags. First, in the public sector, markets are zero sum. As spending is capped, more spent on one procedure means less on another. Second, consumers (patients) are not informed, and they are not attempting to 'buy' a desirable good. No-one in their right mind would positively desire a major operation! The patient is by definition anxious and frequently not in a fit state to take an informed decision.
- *The barter economy* – this most clearly operates between the NHS and social services. Partnerships here are only possible given local give and take and mutual obligations – do me a favour today with patient X and next month I'll do the same for you.
- *The centrally planned economy* – evidence-based medicine, treatment dictated by the National Institute for Health and Clinical Excellence, targets, star ratings, inspections and so on.
- *The gift economy* – this has always existed throughout the public sector and is part of the public service ethos – giving more than is strictly required under contract, for the good of the patient. Hodgkin sees this as being eroded in the NHS, as new contracts become much more restrictive and time-based. A classic example of the gift economy which Hodgkin does not mention was identified in the NHS many decades ago – the totally free and voluntary UK blood donor scheme (Hodgkin 2007).

MARKET STRUCTURES

Economists classify market structures by the number of firms within the market (and to a lesser extent the number of purchasers).

The main classifications are:

- perfect competition
- monopolistic competition
- monopoly
- oligopoly.

There are also two other less commonly found firms:

- monopsony
- bilateral monopoly.

PERFECT COMPETITION

This is a market where no one producer has an advantage over any other producer. There are many producers, none of whom has a sufficient share of the market to be able to influence the market price. They are known as price-takers. Similarly, there are a large number of buyers, who are also price-takers. The price in the market is set by supply and demand.

Demand measures the amount of the good or service which buyers are willing to buy at a given price (note not the amount they need – demand is based on willingness to pay). Broadly speaking, the lower the price the greater the quantity which buyers will demand. This enables us to plot a demand curve – in practice plotted as a straight line (Figure 3.2).

Figure 3.2 A typical demand curve

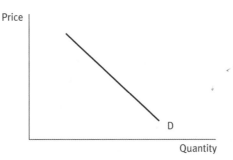

If the price rises, the quantity which buyers are prepared to buy will fall. This is known as a fall in quantity demanded. On the other hand, some external event may mean that buyers are prepared to buy more of the product at all prices – perhaps their incomes have increased. This is known as a rise in demand, and is illustrated on our diagram by a shift of the demand curve to the right (Figure 3.3). Similarly, a fall in demand is shown by a shift of the curve to the left.

Figure 3.3 An increase in demand

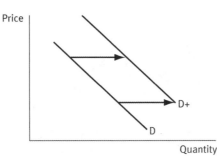

The same principles apply to supply. Broadly speaking, the quantity of a good which producers are prepared to supply is higher the higher the price, producing a supply curve (Figure 3.4). Again, a movement along this line is known as a change in quantity supplied; a shift of the curve rightwards or leftwards is known as an increase or decrease in supply.

Figure 3.4 The supply curve

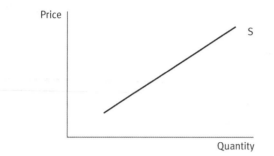

If we put together the supply curve and the demand curve, we get Figure 3.5. This shows that there is one unique combination of price and quantity where the two lines intersect (point E). This sets the price that will be charged in that market and the quantity which will be bought and sold, and crucially this is an outcome which is equally acceptable to both buyers and sellers.

Figure 3.5 Supply, demand and equilibrium

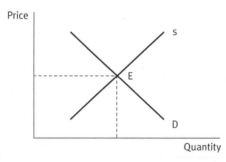

REFLECTIVE ACTIVITY 3.2

Oil prices

In 1973, Opec quadrupled the world price of oil overnight. The result was a severe bout of stagflation for the world economy – simultaneous rising inflation and unemployment. In 1990–91, the oil price again rose rapidly in the build-up to the first Gulf War. However, after the war, oil prices quickly fell back, and by the late 1990s were at their lowest level for many years. In 2003, oil prices again rose rapidly in the build-up to the second Gulf War, but this time, after a brief fall in the immediate aftermath of the war, they have continued to rise, and on 2 January 2008 reached $100 a barrel, five times their low in the late 1990s. Despite this, world inflation has stayed relatively low and economic growth has stayed high. Oil prices eventually peaked at around $150 a barrel, before collapsing after the onset of the world recession in mid-2008. After falling to around $35, they then recovered to stabilise at around $70 in mid-2009, although by 2011–12 they had risen again to around $100.

Questions

1   Why were oil prices so high from the war in 2003 to mid-2008?

2   Why did the increase in the price of oil after 2003 not lead to stagflation, as in the mid-1970s?

3   Why have oil prices risen since the start of
    the recession, although many economies
    have not recovered to their 2008 levels?

The product sold in a perfectly competitive market is assumed to be identical – thus there is no reason to favour one seller over another on grounds of quality or special features or service. It is also assumed that all players in the market are extremely well informed and capable of reacting very quickly to any changes. There is thus no point in advertising – all products are identical and buyers know them to be identical. Buyers will react very quickly to any change in price, while sellers will very rapidly copy any innovation introduced by one of their rivals. Entry to the market is also completely free – anyone can enter or leave the market at any time.

Because of the nature of the market, there is no incentive for any one seller to cut his price – remember he can sell as much as he likes at the current market price. Conversely, if he raises his price even a fraction above the market level, he will sell nothing, because there is no incentive for his customers to stay loyal.

Economists freely admit that perfect competition is extremely unlikely to exist in the real world – its assumptions are too restrictive. Why spend so much space describing it, you may say? The reason is that it is a classic example of an economic model – it is a stylised attempt to explain behaviour, rather than a prescription for managers who want to make sound decisions. Models simplify the real world and cut it down to its bare essentials, and on the basis of these bare essentials they make logical predictions. Thus the essence of the perfect competition model is to say that if the real world was like this, certain predictions would logically follow from it.

One consequence of the model is that it would lead to an efficient use of resources in the economy. Market forces would push production costs down to the minimum and ensure that the most efficient production methods are used. Any firm which did not use them would be forced out of business. Profits would also be forced down to the minimum level required to keep firms in business. Any firm which made more profits than the minimum in the short term would be unable to sustain this position in the long term. Unfortunately, this also writes economic progress out of the model. There is no incentive to innovate or develop new products, because any advantage will be immediately wiped out through perfect knowledge.

It is also possible to apply the perfect competition model to labour markets. The lower the wage, the higher the number of workers which will be demanded by employers, while the higher the wage, the greater the incentive to work in that industry. The only difference is that people's labour services are being sold, rather than, say, apples. Again, the result will be a market equilibrium – exactly the number of workers who are prepared to work for the equilibrium wage will be employed. The labour market will be examined in more detail later in this chapter.

MONOPOLISTIC COMPETITION

Rather more likely is that many firms will compete in a market, but each will sell a slightly different product. This type of market is classified as monopolistic competition. As the product is differentiated, the firms in the market have slightly more freedom in setting their prices. They can decide to charge a slightly higher price and sell a slightly lower volume of goods, and vice versa. To a small extent they are price-makers. They can build up customer loyalty and loyal customers will be prepared to pay a higher price for what they perceive as higher quality, or a closer match with their precise requirements, either in the product itself or in the services which surround its delivery. Each firm is thus seeking to obtain a mini-monopoly for its product.

Not that a real difference in product is not necessary – what is required is that consumers perceive there to be a difference. Firms in monopolistic competition frequently advertise in order to differentiate their product, while firms in perfect competition do not, as they can sell all they wish anyway.

MONOPOLY

Theoretically, a firm has a monopoly if it is the only firm supplying a market – ie it has 100 per cent of the market. This is very rare in practice, particularly if one defines a market widely. The Post Office has a monopoly in the UK for delivery of letters of a certain weight, but we also need to include close substitutes for letters in our definition of this market. Once we do this, it is clear that the Post Office faces competition in information transfer from a host of organisations and services, including email, faxes and courier services. Virtually the only organisation with anything approaching a worldwide monopoly is Microsoft, whose operating systems have about 90 per cent of the PC market. Even here, in practice the monopoly is weakened by software piracy, with some estimates saying that half of all software in the UK is illegally copied.

In practice economists tend to define monopoly functionally – a firm is in a monopoly position if it is able to control the market price of the product it produces. This depends on the size of the firm relative to that of other firms in the industry. If firms in the industry tend to be large, the market leader may need to have perhaps half the market in order to dominate, but in an industry characterised by very small firms, 20 per cent of the market may be enough.

Because it has some control over price, a monopoly can manipulate the price and the quantity which it produces in order to maximise its own profit. Thus price will tend to be higher and quantity produced lower than in a competitive market. This does not necessarily mean that a monopoly will make an excessive profit. If no one wants to buy the product sold by the monopoly, there will be no excessive profit. Being the only producer of horse-drawn hansom cabs is not the best shortcut to a fortune!

However, monopoly does have a tendency to excess profit, as well as other disadvantages. It encourages inefficiency in management and production, as there is no competition to force efficiency, and, most crucially, monopoly leads to a misallocation of resources in the economy as a whole. This would tend to suggest that monopoly will not be in the best interests of consumers and therefore should be at worst controlled, at best banned. This is broadly the approach taken by anti-trust legislation in the US.

In practice things are not so simple. Often monopolists can gain significant cost advantages (economies of scale) purely because they are big and the end result might be both higher profits for the monopolist and a lower price for the consumer. As we will see later, this argument is put forward by supermarkets in the UK. This argument (the natural monopoly argument) has been put forward to oppose the break-up of British Rail at privatisation. Similarly, it may be judged desirable for a company to have a monopoly in the UK market, if the result is that it is big enough to compete efficiently on the world market. As a an example, the Monopolies Commission in the 1970s and 1980s was prepared to tolerate both British Airways' dominant position in the UK market and its takeover of competitors like British Caledonian and Dan-Air.

There is also a view that monopolies and monopoly profits may well be a necessary part of the competitive process (Schumpeter 1950). Entrepreneurs are continually trying to exploit new opportunities. If they do so, they will achieve a temporary monopoly. Unless this monopoly arises from the sole ownership of a resource for which there is no substitute, the monopoly will be temporary because other firms will recognise the opportunity and enter the market, or they will devise substitute products. Schumpeter called this process 'creative destruction'.

Profits may thus be true monopoly profits, based on ability to restrict entry to the industry; windfall profits, based on short-term fluctuations in the environment and which in different circumstances could be windfall losses, and entrepreneurial profits, based on superior foresight or management, exploiting opportunities which were open to all. This view is supported by the law on patents. Anyone may invent a new process or product, but the reward for doing so is to be granted a temporary monopoly by the state, in return for the entrepreneurial risk and research and development expenses which have been incurred. Patent protection is the driving force behind industries like pharmaceuticals.

Following this view, the key element in assessing monopoly power is not market share but barriers to entry. This has led to the development of the concept of contestable markets (Lipsey and Chrystal 1999). Markets are contestable if entry is easy, entrants can compete on equal terms with incumbents and they are not deterred by the threat of retaliatory price-cutting by incumbents. The threat of entry to the market can be as effective as actual entry.

OLIGOPOLY

An oligopoly exists when a few large producers control a market between them. The number of firms may vary between two (a duopoly) and about a dozen, and the products can be homogeneous or diversified. Oligopolies are also known as complex monopolies, and it is the latter term which is used by the UK competition authorities. In all cases, the firms in the industry are interdependent. The performance of each firm depends not only on its own actions, but also on the actions of the other firms in the industry. Thus, for example, before an oligopoly takes the decision to raise its prices, it must decide whether the other firms are likely to follow, or to keep their prices down and aggressively push to increase their market shares.

Oligopoly is extremely common in the UK. Indeed, think of any major consumer good or service, and it will almost certainly be supplied by oligopoly firms – cars, petrol, banks, cigarettes, soap powder, instant coffee, chocolate, baked beans, etc.

One way of measuring oligopoly is by calculation of the five-firm concentration ratio. This is simply the share of the market in percentage terms held by the five largest firms. The higher this figure, the higher the degree of oligopoly.

Table 3.1 UK concentration ratios, 2004

Industry	Concentration ratio
Five most concentrated	
Sugar	99 per cent
Tobacco	99 per cent
Gas distribution	82 per cent
Oils and fats	88 per cent
Confectionery	81 per cent
Five least concentrated	
Metal forging	4 per cent
Plastic products	4 per cent
Furniture	5 per cent
Construction	5 per cent

Industry	Concentration ratio
Structural metal products	6 per cent

Source: National Statistics Economic Trends: Concentration Ratios 2004

Remember that these figures only cover UK producers. As a result of globalisation, all manufacturers are subject to greater and greater international competition, and only in tobacco, of the industries listed in Table 3.1, can the UK be considered world class. Real oligopoly power is higher in services, where there is less chance of competition from imports. The five-firm ratio in food retailing in 2004 was 75, and this has become a four-firm ratio since the takeover of firm number four (Safeway) by Morrisons (number five). In the case of food production and retailing, we have a bilateral oligopoly. Many branded goods are produced by oligopolies and then sold through oligopolies.

Firms in an oligopoly market have a choice between a number of broad types of behaviour:

Collusion

One possible outcome is that the firms in the industry join together and collectively behave as if they were a monopolist. They can then collectively exploit any monopoly profits which are available. An extreme form of this type of behaviour is a cartel or price ring such as OPEC (the Organization of the Petroleum Exporting Countries). Unfortunately from the point of view of potential cartel members, in most countries cartels and other forms of collusive behaviour are illegal. Cartels also tend to be unstable. They must have some mechanism for dividing up production and market quotas among their members, and this is fraught with difficulty. There is also a great temptation for individual members to cheat on their quotas. The cartel may be undercut by new producers (such as UK oil in the 1970s), or new substitutes may be developed (as happened to a limited extent after the oil price hikes of 1973 and 1979).

Price war

An opposite possibility may be a price war, with the aim of driving the competition out of business and eventually emerging with a single-firm monopoly, which can then be exploited. The enormous risk, of course, is that you might lose and yourself be forced out of business. In nearly all cases, the stakes are simply too high and the risks too great. Indeed, in many cases it is only the market leader which can afford the risk of a price war and it is the market leader which has the least need of one. In practice, most apparent price wars are extremely limited and are used by the market leader as a sharp shock to the rest of the industry to stay in line. There are also risks in winning a price war. Driving a weak competitor out of business may just create a vacuum which can be filled by a much more formidable rival. A parallel would be the decision taken by the US to disband the Iraqi army after victory in the Iraq war in 2003. This left a military and political power vacuum which was quickly filled by sectarian militia groups and by Al-Qaeda.

Non-price competition

Rather than risk an all-out price war, firms will frequently engage in non-price competition – they will compete on everything except price. This might include competitions, quality, individual features, BOGOF (buy one get one free – for a limited period). The aim is not to drive the competition out of business, but to gain a marginal increase in market share. All participants understand the rules of the game and know very well that the war is limited, not total. Another possible form of non-price competition is complexity. In the old days, there was one mortgage rate, charged by all mortgage lenders on all mortgages. Now there are a multiplicity of different types of mortgage, each with its own terms and conditions, with the result that it is almost impossible to compare rates. The same thing has happened with utility pricing.

OLIGOPOLY AND THE CUT-PRICE AIRLINE INDUSTRY

The cut-price airline industry has developed in the UK since the mid-1990s, on the lines pioneered in the US by Southwest Airlines. It is based on providing a no-frills service at low cost. It is dominated by two firms, Ryanair and easyJet, who between them control half of the total European low-cost market. Both Ryanair and easyJet are constantly engaged in sniping at each other, with each claiming that it has the lowest fares and that the other is inefficient, incompetent or worse. There appears to be every sign of a constant price war, with both companies sometimes in effect offering free flights and offers of twice the fare back if a customer can find the same flight cheaper elsewhere. However, appearances can be deceptive. Until 2003, the main target of Ryanair's knocking copy was its *bête noire*, the Irish state airline Aer Lingus (which it unsuccessfully tried to take over in 2007), while easyJet's prime target was British Airways, and particularly its low-cost subsidiary Go. Neither has the serious intention of driving the other out of business. Direct competition between them (in the sense of flights to and from the same airport) is limited. On a strict definition, Ryanair and easyJet are direct competitors on only one route, London Stansted to Rome Ciampino. As a result, the 'price guarantee' is almost meaningless. The price war is aimed much more at deterring new entrants to the industry (both Ryanair and easyJet have each taken over one of their main competitors, Buzz in the case of Ryanair and Go in the case of easyJet), and to squeeze better terms out of airports (who gain from a big throughput of passengers).

Price leadership

Here one firm within the industry is regarded unofficially as the price leader. If the leader changes its prices, the other firms in the industry are likely to follow suit. In order to be legal, it is essential that there is no collusion between the firms.

Game theory

Here the firm makes assumptions about the nature of the environment and the behaviour of competitors. Game theory is a huge area, but two simple strategies which can be followed are *maximax*, where the firm assumes that the best possible combination of circumstances will happen and chooses the strategy which will maximise its position in this favourable set of circumstances, and *maximin*, where the firm assumes that the worst will happen and chooses the best (or least bad) strategy on these pessimistic assumptions.

MONOPSONY AND BILATERAL MONOPOLY

Monopsony is a market form where there is a monopoly buyer. Normally the monopsonist is the Government or one of its agencies. For example, for all practical purposes the NHS is a monopsony buyer of pharmaceuticals in the UK. If we have a market where a monopoly is selling to a monopsony, we have a bilateral monopoly. This applies where the NHS buys a particular patented drug from one pharmaceutical company. Monopsony will be important in our later discussion of the labour market (as well as the buyer version of oligopoly, known as oligopsony!).

PRICING STRATEGY

A fundamental distinction in economics is between price-takers (who have no control over the price which they can charge) and price-makers (who have some degree of control over their prices). As we have seen above, price-takers are characteristic of perfect competition, while price-makers have some degree of monopoly power. If we argue that perfect competition does not exist in the real world, all sellers are to some degree price-makers, with the level of their control over prices dependent on their degree of monopoly power.

However, the degree of control over price depends not just on the position of the seller, but also on the perceptions of the buyer. Nagle and Holden (2002) identify nine factors that influence how price sensitive a buyer is likely to be:

1   reference price effect – price sensitivity for a given product increases the higher the product's price relative to alternatives

2   difficult comparison effect – price sensitivity decreases when it is difficult to compare the product with alternatives

3   switching costs effect – the higher the investment a buyer must make to switch suppliers, the less price sensitive the buyer will be (for example, older consumers and utility prices)

4   price-quality effect – buyers are less sensitive to price the more that higher prices signal higher quality

5   expenditure effect – the higher the percentage of budget accounted for by the purchase, the more price sensitive the buyer will be

6   end-benefit effect – the smaller the given component's share of the total cost of the end benefit, the less sensitive the buyer will be to the component's price (think cigarettes and matches for a smoker)

7   shared cost effect – the smaller the proportion of purchase price buyers must pay for themselves, the less price sensitive they will be

8   fairness effect – buyers are more price sensitive when the price is higher than they perceive as 'fair'

9   framing effect – buyers are more price sensitive when they perceive the price as a loss rather than a foregone gain.

ALTERNATIVE PRICING STRATEGIES

Different pricing strategies are appropriate in different circumstances. Here we examine some of the more popular:

- *premium pricing* – used where there is a unique brand and a substantial competitive advantage – top-end cruises or first-class air travel
- *economy pricing* – the opposite of premium pricing, a no-frills low price – this is typical of budget airlines and of many supermarkets (see Case Study 3.3)
- *promotional pricing* – money-off vouchers, sales or BOGOFs (see Case Study 3.3)
- *optional product pricing* – charging more for optional extras – the budget airline Ryanair is a past master at this, even charging extra for things which few would see as optional, such as buying a ticket!

- *captive product pricing* – where products have complements, charging a premium price for the complement as the consumer has no choice – the classic example is razors and razor blades, but the same is true of computer printers and toners/ink cartridges
- *penetration pricing* – the price charged for a new product is set artificially low in order to gain market share, and once this is achieved, the price is increased – this strategy was used by satellite TV companies in the UK
- *skimming* – a company charges a higher price for a new product because it has a substantial but short-term competitive advantage – it skims the cream off the market before competitors move in; new product pricing strategies were discussed by Joel Dean in a classic *HBR* article (Dean 1950, 1976)
- *price discrimination* – charging different consumers different prices for the same product – a classic example – the pricing strategy of the budget airlines – is discussed in Case Study 3.4. In order for price discrimination to work it is essential that the seller must be able to prevent arbitrage – the development of a secondary market in which the product or service can be resold. In the case of the airlines, tickets are non-transferable.

CASE STUDY 3.3 · SUPERMARKET PRICING STRATEGY

Supermarkets in the UK are in intense competition with each other and pricing strategy is one element of this competition. They have a choice of three basic strategies:

- everyday low pricing (EDLP), where low prices are consistently maintained
- promotion pricing, where the general level of price is higher, but there is a rolling programme of special offer promotions, often BOGOFs (buy one, get one free)
- combination pricing, combining both EDLP and promotions.

Historically, the main proponents of EDLP have been Asda and Morrisons, while Sainsbury's led on promotions and Tesco on the mixed strategy.

A survey by the Institute of Grocery in 2003 found that 60 per cent of shoppers preferred EDLP, while 40 per cent preferred promotions. EDLP was particularly favoured by lower-income shoppers and those in the north of England. BOGOFs were more favoured by larger households, shoppers who were not working and those in the south-east. However, even those who favoured EDLP felt that it took much of the interest out of shopping. As Joanne Denney-Finch, the chief executive of the IGD, put it, 'It is... clear that promotions are not just about reducing the overall cost of shopping, but are liked because they bring variety and excitement to what can be a routine task.' It is probably significant that the most successful supermarket of the 2000s, Tesco, consistently follows a mixed strategy (Food and Drink Europe 2003).

Attitudes may have changed with the onset of the recession. EDLP seems to have become much more popular with shoppers. All the major retailers now emphasise low prices and price-matching with their competitors, particularly with Tesco. This is true of Waitrose, which traditionally has emphasised quality rather than price, and of Budgens, which has relied heavily on fortnightly promotions backed by heavy local distribution of flier leaflets. Both now consciously price-match with Tesco on many products.

It should also be borne in mind that consumers may not be as price sensitive as supermarkets assume. A study in Florida found that fewer than half of supermarket shoppers knew the price of the article which they had just selected. Most underestimated the price and 20 per cent could not even guess at the price (Skapinker 2004).

EASYJET AND DYNAMIC PRICING

The classic way to price a product is to charge each consumer exactly the same price. Tesco and Sainsbury's do not haggle with their customers – a price is published and the customer takes it or leaves it. However, supermarkets do reduce prices as goods approach their sell-by date or perishable goods are unlikely to keep until the next day. This is an example of dynamic pricing or yield management – if the alternative is to throw the good away, any price for it is better than nothing.

A much more sophisticated use of the dynamic pricing model is common in the airline industry. Taking advantage of its computerised reservations system and the deregulation of airlines in the US in the late 1970s, American Airlines introduced dynamic pricing in the early 1980s, charging different customers different fares, depending on when they booked their flight. This is much easier to do online than in the physical market, as the costs involved in changing prices are much lower. American is alleged to make up to $500 million a year through its dynamic pricing system. It changes half a million prices each day, an enormous number, as it only carries 50,000 passengers a day (McAfee and te Velde 2005). The model is widely used by the low-cost airlines in the UK and has been copied by full-cost carriers such as British Airways. The result is that theoretically each passenger on a particular flight might have paid a different fare, although they are all consuming the same product – a flight from A to B.

The economic theory underlying dynamic pricing is price discrimination – the idea that different consumers will place a different value on the same product and that, if possible, the seller will strive to extract as much of this value as possible from each customer (Weiss and Mehrotra 2001).

The classic model for dynamic airline pricing is that the price will start low for a flight which is several weeks or even months ahead. This will attract the tourist or leisure market, where customers are not prepared to pay a premium price but are prepared to book some time ahead of the flight. As the date of the flight approaches, the price will rise, attracting business travellers, who are less price sensitive and who may well have to fly at relatively short notice. As the date of the flight approaches, the price will fall if there are still a large number of seats unsold or will rise if the plane is nearly full.

To test the model, I plotted the prices charged by easyJet on one particular flight, flight 211 from London Stansted to Glasgow, departing on 3 July 2007 at 11.25am. I checked the price being charged on the easyJet website once a day from 3 June 2007 until the day of take-off on 3 July (easyJet 2007).

The results confirmed the classic model. The price on 3 June was £4.99 and remained at this level until 13 June, when easyJet started its summer sale, and the price fell to £2.99. It stayed at that price until 20 June, when it rose to £7.99, but it was back to £2.99 on the next two days. It then started a steady rise – £7.99 on 23 June, £11.99 on 24 June and £16.99 on 27 June. The price remained at £16.99 until 1 July, when it rose to £30.99 and then to £38.99 on 2 and 3 July.

Stelios Haji-Ioannou, the founder of easyJet, is a passionate advocate of dynamic pricing, and he has applied the concept in at least two other of his many ventures, easyCinema and easyInternetcafe. However, both of these projects were failures. Part of the problem was a general lack of demand for the products, but there was also a fundamental flaw in the dynamic pricing model as applied to these products. Although the supply conditions were appropriate for value management, this was not true of demand conditions. In the case of the airline, price discrimination is possible because different customers do value a flight differently, but this does not really apply to a cinema seat or an hour in an Internet café (*Economist* 2003).

REFLECTIVE ACTIVITY 3.3

The Serengeti National Park – an example of price discrimination

The Serengeti National Park in northern Tanzania is generally regarded as the finest game reserve in Africa. With an area of 15,000 square kilometres, it is three-quarters the size of Wales, it is estimated to contain 2 million wildebeest, half a million zebra, and 3,000 lions (Briggs 2009). The park effectively continues over the Kenyan border as the Maasai Mara National Park and it straddles one of the major road routes between Tanzania and Kenya.

Entry charges to the national park vary enormously depending on nationality. Citizens of the five East African Community countries (Tanzania, Kenya, Uganda, Rwanda and Burundi) pay 1,500 Tanzanian shillings a day (approximately $1 at summer 2012 exchange rates), while foreigners pay $50 a day (Tanzania National Parks 2009).

Questions

1   Can the enormous differential in entry charges be justified?

2   Why not let Tanzanian citizens into the park for nothing?

COMPETITIVE STRUCTURE

MICHAEL PORTER'S FIVE FORCES MODEL

The economic theory of market structure, distinguishing perfect and monopolistic competition, monopoly and oligopoly, provides a powerful but inevitably simplified model. The real industrial world is much more complex. One important model which attempts to match this complexity is Michael Porter's Five Forces model of competitive rivalry (Porter 1980).

According to the model, the structure of competition in an industry can be described in terms of five major forces. These are:

1   the threat of entry of new firms

2   the power of buyers

3   the power of suppliers

4   the power of substitutes

5   the intensity of rivalry among existing firms.

Each of the five forces is itself determined by a number of different factors. When the five forces are completely analysed, this determines how attractive the industry is to firms within it and to those who might wish to enter it.

Unlike economic models, the value of this model lies not in its predictive ability, but in the way in which it provides a checklist whereby particular firms can clearly analyse and define their own position in relation to their own industry. It is a tool which can be used as the first stage of strategic analysis.

The threat of entry

The threat of entry of new firms to an industry depends on the extent of barriers to entry. These include:

- *Economies of scale* – some industries have very high economies of scale – unit costs of output fall considerably as output increases, as in the car industry or the aircraft industry. Others have very low economies of scale, for example estate agency. A new firm seeking to enter an industry with big economies of scale must either buy a high market share on entry or suffer a cost disadvantage. Economies of scale are measured by the concept of minimum efficient scale (MES), or the market share which is necessary to compete at minimum unit cost. It is also possible to calculate the cost penalty incurred by producing at below this volume. However, note first that globalisation has meant increasingly that what is significant is not share of the UK market, but share of a world market, and second, that lean production and flexible manufacturing techniques like 'just in time' (JIT) have somewhat reduced the importance of economies of scale.
- *Capital requirements* – capital-intensive industries such as the car industry have a very high cost of entry, while an online consultancy operating from home has a very low cost of entry.
- *Access to distribution channels* – a new entrant must establish its own distribution channels. For example, it is difficult to persuade supermarkets to stock new products in competition with existing brands. Reforms in the tied house system, and the spread of the concept of guest beers, have made it easier for small real ale brewers to gain a foothold in the beer market.
- *Absolute cost advantages* – established firms in an industry frequently gain from a learning curve effect, which gives them a cost advantage over new entrants. In other cases incumbents may use a technology or process which is protected by patents.
- *Expected retaliation* – the likely reaction of existing firms is key. If incumbents are expected to retaliate to defend their markets, entry becomes more difficult.
- *Government policy* – in some cases, the Government might restrict entry (commercial television and radio). In other cases, government policy might open up a market to competition (the telephone directory enquiries service).
- *Differentiation* – if existing operators have established a strong brand image for their products or services, this effectively deters new entrants. Existing operators often produce a wide range of brands to plug all possible niches in the market.
- *Switching costs for buyers* – if it is very expensive for buyers to switch to a new supplier, this will deter new entrants to the market. For example, if you have a gas central heating system, it is very expensive for you to switch to electricity, but very cheap to switch to a new gas supplier.

The power of buyers

Buyer power will depend on:

- *Concentration of buyers* – if there is only a small number of buyers, buyer power will be high, particularly if the volume purchases of the buyers are high. For example, although cola drinks are sold through a multiplicity of outlets, high-volume sales are dependent on the big supermarket chains, and even Coca-Cola does not have the muscle to dictate terms to them.

- *Alternative sources of supply*– if the buyer is able to shop around, this will increase his power. This may come about because deregulation of markets has produced new competitors. For example, when the gas industry was privatised and deregulated, consumers became able to buy gas from a large number of possible suppliers, not just British Gas. Similarly, the ending of pre-entry trade union closed shops has helped buyers of labour such as the newspaper industry.
- *Component cost as a percentage of total cost* – if materials form a high percentage of the total cost of a finished product, there is a greater incentive for buyers to shop around. Thus the provision of power to a steel works forms a high percentage of cost, while the provision of paper clips to a management consultancy forms a very low percentage.
- *Possibility of backward integration* – if there is a risk that the buyer may be in a position to set up his own supply operation, this increases the buyer's power.

Power relationships between buyers and suppliers can be changed as a result of deliberate strategic decisions. For example, car manufacturers since the 1980s have followed a deliberate strategy of reducing the number of their suppliers. Suppliers have gained bigger orders and greater security, but at the cost of strict adherence to quality and JIT requirements.

Power of sellers

Seller power will depend on:

- *Number of suppliers* – the smaller the number of suppliers, the greater their power, as in any other monopoly or oligopoly situation.
- *Switching costs* – if switching costs to another supplier are high, this will increase seller power, particularly in a situation where the product supplied is highly specialised and the supplier is integrated into the production process, for example in a JIT environment.
- *Brand power* – if the supplier's brand is powerful, this will give them more bargaining power. For example, Heinz or Kellogg's, who do not produce own brands, can exercise influence over supermarkets, who have to stock the brand leader.
- *Possibility of forward integration* –if there is a risk that the seller may be in a position to set up his own distribution operation, this increases the seller's power.
- *Dependence on customer* – if the supplier is not dependent on selling a high volume of output to a particular customer, and his individual customers are generally small, this will increase seller power.
- *Threat of substitutes* – the threat of substitution can take many forms. There could be technological substitution of one product for another – the fax for the letter, then the email for the fax. In the last resort all goods are substitutes for each other, because they are all competing for consumer spending. This is particularly true of non-essential goods, where there is the ultimate substitute of doing without.

Key questions that need to be addressed are:

- *Relative price and performance of substitutes*–if substitutes are available that offer similar performance at comparable prices, the threat of substitution is very strong and limits are put on the ability to charge high prices – for example brands of pet food.
- *Switching costs* – the cheaper it is for consumers to switch to other products, the higher the threat of substitutes. Switching costs for pet food appear to be zero, as long as the pet is prepared to eat the substitute!
- *Buyers' willingness to substitute* – if an article is both low cost and an infrequent purchase, little effort is likely to be put into shopping around. No-one shops around for the best-value box of matches.

Competitive rivalry

Competitive rivalry is to some extent a function of the other factors. However, there are other special factors:

- *Industry growth* – if the industry is growing rapidly, there is plenty in the cake for everyone so competition does not need to be intense. As an industry moves into the maturity phase of its lifecycle, competition will become more intense.
- *High fixed costs* – this is likely to lead to a high break-even point, and the likelihood of price wars in times of depression to maintain turnover. See for example the steel wars of the late 1990s, when the US and the EU each accused the other of dumping steel on export markets.
- *Volatile demand* – this is likely to lead to intermittent overcapacity, with resultant price wars – steel again.
- *Product differentiation* – the more homogeneous the product, the more intense the rivalry – steel yet again.
- *Extra capacity in large increments* – the competitor making such an addition is likely to create at least short-term overcapacity. For example, in the late 1980s, the Japanese car firms Nissan, Toyota and Honda all built new car assembly plants in the UK.
- *Balance of firms* – if the number of firms is large and/or firms are of a similar size, the risks of aggression may appear acceptable and rivalry will be intense, although probably not lethal. Conversely, a clear market leader can enforce discipline in the industry.
- *High exit barriers* – if there are high exit barriers, excess capacity is likely to persist and rivalry to be intense. This would apply, for example, if there were high pollution clean-up costs associated with decommissioning a plant.

Bear in mind when using Five Forces that it is an analytical technique which can tell you where you are now, probably why you are there, but not how to get to where you want to get. There is also a danger in carrying out more and more detailed analysis – paralysis by analysis!

CRITICISMS OF FIVE FORCES

It must be remembered that Porter takes an economist's approach to his analysis. As a result, his model is oversimplified and makes some basic assumptions. In particular, it is a static analysis. It assumes that change will be slow and that, as a result, the firm can take a planned approach to strategy once it has carried out its Five Forces analysis. This view is challenged by more recent writers on strategic management, who advocate a much more experimental emergent approach to strategic management (see Chapter 10).

There are also some serious gaps in the Five Forces analysis. It ignores the influence of government, and of regulation, which restricts the freedom of organisations to act as they might like. It is very much a private sector model and so much less relevant to the public or not-for-profit sectors. It also assumes that competition is a zero-sum game – if one organisation wins, another must lose. However, it does not take account of co-operation-based strategies such as strategic alliances or joint ventures (Lynch 2006).

The Five Forces analysis was a product of its time. Porter was writing before the economy was transformed by mass computerisation and the Internet. In a comprehensive critique of Five Forces, Larry Downes (1997) identified three new forces which had to be taken into account:

- *Digitalisation* – the development of the Internet means that all players now have instant access to enormous amounts of information. As a result, change has become much more rapid than in the late 1970s and the environment much more unpredictable. As a result, new competitors can appear extremely quickly and from outside the conventional definition of an industry. Examples would be the way in which the bookselling industry has been transformed by the rise of Amazon and the travel agency industry by the rise of online bookings.

- *Globalisation* – businesses now operate on a global scale and customers, using the Internet, can shop around and compare prices on a global scale. A Five Forces analysis must now take account of global as well as of national trends.
- *Deregulation* – in the UK, the US and the EU, many industries have been radically deregulated since Porter wrote about the Five Forces. Again, the effect is to make the environment more dynamic, complex and unpredictable. An example is the explosive growth of low-cost airlines such as Ryanair and easyJet and the effect which they have had on the environment facing full-cost airlines such as British Airways.

Remember, though, that just as Porter was a product of his time, so was Downes. He was writing in 1997, approaching the peak of the dot-com boom. Since the dot-com crash in 2000, views on the future of the Internet are perhaps less gung-ho than in 1997.

One study examined Dutch retailing between 1982 and 2000, in an attempt to evaluate whether Five Forces-style competitive analysis or Blue Ocean-type innovation was more effective. To their surprise they found evidence that a Blue Ocean strategy was sustainable. They suggested that a blended strategy might be optimal: 'by slowing down profit erosion with an effective competitive strategy for an existing market, they can increase the funds available for blue-ocean investments and thus their chances of finding an untapped market with plenty of consumers' (Burke et al 2010, p28).

Sarah Coles re-examined Five Forces in 2009. Her main criticisms are that Five Forces:

- does not consider the role of the Government, corporate social responsibility or business ethics
- provides a snapshot of the competitive position, rather than a dynamic picture
- doesn't explain how to define an industry
- doesn't consider internal factors such as company history or culture
- can become a tick-box exercise.

Other criticisms have been made of the model:

- Not only does it ignore the general influence of government, it also does not consider the importance of regulation as a restraining factor on the corporation. It is also very much a private sector model and so much less relevant to the public and not-for-profit sectors – a reflection of its US origins, perhaps.
- It assumes that competition is a zero-sum game – if one side wins, the other loses. This ignores the more recent development of co-operative strategies such as strategic alliances or joint ventures.
- It stresses efficiency at the cost of effectiveness and so may discourage innovation. Sumantra Ghoshal (2000) has developed this point. He argues that an excessive preoccupation with competition and market forces, by stressing efficiency at the cost of effectiveness, will discourage innovation.

Porter's response (2008) follows logically from his background as a classically trained economist. He says, 'in essence, the job of the strategist is to understand and cope with competition'. Given this concern with competition, factors such as the Government, regulation and ethics are not relevant, although they may be key for other aspects of strategy-making. 'Government is not best understood as a sixth force because government involvement is neither inherently good nor bad for industry profitability. The best way to understand the influence of government on competition is to analyse how specific government policies affect the five competitive forces.'

He argues that what he calls complements (reflected in strategic alliances) are already built into the model and are important only to the extent that they affect the five forces.

He recognises that industry structure and the five forces should not be static, but again he argues that change can be built into the model.

He recognises that it is possible to define the boundaries of the industry incorrectly:

> Defining the industry too broadly obscures differences among products, customers or geographic regions that are important to competition, strategic positioning and profitability. Defining the industry too narrowly overlooks commonalities and linkages across related products or geographic markets that are crucial to competitive advantage... fortunately, even if industry boundaries are drawn incorrectly, careful five forces analysis should reveal important competitive threats.

Finally, Porter identifies common pitfalls in Five Forces analysis:

- defining the industry too broadly or too narrowly
- making lists instead of engaging in rigorous analysis
- paying equal attention to all of the forces rather than digging deeply into the most important ones
- using static analysis that ignores industry trends
- confusing cyclical or transient changes with true structural changes
- using the framework to declare an industry attractive or unattractive rather than using it to guide strategic choice.

In conclusion, it can be said that Five Forces is still a necessary technique, although it is not a sufficient one. As one of a range of analytical tools, it is invaluable.

COMPETITOR ANALYSIS

Porter's Five Forces is a valuable technique, but as it is industry-wide, it does not necessarily tell a firm a great deal about its direct competitors. Here it is useful to identify strategic groups. These are organisations within an industry or sector with similar strategic characteristics, following similar strategies or competing on similar bases. In grocery retailing, for example, Johnson et al (2011) identify supermarkets, corner shops and convenience stores as different strategic groups. They suggest two key characteristics of strategic groups – the scope of an organisation's activities (product range, geographical coverage) and resource commitment (brands, marketing spend, etc).

The strategic group concept is valuable in three ways:

1   understanding competition

2   analysis of strategic opportunities

3   analysis of mobility barriers.

PORTFOLIO ANALYSIS

In the 1970s and early 1980s, strategic emphasis was on organisations building up a balanced portfolio of activities, or strategic business units (SBUs). Several techniques were developed to assist with analysis of portfolios of SBUs.

BOSTON MATRIX

This technique was developed in the 1970s by the Boston Consulting Group and plots SBUs according to their rate of market growth and their market share (Figure 3.6).

Figure 3.6 The Boston Matrix

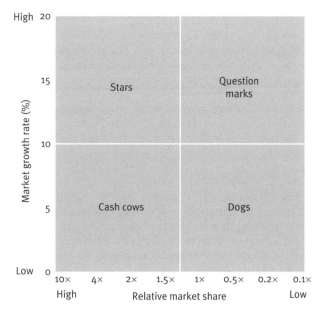

Market growth rate is arbitrarily divided into high growth and low growth, ranging between 0 and 20 per cent per annum. Market share is assessed as share relative to that of the largest competitor, with a high of ten times the nearest rival and a low of one-tenth. SBUs are plotted on the matrix, with their precise position within a cell depending on their exact market share and market growth rate.

The significance of the Boston Matrix is that an SBU's position on the matrix has an impact on its profits and its cash flow. One of the main selling points of the technique is the colourful names attached to the various cells (Joyce and Woods 1996):

- *Dogs* – they have a weak market share in a low-growth market. They generate a very low profit or even a loss, and also may well have negative cash flow. They absorb management resources and the organisation must decide whether they are worth keeping in the long term, closed down or sold off.
- *Stars* – they have a high market share in a high-growth market. Production will be at relatively low cost because of economies of scale and profits are likely to be sound. However, because the market is growing rapidly, heavy investment will be needed to sustain market share. Cash flow is therefore likely to be at best neutral.
- *Question marks* – they have a low market share in a high-growth market. This means that like the stars they need heavy investment, but as they are not the market leader they cannot fully exploit economies of scale. Cash flow is likely to be negative, but profits may well be positive. Management has to take hard decisions – either close down (on the assumption that the question mark may turn into a dog) or sit it out (on the assumption that it will turn into a cash cow).
- *Cash cows* – they have high market share in a low-growth mature market. In the short and medium term this is an ideal position. Because the product is a market leader, it will be low cost and it does not need heavy investment to cope with market growth. It is therefore likely to produce both profits and positive cash flow, which can be milked.

Two further types have also been identified off the bottom of the matrix. These are *war horses* (high market share and negative growth – a cash cow on its last legs) and *dodos* (low market share and negative growth – dead dogs!).

The strategic implications are that an organisation should aim for a balanced portfolio of SBUs, which should include products which can evolve through the sequence of question mark – star – cash cow. Some organisations, particularly at the height of the popularity of conglomerates in the 1980s, became extremely successful by identifying and exploiting cash cows.

One such was Hanson Group, whose strategy was to purchase cash cow products/companies (Imperial Tobacco in cigarettes, London Brick in bricks, Ever Ready in batteries), put in the minimum level of new investment and exploit the cash-generating potential of the products.

The ideal types identified in the Boston Matrix also have implications for HR practice. The dog business will be mainly concerned with redundancy and redeployment. Star businesses are growing rapidly, so the HR priorities are recruitment and flexibility. Question marks ideally should be converted into stars, which will require a willingness to embrace change and an emphasis on training and development. Cash cows place an emphasis on efficiency and effectiveness, and on customer service, which will require an emphasis on training, motivation and reward (Christy and Christy 2009).

There are, however, some weaknesses in the Boston Matrix approach. One is that there is no clear-cut way to define markets. If the market is defined too narrowly, the organisation will overstate its market strength and so tend to ignore 'over the horizon' competitors, who may be quietly building up their strength in a related market. Possibly more serious is that the matrix ignores any synergy factors. Synergy is defined as the way in which the whole organisation is greater than the sum of its parts. SBUs are not totally self-contained – they often provide each other with benefits, such as sharing production processes or distribution channels, or being part of a balanced catalogue of products. As a result, if an organisation decides to kill off a dog product, this may have adverse impacts on its other products. A final weakness is that it assumes a simple relationship between market leadership and profitability. This ignores the way in which many organisations have prospered long term by exploiting small niche markets. Despite these weaknesses, however, the Boston Matrix has been used successfully by a number of companies, including Black & Decker Europe, although alongside other techniques (Walker 1990).

SHELL DIRECTIONAL POLICY MATRIX

This technique, developed by the Shell Chemical Company, meets some of the criticisms of the Boston Matrix. Rather than using market share as a variable, it uses the enterprise's competitive capabilities, assessed as weak, average or strong. This can take into account factors such as managerial skill, possession of appropriate technology and competencies, etc, as well as market share. Market growth rate is replaced by prospects for sector profitability, which again can include other factors. Finally, the analysis is made more discriminating by being based on a 3x3 matrix rather than the Boston Matrix's 2x2 (Figure 3.7).

Figure 3.7 The Shell Directional Policy Matrix

Prospects for sector profitability

		Unattractive	Average	Attractive
Enterprise's competitive capabilities	Weak	Disinvest	Phased withdrawal	Double or quits
	Average	Phased withdrawal	Custodial growth	Try harder
	Strong	Cash generation	Growth leader	Leader

REFLECTIVE ACTIVITY 3.4

Killing the dog

The board at Gamma Manufacturing was deeply divided. Under discussion was Product X, which had been a source of argument within the company for years past. The finance director wanted Product X dropped. He argued that it had absorbed considerable development funds over the years, but had never fulfilled its original promise. It tied up valuable production capacity in the factory and wasted a lot of management time. 'It's a dog,' he said. 'We should put it out of its misery now.'

The marketing director disagreed. She argued that a lot of time, energy and money had been put into the product and it would be a shame to waste all of this just at the point when it might be about to take off. She also made the point that it filled a hole in the product mix. With some customers, it was important to be able to offer a complete product line, including Product X. 'If we haven't got X, I can name at least two big customers who will go straight to the competition,' she said.

Question

1   If you were the managing director, how would you evaluate the arguments put forward by the finance and marketing directors?

THE WORKING OF THE LABOUR MARKET

The same supply and demand analysis which we discussed earlier in relation to goods can be applied to labour, although, as we will see, there are some important differences.

DEMAND FOR LABOUR

Demand for labour is a derived demand. No employer will demand workers purely because he enjoys employing them. They are demanded because the output which they will produce is valuable to the employer. Demand for labour is thus derived from the demand for the goods or services which they produce.

To understand the demand for labour, we have to consider the law of diminishing returns. This states that marginal output (the addition to total output resulting from the employment of one more worker) will fall as more and more units of labour are combined with a fixed quantity of other factors of production (land and capital). The classic example is an allotment of, say, one acre, which has a fixed quantity of gardening tools. One worker will grow very little on the plot, as he has to handle all the tools. Two workers are likely to produce more than twice as much as one worker, because they can specialise (one may be best at digging, the other at weeding). There are increasing returns to scale. Adding a third worker may well add more again. But employing a fourth worker causes co-ordination problems, particularly if there are only three spades available. The fourth worker adds less to total output than the other three. There are diminishing returns. Things get even worse with five workers. A typical situation is illustrated in Table 3.2.

Table 3.2 Diminishing returns to scale

Labour input (workers)	Total output product (units)	Marginal physical product (units)	Price of product (£)	Marginal revenue (£)	Wage rate (£)
1	8	8	10	80	70
2	17	9	10	90	70
3	25	8	10	80	70
4	32	7	10	70	70
5	38	6	10	60	70
6	43	5	10	50	70
7	47	4	10	40	70

At a wage rate of £70, it is just worth employing the fourth worker, but not the fifth, because this would lose the firm £10. If the wage rate rises to £80, it is only worth employing three workers, while if it falls to £60, it becomes worth employing five workers. Plotting this on a graph gives us the familiar downward-sloping demand curve (Figure 3.8). Demand thus equals marginal revenue product.

Figure 3.8 The demand curve for labour

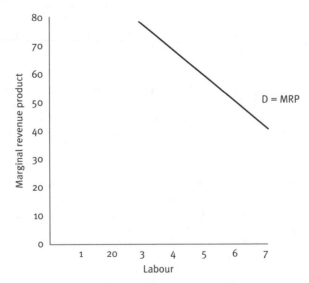

The demand curve for labour can shift to the left or right if the marginal revenue product of a given quantity of labour changes. The curve will shift to the right (an increase in demand for labour) if either marginal physical product increases (a rise in productivity per worker) or the price of the product increases.

THE SUPPLY OF LABOUR

From the point of view of an individual worker, as wage rates rise, the average worker is prepared to work more hours per week. The extra money earned, and the purchases of goods and services which it represents, is more attractive than extra hours spent in bed. Workers substitute work for leisure as wages increase. However, beyond a point, high wages do not tempt a worker to put more hours in. It is more attractive to work fewer hours and spend more time on leisure. This is known as the income effect. At high levels of income, the positive substitution effect of a wage increase is more than offset by the negative income effect. The result is an individual supply curve like that in Figure 3.9.

Figure 3.9 The supply curve for an individual worker

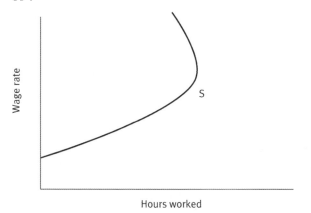

The supply of labour to a firm depends on assumptions which we make about the type of labour market facing the firm. If we assume that the labour market is perfectly competitive, there are many firms hiring many individual workers. In these conditions, an individual firm can hire an extra worker at the existing wage rate. In other words, the supply curve for labour facing that firm is perfectly elastic, as shown in Figure 3.10.

Figure 3.10 Supply of labour to a firm in perfect competition

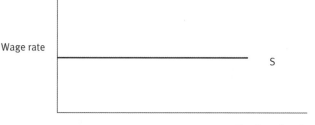

However, things are very different if we assume that the employing firm has some monopoly power (that is, that it is a monopsonist, or a monopoly purchaser). The supply

curve facing this firm will be upward-sloping, which means that to employ more workers, it needs to offer a higher wage. The cost of employing an extra worker (the marginal cost) will be higher than the wage rate the firm has to pay the extra worker. This is because it has to pay the higher wage to all its other employees as well. This is illustrated in Table 3.3 and Figure 3.11.

Table 3.3 Labour costs facing a monopsonist employer

Units of labour	Cost per unit (£)	Total cost (£)	Marginal cost (£)
0		0	
1	20	20	20
2	40	80	60
3	60	180	100
4	80	320	140

Figure 3.11 Supply curve and marginal cost curve of labour facing a monopsonist employer

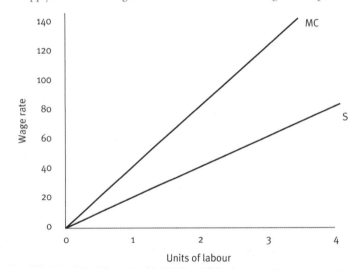

WAGE DETERMINATION

Putting together our demand and supply models helps us explain how wages are determined.

First, assume that there is a perfectly competitive market for labour. Supply and demand would be as shown in Figure 3.12.

Figure 3.12 Employment and wage rates, perfectly competitive market

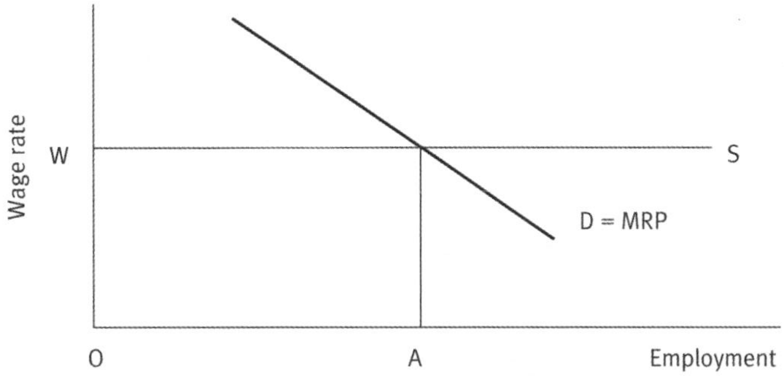

The wage rate, W, is set by the industry as a whole. The firm will employ OA workers at this wage rate.

As you would expect, the situation with a monopsony employer is more complex. Here the number of workers who will be employed is dependent on the firm's marginal cost curve (MC), not its demand curve (Figure 3.13).

Figure 3.13 Wage determination under monopsony

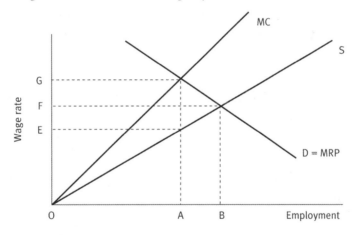

A monopsonist will only recruit labour if the marginal revenue product of that labour is equal to its marginal cost (that is, point OA). However, it does not have to pay a wage OG. The wage rate depends on the supply curve, not the MC curve. It will therefore pay only OE.

If the market were perfectly competitive, OB workers would be employed and they would be paid a wage OF. A monopsonist drives down both wages and employment compared with a perfectly competitive market.

WAGE DETERMINATION WITH TRADE UNIONS

The aim of a trade union in a labour market is to increase the bargaining power of labour. Rather than being an individual selling his or her labour to a monopoly employer, the union member becomes a part of a monopoly supplier of labour.

What the union does is to fix minimum price for labour. The result is to kink the supply curve for labour, as shown in Figure 3.14.

Figure 3.14 Trade unions in a competitive market

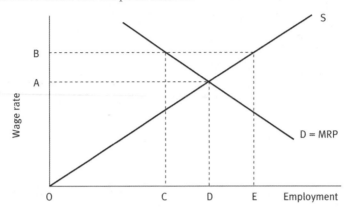

Here the union has set a floor for wages at OB. At this wage, the firm will employ OC workers. If there had been no union, the wage rate would have been lower, but employment would have been higher, at OD. At wage rate OB, OF workers would have chosen to work, but only OC can do so. As a result, there will be unemployment equal to CD.

The situation is totally different if the labour market is monopsonistic, as shown in Figure 3.15.

Figure 3.15 Trade unions in a monopsonistic market

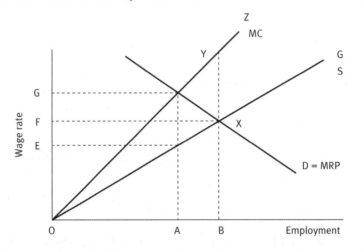

The union sets a floor wage of OF. The result is that the supply curve is now FXG, while the marginal cost curve is FXYZ. The result is that not only is the wage rate higher, at OF rather than OE, but the level of employment has also increased, from OA to OB – the total opposite of the perfect competition case. Workers are better off and more are employed, and the only loser is the employer, who will lose some of his monopoly profits.

It can be argued that unions are not only good for workers; they are also good for employers. This is because unions can exert discipline over their members. If an employer wishes to introduce change, and it is not unionised, it will need to negotiate individually with all workers, which will be expensive and potentially disruptive. On the other hand, if it can persuade the union to support the change, its introduction will be much easier. This is the reasoning which underpins the TUC's New Unionism project and the moves towards social partnership, which are discussed below.

For an extensive discussion of wage determination see Anderton (2006, pp461–515), or for a more scholarly approach, see Manning (2003).

CASE STUDY 3.5

THE IMPACT OF THE NATIONAL MINIMUM WAGE

The National Minimum Wage (NMW) was one of the major labour market reforms of the first New Labour Government, introduced in April 1999 at a rate of £3.60 an hour. The rate is set annually by the Low Pay Commission, an independent body with three employer representatives, three workers and three independents.

Successive increases have seen it rise to £5.80 in October 2009. This represents an increase of over 60 per cent in nominal terms and over 30 per cent in real terms (after adjusting for changes in the Retail Prices Index). The NMW has risen faster than average earnings. Between 1999 and 2007 it rose from 47 per cent to 52 per cent of median earnings. The increase in 2009 is minimal (only 7p an hour) but this has to be set against a fall in the Retail Prices Index and a very small increase in average earnings. By October 2012 the adult rate was £6.19 an hour, a small rise since 2009, but significant when set against the 1 per cent cap on public sector wages over most of this period.

It is clear that the NMW has had an impact on wages. When it was first introduced, it raised the pay of between 5 and 6 per cent of workers (1.2 to 1.3 million workers) by about 15 per cent on average. The effect was much more marked for women, 8.5 per cent of whom gained in 1999, compared with 3.2 per cent of men.

The effect on employment is much less clear-cut. As we found earlier in relation to trade unions, there are two conflicting theoretical perspectives. Just like a trade union, the NMW sets a floor to wages. One perspective is the classical (perfect competition) model, which argues that the result will be a fall in employment. The other is the monopsony (imperfect competition) model, which argues that employment will increase as a result of a squeeze on employers' profits.

The former view was taken by the Conservative Party in the 1990s. In 1991, the then Employment Secretary, Michael Howard, argued that a minimum wage would cost 2 million jobs. This would be caused both by the classical theory model and by a knock-on effect, where higher-paid workers demanded compensation in order to maintain their wage differential over the low paid, which would have the effect of increasing inflation and interest rates in the economy as a whole. The monopsonist view was taken by the Labour Party, following a long socialist tradition dating back to the first call for a minimum wage by the Fabian Society in 1906.

In practice, the effect of the NMW on employment has been complex.

In some cases, the monopsonist model has applied, and both wages and employment have risen.

In other cases, marginal firms have gone out of business as a result of the NMW, leading to a fall in employment.

In cases where there is a large number of small employers, such as the care home sector, the market approximates more to the perfect competition than to the monopsony model, and there has been a small fall in employment.

In some cases the NMW has led to an increase in training, aimed at increasing the productivity of workers to compensate for the higher wage.

There has also been some evasion of the NMW. One study suggested that 20 per cent of workers who should have been paid at the minimum wage were actually paid below it in 2000.

The above effects seem to broadly cancel each other out and the overall impact on employment has been minimal. As a result, there is now a political consensus on the NMW, and in the 2005 General Election, the Conservative Party pledged to keep it.

Finally, the NMW has to be put in a wider context. First, it is part of a wider package of welfare-to-work measures introduced by Labour, including the Working Families Tax Credit. Second, many of the poorest householders do not benefit from the NMW because they have no-one in employment – pensioners, the disabled, many single parents, and so on.

Sources: Metcalf (2007); Draca and Dickens (2005)

CASE STUDY 3.6

WAGE SUBSIDIES – ARE THEY AN EFFECTIVE WAY TO SAVE JOBS?

Are wage subsidies an effective way of saving jobs during a recession? The Welsh Assembly says yes, and so does Germany, France, Italy and Spain, but many labour economists and the UK Government say no.

In November 2008, the Welsh Assembly agreed a wage subsidy scheme called ProAct, which came into force in January 2009. The scheme pays a subsidy of £4,000 per worker to firms on short-time working, of which half goes towards training and half is a wage subsidy. By August 2009, the scheme had paid out to 90 employers and safeguarded over 5,500 jobs. The scheme costs £48 million, of which £30 million comes from the EU's European Social Fund and £18 million from the Welsh Assembly. There is a much bigger scheme in Germany, costing €6 billion. By August 2009, Germany had already officially moved out of recession, while Wales is the only region of the UK where unemployment is falling. There is no direct evidence that either of these happy outcomes is a direct result of wage subsidies, but the coincidence may be suggestive.

A larger-scale scheme for the UK as a whole had been proposed by the TUC and the Federation for Small Businesses. They propose a scheme costing £3.3 billion a year, based on paying 600,000 workers 60 per cent of median wages for up to six months. They estimate that the gross cost would be offset by savings of £1.2 billion in reduced unemployment benefit and £850 million in increased income tax receipts, giving a net cost of £1.25 billion.

The schemes sound ideal, so why would anyone oppose them? The main argument made against wage subsidies is the deadweight cost or moral hazard argument, that subsidies would be paid to firms which would not have laid off workers anyway, putting public money in their pockets with no social return. One survey estimated that deadweight spending on wage subsidies in Ireland in the early 2000s had been between 40 and 80 per cent, and in Belgium in the late 1990s between 46 and 62 per cent. The TUC/FSB proposal suggested that moral hazard could be overcome by making access to the scheme contingent on long-term business viability and genuine need, as assessed and agreed by union, employer and government representatives.

There is also some evidence that employers are lukewarm towards the idea of work subsidies. The spring 2009 CIPD *Labour Market Outlook* found that only 28 per cent of employers would pursue a short-time working subsidy, while 29 per cent would not. Two in five were 'don't knows'.

UK government policy has concentrated on getting the unemployed back to work, rather than on preserving existing jobs. There are three schemes:

- government-funded apprenticeships
- government-funded internships for graduates
- a recruitment and training subsidy of £2,500 to recruit the long-term unemployed.

In addition, the CIPD has called for a six-month work placement subsidy of £1,250 for the young unemployed.

Sources: Connecting Industry (2009); Bailey (2009); CIPD (2009a); *People Management* (2009a); Girma et al (2007)

REFLECTIVE ACTIVITY 3.5

The lemon

In 1970 the economist Akerlof discussed the case of the used car market as an example of imperfect information (Akerlof 1970). In the used car market, sellers have much better information than buyers. In particular, sellers know whether there is something wrong with the car they are selling – whether it is a lemon. Because the buyer knows that some cars being sold are lemons, but not which ones, the price in the market will be an average of the values of good cars and of lemons. If a particular car is a good one, the buyer will get a better deal than the seller. The opposite happens with a lemon. As a result, owners of lemons will be willing to sell, but owners of good cars won't. As a result, the proportion of lemons in the market will increase, the more suspicious buyers will be and the more prices will be pushed down. The whole used car market will spiral downwards.

It is in the interests of potential sellers of good cars to do something to improve information in the market and so to get better prices. There are many ways of doing this. One is to offer warranties on used cars, as is done by Ford through its dealers, for example. Another is to encourage buyers to get the car checked by an independent third party, such as the AA.

From the point of view of the buyer, it is essential to know the reputation of the seller. Large, established main dealers of the major car brands are likely to have a better reputation than the back-street garage or cars sold through small ads in newspapers.

The lemon problem is really a modern application of Gresham's law, which dates from the sixteenth century. This law – 'bad money drives out good' – was invented by Sir Thomas Gresham, treasurer to Queen Elizabeth I. Governments at the time were notorious for debasing the currency – mixing cheaper material into the gold and silver used to make coins. The Government made a profit on this, as the coin cost less to make than its face value. If you had two coins, one of which you knew to be good (of full gold content) and the other to be debased, you would hoard the good one and spend the bad one – bad money drives out good. Unfortunately, everyone else would know that only bad coins would stay in circulation and as a result prices would go up. Gresham advised Elizabeth to avoid inflation by resisting the temptation to debase the currency.

Questions

1   Do you think the lemon model is relevant to wage determination?

2 Find out how eBay, the online auction site,   very little about the reputation of sellers on
   gets around the problem that buyers know   the site.

TRENDS IN EMPLOYMENT

CHANGES IN THE INDUSTRIAL STRUCTURE

In 1951, manufacturing accounted for a third of GDP and nearly 40 per cent of employment. By 2001 employment in manufacturing had fallen to 14 per cent of the workforce, although as the size of the workforce has increased considerably, the number working in manufacturing has only fallen from 8.7 to 3.7 million. Part of the reason for this fall is the shift of manufacturing jobs to eastern Europe and the Far East, a consequence of globalisation. Another reason is peculiar to the UK – the chronic overvaluation of the pound since the late 1970s, which made UK manufacturing uncompetitive and which triggered recessions in the early 1980s and early 1990s. The trend continues – before the recession of 2008 there was much talk of an over-strong pound and a two-speed economy – booming services and recessionary manufacturing. By 2008, the number of manufacturing jobs was down to 2.8 million (10 per cent of the workforce), a fall of nearly 1 million in seven years (Clancy 2009). Where manufacturing has survived, the nature of work within it has changed, from skilled and semi-skilled manual work to much more knowledge-based and less manual work.

The fall in mining and quarrying has been even more marked, from 880,000 workers in 1951 to 76,000 in 2001 (Philpott 2002). The share of public services in GDP has fallen markedly since the early 1950s, although employment has remained more or less constant at around 5 million. Falls in privatised public corporations and the armed forces have been matched by growths in education and the NHS. Services of all kinds have boomed and have grown from about half of employment in 1966 to 83 per cent in 2008 (Clancy 2009).

There have also been changes in the occupational level of the workforce. The share of manual workers in the workforce fell from 64 per cent in 1952 to 38 per cent in 1991, with the biggest proportionate fall among unskilled manual workers, whose percentage has fallen by nearly two-thirds. Skilled manual workers have fallen from 25 per cent of the workforce in 1951 to 12 per cent in 2001, while the managerial professional and technical workforce has risen from 12 per cent in 1951 to nearly 40 per cent in 2001, and relatively poorly paid service sector jobs have also increased.

The above trends are typical of most of western Europe, although the proportion of workers in manufacturing is higher in Germany and Italy, and the proportion working in services higher in the Netherlands (Gallie 2000).

THE IMPACT OF THE RECESSION ON HR

Clearly one of the major impacts of the recession on HR has been the level of redundancies which have been imposed. Between quarter 1 of 2008 (effectively the start of the recession) and quarter 4 of 2011, the number of people in employment has fallen by 463,000 at a time when the size of the potential workforce rose by 614,000. The fall in the number of employees is even greater, at 650,000, as the number of self-employed went up by nearly a quarter of a million. Redundancies have been running at half a million a year. The number of people working part-time because they cannot find full-time work has doubled from 0.67 million to 1.34 million, while two-thirds of those who were made redundant and found a new job suffered a pay penalty of 28 per cent. On average, the cost to an employer of making a redundancy is £13,000, suggesting that redundancies since 2008 will have cost UK employers around £35 billion (Philpott 2012).

Ben Willmott and Cary Cooper discussed the HR implications of redundancy in a CIPD podcast in 2009 (CIPD 2009f). Willmott argued that the increased risk of redundancy would lead to increasing work intensity, stress conflict and bullying in the workplace, while Cooper argued that survivors of redundancy would be likely to turn to unproductive presenteeism in an effort to preserve their jobs from the next round of redundancy. Both agreed that the good practice built up in HR over recent years could be at risk as management becomes even more obsessed with the bottom line.

A major study on HR in recession was carried out for the Irish Labour Relations Commission, reporting in January 2011 (Roche et al 2011). Ireland is significant because it went into recession before the UK and has suffered more severely. Virtually all firms surveyed had implemented general HR retrenchment programmes, comprising pay freezes, recruitment freezes, curbs on overtime, short-time working, redundancies and more rigorous work regimes, including more rigorous management of performance and disciplinary issues. This approach was generally allied with an emphasis on improved communication with both employees and unions – perhaps made easier by the longstanding Irish agreements on social partnership between employers, the Government and the unions (see Chapter 4) – and an emphasis on maintaining employee engagement and commitment.

An interesting, though perhaps atypical, example is the estate agent Sherry Fitzgerald (pp27–9). Property bore the brunt of the Irish recession, with the volume of transactions down by 40 per cent. The initial reaction of the firm was to opt for salary cuts, weighted towards the better paid, employment protection and job security. Recruitment was frozen and career breaks, reduced working weeks and redeployment were offered to staff. However, as the recession deepened, 31 compulsory redundancies became inevitable and a second round of salary cuts followed in 2009. Interestingly, the reaction this time was across the board with no protection for those on the lowest salaries. This arose from staff feedback that insulating any groups from the pay cuts was unfair. HRD was maintained but spend was reduced and employee engagement was identified as an area of future activity. The HR function was seen as central to the response. It was seen as operating in a partnership role with senior managers. It led the communication efforts and maintained an open-door policy for all staff.

Senior managers felt that the company had experienced no significant fall in morale and 'staff in general appeared to have formed the view that changes introduced in pay and conditions were unavoidable, appropriate and fair' (p29).

CASE STUDY 3.7

REDUNDANCY – COSTS AND ALTERNATIVES

Costs of redundancy

Redundancies are a fact of life in a recession, such as that experienced in the UK from 2008 onwards. The CIPD *Labour Market Outlook* for summer 2009 showed that redundancy intentions among employers peaked in spring 2009. The *Outlook*'s net employment intentions figure – the difference between the proportion of employers who expect to increase their staff numbers and those who expect to decrease them – has been negative since winter 2008–09, when it was a net –9. This rose to a peak of –19 in spring 2009, but fell back to –10 in summer 2009, with 34 per cent expecting to decrease their staff numbers (CIPD 2009b).

Within the figures there has been a dramatic shift between sectors. The net employment figure for the private sector has improved between spring and summer 2009 from –30 to –2, while for the public sector it has worsened just as dramatically, from –3 to –28.

Thirteen per cent of public sector organisations expect to reduce their workforce by more than 10 per cent. Optimism in the voluntary/not-for-profit sector has also worsened, with 30 per cent expecting to make redundancies.

As unemployment is a lagging indicator (it is slow to rise in a recession, but continues to rise after a recession is technically over), redundancies continued on a significant scale through 2010 and 2011, and intensified as the economy went into a double-dip recession in late 2011.

In the February 2009 edition of *Impact*, the CIPD research journal, John Philpott discussed the cost of redundancy (Philpott 2009a). Although redundancies can sometimes be inevitable, employers should always remember that there are significant costs associated with them. Philpott calculated the following average costs for a redundancy:

● *Redundancy payments* – any employee made redundant after two years' service is entitled to statutory redundancy pay. Many employers pay more. The average redundancy payment in autumn 2008 was £10,575.
● *Hiring costs* – after the recession ends, it is likely that new workers will have to be hired. The average cost of recruitment in 2008 was £4,667.
● *Training costs* – new-hires will have to be trained, at an average 2008 cost of £1,133.

Survivor syndrome

1   There is likely to be a decline in morale among those left employed (survivors). The CIPD *Employee Outlook: Job-seeking in a recession*, summer 2009 (CIPD 2009c), found that seven out of ten employees whose organisations had made redundancies reported a fall in morale, while 27 per cent said they were personally less

motivated in their jobs. On the other hand, half of employees feel under increased pressure to perform after redundancies. The cost of a fall in morale was calculated by multiplying the reduction in output of survivors by their average earnings.

2   Increased turnover as a result of redundancies – this measures the cost of additional hiring and training costs if turnover increases as a result of redundancies. However, this effect may be small during a recession, when there are few other jobs to go to, although turnover may shoot up once the recession is over and alternative jobs become available. A CIPD survey in August 2009 found that 22 per cent were so unhappy with the way that redundancies had been handled that they were planning to change jobs as soon as the labour market improved (Churchard 2009a).

If we ignore survivor syndrome costs as being indirect and very difficult to quantify, we are still left with an average figure per redundancy (on CIPD figures) of between £10,575 (where redundant workers are not subsequently replaced) and £16,375 (where new-hires need training). Put another way, it costs roughly six months' wages (at the average wage) to make a worker redundant.

Alternatives to redundancy

Most employers have some idea that redundancies cost money and most also feel a sense of responsibility to minimise suffering to their workforce. Hence a search for alternatives to redundancy, discussed by John Philpott in a follow-up to his *Impact* article quoted above (Philpott 2009b).

One possibility is to use voluntary rather than compulsory redundancy. This has the advantage that it is likely to be more attractive to employees and so may marginally reduce survivor syndrome costs, but its direct costs are the same as compulsory redundancy and there is the added disadvantage that as the employer does not choose who is made redundant, the organisation might inadvertently lose key workers. Much the same is true of early retirement, where there is again a loss of control, as well as additional pension costs.

Philpott identifies six common alternatives to redundancy and their rate of use by employers:

Use of main alternatives to redundancy 2009 (per cent)

Recruitment freeze	50
Termination of temporary contracts	44
Flexible working	19
Cutting bonuses	17
Short-time working	15
Cutting pay	7

Recruitment freeze – this reduces the headcount through natural wastage and has the advantage of being cheap, but like voluntary redundancy, the wrong people may be leaving. The recruitment freeze may need to be combined with redeployment to ensure that key tasks are covered.

Terminating temporary contracts – this is attractive, as temporary workers can be terminated without redundancy pay, but the effect for the temporary worker is the same as a redundancy – he or she is out of a job.

Flexible working – this may be desirable in its own right, but is not usually an alternative on its own to redundancy.

Cutting bonuses – this is usually simple and straightforward, as there is rarely a contractual right to a bonus. However, by definition, it is only possible if a bonus is already being paid.

Short-time working – a number of possibilities are available here:

- *Lay-offs* – here the worker is told to stay at home for a specified period of time, during which time they are likely to be unpaid or paid at a reduced rate. If the lay-off is without pay, employers are required to pay statutory guarantee pay of £21.50 a day for a maximum of five days in a three-month period (Directgov 2010).
- *Short-time working* – here hours are reduced (for example a four-day week), usually with a commensurate pay reduction.
- *Sabbaticals* – this is in effect a form of lay-off, where employees are offered an extended period of (usually) unpaid leave while retaining all their employment rights.

Unless there is a specific right written into the contract of employment, all of the above are dependent on the agreement of the employee. If they are introduced without agreement, this is breach of contract.

Pay cuts – again, these will need to be agreed. However, they are cost-effective. If one reckons that a redundancy costs half a year's pay, a 5 per cent pay cut for ten workers is the equivalent of one redundancy and can be sold to the workforce as a fair way of spreading the pain, particularly if managers take a bigger pay cut than workers.

One interesting proposal has been put forward by the CBI. Known as *alternative to redundancy (ATR)*, this would involve a six-month delay to redundancy, during which time the employee would not work, but would receive an ATR allowance worth twice the rate of jobseekers' allowance, half paid by the Government and half by the employer (Churchard 2009b).

Philpott calculates the savings from the various alternatives to redundancy. He finds a recruitment freeze and terminating temporary workers to be the most cost-effective. Other measures save less than redundancy, but they have the advantages of retaining talent and of having less impact on survivor morale.

REFLECTIVE ACTIVITY 3.6

Alternatives to redundancy

Xilinx

Xilinx is a medium-sized US semiconductor company with about 2,600 employees. In 2001, it was hit hard by the collapse of the dot-com boom, with its revenues falling by 50 per cent in six months. Other firms in the industry reacted by introducing redundancy programmes, but the Xilinx management wanted to avoid this if possible. They understood the cyclical nature of the industry and the need to hold on to skilled staff ready for the upturn.

In 2001, they implemented a programme of pay cuts, ranging from zero for the lowest-paid workers to 20 per cent for the CEO, and a two-week shutdown. Employees were given the choice of taking the shutdown without pay, using paid leave entitlement, or 'borrowing' future leave entitlement if they had not accrued enough leave to cover the shutdown. The CEO announced that lay-offs would only be considered as a last resort.

As the market continued to deteriorate, employees agreed to take an additional 7.5 per cent pay cut, with the choice of taking stock options in lieu of pay. However, the events of 9/11 then hit the industry and even further measures were needed. After extensive consultations throughout the company, two additional programmes were agreed:

- voluntary redundancy and early retirement, taken up by 82 employees
- a one-year sabbatical leave, with two months' pay, an education bonus of $10,000 and/or a bonus of $10,000 for working as an executive on loan to a local non-profit organisation – the employee could return with no loss of benefits, seniority or stock options. This was taken up by 41 employees.

In 2002, the market recovered and the pay cuts were restored. By 2003, Xilinx had increased its market share from 30 per cent to 52 per cent, and it was making profits which exceeded that of its three major competitors combined (Cascio and Wynn 2004).

Honda and British Airways

Both Honda and British Airways were hard hit by the 2009 recession and both took imaginative measures to cope. Honda decided that it had to reduce production at its Swindon car factory from a planned 218,000 vehicles to 113,000, which in effect made half its 4,700 staff surplus to requirements. The first step was a voluntary redundancy programme, taken up by 1,300 workers.

However, the company still felt that it had 490 more workers than it needed, but it did not want to lose them as they would be needed when the economy picked up in 2010. Two major programmes were agreed with the union, Unite. One was a four-month shutdown, ending in June 2009. Staff got full pay for the first two months of the shutdown and 60 per cent for the second two months. The second was a pay cut, of 3 per cent for employees and 5 per cent for managers, for ten months from June 2009 to April 2010, with six extra days of paid leave. In Japan, pay cuts of 10 per cent and 15 per cent respectively had been agreed. The pay cut was agreed to by 89 per cent of Honda employees, and the Unite regional officer Jim D'Avila said, 'In true solidarity the workers at Honda are standing together during difficult times to protect hundreds of jobs.' In addition, some of the surplus workers were found jobs in Honda's nearby suppliers (Pidd 2009; Stewart 2009;Churchard 2009c).

In June 2009, British Airways was reported as asking staff to work a month for free. Willy Walsh, the CEO, set an example by foregoing his pay for July, a total of £61,000. However, there were media reports that undue pressure was being put on workers to agree to the proposal and cabin crew and ground staff were reported to be considering industrial action. BA then widened the proposal to a range of options including unpaid leave and a temporary switch to part-time work as well as unpaid work, while making it clear that employees who took up the unpaid work option would still receive allowances and shift pay.

In the end the take-up for the company's proposals was small. Total take-up was 8,000, or 20 per cent of the company's workforce, while the unpaid work option was only accepted by 800 workers, or 2 per cent (*People Management* 2009b; Churchard 2009d; McCarthy 2009).

Question

1   Why do you think the programmes at Xilinx and Honda were successful, while that at BA was a relative failure?

THE FEMINISATION OF THE WORKFORCE

Male participation rates (the proportion of the population of working age who are in employment) have fallen steadily since 1951 (and indeed since 1911). They were 88 per cent in 1951 and had fallen to 71 per cent in 1998 (Gallie 2000). The fall is explained by early retirement and greater levels of sickness incapacity. However, by 2008, this had risen to 78 per cent, mainly because of an increased participation rate among the over-50s (Kent 2009). Female rates over the same period have risen from 33 per cent to 70 per cent in 2008. As a result the share of women in the labour force has risen from 30 per cent to 48 per cent. All of the gain in female employment has come about as a result of an increased participation in the labour force of married women. The single participation rate has fallen from 73 per cent in 1951 to 64 per cent in 1991, while the married women participation rate has risen from 22 per cent to 53 per cent. It is difficult to remember that in the early 1950s women in occupations like the civil service were routinely expected to resign when they married! The overall percentage working part-time has risen from 23.6 per cent in 1992 to 25.5 per cent in 2008. This increase has been driven by men, who are more likely to work part-time in 2008 than in 1992, while women are less likely to do so. Overall, 42 per cent of women in employment were working part-time, compared with 11.6 per cent of men (Kent 2009).

Women are under-represented in the higher professions, managers and administrators, and manual work, while they are over-represented in lower professionals and technicians (primarily education and the NHS), clerical work, and sales and personal service.

Why has the workforce become feminised? Giddens (2006) puts forward three main reasons:

- *Demographic trends* – the birth rate has declined and women are having children at a later age. As a result, they work for longer before they have children. As families are smaller, it is easier for them to return to work after having children. Domestic housework has also become much less labour-intensive and men are at last tending to take a greater share of it. Women spend nearly three hours a day on housework, but men spend 1 hour 40 minutes (ONS 2005).
- *Financial pressures* – single mothers often have little choice but to work and increasingly this is being encouraged by the working of the welfare support system. Even two-parent families often find they need two incomes to maintain their desired standard of living.
- *Personal fulfilment* – the women's movement in the 1960s and 1970s increased women's self-esteem and a desire among women for more independence.

A fourth reason could be that women workers are particularly attractive to employers, because they are much more likely to want to work part-time. In 2004, there were 5.2

million women in the UK in part-time employment, as against only 1.2 million men. Part-time workers are much more flexible than full-time ones and this gives a considerable advantage to employers.

The reasons for women taking part-time work in 2004 were identified as (Manning and Petrolongo 2005):

- in education or training (3 per cent)
- disabled (2 per cent)
- caring for children or other family member (36 per cent)
- found no full-time job (7 per cent)
- did not want full-time job (19 per cent)
- other (34 per cent).

CASE STUDY 3.8

THE FEMINISATION OF MANAGEMENT

The National Management Salary Survey has been carried out by the Chartered Management Institute and Remuneration Economics for 36 years. The 2005 and 2006 surveys throw interesting light on the feminisation of management.

The 2005 report found that women made up 35.7 per cent of managers and directors, up from 31 per cent the year before. Women were a majority of managers under the age of 29, although female representation fell rapidly after that age. Between 35 and 39, women made up only a third of managers, and only 11 per cent of those aged 50 or more (CMI 2006). Women

received more rapid promotion than men, however. The average female team leader was 37, the average male team leader 42. For department heads, the corresponding ages were 40 and 43 (CMI 2007).

For ten years up to 2005, the pay gap between male and female managers had narrowed. The gap was 13.6 per cent of earnings in 2003 and had narrowed to 11.8 per cent in 2005, but in 2006, it rose to 12.2 per cent. In 2007–08, female salaries went up marginally more than male, 6.8 per cent versus 6.6 per cent. At this rate pay equality for managers would be reached in 2195 (CMI 2009).

WORK ORGANISATION

THE FLEXIBLE ORGANISATION

The idea of the flexible firm was first identified by Atkinson (1984) and the concept was refined by Handy (1991). Atkinson identified four types of flexibility:

1 *numerical flexibility*, achieved by altering working hours or altering the number of workers employed through part-time working, etc

2 *functional flexibility*, achieved by training workers to perform a wider range of tasks (multiskilling) and breaking down barriers to deploying workers on different tasks (demarcation)

3 *distancing*, replacing employees with sub-contractors

4 *pay flexibility*, switching from centralised collective bargaining and rigid pay scales to individually negotiated pay and benefits.

The result is a segmentation of the workforce into core and peripheral workers. Core workers are those key workers who are central to the organisation's core functions. They will be long-term employees, possibly with guaranteed employment, and highly trained. They will be committed to the organisation and the organisation will be committed to them. Peripheral workers will be those performing non-core services, often as sub-contractors. They will be hired and fired as required and will serve as a buffer protecting the core workforce from fluctuations.

Handy developed the core–peripheral concept into his Shamrock concept. This type of organisation has three interlocking leaves consisting of three distinct groups of workers who are treated differently and have different expectations – specialist core workers; a contractual fringe, who may or may not work exclusively for the organisation and who are paid a fee based on results rather than a wage based on time taken; and a flexible workforce, who are likely to be employed on a temporary or casual basis.

Remember, however, that what Atkinson and Handy are discussing is a theoretical model of organisations. Although many organisations have moved towards this kind of structure, many have not. As with other new management techniques, British management tends to be conservative and reluctant to adopt new ideas (Marchington and Wilkinson 2008).

One theoretical justification for increasing the flexibility of the labour market is that the more competitive the labour market is, the more efficiently it should operate (on the analogy of perfect competition). This has led to moves to deregulate the labour market and to Margaret Thatcher's attacks on the trade unions in the 1980s. However, as we have seen above, the working of the labour market is extremely complex and the results of deregulation in another important sector of the economy, the finance industry, have been disastrous, as we will see in the next chapter.

A recent report by the venture capitalist Adrian Beecroft examined whether changes in employment law would make the labour market more flexible. One change which he recommended was to relax the laws on unfair dismissal by introducing the concept of compensated no-fault dismissal. Here an employee could be dismissed at any time, even in circumstances which would at present constitute unfair dismissal, as long as compensation was paid equal to that which would have applied in the case of redundancy (Beecroft 2011). This is akin to the concept of dismissal at will, which applies in many US states.

Beecroft produced no hard evidence to back his proposal and reaction generally has been lukewarm. The Government has already increased the qualifying period for unfair dismissal from one year to two, in April 2012, and in response to Beecroft it announced a very short consultation period on the introduction of compensated no-fault dismissal, but only for micro companies (those with up to ten employees). The CIPD in its response was dismissive – 'we do not believe that a deregulation drive will lead to employers creating more jobs and thus stimulating economic growth'. They pointed out that the UK already had the third least regulated labour market in the OECD. They also said, 'the encouragement that [it] would give to bad practice would also tend to suggest to many that the typical micro business was a "rogue employer" and so make it harder for them to recruit' (CIPD 2012). The chances of the change being enacted by government seem very remote as long as the Liberal Democrat Vince Cable remains as Secretary of State for Business, Innovation and Skills. He issued a ministerial statement when the report was published which said, 'at a time when workers are proving to be flexible in difficult economic conditions, it would almost certainly be counter-productive to increase fear of dismissal' (Cable 2012).

Allied to the concept of flexible organisations is that of flexible working. While the flexible organisation primarily benefits the employer, flexible working primarily (although not exclusively) benefits the employee. The Family Friendly Working Hours Taskforce, reporting in March 2010, found a compelling business case for flexible working:

- falling absenteeism and higher retention leads to a reduction in costs
- increased productivity
- increased ability to recruit from a wider talent pool
- greater loyalty among staff (CIPD 2010).

REFLECTIVE ACTIVITY 3.7

The challenges of flexible working

What problems are posed by the movement towards more flexible ways of working?

THE PSYCHOLOGICAL CONTRACT

All employees have a legal contract of employment, but for the employee this is usually presented as a 'take it or leave it' situation. The employee has to accept it or leave. The psychological contract is different. It is implicit rather than explicit, individual rather than collective, tacit rather than written (although elements of it may be incorporated into a social partnership agreement with a trade union) (CIPD 2005). There are dangers in making it too explicit, as organisational and environmental changes may make it impossible to deliver on an explicit contract (Briner and Conway 2001). It can be defined as 'the perceptions of the two parties... of their mutual obligations towards each other' (Guest and Conway 2002). By its very nature, the psychological contract is dependent on trust between the employer and the employee.

Ian Wilson identified eight elements in his 'new social contract' (Wilson 2000):

1   a vision and sense of shared purpose

2   inspiring leadership

3   empowerment

4   customisation of work

5   a climate of equity, respect and due process

6   reduced volatility in employment patterns

7   increasing employability

8   good on-site amenities and services.

Wilson's elements link with the view of the psychological contract that it has changed from an 'employment security' contract to an 'employability' contract. This reflects the shift from the monolithic to the flexible organisation, which we discussed above. Under the employment security contract, the employee offered time and loyalty in return for security of employment and the possibility of promotion (Kimberly and Craig 2001).

As redundancy and downsizing became more common, employers could no longer guarantee their side of the bargain, and gradually it was replaced by the employability contract – employees would still offer time and loyalty, but in return the employer would ensure that they received the work experience and training that would enable them to get another job elsewhere. This has been described as the 'new deal' at work and as producing a 'free agent' mentality among workers.

If this model is correct (and there is some doubt about this – the 'old' psychological contract often still exists, and where it has gone, it has not necessarily been replaced by an employability contract), loyalty may not be enough to keep the free agent employee on board. The organisation may have to offer more, including possibly empowerment. If workers are to be trusted, they expect trust back from the organisation.

Rousseau (2004) distinguished between relational contracts, based on give and take and on trust in the employer, and transactional contracts, which are more short term in approach and concentrate on pay and conditions. The CIPD (2005) points to a suggestion that there has been a shift in recent years from relational to transactional, as trust in employers has declined, but refutes this, saying that employee commitment is broadly stable.

Other implications of the new psychological contract suggested by the CIPD include:

- *process fairness* – employers need to put in processes which ensure that employees see the way in which decisions are made as being fair
- *communications* – communication mechanisms have to be set up to ensure that employers are aware of the employee 'voice' (this is reflected in the EU information and Consultation Directive)
- *management style* – employees expect to know what is going on – management style needs to change from 'top–down' to 'bottom–up'
- *managing expectations* – managers must be seen to be fair, honest and open
- *measuring employee attitudes* – managers need to know what their employees are thinking.

The employability and free agent approaches in many ways put a lot of pressure on employees. They are forced to take responsibility for their own future in a way which, while attractive to many, does not suit everyone. Many people want security rather than opportunity. Those who really crave opportunity may well have shifted to self-employment already (the self-employment rate in the UK is currently around 12 per cent of the workforce – Philpott 2012). Increasingly employers have to offer something else as part of their side of the psychological contract. This is work–life balance, which we discuss in the next section.

WORK–LIFE BALANCE

Changes in social structure have increased pressure on people in work:

- In the 1950s and even into the 1960s, women routinely gave up work on marriage, and so were at home to care for children. People married young and had children young, with most families being completed by the age of 30. At the time when children were dependent, many parents also had an extended family to draw on and relatively young grandparents, who probably lived nearby.
- In the 1990s and 2000s, over half of all married women were in work, whether or not they had children, and families had come to expect and need two incomes. The age of marriage had risen and many women had not had their first child by 30. The extended family had broken down and by the time the family needed support, grandparents were too old, did not live locally and increasingly needed care themselves.
- The increase in the rate of marriage breakdown meant that increasing numbers of single parents with children, particularly women, needed to work to support their families, but had no external support networks to draw on. In 1991, 20 per cent of dependant children lived in single-parent families.
- Millions of women in their fifties have to care for an elderly dependant parent.
- An increased desire on the part of employers as well as employees for a more flexible workforce.

An Institute of Management survey in 2001 highlighted the extent of the problem (*Professional Manager* 2001):

- 46 per cent of female managers have children
- 26 per cent care for others such as elderly parents
- 27 per cent cite family commitments as a career barrier (up from 17 per cent in 1992).

In 2003, 9 per cent of males and 33 per cent of females had at some time given up work to care for somebody (*Social Trends* 2004).

In addition, people without caring responsibilities also feel that they are entitled to a life outside work. One in five people take work home almost every day and one in ten work more than 48 hours a week (CIPD 2009d).

There are some legal requirements on employers to meet the needs of their employees for work–life balance. These are mainly concerned with the right to time off to cope with one-off situations or emergencies, and full details are given in the CIPD factsheet, *Work–life balance* (CIPD 2009d). In addition, from 2003 (under the Employment Act 2002), employees with children under 6 (18 if disabled) can request a change in their hours, time or place of work. The employer must consider such a request and can refuse it, but only after following a detailed procedure and basing their decision on specified business grounds. This was extended in 2007 to employees with children under 17, as a result of the Work and Families Act 2006 (CIPD 2009d).

Although only parents of young children have the right to request flexible working, any other employee can ask for flexible arrangements and many employers have granted this. The latest figures (for 2009) are that 18 per cent of men and 29 per cent of women working full-time have some kind of flexible working arrangements, but the most common arrangements are shown in Table 3.4.

Table 3.4 Most common flexible working arrangements

	Per cent	
	Males	Females
Flexible working hours	10.9	15.3
Annualised hours	4.9	4.9
4½-day week	1.2	0.5
Term-time work	1.2	6.7

Source: National Statistics (2010)

There are similar patterns for part-time workers, with flexible working hours and term-time working being the most used options. Twenty-six per cent of males and 47 per cent of females had changed their hours or working arrangements to look after someone.

REFLECTIVE ACTIVITY 3.8

Work–life balance

1   Our discussion above has been in terms of flexible working hours or time off. What other family-friendly arrangements could employers offer?

2   What business case could you put to your employers to persuade them to adopt family-friendly policies?

3   Among your workforce are two workers: Anne, who is a single parent with a daughter aged four, who has asked to work

school hours only; and Peter, who is the sole family carer for his elderly mother, who has Alzheimer's disease. He has asked to work a 30-hour week, instead of the normal 35, and to leave work one hour early in order to get home before his daytime carer leaves. What response would you make to each worker?

WORKFORCE PLANNING

Like much in our current world, workforce planning was a product of the Second World War. In 1942 the Government drew up the first Manpower Budget to ensure there was enough labour to meet the needs of war production and was shocked to discover that there was a shortfall of 1 million workers. This led to a realisation that the recruitment, retention and training of workers needed to be planned (Turner 2010). Like classic strategic planning, workforce planning (or manpower planning, as it was then called), reached its peak of popularity (and complexity) in the 1960s, but then became discredited as the environment became more turbulent from the 1970s onwards. However, the recession from 2008 onwards has led to a resurgence of interest in workforce planning as a key tool in managed downsizing, but as a bottom–up tool with heavy input from line management, rather than the top–down approach of classic manpower planning.

The CIPD defines workforce planning as 'a core process of human resource management that is shaped by the organisational strategy and ensures the right number of people with the right skills, in the right place at the right time to deliver short- and long-term organisational objectives' (CIPD 2010). As the CIPD's Angela Baron wrote: 'the public sector in particular is looking at how it can ensure that the current round of cuts fall in the right places and do not minimise their ability to provide core services efficiently and effectively. The private sector is looking for innovative ways to keep costs under control while maintaining engagement and holding onto their best talent' (Baron 2010).

The importance of effective workforce planning was starkly illustrated in July 2012 when the CEO of the world's biggest security company, G4S, Nick Buckles, was forced to admit to a Commons Select Committee that his company's planning for the Olympic Games had been a 'humiliating shambles'. G4S had been contracted to supply 10,000 security guards for the Olympics, but was forced to admit two weeks before the Games started that it would miss its target by thousands of workers, leaving a security gap which had to be hurriedly plugged by the calling up of an additional 3,500 members of the armed forces (BBC 2012).

REFLECTIVE ACTIVITY 3.9

Teachers and workforce planning

Intuitively you would think it would be easy to plan the supply of teachers. After all, you know how many children are born each year and where they are born, because all births have to be registered. Then you just project four years ahead (for primary schools) and 11 years ahead (for secondaries), and you know how many children will be entering each level of school in each year. Adding up the years gives you a total school population. Divide this by your planned pupil–teacher ratio and you know exactly how many teachers you need in each year.

Unfortunately, of course, it doesn't work like that. Over the period 1946–2001, there was a shortage of teachers (an excess demand) for all but ten years, reaching a peak of 80,000 in the early 1990s. There was a surplus (excess supply) for ten years from the mid-1970s to the mid-1980s, peaking at about 15,000 (Dolton 2005).

Question

1   Why is it so difficult to plan the supply of teachers?

TRADE UNIONS

So far in this section on work organisation we have concentrated on the position of individuals. We conclude by analysing the collective – the role and position of trade unions.

Trade union membership peaked in 1979 at more than 13 million. Since then it has nearly halved, to around 7.5 million in the late 1990s. It has since stabilised, helped by legislation on union recognition in 1999. The nature of trade union membership has also changed. Union density (the proportion of workers who are union members) has fallen from 54 per cent in 1979 to 29 per cent in 2003, but for women it has only fallen from 37 per cent to 29 per cent.

Density is also affected by age. Density among the over-50s is 33 per cent, while for the age group 25–34 it is 25 per cent (*Social Trends* 2004). Density among full-time workers is 32 per cent, among part-time workers only 21 per cent. Density among professional and associate professional workers and personal service workers is higher than among manual workers. Density in the public sector is 60 per cent, while in the private sector it is only 20 per cent.

In 1979 the typical union member was a male manual worker in heavy industry – a miner or a steel worker. By 2003, the typical union member was a female teacher or NHS worker.

Many reasons have been put forward for the decline in union membership. These include:

● the decline of traditional highly unionised sectors of industry
● the anti-trade union legislation of the Conservative governments between 1979 and 1997
● the recessions of the early 1980 and 1990s
● the growth of a flexible workforce, which is more difficult to unionise
● the growth of pay review bodies in the public sector
● the spread of performance-related pay and individualised HRM systems
● the fall in the size of firms
● defeat in highly publicised set-piece disputes such as the miners' strike.

The response of the trade unions, led by the TUC, was to change their orientation. The traditional perspective taken by unions was a pluralist one – that management and unions have some common aims, but many more conflicting aims, within the employment relationship. Collective bargaining was seen as managing the balance between the interests of management and workers, and would frequently be adversarial. Many individual union leaders took a more radical Marxist perspective and saw the management–labour relationship as an exploitative one.

In the early 1990s, unions in America had developed a different approach, known as New Unionism, based much more on a co-operative relationship, recognising that management and unions have basic agreement in wanting the employment relationship to work more smoothly, and that both sides benefit from a high-wage high-productivity environment. New Unionism also recognised that the approach of union members and potential members is an instrumental one – they want a union to protect their individual interests. They buy union membership like they buy a foreign holiday – they want value for their money.

In 1996, the TUC adopted New Unionism. The emphasis in future was to be on developing social partnerships with willing employers and on stressing casework for individual members (Barber 1998). To further New Unionism, the TUC set up an academy in 1998 to train union representatives. The typical academy student was female and from an ethnic minority.

CASE STUDY 3.9

👁 SOCIAL PARTNERSHIP AT VERTEX

Vertex is an outsourced services company, part of United Utilities, formed in 1996 when North West Water merged with North West Electricity. In five years, it has moved from collective bargaining to union derecognition to non-union consultation to collective bargaining based on partnership.

The head of employee relations, Tony Stark, said, 'I'd had a bellyful of trade unions after working in the car industry and the docks in Liverpool.' However, he was to lead negotiations with Unison which led to partnership. Even when the union was derecognised, union officials were elected onto the company-wide employee consultation forum and proved constructive partners.

After the passing of the Employee Relations Act, Unison applied for a ballot on recognition. Rather than fight the request, Vertex set up a working party with the union, which produced agreement on recognition and social partnership. The company and the union put in a successful bid to the DTI's Partnership Fund, which aims to make organisations aware of best practice in partnership. This funded six months of workshops, facilitated by Ruskin College.

The partnership has produced tangible results, including a pay progression agreement, which has helped the company to achieve a retention rate much higher than that prevalent in the call centre industry. The partnership has also helped the company to win contracts with the public sector (Walsh 2001).

New legislation introduced by the Labour Government supported the new approach. Under the Employment Relations Act 1999, all workers have the right to be accompanied by a fellow worker or union official to disciplinary proceedings. The Employment Act 2002 set out the statutory rights of union learning representatives, who have a key role in helping to promote learning and development within organisations which recognise unions.

Perhaps most important, the 1999 Act introduced a statutory right to union recognition through ballot, as long as 50 per cent of workers vote in favour of recognition and at least 40 per cent of those eligible to vote are in favour. This ensures that a small minority of the workforce cannot force through recognition.

Crucial recognition agreements were those with Honda and Sheerness Steel in 2001. Honda is a classic example of the 'good' company which feels that because it is a good company, unions are not needed (Clement 2001), while Sheerness Steel was the scene of a bitter derecognition dispute in 1992 between the ISTC and the then owners, CoSteel (Gall 2001).

REFLECTIVE ACTIVITY 3.10

Union recognition

What do you think are the advantages and disadvantages to employers of recognising trade unions?

HR RESPONSES TO CHANGES IN THE COMPETITIVE ENVIRONMENT

We illustrate this section with a reflective activity and a case study which analyse examples where environmental change had to be met with HR responses.

REFLECTIVE ACTIVITY 3.11

British Airways

After privatisation in the 1980s, British Airways was extremely successful under the leadership of Sir Colin (later Lord) Marshall. Marshall's strategy was to emphasise customer care and employee empowerment in a (largely successful) attempt to build the 'World's Favourite Airline'. He shed the airline's previous quasi-RAF culture and ensured that the old nickname of 'Bloody Awful' became a thing of the past.

In 1996, Marshall became chairman and was replaced as chief executive by Bob Ayling, who had a very different vision. He saw BA as overstaffed and bloated, with an excessive cost base. Although profits were still high, as a result of the airline boom which followed the recovery from the first Gulf War in 1991, he initiated an ambitious cost-cutting programme, which inevitably involved redundancies.

In practice, few redundancies were actually carried through, but the result was labour unrest in 1997 which cost BA £130 million. By 2000, BA had slumped into a loss and morale was at rock bottom. In March 2000, Ayling was sacked and replaced by the Australian Rod Eddington, who had previously run Qantas.

Before Eddington could impose his own personality on the company, BA, like other world airlines, was hit by the hammer blow of the 11 September 2001 attacks. BA reacted very quickly and announced 12,000 redundancies (about 20 per cent of staff). Twenty per cent of all Heathrow flights were scrapped.

The recovery from 11 September was slow, but by 2004 BA was back in profit. It was then hit by the side-effects of the redundancy programme. It found itself under-staffed, particularly among check-in staff. The result was long waits for check-in, rising tempers among customers, stress for staff and a soaring absenteeism rate. Over the August Bank Holiday, BA was forced to cancel many flights, leading to furious travellers and much adverse publicity (Harper 2000; Kim and Mauborgne 2001).

Questions

1   Given that the cost-cutting programme was necessary, what steps should BA have taken to ensure that it was carried out more effectively? Could the crisis in 2004 have been avoided?

2   What do you feel are the HR implications of the introduction of a more market-orientated culture in the public services?

TALENT MANAGEMENT

The CIPD defines 'talent' as 'those individuals who can make a difference to organisational performance, either through their immediate contribution or in the longer term by demonstrating the highest levels of potential', while 'talent management' is 'the systematic attraction, identification, development, engagement, retention and deployment of those individuals who are of particular value to an organisation' (CIPD 2009e). Capelli has a simpler definition of talent management – 'a matter of anticipating the need for human capital and then setting out a plan to meet it' (Capelli 2008).

Capelli argues that talent management, at least in the US, is in a mess. One approach is to do nothing internally and to rely on hiring talent in from outside as needed. This poaching model is dependent on someone else developing the talent and is ultimately self-defeating. The alternative approach harks back to the heyday of detailed quantitative strategic planning in the 1950s, when the environment was much more stable and benign. The problem with this approach is that all plans fail in a turbulent environment and the organisation will end up with either a surplus or a deficit of talent. A deficit is not so serious, as the shortfall can always be met by hiring in. A surplus means that talented and qualified individuals have no role to perform. An example he quotes is that of Unilever India, which found itself with 1,400 well-trained managers in 2004, 27 per cent up on 2000, despite the fact that its demand for managers had fallen after the 2001 recession.

Capelli's approach is to apply the just-in-time principles of supply chain management to talent management:

- Aim to undershoot in internal talent development and to buy in any shortfall.
- Break up development programmes into smaller segments. Rather than recruiting graduates once a year, for example, plan for two intakes instead. Break down a development programme into smaller modules, so that needs can be re-assessed at the end of each module. Concentrate on general management rather than functional skills in the early modules.
- Share the cost of development with trainees. Common in the UK, this is apparently rarer in the US.
- Keep in touch with leavers. Deloitte, for example, informs former employees of important developments in the firm.
- Involve the employee in talent management. Rather than relying on detailed succession plans, throw promotion posts open to internal competition.

In a 2009 report, *Fighting Back Through Talent Innovation* (McCartney 2009), the CIPD identified a number of strategies organisations can use to manage their talent through the recession:

- Build up the employer brand. This will make it easier to acquire talent when the economy turns.
- Acquire talent from other organisations. Some organisations are making talented individuals redundant, making more talent available on the market. Both Tesco and Standard Chartered are actively recruiting talent.
- Keep talent warm for the future. Interest potential future recruits in the company, even if there are no vacancies at present.
- Increase your focus on talent performance, engagement and retention. It is vital that talented

- employees are fully engaged and motivated.
- Review the effectiveness of current talent management programmes.
- Maximise any available funding opportunities. Management is not the only type of talent. A flow of skilled workers is also vital. The Government has increased funding for apprenticeships and this has been exploited by the Borough of Tower Hamlets and National Express.
- Encourage line managers to be less risk-averse and provide support for stretch assignments. Recruitment freezes force line managers to make better use of internal talent.
- Ask for innovative suggestions by talent pools. The talent is there – make best use of it.

- Experiential-based learning – on-the-job learning need not be expensive and can give a quick pay-off.
- Set up a leadership exchange group and partner with other organisations. Talent management across firms on a partnership basis can provide a wider range of experiences. Second managers to a charity, for example.
- Build a sense of community. People in talent pools progress faster if they can learn, share ideas and network with each other, and if they know this is actively encouraged by the organisation.

STRATEGIC RESPONSES

A later chapter on developing and implementing strategy will consider this issue in greater depth, but here we will consider strategic response in more general terms. Basically, an organisation can make only two responses if it is in an industry where it does not have monopoly or oligopoly power, and so is not in a position to manage its competition and its environment. It can opt for low price or it can opt for differentiation. In the supermarket industry, Aldi and Netto have opted for low price, albeit at the cost of low perceived quality, and have seized a somewhat precarious niche by doing so. Differentiation could include high quality, innovation or specialisation. The seminar activity at the end of the chapter examines other strategies adopted in the supermarket industry.

A firm in an oligopoly market has more freedom of manoeuvre, but it is constrained by the need to consider how its competitors will react to a change in its tactics. If it increases its price and its competitors follow, the chances are that all firms in the industry will increase their profits, although if there is a suspicion of collusion, the competition authorities may intervene. However, if our firm increases its price and the competition does not follow, our firm will lose sales and almost certainly lose profit, while the competition will gain. A monopoly has a simpler decision to make. In principle it can choose whichever combination of price and quantity produced and sold will maximise its profits, although in practice its ability to do this is constrained by the ability of new firms to enter the market (contestability).

SUMMARY

This chapter has analysed the nature of the competitive environment, explored various models which can be used and examined the responses which organisations can make to the competitive environment. A different approach to the competitive environment is given in Chapter 5 on regulation. In addition, this chapter has analysed the working of the labour market.

KEY LEARNING POINTS

- The fundamental economic problem is how to reconcile scarcity and choice. Market and mixed economies tackle these problems in slightly different ways.
- Market economies are underpinned by the concepts of supply and demand, and their interaction to create equilibrium.
- Perfect competition is an unrealistic but ideal model. Other models of the market are measured by their deviation from perfect competition.
- The extent of monopoly power can be measured either by market share or by the degree of contestability of the market in which they operate.
- Performance in oligopoly markets depends on an interaction between the firms operating in the market.
- Porter's Five Forces model is a powerful way of analysing the competitive forces operating in an industry.
- Portfolio analyses, including the Boston Matrix and the Shell Directional Policy Matrix, are valuable but must be used with care.
- The perfect competition and monopsony models are alternative ways of explaining the working of the labour market.
- Since the 1970s, manufacturing has declined rapidly in the UK, along with a growth in employment in services. This has helped to lead to an increasing feminisation of the UK workforce. Globalisation and computerisation have also led to the growth of flexible forms of work organisation.
- The labour force in the UK has increasingly been feminised, although inequality of opportunity between men and women still persists.
- The psychological contract has evolved from an emphasis on job security, to employability, and to work–life balance.
- Workforce planning has returned as a key tool in HR responses to the recession.
- Trade union membership in the UK has almost halved as a result of changes in social and industrial structure. The response of the unions has been to develop the concept of New Unionism.

QUESTIONS

1   What would you say are the differences between a pure command economy and an economy with a command mentality?

2   What do you understand by the concept of dynamic pricing?

3   What are the differences between oligopoly and monopolistic competition?

4   Why is non-price competition a favoured strategy in an oligopolistic market?

5   What are the Five Forces identified by Porter in his model?

6   What criticisms have been made of the Five Forces model?

7   Why might a firm decide not to drop a 'dog' product, as identified in the Boston Matrix?

8   How well do you think that the perfect competition model of the labour market explains wages and employment?

9   Under what circumstances can trade union activity increase both wages and employment?

10   Why do you think that the share of manufacturing in the UK's GDP has fallen?

EXPLORE FURTHER

FURTHER READING

The theoretical background to this chapter is covered in any good economics textbook, such as Lipsey and Chrystal's *Principles of Economics* (Oxford University Press) or Alain Anderson's *Economics* (Causeway Press/Pearson).

Each edition of *Impact*, the CIPD's quarterly update on policy and research (available to members through the CIPD website), has an article by John Philpott, the CIPD's Chief Economist until 2012, on some aspect of the labour market.

There is a useful guide from the CIPD and ACAS, *How to Manage Your Workforce in a Recession*, published in February 2009 (CIPD/ACAS 2009).

USEFUL WEBSITES

As a manager you need to be able to apply the theory to contemporary examples and situations. The best way to do this is to make sure that you regularly read *The Economist* and at least one of the quality broadsheet newspapers – preferably two, one broadly liberal, such as the *Guardian* or the *Independent*, and one broadly conservative, such as *The Times* or the *Daily Telegraph*. The *Financial Times* is also very useful and easier to read than you might think. All of these have their own websites on which you can access their archives, but only the *Guardian* website (www.guardian.co.uk), which also includes the *Observer*, is free. You can access *The Economist* via the CIPD website. Most local libraries provide free access to the Thomson newspaper website, which includes all the newspapers mentioned above. Both our local libraries (Essex and Hertfordshire) provide this service. You should certainly check your own local library website.

AUDIO AND VIDEO MATERIAL

The CIPD produced two excellent podcasts on redundancy in March 2009. The first (Podcast 29 Part 1) discusses managerial issues around redundancy, while the second (Podcast 29 Part 2) discusses practical and legal issues.

Michael Porter has a *Harvard Business Review* video on YouTube (www.youtube.com/user/HarvardBusiness), *The Five Competitive Forces that Shape Strategy*, which supports his *HBR* article with the same title (Porter 2008).

SUPERMARKETS: AN OLIGOPOLISTIC INDUSTRY

Introduction

The supermarket industry has come a long way since Sainsbury's opened the first self-service supermarket in the UK in 1951. Until the 1970s, the industry was fragmented, with a large number of supermarket groups mostly operating small stores, and over 100,000 independent grocery outlets of various types. Economies of scale were low, with deliveries being made direct by wholesalers or manufacturers to individual stores. Supermarkets were in town centres and most people shopped regularly several times a week.

By the late 1970s, two leaders had emerged from the pack – Sainsbury's and Tesco. Sainsbury's was a private family company until 1973. It was concentrated in London and the south-east, with a mainly middle-class clientele. Tesco was a much younger company, founded by Jack (later Lord) Cohen, who was responsible for the notorious slogan 'pile 'em high, sell 'em cheap'. In the late 1970s, Tesco began the slow and at times painful move upmarket that has continued ever since. The two firms were neck and neck in the market until 1995, when Tesco took the lead for the first time.

Tesco is now way out in front, with a market share of 30.4 per cent in 2006 (Competition Commission 2007). Sainsbury's, with 15.9 per cent, is neck and neck with Asda (16.5 per cent), which was a northern-based also-ran until it was taken over by the biggest grocer in the world, Walmart of the US, in June 1999. In fourth place is Morrisons, which again was a long-established northern chain which came from nowhere to take over the struggling but larger Safeway group in 2004. It had 10.3 per cent of the market in 2006, but is having trouble in digesting its prey. Its market share was significantly higher immediately after the takeover.

Between 2000 and 2006, total supermarket grocery sales rose by 26 per cent in real terms, although there was a small fall in the total number of stores. Supermarkets had increased their share of grocery sales over this period from 67 per cent to 72 per cent. Convenience stores held their market share at 20 per cent, while other grocery outlets, including specialist grocery stores, fell from 13 per cent to 8 per cent (Competition Commission 2007).

Superstores

In the late 1970s, the UK supermarket groups started to adopt the French concept of hypermarkets – huge out-of-town stores. In the UK they became known as superstores. A superstore was defined as a store with at least 25,000 square feet of selling space, at least 20 checkouts and selling at least 16,000 lines. In theory, a superstore can be located anywhere, but increasingly they came to be purpose-built buildings on green or brownfield sites either on the edge of towns or out of town, with their own extensive and normally free car parking. Increasingly, they also included a petrol station selling cut-price petrol, rapidly making the supermarket chains the biggest retailers of petrol in the UK. Evidence suggested that people were prepared to drive up to ten miles to visit a superstore. By 1993 there were 750 superstores, taking half of all grocery sales. Superstores yielded very high economies of scale. They were supplied from huge centralised depots, which minimised distribution costs, and the huge superstore buildings were very cheap to maintain. Increasingly, the big groups used new technology to improve efficiency and lower costs.

Electronic point of sale (EPOS) was used by all the big groups. This enabled the store to re-order automatically from the till, to minimise on warehousing, to maximise use of shelf space as less stock needed to be on the shelves, and to react almost instantaneously to changed circumstances. Combined with EFTPOS (electronic funds transfer at point of sale), transaction costs were lowered. Both EPOS and EFTPOS, although very cost-effective, were extremely expensive to install and stretched the financial resources of the smaller groups.

By the mid-1990s, the explosive growth period of superstores was over. Most of the best sites had gone and the Government was tightening up the planning controls on new development. The response of the supermarkets, particularly Tesco, was fourfold:

- *Extended opening hours* – many of the larger stores are now open 24 hours a day and only close (very reluctantly) on Christmas Day.
- *a move into e-commerce*, with grocery deliveries co-ordinated from the local store
- *a move back into town centres* – Tesco started to develop its Tesco Metro chain and Sainsbury's started Sainsbury's Central. Both aimed particularly at lunchtime and commuter shoppers, selling a more restricted range of convenience goods.
- *introduction of new services*, such as pharmacies, film processing and in some cases dry cleaning.

Diversification

Another growth route for the supermarkets was diversification. Both Tesco and Sainsbury's accelerated their movement into the convenience store market through takeovers. Tesco took over T&S Stores in 2004, acquiring 850 stores, and Sainsbury's took over Jacksons Stores (110 stores)

(Wheatcroft 2004). Even the Co-op got into the act, taking over Alldays, doubling its number of convenience stores to over 2,300. At the end of 2006, Tesco owned 1,150 convenience stores and Sainsbury's 287, together making up 3 per cent of the national convenience stores total (Competition Commission 2007). The big groups also moved heavily into non-food sales, which now make up more than 10 per cent of their total sales (Hiscott 2004). One pound in every eight spent in the UK goes to Tesco. It sells more DVDs than HMV and more shampoo than Boots (Purvis 2004). In the summer of 2004, it was reported that Asda had become the UK's biggest clothing retailer, overtaking Marks & Spencer. Sainsbury's for a long time owned the DIY store Homebase.

Diversification has also been global, particularly by Tesco. They have moved into France, Hungary, Poland and Thailand, and are poised to move into China. They are thus excellently positioned to exploit the expansion of EU membership into central Europe in May 2004. Sainsbury's has made less good strategic decisions by opting for expansion in the US, a saturated market. Asda has gone the other way. It has been expanded into by Walmart, with its huge purchasing power, which gives Asda a bigger influence on the market than its market share would suggest.

Price wars

Supermarkets are notorious for their price wars. These are launched by all the groups at regular intervals with a fanfare of publicity. The reaction of customers to price wars tends, probably rightly, to be cynical. Market research in the summer of 1993, during a particularly intense period of price-cutting, showed that more than half of shoppers regarded price cuts as gimmicks, 20 per cent said they took no notice and only 22 per cent believed they were genuine. Price cuts always tend to be concentrated on known value items (KVIs) – the 200 or so items, such as tea, butter and coffee, where customers remember prices. The great bulk of the 20,000 lines stocked by the average superstore are not affected by price cuts. The analysts Smith New Court estimated that the 1993–94 price war would have saved on average 1.5p on a £100 shopping trolley. Remember also that in the main it is not the supermarkets who pay for the price cuts – it is the suppliers.

All the major supermarkets engage in below-cost selling (selling goods below their cost price), representing up to 3 per cent of total revenue. Below-cost selling is concentrated on dry groceries, alcohol and CDs, DVDs and books. A case study example, of Harry Potter books (Chapter 10), is discussed elsewhere in this book. The Competition Commission does not think that below-cost selling is part of a predatory policy aimed at excluding rivals, but does think that it could unintentionally harm smaller grocery retailers and specialist stores (bookshops in the case of Harry Potter). If it leads to these shops exiting the market, this could harm consumers (Competition Commission 2007).

After an investigation of the industry, the Office of Fair Trading in 2002 brought in a 'voluntary' code of practice governing how supermarkets treat their suppliers, particularly farmers. A review of the working of the Code of Practice in 2005 found that on the whole the supermarkets had complied with its terms (Competition Commission 2007).

Competition

In the mid-1990s, supermarkets appeared for the first time to be facing serious new competition. On the one

hand this came from the American warehouse club operation Costco, a giant cash and carry, which opened its first store in the UK in 1993. Tesco, Sainsbury's, and the then number three in the market, Argyll, brought a joint High Court action claiming that Costco was really a retailer, not a wholesaler, and so should have been subject to the tougher retail planning controls. They lost, in a welter of bad publicity (Cohen 1993). However, the warehouse club concept failed to take off in the UK.

The other new competition came from the entry into the market of discount stores from the continent, particularly Aldi and Netto, which had been very successful in Germany and the Netherlands. They stocked a very limited range, mainly of tertiary brands (brands which no-one had ever heard of), and at rock-bottom prices. Although much feared at the time, they seem only to have affected the bottom end of the market, particularly Kwik Save.

Supermarkets and the recession

Like the rest of the economy, supermarkets were hard hit by the recession that started in 2008, which coincided with a spike in food price inflation to 13 per cent. The first impact was a significant trading-down by consumers. In the summer of 2008, the 'hard discounter' Aldi was achieving annual sales growth of 17 per cent, with a 25 per cent increase in footfall and a 17 per cent increase in customers from the ABC1 social groups. By Christmas 2008, Aldi's growth rate was up to 25 per cent. By contrast, Tesco's year-on-year growth, at 4.6 per cent, was below the market average of 6.2 per cent (Finch 2009a). The other big losers were the upmarket Waitrose and Marks & Spencer.

By the summer of 2009, the big retailers had recovered their nerve and were hitting back hard against the hard discounters. Tesco launched its own 'discounter' range and rebranded itself as 'Britain's biggest discounter'. Asda went for a 'round pound' promotion, selling hundreds of goods for £1. Sainsbury's went for 'switch and save', showing the saving in switching from branded products to its own brands, while its advertising frontman, Jamie Oliver, showed how to feed a family for a fiver. Even Waitrose launched a new budget range called Essentials, which now accounts for 15 per cent of its turnover.

The result was that the explosive growth of the hard discounters was stopped in its tracks. In the year to July 2009, Aldi's sales were up 8.3 per cent, but this was beaten by Morrisons at 9.5 per cent and virtually equalled by Asda, Sainsbury's and Waitrose. The only group unable to show a strong comeback was the market leader, Tesco, with growth of just 4.5 per cent. The result was a fall in its market share, down from a peak of 32 per cent to just 30.6 per cent (Finch 2009b). In August 2009, it announced that its was doubling the value of the Clubcard reward scheme, from 1 per cent to 2 per cent, in effect a further price cut of 1 per cent on all purchases (Baker 2009).

There was also significant further restructuring in the industry. One significant change to the structure of the market was the demise of Somerfield, taken over by the Co-op in March 2009. The Competition Commission required more than 100 ex-Somerfield stores to be sold off, of which 22 were bought by Waitrose. The new Co-op has a market share of around 7 per cent, putting it firmly in fifth place, well ahead of Waitrose and Aldi (*Retail Week* 2009). In 2010, Asda/Walmart took over the UK operations of the Danish cut-price retailer Netto in an attempt to get a foothold in the convenience store sector of the market, previously dominated by Tesco, and to a lesser extent by Sainsbury's and the Co-op (*Independent* 2010).

The market was then stunned in January 2012 by a profit warning from Tesco, the first for 20 years. The company announced that underlying sales were down by 2.3 per cent for the six weeks to 7 January (covering the key Christmas and New Year trading period), while Sainsbury's grew by 2.3 per cent and Morrisons by 0.7 per cent over the same period. Even more seriously, Tesco announced that profit growth for 2012–13 would be 'minimal', compared with the 8–10 per cent expected (Thompson 2012).

The shortfall in performance was blamed on the way in which Tesco had used its UK business as a cash cow to finance its expansion in the US and the Far East. Between 2007 and 2012, the average number of workers in a typical 40,000 square feet superstore fell from 275 to 226, with a resulting fall in customer service (Wood 2012). In the short term Tesco was also hit by the failure of its Big Price Drop discounting campaign, financed largely by cutting the rewards paid on its Clubcard scheme (Moore 2012).

In April 2012 Tesco announced its Build a Better Tesco programme. Its key points were to recruit 20,000 more staff in the UK (cost £350 million), improve training, revamp existing stores (£300 million) and boost the online business (£200 million). The future emphasis was based on opening more, smaller Metro-style stores and an end to the hypermarket building programme, which would save £300–400 million a year. Hypermarket sales were particularly hardhit, as non-food sales were increasingly going online. Tesco was also hit by a downgrading of its credit rating by Moody's from A3 to Baa1 (Felsted 2012a, 2012b, 2012c).

By the summer of 2012 there was no clear evidence that the Build a Better Tesco programme was working. Underlying sales at Tesco were still falling, and with the double-dip recession, sales were once again shifting both to the upmarket Waitrose and to the discounters Aldi and Lidl (*Guardian* 2012, Felsted 2012d). On a positive note, Tesco dominated the rapidly growing online grocery business, with a 48 per cent market share (Moore 2012). In December 2012 Tesco announced that it was withdrawing from the US, at a cost of £1.5 billion.

The whole of the sector was also coming to realise that their rush into online trading had perhaps been a mistake. Figures released in early 2013 suggested that while it cost a supermarket around £20 to assemble and deliver an online order, the highest charge which it appeared the market could bear was £5. The result was that the three supermarkets which had gone heavily into online (Tesco, Asda and Sainsbury's) were to a large extent cannibalising their own sales rather than gaining from each other, while the fourth, Morrisons, was losing market share because it had not gone heavily online. None of the four was a clear winner from e-commerce (Pratley 2013).

Questions

1. Why do you think the competition authorities allowed Tesco to take over T&S Stores, even though Tesco had a market share over the 25 per cent which would make it a monopoly under UK law?

2. In what ways does the behaviour of the supermarkets fit with the theory of oligopoly?

3. Carry out a Five Forces analysis of the UK supermarket industry.

4. Tesco has a full-time equivalent UK workforce of 194,000. How can such a huge organisation keep track of its talent?

5. Why would a large supermarket chain be interested in local pay bargaining? Why would the union (USDAW) be opposed to this?

REFERENCES

Akerlof, G. (1970) The market for lemons: quality uncertainty and the market mechanism. *Quarterly Journal of Economics*. Vol 84, August.

Anderton, A. (2006) *Economics*. 4th edition. Harlow: Pearson.

Atkinson, A. (1984) Manpower strategies for the flexible organization. *Personnel Management*. August.

Bailey, D. (2009) *How to plan for economic restructuring, redundancies and/or closure*. Birmingham: Centre for Urban and Regional Studies, University of Birmingham.

Baker, R. (2009) Tesco extends double points offer as market share dips. *Marketing Week*. 20 August.

Barber, B. (1998) Speech to the New Labour and the Labour Movement Conference. 19–20 June.

Baron, A. (2010) What's the future for workforce planning? *Impact*. Vol 33. October.

BBC. (2012) London 2012: Nick Buckles regrets taking contract. 12 July. Available at: www.bbc.co.uk/news/uk-18866153 [Accessed 21 July 2012].

Beecroft, A. (2011) *Report on employment law*. London: Department for Business, Innovation and Skills.

Briggs, P. (2009) *Northern Tanzania*. 2nd edition. Chalfont St Peter: Bradt.

Briner, R. and Conway, N. (2001) *Understanding psychological contracts at work: a critical evaluation of theory and research*. Oxford: Oxford University Press.

Burke, A., van Stel, A. and Thurik, R. (2010) Blue ocean vs five forces. *Harvard Business Review*. Vol 88, No 5. May.

Cable, V. (2012) *Statement by Vince Cable on the Beecroft Employment Law Report*. London: Department for Business, Innovation and Skills.

Capelli, P. (2008) *Talent on demand: managing talent in an age of uncertainty*. Cambridge, MA: Harvard Business School Press.

Cascio, W.F. and Wynn, P. (2004) Managing a downsizing process. *Human Resource Management*. Vol 43.

Chartered Management Institute. (2006) *National management salary survey*. London: CMI.

Chartered Management Institute. (2007) *National management salary survey*. London: CMI.

Chartered Management Institute. (2009) *National management salary survey*. London: CMI.

Christy, R. and Christy, G. (2009) The strategic context. In C. Rayner and D. Adam-Smith (eds) *Managing and leading people*. 2nd edition. London: Chartered Institute of Personnel and Development.

Churchard, C. (2009a) 'Survivor syndrome' hits UK workforce. *People Management*. 7 August.

Churchard, C. (2009b) CBI proposes alternative to redundancy scheme. *People Management*. 6 July.

Churchard, C. (2009c) Honda staff vote for 3% pay cut to save jobs. *People Management*. 16 June.

Churchard, C. (2009d) Voluntary measures will secure BA's future, says HR chief. *People Management*. 17 July.

CIA. (2012) *The world factbook*. Available at: www.cia.gov/library/publications/the-world-factbook [Accessed 1 July 2012].

CIPD. (2004) *Frequently asked questions: parental rights and other family-friendly provisions*. London: Chartered Institute of Personnel and Development.

CIPD. (2005) *Managing the psychological contract*. Factsheet. London: Chartered Institute of Personnel and Development.

CIPD. (2009a) *Labour market outlook*. Spring. London: Chartered Institute of Personnel and Development.

CIPD. (2009b) *Labour market outlook*. Summer. London: Chartered Institute of Personnel and Development.

CIPD. (2009c) *Employee outlook: job-seeking in a recession*. London: Chartered Institute of Personnel and Development.

CIPD. (2009d) *Work–life balance*. Factsheet. London: Chartered Institute of Personnel and Development.

CIPD. (2009e) *Talent management: an overview*. Factsheet. London: Chartered Institute of Personnel and Development.

CIPD. (2009f) *Managing redundancy, parts 1 and 2*. Podcast 29. London: Chartered Institute of Personnel and Development.

CIPD. (2010) *Resourcing and talent planning*. Survey report. London: Chartered Institute of Personnel and Development.

CIPD. (2012) *Dealing with dismissal and compensated no-fault dismissal for microbusinesses: submission to BIS*. London: Chartered Institute of Personnel and Development.

CIPD/ACAS. (2009) *How to manage your workforce in a recession*. London: Chartered Institute of Personnel and Development.

Clancy, C. (2009) The labour market and the economy. *Economic and Labour Market Review*. February.

Clement, B. (2001) Honda workers vote for union recognition. *Independent*. 11 December.

Cohen, N. (1993) Thurrock, Essex, USA. *Independent on Sunday*. 31 October.

Coles, S. (2009) Are we still feeling the Five Forces? *Long Range Planning*. November.

Competition Commission. (2007) *Groceries market investigation: emerging thinking*. 23 January.

Connecting Industry. (2009) CBI outlines new employment measures to help business through critical recovery period. 13 July.

Dean, J. (1976) Pricing policies for new products. *Harvard Business Review*. Vol 54, Nov/Dec (first published November 1950).

DirectGov. (2010) Statutory guarantee pay. Available at: www.direct.gov.uk/en/Employment/Understandingyourworkstatus/Temporarylayoff/DG_177591 [Accessed 12 April 2010].

Dolton, P. (2005) *The labour market for teachers: a policy perspective*. London: Office of Manpower Economics.

Downes, L. (1997) Technosynthesis: beyond Porter. *Context*. Available at: www.contextmag.com/archives/199712/technosynthesis.asp

Draca, M. and Dickens, R. (2005) The employment effects of the October 2003 increase in the National Minimum Wage. *CEP Discussion Paper*. June.

easyJet. (2007) *easyJet website*. www.easyjet.com [Accessed June–July 2007].

Economist. (2003) The big easy: economics and reality. 31 May.

Family Friendly Working Hours Taskforce (2010) *Flexible working: working for families, working for business*. London, CIPD.

Felsted, A. (2012a) Tesco, every little revamp helps. *Financial Times*. 7 March.

Felsted, A. (2012b) Tesco to focus on smaller stores. *Financial Times*. 12 April.

Felsted, A. (2012c) Tesco rating cut as it reveals recovery plan. *Financial Times*. 21 April.

Felsted, A. (2012d) Clarke puts a brave face on Tesco sales slip. *Financial Times*. 12 June.

Finch, J. (2009a) Morrisons beats rivals with bumper Christmas sales. *Guardian*. 23 January.

Finch, J. (2009b) Supermarkets: big four fight back in discount food feud. *Guardian*. 25 July.

Food and Drink Europe. (2003) Flexible pricing strategy keeps shoppers happy. 11 December. Available at: www.foodanddrinkeurope.com/Retail/Flexible-pricing [Accessed 3 July 2012].

Gall, G. (2001) ISTC wins in recognition vote. *People Management*. 22 November.

Gallie, D. (2000) The labour force. In A.H. Halsey and J. Webb (eds) *Twentieth-century british social trends*. Basingstoke: Macmillan.

Ghoshal, S. (2000) Value creation. *Executive Excellence*. Vol 17, No 11. November.

Giddens, A. (2006) *Sociology*. 5th edition. Cambridge: Polity Press.

Girma, S., Goyt, A., Strobl, E. and Walsh, F. (2007) *Creating jobs through public subsidies: an empirical analysis*. IZA Discussion Paper 3168. Bonn, Germany: Institute for the Study of Labour.

Grimshaw, D., Ward, K., Rubery, J. and Beynon, H. (2001) Organisations and the transformation of the internal labour market. *Work, Employment and Society*. Vol 15, No 1.

Guardian. (2012) Tesco loses more market share. *Guardian*. 24 April.

Guest, D.E. and Conway, N. (2002) *Pressure at work and the psychological contract*. London: Chartered Institute of Personnel and Development.

Handy, C. (1991) *Inside organizations*. London: BBC.

Harper, K. (2000) Frustration at the world's favourite airline. *Management Today*. January.

Hiscott, G. (2004) Big chains strengthen hold on Britain's shoppers. *Independent*. 10 August.

Hodgkin, P. (2007) Gift rap. *Guardian*. 5 September.

Hoyos, C. (2006) Opec vows to defend minimum $60 for oil. *Financial Times*. 20 October.

Hutton, W. (2012) The American election is really a battle for the future of capitalism. *Observer*. 22 July.

Hyman, R. (1987) Strategy or structure: capital, labour and control. *Work, Employment and Society*. Vol 1, No 1. p30.

Independent. (2010) Asda to take over Netto stores. *Independent*. 27 May.

Johnson, G., Whittington, R. and Scholes, K. (2011) *Exploring corporate strategy*. 9th edition. Harlow: Pearson.

Joyce, P. and Woods, A. (1996) *Essential strategic management: from modernism to pragmatism*. Oxford: Butterworth-Heinemann.

Kay, J. (2003) *The truth about markets*. London: Allen Lane/The Penguin Press.

Kent, K. (2009) Employment changes over 30 years. *Economics and Labour Market Review*. Vol 3, No 2.

Kim, C. and Mauborgne, R. (2001) How to earn commitment. *Financial Times*. 22 October.

Kim, C. and Mauborgne, R. (2005) *Blue ocean strategy*. Cambridge, MA: Harvard Business School Press.

Kimberly, J. and Craig, E. (2001) Work as a life experience. *Financial Times*. 5 November.

Lipsey, R. and Chrystal, A. (1999) *Principles of economics*. 9th edition. Oxford: Oxford University Press.

Lynch, R. (2006) *Corporatestrategy*. 4th edition. Harlow: FT Prentice Hall.

Manning, A. (2003) *Monopsony in motion: imperfect competition in labour markets*. Princeton, NJ: Princeton University Press.

Manning, A. and Petrolongo, B. (2005) The part-time pay penalty. *Centrepiece*. December.

Marchington, A. and Wilkinson, A. (2008) *Human resource management at work*. 4th edition. London: Chartered Institute of Personnel and Development.

McAfee, R. and te Velde, V. (2005) *Dynamic pricing in the airline industry*. Los Angeles: California Institute of Technology.

McCarthy, T. (2009) BA staff shows blitz spirit. *People Management*. 30 July.

McCartney, C. (2009) *Fighting back through talent innovation*. London: Chartered Institute of Personnel and Development.

Metcalf, D. (2007) Why has the British National Minimum Wage had little or no impact on employment? *CEP Discussion Paper*. April.

Moore, J. (2012) Tesco certainly has big issues, but critics must be mad to say it's in a real crisis. *Independent*. 19 April.

Nagle, T. and Holden, R. (2002) *The strategy and tactics of pricing*. London: Prentice Hall.

National Statistics. (2010) *Social trends*. Vol 40.

Office for National Statistics. (2005) *Time use survey* [refers to 2003]. London: Office for National Statistics.

People Management. (2009a) CIPD calls for subsidy for young jobseekers. 24 August.

People Management. (2009b) British Airways staff asked to work for free. 16 June.

Philpott, J. (2002) HRH – a work audit. *CIPD Perspectives.*Summer.

Philpott, J. (2009a) The cost to employers of redundancy. *Impact.* Vol 26, February.

Philpott, J. (2009b) Labour cost savings from alternatives to redundancy. *Impact.* Vol 27, May.

Philpott, J. (2012) Counting the cost of the jobs recession. *Impact.* Vol 39, July.

Pidd, H. (2009) Honda's Swindon factory reopens. *Guardian.* 1 June.

Porter, M. (1980) *Competitive strategy: techniques for analyzing industries and competition.* London: Macmillan.

Porter, M. (2008) The five competitive forces that shape strategy. *Harvard Business Review.* Vol 86, No 1, January.

Pratley, N. (2013) Online shopping: supermarkets eating themselves. *Guardian.* 5 January.

Professional Manager. (2001) Focused females forge ahead. November.

Purvis, A. (2004) Why supermarkets are getting richer and richer. *Observer.* 25 June.

Retail Week. (2009) Co-op reports record full-year profits. 6 May.

Roche, W., Teague, P., Coughlan, A. and Fahy, M. (2011) *Human resources in the recession: managing and representing people at work in Ireland.* Dublin: Labour Relations Commission.

Rousseau, D. (2004) Psychological contracts in the workplace: understanding the ties that motivate. *Academy of Management Executive.* Vol 18, No 1, February.

Schumpeter, J. (1950) *Capitalism, socialism and democracy.* 3rd edition. New York: Harper and Row.

Skapinker, M. (2004) The psychology of consumption. *Financial Times.* 31 March.

Social Trends. (2004) Chapter 13: Lifestyles and social participation. Vol 34. London: HMSO.

Stewart, H. (2009) Union says yes to Honda pay cut. *Guardian.* 22 June.

Tanzania National Parks. (2009) *Tariffs November 2009.* Available at: www.tanzaniaparks.com/parkfees/Tariffs-New-Dec11 [Accessed 1 July 2012].

Thomas, T. (2009) Tesco eyes loyalty value with Clubcard relaunch. *Marketing.* 13 May.

Thompson, J. (2012) Supermarket giant says Christmas was disappointing and warns that growth in year ahead will be minimal. *Independent.* 13 January.

Turner, P. (2010) From manpower planning to capacity planning – why we need workforce planning, in CIPD, *Reflections on workforce planning*. London: Chartered Institute of Personnel and Development.

Walker, R. (1990) Analysing the business portfolio in Black & Decker Europe. In B. Taylor and J. Harrison (eds) *The manager's casebook of business strategy*. Oxford: Butterworth-Heinemann.

Walsh, J. (2001) A happy reunion. *People Management*. 8 November.

Weiss, R. and Mehrotra, A. (2001) Dynamic pricing and the future of e-commerce; an economic and legal analysis. *Virginia Journal of Law and Technology*. Vol 11, Summer.

Wheatcroft, P. (2004) Supermarkets take a convenient route. *The Times*. 17 August.

Wilson, I. (2000) *The new rules of corporate conduct*. Westport, CT: Quorum Books.

Wood, Z. (2012) Tesco calls time on megastores after profit warning shock. *Observer*. 15 January.

Government Policy

INTRODUCTION

In this chapter we will analyse the evolution of government policy in social, economic and industrial fields, and the impact of government policy on organisations. As developments in the UK are heavily influenced by the actions of the EU, we will be concerned with both UK and EU policy. We start with formal legislative procedures in the UK and the EU, and then go on to consider informal influences on the evolution of policy. We then consider recent developments in policy in the UK.

THE LEGISLATIVE PROCESS IN THE UK AND THE EU

THE UK

Most legislation originates in government departments and is directly sponsored by the Government. Some legislation, particularly on matters of conscience, starts as a private member's bill. Most of these fail. Normally they only pass with substantial cross-party support, and support, or at worst neutrality, from the Government.

Indeed, frequently the purpose of a private member's bill is not actually to pass a new law, but to bring public attention to an issue which is important to an individual MP and those pressure groups who support him or her. In this section, we are only going to look at government bills.

At least for bills published relatively early in the life of a parliament, the general subject matter of the bill will appear in the governing party's election manifesto – 'we intend to bring in legislation to put right the long-standing grievances concerning...'

The next (optional) stage is a green paper. This is a consultative document setting out the case for the forthcoming legislation and the pros and cons of various approaches to legislation. This does not commit the Government to anything, but forms a basis for discussion with interested parties and pressure groups. After consultation on the green paper, the Government may choose to:

- follow it up with a white paper
- go straight to legislation
- drop the proposal.

A white paper firms up on the proposal, but again does not commit the Government on detail. A lengthy period of consultation may then follow.

The parliamentary session normally starts in November, with the Queen's Speech, where the Queen sets out the programme of legislation for the coming year – 'my government intends to introduce legislation on...' The Government will then publish a bill, drafted by specialist parliamentary lawyers. The bill then goes through a number of formal stages:

- first reading – a formal presentation of the bill to the Commons
- second reading – a full debate on the principles of the bill rather than the details
- committee stage – the bill is then scrutinised in detail by a standing committee of the Commons, consisting of between 15 and 20 MPs, with a government majority; the bill will be debated and voted on clause by clause, and some provisions may be amended
- report stage – the amended bill goes back to the full Commons, where the Government has an opportunity to reverse any amendments forced on it at the committee stage
- third reading – this is formal, and not usually debated
- the bill then goes to the House of Lords, and repeats the same stages as in the Commons. The Lords can amend the bill or reject it. If they reject it, this delays the bill for one parliamentary session. Having passed through the Lords, the bill goes back to the Commons, which can reject any amendments made by the Lords
- royal assent – the Queen then agrees to the bill, which becomes an Act. In theory the Queen could reject the bill, but this has not been done for 300 years.

As a legal document, every word of an Act matters, and it is subject to interpretation by the courts.

THE EU

This is very different from the process in the UK. Initial proposals for legislation are drawn up by the Commission, and must be based on one of the EU treaties (Rome,

Maastricht, Amsterdam, Nice, etc). Each treaty has to be unanimously ratified by the member states. By contrast, in the UK the Government has a free hand to legislate on anything that it chooses (including leaving the EU).

At this stage, the proposal is known as a draft framework law or a draft directive. The draft then goes out for consultation to the Council of Ministers, the European Parliament, and the Social Partners (the two employers' bodies UNICE, CEEP and the trade union body ETUC). The Commission then revises its proposals, which are then formally presented to the Council of Ministers, which will take a decision on unanimity or qualified majority voting, depending on the nature of the legislation. The European Parliament has the right to debate and to comment on the proposed directive, but until the Lisbon Treaty is adopted, no right to amend or reject it. Under the Lisbon Treaty (which replaced the ill-fated EU Constitution), the European Parliament will have the right to reject or amend the proposal, but only by a majority of more than half of all MEPs (not just those who vote).

The law will be adopted if:

● both the Parliament and the Council of Ministers approve it (by either unanimity or qualified majority, depending on the type of legislation)
● the Council of Ministers approves the Parliament's amendments. (If the Commission opposes an amendment, it must be approved by a unanimous vote of the Council of Ministers.)

The directive then has to be implemented by member states – ie EU directives become law in the UK through a UK Act of Parliament. At the end of 2003, there were about 2,500 EU directives, and the compliance rate by member states ranged between 96 and 99 per cent (Mulvey 2003).

REFLECTIVE ACTIVITY 4.1

UK and EU legislation

1   What are the differences in passing legislation between the UK and the EU?

2   Which system do you think is more democratic?

INFORMAL INFLUENCES ON POLICY

Political parties

Traditionally the electoral system in the UK has ensured a predominantly two-party electoral system (plus regional and/or nationalist parties representing Scotland, Wales and Northern Ireland) – a broadly 'right-wing' party in favour of maintaining the status quo (the Tories in the early nineteenth century, the Conservatives from the late nineteenth century onwards), and a broadly 'left-wing' party in favour of change (the Whigs in the early nineteenth century, the Liberals in the late nineteenth century, Labour from the 1920s). The two wings broadly represented different class interests – the right wing the 'haves' who resisted change (the ruling class, and later the middle class), and the left wing the 'have-nots', those seeking change (the working class). Thus ideology and social class were seen as underpinning the UK party system. In Reflective Activity 4.2 you will explore how far this is still true.

The influence of members of political parties, even MPs, over government policy-making is small, and probably getting smaller. MPs are subject to party discipline, and although they can and do vote against their own government on occasions, every MP knows that if he votes to bring down his own government, his party career will be finished. Even massive revolts are unlikely to change government policy, as can be shown by the Labour revolt on university fees, and on the Iraq war, where even the resignation of a leading Cabinet member, Robin Cook, had no influence on policy.

Party conferences can pass resolutions critical of government policy, but governments have never had to take much notice of these. Policy is nowadays decided much more by focus groups and think tanks. MPs do have the power to force an election for the post of party leader, and when the Conservatives ousted Margaret Thatcher and replaced her with John Major, the decision was taken solely by Conservative MPs. However, the Conservative Party, like the Labour Party, now elects its leader through a complicated electoral college system, where MPs, peers, MEPs and party members all have a weighted vote.

REFLECTIVE ACTIVITY 4.2

Political parties

1   What arguments would you put forward if asked to support the argument that ideology and class no longer underpin the present party system?

2   David Farnham argues that there are two crucial differences between a political party and a pressure group (Farnham 1999, p137):

- Parties try to win political control to use political power. Pressure groups seek to influence political decisions not to get in a position where they can make those decisions themselves.
- The political programmes of parties are broad-based, while pressure groups tend to concentrate on a single issue.

Given the above, would you say that the UK Independence Party (UKIP), which won many seats in the EU elections in 2009, but failed to win any seats in the 2010 general election, is a political party or a pressure group? What about the Scottish National Party?

CASE STUDY 4.1

EASYCOUNCIL

Conservative-controlled local authorities are providing evidence for a radical new approach to the provision of local services. Hammersmith and Fulham, for example, is raising the rents for its social housing to market levels, and has suggested an end to the 'tenure for life' held by social housing tenants. Essex has suggested that social security benefits should be set and administered locally.

The most radical changes are coming from Barnet Council in north London, which includes Margaret Thatcher's old constituency of Finchley. The council has consciously modelled itself on the low-cost airlines easyJet and Ryanair. The key to the low-cost airline business model is that you get what you pay for. The *Guardian* quotes the example of a Ryanair flight from Stansted to Perugia where the fare is £2.99, but once you add in online booking (£5 – cheaper than checking in at the airport), taxes, priority booking and two bags of luggage, the cost rises to £69.26. Ryanair argues that this extends customer choice, as customers choose the level of service they need and pay accordingly.

Barnet is extending this model to local authority services. It is proposing a charge for 'jumping the queue' on planning applications. Recipients of adult social care will be given a personal budget, which they can spend how they wish, including perhaps a weekend in Eastbourne, rather than the council saying 'you need help with shopping, cleaning and meals on wheels' whether the clients wanted that package or not.

Another controversial proposal is to remove live-in wardens from sheltered housing and to replace them with mobile (and outsourced) wardens who can be summoned through alarm buttons. As the leader of Barnet Council says, 'It is surprising how able even so-called vulnerable people are. Helping people help themselves, that's the new Conservatism.' A council document, *Future Shape*, says the goals of the proposed reforms are 'facilitating self-help through behaviour change' and 'more services delivered by organisations other than the council'. Outsourcing services such as street cleaning, parking, planning and residential care is expected to save up to £15 million a year.

The programmes of councils such as Barnet present a dilemma for the Conservative leadership. David Cameron has worked hard to change the image of the Tories as the 'nasty party', but at the same time, there is a considerable attraction for a Conservative government in having cuts administered locally, where they are less visible to the general public. Hammersmith and Fulham's 3 per cent

reduction in council tax has received more attention outside the borough than its spending cuts. Indeed, the shadow Chancellor, George Osborne, said in a major speech in September 2009 that a 'Conservative government will have much to learn from Conservative local councils'. Charges for jumping the queue on NHS waiting lists, perhaps?

Labour has hit back with a 'John Lewis council' proposal – to run Lambeth Council in London as a co-operative. Suggestions include:

- an 'active citizens' dividend', whereby those involved in community organisations would get a council tax rebate
- turning local services like primary schools into citizen-led mutuals
- turning council housing estates in co-operatives.

The early evidence from Barnet is not encouraging. In the financial year 2010–11 the council spent £1.5 million to achieve savings of £1.4 million. The policy is now known as 'One Barnet' and involves the outsourcing of 70 per cent of the council's functions in two ten-year private sector contracts, worth a total of £1 billion. The ten-year life of these contracts has severe implications for local democracy, as London boroughs such as Barnet operate on a four-year electoral cycle.

Sources: Mulholland (2009); Travers (2009); Burgess (2009); Booth (2009a, 2009b, 2009c, 2010); Harris (2012).

Pressure groups

A pressure group is 'any group in society which, through political action, seeks to achieve changes which it regards as desirable or to prevent changes which it regards as undesirable' (Forman and Baldwin 1999, p128). They can broadly be classified into two main types:

- interest or sectional groups
- attitude or cause groups.

Interest groups are those pressure groups which have a common interest and they exist to promote the interests of that group. Classic examples are trade unions and employers' associations, but interest groups also include professional bodies, the Royal British Legion and the AA, the last of which started as a members' organisation but later became a public company and later still was acquired by a private equity group.

Attitude groups are those pressure groups whose members have attitudes or beliefs rather than material interests and they seek to advance particular causes. Examples include the National Trust, Oxfam, Greenpeace, Liberty, the RSPB. Some pressure groups appear to be hybrids. The Countryside Alliance, for example, would see itself as an attitude group, while its opponents would see it as an interest group.

Pressure groups have a number of important functions:

- *Intermediaries between the government and the public* – the prime role of a pressure group is obviously to apply pressure on the Government (or sometimes on other political bodies such as the EU, the IMF or a foreign government). They channel and express public opinion on key issues. Some pressure groups use professional lobbying organisations to put forward their point of view to decision-makers. American gaming interests are alleged to have spent £100 million in 2004 in support of the Gambling Bill which would introduce Las Vegas-style 'super-casinos' to the UK (Mathiason 2004). For a detailed analysis of the tactics used by the lobbyists in this case, see Hencke (2004).
- *Opponents and critics of government policy* – party discipline prevents governing party MPs from opposing government policy, while criticism from opposition parties tends to be ignored because everyone expects the Opposition to oppose. Pressure groups can provide detailed and (hopefully) constructive criticism of policy. Indeed, on some occasions pressure groups in effect write government policy for it.
- *Agents of government* – this is controversial. Increasingly, pressure groups which themselves provide services, particularly charities, receive government grants towards providing those services, which some feel may compromise their independence.
- *Publicists* to promote an interest or defend a standpoint.

REFLECTIVE ACTIVITY 4.3

A question of influence

Make a list of the ways in which pressure groups can influence the Government.

THE GOVERNMENT AND THE ECONOMY

SOME KEY DEFINITIONS

Before we can examine ways in which the Government can manage the economy, we need to define some key concepts.

Gross domestic product

The most common method of measuring the output of an economy is gross domestic product (GDP). This is the measure of the country's total annual output of goods and services. This is not the same as the sum of the outputs of all organisations in the economy, as this would involve double counting. For example, sales of cans of baked beans made by a supermarket are counted, but not sales of the tinplate for the cans made by a steelworks. When calculating GDP:

- indirect taxes and subsidies (such as VAT) are normally ignored
- exports are included, because they form part of the output of the UK
- imports are excluded, because although they are consumed in the UK, they are part of the output of other countries.

John Maynard Keynes defined GDP (or Y) in terms of an equation, as follows:

$$Y = C + G + I + X - M$$

where C is consumption, which is a function of disposable income (Y – T (taxation)), less savings, plus borrowing; G is government current spending, I is investment on long-term capital items by industry or the Government (mainly dependent on interest rates and the prospect of making a financial return), X is exports (dependent on productivity and the exchange rate), and M is imports (dependent on exchange rates and the level of national income). To stress Keynes' understanding that demand is the main driver of GDP, he argued that Y = aggregate demand (Sexton and Fortura 2005). It follows that if any of the components of aggregate demand (C, G, I and (X – M)) fall, GDP will fall. This will be important in our later discussion of current economic policy.

An important distinction to make is between GDP and the standard of living or quality of life. Governments are concerned to achieve economic growth, defined as an increase in GDP over time. Individuals are much more concerned with their own standard of living.

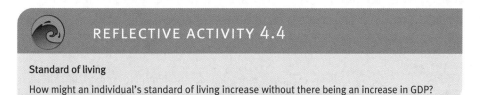

REFLECTIVE ACTIVITY 4.4

Standard of living

How might an individual's standard of living increase without there being an increase in GDP?

Business cycles

The economy tends to move in a series of ups and downs in the short term, although the long-term trend is for the size of GDP to grow. These fluctuations, over a five- to ten-year period, are known as the business cycle. Governments attempt to dampen the effects of these cycles, but have not succeeded in abolishing them entirely. The top of a cycle is known as a peak, the bottom as a trough. In the period between a peak and a trough, economic growth may merely slow down, as in the period 2001–03, following the terrorist attacks of 11 September 2001, or GDP may actually fall. If GDP falls for two consecutive quarters, this is technically known as a recession, as the UK experienced in 1973–75, 1979–81, 1990–92, 2008–09 and 2012. If two recessions follow each other in quick succession, as in 2008–09 and 2012, this is known as a double-dip recession. If a recession is both deep and long-lasting, it is known as a depression, as with the Great Depression of 1929–33 following the Wall Street Crash.

Unemployment

Unemployment is a surprisingly complex concept which has significant social as well as economic consequences. It is not even simple to define unemployment. A person can only be unemployed if he or she is out of work and seeking work. But what about someone who is:

- working part-time but would rather work full-time?
- apparently seeking work, but has totally unrealistic expectations about the sort of job which he or she could obtain?

There are two main ways of measuring unemployment:

- *Count those people who are claiming unemployment benefit (the claimant count)* – this means that those who do not have work, and are seeking work, but who do not qualify for benefit, are excluded. On the other hand, some people who are not genuinely seeking work may be included.
- *Carry out a survey and ask people whether they are employed or unemployed* – this is carried out through the Labour Force Survey, using internationally agreed definitions provided by the International Labour Organization (ILO). Here someone is classified as unemployed if they are

  - out of work
  - have been seeking work within the last four years
  - available to start work within two weeks.

The ILO method is now the Government's preferred measure, but both are regularly published in the UK. The ILO figure comes out higher than the claimant count measure, mainly because it includes large numbers of women who are ineligible for unemployment benefit.

Inflation

Inflation is a general rise in the level of prices. In the UK it is measured in three ways:

- *RPI – the Retail Price Index.* This is calculated by measuring monthly changes in the price of a basket of goods which is meant to represent the spending pattern of the average family. This is the measure used to assess yearly increases in pensions and some state benefits.
- *RPIX – the Retail Price Index excluding mortgage interest.* Until November 2003 this was the Government's preferred target measure, as it represents the underlying rate of inflation in the economy (mortgage interest rates depend on the general level of interest rates, set by the Bank of England).
- *CPI – the Consumer Price Index.* This is the agreed measure of inflation used throughout the European Union, and was adopted as the official inflation target in the UK in November 2003 (when it was known as the Harmonised Index of Consumer Prices – inevitably called hiccup!). It is now used to assess yearly increases in most state benefits excluding pensions.

Balance of payments

The balance of payments is a measure of flows of money into and out of the UK economy. It is extremely complex as it has a number of different components. The most commonly used elements are:

- *The balance of trade* – this measures imports and exports of goods.
- *The balance of payments on current account* – this measures imports and exports of goods and services.

ECONOMIC OBJECTIVES

All governments, whatever their political complexion, are basically trying to achieve four main economic objectives:

- *Economic growth* – since the 1990s this has increased by an average of around 2–2.5 per cent, with some periods of falling GDP, and others when the growth rate in the short term has gone as high as 4 per cent.

- *Full employment* – this does not mean that nobody is unemployed, but that there are in theory jobs available for those seeking them, at current wage rates. In practice, this means that full employment is achieved if the number out of work is matched by the number of unfilled vacancies.
- *Stable prices (or low inflation)* – again there is some dispute about the optimum level of inflation, but most economists would agree that it is around the Labour Government's target of 2.5 per cent on the RPIX in the late 1990s (restated as 2 per cent on the CPI in November 2003).
- *Equilibrium in the balance of payments* – that is, that the value of goods and services exported should roughly equal the value imported. This has deteriorated in recent years, with the trade deficit expected to be around £99 billion in 2011, although this is offset to some extent by a strong surplus on the balance on services.

The New Labour Government since 1997 has been more successful than most governments, at least until 2007, achieving full success on economic growth and inflation, and considerable success on full employment. The only blot on its record was a worsening balance of payments, but of course it was blown seriously off course by the onset of the credit crunch recession in 2008.

In addition, governments will have policies on other economic objectives. These might include:

- *Redistribution of income* – this is seen as a social objective in its own right, but its prime economic function is as a means to achieve economic growth. Traditionally the objective was to use the tax system to redistribute from the rich to the poor, but increasingly the distribution of income favours the rich.
- *Exchange rates* – the exchange value of the pound is seen as a political virility symbol, but it is primarily important as a means of managing the balance of payments. UK entry to the euro is of course a long-running contentious political issue.
- *The level of taxation and the level of government spending* – both in terms of their absolute level in the economy and of the balance between them.
- *Interest rates* – these are seen either as a means of controlling inflation or of managing growth.
- *Money supply* – in the 1980s this was seen as an objective in its own right, but is now seen as a means of achieving other objectives.
- *Privatisation (or nationalisation)* – linked with this is more general regulation or deregulation of the economy.

As you will see from the above list, economics is not value-free. Managing the economy inevitably has strong political and social, as well as economic, elements.

THE TOOLS OF GOVERNMENT POLICY

A range of tools are available to the Government in its objective of managing the economy.

Fiscal policy

This involves a manipulation of the level of taxation and/or government spending. The theory underpinning this was established by the economist John Maynard Keynes in the 1930s. If there is a persistent level of unemployment in the economy, he argued that this is fundamentally due to a lack of demand. In order to increase demand in the economy, the Government can inject demand into it, either by increasing its own spending, which will directly lead to a higher demand for goods and services, or by cutting taxation, which will put more money into the hands of consumers and so enable them to demand more goods and services. However, changes in taxation or public spending are subject to long time lags before they take effect and, increasingly, Chancellors of the Exchequer have not seen fiscal policy as an appropriate tool for short-term management of the economy. Instead, they have taken the view that the level of spending and taxation are much more issues of political rather than demand management policy. Gordon Brown expressed this in his Golden Rule, which states that over an economic cycle, the Government should aim for a balanced budget, that is, the revenue raised through taxation should equal the amount spent on current goods and services. This policy does allow for some flexibility, that is, for expenditure to exceed taxation during the trough phase of the cycle, as long as this is balanced by a surplus at the peak. However, the Golden Rule, and its accompanying more general policy, prudence, were torn up when the full impact of the credit crunch became apparent in the autumn of 2008.

Monetary policy

Monetary policy was strongly in vogue during the 1980s, at the height of the power of Margaret Thatcher and under the influence of the American economist Milton Friedman, who argued a direct causal link between the supply of money and the level of inflation. Policies were therefore implemented directly to control the supply of money. However, as the leading monetarist economist Sir Alan Budd, who was chief economic adviser to the Treasury between 1991 and 1997, says, 'I hope I can say without offending anyone that the experiment in seeking to control inflation by setting quantitative monetary targets did not match the hopes of its most enthusiastic supporters (among whom I am willing to count myself)' (Keegan 2004a). One of the main problems was not the existence of the link between money supply and inflation, but the difficulty in producing a watertight definition of money at a time of great technological change, including the explosive growth in the use of credit cards (which enable people to spend money they do not possess, and which does not exist until they spend it).

Monetary policy is now much simpler. It consists of control over interest rates, set by the independent Bank of England. The way in which this works will be explored in considerable detail below.

Competitiveness (supply-side) policy

Policy here is linked to the concept of NAIRU (the rate of unemployment which ensures a stable level of inflation). If the economy can be made more competitive, the rate of NAIRU should fall and the economy will be able to operate at lower levels of inflation and unemployment. This involves deregulating the markets for both goods and services and for labour, through policies including privatisation and rigorous control of monopolies and cartels. It also involves a concerted drive to increase the rate of growth of productivity in the economy, by encouraging investment in research and development, and in the enhancement of worker skills. Again, this policy will be examined in depth below.

Exchange rate policy

It is possible to manipulate the exchange rate in order to achieve economic objectives. For example, if an exchange rate is set at a level below that justified by market forces, the currency will be undervalued. This will stimulate exports, which will be artificially lowered in price, and discourage imports, which will be artificially highly priced. An overvalued currency will have the opposite result. However, there are two major snags with this.

Manipulation of the exchange rate is only seriously possible if the exchange rate is fixed. However, since the 1970s, most currencies have floated, that is, been subject to market forces. Even in a fixed exchange rate system, it is very difficult in the long term to maintain an exchange rate markedly different from that implied by market forces.

The other key issue in exchange rate policy is of course the euro. Should the UK join or not? At the moment, the UK has an opt-out from Economic and Monetary Union, and thus from the euro. However, the UK is qualified to join EMU if it chooses. In 1997, the Chancellor of the Exchequer postponed a decision on entry, saying that the UK would only consider joining if five economic tests were met: These were:

- Are business cycles and economic structures compatible so that the UK can live with euro interest rates?
- Is there sufficient flexibility to deal with any problems which might arise?
- Will joining EMU create better conditions for firms making long-term decisions to invest in the UK?
- What impact will entry have on the competitive position of the City of London?
- Will joining the euro promote higher growth, stability and a lasting increase in jobs?

If the Government decided that these tests were met, it would recommend entry to the euro, but the final decision would be taken by a referendum. Public opinion in the UK appears to be heavily against euro entry and entry is opposed by the Conservative Party and by significant elements in industry. In the last resort any decision on entry is likely to be political rather than economic. Labour may be in favour in principle, but will only hold a referendum if it is sure it will win. Most voters will probably make their decision on gut feeling, rather than the detail of the economic arguments. To no-one's surprise, the Government decided in 2003 that the Five Tests had not been met and, as a result, any decision in favour of entry has been postponed indefinitely – to the great relief of virtually everybody in the UK as the crisis in the eurozone developed from 2010 onwards. This will be discussed more fully in Chapter 6.

CASE STUDY 4.2

INFLATION AND INTEREST RATES

The impact of inflation

We have already defined inflation as a general increase in the level of prices in the economy, measured in various ways – RPI, RPIX or CPI. In the last resort this is caused by excess demand in the economy, basically when the amount of goods and services which people want to buy is greater than the productive potential of the economy – 'too much money chasing too few goods'. The generally accepted view is that inflation is harmful, and it follows from this that low inflation is beneficial, for the following reasons:

- *Increased price competitiveness for UK goods* – the important factor here is relative inflation – in order for UK goods to be competitive, UK inflation must be rising at a slower rate than that of our international competitors. Of course, if UK inflation is very rapid, it is likely that the value of the pound will fall, but this itself could generate further inflation, as import prices will rise.

- *Distribution of income will be less distorted* – high inflation benefits borrowers, particularly those with outstanding mortgages, which fall in value in real terms as the value of their houses tend to rise. In addition, the gap in money terms between wage settlements obtained by strong unions as compared with weak ones tends to be greater in times of rapid inflation.

- *Reduced uncertainty* – the more rapid the rate of inflation, and particularly the more variable it is, the more unpredictable the environment becomes for business and individuals. As a result, investment will be discouraged, as firms do not want to take risks, and the result could be falling output and rising unemployment.

- *High inflation means high nominal interest rates* – this puts pressure on the cash flows of borrowers if their main source of income is interrupted, for example by unemployment.

REFLECTIVE ACTIVITY 4.5

Deflation

If the effects of high inflation are adverse, would it be better to have falling prices (deflation), as in 2008–09?

THE LINK BETWEEN UNEMPLOYMENT AND INFLATION

In the late 1950s, Professor Phillips identified that over the previous 100 years there was an inverse relationship between the rate of change of money wages and the level of unemployment. In the short term this intuitively makes sense. If unemployment is low, workers can demand higher wages, and vice versa. As wage inflation is a very important component of general inflation, it could thus be argued that there was an inverse relationship between unemployment and inflation – if unemployment rose, inflation would fall, and vice versa. This implied that governments could in principle choose the trade-off between inflation and unemployment which best suited their overall objectives.

Unfortunately, almost as soon as Phillips identified the relationship, it ceased to apply. Throughout the 1970s, both inflation and unemployment rose steeply at the same time, giving rise to a phenomenon known as stagflation. Gradually over the 1980s, inflation was squeezed out of the system through strict control of the money supply, but only at the cost of continuing high levels of unemployment. Since 1992, unemployment has fallen considerably, while inflation has stabilised at the 2–3 per cent level.

Clearly the simple concept of the Phillips curve no longer applies, but it has been replaced by the concept of NAIRU (non-accelerating inflation rate of unemployment). This is the level of unemployment at which inflation will be stable. NAIRU appears to have been about 7–8 per cent in the 1970s, but to have fallen to around 3–4 per cent (on the ILO measure) by the early 2000s. One prime objective of governments is to continue to improve the trade-off between inflation and unemployment by lowering the level of NAIRU. This can be done through making the labour market more competitive.

However, as the Bank of England says, 'The level of the NAIRU cannot be determined with any precision for the purposes of setting monetary policy. … It is easier to construct plausible estimates after the event – ie once we have observed inflation – rather than in anticipation of it' (Bank of England 2004a). NAIRU appears to be much lower in the UK and US, with largely deregulated labour markets, than in the eurozone, where labour markets are much more heavily regulated. Of course, there is a political and social, as well as an economic, trade-off here – which is preferable, a higher risk of unemployment in the eurozone or the higher level of benefits which accompany unemployment there?

INTEREST RATES

An interest rate is simply the price of money. However, unfortunately the real world is more complicated. As an individual, you are almost certainly paying and receiving several different rates of interest – on your bank current account, on your building society account, your Internet savings account, your mortgage, your credit card, your hire-purchase agreement. Ultimately these come back to one rate, the official rate set by the Bank of England, and at which it will lend money to the banks and other financial institutions. This is set monthly by the Bank's Monetary Policy Committee.

If this official rate changes, the banks and building societies will change the rates for their own savers and borrowers. Equally importantly, an increase in interest rates affects expectations. If interest rates start to rise after a period when they have been static or falling, the expectation is that they will continue to rise in the near future. The Bank of England used this to great effect in 2004, when it made a series of quarter-point increases in interest rates, none of which was particularly serious on its own, but which had a big effect on expectations. A series of aggressive interest rate cuts in 2008–09 signalled the seriousness of the credit crunch crisis.

INTEREST RATES AND DEMAND

When interest rates are changed, demand can be affected in a number of ways:

- *Spending and saving* – an increase in interest rates makes saving more attractive and spending less attractive. Consumer spending is likely to fall. At the same time industrial investment will fall, as the margin between what an investment costs and the profit which it will produce becomes narrower.
- *Cashflow* – higher interest rates mean higher mortgage rates – normally paid monthly – and higher rates of interest on savings – normally paid annually. The short-term effect on the cashflow of individuals is likely to be negative, reducing demand.
- *Asset prices* – a change in interest rates affects the price of stocks and shares. If interest rates go up, the price of stocks and shares tends to fall, as it becomes more attractive to hold cash. There will be a similar effect on house prices. An increase in interest rates thus marginally reduces individuals' wealth, again making them more reluctant to spend.
- *Exchange rates* – at the same time, the exchange rate is likely to rise marginally, as it becomes more attractive to hold pounds rather than other currencies. This makes export prices higher, which again reduces demand. At the same time, import prices become cheaper, which immediately reduces inflation (Bank of England 2004b).

An increase in interest rates thus clearly reduces demand in the economy, which will lower the rate of inflation. However, as with everything in economics, this is subject to time lags. Some effects are almost immediate, such as the impact on the exchange rate; some take a matter of weeks, such as the impact on mortgage and savings rates; while others are long term, such as the wealth effect of falling share prices. The Bank of England calculates that it takes up to two years for the full impact to work through the economy. In making its interest rate decisions, the Bank of England thus has to make estimates of the level of inflation two years hence. This produces the apparently perverse result that the Bank can sometimes cut interest rates at a time when current inflation is above target, or vice versa.

CENTRAL BANKS AND INTEREST RATES

The Bank of England

The Bank of England has been involved in setting interest rates for many years and this system was formalised in the mid-1990s by the 'Ken and Eddie Show', when interest rates were set at a monthly meeting between the Chancellor, Kenneth Clarke, and the Governor of the Bank, Eddie George. However, in the last resort, the decision was the Chancellor's. This was changed in the first act of the incoming Labour Government in May 1997. To great surprise, Gordon Brown announced the granting of operational independence to the Bank. In future, interest rate decisions would be taken monthly by the Monetary Policy

Committee, chaired by the Governor, which consists of both Bank and government nominees (a total of nine members).

Interest rate decisions were to be taken in line with the Government's inflation target – initially set as 2.5 per cent on RPIX, subject to a margin of plus or minus 1 per cent. The target was thus a symmetrical one, unlike the previous Conservative target, which was 2.5 per cent or less.

Under the Bank of England Act 1998, the Bank's remit was to:

- maintain price stability and
- subject to that, to support the economic policy of the Government, including its objectives for growth and employment.

In its remit for the Monetary Policy Committee, this was interpreted as 'The Government's central economic policy objective is to achieve high and stable levels of growth and employment. Price stability is a precondition for these high and stable levels of growth and employment, which will in turn help to create the conditions for price stability on a sustainable basis' (Bank of England 2003).

In December 2003, the target inflation rate was changed to 2 per cent on CPI, again plus or minus 1 per cent. This was a slightly looser target, as 2 per cent on CPI roughly equates to 3 per cent on RPIX.

If inflation moved away from target by more than one percentage point in either direction, the Governor was required to send an open letter to the Chancellor, setting out:

- the reasons why inflation has missed the target
- what the Bank is doing about it
- the time span for remedial action
- how the remedial action meets the Government's monetary policy objectives.

It is a measure of the success of the policy that such a letter was only required once before the onset of world recession, when inflation became much more volatile.

The European Central Bank

The ECB was set up in 1998 to manage Economic and Monetary Union, including setting interest rates for the eurozone. Interest rates are fixed on a monthly basis by the Executive Board of the ECB, which consists of six members appointed by the 17 eurozone countries, headed by the President of the ECB, Mario Draghi.

The ECB is totally independent and sets its own inflation target. The prime objective of the ECB is to maintain price stability, originally defined as 2 per cent or less on CPI. In 2003, this was slightly but significantly modified to 'close to 2 per cent over the medium term' (*Guardian* 2003a). This was slightly less deflationary. The objective was modified again in 2004, when the ECB said that, 'without prejudice to the objective of price stability', the eurosystem will also 'support the general economic policies in the Community', including 'a high level of employment' and 'sustainable and non-inflationary growth' (ECB 2004).

The Federal Reserve

The central bank of the US is the Federal Reserve Board, currently headed by Ben Bernanke. It has no specific inflation target, but its remit is laid down by the Federal Reserve Act as to 'promote effectively the goals of maximum employment, stable prices and moderate long-term interest rates' (Federal Reserve 2004). Interest rates are set monthly by the Federal Open Market Committee.

THE CREDIT CRUNCH CRISIS OF 2008–09

In October 2008, the world financial system came within a whisker of complete meltdown. In September 2008, the US Government had decided to allow the investment bank Lehman Brothers to go bust, and in October the UK Government nationalised the Royal Bank of Scotland (RBS) and Bradford & Bingley, and forced Halifax Bank of Scotland (HBOS) into a shotgun takeover by Lloyds, funded by government money. Also in October, the US Government nationalised the massive insurance group AIG. Meltdown was avoided, but the world moved rapidly into recession, with an almost complete shutdown of bank lending and rapidly rising unemployment.

What went wrong? The immediate seeds of the crisis were sown with the terrorist attacks of 11 September 2001. The US economy was already slowing before the attacks, and Alan Greenspan, the head of the US Federal Reserve, felt that decisive monetary action was needed to avoid outright recession. He quickly slashed US interest rates to an unprecedented 1 per cent, and the Bank of England and the European Central Bank followed, although not to the same extent. US interest rates were held at this low level for several years.

With hindsight, it is clear that Greenspan went too far too fast. The economic impact of 9/11 proved to be short-lived, and by 2004, the US economy was back in boom. In normal circumstances, such a loose monetary policy would have rapidly led to a rise in inflation, but retail prices in the US, the UK and the eurozone were kept down by the boom in cheap imports from China. Instead, inflationary pressures built up on asset prices, particularly house prices.

There were also long-term trends which contributed to a build-up of pressure on the economic system. Real incomes for workers in the US had been stagnant or falling for decades, for all income groups except the very rich (Elliott 2012), and research by the Resolution Foundation showed that the same had been happening in the UK since 2001. The median male worker's real wage in 2011 was only 96 per cent of that in 2001, while a male worker in the bottom 10 per cent of the wage distribution received a real wage 94 per cent of that in 2001. Even male workers in the top 10 per cent had seen stagnant real wages. Average income of the top 0.1 per cent, on the other hand, grew by 63 per cent over the same period. The average household's income was only maintained through tax credits, through a second income if that was available and, increasingly, through borrowing, which often took the form of equity withdrawal from the increased value of houses (Resolution Foundation 2012). The debt to income ratio of the average household rose from 95 per cent in 1997 to 160 per cent in 2008 (Lansley 2009). As early as 2004, *The Economist* was already concerned about the danger from the credit explosion, reporting that household debt had passed £1 trillion (*The Economist* 2004).

The combination of stagnant real incomes, rising debt and rising house prices produced a toxic mix. Mortgage lenders in the US started an aggressive lending programme, buoyed by the expectation that house prices would continue rising indefinitely. Many specialised in lending to so-called 'ninja' borrowers – no income, no job, no assets – in the so-called sub-prime market. In the UK the ex-building society Northern Rock followed a similar policy, lending on mortgages of 125 per cent of the value of a property, financed by its own borrowing from the wholesale money markets. The money markets themselves became contaminated. In order to spread their risk, the US mortgage lenders packaged up their mortgages (a process known as securitisation), into so-called collateralised debt obligations (CDOs) – a package of mortgages sold as a bond to other institutions. By 2007, CDOs in the US were valued at $1.3 trillion, and this was only the tip of an enormous syndicated debt iceberg worth $14 trillion in the US, 7 per cent of total US GDP. The securitised bundles were so complex that an individual bank found it almost impossible to assess the risk they were running.

Like any pyramid scheme, the whole thing only worked as long as house prices continued to rise. Unfortunately, as US interest rates began to rise again, the ninja borrowers were no longer able to meet their mortgage obligations. US house prices peaked in summer 2006 and fell 25 per cent over the next year.

The first victim of the crisis was Northern Rock, which failed in September 2007 and was eventually nationalised by the UK Government. In March 2008, the US Government rescued the investment bank Bear Stearns and in July it rescued the two major US mortgage providers, Fannie Mae and Freddie Mac. As explained above, the crisis then reached its peak in September–October 2008.

An underlying contributory factor was the very loose supervision of financial institutions in the UK, and to a lesser extent in the US. As Vince Cable points out, the Financial Services Authority 'to the end remained supportive of Northern Rock's business model' (Cable 2009, p13).

The result of the bank crashes was that inter-bank lending totally dried up, as no bank could be sure how safe its fellow bank was. This was passed on to customers, who found it increasingly difficult to obtain loans. Many totally viable companies with temporary cashflow needs were forced into bankruptcy. Spending dried up, unemployment rose and the economy spiralled downwards, rapidly moving into recession (two successive quarters of negative GDP). Mervyn King, the Governor of the Bank of England, described this bank behaviour as individually understandable but collectively suicidal (Cable 2009, p57).

The UK Government's reaction to the crisis was swift and decisive. HBOS and RBS were bailed out to the tune of £35 billion, VAT was cut from 17.5 per cent to 15 per cent, interest rates quickly slashed to 0.5 per cent, and a fiscal expansion package worth 1 per cent of GDP introduced. The Bank of England also undertook a programme of quantitative easing, in effect printing more money. All of these policies were generally applauded, except by the Conservative opposition, quickly followed by the US and endorsed by the G20. However, each policy had risks:

- The bail-out of the banks risked moral hazard, where in effect the banks were shielded from the effects of their folly.
- The VAT cut was widely seen as minimal and unlikely to stimulate spending.
- If interest rates were held down for too long, there was a risk that inflationary pressures could build up in the long term. The same was true of the quantitative easing. However, as Keynes said, in the long run we are all dead.
- The fiscal stimulus, coupled with the bailout of the banks and a natural fall in tax receipts and rise in government spending due to unemployment, ran the risk of driving the government deficit to unacceptable levels. However, as the Government pointed out, the UK deficit before the crisis was on the low side compared with the rest of the G7, and even after all the extra spending would still be relatively low by historical standards.

The crisis seems to have developed in a way uncannily like that suggested by Karl Marx in *Das Kapital* in the late nineteenth century. Marx predicted that the inherent conflict between capital and labour would manifest itself as companies' pursuit of profits and productivity naturally led them to need fewer and fewer workers, creating an 'industrial reserve army' of the poor and unemployed: 'Accumulation of wealth at one pole is, therefore, at the same time accumulation of misery' (Marx 1867, 2004).

Marx also pointed out the paradox of overproduction and underconsumption: the more people are relegated to poverty, the less they will be able to consume all the goods and services companies produce. When one company cuts costs to boost earnings, it's smart, but when they all do, they undermine the income formation and effective demand on which they rely for revenues and profits. As noted above, the fall in real wages predicted by Marx was concealed to some extent by the easy credit available in the early

2000s, but Marxists would see this as a cynical move by the capitalist class to protect their own interests (Magnus 2011).

In the US, the share of GDP going to profits in 2011 was 12.6 per cent, the highest since 1950, while the share going to wages was 54.9 per cent, the lowest since 1955 (*Wall Street Journal* 2011). The fall in the share of GDP going to wages is not as extreme in the UK, but the trend is similar. Wages took around 58 per cent of GDP in the 1950s and 1960s, and briefly peaked at 65 per cent in 1975, at the height of trade union power. Between 1977 and 2008, the share going to wages fell from 59 per cent to 53 per cent, while the share going to profits rose from 25 per cent to 29 per cent (Elliott 2012).

After bottoming at 52 per cent in 1996, after Margaret Thatcher had neutralised the countervailing power of the unions, the wage share rose slightly under the Labour Governments after 1997, before falling to 53 per cent in 2008 (Willow 2011; Weldon 2012). As Marx put it in *Das Kapital*: 'The ultimate reason for all real crises always remains the poverty and restricted consumption of the masses.'

For a concise and relatively impartial account of the crisis, see the then Liberal Democrat shadow chancellor, Vince Cable's, book *The Storm: The world economic crisis and what it means* (2009). Cable is now (November 2012) the Secretary of State for Business, Innovation and Skills in the Coalition Government.

REFLECTIVE ACTIVITY 4.6

Gordon Brown and the recession

The Conservative Party blamed Gordon Brown for the recession in the UK in 2008–09. Is this fair?

THE UK ECONOMY SINCE 2010

By the middle of 2010 there were signs that the UK was moving into a sustained recovery from the recession. In quarter 2 of 2010 the economic growth rate was 1.1 per cent, and government net borrowing was falling slightly (Pettiger 2012a). The reduction in interest rates and the cut in VAT were having an impact.

After the UK general election of May 2010, a Coalition Conservative/Liberal Democrat Government was formed, with the primary economic objective of attacking the budget deficit. The deficit in 2009–10 was £167.4 billion, about 11 per cent of GDP, way above the generally accepted target of 3 per cent. Total national debt was around 65 per cent of GDP, again well above the generally accepted target of 40 per cent, but well below the 180 per cent of the late 1940s and below that in Japan (194 per cent), Italy (100 per cent plus) and the US (75 per cent) (Pettiger 2012a).

George Osborne, the Chancellor the Exchequer, set two targets for the budget deficit and the national debt:

- to eliminate the structural budget deficit by 2014–15 (the structural deficit is that part of the deficit which persists even with full employment) – the Government estimated that this was around 80–90 per cent of 2009–10 borrowing
- to reduce the national debt as a percentage of GDP by 2015–16 (Treasury 2010).

The Labour Party agreed that the deficit must be reduced and had already published its own deficit reduction programme, but disagreed on two key issues:

- *The speed of the reduction programme* – they claimed that the Government's programme was much too rapid, and could lead to a further recession.

- *How the deficit would be reduced* – two options were available – cutting government spending and increasing taxation. Both sides called for a balance between the two, but the Government preferred cutting spending, while the Opposition favoured increasing taxation.

The conventional Keynesian approach to the deficit was to deal with the recession first and lead the deficit to take care of itself. As the economy recovered from recession, tax receipts would rise and payments such as unemployment benefit would fall, thus gradually reducing the deficit. Cutting the deficit during a recession would be self-defeating, as this would make the recession worse. To understand this, we need to go back to the Keynesian national income equation which we discussed on page 161:

$$Y = C + G + I + X - M$$

Cutting government spending would reduce G and thus, by definition (other things being equal), reduce Y (national income). Increasing taxation would lower disposable income, a main component of consumption, which would reduce C, and hence again reduce national income.

The Keynesian approach was not without risk, however. There would be a time lag before the deficit began to fall, and in the short term stimulating the economy could increase the deficit.

The Government used two main arguments to justify its aggressive deficit reduction programme. One was the household analogy, beloved of Margaret Thatcher – just as a household in debt will rationally cut its spending in order to reduce its debt, so should the Government. The fallacy in this argument is that what is rational for a household is not rational for a government. If a household cuts its spending, this has virtually no impact on other households, whereas if a government cuts its spending, this impacts on all other parts of the economy.

The second argument was a much better one. Back to the Keynesian equation again. Cutting government spending would free resources for the private sector. Lower government spending would mean less state borrowing, which would lower interest rates and so encourage the private sector to invest. This would increase I and so increase national income. Lower government spending should also increase exports, as again resources would be freed. Higher exports would again increase national income. Their ideal combination economic policy was tight fiscal policy combined with loose monetary policy.

The Coalition Government started its deficit reduction programme very quickly. Value added tax was increased from 17.5 per cent to 20 per cent in January 2011, and plans announced for big cuts in government spending, concentrating on welfare payments and local government spending.

For two years the deficit reduction programme seemed to proceed well. The deficit in 2010–11 was down to £145 billion, and in 2011–12 down to £111.9 billion. The biggest cause of the drop was a fall in public sector net investment of around £20 billion, partly as a result of cuts already planned by the previous Labour Government and partly as a result of coalition cuts, for example in the school rebuilding programme (Pettiger 2012b). However, the onset of a double-dip recession in the fourth quarter of 2011 started to push borrowing up again, and the deficit for 2012–13 was forecast to be £127 billion, an increase of £15 billion over 2011–12 (Pettiger 2012a).

The effect on economic growth was as the Keynesians had forecast. After inheriting a growth rate of 1.1 per cent in quarter 2 of 2010, economic growth was negative by quarter 4 and anaemic throughout 2011. By the first quarter of 2012 the economy was back in a double-dip recession (two quarters of negative growth), which persisted into quarter two of 2012. Only in the third quarter of 2012 was there a significant bounce-back, to growth of 1 per cent, helped by the boost given by the London Olympics. Total growth in the first two and half years of the Coalition Government has been little more than 1 per cent and the economy is still well below its peak in 2008 (unlike the US and Germany, both of which now have output higher than 2008, and China, whose economy is now half as much again as it was in 2008). If one takes account of four years of lost growth at the long-run average of 2.5 per cent a year, the economy is something like 13 per cent smaller than it should have been by 2012.

Private sector investment had not increased as the Government had hoped. Small firms were unable to obtain bank funding and the private sector was not prepared to invest purely because interest rates were extremely low. They calculated (probably correctly) that because aggregate demand was down, there was little prospect of selling the extra goods resulting from extra investment. They also built in the risk involved in new investment, particularly once the economy went into a double-dip recession.

Pressure increased on George Osborne to change his deficit reduction policy and adopt a less deflationary Plan B. In June 2011, 52 signatories, including many leading UK economists, called for a Plan B (Stewart and Boffey 2011). In August George Osborne hit back, saying that 'the alternative of more spending and yet more borrowing... places those who advocate it "to the ludicrous outer fringe" of economics' (Osborne 2011). Among those advocating just such a policy were four winners of the Nobel Prize for Economics – Paul Krugman, Amartya Sen, Jospeh Stiglitz and Christoper Pissandes (Chu 2011). In January 2012 the heads of 11 world economic bodies, including the IMF, the World Bank and the WTO, warned of the dangers of austerity (Elliott 2012). Osborne countered that he was right and that the worsening situation in the UK was caused not by his policies, but by the eurozone crisis, which was driving our main trading partners into recession. However, although exports to the eurozone were slightly down, the export situation was generally quite strong. 'The big picture is that the external sector is still holding up quite well given the euro-zone debt crisis,' said Vicky Redwood, chief UK economist at Capital Economics (Billington and Thomson 2012). Time will tell whether George Osborne or the Keynesians were correct in their reading of the UK economy.

REFLECTIVE ACTIVITY 4.7

The UK deficit

Critically examine each of the following statements on the UK deficit:

'The central point is that the country must not get stuck on a downward escalator where slow or no growth means bigger deficits leading to more cuts and even slower growth. That is the way to economic disaster and political oblivion.'

Vince Cable MP (Lib Dem), Secretary of State for Business, Industry and Skills, speaking to the Liberal Democrat Party Conference, 24 September 2012.

'Families across Britain are trying to live within their means. The Coalition Government must do the same... The most important question of our

time is how government can improve people's lives without simply borrowing more money.'

Philip Clarke, ex-CEO of Tesco, quoted in William Keegan, Every little helps? Not in an economic crisis as big as this. *Observer*. 23 September 2012.

'It has been suggested that the deficit reduction programme set out by George Osborne in his emergency budget should be watered down and spread over more than one Parliament. We believe that this would be a mistake. Addressing the debt problem in a decisive way will improve business and consumer confidence. Reducing the deficit more slowly would mean additional borrowing every year, higher national debt, and therefore higher spending on interest payments.'

35 business leaders writing to the *Daily Telegraph*, 18 October 2010.

'Both those who deny the need to cut the deficit and those who refuse to say how to do it are placing themselves outside of the domestic and international debate. In becoming deficit deniers they are saying that they would set the economy on a road to economic ruin.'

George Osborne MP (Conservative), Chancellor of the Exchequer, quoted in James Kirkup,

George Osborne attacks 'deficit deniers'. *Daily Telegraph*. 17 August 2010.

'The budget deficit that we are tackling now is predominantly the result of the financial crisis. In particular, the fall in GDP has, by definition, caused the deficit as a share of GDP to rise. But to bring down the debt and deficit burden requires not a "slash and burn" approach, but a strategy for growth.'

Rachel Reeves MP (Labour), Shadow Chief Secretary to the Treasury, The politics of deficit reduction. *Renewal.* Vol 18, No 3/4. 2010.

In October 2012 the former Conservative Deputy Prime Minister Lord Heseltine published a report, commissioned by the Government, on how to stimulate economic growth in the UK. His main recommendation was that £49 billion of public spending should be devolved from central government to the regions. He claimed that cities were 'pulsing with energy' which should be harnessed (BBC 2012).

REFLECTIVE ACTIVITY 4.8

Unemployment

In the September–November quarter of 2011, unemployment was 2.68 million, or 8.4 per cent of the workforce, while in September–November 2012 it was 2.49 million or 7.7 per cent (ONS 2012, 2013). In 2012, there were three quarters of recession and one quarter of

growth, and overall over the year the economy did not grow at all.

Question

1   Given the flatlining economy, why do you think that unemployment fell?

PUBLIC OWNERSHIP AND PRIVATISATION

PUBLIC OWNERSHIP

When most people think of public ownership, they think of the nationalisations of the Labour Government in the late 1940s. But public ownership goes back a lot further than that. The beginnings of a state system of welfare came with the Elizabethan Poor Law in the sixteenth century. The Post Office dates back to the seventeenth century and developed telegraph services in the nineteenth (the precursor of British Telecom). The Metropolitan Police was founded in 1829, while a primitive system of policing through parish constables goes back hundreds of years before that. A state system of education dates from 1870, and in the 1840s Gladstone gave the state reserve powers to nationalise the railways if necessary. In the late nineteenth century, gas, electricity and water services were developed by local authorities ('municipal socialism').

During the First World War, the state obtained a controlling interest in what later became BP, in 1919 the Forestry Commission was set up to manage Britain's woodlands and the BBC came into public ownership in the 1920s.

These early examples illustrate some of the driving forces behind public ownership:

- to ensure adequate coverage of services (Post Office, Poor Law, schools)
- to safeguard interests vital to the state (BP, Forestry Commission, BBC)
- to control natural monopolies (police).

The nationalisations of the 1940s added a further motive, a socialist desire to control the 'commanding heights' of the economy in the interests of the state. But even here things were not entirely straightforward. When the Bank of England was nationalised in 1946, it had been effectively under total state control for at least a hundred years. The nationalisations of water, gas and electricity involved taking over municipally owned companies rather than private ones. The railways were in private hands, but had been subject to compulsory amalgamations in the 1920s. The NHS took over Poor Law hospitals, by this time under local authority control, as well as charity hospitals. The truly socialist thing about the NHS was the concept of services free at the point of use, rather than ownership. Perhaps the only truly socialist nationalisation was the National Coal Board, which took over from the generally hated coal owners. Generally, the force behind the 1940s nationalisation could be seen equally as a desire to exercise effective centralised planning (Kay 2003).

The nationalised industries had a mixed record of performance, but suffered from a number of systemic flaws:

- John Kay has argued that in order for any type of organisation to operate efficiently and effectively, it must be subject to 'disciplined pluralism'. Because there was no requirement to make a profit, there was little pressure to achieve greater efficiency, that is, no discipline. And because the nationalised industries were monopolies, there was also no pluralism (Kay, quoted in Palmås 2005).
- Although day-to-day management was given to the public corporations who controlled the industry, there was a great temptation for governments of all hues to interfere, and government also strictly controlled the level of investment. Nationalised industries thus tended to be used as an instrument of macroeconomic policy, with their investment levels moved up or down depending on the state of unemployment or inflation.
- Nationalised industries were at their height in an era before most businesses, public or private, gave much attention to customer service. As a result, allied with the strength of trade unions, nationalised industries tended to be run in the interests of staff rather than the customer – television in the 1970s loved to expose 'jobsworths' in the nationalised industries and local government. On the other hand, public sector staff did tend to share a 'public service ethos', which in the case of the railways, for example, led to a high emphasis on safety, and a determination to 'muddle through'. Thus trains kept running during the terrible winter of 1963 in a way which in many cases they failed to do during the floods of 2007.

PRIVATISATION

The Thatcher/Major governments between 1979 and 1997 embarked on an extensive programme of privatisation, starting with British Telecom in 1982 and ending with British Rail in 1996. Most of the big privatisations were public offers of shares to the general public, while others, like the National Freight Corporation and National Bus, were trade sales.

The arguments for privatisation were partly financial and partly political. Privatisation raised very large sums of money for the Treasury and so permitted tax cuts (memorably criticised by Harold Macmillan as 'selling the family silver'). It also reduced the role of the state (a key element in Thatcherism), which hopefully would give managers more autonomy to manage efficiently. By making the privatised businesses leaner and meaner, they would be better able to compete effectively in a globalised economy. Privatisation was also intended to stimulate personal share ownership. To ensure that the privatised companies did not exploit their monopoly positions, they were subject to detailed regulatory controls, particularly over pricing, which were intended to force efficiency.

However, just as with nationalisation, flaws in the model gradually become apparent. First, there is no evidence that personal share ownership was significantly expanded. The small investors who bought shares in the privatised companies usually have no other equity investments.

In most cases, prices to the consumer have been reduced, but it is impossible to say whether this is the result of privatisation. In the case of BT, for example, privatisation coincided with a period of rapid technological advance and globalisation in telecommunications. It appears more likely that it is intense competition which has transformed BT rather than privatisation. Privatised industries which are not subject to competition, such as water and railways, have been much less successful.

There is also the problem that once an industry is privatised, the state loses effective control over it. One way to try to alleviate this was the system of golden shares – a single share, held by the state, which gave it veto powers over the ownership of the privatised company. For example, the state retained a golden share in the airport operator BAA, which capped a single shareholding at 15 per cent. In other words, the state could veto any takeover of BAA. This was declared illegal by the European Court of Justice in 2003, as it was against EU rules on free movement of capital (Osborn 2003). The hostile takeover of BAA by the Spanish company Ferrovial duly followed in 2006. Other privatised industries which did not have a golden share, such as water and electricity distribution, are now effectively in the hands of French and German companies, including the state-owned Électricité de France. Surely if a key part of the economy is to be in public hands, those hands should be British rather than French!

A fourth problem is what happens when a privatised company fails. By definition, the services provided by a privatised company are vital and it is important that there is continuity in their supply. Two examples where this happened, Railtrack and Metronet, are discussed below.

Finally, although often regarded with amused contempt, the nationalised industries had a fund of goodwill from the public. When things went wrong, as with train crashes under British Rail, these tended to be regarded as 'acts of God' rather than the fault of the company. The privatised companies have not been successful at building up a similar fund of goodwill. Thus the drought in Yorkshire in 1996 was widely, if unfairly, seen as the fault of the (privatised) Yorkshire Water (Kay 2002).

THE PUBLIC AND VOLUNTARY SECTORS

Broadly speaking, three types of organisation operate in the UK today – businesses, which produce goods and services with the aim of making a profit; the public sector, which supplies goods and services which cannot be supplied at a profit; public goods (where the whole of society benefits from a service such as public health, whether they pay for it or not) and natural monopolies. The voluntary sector meets the needs of its members (clubs, mutual organisations or professions), its clients (charities) or campaigns on issues (Greenpeace, RSPB).

Unfortunately, these distinctions are not as watertight as they were 30 years ago. Some public goods and natural monopolies are now supplied by privatised businesses; the private and voluntary sectors provide some services, such as refuse collection and welfare services, on behalf of the public sector. Many public sector and voluntary bodies have commercial arms (like BBC Enterprises and CIPD Enterprises) which operate in competition with the private sector. One organisation, Railtrack, has changed in a five-year period from being part of a nationalised industry (British Rail), to being a privately owned company on privatisation, and then to a non-profit-making trust (Network Rail), when Railtrack collapsed in 2001.

A growing trend is social enterprise. Social enterprises are profit-making, but plough their profits back into society rather than primarily paying dividends to shareholders. Examples include Jamie Oliver's Fifteen restaurants, the *Big Issue* and Divine Chocolate. There are 62,000 social enterprises in the UK, with a combined turnover of £27 billion (Harding 2004; Lucas 2009).Officially known as community interest companies (CICs), they were recognised legally by the 2006 Companies Act. They have two main legal features:

- Assets owned by the company are held in an asset lock which ensures that they are used for the good of the community and which protects the CIC from takeover.
- There are limitations on dividend and interest payments to ensure that the primary focus remains on achieving benefit for the community (CIC Association 2012).

The three sectors also have more similarities than differences in how they are managed. They all:

- spend money
- need income to carry out their activities
- produce a product or service
- have consumers of their good or service (whether or not the consumers directly pay for this)
- need people to staff their operations
- use the same range of management services – accounting, IT, personnel, etc.

This all suggests a convergence. This view would be supported by the former Prime Minister, Tony Blair. His Third Way philosophy argues that what is important is not ownership (public or private), but how efficiently services are delivered, along with accountability.

Lawton and Rose (1994) distinguish four different cultures which they see as prevalent in the public sector:

- *Political culture* – particularly prevalent in local government, where council officers are in almost day-to-day contact with the politicians to whom they are answerable. Also true in the sense that the whole of the public sector is ultimately politically directed.
- *Legal culture* – public bodies are only permitted to do what is specifically allowed to them by statute. Any other action is *ultra vires* (beyond their powers) and is subject to judicial review. Private sector companies are in theory limited in their activities by their articles memorandum of association, but the control is much less strict.
- *Administrative culture* – concerned with rules, roles, and authority – the 1960s and 1970s caricature of the local authority 'jobsworth'.
- *Market culture* – where public sector organisations are exposed to the market through competitive tendering, best value, contracting out, internal markets, etc.

They argue that the last of these, the market culture, is becoming predominant and that, as a result, running the public sector is becoming much more an issue of management and much less an issue of administration.

The distinction between the sectors is becoming more and more blurred:

- Many local authority services which may previously have been free are now charged for and often contracted out to the private sector (leisure centres, for example). This has involved the development and application of legal systems such as TUPE.
- Much of the long-term finance for the public sector is now provided by the public sector, through the private finance initiative (PFI) and public–private partnerships (PPPs). The biggest of these is London Underground, where train services continue to

be provided by the public sector, but where all the maintenance of and investment in improving the lines is carried out by three private sector consortia.

- There is a growing realisation that the private sector, almost as much as the public sector, operates in a political environment and that the activities of the private sector are heavily constrained by the legal environment.

- The Government is keen to increase the involvement of the voluntary sector in the delivery of public services, partly to move the debate away from a head-to-head clash between the public and private sectors (Ward 2000). Not-for-profit trusts are the Government's preferred option for failing public services. They can borrow private cash without this counting as public borrowing and they can also reinvest any surpluses into service improvement (Weaver 2001). The voluntary and social enterprise sector is at the core of both David Cameron's Big Society and Ed Miliband's One Nation approaches.

CASE STUDY 4.3

MANAGING VOLUNTEERS

One major issue for the voluntary sector is how to manage staff, both paid and volunteers. Paid staff are likely to have a high commitment to the objectives of the organisation and thus likely to be prepared to work for less than the current market wage, but in return want a high degree of autonomy. The psychological contract is highly important and any move by management to alter the contract will lead to resentment and perhaps staff moving to other organisations.

The issue is even more crucial with volunteers. By definition, volunteers can move to other organisations at any time. Volunteers want autonomy, the ability to put their knowledge and skills to best use, and a sense of being valued. They do not want to be seen as having a lower status compared with paid staff and they do not want to be over-regulated.

Moreton (2006) suggests that the ideal management style for managing volunteers is the team management style on the Blake and Mouton Management Grid. This has a high concern for production combined with a high concern for people. It is characterised by work accomplishment through committed people and interdependence through a common stake in organisation purposes that leads to relationships of trust and respect.

All organisations need some degree of bureaucratic management systems, if only to conform with the law and regulation, but Moreton recommends that these should be disguised so that volunteers are as far as possible unaware of them. He quotes the analogy of the swan, which appears graceful to the onlooker, but is actually paddling furiously under the surface.

This case study is based on material kindly supplied by Stephen Moreton of the charity Attend, which is gratefully acknowledged.

PUBLIC INTEREST COMPANIES

The advent to power of the New Labour Government in 1997 revived interest in a third way of delivering public services, which was neither a nationalised industry nor a privatised company. This was the public interest company (PIC). These had three main characteristics:

- They do not normally have shareholders.
- They are independent from the state.
- They deliver a public service.

Legally the public interest company is normally a company limited by guarantee. A typical PIC was a housing association, providing and managing social housing.

As Maltby points out, it has always been an oversimplification to see a simple dichotomy between privatised companies and nationalised industries. In fact, there is a continuum of types (Maltby 2003). Going from pure public sector to pure private sector, we have:

- nationalised industries
- public PLCs, where a company operates as though it is in the private sector, but is wholly owned by the state – a good example is the Post Office
- public interest companies
- public–private partnerships, including private finance initiative contracts (see below)
- regulated private companies – typically privatised companies
- private companies – ordinary PLCs.

Public interest companies appealed to New Labour for two main reasons:

- They represented a Third Way between nationalisation (socialism) and privatisation (capitalism).
- They provided an opportunity to give formal influence to stakeholders.

As Palmås argued, PICs combined the management freedom, efficiency and innovativeness of the traditional PLC, the public interest ethos of the public sector, and the stakeholder governance of mutuals and the voluntary sector (Palmås 2005).

DwrCymru Welsh Water is a leading example. Originally privatised, it has been owned and managed by GlasCymru as a PIC since 2001. All financial surpluses are reinvested for the benefit of customers, and since 2001 it has returned £98 million to customers as 'customer dividends'. It has also reduced its level of borrowing from 91 per cent to 75 per cent, so lowering its level of risk (Article 13 and CBI 2007).

An opportunity to experiment with the PIC model on a large scale came with the collapse of Railtrack in 2001. Railtrack had been set up as a result of rail privatisation in 1996, with responsibility for running the rail infrastructure (train services were provided by train operating companies such as Virgin or GNER, which rented track use from Railtrack).

At first Railtrack was very successful in financial terms, mainly because it laid off 65 per cent of its staff and outsourced most of its maintenance. It was then hit by a series of accidents, culminating in the Hatfield crash of 2000, caused by a broken rail. In response to public pressure, Railtrack was forced to impose drastic speed restrictions on the network while rails were checked. As a result, Railtrack's profits were shattered, leading to a £534 million loss in 2001. However, Railtrack then paid out a dividend of £137 million.

Railtrack's fortunes continued to decline, and in October 2001, the company was put into administration. By this time its share price had dropped from a peak of £17 to 280p. Eventually, in the spring of 2002, the Government effectively bought Railtrack at a price of 250p a share and handed its management to a new PIC, Network Rail (Palmås 2005).

Network Rail's governance was in the hands of a large group of individuals representing major stakeholders, including 30 drawn from companies already heavily involved in rail, including Amey, Jarvis and London Underground, 34 public members drawn from a range of organisations ranging from Eurotunnel to the National Farmers Union, and 51 individual members selected by a membership panel and who were mostly drawn from 'the great and the good' who frequently appear on the boards of quangos (*Guardian* 2003b).

The Government argued that the members of Network Rail represented a fair cross-section of those with an interest in the railways, but it could be argued that too many represented vested interests. It is also unclear exactly what influence the members have on the operation of Network Rail. There is an argument that Network Rail is effectively answerable to no one. In these circumstances, argues Jeremy Warner, 'the engineers are taking over', and 'all [they] want is a shiny new train set' (Warner 2003). However, because Network Rail did not have to distribute profit to shareholders, it was unlikely to be as obsessed in the short term as Railtrack.

THE PRIVATE FINANCE INITIATIVE AND PUBLIC–PRIVATE PARTNERSHIPS

Public–private partnership (PPP) refers to any financial collaboration between the public and private sectors. For example, in the 1980s, local authorities were forced to put many of their services out for tender to the private sector under the compulsory competitive tendering system. The result today is that the council dustman has virtually disappeared. Instead, they are employed by private waste disposal companies, although their job is still to collect people's rubbish.

Other examples include the use by schools of private security companies, or the way in which the BBC uses private production companies to produce many of its TV programmes. Some PPPs are really public voluntary partnerships – the transfer of local authority social housing to housing corporations, for example, since 1989 (Ward 2000).

The private finance initiative (PFI) is a specialised type of PPP. Set up by Norman Lamont in 1992 after the UK was forced out of the EU Exchange Rate Mechanism, it was seen as a way simultaneously to stimulate the economy and to hold down public spending. Say the NHS wants to build a new hospital. Under the old system, the capital cost of the hospital was financed by the state, and so increased public borrowing. Under PFI, the private sector provides the cash, which is repaid with interest once the new hospital opens. The NHS (and the Government) avoids a high capital payment up front, but it is committed to monthly payments for the next 25–30 years, which will amount to much more than the hospital would have cost in the first place. Deals will include penalty clauses if the terms of the contract are not met – if the heating system fails, for example. The private sector company will gain a guaranteed flow of income for 25–30 years, but takes the risk if there are cost over-runs.

Many PFI deals went much further. Not only would the contractor in effect lease the hospital to the NHS, but the contract also included the provision of ancillary hospital services, typically catering, cleaning and security. This included the transfer of NHS jobs to the private sector, where they were subject to the EU Transfer of Undertakings (TUPE) regulations.

When New Labour came to power in 1997, it was at first thought that the days of PFI were numbered. Instead, the system was expanded. The opportunity for Gordon Brown to keep public sector capital spending off the public sector borrowing requirement was too good to miss. However, Labour did bring in some safeguards. The system of compulsory competitive tendering for local authorities was changed to best value, where the local authority could continue to provide services in-house if it could establish that it provided as good value as outsourcing. PFI was also stopped for small projects, where the cost of the tendering process outweighed any financial savings, and for IT projects, where many contracts had proved expensive failures. It was also stressed that PFI could only be used where it did not come at the expense of employees' terms and conditions.

Several possible models for PFI/PPP were identified by the Institute for Public Policy Research in 2001. These were:

- *Public sector default* – the public sector provides all services – broadly the position for police and fire services.

- *Private sector rescue* – the private sector acts as provider of last resort only if the public sector is seen to be underperforming – for example, some failing local education authorities have been taken over by the private sector.
- *Level playing field* – equal treatment between different organisations seeking to deliver public services – broadly the position with local authority best value.
- *Public sector rescue* – the public sector acts as provider of last resort only if the private sector is seen to be underperforming – the replacement of Railtrack by Network Rail.
- *Private sector default* – the private sector provides all services – the building and operation of new prisons (IPPR 2001).

The Treasury stressed that one of the main benefits of PFI was that it transferred risk to the private sector. The public authority received the certainty that specified services would be delivered at the cost at which they were contracted. In 2006 the Treasury estimated that PFI would total 10–15 per cent of total investment in public services, and in the five-year pipeline were 200 projects worth £26 billion.

In 2003, Tony Blair seemed to herald a big expansion of PPP into clinical services in the NHS. He said, 'We are anxious to ensure that this is the start of opening up the whole of the NHS supply system so that we end up with a situation where the state is the enabler, it is the regulator, but it is not always the provider' (Carvel 2003).

Treasury research in 2006 also established that on the whole the public sector was satisfied with the results of PFI:

- 79 per cent said service standards are delivered always or almost always
- overall performance of 96 per cent of projects was at least satisfactory
- 70 per cent of public sector mangers believe relationships with private sector partners are good or very good.

Only 20 per cent of PFI projects are late, compared with 70 per cent of non-PFI contracts, while 20 per cent are over budget, compared with 73 per cent of non-PFI projects (Treasury 2006).

However, there are many criticisms of PFI:

- They lock the public sector into contracts that are too long. It is very difficult to forecast demand for facilities as far ahead as 30 years. Schools, for example, are frequently surplus to requirements long before 30 years because of changes in local population. Government NHS policy is to shift significant portions of the work of hospitals into the community. This again puts in doubt 30-year contracts (Batty and Weaver 2006).
- A PFI contract may deliver on time, but this does not take into account the length of time required to finalise contracts – frequently a matter of years. The contracting process itself is also extremely expensive and the contracts frequently too restrictive. The process also creates a 'contract culture', with endless arguments over exactly what the contract does and does not require.
- PFI threatens the public sector ethos. For example, when cleaners in hospitals were employed by the NHS, they were driven by a desire to produce the best possible service for the patients. When the same people are employed by the private sector under PFI, they are ultimately contract and profit driven – they are not permitted to go beyond the terms of the contract because this will cost their employer money.
- Many PFI companies are moving into areas well away from their core expertise. The leading firms involved in educational administration are Jarvis and Atkins, both primarily civil engineering specialists, and VT Education, the service arm of defence and shipbuilding firm Vosper Thorneycroft. In a Fabian Society report, Colin Crouch argued that the main expertise of these companies lies in their experience in lobbying and negotiating large contracts with the Government (Woodward 2003).

- PFI drains public services of current spending power. At the end of 2006, £8billion worth of NHS hospital PFI schemes were operational or under construction in England. On these, the NHS would have to pay £37billion in debt payments over the next 30 years. It is estimated that 50 per cent of NHS trusts with major PFI schemes are in financial difficulties, much higher than the average across the NHS. Some, like South Tees and Queen Elizabeth Woolwich, both in substantial deficit, are paying 20 per cent of their turnover to PFI partners (Hellowell 2006). In the case of Queen Elizabeth, the PFI deal cost £9 million a year more than an equivalent hospital built with money borrowed directly from the Government (Batty and Weaver 2006).

- In practice, risk is not completely transferred to the PFI partner. In 2004, the PFI contractor Jarvis was in severe financial difficulty following its involvement in the Potters Bar train crash, where it was responsible for track maintenance. At the time Jarvis was responsible for 14 PFI projects, all of which ground to a halt as the City sorted out a rescue package for Jarvis. Part of the problem appeared to be that Jarvis had been 'lowballing' – bidding too low in order to secure bargain basement PFI contracts – and then running into trouble when unexpected problems appeared. At the very least, Jarvis's failure led to delays and waste for its public sector partners; at worst, contracts would have to be renegotiated with another partner, leading to higher costs than originally budgeted (Hirst 2005).

COMPETITIVENESS

In the 1970s, the UK was widely seen as a failed economy. It was subject to wide fluctuations in economic performance and suffered from high inflation and unemployment. Taxation was high, the economy was heavily regulated and trade unions were widely seen as too powerful. Some of these shortcomings were tackled by the Thatcher Governments between 1979 and 1991, which lowered taxation, cut back on regulation and attacked the power of the trade unions. The result was an increase in the efficiency of the economy, although this was largely a function of the contraction of manufacturing. The manufacturers which survived were inevitably more efficient than those which had failed.

However, the impetus behind the reforms of the Thatcher Governments was as much political as economic. Policy changed with the advent of the Major Government in 1991. This was much less ideological. Policies were to be followed because they were effective, rather than because they were politically correct.

This approach was continued by New Labour in 1997, with an almost seamless transition from Ken Clarke to Gordon Brown as Chancellor of the Exchequer. Competitiveness became the watchword and pragmatism the policy. The aim was to reform the British economy so that it could compete with the best in the world.

PRODUCTIVITY

Competitiveness has a large number of facets, from a tightening of anti-trust legislation to the promotion of a higher skills base in the UK and stabilisation of macroeconomic policy. What ties them all together is the concept of productivity. This is a measure of how much the economy is producing per worker employed. This is dependent on both the efficiency of the worker and on the hours worked, so a better measure is probably output per worker hour.

In 2002, productivity measured by output per worker was 39 per cent below the US, 15 per cent below France and 7 per cent below Germany. However, France and Germany work fewer hours than the UK and the US works more, so on the better measure, output per worker hour, the UK is 26 per cent behind the US, 24 per cent behind France and 11 per cent behind Germany. This is known as the productivity gap (Philpott 2002).

The 2002 figures represented a considerable improvement on the position in 1991, when the UK was 35 per cent behind France on output per worker hour and 30 per cent behind Germany (Daneshkhu 2007a). The improvement continued after 2002, and by 2007, the UK was 18 per cent behind the US and 20 per cent behind France, although the gap with Germany had widened slightly to 13 per cent (Daneshkhu 2007b). Between 1995 and 2006, UK labour productivity growth was 2.1 per cent per annum, France's 1.9 per cent, Germany's 1.7 per cent and Italy's 0.4 per cent (Giles 2007).

Since the 1950s, the underlying rate of growth of productivity in the UK has been around 2 per cent. Government policy is to try to increase this underlying rate, with a wide range of detailed polices put forward in two white papers, *Building the Knowledge Driven Economy* in 1998 (www.dti.gov.uk/comp), and *Opportunity for All in a World of Change* in 2001 (www.dti.gov.uk/opportunityforall/index.html). Success in doing so would increase the UK's long-term rate of economic growth and would also lower NAIRU, allowing the UK economy to control inflation at a lower level of unemployment (Philpott 2002). A similar programme was launched by the EU at the Lisbon Summit in 2000 (EU 2004), which set the objective of becoming the most competitive, dynamic, knowledge-based economy in the world by 2010. Its detailed proposals included creating an environment which was conducive to business start-ups, a fully operational internal market, education and training suitable for a knowledge society, and a raising of the EU employment rate from 61 per cent in 2000 to 70 per cent in 2010, thereby creating 20 million new jobs. Of these, 5 million had been created by 2003 (Philpott 2003).

In 2004, a group appointed by the EU, under the chairmanship of the former Dutch Prime Minister, Wim Kok, reported on progress (Hutton 2004). They proposed:

- EU members should spend 3 per cent of GDP on research and development (the UK at present spends 1.9 per cent).
- There should be a European Research Council supporting centres of scientific excellence.
- Degrees and qualifications should be mutually recognised, in order that researchers can develop career paths within the EU rather than joining the brain drain to the US.
- There should be an EU-wide patent law.

However, in 2005, *The Economist* pointed to slow progress towards the Lisbon targets and blamed this on the failure of Germany, France and Italy to open up their economies to competition, citing their opposition to the EU Services Directive, intended to liberalise cross-border trade in services (*The Economist* 2005).

An increase in productivity depends on changes in a number of factors. These include:

- *Capital investment* – the more modern the equipment with which people work, the more efficient they will be. Historically, investment in the UK has been low and increases in productivity have come more through the shutdown of the most inefficient plant rather than the building of a new plant. A telling comparison with the US is that while the UK produces the same volume of manufacturing output with half the capacity of the 1970s, the US produces twice the output with the same capacity.
- *Economic stability* – one key factor which deters investment is economic instability. Investors need to be convinced that there will be a consistent demand for what they produce and that inflation will be stable. Here the UK has made great advances over the last decade. De Grauwe has argued that a comprehensive and reliable welfare state is also necessary, although this does not seem to be required in the US (De Grauwe 2001).
- *Research and development (R&D)* – the UK is excellent at scientific research but much less good at the applied R&D needed to convert this into practical products and processes. It is significant that the UK's only world-class industry, pharmaceuticals, is the heaviest investor in R&D.

- *IT and the Internet* – during the dot-com boom of the late 1990s, the Internet was seen as the Holy Grail of productivity, and some US economists put forward the concept of a New Economic Paradigm, where the business cycle was abolished and growth would continue indefinitely. This rosy view was shaken by the dot-com crash in early 2000, and shattered by 11 September. Of the dot-com companies, virtually only Amazon, eBay and a few business-to-business (B2B) companies are profitable.
- *Restrictive practices* – restrictive practices by the trade unions were tackled by the Thatcher Governments, so the main concern is restrictive practices by industry. The UK has anti-trust laws (covered in more detail in Chapter 5 on regulation), but they are much less tough than in the US. One change here has been to make participation in price-fixing activities a criminal offence, subject to imprisonment – a measure in force in the US since 1890 (Lennan 2001).
- *Management* – the quality of management in the UK is widely perceived as being poor, despite the spread of management qualifications such as the MBA. As with the whole of UK industry, there are some very good examples of management practice, but a very long tail of poor performers. The average standard needs to be raised to be nearer the best. Two main failings are a short-termist approach, which discourages long-term investment and development, and a failure to introduce modern management practices such as 'just in time' and continuous improvement. Many sectors of industry still experience high levels of stress and alienation, and many managers refuse to consider a partnership approach with their workers.
- *Infrastructure* – the UK has the most congested roads in the EU. This adds to business costs and makes the operation of techniques such as JIT more difficult.
- *Flexibility* – industry must become more flexible in order to optimise its use of resources. This involves being:
  - *Numerically flexible* – working time must adjust to meet customer demand – 'the 24/7 society'. This involves the use of techniques such as annual hours.
  - *Functionally flexible* – skills levels must be improved and these skills fully utilised.
  - *Occupationally flexible* – workers must become multi-skilled.
  - *Wage flexible* – reward must be used as an incentive to higher productivity.
  - *Mindset flexible* – diversity must be encouraged in order to tap all available talent and organisations must be family-friendly in order to encourage diversity (Philpott 2002; Merrick 2001; Briner 2001).
- *Education* – a key element is the need to develop workforce skills. The UK has a higher proportion of low-skilled workers than other comparable economies. A whole series of initiatives has been introduced, ranging from NVQs to TECs, ILAs to LSCs. The result has been an alphabet soup, without a great deal of impact on the skills base. As usual, the UK pattern is one of excellence at the top, with very effective degree-level provision, a gap in the middle, where technician-level skills are poorly developed, and a long tail of functional illiteracy and innumeracy. However, it is becoming clear that workforce development is a dual responsibility, with the Government responsible for developing the basic skills of numeracy, literacy and IT (as stressed in the Tomlinson Report on the reform of 14–19 education in October 2004), and industry being responsible for the development of workplace-specific skills.

The best that can be said at present about the effectiveness of competitiveness policy is that the UK is holding its own and not falling further behind its main competitors. Short-term gains are unlikely and these policies should be seen as essentially long term.

In 2003, Michael Porter and Christian Ketels carried out a study for the DTI on the UK's competitiveness (Porter and Ketels 2003). Their conclusions were rather more optimistic. They said that successive governments have 'fundamentally changed the macroeconomic, and, more importantly, the microeconomic context for competition'. They identified what they saw as the strengths of the UK business environment: its openness to international trade and investment, its very low regulatory barriers to national-level competition and its sophisticated capital markets; but also identified weaknesses, particularly a deteriorating physical infrastructure, skills deficits, and low levels of R&D and innovation despite a strong science base. The challenge for the future was to manage the transition from an economy based on low cost to one based on unique value and innovation.

However, the Porter report has been criticised for its emphasis on economic issues at the expense of behavioural ones. For example, US-owned firms in the UK have higher productivity than UK-owned ones. Andrew Pettigrew of the University of Warwick points out that the most obvious explanation for this lies in the 'varying abilities of managers to perceive, incorporate or even change [environmental] conditions' (quoted in Caulkin 2003).

It is also important to remember that productivity per head is not the only driver of economic growth. As William Keegan pointed out in October 2004 (Keegan 2004b), superior economic growth in the US is largely caused by factors such as:

- a growing labour force, driven by high rates of immigration – this tends to lower the average age of the workforce and also forces a high rate of investment to keep pace with the demand created by a growing population
- long hours and short holidays
- generally expansionary macroeconomic policies.

CASE STUDY 4.4

SKILLS POLICY

In 2006, Lord Leitch identified the skills weaknesses of the UK (Leitch 2006). He discovered that only 85 per cent of adults had basic literacy skills and 79 per cent basic numeracy. Only 69 per cent of adults had gained at least a level 2 qualification (equivalent to five GCSEs at A*–C grade) and 29 per cent had a higher education qualification (Level 4 or above). In order to be in the top 25 per cent of OECD countries by 2020, these figures would have to be considerably improved:

- basic literacy up from 85 per cent to 95 per cent
- basic numeracy up from 79 per cent to 95 per cent
- level 2 qualifications up from 69 per cent to 90 per cent
- level 4 qualifications up from 29 per cent to 40 per cent
- apprenticeships to reach 500,000 a year in England.

The Leitch proposals were accepted in full by the Government in July 2007

(DIUS 2007) and the Government also set out intermediate targets:

By 2011:

- 89 per cent of adults to achieve basic literacy and 81 per cent basic numeracy
- 79 per cent of adults qualified to level 2
- 56 per cent of adults qualified to level 3 (two A-level equivalent).

By 2014:

- 36 per cent of adults qualified to level 4.

The Leitch review stressed that the emphasis in the skills strategy should be on adults, as 70 per cent of the 2020 workforce was already beyond the compulsory education age in 2006.

As significant as the targets were the mechanisms by which Leitch felt they should be achieved. He stressed a demand-led approach, with employers and workers given funding to commission their own training. In the case of employers, funding would be channelled through the Train to Gain programme, which was forecast to rise from £440 million in 2007–08 to £900 million in 2010–11. Funding for individual training would come through a new scheme of Skills Accounts.

The Leitch proposals were broadly welcomed by interest groups. The TUC welcomed the proposal to create a statutory right to workplace training to level 2, but questioned the emphasis on an employer-led approach. It felt that a social partnership approach between both employers and employees would be more appropriate and that more emphasis should be given to the role of union learning representatives. It also questioned whether employers would actually take up their responsibility to lead on training (TUC 2008). The CBI welcomed the employer-led approach and stressed the cost of low skills to business. Low basic skills cost a typical SME with 50 employees £165,000 a year, and the cost to the whole UK economy was £10 billion a year (CBI 2005).

The CIPD pointed out that the Government should not put all its efforts into improving basic and low skills. They stressed that the productivity gain from boosting basic skills is only 1 per cent, whereas higher-level skills would boost productivity by 4.4 per cent (CIPD 2008). The Conservative Party has attacked the emphasis on Train to Gain, which it regards as wasteful and bureaucratic (Conservative Party 2008).

The skills strategy produced some early successes. Between 2001 and 2007, the percentage of establishments with any staff who were not fully proficient fell from 23 per cent to 15 per cent, while the percentage of staff not fully competent fell from 9 per cent to 6 per cent. The number of vacancies caused by lack of skills fell from 25 per cent in 2005 to 21 per cent in 2007. The National Employers Skills Survey 2007 identified the main causes of skills gaps as lack of experience/newly recruited (68 per cent), staff lack motivation (28 per cent), failure to train and develop staff (20 per cent), and inability of the workforce to keep up with change (19 per cent) (LSC 2008).

CASE STUDY 4.5

INVESTORS IN PEOPLE

Investors in People (IiP) was introduced in October 1991. It is one of the key competitiveness-promoting initiatives which has been truly non-political, enthusiastically backed by both the Major and the Blair Governments. By 2001, 25,000 organisations had qualified for the standard, employing 24 per cent of the UK workforce.

Research carried out for IiP suggests that 73 per cent of organisations awarded the standard more than 12 months ago feel that it has increased their productivity. However, there is a counter view, put forward by Scott

Taylor of the Open University, that IiP frequently has little impact on performance (Brown 2001), and this is supported by research from the Institute of Directors, where only 15 per cent of 275 company directors felt that IiP had increased profitability, and a quarter thought it had increased productivity (Nelson 2001).

Arguments in support of Taylor's contention could include:

● Some organisations see IiP as a marketing exercise. The standard is

- treated as 'just another badge on the wall' rather than a development tool.
- Achievement and maintenance of the standard involves considerable amounts of management and worker time. These have to be offset before there can be any overall improvement in productivity.
- There is considerable emphasis on measurement of outputs. There is a risk that too much emphasis may be put on the targets rather than the processes. To many people, the present government seems obsessed with targets, which can cause distortions. In a recent case, patients waiting for accident and emergency assessment were held in ambulances outside an A&E department because there is a target for maximum waiting times in A&E, but the clock does not start ticking until the patient actually enters the building (Bowcott 2004).
- More generally, IiP can only succeed where it is seen not as a box-ticking exercise, but as a fundamental change in values and attitudes. As with similar initiatives such as total quality management, a belief in the virtues of development must be internalised in the organisation and become an integral part of its culture. Many organisations of course do this, and it is clear that in many cases IiP has been a total success.

HR ISSUES IN THE PUBLIC SECTOR

The final section of this chapter, on HR issues in the public sector, consists of a case study on recruitment of social workers.

BABY P AND THE RECRUITMENT OF SOCIAL WORKERS

CASE STUDY 4.6

Child protection social work must be one of the most stressful jobs imaginable. Not only are interactions with difficult, evasive and often violent or abusive clients emotionally draining, but social workers know they are constantly walking a tightrope. If they make a mistake and, at worst, a child for whom they are responsible dies, they will be vilified by the tabloid press as murderers, while if they err on the side of caution and take children too readily into care, they will be condemned by the same tabloid press as callous family-breakers. In addition, social work, like teaching, the police and the NHS, is a victim of the Government's target culture for the public services, which has resulted in an increase in time-consuming bureaucracy (Hudson 2009; Kirkpatrick and Ackroyd 2003).

As a result, the level of unfilled posts in local authority social services departments is high. The national average for social work vacancies in June 2009 was 12 per cent, while some authorities had much greater problems – Sandwell, in the West Midlands, had a vacancy rate of 39 per cent, Waltham Forest in East London 34.9 per cent, Hounslow in West London 31 per cent and Essex 28.1 per cent (Bowcott 2009a). There is also some concern over the quality of social workers. Like teaching and nursing, social work is an all-graduate profession, with qualification through a bachelor's degree in social work or a postgraduate qualification. A Commons committee found that since 2003–04, the failure rate of students is only 2.62 per cent, much lower than for other degree courses. The entry level of students is also lower than average. In 2006–07, nearly half the students admitted to social work degree courses had fewer than 240 points, which is the equivalent of three C grades at A-level (Newman 2009). The social work qualification is a generic one. There are no specialist degrees in child protection.

Already suffering from severe recruitment problems, social work was then hit by the Baby P case. Baby P (Peter) was born in Haringey in March 2006. In December 2006, he was placed on the Haringey child protection register for physical abuse and neglect. Despite extensive contacts with social services, the NHS and the police, it was decided in July 2007 that the case did not meet the legal threshold for care proceedings. On 3 August 2007, Peter was taken to hospital but pronounced dead on arrival. In November 2008, his mother, his mother's boyfriend and a lodger were found guilty of causing his death.

A review by Lord Laming declared Haringey's child protection services to be exceptionally inadequate. The council leader and cabinet member for children and young people resigned. The director of children's services was summarily dismissed on the direct instructions of Ed Balls, the Children's Secretary. Later Haringey dismissed a social worker and three managers. A hospital consultant who examined Peter just before his death but found no cause for concern was suspended, as was Peter's GP, who had seen him 14 times before his death. No action was taken against any of the police involved in the case (Batty 2009).

In May 2009, Ed Balls announced a series of measures designed to improve recruitment and retention. These included:

- a recruitment campaign designed to attract 500 social workers who have left the profession to rejoin it, supported by refresher training

- sponsoring 200 university places to encourage 'the highest achieving graduates, from any disciplines' to take social work conversion courses
- improvement of supervision for newly qualified social workers in their first post
- a new master's degree in social work
- advanced social work status – at present the only progression route for social workers is to go into management. As with teaching, the proposal would provide for a practitioner progression route, as well as a managerial one
- simplification of the Integrated Children's System software system for recording social workers' interactions with children and families.

Balls said he expected these initiatives to cost £58 million (Carvel 2009).

Other measures which emerged later included:

- a national social work college, to give support, leadership and enhanced status to the profession (Brindle 2009)
- an advertising campaign to raise the image of social workers by highlighting success stories, featuring, among others, the Oscar-nominated actor Samantha Morton, who was herself in care as a child (Samuel 2009)
- Haringey has recruited 22 social workers from the US and Canada, after failing to recruit in the UK (Bowcott 2009b).

The Government has so far refused to implement two of Lord Laming's key recommendations:

- ring-fencing of spending on child protection
- specialist undergraduate programmes in child protection (Carvel 2009).

Nothing, of course, has been done about what one commentator described as the 'vicious reporting' of the tabloids (Sawford 2009).

SUMMARY

This chapter has analysed the legislative process and influences on policy formation in the UK and the EU. The key components of the economy were analysed, as were the objectives of government policy and the tools which the Government can use to achieve them. Detailed case studies of inflation and interest rates were also analysed.

The chapter also analysed the public and voluntary sectors, and relationships between the public and private sectors. A study was also made of competitiveness and productivity, and of the role of skills policy.

KEY LEARNING POINTS

- Legislation in the UK is normally initiated by the Government, whereas in the EU it is initiated by the Commission. The role of Parliament is much greater in the UK than in the EU.
- Political parties and their members have some influence on policy formation, but this influence is tending to decrease.
- Pressure groups are of two main types: interest or sectional groups and attitude or cause groups. They have considerable influence both on the evolution of government policy and on its implementation.
- There are crucial differences between gross domestic product and standard of living or quality of life.
- All governments, of whatever political colour, are striving to achieve economic growth, full employment, stable prices and equilibrium on the balance of payments.
- Policy instruments available to governments include fiscal policy, monetary policy, competitiveness policy and exchange rate policy.
- Interest rates in the UK are set by the Bank of England, subject to an inflation target set by the Government.
- The inflation target in the UK is symmetrical and therefore less restrictive than that of the European Central Bank.
- A drive to increase productivity and competitiveness is a key aim of both UK and EU economic policy, but does not lead to quick results.

QUESTIONS

1 What is the difference between a green paper and a white paper?

2 Through what stages does a bill pass in the UK before it becomes an Act?

3 What are the differences between an interest and an attitude pressure group?

4 What are the differences between RPI, RPIX and CPI? Which do you think is the best measure of inflation?

5 What are the five tests on whether the UK should join the euro?

6 What were the main causes of the credit crunch recession of 2008–09?

7 What is a public interest company?

8 What is the difference between PFI and PPP?

9   What major competitiveness weaknesses of the UK economy were identified by Michael Porter?

10   What were the main recommendations of the Leitch Report?

EXPLORE FURTHER

FURTHER READING

For the underlying economic theory, see Lipsey and Chrystal (recommended in Chapter 3).

John Philpott, the CIPD's chief economist until 2012, produced an occasional series for the CIPD entitled *Perspectives*, which is invaluable, as are his articles in the CIPD's magazine *Impact*.

For updating on economic events, serious newspapers such as the *Financial Times, The Times,* the *Guardian* and *The Economist* are essential.

USEFUL WEBSITES

For the evolution and application of policy, the Bank of England (www.bankofengland.co.uk) and the Department for Trade and Industry (www.dti.gov.uk) websites are useful. For current political party policy, you should check out the main party websites (www.conservatives.com, www.labour.org.uk, and www.libdems.org.uk), and for the reaction from the major political interest groups see the TUC (www.tuc.org.uk), CBI (www.cbi.org.uk) and CIPD (www.cipd.co.uk) websites. The BBC News website (www.bbc.co.uk/news) frequently has background articles on economic policy. Those by the BBC economics correspondent, Stephanie Flanders, are excellent.

AUDIO AND VIDEO MATERIAL

Two videos are useful. One, by (Lord) Robert Skidelsky, the biographer of Keynes, on *A Keynesian Response to the Crisis*, 6 September 2012, puts the orthodox Keynesian point of view (www.youtube.com/watch?v=8R1lEVY5T_c). The other, by Deanne Julius, an ex-member of the Bank of England's Monetary Policy Committee (A reduction of UK deficit targets seen as risky, 11 October 2012), is a more monetarist view (www.onenewspage.com/video/20121011/1079138/Reduction-of-Deficit-Targets-Seen.htm)

ECONOMIC DEVELOPMENT IN INDIA AND CHINA

Between 1985 and 1995, GNP growth in the developing world averaged 6 per cent a year, more than twice that of the developed world (World Bank 2000). This suggests that the developing world will soon catch up with the developed world. Unfortunately, this hopeful forecast ignores two key factors. One is the rapid rate of population growth in the developing world. When this is stripped out, and growth converted to GNP per head, the growth rate per head in the developing world falls to 3.8 per cent, while that of the developed world falls to 2.1 per cent.

Second, the developing country figures are distorted by the outstanding success of the two most populous countries, India and China. In the period 1985–95, India's GNP per head rose by 3.2 per cent a year and China's by an impressive (although possibly unreliable) 8.3 per cent a year. Stripping out India and China from the figures, the rest of the developing world actually had a GNP per head which fell by nearly 1 per cent a year. Since the 1990s, growth in both countries has accelerated, to 10 per cent or more in China and 8 per cent in India.

China's success has been particularly remarkable. It took England 58 years to double its GDP after 1780, the US 47 years from 1839, Japan 34 years from 1885, and South Korea 11 years from 1966 (Meredith 2007). It took China nine years from 1978. It then doubled again by 1996 and doubled yet again by 2006 (Hutton 2007).

Why have India and China done so well? To some extent both countries are returning to their historic position in the world economy. At the time of the Roman Empire, China had 26 per cent of the world's economy and India had 33 per cent. Even by 1820, China had 33 per cent, India 16 per cent (compared with western Europe at 24 per cent and the US at 2 per cent)(Smith 2007b). It was only in the nineteenth century that the Indian and Chinese economies collapsed. China's GDP per head in 1950 was only three-quarters of its 1820 value. By the early 1970s, China's share of world output was only 5 per cent and India's 3 per cent, compared with western Europe's 26 per cent and the US and Canada's 25 per cent.

India and China have some distinct similarities in their economies. Both had their year zero in the 1940s, when their political and economic status was transformed – India's by independence in 1947, China's by the victory of Mao and the Communists in 1949. Both have huge populations and a dominant agricultural sector, employing more than half of the population. Both went through the same sequence of economic development, of emphasis on heavy industry and a planned economy, followed by agricultural reform, followed by export-led growth, with greater emphasis on the market (Goyal and Jha 2004).

The main difference comes in their political systems. China has been a unitary state since the time of the first emperor (he of the terracotta warriors) in the second century BC. Throughout most of its history, India has been a cultural rather than a political entity, and has only been a single state under foreign conquerors, from the Mughals in the fifteenth and sixteenth centuries to the British in the eighteenth to twentieth centuries. China is a one-party state with power centralised in the Communist Party; India is a multi-party democracy. China is relatively homogeneous racially, with few religious or racial minorities, except for Muslims in the far west, while India is a heterogeneous state both racially and religiously, with a very large Muslim minority population (India has a bigger Muslim population than Pakistan) and significant numbers of Sikhs, Buddhists, Jains and Christians.

Both initially made economic mistakes, but both laid the foundations for their future success immediately after their respective year zeros. Mao took over a state where illiteracy was rife, with a male illiteracy rate of 70 per cent and female illiteracy up to 99 per cent in rural areas (Hutton 2007, p76). Mao immediately instituted a crash programme of primary education and by the mid-1990s adult literacy was up to 80 per cent. It is forecast that by 2025 there will be more English speakers in China than there are native English speakers in the rest of the world (Smith 2007b, p100). China's economic policy was eccentric and destructive until the 1970s. The Great Leap Forward between 1958 and 1961 tried to industrialise China through village communes, which predictably proved to be a failure, while the whole Chinese economy was torn apart by the Cultural Revolution between 1966 and 1976.

India after independence went for a moderate socialist economy similar to that constructed in the UK in the 1940s, with extensive nationalisation of key industries, and also, following the ideas of Gandhi, opted for economic self-sufficiency (autarky). Small industries were encouraged and tariff barriers were high. The economy was also highly bureaucratic (known as the Permit Raj) and this discouraged entrepreneurialism. However, many small to medium-sized firms prospered under this benign and protectionist regime and India developed skills in small-scale manufacture.

The first prime minister of India, Pandit Nehru, was also, like Mao, committed to education. His legacy was the foundation of a group of seven Indian Institutes of Technology (IITs), founded in 1947. Although small, these were excellent, rated in 2005 as the third best institutions of technology in the world, behind only MIT and the California Institute of Technology. Graduates from the IITs were later to develop the Indian software industry, as well as much of Silicon Valley.

China's switch to a high-growth economy began in 1978, when the veteran communist Deng Xiaoping came to power. Deng realised that results were more important than ideology. One of his sayings is 'it doesn't matter whether a cat is black or white as long as it catches mice'. Deng dismantled the rural communes, giving land back to the peasants, which immediately led to a rise in agricultural output. He ensured that state enterprises were run by managers rather than party bureaucrats, and he set up Special Economic Zones, tax-free enclaves which welcomed foreign investment, initially from the Chinese diaspora in Hong Kong, Singapore and Taiwan, but later from the West, particularly the US. He cut tariffs on imports and launched a huge programme of infrastructure investment, with tens of thousands of miles of motorway and dozens of new international airports being built. The combination of good infrastructure and plentiful, cheap but well-educated labour proved irresistible to foreign investors. By 2008, China made two-thirds of the world's photocopiers, shoes, toys and microwaves, half the DVD players, digital cameras and textiles, a third of the desktop computers, and a quarter of the mobile phones and TVs (Jacques 2009). China's manufactured exports have boomed, although there has been some criticism that the result is that goods are 'made in China', but not 'made by China' (Hutton 2007, p114). There are very few major Chinese-owned companies and none which are truly world-class. However, the success of Chinese companies like Galanz (see Reflective Activity 1.4) suggests that this will soon change. In addition, as Hout and Ghemawat (2010) argue, increasingly China is insisting that one requirement for western companies entering into joint ventures in China is that they transfer advanced technology know-how to their Chinese partners. They cite the case of the development of the Chinese high-speed rail system. In the early 2000s this was dominated by Alstom, Siemens and Kawasaki, and Chinese firms only manufactured simple components. In 2009 the Chinese Government announced that in future the foreign rail companies must form joint ventures with the Chinese rail equipment companies CSR and CNR, and share their latest technologies.

China's industrial policy concentrated on developing clusters and exploiting external economies of scale, as suggested by Michael Porter (1990). The small town of Qiaotou (population 64,000) has 380 factories that manufacture 70 per cent of the buttons used in China. Datang manufactures a third of the world's output of socks, Shenzhou 40 per cent of the world's neckties (Hessler 2010). On a larger scale, the city of Wuhan in Hubei province in central China is a world leader in optoelectronics and produces 25 per cent of the world's optical fibre. This is supported by 80 universities and 100 high-tech research institutions. The city also has the fourth biggest air hub in China and a high-speed rail link to Beijing (1,200 kilometres in four hours) (Li 2012; Zhang 2012; Hao 2012). It is interesting that the main driver for investment in Wuhan is not the central government, but the city of Wuhan and the provincial government of Hubei.

Potentially the Chinese economy was at severe risk from the onset of world recession in 2008, because one of the first manifestations of the recession was a collapse in world trade. This hit China hard, as its economy was crucially dependent on exports of manufactured goods, particularly to the US. However, the Chinese Government took quick and decisive action, putting a fiscal stimulus of four trillion yuan (about £400 billion) into the economy and switching production to the home market.

China's economy again came under pressure in 2012 as a result of the euro crisis and the double-dip recession in the UK. Growth slowed to around 7 per cent (seen as the equivalent of a recession in China) and exports of manufactured goods slowed down again. The response of the Chinese Government was to introduce another economic stimulus, this time of one trillion yuan, as usual mainly aimed at infrastructure investment, but also aimed at stimulating domestic consumer demand, for example through reducing tax for farmers (Rapoza 2012). It is interesting to compare the various economic stimuli in China with the programmes of quantitative easing implemented in the UK and US. In the case of China, the money is spent, while in the UK and US quantitative easing has mainly been used to improve bank balance sheets rather than for real investment.

For over 40 years, India bumbled along, with some economic growth but not sufficient to cut rural poverty significantly (what J.K. Galbraith described as 'functioning anarchy') (Smith 2007b, p172). Despite the success of the IITs, illiteracy, especially in rural areas, remained high, and India was also held back by its caste structure. Since independence, discrimination against *dalits* (untouchables) has been illegal, but in practice it persisted. Only 20 per cent of rural residents are *dalits*, but they make up 38 per cent of the very poor. A further 11 per cent are *adavasis* (members of tribal groups), but they are even poorer, making up 48 per cent of the very poor (Meredith 2007, p119).

India's point of change came in 1991, when the country faced a financial crisis. This led to reforms introduced by Manmohan Singh, the finance minister, and now (2007) Prime Minister of India. He liberalised external trade and deregulated the domestic economy, copying Deng's concept of Special Economic Zones. The growth rate accelerated, reaching 8 per cent by 2000. India built on its strength in small and medium-sized manufacturing, backed by highly skilled craftsmen.

Whereas China was the country of choice for mass production, India concentrated on short, highly specialised production runs. More importantly, India latched on to the boom in new technology in the 1990s. Not only did it scoop the market in call centres and business process outsourcing, by the 2000s taking a 48 per cent share of the world market (Smith 2007b, p132), but it also developed a world-class software industry, centred on the southern city of Bangalore, where Infosys and Wipro are world-class and rapidly growing software companies. The software for Apple's highly successful iPod was developed in India (and the product assembled in China) (Meredith 2007, p102). Services now account for more than half of India's GDP (Rudiger 2008). Older industry also started to flourish, led by the long-established conglomerate Tata, which now owns Corus (the ex-British Steel) as well as a range of Western companies including Tetley Tea. It subsequently bought Jaguar and Land Rover from Ford in 2008 for $2.3 billion. In 2007, India became the world's 12th largest economy (De Vita 2009). India seems to have weathered the world recession without too much damage and expects economic growth soon to return to the pre-credit crunch figure of 9 per cent.

India also had great institutional strengths – the English language (although China now teaches English from the primary school stage), a vibrant democracy, a free press and universal acceptance of the rule of law. Hutton sees these soft attributes as key. However, like China, India has weaknesses. Its literacy rate lags well behind China and its physical infrastructure is very weak. Its roads, with a few exceptions, are appalling, and anyone who has experienced Agra airport will know that the same can be said for most of its airports.

Each of the 28 Indian states has its own border controls and regulations. Smith describes a lorry journey from Kolkata (Calcutta) to Mumbai (Bombay), a distance of 2,150 kilometres, which took eight days, including 32 hours waiting at border toll booths (Smith 2007b, p164). However, the latest Five Year Plan (2007–12) has earmarked $500 billion for infrastructure improvement.

Like China, India also suffers from endemic corruption. In 2007, Andrew Wileman described an attempt to transport a bull elephant from Kerala to Bangalore in order to take part in a Hindu ceremony at one of the IT companies, Aditi. The 300-mile journey involved the payment of £250 in bribes at every state border to and from Bangalore, because 'elephant transportation papers were not in order'. He also tells the story of the auto-rickshaws in Delhi. Apparently there are 500,000 of these, but only 100,000 hold official licences. The other 400,000 stay in business by paying regular 'fines' to the traffic police (Wileman 2007).

The latest move to lessen the grip of the bureaucratic 'permit raj' came in September 2012 with the decision to allow foreign supermarket chains to enter India. However, being India, this was hedged with restrictions. The foreign chains had to form joint ventures, they were only allowed into cities with a population of more than 1 million (46 cities) and they must invest $100 million over three years. The reforms are opposed by the nationalist opposition BJP party, traditionally the party of small shopkeepers, and by left-wing parties, including that which controls the state of West Bengal. This means that Kolkata, the capital of West Bengal and one of India's biggest cities, will be excluded (Jack 2012).

As a democracy, India is relatively slow to take decisions and to make major shifts in policy. On the other hand, decisions in India have democratic legitimacy. China can take quick decisions and tends to be better at taking long-term decisions, as its government is not answerable to an electorate, while decisions in India are shorter term and geared to the electoral cycle. As a result, China was better placed to make long-term investments in its education and health programmes and to steamroller through its infrastructure improvements. Despite its centralised political system, China has been very effective at decentralising economic decision-making. It has given a great deal of economic autonomy to the growth areas of Shanghai, Quangdong and Hong Kong.

China has also been more effective at opening its economy to the West and at encouraging foreign direct investment through a stable exchange rate and low real interest rates. India has gained through the widespread use of English in its higher education system, which has led to the outsourcing of large numbers of service jobs from the West. China has tended to gain from the outsourcing of manufacturing rather than service jobs. This has led to a big increase in Chinese exports, particularly to the US and Japan.

Both countries clearly have economic systems which are highly effective at generating economic growth. As an authoritarian state, China has been able to be more single-minded in its pursuit of growth and as a result has achieved a higher rate of growth. However, there are costs in the Chinese system. As the development economist Amartya Sen has pointed out, no democratic country has experienced a devastating famine, whereas authoritarian states like China have (Steele 2001).

It appears that a combination of authoritarian political control and a decentralised market-run economic system seems to be highly effective at producing economic growth, but with accompanying costs such as loss of freedom, economic inequality and social disruption.

However, it is possible to over hype the success of China (Hilton 2004). It took until 1993 before China's exports were back at the level they reached in 1928, before the Japanese invasion, and despite its vast population, China's GDP in 2000 was only a quarter of that of Japan. The dash for growth has also caused enormous environmental degradation. China has 16 of the world's 20 most polluted cities.

Question

1 Which do you think is more likely to sustain its economic growth in the long term, India or China?

There are three excellent books, all published in 2007, which provide background material for this Seminar Activity. Two are journalistic accounts of the economic rise of India and China. David Smith's *The Dragon and the Elephant: China, India and the new world order*, examines the issues from a UK perspective. Robyn Meredith's *The Elephant and the Dragon: The rise of India and China and what it means for all of us*, covers much the same ground from a US perspective. Will Hutton's *The Writing on the Wall* takes a more analytical approach, concentrating on China, and is as much a critique of the West as it is of China. A further book, published in 2009, is Martin Jacques' *When China Rules the World,* which takes a mainly cultural perspective on the rise of China.

REFERENCES

Article 13 and CBI. (2007) DwrCymru Welsh Water. *CBI-CSR Case Studies.* September.

Bank of England. (2003) *Remit for the Monetary Policy Committee of the Bank of England and the New Inflation Target.* www.bankofengland.co.uk/education/Pages/targettwopointzero

Bank of England. (2004a) The labour market. Available at: www.bankofengland.co.uk/education/Pages/targettwopointzero

Bank of England. (2004b) How do www.bankofengland.co.uk/targettwopointzerointerest rates affect inflation? Available at: www.bankofengland.co.uk/targettwopointzero

Bank of England. (2007a) *Treasury Committee Inquiry into the Monetary Policy Committee of the Bank of England: ten years on. The Bank of England's submission regarding the economic context.* www.bankofengland.co.uk

Bank of England. (2007b) *Governor's Open Letter to the Chancellor of the Exchequer.* 16 April. www.bankofengland.co.uk

Batty, D. (2009) Timeline: the Baby P case. *Guardian.* 22 May.

Batty, D. and Weaver, M. (2006) Q&A: private finance initiative. *Guardian.* 3 May.

BBC. (2012) Heseltine report calls for action to stimulate growth. 31 October. Available at: www.bbc.co.uk/news/business-20142837 [Accessed 19 November 2012].

Benati, L. (2006) *UK monetary regimes and stylised macroeconomic facts.* Bank of England Working Paper no 290. www.bankofengland.co.uk

Billington, I. and Thomson, A. (2012) UK trade data more upbeat than wider deficit implies. *Wall Street Journal.* 14 March.

Booth, R. (2009a) Welcome to Barnet, the Tory test-pilot of no-frills government. *Guardian.* 27 August.

Booth, R. (2009b) Tory-controlled borough of Barnet adopts budget airline model. *Guardian.* 27 August.

Booth, R. (2009c) The Ryanair pricing model that could be a route to budget care in Barnet. *Guardian.* 27 August.

Booth, R. (2010) Barnet's 'easyCouncil' finds it hard to cut with £1.5m spent, £1.4m saved. *Guardian.* 26 October.

Bowcott, O. (2004) Transcript reveals doctor's pleas for dying teenager. *Guardian.* 18 October.

Bowcott, O. (2009a) Social work vacancies as high as 39%. *Guardian*. 17 June.

Bowcott, O. (2009b) Baby P council looks to US for social workers. *Guardian*. 3 October.

Brindle, D. (2009) Ministers back plan for a national social work college. *Guardian*. 29 July.

Briner, R. (2001) Why family-friendly practices can also be performance-friendly. *People Management*. 8 November.

Brown, K. (2001) Standard that has delivered. *Financial Times*. 30 October.

Burgess, J. (2009) The budget airline model won't work for councils. *Guardian*. 2 September.

Cable, V. (2009) *The storm: the world economic crisis and what it means.* London: Atlantic Books.

Carvel, J. (2003) Blair puts NHS out to tender. *Guardian*. 14 May.

Carvel, J. (2009) Government pledges £58m to recruiting top quality social workers following Baby P case. *Guardian*. 6 May.

Caulkin, S. (2003) Wanted: one kick in the pants. *Observer*. 18 May.

CBI. (2005) *CBI response to Leitch Review of Skills*. London: Confederation for British Industry.

Chu, B. (2011) George Osborne's outer fringes. *Independent*. 8 August.

CIC Association. (2012) What is a CIC? Available at: www.cicassociation.org.uk/about/what-is-a-cic [Accessed 18 November 2012].

CIPD. (2008) *The skills agenda in the UK*. London: Chartered Institute of Personnel and Development.

Conservative Party. (2008) *Building skills, transforming lives: a training and apprenticeships revolution.*

Daneshkhu, S. (2007a) The quest for improved productivity. *Financial Times*. 22 May.

Daneshkhu, S. (2007b) Output still trails other large countries. *Financial Times*. 26 June.

De Grauwe, P. (2001) Competitiveness and compassion. *Financial Times*. 8 November.

Department for Trade and Industry. (1998) *Building the knowledge driven economy*. Available at: www.dti.gov.uk/comp [Accessed 29 August 2004].

Department for Trade and Industry. (2001) *Opportunity for all in a world of change*. Available at: www.dti.gov.uk/opportunityforall/index.html [Accessed 29 August 2004].

De Vita, E. (2009) Fast track India. *Management Today*. August.

Dillow, C. (2011) The wage squeeze. *Investors Chronicle*. 26 January.

DIUS. (2007) *World class skills: implementing the Leitch Review of Skills in England*. Cm 7181. London: Department for Innovation, Universities and Skills.

ECB.(2004) *Objective of monetary policy*. Available at: www.ecb.int

Economist. (2004) Debt threat. 24 April.

Economist. (2005) From Lisbon to Brussels. 19 March.

Elliott, L. (2004) The outlook is not so nice when hidden hazards are exposed. *Guardian.* 18 October.

Elliott, L. (2012) Why more jobs may reflect hard times for workers. *Guardian.* 3 December.

Elliott, L. and Stewart, H. (2011) IMF warns that world risks sliding into a 1930s-style slump. *Guardian.* 15 December.

European Union. (2004) *European performance in competitiveness and innovation.* Available at: www.europa.eu.int [Accessed 18 September 2004].

Farnham, D. (1999) *Managing in a business context.* London: Chartered Institute of Personnel and Development.

Federal Reserve. (2004) *Frequently asked questions: monetary policy.* Available at: www.federalreserve.gov

Forman, F.N. and Baldwin, N.D.J. (1999) *Mastering British politics.* 4th edition. Basingstoke: Macmillan.

Giles, C. (2007) Productivity loses steam under Labour. *Financial Times.* 23 January.

Goyal, A. and Jha, A. (2004) Dictatorship, democracy and institutions: macro policy in China and India. *Economic and Political Weekly (India).* 16 October.

Guardian. (2003a) Duisenberg decorated but still dithering. 10 May.

Guardian. (2003b) Accountability vacuum. 3 May.

Hall, S. and Henry, S. (2006) An independent Bank of England: is that enough? *National Institute Economic Review.* April.

Hao, N. (2012) Wuhan's development picking up steam. *China Business Weekly.* 15 October.

Harding, R. (2004) Social enterprise: the new economic engine. *Business Strategy Review.* Winter.

Harris, J. (2012) Outsource to easyCouncil? Not in our name. *Guardian.* 12 November.

Hellowell, M. (2006) Alive and kicking. *Public Finance.* 17 November.

Hencke, D. (2004) Big players lobbying for piece of the action. *Guardian.* 27 October.

Hessler, P. (2010) *Country driving.* New York: Harper.

Heywood, A. (2008) *Essentials of UK politics.* Basingstoke: Palgrave Macmillan.

Hilton, I. (2004) A rampaging market, but a long way from global power. *Guardian.* 13 November.

Hirst, J. (2005) The awkward age. *Public Finance*. 14 January.

House, J.D. and McGrath, K. (2004) Innovative governance and development in the new Ireland: social partnership and the integrated approach. *Governance*. Vol 17, No 1.

Hout, T. and Ghemawat, P. (2010) China vs the world: whose technology is it? *Harvard Business Review*. Vol 88, No 12. December.

Hudson, B. (2009) Captives of bureaucracy. *Community Care*. 9 April.

Hutton, W. (2004) We must dare to be dynamic. *Observer*. 7 November.

Hutton, W. (2007) *The writing on the wall*. London: Little Brown.

IPPR. (2001) *Building better partnerships*. London: Institute for Public Policy Research. June.

Jack, I. (2012) Centuries of Indian life could be extinguished by the arrival of Walmart. *Guardian*. 21 September.

Jacques, M. (2009) *When China rules the world*. London: Allen Lane.

Kay, J. (2002) The balance sheet. *Prospect*. July.

Kay, J. (2003) *The truth about markets – their genius, their limits, their follies*. London: Allen Lane.

Keegan, W. (2004a) Erm, there's a danger in paradise. *Observer*. 17 October.

Keegan, W. (2004b) Keeping an eye on the competition. *Observer*. 31 October.

Keegan, W. (2012) Every little helps? Not in an economic crisis as big as this. *Observer*. 23 September.

King, M. (2007) *The MPC ten years on: a speech to the Society of Business Economists*. 2 May. www.bankofengland.co.uk

Kirkpatrick, I. and Ackroyd, S. (2003) Transforming the professional archetype?: the new managerialism in UK social services. *Public Management Review*. Vol 5, No 4.

Kirkup, J. (2010) George Osborne attacks 'deficit deniers'. *Daily Telegraph*. 17 August.

Lansley, S. (2009) *Unfair to middling*. London: Trades Union Congress.

Lawton, A. and Rose, A. (1994) *Organisation and management in the public sector*. Harlow: FT/Prentice Hall.

Leitch, Lord. (2006) *Leitch review of skills: prosperity for all in the global economy – world class skills*. London: HM Treasury.

Lennan, D. (2001) Cartel crooks belong in jail. *Financial Times*. 2 November.

Letter to the Editor. (2010) The cuts will strengthen Britain's economy by allowing the private sector to generate more jobs. *Daily Telegraph*. 18 October.

Li, F. (2012) Hubei's capital poised to grow. *China Business Weekly*. 15 October.

Lipsey, R.G. and Chrystal, K.A. (1999) *Principles of economics*. 9th edition. Oxford: Oxford University Press.

LSC. (2008) *National employers skills survey 2007: key findings*. London: Learning and Skills Council.

Lucas, E. (2009) Businesses that 'put back' are bucking the trend. *Professional Manager*. September.

MacCormaic, R. (2008) Twenty years of social partnership agreements. *Irish Times*. 4 August.

Magnus, G. (2011) Give Marx a chance to save the world. *Bloomberg View*. 29 August. Available at: www.bloomberg.com/news/2011-08-29/give-marx-a-chance-to-save-the-world-economy-commentary-by-george-magnus-html [Accessed 6 November 2012].

Maltby, P. (2003) *Public interest companies: fad or permanent fixture?* London: Institute for Public Policy Research.

Marx, K. (1867, 2004) *Capital: a critique of political economy*. Harmondsworth: Penguin.

Mathiason, N. (2004) Casino bill derailed by bitter split in Cabinet. *Observer*. 24 October.

Meredith, R. (2007) *The elephant and the dragon: the rise of India and China and what it means for all of us*. New York: Norton.

Merrick, N. (2001) Minority interest. *People Management*. 8 November.

Moreton, S. (2006) *Are 'professional' HR practices compatible with volunteer management?* London: Attend.

Mulholland, H. (2009) We will follow example of efficient Tory councils, says Osborne. *Guardian*. 10 September.

Mulvey, S. (2003) The EU law that rules our lives. *BBC News Online*. Available at: www.bbc.co.uk/news [Accessed 15 May 2013].

Nelson, P. (2001) Does IIP still make the grade? *Personnel Today*. 13 November.

Newman, M. (2009) Social work degrees difficult to fail, MPs told. *Times Higher Education*. 6 August.

Office for National Statistics. (2012) Labour market statistics. January. Available at: www.uk/ons/rel/lms/labour-market-statistics/january-2012/index/html [Accessed 1 February 2013].

Office for National Statistics. (2013) Labour market statistics. January. Available at: www.uk/ons/rel/lms/labour-market-statistics/january-2013/index/html [Accessed 1 February 2013].

Osborn, A. (2003) State's golden share in BAA is illegal. *Guardian*. 14 May.

Osborne, G. (2011) Britain is leading the way out of this crisis. *Daily Telegraph*. 7 August.

Palmås, K. (2005) The UK public interest company: the idea, its origins, and its relevance for Sweden. *CbiS Discussion Paper 1*. Göteborg University, Sweden.

Pettiger, J. (2012a) UK national debt. *UK Economics*. 22 October. Available at: www.economicshelp.org/blog/category/uk-economy/ [Accessed 3 November 2012].

Pettiger, J. (2012b) How the budget deficit was cut by 25%? *UK Economics*. 23 October. Available at: www.economicshelp.org/blog/category/economics/ [Accessed 3 November 2012].

Phillips, A.W.H. (1958) The relationship between unemployment and the rate of change of money wage rates in the UK 1861–1957. *Economica*.Vol 25, No 2.

Philpott, J. (2002) Productivity and people management. *Perspectives*. Spring. London: Chartered Institute of Personnel and Development.

Philpott, J. (2003) Europe. *Perspectives*. Summer. London: Chartered Institute of Personnel and Development.

Porter, M. (1990 *The competitive advantage of nations*. New York: Free Press.

Porter, M. and Ketels, C. (2003) UK competitiveness: moving to the next stage. *DTI Economics Paper No 3*. DTI/ESRC. May.

Rapoza, K. (2012) New China stimulus package coming. *Forbes*. 24 May.

Reeves, R. (2010) The politics of deficit reduction. *Renewal*. Vol 18, No 3/4.

Resolution Foundation. (2012) *Gaining from growth: the final report of the Commission on Living Standards*.

Rudiger, K. (2008) *The UK and India: the other 'special relationship'?* The Work Foundation Provocation Series. Vol 4, No 3.

Samuel, M. (2009) Celebrities back social work in government recruitment push. *Community Care*. 1 September.

Sawford, A. (2009) How Whitehall betrayed social workers. *Guardian*. 12 March.

Searjeant, G. (2007) Bank Governor hits back at criticism over inflation. *The Times*. 25 April.

Sexton, R. (2012) *The exploration of economics*. 6th edition. Cincinnati, OH: South-Western College.

Sexton, R. and Fortura, P. (2005) *Exploring economics*. Scarborough, Ontario: Nelson.

Smith, D. (2007a) We still have a grip on inflation, says Bank. *Sunday Times*. 22 April.

Smith, D. (2007b) *The dragon and the elephant: China, India and the new world order*. London: Profile.

Steele, J. (2001) Food for thought: Amartya Sen. *Guardian*. 31 March.

Stewart, H. and Boffey, D. (2011) George Osborne plan isn't working, say top UK economists. *Observer*. 5 June.

Stratton, A. (2010) Labour's plan for the first 'John Lewis' council. *Guardian*. 18 February.

Tomlinson, M. (2004) *14–19 curriculum and qualifications reform.* London: Department for Education and Science.

Travers, T. (2009) Osborne shows he is a true blue. *Guardian.* 10 September.

Treasury. (2006) *PFI: strengthening long-term partnerships.* London: HM Treasury. May.

Treasury. (2007) *Chancellor of the Exchequer's reply to the Governor of the Bank of England.* HM Treasury. 17 April. Available at: hm-treasury.gov.uk

Treasury. (2010) *Budget report.* London: HM Treasury.

TUC. (2008) *After Leitch: implementing skills and training policies: TUC submission to the Innovation, Universities and Skills Committee Inquiry.* London: Trades Union Congress.

Wall Street Journal. (2011) Corporate profit's share of pie most in 60 years. *Wall Street Journal.* 29 July.

Ward, S. (2000) Brown to gamble on 'spend more' call. *Guardian* 10 November.

Warner, J. (2003) Network Rail spends away, but is it really value for money? *Independent.* 8 May.

Warner, J. (2007) Governor's letter should not be seen as a non-event. Rather, it highlights policy failings. *Independent.* 18 April.

Weaver, M. (2001) Labour chooses third way to improve failing services. *Guardian.* 22 October.

Weldon, D. (2012) Profits before pay. *BBC Radio 4 Analysis.* 26 February. Available at: www.bbc.co/iplayer/episode/b)1c7nd5/Analysis_Profits_Before-Pay   [Accessed   7 November 2012].

Wileman, A. (2007) India rising. *Management Today.* July.

Willow, C. (2011) The wage squeeze. *Investors Chronicle.* 26 January.

Woodward, W. (2003) School firms' forte is 'lobbying for work'. *Guardian.* 5 May.

World Bank. (2000) *Beyond economic growth: meeting the challenges of global development.* Geneva: World Bank. Available at: www.worldbank.org/depweb/beyond/beyondco/beg_04.pdf

Wright, R. (2007a) Cost rises in the first three years. *Financial Times.* 16 July.

Wright, R. (2007b) Working relationship proved dear. *Financial Times.* 18 July.

Zhang, Z. (2012) Economic powerhouse rising in Central China. *China Business Weekly.* 15 October.

Regulation

INTRODUCTION

The *rule of law* that applies in democratic societies is one of the key features that differentiate democracy from dictatorship and tyranny. Legal decisions cannot be taken capriciously or for small special interest groups but for the long-term benefit of society as a whole. Laws, as determined by an elected parliament and interpreted by the independent judiciary, are fundamental to a well-governed and stable society.

The last time that this was tested was in March 1984 when Arthur Scargill led the miners' union into a national strike to try to improve working conditions in the mines and to prevent a massive programme of pit closures. He dismissed the legislation passed two years earlier requiring a ballot before strike action could go ahead, taking the view that 'bad laws should be ignored', just as the trade union movement had successfully done in 1972 against earlier Tory trade union legislation. In a defining moment of the Thatcher administration, the Government brought the full force of the establishment – police, army, public opinion – to restore the '*rule of law*', supporting the concept that laws passed in a proper democratic process must be obeyed by individuals and organisations. The view was widely promulgated that 'societies where the rule of law can be flouted with impunity cannot survive' and it was the almost unanimous support of this view across the UK that ultimately sealed the miners' fate.

The legal system, then, is at the heart of a democratic society. It sets out the rules within which people and organisations live and do business with each other; it reflects the current views on morality held by the majority of its citizens; it defines the punishments for breaking these rules; it establishes the nature of the contracts between the individual, the organisation and the state whereby the state is paid (through taxation) to protect the interests of all parties in a fair and impartial way. It allows everybody to plan their lives with the fair certainty of foreseeing what actions and behaviour are allowed and what is forbidden.

This chapter provides a general introduction to the structure of UK law, details some of the specific legislation that sets out a level playing field for business and the consumer, indicates the main protection for employees in the workplace, examines how law regulates particular sectors and labour markets and suggests ways that employers can respond to new legislation. There is a detailed examination of the role of government in regulating business activity, from health and safety to the size and compensation of bankers' bonuses.

Law is a complex subject and organisations and individuals regularly call on experts to advise them, so the outline provided in this chapter is primarily to raise awareness of the legal framework together with a good number of working examples.

LEGAL CONTOURS

LEGAL CONCEPTS

There is a clear *division of authority* between the judiciary and the executive, a factor that distinguishes true democracy from a dictatorship. Judges are independent and, once appointed, cannot be dismissed, except in extreme cases such as where they are convicted of corruption or another serious offence. If they take decisions that the Government does not like (and this is increasingly happening with the increased use of judicial review), the Government simply has to accept their decisions.

Precedent requires courts to follow decisions laid down in earlier cases where the facts are broadly similar. To give an example, in decisions made on unfair dismissal claims soon after the Industrial Relations Act was passed in 1972, higher courts confirmed the circumstances under which an employee could claim *constructive dismissal*, including the need for the individual to immediately resign and leave the employment once the incident had occurred. If a claim reaches a tribunal today and the claimant delayed by a few weeks in leaving the employment after the incident occurred, the tribunal would be required to follow the precedent and throw out the claim.

When lawyers are advising on a case, then, they need to be well read not just in the law itself, but in the way it has been interpreted by the courts as shown in the precedents involved. They need to read the '*obiter dictum*', which are the judge's recorded comments justifying their decisions. Faced by precedents which indicate that a case would be unsuccessful, a lawyer would either advise their client to withdraw or the lawyer would try their best to argue that the facts of the case were significantly different so the precedent did not apply.

That is not to say that precedents cannot be changed. One of the duties of the Court of Appeal is to examine precedents argued before them and judge whether such precedents are out of date for changing social times or preserve a system which is clearly unfair. In such cases, they may decide they need to be altered at the margins or completely reversed. A well-known example of reversal was the *Walker v Northumberland County Council* case (see Case Study 5.1).

CASE STUDY 5.1

CHANGING A PRECEDENT

John Walker was a social work manager who returned to work having had a mental breakdown brought on through an excessive workload. He requested a reduction in his duties and additional resources to allow him to cope with his responsibilities and serve the community. His employer did very little to help him and he subsequently suffered a further extended breakdown which ended his career. Prior to this case, the precedent had been that the employer had a clear duty of care in respect of preventing foreseeable physical illness but not mental illness brought on by stress. The Court of Appeal confirmed that this duty of care should be extended to foreseeable mental illness because there was no logical reason why it should be excluded from the scope of the Health and Safety at Work Act. Walker was awarded £175,000 in damages and this decision established a change in precedent. Consequently, employers have had to give much more careful consideration to the issue of foreseeable stress and subsequent mental illness among their staff.

Source: *Walker v Northumberland County Council* 1995 IRLR 35/95

In serious criminal cases (and, surprisingly, civil cases for libel or slander), the final decision is made by a jury – one is *judged by one's peers*. In jury trials, even the judge's advice can be overturned under the belief that it is a matter of whose word can be trusted and a jury of 12 people is the best way to test this.

TYPES OF LAW

The law is divided into two main divisions.

Civil law

The ground rules dealing with relationships between individuals and between an individual and an organisation are laid down under civil law. Where one side believes that the law has been broken, they will take the case up in the civil courts and aim to have the wrong righted and/or obtain compensation. The main areas under which civil cases are brought are *breach of contract* (where it is claimed that one party has broken the terms of a legally enforceable contract) and *torts*, which are civil wrongs independent of contract, such as negligence, nuisance or defamation (see Case Study 5.2).

CASE STUDY 5.2

EXAMPLE OF A TORT

Your next-door neighbour has allowed a tree to grow so large that parts are overhanging your small garden and takes away most of your light. You have asked him politely to take some action but nothing happens. You therefore bring a case claiming *nuisance*. Before the case comes to court, a gale brings down a large branch which smashes your fence and greenhouse. You therefore add a further claim for *negligence* to the case.

The remedies you can obtain are:

- *compensation (damages)* – but only to the extent of your proven losses, plus costs you have expended
- *specific performance* – where the court instructs the plaintiff to carry out an action (see Case Study 5.3)
- *injunction* – where the court instructs the plaintiff to *not* carry out an action, such as demolishing a listed building.

CASE STUDY 5.3

SPECIFIC PERFORMANCE

You have successfully bid for an original painting at an auction but you learn subsequently that the owner decided to withdraw the painting for sale. You believe you have a valid contract and you successfully ask the court to instruct the owner to complete the contract and deliver the painting to you. You have set your heart on obtaining that unique painting and no alternative or compensation would satisfy you.

Criminal law

Here offences (crimes) are defined which society believe need punishing. The court case is a result of a police investigation and a case brought by the Crown Prosecution Service. Very occasionally, a private prosecution takes place, such as by the parents of the victims of the Hillsborough stadium disaster in the 1990s. In general, however, these have a very low success rate and can be stopped by the Attorney General if they are not regarded as in the public interest.

Cases are divided into *indictable offences*, generally serious crimes – murder, rape, serious fraud – where conviction can result in imprisonment – and *summary offences* – parking, petty theft – which are less serious and where conviction brings a fine.

REFLECTIVE ACTIVITY 5.1

In February 2010, Cotswold Geotechnical Holdings was charged with gross negligence manslaughter over the death of a geologist. He was taking small samples from a development site when the pit he was working in collapsed, killing him.

Look up the Corporate Manslaughter Act 2007 and trace the outcome of this case, which was the first such case brought under this legislation. The outcome will indicate under what other circumstances an organisation can commit a criminal offence.

FROM WHERE DOES THE LAW ORIGINATE?

We are so used to a flood of new legislation (*statute law* as explained in Chapter 4), emerging from parliament each year that it is a common fallacy to believe that this process is the only source of law. However, there are two other main sources.

Common law

Up until the nineteenth century, most law was 'common', which meant that it had come into effect through judges recognising custom and practice (and common sense) and this was spread around the country by judges on their circuits. These decisions made up the precedents. In most areas today, common law decisions have been incorporated into statute, but there are a number of fundamental common law concepts that remain, such as those relating to the law of contract and employee rights (see later in the chapter). There also remain some more isolated specific rights under common law, such as grazing rights held by New Forest Commoners.

Codes of Practice

Although not technically law, formal codes have a strong influence on decisions taken by the courts. For example, an organisation facing a tribunal claim for unfair dismissal that has not followed closely the Acas Code on Disciplinary and Grievance Procedures is less likely to make a successful defence. Similarly, an employer facing an equal pay claim should ensure that the Equality and Human Rights Commission's Code on Equal Pay has been incorporated into their procedures.

It should also be noted that much of the statute law originates from the *European Union*, whose legislative processes were also set out in Chapter 4.

COURTS SYSTEM

In Figure 5.1, the courts system for England and Wales is set out (Scotland has had its own, somewhat different system for more than 500 years). Courts are distinguished through their regulation of civil or criminal law and whether they are courts of first instance or whether they hear appeals or both.

Figure 5.1 Court system in England and Wales

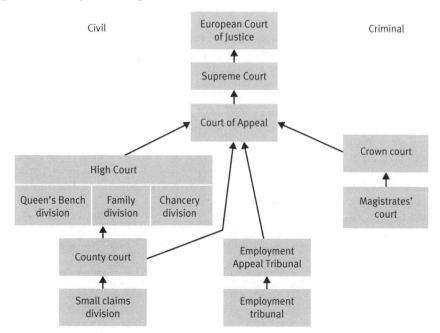

Note: the tribunal route indicates the process for employment law only.

CIVIL CASES

Claims start in the county court or, if the amount at issue is less than £5,000, the small claims division. Speed, accessibility and informality are the keynotes here, with representation frowned upon and costs normally limited to the value of the summons. The judge acts alone as the arbitrator. It provides an opportunity for businesses and individuals to claim small debts and torts to be examined and resolved. One day it may be resolving the overhanging tree dispute, the next, dealing with a claim from an ex-employee for unpaid overtime. There are around 200 county courts situated in cities and market towns with judges still going on 'circuits' to try to ensure a degree of consistency, although small claims courts are overseen by a registrar.

County courts deal with actions for less than £15,000 together with some others up to £50,000 by agreement with the parties, depending on their complexity (although this can vary depending on the nature of the claim). Additional subject areas at the county courts, apart from contract and tort cases, include probate disputes, bankruptcy, undefended divorce, consumer credit issues and some land questions. Around 1.5 million summonses a year are taken out at county courts, but only around 5–10 per cent arrive in court and an even smaller percentage are actually defended.

Summonses valued at over £50,000 go directly to the High Court. This has three divisions which deal with cases of first instance and appeals from lesser courts. The *Queen's Bench* division is the busiest, with jurisdiction over high-value contract and tort cases, and a special commercial court dealing with banking, insurance and other financial services cases. It also has an admiralty court to hear cases involving ships and aircraft, while it also hears some appeals from the county court and a comparatively small number of criminal appeals from crown courts. The *Family* division handles matrimonial cases, including wardship, adoption and custody claims. Finally, the *Chancery* division, the oldest court of all, has jurisdiction over high-value tax cases, trusts, partnership disputes, patent and copyright actions and land disputes.

CRIMINAL CASES

The *magistrates' courts* manage most of the criminal cases, determining around 98 per cent of all crime. Motoring offences make up around half of it (1.5 million cases). It handles all forms of petty crime with the maximum penalty it can apply being a six months' prison sentence, although few prison sentences are awarded. It has special arrangements to handle juvenile cases and it acts as a preliminary hearing in serious crime cases, deciding on 'committing' to a crown court and agreeing bail/custody arrangements. There are 400 magistrates' courts, with a total of 30,000 magistrates who hear the cases. They are a mixture of stipendiary (paid) officials and unpaid appointees. Stipendiary magistrates can sit alone. It is possible for those accused at a magistrates' court to decide to be heard in front of a jury at a crown court, usually in the hope that juries convict less often than hardened magistrates. Appeals (there are few) go generally to the crown court.

There are 91 *crown courts*, the most famous being the Central Criminal Court (Old Bailey). Cases are heard by juries, although the judge has a strong influence through control of the proceedings, interventions to clarify issues and the summing up. The number of crown court cases increased to a peak in 2010 at 152,000 but dropped by over 10 per cent by the middle of 2012.

From 2010, a number of serious cases may be heard by a judge sitting alone where jury tampering may be a serious threat.

HIGHER COURTS

The *Court of Appeal* hears both criminal and civil court appeals with three to five judges in attendance and a majority decision prevailing with each judge's reasons published. Their judgments are extremely influential, much used to clarify the law and to set the ultimate precedent. Cases are sometimes referred to this court when new evidence has come to light that casts doubt on the validity of criminal convictions, cases that may have been held as long as 20 years or more ago. The appeal to the *Supreme Court* can only be on a legal issue and the decision is final, except where the case comes under European law, where much of employment law resides. If so, the case is heard by *the European Court of Justice*, which gives a ruling and then refers the case back to the UK court for implementation.

TRIBUNALS

The most well-known tribunals are those in employment areas, such as unfair dismissal and sex, race and disability discrimination. However, there are numerous tribunals set up by statute in other areas. There are rent tribunals, set up to help protect tenants from unscrupulous landlords, social security appeal tribunals, to provide an opportunity for citizens to questions decisions made about their right to benefits, such as unemployment and sickness, and various tribunals related to appeals over taxation. They all have the same intention, which is to provide a formal yet accessible process for the aggrieved citizen to have their cases heard fairly, impartially and thoroughly by persons not involved in the original decision. The accessibility comes about through, first, some discouragement of legal representation, as with the small claims court, by generally not awarding costs, and second, by ensuring that help in the initial stages is provided by the tribunals themselves and by volunteer bodies such as the Citizens Advice Bureau.

In the employment area, the tribunals are bound by rules of evidence and precedent but the three-member tribunals are allowed to operate a much more informal and inquisitive approach than the higher courts. Appeals to the employment appeal tribunal and subsequent appeals to higher courts can only be on the basis of law.

OMBUDSMEN

A final grouping of quasi-legal intent are the sets of ombudsmen, set up by legislation to investigate complaints of maladministration, mostly in the public arena. There are a number of commissioners (ombudsmen) in areas such as local government, the National Health Service and parliament whose reports have no precise legal standing but put pressure on the bodies concerned to rectify mistakes and improve their services. An example of a case where the work of the ombudsman led to substantial costs to the Government is set out in Case Study 5.4.

PARLIAMENTARY OMBUDSMAN REPORT ON PENSION LOSSES

Between 1997 and 2005, 400 private sector pension schemes were closed with outstanding deficits. The main reason for the closures was the demise of the company or its financial inability to continue contributing to the scheme. The outcome was that 85,000 employees, ex-employees and pensioners did not receive the pensions they had been promised under the scheme. Some, indeed, lost all of their pension entitlement.

In 2005, the Parliamentary Ombudsman was asked to investigate the Department for Work and Pensions' (DWP) role in encouraging employees in this debacle. In March 2006, Commissioner Ann Abraham reported that the DWP had been guilty of maladministration. Its official guidance to employees was 'inaccurate, incomplete, unclear and inconsistent'. Much of the criticism was directed at government information leaflets which gave a misleading impression of the security of the schemes. They had not given sufficient warnings of the possibility of scheme closures and loss of pension rights.

The Government responded that they dismissed the report, pointing out that employees did not rely exclusively on these leaflets as a basis for their financial decisions. The minister responsible declared that the Government could not take on the heavy financial responsibility for the failure of private pension schemes. They were not obliged under legislation to take any further action and would not do so.

Pension campaigners then took the matter to the High Court and, in 2007, obtained a decision that the Government had wrongly rejected the ombudsman's findings. It confirmed that the DWP had committed maladministration in its advice on the schemes.

This put additional pressure on the Government, which was forced, in April 2007, to make concessions in terms of compensation to many of those who lost out. The Government agreed to cover 80 per cent of the losses at a cost of around £2 billion.

LAW OF CONTRACT

Introduction

Contracts are at the heart of all business and employment activity and the common law governing their operation goes back further in time than most other law. For centuries, the judges interpreted the law in a way that reflected the 'laissez-faire' approach to all business, with the state interfering very little and people in business and employment were left alone to run their affairs. This was partly to preserve the inequality of the 'master and servant' relationship and partly because most business contracts were on a relatively equal basis. To buy a pair of shoes, a customer went to the local cobbler and negotiated a price on a fairly equal basis. However, this was to change by the mid-nineteenth century as the industrial revolution and the development of capitalism had created large enterprises in commerce and industry which produced many unequal bargaining situations. In the next section, we shall see how the state intervened over the last 100 years by introducing legislation to provide a more balanced situation.

The essence of a contract is to provide a legally binding format to a set of mutual promises. In general, the contract involves one party providing goods or a service and the other paying for them and a typical organisation will have scores of contracts with suppliers, customers, service providers, intermediaries, staff and contractors. These contracts do not have to be in writing to be legally binding (apart from those related to land), although for clarity and certainty, most of them are confirmed in this way. However, any informal changes that both parties agree to, even if not confirmed in writing, will supersede those written into the contract as long as one side can produce compelling evidence that such an informal arrangement took place.

Interestingly, there are some very important contracts where the parties have to agree that they are not legally binding. These are agreements between employers and trade unions where, by tradition, both sides reserve the right to go back on the deals they make should they choose to do so. This is an interesting reflection on the trust between the parties under British employment relations.

There are six main elements in any contract:

Offer and unconditional acceptance – for each contract, the offer must state all the terms, be communicated effectively and must be clear and unambiguous. It is different from what is known as an *'invitation to treat'*. When shops first started putting prices in their shop windows, the courts were asked to intervene to distinguish between what appeared to be a legal 'offer' and what was merely an invitation to people to come into the shop and start negotiating. They decided that the prices marked on goods in the shop window or in advertisements are not 'offers' (or even 'special offers') and a potential customer cannot go into the shop and demand the legal right to buy the goods at the prices shown. It needs the shopkeeper's acceptance to make this a contract.

Acceptance must be unconditional and within the stipulated (or reasonable) time. An offer can be withdrawn at any time prior to acceptance. If the acceptance stipulates conditions, this becomes a counteroffer. If both parties act as if they are working under an agreement, a contract is deemed to have been agreed.

An area that still provides some difficulties with the courts is that of standard terms and conditions. One business will ask for tenders for providing goods (an invitation to treat). Another company will respond, making an offer on documentation which has its standard terms and conditions of trading printed on the back. The first company then accepts the offer on documentation with its own standard terms and conditions on the back. If the terms differ, it could be held to be a counteroffer, of course. If there is a dispute over some small detail which differs between the companies, the courts have tended to decide that the last set of documentation applies, but will be influenced by the actions of the parties and any evidence that can be offered to support the view that a particular term applied. It still does lead to problems, however, which are regularly resolved by an arbitration service.

There must be ***genuine agreement*** – each party must have the same understanding of what makes up the contract and there must be no misrepresentation. For example, if the car seller knowingly indicates a mileage that is not genuine, the contract will be void and the buyer can claim damages. What often needs to be clarified under this heading is what were 'representations' ('I think this is a most reliable motor') and what were actual terms of the contract ('the tyres are three months old'). A buyer acting on representations has no redress. Contracts must not be entered into under duress or undue influence, including drink or drugs. If this is the case, the contracts can be voided.

The parties must have the ***capacity to contract*** – so minors are excluded, except for necessities (such as sweets and bus journeys!), but not for larger items. The same applies to those of an unsound mind. An interesting area is that it can be assumed that employees of an organisation who appear to have the authority to contract do in fact have this authority. This is to avoid the situation where an organisation can go back on a contract they subsequently decide is not in their favour.

There must be an ***intention to create legal relations*** – in general, legal relations between close relatives are rarely upheld by the courts, unless there is clear evidence to the contrary. The opposite applies to all business relationships where the presumption is that there is an intention present.

The contract must be for ***legal purposes*** – a contract is void if, for example, payment is made as 'cash in hand' where National Insurance should be paid or any contracts set up which are purely to evade taxation.

There must be ***consideration*** – this is normally money, although it can be any right or benefit which can be held to be of monetary value either currently or in the future and contracts of barter are legal (that is, international contracts of grain in exchange for oil). Without consideration, as in an agreement to paint the house of a friend for nothing, there can be no enforceable contract. In the voluntary world, this still provides some problems of course. The payment must refer to the future and not to some past payments or obligations. Finally, the payment does not have to be adequate, fair or reasonable – that is up to the parties concerned.

A *contract of employment* arises directly out of contract law. A job must be offered and unconditionally accepted; there must be genuine agreement with no misunderstanding of the essential terms and conditions, such as the need to work night shift or the type of company car; the contract must be legal, with no illegal activities such as 'cash-in-hand'; there must be consideration, a wage or salary, as voluntary work is not enforceable and only those over 13 can have an employment contract, with strict regulations relating to the employment of those under 18. Interestingly, the courts recognise the employment of wives and husbands as long as there is clear evidence of a contract existing.

There are more details on employment law later in the chapter.

REGULATING BUSINESS AND PROTECTING THE CONSUMER

On a hot summer's day in 1930, a bottle of ginger beer was bought at the end of a walk by a young man for his lady friend. She gratefully drank up but, in finishing the opaque bottle, the remains of a decomposed snail appeared and, not surprisingly, she became very ill. On recovering, she wanted recompense for her unhappy experience but she could not sue the shopkeeper because she had no contract with him, nor could she sue her boyfriend because there was no consideration – the bottle was a gift. Nor did she have a contract with the manufacturer. However, a lengthy legal case was commenced which, two years later, appeared at the House of Lords (*Donaghue v Stevenson*), where the landmark decision was reached that manufacturers can be guilty of the tort of negligence.

Prior to the case, 'caveat emptor' (let the buyer beware) applied in all consumer purchases but *Donaghue v Stevenson* established that manufacturers have a duty of care to their customers not to be negligent and to avoid any acts or omissions which can be reasonably foreseen to kill, injure the consumer or member of the public or to damage property. Subsequent cases have clarified guidelines, such as drug manufacturers having a greater duty of care than newspaper publishers because the consequences of faulty goods are far more serious.

Donaghue v Stevenson was an important case and the outcome was a distinct improvement in the degree of protection for consumers. By the late 1960s, however, governments started to take a more supportive view for the consumer. There were a number of reasons for this:

- The growth of huge multinational corporations made it much more difficult for the view to be held that a contract was made between equal partners.

- Mergers and acquisitions were growing to the stage that some companies had control of substantial sectors of the marketplace and could dictate terms.
- There was a growth in practice of large organisations inserting 'small print' into contracts where special conditions were inserted and liabilities excluded to the detriment even of the observant consumer.
- Pressure had developed from consumer organisations, such as *Which?* magazine, which helped develop consumer awareness of shady practices and politicians appreciated they needed to take notice of this pressure.
- Britain decided to join the European Union in the early 1970s and some legislation was required to bring the UK in line with European law.
- Trading practices were changing in line with technological and monetary developments and there were gaps in the law in these areas.

The legislation can be divided into the macro area – to control and enhance competition generally – and in the micro area – where specific unfair business practices are made illegal.

CONTROLLING AND ENHANCING COMPETITION

Fair Trading Act 1973

It was considered essential that a watchdog with wide powers of investigation should exist to champion the consumer interest and provide independent advice to the Government. The Office of Fair Trading (OFT) took this role and its powers have been increased with subsequent legislation, including the Competition Act 1998 and the Enterprise Act 2002. The Director-General of Fair Trading has responsibility to investigate commercial activities which may appear to be against the interests of consumers and advise the Government if it believes action is necessary. The scope of activities investigated is wide, covering all sectors, businesses large and small, and dealing with contract terms, selling methods, packaging and promotion. Although its powers have limits, the fact that an investigation can take place and that it can seek orders from the Government to stop certain activities are, in practice, strong deterrents and have often changed the way business is carried out. In its early days, it investigated pyramid selling and ensured its abolition.

Restrictive Trade Practices Act 1976/Competition Act 1998

This legislation was passed to prevent the use of monopoly power either by individual companies or groups of companies colluding. A restrictive practice is defined as collusion on prices, terms of supply, manufacturing processes and any activity that is likely to have the effect of restricting, distorting or preventing competition. The OFT has the right to enter premises and demand documents and to enforce restrictions on movement or destruction of evidence. If an organisation refuses to co-operate, it can be penalised to the extent of 10 per cent of turnover.

When a practice is found to exist, it can only be successfully justified by the argument that it:

- protects the public from injury
- is a counterweight to another monopoly (such as in negotiations with the Royal Mail)
- provides extensive benefits to exports.

Examples of investigations in recent years include extended warranties (see Case Study 5.5), operation of small pharmacies and the major chains, private dentistry, consumer IT services and estate agencies. It has also investigated some business methods, including doorstep selling and public sector procurement. A number of investigations were carried out in the 1980s and 1990s regarding price-fixing by colluding cement companies (see Chapter 3 for a discussion of the economic aspects of collusion), which eventually resulted in the cartel being broken up and cement prices substantially reduced.

CASE STUDY 5.5

COMPETITION COMMISSION REPORT ON EXTENDED WARRANTIES

In 2003, the Competition Commission carried out an investigation into the £500 million market in extended warranties, following on from a referral from the OFT, chiefly for electrical goods. They found that the bulk of warranties were purchased at the point of sale of the goods and could add 50 per cent to the price of the product and were generally poor value. Bad practice reported included:

- Sales staff emphasised the risk of product failure.

- Customers were told that independent repairs were difficult to obtain and were expensive.
- The consumer was not encouraged to shop around.

It was also reported that self-regulation had not worked and that the large electrical retailers were exploiting their monopoly situation to the detriment of consumers.

Source: Competition Commission (2003)

The OFT reports to the Government, which can decide to refer the matter to the Competition Commission either for a decision or, in the case of an impending merger where the organisation will have 25 per cent or more of the market, a fuller enquiry to decide if the merger is in the public interest and under what terms the merger would be allowed to progress. Full-scale investigations by the Commission in recent years have included one into the position of Nestlé (where it found it did not have excessive monopolistic power on coffee prices), video games (where it recommended the abolition of licence controls) and UK car prices (where it found that the exclusive dealership system operated against the public interest).

Investigations of potential wrong-doing, or the threat of referral to the OFT or the Competition Commission, have a huge impact on organisations or their future planning of possible mergers. A raid by the OFT on premises can cause the company's share price to drop 10 per cent and many mergers have been decided by the policy of the Competition Commission.

Two investigations in 2011 demonstrated the balance it needs to hold between encouraging effective competition and the consideration it must give to the changing business and technological environment. In the first case, the examination of local bus services, it found that there was a high level of concentration, large barriers to entry and operators avoiding competing with each other in one operator's 'core territory', leading to geographic market segregation; all such activities lead to harmful effects on consumers. A number of requirements to improve the competitive framework were set out by the Commission. On the other hand, it cleared a proposed merger of the travel and leisure interests of Thomas Cook and the Co-operative Group because, although it led to much more limited competition in the field of travel agents, the development of Internet travel and leisure compensated such a restriction in the marketplace.

In 2014, the OFT and the Competition Commission will be merged into the Competition and Markets Authority (CMA).

A direct effect on the resourcing aspect of human resource management is shown in Case Study 5.6.

CASE STUDY 5.6

COLLUSION BY RECRUITMENT AGENCIES

In 2009, six recruiting agencies were fined £40 million by the OFT for operating a cartel that fixed fees and boycotted a rival. The biggest company involved, Hays Recruitment, was fined £30 million, equivalent to more than 2 per cent of its turnover. The agencies, acting together as the Construction Recruitment Forum, met five times over two years to fix prices to allow higher profits. At the same time, they organised an effective boycott of contracts where a competitor, Parcs (which was not part of the cartel), was offering cheaper rates. Two other companies that took part in the cartel were offered immunity in return for providing evidence against the six companies.

Source: Mathiason (2009)

REFLECTIVE ACTIVITY 5.2

The OFT carried out a survey of doorstep selling in response to complaints from the Citizens' Advice Bureau. Their report in 2004 recommended that legislation needs to be updated to combat the psychological tactics employed by many salespeople.

The study into the practice of selling goods and services on the doorstep and in the home, worth at least £2.4 billion a year, found that a range of sales tactics and influencing techniques can lead consumers to make inappropriate purchases which they later regret. This highlights a gap in consumer protection. The current legislation gives consumers who are cold-called a seven-day period in which to cancel a contract. This protection does not apply to consumers who asked for the visit.

Buying in the home provides a unique setting for a business transaction – salespeople effectively have a captive audience. Nearly 40 per cent of consumers have bought goods or services in the home. While 70 per cent of those were satisfied, a significant minority of 30 per cent experienced problems: at least 15,000 complaints a year are made to trading standards departments regarding doorstep sales. Most respondents to the OFT's consumer survey said they felt buying in the home was more pressurised than other settings.

The OFT recommends that the Government should extend the legislation to give cancellation rights to solicited visits as well as unsolicited. The OFT will also run a consumer education campaign in conjunction with interested groups to raise awareness of consumers' rights and alert them to the psychological techniques used and how to combat them.

Look up the Office of Fair Trading's website and examine two more of its recent investigations, including the remit to the OFT, the decisions it has made and the justification for those decisions.

CONSUMER PROTECTION

Economic theory would argue that rational behaviour by consumers makes their protection unnecessary. Poor-performing products would not survive and consumers simply walk away from poor service. To a large extent that is true, but the consumer is not always in a position to behave rationally. They may not have sufficient information about the product (hence the need for product description on the label), they may not have a choice of products if an uncontrolled monopoly exists and they may not be able to challenge a large and unscrupulous supplier. So a whole raft of legislation has been passed in recent years covering all business–consumer relationships and attempting to tighten up on legal loopholes. Much of the legislation encoded the common law in place and then extended it. Here is a brief summary of the key features.

Trade Descriptions Act 1968/Consumer Protection Act 1987

These two Acts protect against traders who deliberately give false descriptions in the price, quality and nature of service. These are criminal offences and can result in fines and even imprisonment for repeated offences. The Act is policed by local government Trading Standards officials, who, incidentally, also assist the Office of Fair Trading in gathering information. Examples of cases include:

- advertisements showing massive price reductions when the prices had only been increased the day before – regulations now state that goods must have been at the pre-reduction price for 28 continuous days during the previous six months
- cars being advertised with 'one owner' which was a leasing company who had leased the car out for long periods to five different drivers
- prices being advertised but no indication that VAT is to be added.

CASE STUDY 5.7

MISLEADING VALUATIONS

The Office of Fair Trading carried out an investigation in 2011 into the activities of the website Webuyanycar.com, following complaints from customers and consumer support groups. Consumers were given the impression that they would be paid the full online valuation if the company's inspection matched the condition of the car entered by the seller on the website. However, customers found that other factors reduced the original online valuation, including 'market conditions', and that vehicle inspectors were set targets regarding the purchase price of vehicles, sometimes to reduce the online valuation by as much as 25 per cent.

As a result of the investigation, the company gave undertakings to change their methods of operation in line with OFT requirements.

Source: www.oft.gov.uk press release (April 2011)

The Consumer Protection Act also places strict (but not absolute) liability on suppliers for damage and death/injury caused by defects in their products. There is no need to prove negligence or a contractual relationship, but there is a defence that the state of scientific and technical knowledge at the time the product was supplied was not sufficiently advanced for the defect to be recognised (the 'state of the act' defence).

Unfair Contract Terms Act 1977

Introduced to prevent 'small print' removing consumers' rights, generally without their knowledge, the Act has two parts. First, the seller cannot remove the liability for death or injury through negligence under any circumstances. Second, a trader cannot enforce a contract term that the courts hold to be unfair. For example, a coach company advertised a tour by luxury coach with videos, toilet, etc, but added in their small print that they reserved the right to substitute a coach of inferior quality. The courts held this to be unfair as it gave too much leeway to the coach company and most customers would not have picked up this particular item among the small print. The claimant was awarded compensation. Most decisions in this area are now dealt with by the OFT through an 'informal undertaking' agreed with the company. A 2007 example of this is set out in Case Study 5.8.

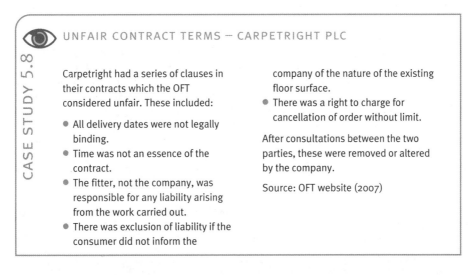

CASE STUDY 5.8

UNFAIR CONTRACT TERMS – CARPETRIGHT PLC

Carpetright had a series of clauses in their contracts which the OFT considered unfair. These included:

- All delivery dates were not legally binding.
- Time was not an essence of the contract.
- The fitter, not the company, was responsible for any liability arising from the work carried out.
- There was exclusion of liability if the consumer did not inform the company of the nature of the existing floor surface.
- There was a right to charge for cancellation of order without limit.

After consultations between the two parties, these were removed or altered by the company.

Source: OFT website (2007)

A number of well-publicised cases and the constant vigilance of consumer societies and other pressure groups have resulted in much greater honesty in communicating the real (and generally reasonable) contract terms by suppliers since this Act was passed.

Sale of Goods Act 1979/Supply of Goods and Services Act 1982

These Acts enable dissatisfied customers to take civil action against the supplier. The Acts require that:

- Goods and services must match the description.
- Goods and services must be of merchantable quality – in appearance, finish and durability.
- Goods and services must be fit for the purpose.
- Services provided must be carried out with reasonable skill and within a reasonable time.

As the Act has been interpreted, the issue of reasonableness is key. A very cheap pair of canvas shoes is fit for purpose if they last six months, while a pair of expensive, hand-made leathers would not be fit if they wore out after four years' light wear. In essence, it has been for the court to decide what are the bounds of reasonableness and we shall see this again in the field of employment law.

If the product fails to meet the tests under the Act, the consumer has the remedy of the right to their money back, or receive a credit note, or for the goods to be replaced free of charge or the consumer can take the goods at a reduced price.

Consumer Credit Act 1974

This Act was introduced following the boom in hire purchase and credit agreements in the 1960s and 1970s, which led to high-pressure selling, especially in people's homes, and high rates of interest. The Act took two main directions. First, it aimed to clean up the industry by enforcing licensing of lenders for all credit activities, including credit cards. The licensing involves an inspection regime and a requirement for effective staff training and proper funding of the business.

The second direction was to ensure that contracts were not oppressive. All credit contracts and all contracts signed outside of business premises have a seven-day 'cooling-off' period where the consumer can cancel without loss to either party. The terms of the credit can be altered by the courts if they regard the rate of interest as excessive. The consumer has the right to full details of the agreement before signing, including the annual rate of charge (calculated by means of the OFT current formula), the full cost of the loan, the debtor's right to pay the loan off early and the terms under which they would do so. The Act does not apply to loans over an upper limit, currently £25,000, and only applies to consumer credit, not corporate credit.

Additional EU-wide consumer protection has been introduced for ordering on the web (Electronic Commerce Regulations 2002) and mail order (Consumer Protection (Distance Selling) Regulations 2000).

Later in the chapter we will look in more detail at the effect these laws and additional regulations have in specific sectors and industries.

EMPLOYMENT LAW

The regulation of employment relationships has changed beyond all recognition over the last 40 years. Originating from the individual 'master–servant' contract, the fundamental inequality of the parties to the relationship became clear by the mid-nineteenth century and a political party (the Labour Party) was set up essentially with the aim to rectify these inequalities through legislation by establishing employee rights and removing legal restraints on collective bargaining. It was clear that there was a major difference between a conflict over an employment contract, which can lead to unemployment and suffering abject poverty, and a difference over buying a pair of shoes. Moreover, the evidence of unscrupulous use of dominant employer power was widespread.

Although much progress was made in these areas in the early twentieth century, especially in the collective bargaining field, the stimulus to enacting more radical and extensive employee protection has come from the European Union. At the same time, the political consensus in recent times has been that the rights granted to trade unions in the collective bargaining field went too far and they have been reined in by Conservative Governments in the period between 1980 and 1997 and have been subject to further tightening in the Coalition Government since 2010.

SOURCES OF THE EMPLOYMENT CONTRACT

The terms of an employment contract come from a surprising number of sources. It is not just the *express terms*, which are those specifically included in the contract (usually set out in the offer letter), such as salary, notice and holiday entitlement. Other sources are of equal importance:

● There are a number of *implied terms* originating from common law. These include the duty of the employee to co-operate with the employer in such areas as reasonable changes to the job, exercise due care in looking after the employer's goods and property, and show loyalty demonstrated by not disclosing confidential information. The employer also has duties, such as to exercise due care over the employee's health, safety and well-being (see pages 231–235), to provide work, indemnify the employee if he or she incurs loss, expense or liability in carrying out the employer's instruction and to pay wages on time and correctly.

- Many contracts incorporate *collective terms* negotiated between the employer(s) and union(s) either at a local or national level. These may deal with issues such as overtime payment, holidays and disciplinary procedures.
- Contract terms are also incorporated through the *employee handbook*, which sets out rules and policies set out by the employer that the employee must sign up to.
- Many more unwritten contract terms reflect *employment laws* covering employee rights and benefits (see pages 222–223).

An additional complication is that the *contract terms do not need to be written down*. Rules relating to, say, employees swapping shifts, which have operated informally for some years (that is, through custom and practice) with the full knowledge of management, become part of the contract. In claims for unfair dismissal, the tribunal is very keen to establish whether terms written into contracts are those that actually operate in practice. For example, if an employee is dismissed for fighting (as clearly laid out in the employee handbook) but it comes to light that on the last two occasions when a similar incident occurred the employees were merely warned, the tribunal can take the view that custom and practice is that dismissal is not the normal punishment under the contract.

That is not to say that contractual terms cannot be changed by either party. An individual employee can request changes to his or her holiday arrangements which are different from the standard contractual terms. Or changes can be negotiated on a collective basis, usually through unions but sometimes through a works council. An employer can change shift arrangements and introduce different work practices and systems. In doing so, they should consult with the workforce, be able to justify the changes for business reasons and ensure they are published widely. They do not need to get every individual's signed agreement to the changes. An employee who continues to work under the changes is deemed to have accepted the changed contract.

A further complication is differentiating between the normal employee contract, called a *contract of service*, and the contract for the self-employed, who work under a *contract for services*. The legal implications are great in that a different tax regime applies (hence considerable interest by the Inland Revenue in this area) and the self-employed have none of the rights and benefits detailed below. Legal tussles have occurred in areas such as commission-only salespeople and those providing occasional but regular services, such as consultants. Although a complex area, the courts examine the degree of control and the nature of exclusivity of contract which can sometimes overcome the apparent clarity of the payment and tax arrangements.

Under the Employment Rights Act 1996, employers are required to give to each employee within two months a statement of certain contract terms under 16 headings, which includes details such as the date that continuous employment started, hours of work and holiday entitlement. This is called the 'principal statement' but, to repeat, it is not the actual contract of employment.

EMPLOYEE RIGHTS

The bulk of employment law since the 1970s has been enacted to improve the minimum level of benefits for employees and to protect them from potential employer abuse. There was some earlier legislation in this area, such as the prohibition of child labour and the nine-hour working day in the coal mines from the nineteenth century, but the recent legislation has taken the process much further and allowed employees to benefit extensively from the changes.

Employee protection has been enhanced in the following areas:

Protection from discrimination

Since the 1970s, groups seen as vulnerable in the employment field because of well-evidenced discrimination, harassment and bullying have been given legal protection. The various Acts make it unlawful to discriminate on the grounds of sex, ethnic origin, disability, age or religion. Discrimination has taken two forms:

● *Direct discrimination* – an instance here would be to advertise for a 'Girl Friday' or to use different criteria for selection for promotion. In the case of race discrimination, it may relate to an employer indicating to a recruitment agency that they do not want black casual workers; or an employer may turn down a deaf or partially sighted applicant specifically because of this disability. In each case, an individual or group is treated less favourably than another on the grounds of sex, race or disability. The employer has no defence even if they genuinely believe that what they are doing is right. The motives are irrelevant.

● *Indirect discrimination* – this occurs where the employer treats all applicants or employees the same but a practice, condition or policy adversely affects one sex or race more than another, or it affects the disabled more than the able-bodied or the elderly more than the young. The way it normally adversely affects that group is because the proportion of people from a particular group able to meet the condition or policy is considerably smaller. Moreover, the employer cannot objectively justify the practice, policy or condition. If the employer cannot convince the tribunal that the defence is genuine and substantial, the employer will lose the case. Tribunal cases have included:

  – the requirement to restrict applicants geographically by residence to a specific area, which discriminated against ethnic minorities whose representation in that area was slight

  – recruiting only through word of mouth in an employment site dominated by white males

  – promoting internally when the workforce is unbalanced.

The Equal Pay Act 1970 prohibits discrimination in pay and benefits between men and women, where work is 'like' or rated as similar under a job evaluation scheme. In addition, an employee can claim that their work is of 'equal value' as another employee of the opposite sex.

Harassment and bullying

Described as 'unwanted behaviour which a person finds intimidating, upsetting, embarrassing, humiliating or offensive', the courts have increasingly punished harassment and bullying, using both the concept of an employer's duty of care and discrimination legislation, supported by the EU Equal Treatment Directive (amended in 2000). This reflects the changing social attitudes in society where a predominantly male, white culture in workplaces, where power may be exercised over staff in a vulnerable position, is no longer acceptable in a modern state. It has been accepted by the courts that the judgement as to whether behaviour is acceptable or not comes from the subject(s) of the harassment. There can be additional compensation awarded for 'loss of feelings'.

No service requirement is necessary in any area of discrimination. Protection applies from day one of employment.

Protection from unfair dismissal

Since 1972, employees have been protected from arbitrary and unfair dismissal. From 2012, employees need two years' service to qualify for this protection, except in the case of trade union, equal opportunities or health and safety issues. To successfully defend a claim, the employer has to show that they have a justifiable reason (usually based on poor performance, conduct or redundancy) and that they have carried out the dismissal using the correct procedures. If they fail, the tribunal awards compensation up to a maximum of £74,200 (2013) and, occasionally, can order the employer to reinstate the employee.

Acas has provided codes of practices in dealing with dismissal and redundancies which organisations need to observe to defend claims successfully. For example, where the offences are deemed to be misdemeanours (timekeeping, attendance, poor performance), warnings are required, whereas with gross misconduct (theft, violence), instant dismissal is permitted. Employees' rights, including that of a fair hearing, a colleague to help support their case and a fair appeal procedure, must be observed.

From July 2013, applications to a tribunal will cost £160, with an additional cost of £80 if the claim goes to a hearing and higher costs for more complex cases.

The same protection is also afforded against dismissal due to pregnancy or for being a union activist (see Case Study 5.9).

CASE STUDY 5.9

DISMISSAL BECAUSE OF PREGNANCY

In *Hildreth v Perdu* (2006) UKEAT 0533/06, Hildreth, a finance manager, endured a campaign of harassment, intimidation, embarrassment and verbal abuse by the company owners after she had told them she was pregnant. They indicated strongly that they would not want to continue to employ her in a pregnant state. Her position had become so difficult that she resigned and successfully claimed constructive dismissal, receiving £8,000 in compensation.

Protection from working excessive hours

Arising from an EU directive and essentially a health and safety measure, the Working Time Regulations 1998 have had a controversial history. They have established that employees cannot be forced to work in excess of 48 hours a week, averaged over 17 weeks. Employees should have 11 consecutive hours of rest in any 24-hour period and a 24-hour rest in every seven-day period, plus a 20-minute break if the shift exceeds six hours. The Regulations also insist on the provision of 28 days' holiday.

The controversial aspect is that employers and employees can agree to 'opt out' of the Regulations so that they often apply as a voluntary measure. How 'voluntary' they are and whether the opt-out should remain is discussed later.

Protection when being transferred

The Transfer of Undertakings (Protection of Employment) Regulations 1981 (known as TUPE) were introduced as a result of the EU Acquired Rights Directive. The philosophy here is that employees need to be protected when their organisation is sold to or merged with another organisation, or they are outsourced with their work. Prior to these Regulations, employees' terms could be fundamentally and unilaterally altered, with the employees having the choice to accept or leave.

Under the Regulations, all employment terms and conditions are protected (except pensions) and prior service is recognised. This does not stop the new employer having the right to change terms at a later date, but this right is limited by statute. Full consultation must take place with the employees being transferred.

Protection from deductions from pay

Under the Employment Rights Act 1996, employees have the right of an itemised pay statement and deductions can only be made with prior authorisation from the employee in writing.

EMPLOYEE RIGHTS AND BENEFITS

A summary of the minimum benefits introduced through legislation is set out in Table 5.1.

Table 5.1 Employee rights and benefits introduced through legislation

Minimum benefit	Legislation	Summary of key details
Minimum wage	National Minimum Wage Act 1998	Provides a minimum wage (£6.31 for employees aged 22 and over in 2013), includes bonuses and tips, with lower rates for employees under 22. Aims to eradicate exploitative pay in vulnerable sectors, such as home-workers and hospitality.
Holidays	Working Time (Amendment) Regulations 2007	Minimum entitlement, including public holidays, is 28 days.
Maternity pay	Employment Rights Act 1996, amended by Employment Act 2002	Payable by employers for 39 weeks. Six-month qualifying period paid at 90 per cent of average earnings for six weeks then £136.78 per week (2013) for remaining 33 weeks.
Ante-natal care	As above	Right to paid time off during working hours for all ante-natal care and treatment
Maternity leave	As above	On top of paid maternity leave, an additional 26 weeks' unpaid maternity leave can be taken, with the right to the same job back upon return (see Case Study 5.10).
Paternity leave and pay	Employment Act 2002	Six-month qualifying period. Applicable to father of child, mother's husband or partner and be expected to have some responsibility for upbringing of child. Paid for two weeks at £136.78 per week (2013). Government plan to allow sharing of maternity/ paternity leave through the 2013 Children and Families Bill.
Adoption leave	Employment Act 2002	One of the parents can take up to 26 weeks' unpaid leave when an adoption takes place. Six months' qualifying service.
Parental leave	Maternity and Parental Leave Regulations 1999	Parents with children under 5 (or disabled children under 18) can take up to 18 weeks' unpaid leave with the right to return to the same job. One year qualifying service. Shared parental leave is planned for 2015.

Minimum benefit	Legislation	Summary of key details
Time off for dependants	Employment Rights Act 1996	Reasonable unpaid time can be taken off to provide assistance when a dependant dies, falls ill, gives birth or is injured/assaulted, if there are any school problems or disruption to existing care arrangements. It is not applicable simply to provide normal care on a regular basis and only applies for an immediate crisis. In *Qua v John Ford Morrison Solicitors*, the employment appeal tribunal confirmed a fair dismissal when Qua took 17 different days off to look after her child who had medical problems.
Flexible working	Employment Act 2002/ Employment Rights Act 1996 Work and Families Act 2006	Provides the right of a parent of a child under 6 (18 if disabled) to apply for a change in working arrangements, including to work flexibly in order to care for the child. Employers can refuse on the basis of burden of additional costs, detrimental effect on ability to meet customer demand or quality of service, disruption of staff/department. Six-month qualifying period. These rights also cover employees responsible for caring for adults.
Time off for public duties	Employment Rights Act 1996	Reasonable unpaid time can be taken off relating to work as a member of a local authority, health authority or similar.
Time off for trade union duties	TULRCA 1992	Officials of independent trade unions have right to time off with pay during working hours to carry out reasonable and relevant trade union duties and to undertake training, as specified by the Acas Code of Practice.
Statutory Sick Pay (SSP)	Social Security Contributions and Benefits Act 1992/Statutory Sick Pay Act 1994	Employers are responsible for payment of SSP for up to 28 weeks of sickness/injury in any single period of entitlement, payable at £86.70 per week (2013).
Redundancy consultation, time off and pay	TULRCA 1992	Consultation with employees/representatives must take place 45 days before redundancies take effect if 100 or more employees are redundant (30 days if between 20 and 99 employees) and adequate information must be provided by the employer. Redundancy pay entitlement at one week's pay (1.5 weeks at age 41 and over, 0.5 weeks from 18 to 21) for each year of service, up to 20 years. The maximum week's pay is £450 (2013). Reasonable time off with pay must be given to look for alternative work.

Notes: These benefits are correct at the time of writing but are subject to amendment, both in terms of the pay arrangements and in other details.

These are minimum benefits and employers can (and do) improve them by granting pay where there is no entitlement under the legislation, increasing the rates or enhancing the terms and conditions.

CASE STUDY 5.10

RIGHT TO RETURN TO SAME JOB

Blundell, a primary school teacher, was allocated a different class on her return from maternity leave. She claimed she should have returned to teach the same class in the same room. The Employment Appeals Tribunal held her job was to teach at the school, not to teach the same class. The terms and conditions of the job gave the school head discretion in allocating staff, and although staff could indicate a preference, they could not insist on a particular class. The school also pointed out that staff were rotated to different classes and the change in Blundell's class was due to this rotation. But the school lost on its procedure. They did not consult her because she was away on maternity leave (all other staff were consulted) and this was held to be sex discrimination.

Source: *Blundell v St Andrew's Catholic Primary School* UKEAT/0329/06

REFLECTIVE ACTIVITY 5.3

Should the rights and benefits set out in Table 5.1 be applicable in all organisations or should small employers be exempt from some of them? Set out arguments for and against such exemptions.

REGULATION OF CONTRACTS THROUGH COLLECTIVE BARGAINING

In the nineteenth century, government legislation was put in place to stamp out the infant trade unions, who were attempting to interfere with the employment contract. Over the last 200 years, as explained in Chapter 3, the pendulum has swung, first to provide a legal framework for union immunity so union activities are protected in tort, and then back the other way under Thatcherite reforms, where tight restrictions on this immunity were introduced to protect employers from arbitrary union power.

Under a variety of Acts in the period 1980–95, legal immunity is only available for unions in leading their members to break their contracts through strikes or other industrial actions when they:

- have a secret ballot before action is taken (with strict requirements as to notifying the employer, how the ballot should be carried out and who is entitled to vote)
- only take action against their own employer (so-called secondary action against suppliers or customers is not protected)
- carry out picketing only at their own place of work and in very small numbers (to prevent the dangerous and oppressive mass picketing which took place during the 1984 miners' strike)
- do not insist on a 'closed shop' – employees can join or not join a union as they wish
- ensure they elect their full-time officials on a regular basis under strict governance and follow their own rules on disciplining and expelling members.

After the 1997 election of a Labour Government, the pendulum swung somewhat back towards improving the regulation of relationships with the workforce, chiefly through organised labour. First, the statutory recognition procedures in the 1999 Employment Relations Act has served to support union members who wish to formally negotiate in the workplace (see Reflective Activity 5.4). Second, the European-initiated Information and Consultation Regulations 2004 gave rights to employees to be informed and consulted about the business for which they work. Third, the requirement for proper grievance and disciplinary procedures to be in place and operating fairly in all organisations was set out in the Employment Act 2008.

This conferred discretionary powers on employment tribunals to adjust awards by up to 25 per cent if parties have failed unreasonably to comply with a relevant Code of Practice.

Not all attempts at legislation in this field obtained the desired result. For example, the main intention behind the 2004 Dispute Resolution Regulations (predecessor of the 2008 Employment Act) was to cut down on tribunal claims by encouraging employers to set up and follow appropriate procedures and insisting that employees exercised their rights to hearing and appeals under such procedures. Either side would be penalised when they did not follow procedures. However, after three years of operation, the number of unfair dismissal claims actually increased, chiefly due to the number of disputes over the nature and operation of such internal procedures and the legal wrangles associated with such disputes. Cases have taken longer to settle and the whole process was reviewed in 2007, leading to the Regulations being abandoned.

REFLECTIVE ACTIVITY 5.4

Union recognition

An application was made to the Central Arbitration Committee in 2012 by the GMB union for the right for recognition for manual staff at Intersnack, Ltd. The union claimed that they already had 18 members out of the 110 staff and that they had organised a petition that showed a further 37 employees would be interested in joining the union and for the union to act on their behalf. The employer had responded to the request by stating that he had little evidence of interest in union recognition and that he was concerned that the involvement of a union would upset the existing relations with staff and the operation of a successful existing works council.

After fully investigating the union membership claims and considering the ballot that had taken place, CAC found that, 'given the level of union membership and support demonstrated by the petition, and in full consideration of the evidence made available, the panel is satisfied that, in accordance with paragraph 36(1)(b) of the schedule, a majority of the workers in the proposed bargaining unit would be likely to favour recognition of the union'. They therefore approved the union right for recognition for bargaining purposes.

Look up the website for the Central Arbitration Committee and examine a further two decisions that they have taken recently, including the parties involved, the background to the dispute over recognition and the justification for the decision.

IMPLICATIONS OF REGULATION

Earlier in this chapter, the roles of the Office of Fair Trading and the Competition Commission, and their successors, in disseminating, regulating and enforcing commercial and consumer legislation were set out. Additional industry-specific regulation has been put in place over the last 20 years and this section will examine the operation of a selection of these regulators and the implications in the fields of privatised utilities, financial services, communications and areas of the public sector.

INDUSTRY REGULATORS – PRIVATISED UTILITIES

During the period 1980 to 1995, public utilities in the UK were privatised in what is now seen as a momentous and generally successful business revolution. The Labour Party ideology of nationalisation of key industries, which led to coal, steel, gas, electricity, railways and many others coming under state control in the post-war period until 1976, was replaced by the free trade and competition philosophy, promulgated by Milton Friedman (1970). It had become clear that the philosophy of veering towards a centrally controlled interventionist state operation, which had operated for the previous 20 years in the Western economies, had failed to produce the economic success that had been promised. Managers in state-controlled industries complained of constant ministerial interference, starvation of investment and regular changes in strategic direction. At its peak, almost 10 per cent of GDP came under government control. By 2002, after privatisation, this had been reduced to only 1 per cent.

Detailed studies (Martin and Parker 1997; Electricity Association 1998) have shown that labour productivity has risen at an average of 15 per cent, service provision has improved substantially and prices have generally fallen, especially in telecommunications and electricity.

In Chapter 3 you will have read about the issues associated with the privatisation of state monopolies. The model for privatisation was essentially one of attempting to break up state monopolies, introducing a variety of methods to stimulate competition and to keep a measure of control through regulation in the interests of the consumer. Unbundling has involved separating out the potentially competitive areas (for example electricity generation, telecommunication value added services) from the monopoly part (for example transmission and distribution grids, telephone lines to homes). This picture has been repeated across Europe with only a handful of mostly Scandinavian governments owning the state telecommunications company, reinforced by EU directives requiring member states to establish independent regulatory agencies to provide a 'level playing field' for potential competitors (Pollack 1997; Curwen 1997). This policy has continued with EU accession states having to sign up to privatisation of their main utilities.

Regulators

In each sector privatised in the UK, a *regulator* has been appointed to oversee the operation of the business for the benefit of the consumer (business and private) and to try to ensure that the form of privatisation actually worked in practice. The main responsibilities of the regulator are:

● to set out the pricing model (with or without agreement from the participants)
● to establish and monitor service standards
● to encourage the working of a competitive market
● for products such as gas and electricity, to ensure stable sources of supply
● to prevent the exercise of any remnant of monopolistic power
● to ensure the industry meets social and environmental responsibilities.

The regulator is appointed by the Government but is independent of government control. Each industry has been faced by a specific business context and the model of regulation has constantly been changed as the nature of the competitive challenges within each sector has altered. For example, one of the major issues in the telecommunication industry has been the role of the dominant provider, BT, which originally controlled landlines into most UK homes. The challenge was to encourage competition to this control, achieved mainly through encouraging the development of cable and mobile phone systems and through complex agreements allowing other companies access to the landlines to provide alternative services and through acting as a mediator in resolving disputes between the parties, such as the dispute in 2004 over NTS discounts. The telecommunication industry has, in fact, moved from one monopoly provider in 1984 (BT) to over 100 providers in 2011, while the degree of competition in the power industry has extended so far that over 5 million customers switched their electricity supply in 2011. In 2004, Ofgem fined Powergen £700,000 after the company stopped more than 20,000 domestic customers from switching to new gas/electricity contracts.

In another sector, the policy of the water industry regulator, Ofwat, has changed over recent years. At the time of privatising in the early 1990s, the water industry was allowed to make a substantial increase to tariffs to fund the substantial investment required to transform sewage treatment, reduce effluent discharge and thereby improve water quality around the UK coastline. However, in 2009, the regulator drafted a new five-year pricing regime which required water companies to cut prices by 0.2 per cent per year and increase capital expenditure. Since the draft publication, a number of water companies have called a halt to capital projects, which has led to redundancies among engineering companies supplying the water industry (Waples 2009). Despite this pressure, the final decision by Ofwat in November 2009 confirmed tight price controls.

In terms of its policing role, Ofwat fined United Utilities Water £8.5 million in 2007 for breaching rules governing trading arrangements with associated companies and threatened to revoke their licence.

The ability to set pricing models (unsuccessfully challenged in the courts in the mid-1990s by the gas industry) and to discipline players in the industry has given the regulator substantial power over operating companies. However, the need for establishing a fair pricing model has been reduced in recent years as more sophisticated markets have been introduced into gas and electricity, as mentioned earlier, allowing more providers to enter the market and create more competition, while natural competition has developed in the telecommunication industry.

INDUSTRY REGULATION – FINANCIAL SERVICES (FSA/PRA) AND COMMUNICATIONS (OFCOM)

A second strand of regulation covers two industries that the state regards as needing special forms of regulation, namely financial services and communications. These are industries which, generally, have not been government-owned (apart from the BBC and BT), but where there is a strong public interest. This interest is not just to preserve or encourage competition but to inspire confidence in the financial or communication systems, regulate ethical behaviour and to act as a watchdog over technical developments.

Ofcom, set up in 2003, covers activities previously controlled by, among others, the Broadcasting Standards Commission, Radio Authority, Oftel and the Independent Television Authority. In 2011, it took over the responsibilities for regulating the postal service from Postcom, which was abolished. It has a duty to 'balance the promotion of choice and competition with the duty to foster plurality, informed citizenship, protect viewers, listeners and customers and promote cultural diversity'. Its activities include:

- reform of public service broadcasting, the effects of digital television on the BBC's channel provision and the regular licence review
- policy on awarding of radio and television licences
- policy on television advertising under a single terrestrial commercial provider (ITV)
- advising the Government on foreign takeover of major communication players, such as national newspapers

- *protecting small players* – producing codes on the ability of independent programme producers to retain their programming rights
- *technology reviews* – advising on the digital switchover between 2007 and 2012
- *protecting public morals* – advising on television programme content in terms of sex and violence.

Financial Services Authority/Prudential Regulatory Authority

Regulating financial markets has, in recent years, been a key part of government economic activity. Understanding that confidence is at the heart of a country's financial system and, fearful of the 'meltdown' that could occur should this confidence suddenly evaporate, governments have established systems of financial supervision to try to avoid rogue activities. Up until 2013, much of this authority had been shared between the Bank of England and the Financial Services Authority, with a good part of the detailed supervision, investigation and enforcement taken up by the latter. Its main aims had been to:

- protect consumers through vetting firms and individual traders for honesty, competence and financial soundness
- promote public understanding of the financial system
- help to reduce financial crime, including money laundering and insider trading
- maintain confidence in the UK financial system by supervising exchanges, settlement houses and conducting market surveillance and monitoring transactions.

However, the financial crisis which began in 2007 and continued into 2013 – with little sign of abating – demonstrated that the FSA had signally failed to maintain the required level of financial supervision while financial confidence in the UK system had been severely shaken. As indicated in Chapter 4, the FSA had adopted a 'light touch' policy on banking regulation during the period 2000–07 so that it had been unable to forecast the financial crisis of 2007 or to handle it effectively. The FSA was accused of failing to apply enough regulation to bullish financial institutions in the boom years, a failure that contributed to the size of the crisis.

It also failed to give proper protection and redress on various fronts, including the mis-selling of endowments, payment protection insurance and allowing banks to apply sky-high overdraft charges and to sell risky investments to customers looking for safe savings products.

The Coalition Government announced in 2010 that the FSA would be broken up and two new bodies appointed:

- *Prudential Regulatory Authority (PRA)* – under the control of the Bank of England, chaired by its governor and responsible for the supervision of banking and other financial institutions. A much tighter grip on financial activity is likely to ensue and, as part of the Bank of England, financial policies are likely to be better integrated between the micro and macro sides.
- *Consumer Protection and Markets Authority (CPMA)* – an independent regulatory body that promotes confidence in financial services and protects the consumer.

The CPMA will inherit much of the powers of the FSA to investigate and, where necessary, fine organisations and individuals and restrict their activities. For example, during the course of 2012, examples of disciplinary action by the FSA included:

- Fining Peter Cummings, ex-chief executive of the corporate division of HBOS bank, £500,000 and banning him from holding any senior position in a UK bank, building society, investment or insurance firm. This is the highest fine imposed by the FSA on a senior executive for management failings. The FSA judged that between January 2006 and March 2008, Cummings failed to exercise due skill, care and diligence by pursuing an aggressive expansion strategy within the corporate division without suitable controls in place to manage the associated risks. Also, between April and December 2008, Cummings failed to take reasonable care to ensure that the corporate division adequately and prudently managed high-value transactions which showed signs of stress. They found that he was aware that there were significant issues with the corporate division's controls, including: weaknesses in management information; staff being incentivised to focus on revenue rather than risk; and a culture which saw risk management as a constraint on the business rather than an integral part of it. Under Cummings' direction, the division pursued an aggressive growth strategy, despite these known weaknesses in the control framework. This focus on growth peaked in 2007 and continued into 2008, despite Cummings being aware of concerns within HBOS about some of the markets in which the division operated and growing signs of problems in the economy. Rather than taking reasonable steps to mitigate potential risks, he directed his division to increase its market share as other lenders were pulling out of deals.

- Fining BlackRock Investment Management (UK) Limited (BIM) £9,533,100 for failing to protect client money adequately by not putting trust letters in place for certain money market deposits, and for failing to take reasonable care to organise and control its affairs responsibly in relation to the identification and protection of client money.
- Obtaining a successful prosecution of traders Christian and Angie Littlewood for insider trading, which led to custodial sentences and confiscation orders totalling over £3 million.

(source: FSA website)

As a direct result of the financial crisis of 2007–10, the FSA issued a *Code of Practice on Remuneration Practices* in August 2009 which applied to 26 large financial institutions – banks, building societies and investment firms. This code aims to discourage the payment of large cash bonuses for short-term gains, which has been considered as one of the major causes of the recent crisis because this encouraged substantial risk-taking.

The essential features of the code were:

- Bonuses should be based on employees' long-term contributions to minimise the impact of volatility on awards.
- Profits should determine bonus pools, which should be adjusted to reflect current and future risk profiles.
- A proportion of bonuses should be deferred to reflect the long-term aspects of financial performance.
- Firms should be able to explain how individual pay awards have been calculated.
- The practice of agreeing 'guaranteed bonuses' for new employees should be discouraged and limited to a period of one year only.

This code has been criticised by commentators on a number of counts:

- It is only a code and therefore non-binding, except on those organisations where the UK Government has a majority holding. Although the companies affected have signed up to the code, no action can be taken for any subsequent evasions. 'Toothless' is a word that has been often used.
- The FSA has retreated from its original position on the deferment of bonuses. It previously was an important 'principle' but has been converted to 'good practice' in the final version.
- Restriction on bonuses will affect the long-term position of the City of London as the top performers will move to unregulated companies in places such as the Gulf or Hong Kong. In 2009, there were a number of anecdotal examples of this occurring.

This issue is an important example of the difficulty of applying regulation in a global economy. Without international agreement, organisations and individuals will tend to migrate to those countries which have the most amenable forms of regulation.

The splitting up of the responsibilities of the FSA has also been criticised because it may not be easy to divide the 'prudential' aspects from the 'conduct' aspects. As Black and Hopper (2011) explain:

> ... for example the proposal that the CPMA is to make provisions on internal controls for Conduct of Business rules, the PRA on internal controls for capital rules. However, in many firms the risk and compliance functions are merged. In practice, there is an enormous overlap between prudential and conduct regulation. For example, managing compliance with conduct requirements has significant overlap with operational risk management which is of increasing importance to prudential regulation; effective credit risk management and "responsible lending" are intimately connected. There are real dangers of inconsistencies emerging in the internal control and risk management standards required by the two different regulators leading to costly and confusing requirements for firms with no proven beneficial impacts. (p8)

REGULATION AND THE PUBLIC SECTOR

For 30 years, the Audit Commission has carried out a different form of regulation in the public sector. It has been a true 'watchdog', carrying out investigations into the operations of local authorities, health services and government departments. It principally examined issues of efficiency and ethical behaviour, endeavouring to establish realisable targets, examples of best practice and to shame poor performers into change by publicising their faults. Although it had no executive power to change an organisation's policies or practices, the Government takes note of its findings when it takes decisions over funding, especially with local authorities. It has had a degree of success in leading public organisations to carefully examine their methods of operation and benchmark their performance against similar bodies.

However, in 2010, the Coalition Government announced that it would be substantially reduced in size (from 2,000 employees down to around 70) in order to save around £50 million. Local authorities and other public sector bodies would be able to appoint their own auditors. This was a decision criticised by a House of Commons Select Committee:

> The abolition of the Audit Commission will leave a substantial hole in the system of audit and inspection in local government and ministers must not assume that freedoms and market forces will automatically fill it. It is not clear to us that significant savings will result from abolition of the Audit Commission, at least in the short to medium term. (Communities and Local Government Committee Report 2011, pp24, 28)

REGULATION AND OTHER SECTORS

Although most sectors operate without a specific regulator, they are touched by regulation in a number of ways:

- Their practices may be investigated by the OFT and Competition Commission (and their successors), such as the doorstep selling example explained in 'Regulating business and protecting the consumer' (above).
- A planned merger or takeover can be referred to the Competition Commission to decide if it breaches the monopolies guidelines, such as was threatened in the 2003 battle over Safeway PLC.

- Their detailed operations can be constrained by UK or European law in areas such as labelling and packaging, information to consumers or environmental regulations.
- Planning laws have become increasingly intrusive, such as the government policy in 2000 to reject any further out-of-town shopping developments, including supermarkets, because of their effect on traffic growth and decline of the local high street.

CODES OF PRACTICE

Each of the regulators is authorised to produce codes of practices. Ofgem, for example, have produced a code of practice for the action that should be taken when a provider proposes to cut off a consumer's gas or electricity supply, and Ofcom has a Code of Advertising Practice. They do not in themselves have a force of law but they have strong influence on business behaviour. They help to raise standards throughout the industry, stopping organisations from indulging in dubious practices which, although not illegal, give the industry a bad name. Many organisations are happy to accept and influence the production of a code rather than having legal restrictions imposed on them.

REFLECTIVE ACTIVITY 5.5

Benefits of a regulatory system

What are the benefits of a regulatory system, controlled by autonomous bodies, as opposed to a state-controlled system?

HEALTH AND SAFETY REGULATION

The protection of employees in the workplace has been extended in recent years by a substantial collection of legislation emanating from both Europe and the UK. Regulation of health and safety in the UK is very extensive, with over 100 current pieces of legislation. Although there has been a steady decline in the number of deaths and serious accidents over the last decades, over 200 people are killed in accidents at work each year, including nearly 100 members of the public. Not only is this a huge waste of human resources, but it is very costly for the economy. The main aim of the regulation, therefore, is to reduce the number of accidents and resultant ill-health and to ensure that a safety-conscious culture becomes widespread so that business can operate more efficiently.

ROLE OF HUMAN RESOURCES IN HEALTH AND SAFETY

In the majority of organisations where separate human resource departments exist, they either have responsibility for health, safety and welfare issues in that organisation or they play a major part in those activities. The main activities consist of:

Formulating policies and procedures

This activity is more than a formality required by law. It is essential that new employees understand how safety works within a new organisation and the policies and procedures will set out how the safety responsibilities are structured and the requirements from each employee. Specific references to areas (such as responsibility for checking lifting gear, or guards) should be clearly spelled out. The document should give a statement of management intent as to how safety issues will be treated in the workplace. Detailed procedures should be set out for dealing with emergencies, safety training, information arising from the investigations under COSHH, and procedures should be set out for all departments where hazards have been identified. Human resources should ensure that such documents are logical, readable and have been circulated correctly.

Monitoring policies and procedures

At regular intervals, all procedures need examining to see if they need updating to take account of new processes, materials and layouts. By attending management and safety meetings, human resources can ensure such necessary revisions can be identified and put into place.

Advising management and employees on safety legislation

The defining Act has been the Health and Safety at Work Act 1974 but HR practitioners should be aware of other legislation dealing with, for example, Control of Substances Hazardous to Health (1988), Reporting of Diseases and Dangerous Occurrences Regulations (1995) and those relating to manual handling and display screens. New regulations continue to emerge, especially from Europe, with different levels of importance and different implementation dates.

Designing, providing and recording health and safety training

Systematic training is essential if procedures are to operate properly. It should start with induction training to ensure that employees who are involved in any hazardous operation have instruction in key areas before they set foot on the work site. Safety instruction should be incorporated into any new processes or where new materials are introduced onto site. There is a legal requirement to recognise safety representatives and they have the right for time off for training.

Assisting in risk assessments

It is a legal duty for employers to assess and record health and safety risks for all of their operations. Much of this work involves attempting to balance the nature of the risks, their seriousness in terms of likely danger to employees and the cost of implementing protection from these risks.

Identifying and dealing with occupational stress

Stress has become one of the most serious health issues of recent years. A survey by the HSE (2006) estimated that stress cost nearly £10 billion per year in the UK, over 2 per cent of gross domestic product, close to £400 per employee per year. The number of work-related stress cases reaching the courts rose to 6,428 in 2003 (Palmer and Quinn 2004). 12.8 million working days were lost to stress, anxiety and depression in 2004–05 (Yarker and Lewis 2007). Employees aged between 34 and 44 suffer the most, while the problems worsen the longer they stay in the same job.

The causes of occupational stress are numerous. They are associated with perceptions of job insecurity, increase in work intensity, aggressive management styles, lack of effective workplace communication, overt or insidious bullying and harassment, faulty selection for promotion or transfer and lack of guidance and training (Cartwright and Cooper 1997). Employees may be exposed to situations which they find uncomfortable, such as continually dealing with customers, excessive computer work, repetitive or fragmented work or having to make regular public presentations. Probably the most common cause, however, is the constant fear of organisational change through restructuring, takeovers, mergers or business process re-engineering. A lack of control over their work, their environment or their career progression can also be stressful (Rick et al 1997).

When a work environment containing these cultural aspects is added to personal problems, such as divorce or separation, ill or dying relatives, difficult housing conditions or financial problems, it is not surprising that the employer will be faced with a good proportion of employees with stress-related problems.

Stress is manifested not only in high absence levels. Fatigue, increases in infections, backache and digestive illnesses are commonly found. Irritation, hostility, anxiety and a state of panic can arise in the workplace, with knock-on effects on working practices and relationships between employees. The end result may be that the employee is 'burnt out', unable to cope with pressures that previously had been regarded as challenging and stimulating. Employees may also turn to palliatives, such as alcohol or drugs.

The employer who neglects the problem of occupational stress may face legal action. The first legal breakthrough for an employee was John Walker, a social work manager with Northumberland County Council, who, having had a mental breakdown arising from his occupation, returned to his job but received no positive assistance from his employer to help him to cope successfully, as set out on page 205.

Successive cases have included a primary school head who won £100,000 after suffering two nervous breakdowns allegedly caused by stress brought on by bullying and harassment, and an out-of-court settlement which was reached in 1998 between an NHS trust and the bereaved spouse of an employee who committed suicide. In a later case, Birmingham City Council admitted liability for personal injury caused by stress where they moved a 39-year-old senior draughtsman to the post of a neighbourhood housing officer without sufficient training. The nature of the work was so different and the interpersonal demands so great that she had long periods of ill-health leading to early retirement on medical grounds. She was awarded £67,000 (Miller 1999).

Greater clarification as to the employer's responsibility in the case of psychiatric injury based on exposure to unacceptable levels of stress was given by the Court of Appeal in 2002 (*Sutherland v Hatton*). The court held that an employer was entitled to assume that an employee was able to withstand the normal pressures of the job and to take what the employee said about her own health at face value. It was only if there were indications which would lead a reasonable employer to realise that there was a problem that a duty to take action would arise. In terms of whether the injury to health was foreseeable, factors that should be taken into account include whether:

- the workload was abnormally heavy
- the work was particularly intellectually or emotionally demanding
- the demands were greater compared with similar employees.

If the only way of making the employee safe was to dismiss him or her, there would be no breach of duty by letting the employee continue if he or she was willing to do so (IRS 2002).

An organisation's responsibilities for stress reduction was shown in stark outline in 2008 when the HSE issued an improvement notice to United Lincolnshire NHS Trust for 'failing to identify the potential risks to the health and safety of its employees from exposure to work-related stress'. The issue in this case was the complete lack of a work-related stress policy or risk assessment (Scott 2009).

All of these cases show that employers need to carefully consider the way that the work demands affect their employees and ensure that they investigate each case, taking appropriate action to ameliorate potentially health-damaging situations. A further consideration is the level of employees' expectations on welfare provision. It is a sure sign of a sympathetic and caring employer who will make special provision for the personal and individual needs of employees. Finally, a CIPD study (Tehrani 2002) has shown that employers who have some form of 'wellness' programmes incurred annual employment costs of between £1,335 and £2,910 less per employee than employers who did not.

REFLECTIVE ACTIVITY 5.6

You have been brought in as a consultant to carry out a review of the level of stress in an organisation. Having investigated safety and welfare statistics, and carried out an employee attitude survey, you report on the following indicators of stress:

- The absenteeism levels had risen from 6 per cent to 9 per cent over the last three years, of which 3 per cent was reported as being caused by stress-related illnesses.
- The number of staff on long-term sick had increased from 8 to 14, with 6 incidents of stress or other mental problems.
- The level of reported accidents had doubled from 12 to 24 over the same period.
- There had been three incidents of violence inside the site, two alcohol induced. Five employees had been dismissed arising from

these incidents. Two had resulted in claims to employment tribunals.

- The staff attitude survey showed that over 70 per cent considered that they worked excess hours which caused stress 'occasionally' or 'regularly'.
- Twenty per cent of staff found that their relationships with their managers were 'poor' or 'very poor'.
- Thirty per cent believed that urgent improvements in their physical environment were required.

Question

1   What advice would you give to the employer to alleviate the causes of stress in this organisation?

Formulating initiatives that help create a healthy working environment

All the research indicates that a healthy workforce will be a successful one and a higher-performing one, so being proactive in introducing and encouraging initiatives to support health programmes can make a substantial difference to organisational performance, as shown in Case Study 5.11.

IMPROVING EMPLOYEE HEALTH AT KIMBERLEY-CLARKE

CASE STUDY 5.11

Kimberley-Clarke, which makes products such as Kleenex and Huggies nappies, has made cost savings of £500,000 per annum and reduced long-term staff absence from 6.8 per cent to 0.5 per cent after launching schemes in 2002 aimed at improving the health of its 174 UK staff. Under the programme, the company introduced work–life balance coaching sessions, massages for desk workers and sleep

management workshops to improve employees' sleep quality. It also provided free fruit twice a week to promote healthy eating. Evidence that the scheme was getting immediate results was that, after six months, only 19 per cent admitted they suffered sleep problems, which was down from 68 per cent before the scheme started.

Source: Watkins (2003)

The most successful initiatives are those that are shown to be cost-effective as well as improving employee health, an example of which is shown in Case Study 5.12.

CASE STUDY 5.12

PHYSIOTHERAPY FOR NORTH EAST AMBULANCE SERVICE (NEAS) CREWS

Ambulance work is physically demanding, sometimes causing musculoskeletal injuries among staff. NEAS, employing 1,800 ambulance staff, found that the waiting time for an in-house physiotherapist first appointment was over three weeks and crew members were unable to work on full duties during this time, with average individual productivity levels dropping to 36 per cent.

To counter these delays, NEAS hired a private contractor in February 2011 who provided an appointment within three days. The effect was immediate, according to Susan Kaszefko, HR Manager, with an 81 per cent reduction in musculoskeletal absence and a saving in the first year of £532,926 from time that would have been lost in absence. The service cost only £39,563. A similar system for providing an MRI scan (currently with a waiting time of over two months) has also been introduced at a cost of £400 for a scan provided within a week.

Source: Griffiths (2012)

A test of overall success is whether a safety-conscious culture pervades the organisation. This is shown through management operating systems and procedures, not just because of the legal requirements but because they see that it makes good business sense, both in terms of reducing costs arising from accidents and from establishing a caring relationship with the labour force.

TRENDS TO WATCH

Governments of all shape, EU and UK, find it difficult to restrain themselves from introducing legislation, so watch out for developments in the following areas:

- In the *employment law area*, the extension of flexible working rights in the UK beyond working parents and carers and a resolution of the long-standing debate on the rights of what the EU call 'atypical working', such as agency workers.
- In the *consumer protection area*, greater clarification and consistency on the roles of regulators, the OFT and the Competition Commissions, with a more consistent approach across Europe.
- In the *financial area*, the European Union is planning to set up a European-wide system for regulating banking activities.

HOW FAR SHOULD REGULATION EXTEND?

There have been two major debates centred around the extent and development of regulation in recent years. The first covers the *breadth* of the regulation – the degree to which regulation should be local, national or international. The second deals with the *depth* of the regulation – how tightly it should apply and in what detail. We shall deal with each of these in turn.

BREADTH OF REGULATION

Governments in the West have led the way in most areas of regulation, from creating and protecting individual employment rights to enhancing consumer power and protecting the environment. However, this action has been taken at a number of levels, as shown in environmental regulation in the UK (Brooks and Weatherston 2004).

At the local level, local authorities have a number of responsibilities, including food hygiene, pest control and noise pollution. At the national level, a number of enabling laws, such as the Environmental Protection Act 1990 and the Environment Act 1995, cover a wide area of environmental control, including waste disposal and recycling requirements, mostly enforced by the Environment Agency. At the international level, the European Union has taken a number of initiatives through environment action programmes with mixed success to obtain compliance across the EU. Many attempts have been made by governments to agree to international environmental standards, the most well known being the Kyoto Protocol in 1997, which has mixed take-up in the twenty-first century. There have been numerous attempts subsequently to gain worldwide approval to standards of greenhouse gas emissions and systems of carbon emission trading. In the financial area, governments and central banks have made many attempts in recent years to produce effective regulation in the banking area but few have shown much success. For example, the overhaul of banking rules under Basel III has been consistently delayed (currently to be discussed further in 2014) because of disagreement between nations on the measures necessary to regulate capital requirements. Similarly, no agreement has been reached on an overall EU system to encourage women on to boards of EU companies.

In January 2013, however, an agreement was reached at the EU Council of Ministers to limit bankers' bonuses to no more than base salary, or up to twice salary with the explicit approval of shareholders. This decision was widely criticised in some UK business circles because it would drive away the highest talent in banking to centres outside the EU such as Switzerland, Singapore and Hong Kong or, alternatively, banks can circumvent it by simply increasing the base rate of their top bankers (BBC 2013).

The benefits of operating at different levels are:

- It involves all communities at whatever level to get involved in subjects that affect them.
- Without multi-level involvement, it would be difficult to get general support for regulatory action.
- A combination of experimental policies can be tried out in different countries (or within countries) to see which ones can work and to identify the main problems faced.
- It is recognised that international agreement is always problematic, so it is foolish to wait for a complete international solution before acting. Partial success is seen as better than no progress.
- The long-term aim of organisations and countries operating and competing on a level playing field is to be applauded and has been successful in some areas, such as agreements within the World Trade Organization.

The disadvantages of operating at different levels are:

- The raft of regulation can be very confusing for companies trying to operate within the law.
- International companies may choose to locate to the less regulated environments. Most shipping companies, for example, operate with 'flags of convenience' in countries which have little enforcement on labour rights and minimum health and safety. Similar action has been threatened recently by hedge funds.
- There is little optimism that some countries, such as China, will accept international regulation and the slow progress allows them to continue to operate as accepted competitors without having to change their policies in fields such as ecological effects and human rights because there is not the willpower to penalise them.

DEPTH OF REGULATION

There is much debate as to the degree of regulation that is ideal for a society. The current trend is for government to steadily increase the intensity of regulation in all fields, this being their main thrust of legislation. Occasional attempts to reverse the tide, such as Margaret Thatcher's policies on privatisation and encouraging more competition in the financial and other sectors, though having a good degree of success, can be set against the huge amount of additional legislation in recent years in enhancing labour rights, controlling financial activities, increasing planning controls and protecting the environment.

Those who doubt the benefits of additional regulation put forward the following arguments:

- Regulation discourages entrepreneurial activity and therefore restricts job creation, especially in small organisations, which have to cope with an annual collection of laws with which they have to comply, despite having few resources to judge the degree and cost of compliance necessary. Support for this viewpoint from the Coalition Government led to a package of measures introduced in 2013 to cut unnecessary bureaucracy and reduce government regulation which exempted large numbers of low-risk organisations from safety inspections. These included shops, offices, pubs and clubs, unless they had an accident or poor safety track record.

- Regulation is expensive. There are large costs involved in obtaining agreement, especially on the international front, in terms of providing incentives for poorer countries and those less willing to comply, let alone the huge costs of endless international conferences. There are similar large costs in enforcing the regulations. It had been estimated that 50,000 UK staff were employed within financial organisations in 2007 to ensure compliance to regulation set out by the Bank of England and the FSA.

- Some businesses argue that regulation goes too far. In the field of employment law, for example, much lobbying continues to take place to try to ensure the UK National Minimum Wage is kept as low as possible, and French employers have attempted, with some success, to reverse the legislation which introduced the 35-hour working week. The rapid increase in the financial regulation has been hotly opposed by many companies, although the opposition has been much quieter of late following the continuing financial crisis.

KEY LEARNING POINTS

- UK law can be divided into criminal and civil law and originates chiefly from legislation emanating from the European Union, the UK parliament and common law. Courts are bound by precedent.
- The last 30 years has seen a substantial increase in the volume and intensity of legislation to protect employees and consumers with increased regulation of business activity.
- The burden of this legislation has been borne by businesses, which need to adapt their operations to ensure compliance.
- A larger emphasis has been put on organisations carrying out safety audits and risk assessment to ensure accident prevention and a healthier workplace.
- Few sectors now manage to avoid a form of regulation, with a substantial presence in the privatised utilities and the financial and communications sectors, where regulators have considerable legal powers.
- Consumers are also protected through the regulation of markets to prevent the use of monopolistic powers by large organisations.

1   What are the main roles of the Office of Fair Trading?

2   What actions should HR practitioners take to improve health and safety?

3   Set out the main influences on governments which have led to the enhancement of consumer rights through legislation from the 1960s onwards.

4   What are the main sources of the employment contract?

5   Describe the main roles of a regulator in the utilities sector.

6   Give six examples of legislation introduced in the UK to give protection to employees.

7   Trace the path of a tribunal application through the UK/European courts.

8   What is the meaning of the expression 'precedent' under UK law?

9   What are the six main elements in any contract?

10 What are the responsibilities of an employer concerning stress in the workplace?

EXPLORE FURTHER

FURTHER READING

There are large numbers of legal textbooks available dealing with the English legal system. Some cover the whole picture, including criminal and civil law; others specialise in areas such as contract law, commercial law or employment law. It is worthwhile for the HR practitioner to have a general legal textbook on their shelves together with a specialist book on employment law. Current publications of the latter include:

Daniels, K. (2012) *Employment Law: An Introduction for HR and Business Students*. 3rd edition. London: CIPD.

Lewis, D. and Sargeant, M. (2013) *Employment Law: The Essentials*. 12th edition. London: CIPD.

In terms of legal issues relating to discrimination, a good source is:

Connolly, M. (2011) *Discrimination law*. 2nd edition. London: Sweet &Maxwell.

For financial regulation, a good introductory approach is given in:

Davies, H. and Green, D. (2008) *Global financial regulation*. London: Wiley.

SEMINAR ACTIVITY

RACE DISCRIMINATION

In 2004, Mahmood Siddiqui, aged 59, was awarded £180,000 from the Royal Mail arising from a four-year campaign of racial abuse at work. He was repeatedly sworn at, bullied and called a 'Paki' by colleagues at a sorting office in Harlow, Essex. On one occasion, one of them ignited a cigarette lighter in front of him and threatened to burn him. Others daubed offensive graffiti, including the messages 'Siddiqui hang him' and 'Paki scab lover'. His car was vandalised and threats were made to his wife and children.

Despite repeated complaints to his managers, the racial harassment continued with 'tacit support' from his boss. It was only some time later when a hidden camera was installed that the culprits were caught and disciplined. By then, Mr Siddiqui, the only non-white on the night shift, was suffering severe stress. Ill-health forced him to retire in 2002 after 12 years' service. The tribunal commented that 'throughout the case, the word "banter" was used. We consider this to have often been employed as a euphemism for racial abuse for which he alone was singled out.' His award consisted of £104,000 for loss of earnings, plus £20,000 for loss of interest and £8,000 legal costs together with £48,000 for personal injury and injury to feelings.

Questions

Consider the above summarised article and answer the following questions:

1 What action should the organisation have taken when the complaints were first made?

2 What specific steps should HR departments take to try to prevent such action occurring in their organisations?

REFERENCES

BBC. (2013) EU agrees to cap bankers' bonuses. 28 February. Available at: www.bbc.co.uk.

Black, J. and Hopper, M. (2011) *Breaking up is hard to do.* London: London School of Economics.

Brooks, I. and Weatherston, J. (2004) *The business environment.* 3rd edition. London: FT Prentice Hall.

Cartwright, S. and Cooper, S. (1997) *Managing workplace stress.* London: Sage.

Communities and Local Government Committee Report. (2011) Available at: www.publications.parliament.uk/pa

Competition Commission. (2003) *Extended warranties on domestic electrical goods: a report on the supply of extended warranties on domestic electrical goods within the UK.* Available at: www.competition-commission.org.uk/rep/485xwars

Curwen, P. (1997) *Restructuring telecommunications: a study of Europe in a global context.* London: Macmillan.

Dey, I. and Smith, D. (2009) Mr Darling's exceedingly poor fudge. *Sunday Times Business*. 12 July. p7.

Electricity Association. (1998) *Electricity industry review*. London: HMSO.

Freidman, M. (1970) *The counter-revolution in monetary theory*. London: Institute of Economic Affairs.

Griffiths, J. (2012) Taking care of business. *People Management*. 25 September. pp39–42.

HSE. (2006) *2005/6 survey of self-reported work-related illnesses*. London: Health and Safety Executive.

IRS. (2002) *Court of Appeal guidelines for stress at work cases*. Employment Law Review 748. 25 March.

Martin, S. and Parker, D. (1997) *The impact of privatisation: ownership and corporate performance in the UK*. London: Routledge.

Mathiason, N. (2009) Recruitment firm Hays to appeal against £30 million price-fixing fine. *Guardian*. 30 September. p12.

Miller, S. (1999) Council pays £67,000 for stress injury. *Guardian*. 6 July. p4.

Palmer, B. and Quinn, P. (2004) Protracted agony. *People Management*. 6 May. p17.

Pollack, C. (1997) European Union policies. In I. Lewington (ed.) *Utility regulation*. Bath: Centre for the Study of Regulated Industries and Privatisation International.

Rick, J., Hillage, S., Honey, S. and Perrymen, S. (1997) *Stress: big issue, but what are the problems?* Institute of Employment Studies Report 311, July.

Scott. A. (2009) HSE raps health trust for 'failing' on stress. *People Management*. 26 February. p9.

Tehrani, N. (2002) *Managing organisational stress: a CIPD guide to improving and maintaining well-being*. London: Chartered Institute of Personnel and Development.

Wainwright, M. (1994) Mistakes led to chemical plant deaths. *Guardian*. 21 June. p8.

Waples, J. (2009) *Sunday Times Business*. 4 October. p4.

Watkins, J. (2003) Wellness beats output slump. *People Management*. 18 December. p12.

Yarker, J. and Lewis, R. (2007) *Management competencies for preventing and reducing stress at work*. London: HSE.

CHAPTER 6

The World Economy

LEARNING OUTCOMES

By the end of this chapter, readers should be able to understand, explain and critically evaluate:

- the role and functions of the European Union and its major institutions
- debates about the evolution of the European Union (integration and enlargement)
- the eurozone crisis of 2010 onwards
- major international bodies which impact on the business environment of organisations (IMF, World Bank, WTO)
- the causes and extent of globalisation processes
- multinational and transnational organisations, and their HR systems
- major debates about the significance and desirability of globalisation
- the response of governmental organisations to globalisation processes
- the impact of globalisation on markets for goods and services
- the impact of globalisation on employment and labour markets
- globalisation and the recession
- management and HR styles in selected members of the G20
- Geert Hofstede's cultural dimensions.

INTRODUCTION

Should Greece leave the euro? Is globalisation good or bad for the developing world? These are the kinds of issues that will be explored in this chapter on the international economy.

Since the end of the Second World War, the world economy has become more and more integrated. Partly this has been a deliberate, planned development. The International Monetary Fund (IMF), the World Bank and the General Agreement on Tariffs and Trade (GATT) were set up to regulate the world economy and to ensure that the world did not suffer from a recurrence of the Great Depression of the 1930s. The European Economic Community, the predecessor of the European Union, was set up partly to ensure that France and Germany could never again go to war with each other. Other developments were only made possible as a result of technological developments in communication and transport, which enabled the growth of globalisation.

THE HISTORICAL BACKGROUND TO THE EUROPEAN UNION

The origins of the European Union go back to the period just after the Second World War, when there was a strong desire in Continental Europe (particularly France and West Germany) to ensure that a further war would be impossible.

The founding states of the European Economic Community, set up by the Treaty of Rome in 1957, were France, West Germany, Italy, Belgium, the Netherlands and Luxembourg. Britain declined an invitation to join, seeing its economic interests as lying much more with the US and the Commonwealth.

The UK, Ireland and Denmark joined on 1 January 1973, Greece on 1 January 1981, Spain and Portugal on 1 January 1986, and Sweden, Austria and Finland on 1 January 1995. The former East Germany automatically joined on German reunification in 1990. Norway twice negotiated entry, but on each occasion that was rejected by a referendum. Switzerland did not apply to join, citing its long-standing policy of strict neutrality (it is not even a member of the United Nations), but it has close economic relations with the EU.

In 1976, the institution adopted the name European Community, and the Maastricht Treaty of 1992 adopted the name European Union from 1 January 1993.

Up to the end of the twentieth century, the EU was very much a Western European club. With the exception of Greece, Spain and Portugal, which had recent histories of fascist rule, all the members were long-standing stable, prosperous, democratic countries. This changed fundamentally with the next enlargement, from 15 to 25 members on 1 May 2004. This came about with the accession of five post-Communist central European states (Poland, Hungary, the Czech Republic, Slovakia and Slovenia), the three Baltic states of Estonia, Latvia and Lithuania, which had previously been republics within the USSR, and two small Mediterranean islands (Malta and Cyprus). The implications of this expansion for the EU will be considered below.

THE AIMS OF THE EU

The European Union has a number of general aims. These include:

- upholding peace in Europe by integrating national economies
- increasing prosperity by developing a single market
- easing inequalities between people and regions
- pooling the energies of member states for technological and industrial development
- developing an effective means of resolving political disputes
- implementing a Union-wide social policy
- implementing European Monetary Union
- assisting people of the Third World.

These aims reflect a number of different perceptions concerning the future development of the EU (Morris and Willey 1996).

Single market ('European single market')

This sees the EU in economic terms and concentrates on removal of national restrictions which limit the free movement of labour, capital, goods and services. In effect, the EU is seen as solely a free trade area, without a political dimension. Common political institutions should be minimal, and so should the structure of EU law, which should be limited to that necessary to ensuring that the single market functions effectively. The single market concept underpinned the early development of the European Community and reached its fullest expression in the Single European Act 1986, which led to the setting up of the Single European Market in 1993. At least in theory, this ensured the free movement of labour, capital, goods and services. However, this does not fully work in practice. For example, the Schengen Agreement in 1990 eliminated internal border controls within the EU, meaning that travel within the EU was possible without a passport, but the agreement has never been implemented by the UK and Ireland.

Federalist ('United States of Europe')

Here the EU is seen as having the structure of a federal state such as the USA or Germany – a central, or federal, government which sets the general direction of policy and local governments (states in the US, *Lander* in Germany, nation states in the EU) which are responsible for the practical administration of policy. Some political mechanism is needed at the centre to decide on overall policy, but this should be kept to a minimum. The function of EU law is to settle disputes between the central authority and the member states. Central to this perspective is the concept of subsidiarity, which says that as a matter of principle, decision-making in the EU should be taken at the lowest possible level.

Integrationist ('Europe')

The aim here is ultimately a long-term shift of power from member states to EU-wide institutions. The classic example of this is Economic and Monetary Union (discussed in detail in a later chapter), which led to a single currency, the euro, and to control of EU monetary policy passing from member states to the European Central Bank. Subsidiarity may still apply, but the member states would only have those powers specifically delegated to them by the central government. EU law would not only settle disputes between member states and the centre, but would also directly impinge on EU citizens.

The issue of how far to move towards the integrationist model underpins the ongoing argument about an EU constitution, which has occupied much of the EU's efforts since the Nice Summit in 2000, and is also central to an understanding of the crisis surrounding the euro.

REFLECTIVE ACTIVITY 6.1

Models of the EU

1   Which of the models of EU organisation (single market, federalist, integrationist) would best describe the view of the following political parties in the UK?

- New Labour
- Conservative
- Liberal Democrat
- UK Independence Party

2   Why do the other members of the EU feel that true implementation of the Single Market also requires harmonisation of taxation, and why does the UK oppose this?

THE INSTITUTIONS OF THE EU

Responsibility for achieving the aims of the EU rests with four institutions:

- the Commission
- the Council of Ministers
- the European Parliament
- the European Court of Justice

and two auxiliary bodies:

- the European Central Bank
- the Economic and Social Committee.

The Commission

The Commission is the executive of the EU. It is responsible both for proposing policy and legislation, and for implementing policy after it has been agreed. It is completely independent of member states, even though its members are appointed by the member states.

Before the 2004 enlargement, the Commission had 20 members, two each from France, Germany, the UK, Italy and Spain, and one from each of the other member states. Each commissioner was responsible for an area of EU policy. The Commission is headed by a president, appointed by the Council of Ministers. The president is usually a powerful figure in his own right. The president until October 2004 was Romano Prodi, ex-prime minister of Italy, and from late 2004, José Manuel Durão Barroso, ex-prime minister of Portugal.

The Treaty of Nice in 2002 made provision for reform of the Commission after enlargement. Each member was to have one commissioner, a major concession by the large member states, who lost one of their two commissioners.

The responsibilities of the Commission are laid down by the various EU treaties (Rome, Maastricht, Amsterdam, Nice, etc). They include:

- *Initiating legislation* – the Commission tables proposals to the Council of Ministers after wide-ranging consultation with interested parties.
- *Guardian of the treaties* – the Commission has to ensure that the treaties and EU legislation are properly implemented.
- *Implementing policy* – the Commission either directly implements policy itself, or supervises programmes administered by member states under the principle of subsidiarity, which we looked at earlier.

The Commission is collectively answerable to the European Parliament, and can be removed by a vote of censure carried by a two-thirds majority – although there is no procedure for removing individual commissioners. In early 1999, after a report which criticised the then President, Jacques Santer, and several individual commissioners, and after a series of debates in the European Parliament, the whole Commission resigned, and Santer was replaced by Romano Prodi.

The Council of Ministers

The Council is the final decision-making body of the EU. It consists of representatives of the governments of the member states. In practice, the Council is really a series of specialist bodies, dealing with particular areas of policy, and attended by the appropriate ministers from the member states. When the heads of state or government meet, the Council is referred to as the European Council, which meets twice a year. Each member state in turn acts as president of the Council for six months. Council meetings are attended by the president of the Commission, who has a full right to take part in discussions but who does not have a vote.

Until 1986, decisions in the Council of Ministers were taken by unanimity, which meant that each member state had an absolute veto. This was becoming unworkable and would clearly become more so as more countries joined the EU. The Single European Act in 1986 introduced the concept of qualified majority voting (QMV), under which decisions in clearly specified areas could be taken by a majority vote. In practice, this gave the 'big four' states a collective veto, but meant that they could not force a proposal through unless they obtained the support of several of the smaller states.

The European Parliament

This is directly elected by all member states for five years. The most recent elections were in June 2009, with the next elections due in 2014. Its powers are mainly budgetary. It has the final say on all 'non-compulsory' spending (any spending which is not the inevitable consequence of EU legislation, making up 25 per cent of the budget). It can also reject the budget in total and did so in 1979 and 1984.

The Parliament has a right to debate all EU issues, and the Council can reject its views only by a unanimous vote. It cannot initiate legislation (the responsibility of the Commission), nor does it have the final say in passing law (the responsibility of the Council of Ministers), but it can reject measures which were passed by the Council of Ministers through QMV. In October 2004, it came very close to rejecting the whole of the new Commission proposed by the new president, José Manuel Barroso, because of the illiberal views held by the Italian nominee. The crisis was only defused at the last minute when Barroso withdrew his whole Commission for reconsideration and the Italian Government withdrew its nominee.

The European Court of Justice (ECJ)

The ECJ rules on the interpretation and application of EU rules and on disputes between the Commission and member states. Its decisions apply directly in the member states. It consists of judges appointed by the member states. Findings are decided by a simple majority and dissenting opinions are never published. Rulings are binding in all EU member countries, take precedence over all other legal decisions and are not subject to appeal (Osborn 2004).

ECJ decisions have had a huge impact on UK employment law in fields such as equal pay, discrimination, business transfers and working time, as illustrated in Case Study 6.1.

CASE STUDY 6.1

THE WORKING TIME DIRECTIVE AND JUNIOR DOCTORS

The European Working Time Directive was enacted into UK law as the Working Time Regulations from 1 October 1998. The Regulations call for:

- an average of 48 hours' working time each week, measured over a reference period of 26 weeks
- 11 hours' continuous rest in 24 hours – that is, no shift can exceed 13 hours
- 24 hours' continuous rest in 7 days, or 48 hours in 2 weeks – that is, the maximum number of consecutive days of duty is 12
- a 20-minute break in work periods of over six hours
- 5.6 weeks' annual leave, pro rata for part-time staff.

Individuals have the right to opt out of the 48-hour week provision, but cannot be forced to do so, and have the right to opt back in at any time. There is no opt-out from the rest and leave provisions.

Initially junior doctors in training were exempt from the Regulations, although they applied to all other doctors and NHS workers. Junior doctors were notorious for working up to 100 hours a week and often for being on duty for 24 hours or more continuously. The Regulations were extended to junior doctors in 2004, with a maximum average working week of 58 hours, reduced to 56 hours a week by August 2007, and to 48 hours a week from August 2009.

Until 2000, it was thought that when the Regulations were extended to junior doctors, their impact would be less serious because of the on-call system. On-call time was not normally regarded as working time, unless the doctor was actually called on. This was changed by the European Court of Justice in 2000 in the *SiMAP* judgment (*Sindicato de Medicos de Asestencia Publica v Conselleria de Sanidad y Consumo de la Generalidad Valenciana*). The ECJ ruled that on-call time where the doctor is required to be on the premises counted as working time, even if the doctor was actually asleep for part of this time. For doctors on call but not required to be on the premises, working time only started when the doctor responded to a call.

This was confirmed in the *Jaeger* case in 2003 (*Landeshauptstadt Kiel v Jaeger*), which added the additional stipulation that if working hours were exceeded, a rest period should be taken immediately, not at a later date (NHS Employers 2009).

The NHS has recognised that there are particular problems with the 48-hour regulations in some hospitals, and a postponement of implementation (a derogation) was obtained from the EU covering specialities such as paediatrics and obstetrics in 38 trusts, permitting an average 52 hours a week until 2011 (Hope 2009). Opinion within the medical profession was divided. The strongest opposition came from the Royal College of Surgeons (Brockett 2009; House 2009). The surgeons put forward two main arguments against implementation of the 48-hour week:

- Continuity of care would be disrupted, as patients would be seen by more different junior doctors, which would make it more difficult to detect subtle changes in a patient's condition.

- More seriously, training would be disrupted. Surgeon training is still very much based on 'sitting by Nellie', observing consultants at work. A shorter working week would considerably cut the opportunities for this.

The NHS response to the surgeons' concerns on training is that medical education has changed. Greater use is being made of e-learning, simulation and skills labs, leading to less need for the 'sitting by Nellie' approach (NHS Employers 2009, p10).

Nurses were much more favourably inclined to the Regulations. When interviewed by the *Nursing Times*, Wendy Reid, the national clinical lead for the European Working Time Directive, said that it was important not just to tackle the problems of implementation by juggling the rotas of junior doctors. What was needed was a fundamental rethink of skills mix and a reduction of artificial barriers between roles. Many of the jobs carried out by junior doctors could be done as well, if not better, by nurses. She cited the Hospital@Night programme, whereby multidisciplinary teams were used to provide out-of-hours clinical cover. Many of these teams were led by nurses. 'Patients no longer care what your badge says,' she said (Ford 2009).

The main lessons to be drawn from this case are, first, that it is essential that HR thinks holistically outside the box when introducing a change as radical as this one. Merely reducing junior doctors' working hours is not enough. Working practices, training practices and skills mix all have to change as well.

The Economic and Social Committee

This is a consultative body made up of representatives of employers (UNICE – the Union of Industrial and Employers' Confederations of Europe – and CEEP – the European Centre of Enterprises with Public Participation), trade unions (ETUC – the European

Trade Union Confederation), and special interest groups (collectively known as the 'social partners'). It must be formally consulted by the Commission on economic and social proposals.

The European Central Bank (ECB)

The ECB was set up in 1999 to administer Economic and Monetary Union (EMU). It has sole responsibility for setting interest rates in the eurozone. It is headed by a president appointed by the Council of Ministers and representatives from each member of EMU (which does not include the UK).

REFLECTIVE ACTIVITY 6.2

EU institutions and power

1   Why do you think that ultimate power in the EU lies with the Council of Ministers rather than the Commission?

2   You work for a FTSE 100 company. Your company is concerned about a possible change in EU social policy which could lead to legislation in the next few years. How can your company influence forthcoming EU decisions on this change?

EU ENLARGEMENT

The enlargement of the EU which took place on 1 May 2004, from 15 to 25 members, increased the population of the EU by 74 million, ranging from 38 million in Poland to 400,000 in Malta. This enlargement was qualitatively different from any which had gone before:

- The sheer number of new entrants was larger than any before. This in itself will put new strains on the EU's institutions and increased pressure for speedy agreement on the new constitution.
- Some of the new entrants – Latvia, Lithuania and Slovakia, for example – are far poorer than any previous entrant. GDP per head of the new entrants is about 15 per cent of the old EU average.
- The biggest new entrant, Poland, has a massive and under-developed agricultural sector.
- There were fears in some quarters – which proved to be justified – that enlargement would release a flood of immigrants from the new to the old EU states.
- Eight of the new entrants are ex-Communist and three, the Baltic states, were once part of the USSR. Russia will inevitably feel threatened by this, particularly as an outlying part of its territory, Kaliningrad, is now completely surrounded by EU territory (Poland and Lithuania).
- One new entrant, Cyprus, is divided between an officially recognised Greek state, which is in the EU, and a non-recognised Turkish state, which is not.
- Further expansion is inevitable. Bulgaria and Romania joined in 2007. These countries are even poorer than the 2004 entrants. The accession of Croatia and Iceland is likely in the near future.

REFLECTIVE ACTIVITY 6.3

Polish plumbers

On 1 May 2004, 10 new members joined the EU. Eight of these, known as the A8, came from Central and Eastern Europe, the biggest of these being Poland, with a population of about 38.5 million. The UK already had a significant Polish minority, the descendants of the Free Poles who had fought on the Allied side in the war and who had decided not to go back to a Communist Poland. In the 2001 census, there were nearly 61,000 people who had been born in Poland, with a third of these living in London (BBC nd). With their descendants, they made up a population of Polish ancestry of about a quarter of a million.

Under the EU rules on free movement, people from the A8 countries had the right to come to other EU countries, but this did not necessarily extend to the right to work. As part of the accession arrangements, the 15 'old' EU countries had the right to impose restrictions on work for A8 citizens for up to seven years. Only Sweden allowed A8 citizens an unrestricted right to work. The UK and Ireland granted them right to work, but no right to unemployment benefit until they had worked continuously for a year.

It was forecast at the time of accession that 13,000 A8 workers a year would come to the UK. However, this has proven to be a gross underestimate. Denis MacShane, who was Europe minister at the time, claimed that the original figure was based on all 15 old EU members opening their doors to A8 workers (MacShane 2006).

Although it is clear that many more A8 workers, particularly Poles, are working in the UK than originally thought, nobody really knows how many. As Poles and other A8 citizens can enter the EU without a visa, there is no way of telling how many of those who enter the country intend to work and how many are just passing through. The Office for National Statistics carries out random interviews on arrivals to the UK and on this basis estimates that 56,000 Poles entered the UK to work in 2005. However, the Department for Work and Pensions says that 170,000 Poles applied for National Insurance numbers in 2005 (Doward and McKenna 2007).

The other main source of information on numbers is the Worker Registration Scheme (WRS), under which A8 workers are encouraged to register. This is not compulsory, is not required for the self-employed and costs £75. There is also no requirement to deregister if a worker leaves the UK. In May 2005, the BBC reported that 176,000 had registered by March 2005. Of these, 82 per cent were aged between 18 and 34, 96 per cent were working full-time and a third may have been working illegally in the UK before accession and merely regularising their position. Poland was the biggest provider, with 56 per cent of the total, followed by Lithuania with 15 per cent and Slovakia with 11 per cent (BBC 2005a). This is not surprising, as Poland had by far the biggest population of the A8 countries, it had 20 per cent unemployment, wages one-sixth of those in the UK and a well-educated population, many of whom spoke English.

By January 2007, 579,000 had registered under the WRS, of whom 63 per cent were from Poland. The anti-immigration pressure group claimed that this was an underestimate and that the true figure was nearer 600,000, although they admitted that many of these will have left the country (Migration Watch 2007). By December 2007 the number registered had increased to 750,000 (House of Lords 2008) and by 2009 the number was just over 1 million (Travis 2010). However, this is a gross figure. Many are seasonal agricultural workers who come to the UK every summer and re-register.

Some figures are also available from the Polish end of the migration. In 2004, the year of accession, there were fewer movements of Poles out of the country than in 2003 (27.2 million compared with 38.6 million) (Iglicka 2005). However, there is no way of telling how many of these were going out of Poland to work or, perhaps, on day trips to Germany or the Czech Republic. What may be significant, however, is that the number of those leaving by air increased by 37 per cent in 2004 to 1.89

million. Official emigration in 2004 was also lower than in 2003, and only 543 Poles officially emigrated to the UK, compared with 12,646 to Germany.

Rumours and urban myths abound about the number of Poles in the UK. There are said to be 10,000 in Slough, 15,000 in Boston, Lincolnshire, 3,000 in Crewe (Doward and McKenna 2007). According to the 2011 census, about 7,000 of Boston's population of 64,600 came from the A8 countries plus Romania, well below the 15,000 suggested. This has put considerable pressure on local infrastructure such as housing and schools, although it has also been pointed out that the local maternity unit would have closed but for the extra demand from eastern European births (Pidd 2012).

Remember also that despite the myths, most Polish and other A8 immigrants are not plumbers. Among the A8 immigrants, 24 per cent work in distribution, hotels and restaurants, 21 per cent in manufacturing, 14 per cent in construction, and a significant but unstated proportion in agriculture and food processing (House of Lords 2008, p18).

The plain truth is nobody really has any idea how many Poles are working in Britain. Latest estimates are that up to 1 million Poles may have left Poland, although they have not all come to the UK (Barrell et al 2007). If, say, a third have come to the UK, this makes about 400,000. It is thought that most Polish and other A8 workers come to the UK with every intention of going back to Poland and, unlike other immigrant groups, going back is very easy and cheap – £10 on a Ryanair flight. When questioned by the Joseph Rowntree Foundation immediately after accession, only 6 per cent said they intended to stay in the UK permanently. A year later, this had risen to 29 per cent (Spencer et al 2007). In September 2007, 62 per cent of those arriving in the previous 12 months said they intended to stay for less than one year (House of Lords 2008), although the experience of other immigrant groups suggests that more will stay than initially expected to.

With the onset of the recession in 2008, many Polish workers returned to Poland, which was the only country in the EU to experience positive economic growth in 2009. In the year to September 2009, 12,000 more Poles left the UK than entered (Pidd 2011). In May 2011, Germany also opened its borders to Polish workers, as the transition period agreed in 2004 came to an end. It is expected that up to 1 million Poles may emigrate to Germany (Hall et al 2011).

The situation became clearer by 2011. The Office for National Statistics announced that the UK had 545,000 Polish-born residents in 2010, the biggest foreign-born national group (ONS 2011). Of these, 86 per cent were of working age, 80 per cent of these were in work and unemployment was 5.5 per cent. Corresponding figures for the UK as a whole were 60 per cent, 70 per cent and 7.8 per cent. The 2011 Census figure for people born in Poland was 579,000 (BBC News 2012).

Questions

1   What do you think is the likely economic and social impact of the influx of Polish and other A8 workers into the UK?

2   How can trade unions respond to the issues raised by the influx of Polish workers?

TURKEY AND THE EU

Turkey has been an associate member of the EU since 1963 and has sought full membership since that date. It was formally recognised as a candidate in 1999 (Lungesen 2004) and formal accession talks started in October 2005 (Akcapar and Chaibi 2006). However, accession talks were 'part suspended' in December 2006 following a dispute about Turkish recognition of Cyprus (Tisdall 2007).

Should Turkey join the EU?

There are four requirements for new entrants to the EU, known as the Copenhagen Criteria:

- Each applicant must show that it is in sympathy with the fundamental ethos of the EU by demonstrating that it practises liberty, democracy, respect for human rights and fundamental freedoms, and the rule of law.
- Each applicant must create a functioning market economy.
- Each applicant must comply with the body of EU laws and standards (the *acquis communitaire*) – which is 100,000 pages long!
- The applicant must be part of Europe.

Turkey does have a history of military coups and a dubious human rights record in relation to its treatment of its Kurdish minority, but the country argues that it meets the criteria. It is a long-standing democratic country and, since the present government came to power in 2002, it has taken a number of steps to improve its human rights record. It has abolished the death penalty, released some Kurdish activists and started TV broadcasts in Kurdish. Few dispute that it has a functioning market economy. Only a small part of Turkey (Thrace) is technically within geographical Europe, with the rest (Anatolia) being in Asia,

but Turkey has always seen itself as part of Europe. The geographical position of Turkey could be a problem, as it has frontiers with Iraq, Iran and Syria, but the former EU enlargement commissioner, Guenter Verheugen, saw this as an asset, not a drawback. Membership would demonstrate to the Middle East that the EU could work with a Muslim country (Lungesen 2004). As the Portuguese foreign minister said about the negotiations with Turkey, this was a victory for Europe and a bitter defeat for Osama bin Laden. Turkish membership should increase Turkish prosperity and so, paradoxically, decrease rather than increase immigration from Turkey (Kirisci 2007).

There is some opposition to Turkish entry on the grounds that its 70 million predominantly Muslim population would upset the religious and cultural balance of the EU, but Turkey is a fiercely secular state, not an Islamic one, and to say that we don't want Muslims in Europe is an insult to the Muslim minorities in the UK, France, Germany and Spain. However, in April–May 2007 there was considerable unrest in Turkey over the election of a known Islamist as president, with the threat of a military coup to preserve secularism.

One argument against Turkish entry was that Turkey was too poor. However, this is difficult to support, as Turkey's GDP per head on a purchasing power parity basis is almost identical to that of Romania, which joined the EU in 2007 (CIA 2007). Another fear is an increased influx of Turkish workers into the EU, which already has 3 million Turkish-born workers. However, Turkey claims that by 2015 its economic growth will have reached a point where it will itself be a net importer of labour.

The strongest argument against Turkish entry is its sheer size. Its population is just smaller than that of Germany, but it is rising at 1 per cent per annum and will soon overtake Germany. The population of the EU27 is probably already falling. By 2050, Turkey could make up between a fifth and a quarter of the total EU population. This is of particular concern to France and Germany, which see their power base being eroded.

In surveys in 2005, 35 per cent of EU citizens supported Turkish entry, while 52 per cent opposed it. If Turkish entry were approved, Austria would hold a referendum on the issue before agreeing to ratify the accession. Only 10 per cent of Austrians support Turkish entry, which may be a historical folk memory of two sieges of Vienna by the Turkish Empire (Akcapar and Chaibi 2006).

Until recently, Turkish public opinion has been firmly in support of EU membership, but this is now waning due to what the Turks see as the patronising approach of the EU. One Turkish commentator recently said, 'The EU is off the radar. It has confirmed Turkey's worst expectations. At present, it is an irrelevancy,' while another said, 'Europe is not ready for Turkish membership' (Tisdall 2007).

THE EU CONSTITUTION AND THE LISBON TREATY

By the late 1990s, it was clear that the EU was about to undergo a dramatic enlargement and equally clear that the existing structure of EU institutions would not be able to cope with a greatly increased membership – hence the move towards an EU constitution to modernise the EU's structure. A first attempt at modernisation was made at the Nice Summit in 2000, but the arrangements agreed there really satisfied no-one. A Convention under the former French president, Giscard D'Estaing, produced a draft constitution, and eventually, after much haggling and amendment, a new constitution was agreed by the member states in June 2004.

The main points of the Constitution were:

- *The Council president* – the European Council (the heads of state or government of member states) will elect a president of the Council, by qualified majority, for a term of two and a half years, renewable once. The president would have to be approved by the European Parliament. The idea here was to give greater continuity. At present, the presidency rotates through the member states every six months.
- *The foreign minister* – the European Council would appoint a foreign minister, by qualified majority. That individual would speak for the EU on foreign policy. This new post effectively combines two existing posts. However, the foreign minister will not decide policy and will only be able to speak for the EU where the European Council has decided on policy. Most importantly, foreign policy is one of the three areas (the others being defence and taxation) where each member state still has a veto.
- *The Commission* – from November 2004, each member state will appoint one commissioner. This means that the big powers (Germany, France, the UK and Italy) would lose one of their commissioners, as already agreed at Nice. However, it was agreed that by 2014 the size of the Commission will be reduced to two-thirds of the number of member states, although the precise mechanism for doing this has still to be negotiated.
- *The Parliament* – the powers of the Parliament are being significantly increased. It will have powers of 'co-decision' with the Council of Ministers for those policies requiring a

decision by qualified majority. This means that the Parliament will effectively have the right to veto proposed legislation, a very real increase in power.

- *Qualified majority voting* – there are two significant changes to the system of qualified majority voting in the Council of Ministers. First, more areas will now be subject to majority voting. These include asylum and immigration policy and cross-border crime. As we saw above, only foreign affairs, defence and taxation are still subject to veto. Second, the procedure of qualified majority voting will change. Gone is the system where member states had different numbers of votes. Now all will have one vote, but a qualified majority is defined as 'at least 55 per cent of the members of the Council, comprising at least 15 of them and representing member states comprising at least 65 per cent of the population of the Union'.

- *Charter of Fundamental Rights* – this sets out key 'rights, freedoms and principles'. These include the right to life and liberty and the right to strike. This could affect existing UK industrial relations law, but the UK Government feels that national laws on industrial relations will not be affected. This has yet to be tested by the European Court of Justice.

The fact that the member states agreed on the Constitution did not mean that it immediately came into force. The Constitution had to be ratified by each of the 25 member states. A number of states decided that this would only be after a referendum.

The key referenda were those in France and the Netherlands, held in May and June 2005. Both campaigns were very difficult for the national governments and the EU. France voted 54.9 per cent 'no' on 29 May and in the Netherlands, 61.7 per cent voted against on 1 June (Nugent 2006). This was sufficient to kill off the Constitution. In each case, non-EU issues muddied the picture. In polls held by the Commission after the referenda, a third of Dutch people who voted no said it was because of lack of information and 14 per cent said it was because they opposed the ruling party. A third voted no on specifically constitution-related issues – 19 per cent because of a fear of loss of national sovereignty and 13 per cent because they felt Europe was too expensive (the Netherlands is the largest per head contributor to the EU budget). In France, reasons for voting no were predominantly economic – either a fear of negative effects on employment (31 per cent) or that the economic situation was too weak (25 per cent). Another third thought that the Constitution represented an unacceptable move towards Anglo-Saxon models of capitalism or a weakening of the European social model (Church and Phinnemore 2006).

The Constitution therefore had to be renegotiated in June 2007 at the Lisbon Summit and significant changes were made:

- The name 'Constitution' was dropped and replaced by 'Reform Treaty'.
- The constitution proposal for a 'double majority' system of qualified majority voting (55 per cent of member states representing 65 per cent of the EU's population) is maintained, but, to meet Polish objections that this gives too much weight to Germany, it will not be phased in until 2014–17.
- The national veto will be maintained for social security and culture, as well as for defence, foreign policy and taxation.
- The post of EU Council president remains, but the EU foreign minister's title is changed to 'high representative'.
- The UK has obtained an opt-out from the Charter of Fundamental Rights (BBC 2007).

Like the Constitution, the Lisbon Treaty still had to be ratified. The UK Government said that it would not hold a referendum and the treaty was ratified by Parliament. Ireland held a referendum, which voted 'no', but a second referendum voted 'yes' in October 2009. Poland then ratified the treaty, leaving only the Czech Republic refusing to ratify. Here the Treaty had been approved by Parliament, but the eurosceptic president refused to sign the Treaty. After obtaining a last-minute opt-out from the Charter of Fundamental Rights, the

Czech Republic finally signed in November 2009, completing ratification of the Treaty. The Conservative Party in Britain had pledged to hold a referendum on Lisbon if the Treaty was still unratified when they came to power, but this pledge was no longer relevant. Instead, the party pledged to hold a referendum on any future EU treaty (Watt 2009).

THE EURO AND THE EUROZONE CRISIS

The concept of the euro dates back to the Maastricht Treaty of 1992, which established the programme of Economic and Monetary Union (EMU), with the intention to create a single currency by 1999. Under EMU, all EU members agreed to keep their exchange rates within narrow bounds (the Exchange Rate Mechanism (ERM)) and to accept limits on their public spending and borrowing. The UK left the ERM in 1993. The spending limits were formalised in the Stability and Growth Pact in 1997, which said that all countries in the eurozone should keep their annual budget deficit below 3 per cent of GDP and their total public debt below 60 per cent of GDP. If a country broke the rules for three consecutive years, it could be fined by the European Commission.

In 1998, 11 members agreed to fix their exchange rates and handed over their power to set interest rates to the European Central Bank. The UK, Sweden and Denmark refused to join and Greece was not invited to join because it did not qualify under EMU rules (it did join at the last minute in 2001). The 12 countries of the eurozone started to use the euro on 1 January 2002. Of the new members that joined the EU in 2004, Slovenia, Cyprus, Malta, Slovakia and Estonia have adopted the euro. It is also the official currency in the statelets of Monaco, San Marino and the Vatican (James and Sonny 2006, 2012).

The members of the eurozone had voluntarily surrendered two key tools of economic policy – the power to vary their exchange rate and to vary their interest rates. This, and the last-minute decision to admit Greece, were to prove crucial weaknesses when the eurozone crisis started in 2008 and intensified from 2010. EMU also attempted to control fiscal policy through the Stability and Growth Pact, which was designed to control the spending of the weak southern European members. However, in 2003, both France and Germany broke the Pact but avoided punishment by the Commission. Thereafter, the Pact was effectively dead, although a modified version, the Fiscal Treaty, was introduced in 2011. The UK and the Czech Republic refused to sign up to the Fiscal Treaty (James et al 2006, 2012).

The fundamental weakness of the eurozone was that the economies of its members were too diverse. At one extreme was Germany, extremely wealthy, with very high productivity and a pathological aversion to inflation. At the other extreme was Greece, a poor country with low productivity, a tendency to inflation and poorly controlled public spending, and a reputation for tax evasion. For a time, the cracks were papered over. Eurozone interest rates were low, which stimulated runaway housing booms in Ireland and Spain, while Greece fudged its public borrowing to appear to stay within the Stability and Growth Pact. With the onset of the world recession in 2008, the weaknesses of the eurozone became all too apparent. The Irish and Portuguese governments were forced to ask the EU for financial bailouts, but the weakest link, predictably, was Greece.

In February 2010 the EU instructed Greece to cut its public spending and raise its taxes to reduce its debt and the eurozone agreed to lend Greece €80 billion. In May 2010 the eurozone set up a more formal rescue fund, the European Financial Stability Facility (EFSF), a temporary fund with resources of €440 billion (increased to €800 billion in March 2012), which made a second bailout loan of €109 billion to Greece. The crisis eased somewhat after a speech by Mario Draghi, the president of the ECB, in which he said the ECB was 'ready to do whatever it takes' to save the euro (Draghi 2012). Later in 2012, the eurozone agreed that the EFSF could lend direct to banks, rather than only to sovereign states. In November 2012, the EFSF lent €37 billion to four Spanish banks to finance restructuring (Tremlett 2012). The EFSF is being replaced by the permanent European Stability Mechanism in 2013.

In order to qualify for bailout loans, Greece has made savage cuts to its public spending, including pensions and health spending. Greece has found itself caught in the same trap as George Osborne in the UK – savage cuts in public spending increase the budget deficit rather than reduce it.

What can be done to cure the eurozone debt crisis? The normal approach for a country with control over its currency would be to devalue, thereby making its exports more competitive, which in the medium term will stimulate its economy, and also to cut its interest rates. Neither of these is available to Greece, as the European Central Bank controls the euro exchange rate and eurozone interest rates. The only approach available is 'internal devaluation' – making exports more competitive by forcing down wages and prices through public spending cuts. This may eventually work in Greece, but there are no signs that it is yet doing so. The only other remedies available to Greece are two doomsday solutions – leaving the euro, restoring the drachma and then drastically devaluing, or defaulting on debt, as Argentina did in the late 1990s.

One solution open to the eurozone would be to write off at least some of the debts owed to it by Greece. Some very tentative steps were taken towards this in November 2012 as part of the third bailout (Strupczweski and Breidhardt 2012), but this would be seen as a desperate last resort by the eurozone. Other euro countries, especially Germany, are worried about moral hazard – if they let Greece off, they would come under intense pressure to do the same for Ireland, Portugal, Spain and, possibly at a later date, Italy.

Another medium-term solution involves Germany. Greece (and the other southern European economies) cannot compete with Germany. Internal devaluation tries to make countries like Greece more competitive, but an alternative approach would be to make Germany less competitive. This would involve deliberately creating inflation in Germany, but the Germans regard this prospect with horror, as there are folk memories of the hyperinflation which hit Germany in the early 1920s and which contributed to the rise of Nazism. There is also a doomsday solution involving Germany, which is the mirror image of that facing Greece – that Germany should leave the euro, restore the mark and then revalue. This might make economic sense, but it is clearly politically impossible.

In the long term, the only viable solution is fiscal union, which would almost certainly also entail political union. A country like the UK has a single currency, the pound, and rich and poor areas. However, disparities between regions are less marked because the UK has a common taxation system. Poor areas in the UK pay less in taxation, particularly income tax and VAT, but receive more in public spending, such as unemployment benefit. To some extent the EU budget is redistributed from rich to poor countries, but to a much smaller degree. It is possible that in the long term the members of the eurozone might agree to common taxation, but it is inconceivable that the UK would agree.

Meanwhile Greece moves closer to total collapse. It is estimated that Greek GDP will have fallen by 25 per cent by 2014, the biggest drop anywhere since the 1930s. Malaria has returned to Greece for the first time in 40 years, schools are cold because they cannot afford to buy heating oil, the political party leading in the opinion polls in Greece is from the extreme left, while the third-placed party is neo-Nazi, raising the spectre of the Greek civil war of the late 1940s (Smith 2012).

The best source to keep up to date on the euro crisis is the BBC News website (www.bbc.co.uk/news/). A range of sources from this website are in the *References* for this chapter.

REFLECTIVE ACTIVITY 6.4

An in–out referendum	Questions
The UK Prime Minister, David Cameron, has announced that if re-elected in 2015, he intends to renegotiate the UK's relationship with the European Union, leading to an in–out referendum in 2017 on whether the UK should leave the EU (Watt 2013).	1 Put forward a case for the UK (a) leaving the EU and (b) staying in the EU. 2 What would be the likely HR consequences if the UK did leave the EU?

EU EMPLOYMENT POLICY

Employment policy in the UK is influenced by the EU at several different levels.

EU TREATIES

The treaties set out the competencies of the EU. The organisation is only allowed to act in areas set out in the treaties. The various treaties, culminating in the Lisbon Treaty of December 2009, have always been committed to improvements in working conditions. National economic policies must be consistent with the EU's broad economic guidelines, which stress a high level of employment as a major objective. Employment policy was a key element of the Lisbon Strategy on EU competitiveness agreed in 2000. The Lisbon strategy was replaced by the Europe 2020 strategy on 17 June 2010. The Europe 2020 strategy aims to create jobs and encourage 'green' economic growth and create an inclusive society. The strategy's main employment targets include:

- raise EU employment rate from 69 per cent to 75 per cent
- reduce school drop-out rates to less than 10 per cent (Civitas 2010).

The treaties stress a commitment to improved living and working conditions with a view to harmonisation (remember that one of the key EU principles is a level playing field between member states); social protection; dialogue between management and labour; development of HR with the aim of lasting high employment; and combating exclusion. However, the treaties also stress that the EU should avoid placing excessive burdens on small and medium-sized businesses.

An important element in the Lisbon Treaty was the incorporation of the Charter of Fundamental Rights, originally agreed in 2000, but never accepted by the UK. The Charter guarantees a number of individual rights, some of which relate to employment, but as part of the treaty negotiations, the UK and Poland were granted an opt-out from the Charter, joined at the last minute by the Czech Republic.

The Lisbon Treaty also lays down how decisions must be taken on employment matters. Unanimity is required for proposals that concern social protection and social security, and protection of workers' interests on termination of the employment contract. All other employment issues are subject to co-decision, which gives a significant role to the European Parliament and ensures that no one member state can exercise a veto.

EU DIRECTIVES

While the treaties deal with the principles of EU employment policy, details of implementation are enforced through EU directives. HR professionals will be familiar with most of them, including collective redundancies, TUPE, discrimination, equal pay, health and safety, information and consultation, atypical workers, pregnant workers, agency workers and working time. If the requirements of an EU directive set a lower standard than that already existing in national law, member states are not allowed to reduce their level of worker protection.

Social partner agreements

EU employment policy is also made by agreements between the social partners, the European Trade Union Confederation (ETUC), representing trade unions (including the TUC), and UNICE, representing employers (including the CBI). EU-level social partner agreements include parental leave and leave for family reasons, the protection of fixed-term, part-time and teleworkers, and workplace stress. The European Commission also encourages agreements made by sectoral social partners.

For further details, see the CIPD's *Employment Law: EU influence* factsheet, last revised in September 2011 (CIPD 2011).

THE EU AND OTHER REGIONAL BLOCS

The EU is not the only major regional trading group in the world. The North American Free Trade Agreement (NAFTA) covers the US, Canada and Mexico, while the Association of South East Asian Nations (ASEAN) includes the Asian Tiger states of Indonesia, Malaysia, the Philippines, Singapore and Thailand, as well as states including Vietnam and Myanmar, with China, India, Japan and Australia as Dialogue Partners. Both NAFTA and ASEAN are primarily free trade area agreements and thus of much narrower scope than the EU.

All three encourage trade within their own area and thus may indirectly discourage trade between the three blocs. Those of you who have read George Orwell's *1984* may see parallels with his three competing blocs of Eurasia, East Asia and Oceania, who divided up the world between them!

In 2000, the so-called triad of the US, the EU and Japan received 71 per cent of total world inward direct investment and was responsible for 82 per cent of outward direct investment (Williams 2001).

INTERNATIONAL FINANCIAL INSTITUTIONS

THE BRETTON WOODS CONFERENCE

In 1944, the wartime Western allies held a conference at Bretton Woods in New Hampshire which was to shape the economic future of the international economy. Their prime aim was to prevent a repetition of the competitive devaluations and protectionism which had followed the Wall Street crash in 1929 and which had made the ensuing Great Depression even more severe in its impact. The idea was to impose strict controls on the ability of each country to follow beggar-my-neighbour policies and to force international economic co-operation.

Out of Bretton Woods came three great international institutions, the International Monetary Fund (IMF), the International Bank for Reconstruction and Development (the World Bank), and the General Agreement on Tariffs and Trade (GATT).

THE IMF

The main plank of the IMF regime was a system of fixed exchange rates, which all member countries agreed to maintain. In practice this meant that each member state fixed the value of its currency in terms of the US dollar, while the US dollar itself was linked to gold. It was recognised that members might experience problems with their balance of payments in the short term (an excess of imports over exports). In such a situation, the

IMF agreed to make hard currency available to them on a short-term basis to allow the member a breathing space to adjust its economy. Only if the balance of payments problem was long term was the member state permitted to devalue its currency. The system was financed by subscriptions from member countries, with by far the largest contribution coming from the US.

The system worked reasonably smoothly for nearly 30 years, although there were still balance of payments crises and occasional devaluations (most notably in the UK, France and Italy). Most lending was to developed countries and the IMF had little involvement with the Third World. However, the world economic structure changed fundamentally in the early 1970s. Now it was the US which experienced a balance of payments crisis. The IMF system could not cope with this – the absolute stability of the dollar was fundamental. Eventually, President Nixon abandoned the fixed price link between the US dollar and gold – in effect devaluing the dollar. As a result, fixed exchange rates were abandoned and have never been restored on a world level.

The floating exchange rate regime immediately removed the IMF's major role. It still carries out its role of alleviating short-term financial crises, but almost always with developing rather than developed economies – the Asian Tiger economies (Thailand, South Korea, Indonesia) in 1997, Russia in 1998, Brazil in 1999 and Argentina in 2001 – but the IMF also started to develop a wider role of encouraging structural reform in member states (often known as 'mission creep' – a typical example of an organisation broadening its original aims beyond all recognition). An early example of this was the loan to the UK in 1976, which was made conditional on the (Labour) Government cutting public spending and adopting monetarist policies.

This process has now gone much further, and from the 1980s onwards the IMF has followed a policy of imposing Thatcherite, free-market neo-liberal conditions (particularly privatisation) on its support, particularly to Third World countries:

- Tanzania was forced to charge for hospital visits and school fees.
- Ecuador was forced to sell its water system to foreigners and to increase the price of cooking oil by 80 per cent.
- Malawi was told to sell off its strategic reserves of maize, two years before the country was hit by famine.
- Guyana was told to privatise its sugar industry.
- Zambia was told to privatise its banks (Mathiason 2003).

Should the IMF try to impose long-term neo-liberal reform in the Third World, rather than concentrating on lending money to countries in short-term financial difficulties?

There are three main arguments in favour of this policy:

1 State-run sectors in Third World countries tend to be inefficient, corrupt, devourers of resources, and they discourage foreign investment. The state may also spend wastefully and not in the best long-term interests of its population – for instance by excess spending on arms.

2 Moral hazard – the concept that because countries expect to be bailed out if they get into difficulties, they will be reckless in their behaviour, because they know they will never really be called to account for their actions. For example, Brazil has defaulted on its debts five times and Venezuela nine times. In essence, this is the same argument that says that insurance companies should carry out very strict checks before they pay out on policies in order to discourage fraudulent claims.

3 Short-term intervention tends by definition to treat short-term symptoms rather than the long-term illness. The only way to tackle long-term problems is through long-term reform.

There are two counter arguments:

1   While the above may be true in the long run, the short-term effect of privatisation and liberalisation is to increase poverty and inequality in the Third World.

2   By concentrating on the long term rather than the short term, the IMF is moving into areas which should more appropriately be the responsibility of the World Bank (Stiglitz 2003).

The current consensus seems to be that the IMF should concentrate on macroeconomic factors such as budget deficits and inflation, rather than trying to micro-manage the economies of clients. Charles Wyplosz, professor of economics at the Institute of International Studies in Geneva, was quoted in the *Financial Times* in May 2004 as saying, 'when firemen come to your house to put out a blaze, you would not expect them to meddle in your marriage' (Swann 2004).

Ngaire Woods suggests three changes:

1   The IMF should be the cornerstone of global monetary co-operation.

2   The IMF should help countries mitigate or cushion shocks from the global economy.

3   The IMF must command the confidence of all its members (Woods 2007).

The IMF is currently heavily involved, along with the European Union and the European Central Bank, in managing the Greek debt crisis.

THE WORLD BANK

Like the IMF, the World Bank was set up at Bretton Woods and nearly all countries in the world are members. Unlike the IMF, its main role is to provide access to capital for long-term development, particularly in the Third World. It does this partly through direct lending through a number of its own agencies, some of it interest-free, and partly by leveraging investment from the private sector.

It also has a wider social remit than the IMF. It emphasises social services, the environment and gender equality as well as economic growth. However, like the IMF, it has been criticised for the neo-liberal conditions which it tends to attach to its loans and also for over-lending to relatively advanced developing countries such as Brazil and particularly China, which have sufficient clout to be able to borrow to finance their development on a commercial basis. The Bank is also a key component in the so-called Washington Consensus, not least because of the convention that its president is nominated by the US (Woods 2007).

One proposal that has been put forward is that the IMF and the World Bank should merge. There is clear overlap – in practice if not in theory – between the activities of the IMF and World Bank, although in principle their functions are distinct. A merger might therefore seem logical and it might help to prevent mission creep. However, if the IMF had a dominant role in the merged organisation, its neo-liberal agenda might swamp the wider social and environmental principles of the World Bank.

INTERNATIONAL TRADE AND COMPARATIVE ADVANTAGE

Very few countries are self-sufficient, in the sense that they produce everything which they need within their own boundaries. Ever since the Stone Age, societies have traded with each other. The most obvious reason for a country to trade is to obtain something which it is incapable of producing for itself. For example, until the discovery of North Sea oil, the UK had to import oil. However, strictly speaking this only applies to extractive industries. Anything else could be made or grown, at a price. There is nothing to stop the UK growing its own bananas in greenhouses (except common sense!). It is a much more efficient use of resources for countries to concentrate on what they are best at producing and to import other goods. For example, if we compare the UK and the Windward Islands, the UK has an *absolute advantage* in the production of pharmaceuticals, while the Windwards have an *absolute advantage* in the production of bananas. It therefore makes sense for the UK to specialise in pharmaceuticals and to export these to the Windwards, while the Windwards should export bananas to the UK. (As we will see later when we look at the banana war, the real world is a lot more complicated than this simple example suggests.)

Even if one country is better at producing everything than another country, international trade will still benefit both sides. For example, let's stretch our banana example even further. Assume that the UK is four times as efficient as the Windwards at producing pharmaceuticals, but twice as efficient at producing bananas. In this case, the UK has a *comparative advantage* in the production of pharmaceuticals and the Windwards a *comparative advantage* in bananas. Both sides would benefit if the UK specialised in pharmaceuticals and the Windwards in bananas. The mathematics to prove this can be found in any textbook on international economics.

For comparative advantage to work, however, it is essential that there are no restrictions on trade between the countries involved, that is, that there is *free trade*. For example, assume that the UK has a banana industry which is struggling to cope with competition from Windwards bananas, and then assume that the UK banana industry persuades the UK Government to place either quotas (restrictions on quantity) or tariffs (taxation) on imports of Windwards bananas. People working in the UK banana industry would benefit, but everyone else in both economies would lose.

If you think that this example seems totally unrealistic, you are probably right, but bear in mind that Japan, for example, protects its rice growers with a 500 per cent tariff on imported rice.

REFLECTIVE ACTIVITY 6.5

Is comparative advantage good for you?

The theory of comparative advantage suggests that everyone gains from free trade. Why then do so many countries protect their own domestic industries?

THE WORLD TRADE ORGANIZATION (WTO)

After the Second World War, the Allies set up the General Agreement on Tariffs on Trade (GATT), whose remit was to encourage free trade and prevent the destructive protectionism that had blighted the world economy in the 1930s. Its objectives were to:

- eliminate existing trade barriers
- deter the formation of new barriers
- eliminate all forms of trade discrimination.

In 1995, GATT was absorbed into a new body, the WTO, with wider objectives. Its membership now includes virtually the whole world, following the accession of China and Taiwan in the early 2000s. The WTO continues the process of liberalising world trade, but its powers also extend to trade in services as well as goods, and also the regulation of international property rights such as patents and copyright. It also has the power to adjudicate on disputes between members, with the right to impose financial penalties.

CASE STUDY 6.3

THE BANANA WAR

The banana war was one of the most bitter trade disputes of the 1990s and one of a number of disputes between the two dominant trading blocs, the EU and the US. The key to the dispute was the preference that the EU gave to bananas from ex-British and French colonies in Africa, the Pacific and the Caribbean (the APC countries). The EU argument was that without protection, the banana industries in these areas, particularly in the Caribbean, would collapse, devastating the local economies and perhaps pushing producers to alternative less desirable crops such as cannabis or coca. They pointed out that the WTO had an objective to assist developing and transition economies.

The US responded that the EU action was a gross breach of WTO rules. Three US companies – Chiquita, Dole and Del Monte – control two-thirds of world trade in bananas from their huge plantations in Central America (the APC has 4 per cent of the world market).

Legally, the US had an unanswerable case, but it weakened its moral position by imposing punitive import tariffs in 1998 on a range of EU exports to the US in retaliation, before the WTO delivered its judgement. Worse, this was announced shortly after Chiquita gave a big donation to the ruling US Democratic Party.

The WTO ruled in favour of the US and ordered the EU to abolish its protective quotas on APC bananas by 2005. The effects on the Caribbean have been predictably devastating. Between 1993 and 2000, two-thirds of the banana growers in the Windward Islands went out of business, while exports of bananas from St Vincent and the Grenadines fell from $120 million to $50 million (Ryle 2002). By 2009, only 4,000 of the 24,000 Windward Island banana growers in 1993 were still in business. Between 1992 and 2007, UK banana imports almost doubled from 545,000 to 927,000, but the proportion imported from the Caribbean fell from 70 per cent to less than 30 per cent (Doward 2009).

THE WORKING OF THE WTO

The WTO (and its predecessor GATT) works in a series of long trade rounds, initiated at a major conference, and then negotiated and implemented over a long period. The Uruguay Round in the 1990s was primarily concerned with textiles, where the developing world had a comparative advantage but where the developed countries maintained protection of their own textile industries. The developed Western countries agreed to eliminate protection, but only over a ten-year period, with most of the concessions coming in the last year! This tends to be the pattern – the West speaks the language of free trade, is keen to impose free trade on the developing world, but drags its heels when it comes to its own concessions.

Larry Elliott in the *Guardian* in 2004 drew a telling parallel with medieval Europe, where in theory all states owed spiritual allegiance to the papacy and the universal values of the Church, but in practice spent most of their time at war with each other (Elliott 2004).

THE FAILURE OF DOHA

The Doha Round of trade negotiations was launched by the World Trade Organization in 2001 in the wake of the 9/11 terrorist attacks on New York and Washington. The negotiations were specifically designated as a 'development round', aimed at improving the economic position of developing countries as a symbol of world solidarity against terrorism (*Economist* 2003).

WTO negotiations are always difficult, as all agreements have to be unanimous. Unlike the IMF, rich countries do not have disproportionate power. Three main issues of particular interest to developing countries dominated the negotiations: special trade treatment for developing countries, supply of cheap generic medicines for poor countries and liberalisation of agriculture (De Jonquieres 2003).

The deadlines for special trade treatment and generic medicines were missed at the end of 2002 – in the case of generic medicines the only country voting against agreement was the US.

Agricultural liberalisation was a much more crucial issue. When the first Doha meeting was called, it produced a pledge to improve market access for Third World countries, to reduce trade-distorting domestic support and to reduce export subsidies.

Reform was urgently needed. In 2001, assistance to rich-country farmers amounted to $311 billion, compared with $50 billion in development aid. The EU paid subsidies of $913 a year to each EU cow and $8 in aid to each sub-Saharan African. Comparable figures for Japan were $2,700 and $1.47 (Wolf 2005, p215). The EU was the world's largest exporter of skimmed milk powder, sold at half its cost of production, and of white sugar, sold at

a quarter the cost of production (Wolf 2005, p216).

Stuart Harbinson, the WTO chairman for agriculture, proposed a package that would:

- end export subsidies in nine years
- reduce tariffs by 40–60 per cent
- cut trade-distorting farm support by 60 per cent.

It was calculated that these proposals would increase annual global income by $100 billion, with 20 per cent of the gain going to developing countries and 80 per cent to rich countries through lower prices (De Jonquieres 2003).

The US and the Cairns Group of major agricultural exporters (including Australia and Canada) argued that the Harbinson proposals did not go far enough, while the EU and Japan claimed that they were too ambitious. India wanted to maintain its own tariffs to protect its farmers. The ACP (Africa, Caribbean and Pacific) group of developing countries sided with the EU, worried about losing their preferential access to EU markets (see Case Study 6.3).

The key to the negotiations was the attitude of the EU. The European Commission proposed reform of the Common Agricultural Policy which, by phasing out incentives for overproduction and switching to support based on rural development and protection of the environment, would reduce export subsidies but would not make EU markets more open to imports. Meanwhile, France and Germany had reached an agreement to maintain spending on the CAP until 2013.

Under the terms of the negotiations, agreement was required by 31 March 2003, by which time the Iraq war had just broken out, relations between the

US and France were at an all-time low and, ironically, Doha was the military headquarters for the war.

The 31 March deadline was missed. The day after this, Franz Fischler, the EU agriculture commissioner, and Pascal Lamy, the trade commissioner, wrote an article in the *Financial Times* justifying the EU position (Fischler and Lamy 2003). They criticised the Cairns Group, arguing that they wanted nothing more than 'an unlimited right to exploit its members' undeniable comparative advantages'. They also pointed out that the EU is the largest importer of agricultural products and the main importer of food from developing countries, taking in more food imports than the US, Japan, Canada and Australia put together. Lamy became head of the WTO in 2007 – a classic case of poacher turned gamekeeper!

Negotiations staggered on for another three years. In Geneva in August 2004, the WTO agreed that export subsidies should be abolished, but no starting date or timetable has been agreed. The final breakdown came over fundamental disagreement between the EU and the US. The US argued that the EU was not offering big enough reductions in tariffs, while the EU

claimed that the US was not proposing a big enough reduction in subsidies. Eventually the US decided that no deal was better than a weak deal – 'Doha lite', as the US trade representative, Susan Schwab, put it. On 24 July 2006, the Doha Round was formally suspended, with no date set for a resumption (*Economist* 2006a).

Eventually negotiations were reopened. Agreement was nearly reached in 2008, but failed at the last minute due to one outstanding issue between the US and India. Unfortunately the Doha Round is based on the principle that 'nothing is agreed until everything is agreed' (McClanahan 2012). Negotiations will next reopen in Bali in December 2013.

What does the failure of Doha tell us?

- the hypocrisy of the developed world, which is ready to impose trade liberalisation on the developing world, but not to make meaningful concessions itself
- the strength of the farm lobby in both the EU and the US, which prevented any agreement
- divisions among the developing countries and agricultural exports, with diametrically opposing stances being taken by India, the Cairns Group and the ACP.

DEBT RELIEF

One of the most pressing problems of the world economy is the crushing burden of Third World debt. The 52 most indebted countries, mostly in Africa, have debts of $375 billion, most of it unpayable, but on which interest still has to be paid. In 1998, it cost these countries $23.4 billion to service their debt, mostly owed to Western governments, the IMF or the World Bank. In many countries, debt repayment dwarfs welfare budgets. Mauritania pays $63 million to service its debt, but only $51 million on education and $17 million on health (Madeley 2001).

Much of the debt is a product of the Cold War period, when the West was keen to tie the Third World to its side, and much of the money was wasted, either going on armaments or disappearing through corruption, by the likes of the late unlamented Presidents Amin and Mobutu.

Many arguments can be advanced for relieving at least some of this burden of debt. These range from the moral – that debt is denying the inhabitants of these countries the human rights of decent education and health – the economic – that money being spent on debt repayment is not being spent on imports from the West – and the geopolitical – that poverty and discontent create an environment conducive to terrorism.

An international campaign for debt relief was launched in 1996 by the pressure group Jubilee 2000, which has produced some results. The IMF and the World Bank have set up the Heavily Indebted Poor Countries (HIPC) initiative to administer debt relief to the 52 poorest states, the G7 promised the cancellation of $110 billion of debt, while the UK Government agreed to hold debt repayments in a trust for poverty relief, to be released when each country agreed a poverty reduction plan (Madeley 2001).

However, progress has been limited. By the end of the Jubilee 2000 campaign in December 2000, only one country, Uganda, had debt cancelled, with reductions agreed for another 21 and, in line with normal IMF/World Bank policy, stringent conditions were attached.

The Jubilee 2000 campaign was followed by the Make Poverty History campaign, which seemed to have reached success at the Gleneagles conference of the G8 in July 2005, chaired by Tony Blair. This pledged to double development assistance to Africa, including debt relief and aid, to $100 billion a year by 2010. However, in April 2007, the Africa Progress Panel (APP), set up to review progress on the pledge, headed by Kofi Annan, the former UN secretary-general, reported that the G8 was only 10 per cent of the way to reaching its target. The UK, alone of the G8, has met its commitments in full, but Bob Geldof, who is also a member of the APP, singled out Germany and Italy as countries which were significantly failing to meet their commitments. At the same time the OECD reported that after one-off packages of debt relief for Iraq and Nigeria were taken into account, aid flows from the West fell for the first time in a decade in 2006 (Elliott and Connolly 2007).

However, the issue of debt relief and aid is not straightforward. Boone (2005) argues that much aid is ineffective. Countries which received large aid flows did not do better at reducing child mortality than those which received small amounts of aid. Indeed, contrary to popular belief, little aid goes to finance social reform. Only 4 per cent went to health, 12 per cent to education and 6 per cent to emergencies. Countries or regions which were most successful at reducing child mortality were Cuba, Sri Lanka and the Indian state of Kerala. These had very different political systems, but all had put a lot of effort into developing their infrastructure. As a result, aid was spent where it was needed, rather than being wasted on bureaucracy or corruption.

REFLECTIVE ACTIVITY 6.6

Debt relief

Can you put forward any arguments against either the principle or the practice of debt relief for the Third World?

GLOBALISATION

Globalisation is an emotive word. It has inspired violent demonstrations all over the world and also vehement defence. But what is globalisation? There is no single clear definition.

First, it is useful to look at what globalisation is not (Scholte 2000):

- *Internationalisation* – the world has always been international. There were trade links between the Roman and Chinese empires, for example.
- *Free trade* – trade was at least as free in the late nineteenth century as it is now.

- *Westernisation* – Western culture was exported to much of the world as a result of the dominance of Western empires in the late nineteenth and early twentieth centuries.
- *Universalisation* – global lifestyles and ideas are nothing new. Islam spread across half the known Western world in 50 years in the sixth century, and later spread to countries as far apart as Nigeria and Indonesia.

John Gray sees its key features as free mobility of capital and free trade (Gray 1995). Ngaire Woods sees globalisation as much wider, and political and social as well as economic.

She distinguishes three elements (Woods 2000):

- *The expansion of markets* – technological changes like the mobile phone and above all the Internet have speeded up communications to the extent that both financial and physical transactions can be carried out instantaneously, while improvements in transport permit goods to shipped quickly and relatively cheaply anywhere in the world (think of the universal availability in the UK of asparagus from Peru and French beans from Kenya). At the same time, governments throughout the world have been deregulating and reducing their control over their economies, at the same time as the growth of e-commerce has started to erode their control of their tax base. The result has been the spread of transnational enterprises and global brands, leading to what Kenichi Ohmae, the Japanese management guru and one of the early proponents of globalisation, called 'the borderless world' (Ohmae 1990). The knowledge economy also creates a borderless world. Knowledge is not dependent on possession of natural resources and can instantaneously be transmitted via the Internet. As Lester Thurow says, 'knowledge is the new basis for wealth' (Thurow 1999) – hence the outflow of call centre and data-handling jobs from the UK to India.
- *The transformation of politics* – free movement of capital has produced a world financial market which has the potential to swamp any single economy. At the same time, transnational issues have become of increasing importance – global warming, human rights, drugs, world poverty and immigration, terrorism. Increasingly, in order to have any influence, nation states have to join together in regional groupings. The European Union is the best known, but there are other important groupings such as the North American Free Trade Agreement and ASEAN. Just as nation states are handing over power to regional groupings, they are also devolving power internally to regional entities – Scotland and Wales in the UK, Catalonia in Spain.
- *The emergence of new social and political movements* – a global (or American) culture has developed, with US corporations such as McDonald's, CNN, Disney and Nike setting trends across the world. At the same time, counter-movements have developed, ranging from the anti-globalisation movement to militant Islam.

Globalisation is nothing new. An early example came with the Opium Wars in the 1840s, when Great Britain forced China to open its borders to imports of opium in order to finance the early Victorians' obsession with China tea. It has often been argued that the golden age of globalisation was the period 1880–1914, when the world economy was regulated by the universal use of the Gold Standard and there was almost universal free trade and free movement of capital. Indeed, this period had one element of globalisation which does not apply today – free movement of people. Not only could an individual travel without a passport, there was also free movement of labour and very little control on international migration – this is the period when the Statue of Liberty was erected in New York. One commentator even said in 1911 that a major war was now impossible, as the world had become so interdependent (Micklethwait and Wooldridge 2000).

Two dates mark the development of modern globalisation. One is 1973 and the first oil crisis. This led to two things – a realisation that the world economy was inextricably linked through its dependence on oil, and the collapse of the Bretton Woods system of fixed exchange rates, which ushered in a period when world financial markets became much more dominant.

The other is 1989. One factor here was the collapse of communism as a world ideology and the triumph of the US in the Cold War – what the US political scientist Francis Fukuyama called 'the end of history'. The other, much less noted at the time but equally important, was the final bursting of the Japanese 'bubble economy'. Throughout the 1980s, it seems that globalisation was likely to be Japanese – rather than US-dominated. Japanese industrial techniques were sweeping the world and most of the world's biggest corporations were Japanese rather than American. The economic collapse of Japan ensured that globalisation would be US-dominated economically, as well as politically and culturally.

DRIVERS OF GLOBALISATION

A number of drivers of globalisation have intensified in the last 20 years or so:

- *Technology* – the most important developments here are in information and communication technology (ICT), particularly the mobile phone and the Internet. These have transformed the way in which particular industries operate. An example is the insurance industry, which traditionally was staid and conservative, but has been transformed by the application of new technology, which has led to a wave of mergers.
- *Cultural homogenisation* – the universal availability of television and the global audiences for international sporting events such as the World Cup and the Olympic Games, combined with the explosion in overseas travel, has led to a homogenisation of international culture, which permits the development of global brands. However, global brands such as McDonald's still have to be responsive to local cultural differences – no traditional beef Big Macs in India, for example. Two small but telling examples are that since the 2008 Olympics in Beijing, all public lavatories in China are labelled in English as well as Chinese, while in London, Harrods and John Lewis accept Chinese yuan over their counters.
- *Economies of scale* – developments in manufacturing techniques have meant that the minimum efficient scale of operations in many industries has become a significant percentage of the available world market. The most extreme example is the aircraft industry, where the total world market is barely big enough to support two firms (Boeing and Airbus).
- *Deregulation* – deregulation has been driven by bodies such as the WTO and the EU. It reduces the costs of cross-border trade and so promotes the development of global companies.
- *Competition* – if one firm in an industry globalises, it will gain a competitive advantage. In order to stay in touch, its competitors will also be forced to globalise (Segal-Horn 2002).

TWO GLOBAL COMPANIES

Siemens

Siemens was founded in Germany in the mid-nineteenth century and by 1865 was already operating in the UK and Russia. In 1872 it supplied China with its first telegraph. It is now Europe's largest engineering company, operating in 190 countries. Eighty per cent of its sales, 70 per cent of its factories and 66 per cent of its workforce are outside Germany.

Its workforce in China is 36,000 and its annual Chinese sales are €4.4 billion. Like most globalised companies, it uses low-cost countries to manufacture components. But unlike most, it also does a lot of its R&D abroad. For example, a tailor-made low-cost body scanner for use in poorer countries was developed and is manufactured solely in China. Customers are happy to buy the product because they know that they can trade up at a later date to a more sophisticated German-made product using the same software. The company's Medical Solutions Group is investing over €30 million in its Asia Center of Excellence in Shanghai.

In non-medical areas, the company is building 60 high-speed trains in China with its local partner Tangshan Locomotive Rolling Stock Work, in a contract worth €670 million to Siemens. In 2005, Siemens filed over 1,000 patents in China. The company also sees India as key to its world development. It exports railway locomotives to the Middle East, but does so through India, where it employs 15,000 people.

Philips

Philips is smaller than Siemens, employing some 122,000 people in 60 countries. It has also had a much more chequered recent history. It started as a light bulb manufacturer in Holland in 1891. It then moved into x-ray machines and radio equipment. In the 1970s it moved into the record business and also expanded in electronics, including mobile phones and semiconductors.

By 2000, Philips had run into trouble. In most of its markets it was number three, four or worse, and so very vulnerable to competition. In 2001–02, it lost over €3 billion, and shed 55,000 jobs. It cut its 30 separate divisions to five – domestic appliances, lighting, medical, consumer electronics and semiconductors. This turned the company around, but downsizing continued. Philips exited the mobile phone business and sold a majority stake in its semiconductor business to the private equity company KKR.

The company's strategy now is to develop advanced products that are well designed and easy to use. China is key to this. Philips has long had links with China. In the 1920s, it sold an x-ray machine for the personal use of the last Chinese Emperor. It now has 20,000 employees in China, with production there worth €6 billion, half of which is exported. Like Siemens, it carries out R&D in China, at 15 centres employing 900 staff. The CEO, Gerard Kleisterlee, recently said, 'for us China is not just a workshop or a marketplace – it is a centre of innovation for new products and services with global applications'.

The lessons

1   Globalisation leads to constant and rapid change. It makes the environment more turbulent. Both companies, but particularly Philips, are continually restructuring, developing new product ranges and dropping old ones.

2   It is an old-fashioned view of globalisation to see India and China solely as low-cost manufacturing production lines. They are huge, rapidly growing and

increasingly sophisticated markets in their own right. Successful globalisers design products for China, in China (and India).

REFLECTIVE ACTIVITY 6.7

Why do people hate the WTO and globalisation?

Throughout the West, there is deep suspicion, in many cases verging on hatred, of the progress of globalisation in general, and the activities of the WTO in particular. Why do you think this is?

MULTINATIONAL AND TRANSNATIONAL CORPORATIONS

Multinational corporations (MNCs) are companies producing or distributing goods or services in two or more countries. A transnational corporation is an MNC with more than two-thirds of its activities outside its home country. Such companies can locate different activities in parts of the world where they reap the biggest comparative advantage. Thus Rupert Murdoch's News Corporation is controlled through holding companies in the Cayman Islands, a notorious tax haven. The result is that News Corporation pays an average tax rate of 10 per cent.

In another example, the fall in the costs of air transport have led to the centralisation of the world flower industry in the Netherlands. Flowers are flown in from Kenya or India one day, sold at auction and then flown to customers in Europe or the US the next day.

The best-known example of local advantage is low labour costs. This is most obvious in low-wage industries such as textiles, but a high-tech example is that of the Brazilian manufacturer of regional jet airliners, Embraer. Its employment costs in 2002 were $26,000 per employee, as against $63,000 in the regional jet business of its major Canadian competitor, Bombardier (Ghemawat 2003).

Rollinson (2008) suggests a more complex model. The simplest form is the domestic organisation, which supplies only its home market in its country of origin. Next in complexity is the international organisation, which serves home and overseas markets but has a centralised headquarters in its country of origin. The multinational organisation produces goods or services in relatively autonomous overseas subsidiaries. The global organisation operates worldwide through independent overseas divisions, which are co-ordinated rather than controlled by a central headquarters. Finally, there is the transnational organisation, first described by Bartlett and Ghoshal (1991). The transnational corporation (TNC) operates simultaneously as an international, multinational and global organisation. Specialised units could be located anywhere in the world and are managed as a seamless network by footloose managers with a global mindset.

In 2001, there were estimated to be 63,000 TNCs, which had 800,000 foreign affiliates and which controlled two-thirds of world trade. Of the top 100 non-financial TNCs, 91 were based in the US, the EU or Japan (UNCTAD 2001). Of the companies in the 2006 Fortune Global 500 (measured by turnover), 172 were based in the EU, 114 in the US, 70 in Japan and 20 in China (Fortune 2006).

Interbrand identifies its Best Global Brands each year. To qualify as a global brand, the brand must achieve more than a third of its sales outside its home country (which excludes Walmart, most of whose sales are in the US). Interbrand's valuation is based on expected future earnings, rather than on current turnover or profit (Interbrand 2006). It is interesting that only one company (Toyota) appears in the top ten of both the Fortune and Interbrand lists. While there are five oil companies in the Fortune top ten, there are none in Interbrand's.

Not all industries can be globalised. Clark (2005, p413) distinguishes four patterns of industry internationalisation, based on level of international trade in the industry's products and degree of foreign direct investment (Figure 6.1).

Figure 6.1 Patterns of internationalisation

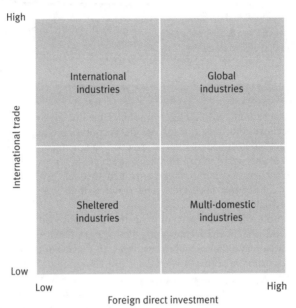

- Sheltered industries supply a domestic market and are not attractive to foreign investment. Typical examples would be hairdressing or railways.
- Multi-domestic industries supply domestic markets, but may do this in a number of countries. Typical examples would be hotels or management consulting.
- International industries supply a world market, but are tied to one country by availability of raw materials (diamond mining or agriculture) or by economies of scale (aerospace).
- Global industries have no national restrictions and can truly be globalised – cars, oil, consumer electronics.

However, even global industries may still be forced to differentiate between national markets. This may be because of:

- laws and regulations – cars must be made either left- or right-hand drive, depending on local regulations
- distribution channels may differ between national markets
- some markets are lead markets – they have a higher level of sophistication and acceptance of innovation
- differences in national culture may affect acceptability of products (Clark 2005, p429).

Perlmutter (1969) identified three major types of multinational companies:

- *Ethnocentric* – where each local subsidiary is expected to conform to the style and culture of the parent company, regardless of local conditions. Managers here are typically expatriates from the home country. This corresponds to Rollinson's international organisation.

- *Polycentric* – where each subsidiary is allowed to manage in its own way and to develop its own culture. For example, IBM Ireland was allowed to recognise unions, although the IBM culture is generally anti-union (Marchington and Wilkinson 2008, p33). Managers in the local subsidiaries are likely to be nationals of that country, with few if any expatriates. This corresponds to Rollinson's multinational and global organisations.

- *Geocentric* – where local subsidiaries focus on worldwide objectives, making a unique contribution based on its local core competencies. Managers would be recruited on a global level, taking the best from anywhere in the world. Pucik (2007) quotes the example of ABB, where Percy Barnevik, the CEO, decided that the company needed about 500 hand-picked global managers – from a workforce of 200,000 – ready to move across countries, functions and businesses. The geocentric organisation corresponds to the transnational corporation.

CASE STUDY 6.6

RETAIL GLOBALISATION IN THAILAND

Retailers in the developed world are increasingly facing saturated markets. Companies such as Tesco and Walmart already dominate their home markets and prospects for further growth are limited. An obvious solution is to expand overseas.

However, retailing is much less globalised than other major industries. Of the world's top 250 retailers in 2006, 104 have no international operations at all. The most globalised retailer, the French supermarket group Carrefour, has stores in 29 countries (*Economist* 2006b). Turn this on its head and Carrefour has no presence in over 80 per cent of the world's countries.

Many retailers have had spectacular failures overseas. Walmart pulled out of Germany in 2006, having previously failed in Indonesia; Marks & Spencer pulled out of continental Europe in 2001; while IKEA abandoned Japan as early as the 1980s (Emmott et al 2002; *Economist* 2006b).

So what is the secret of success as a global retailer? The contrasting experiences of Tesco and Boots in Thailand provide some clues.

To most people in the West, Thailand is little more than an exotic holiday location, but it is actually a significant player on the world stage and is one of the 20 biggest world economies. Its population is 64 million and its GDP per head (on a purchasing power parity (PPP) basis) is slightly higher than that of Brazil or Turkey. The Thai economy on a PPP basis is one-third the size of the UK's.

In the 1980s and 1990s, it was one of the Asian tiger economies which enjoyed the kind of explosive growth experienced by China today. It received a severe setback in the late 1990s (the Asian financial crisis started in Thailand in 1997), but by 2000 it was back on the growth path and in 2003 its growth rate of GDP was 6.9 per cent. Literacy is high at well over 90 per cent, which encourages the rapid dissemination of new ideas, inflation and unemployment are low, and its capital, Bangkok, is one of the major world conurbations (CIA 2007).

The Asian financial crisis provided an ideal opportunity for Western retailers to enter Thailand. During the crisis, the Thai baht collapsed in value by 25 per cent against the dollar, making inward investment much cheaper. Among those retailers taking advantage of the opportunity were Boots and Tesco.

Boots opened its first store in Thailand in 1997, and by 2001 operated 67 stores throughout the country. The stores were very similar to those operated in the UK. Boots own brands represented 60 per cent of the product range, while only 18 per cent, or about 400 lines, were produced in Thailand (Jitpleecheep 2002a). As most lines were imported, they were too expensive for the price-conscious Thais, even though the typical Boots Thai customer was affluent by Thai standards, with average earnings of 17,000 baht a month (about £280).

The stand-alone Boots operation was not a success. Between 1997 and 2001, it had accumulated losses of 700 million baht (about £11 million). In 2001 alone, it lost 388 million baht (about £6 million) on turnover of 1.5 billion baht (about £25 million) (Jitpleecheep 2002b).

Boots ceased new store openings in 2001 and decided instead to sell through dedicated sections in supermarkets. Its chosen partner was the Tops supermarket chain, operated by CRC Ahold, the Thai arm of the Dutch retailer Royal Ahold. For Boots this lowered risk, while it gave Ahold the opportunity to attract more up-market customers (Jitpleecheep 2001). Meanwhile, Boots closed 12 non-performing stores in 2002 (Jitpleecheep 2002a). In 2002, Boots had 20 outlets in Tops stores, with a turnover of around 100 million baht (about £1.6 million) (Jitpleecheep 2002c)

Tesco took a different route. It entered Thailand in 1998 by purchasing the Thai retailer Lotus. Expansion has been rapid. In February 2007, Tesco Lotus had 366 stores open – 57 hypermarkets, 17 Value stores, 23 Talad Lotus stores and 269 Express stores. By 2008, it expected to have up to 500 Express stores opened (Tesco Lotus 2007).

By 2006, Thailand had the third highest sales in the Tesco group (after the UK and South Korea), at just under £1 billion a year (Fletcher 2006). Group sales in Asia grew by over 60 per cent in 2006 (Datamonitor 2006). Information on profits from the Thai operation is not available, but as Tesco Lotus paid over 1 billion baht (about £16 million) in corporation tax in 2006, profits must be substantial.

Why has Tesco done so well in Thailand and Boots so badly? Boots seemed to have cloned a UK operation in Thailand, with little consideration for local conditions or sensibilities. Its style of operation seems to have been aimed at expatriates, tourists and wealthy cosmopolitan Thais. This could have led to a profitable niche operation, but Boots' prices were too high for a mass Thai market.

The company predominantly imported Boots own brand products from the UK. While these had a high reputation for quality in the UK, they were virtually unknown in Thailand. The joint venture with CRC Ahold promised access to a bigger market with lower risk, but still did not tap local Thai expertise. In short, the Boots operation was a typical example of Western-centric globalisation.

The Tesco expansion was different in almost every way. It is a classic example of glocalisation (Swyngedouw 2004). Throughout the process, Tesco was extremely sensitive to Thai conditions. Rather than starting with a greenfield operation like Boots, it took over Lotus, but was careful to retain the Lotus brand name and logo, which were well known in Thailand. It tailored its scale of operations by opening hypermarkets, supermarkets (Value stores) or convenience stores (Express stores) as appropriate to local demand. It even supported small 'Mom and Pop' competitors by selling them 'Club Packs' for resale (Tesco Lotus 2007).

Whereas Boots imported 82 per cent of its products, Tesco sourced 97 per cent in Thailand, and it also facilitated the export of Thai products worth over £100 million a year to Tesco UK. The company also set up a charitable foundation, Tesco for Thais, which although small scale, was valuable in securing goodwill in Thailand.

Both Boots and Tesco gained from the open market policies espoused by the Thai Prime Minister Thaksin Shinawatra between 2001 and 2006. However, there are always losers in globalisation, and Thailand has been no exception. Between 1996 and 2001, the share of retail food sales in Thailand made through traditional markets fell from 75 per cent to 50 per cent, which has severely damaged the earnings of thousands of Thai market traders.

Before he was overthrown by a military coup late in 2006, Thaksin was seriously considering placing curbs on foreign-owned retailers and giving greater support to small shopkeepers. These policies have been taken further by the military government, and this may clip even Tesco's wings in the future (*Economist* 2007a).

This case study illustrates Perlmutter's model of globalisation. Boots' approach was an ethnocentric one, giving very little autonomy to the Thai operation, while Tesco's was polycentric, with the whole operation driven by Thais. Ironically, after getting it right in Thailand, Tesco then got in wrong in the US. Its Fresh and Easy operation in California was ethnocentric, driven from the UK, and ignored a lot of the market research that the company had done on the ground. It was abandoned in 2012, at a loss of £1.5 billion (Butler 2012).

THE GLOBALISATION DEBATE

Aisbett (2003) identifies four main areas of concern over globalisation:

1   An objection not to globalisation in principle, but to the way in which it is skewed in favour of developed countries. This is exemplified by the protectionist agricultural policies of the US and the EU.

2   Loss of sovereignty, to transnational corporations and to institutions such as the IMF and the WTO.

3   Neo-liberal or 'Washington Consensus' policies, as imposed by the IMF on debtor countries – privatisation, welfare cutbacks, etc.

4   The rise of big corporations. Of the 100 biggest economic units in the world, 52 are corporations. They can expand or contract their activities in particular countries in order to maximise their overall profit.

However, Aisbett points out that the debate is no longer between supporters and opponents of globalisation. The anti-capitalist protest movements of the late 1990s have run out of steam and the main arguments are now between enthusiastic and cautious globalisers. Even Oxfam has recognised that globalisation can have some benefits. A similar point is made by Jacobs (2001).

Aisbett identifies areas of agreement between the enthusiastic and cautious globalisers. These include:

● Trade is often a source of economic growth and growth is good for the poor (although the Green Party argues that local production may be more efficient) (Lucas 2001).
● The US and the EU should open their markets to the developing world.
● Safety nets should be provided for the losers from globalisation, and education, health and welfare in developing countries should be safeguarded.

- Income is an inadequate measure of poverty, and social factors should be taken into consideration.
- Excessive corporate power is a problem.
- Political reform is needed in many developing countries.

There are also still important areas of difference, outlined in Table 6.1.

Table 6.1 Alternative views on globalisation

Issue	Enthusiastic view	Cautious view
Attitudes to poverty	Globalisation in all its forms is good for the poor, and reducing poverty is what matters, even at the cost of increased inequality.	Reducing inequality is equally important, and globalisation frequently increases it.
Trade liberalisation	Trade liberalisation is always beneficial.	Totally free trade will often have adverse social or environmental side effects. Decisions should be taken on a case-by-case basis.
Transnational corporations	Their activities should be encouraged as they provide jobs and bring in new technologies.	Big corporations destroy indigenous producers and the net effect may be negative.
Privatisation	Government provision of essential services in developing countries is invariably corrupt and/or inefficient and therefore these services should be privatised.	Only government provision of essential services can ensure that they are available to the poor.
Competitiveness	Opening developing economies to foreign trade and investment improves competitiveness by destroying local monopolies.	Opening developing economies to foreign trade destroys indigenous producers whether or not they were monopolies and further increases the power of transnational corporations.

GLOBALISATION, GROWTH AND POVERTY

The evidence appears to be indisputable that globalisation has led to higher growth in most of the developing world, particularly in China and East Asia. The Asian Tigers, particularly South Korea and Thailand, were early to liberalise their trade and have experienced rapid growth. So has China following its market reforms in the 1980s, and India, where Manmohan Singh, then finance minister, now prime minister, reduced protectionism.

Wolf (2005, p142) quotes World Bank figures from 2002 which suggest that the gains from globalisation have been widespread. In the 1980s less globalised countries had higher GDP per head than more globalised ones, while by 1997 the situation was reversed. Annual growth rates per head in the more globalised countries were 3.1 per cent, in the less globalised ones only 0.5 per cent. Further evidence came from growth of a global middle class (defined as an annual income of between $3,650 and $14,600 a year, at purchasing power parity and 1993 prices). In 1960, 64 per cent of the global middle class lived in high-income Western countries and only 6 per cent in Asia, the Middle East and North Africa. By 2000, only 17 per cent lived in developed countries and 51 per cent in Asia, the Middle East and North Africa (Wolf 2005, p170).

There is some evidence that multinationals in developing countries pay higher wages than local manufacturing employers, although the evidence is rather old, dating from 1994 (Emmott et al 2002). Multinationals in low-income countries paid an average wage of $3,400, while local employers paid $1,700. The ratio of 2:1 between multinational and local wages was higher than that in high-income countries, where the ratio was 1.4:1.

Strong as the evidence seems, there are some caveats. GDP per head is not the same as standard of living, and there were losers as well as winners in the globalising country. Winners tended to work in manufacturing, losers in agriculture and extractive industries (see Case Study 6.3). Workers in developing countries tend to be non-unionised, capital inflows are unstable, multinationals can move out very quickly and the risk of financial crisis increases, as in Thailand in 1997 (*Economist* 2007, p16).

There is also evidence that inequality has increased in globalising countries (Legrain 2003). As Legrain points out, globalisation is no guarantee of economic success. It won't help war-torn countries like Somalia or the Democratic Republic of Congo, it won't cure AIDS (particularly after the collapse of the Doha trade round – see Case Study 6.4), and it won't stop crooked rulers salting money away in Switzerland (Legrain 2003, p52). But while not a sufficient cause for economic growth, it seems to be a necessary one.

MULTINATIONALS AND BRANDS

Are multinationals and their brands too powerful? Foreign-owned multinationals employ one worker in every five in European manufacturing and sell one euro in every four of manufactured goods in Europe (Venables 2005). Aisbett (2003) quoted the claim that 52 of the world's largest economic units are corporations, not states. However, supporters of globalisation such as Legrain dispute this. They point out that this figure compares the turnover of corporations with the GDP of states. This leads to double or triple counting in the case of corporations. The correct comparison is with company value added (after deducting the cost of inputs). On this measure, there are only two corporations in the top 50 (Walmart and Exxon), and 37 in the top 100. The US economy is 200 times bigger than Walmart, Japan 100 times bigger, China 20 times bigger (Legrain 2003, pp139–40).

Corporations are also less powerful than nation-states. They cannot impose taxes or regulations, they cannot go to war, they cannot force people to buy their products and, unlike states, they can go bust.

There are also limits to their mobility, although this tends to benefit their home country rather than the developing world. It is very rare for companies to move their headquarters from one country to another (although Ericsson did it in 1999, when it moved its corporate HQ from Sweden to London to avoid high Swedish taxes) (Legrain 2003, p159). Nokia is happy to stay in very high-cost Finland and Lego in Denmark. On the other hand, the 'branch factory syndrome' seems to apply. When companies downsize, it always seems to be the branch factories rather than those near the headquarters which are closed down first.

Foreign direct investment (which creates multinationals) originates predominantly from developed countries (93 per cent 1998–2000) and also goes to other developed countries (78 per cent). Of the FDI which goes to developing countries, the great bulk goes to China (the 2005 takeover of Rover by China's Nanjing Automotive and the 2007 takeover of Corus by India's Tata Steel are very much the exceptions – for now). Inward investment creates jobs in the host country, but can also force up wages there, which in the long run makes the host less competitive. One country which has avoided this vicious circle is Ireland, which has used the additional wealth brought in by high-tech multinationals to invest in its infrastructure and education, which makes it still attractive even at higher wage levels (Venables 2005).

One clear counterweight to global corporations would be global trade unions. On 1 May 2007, the TGWU and Amicus merged to form the UK's biggest union, Unite, with 2 million members. Its joint general secretaries, Derek Simpson and Tony Woodley, writing in the *Guardian*, said 'the challenges presented by world capitalism... cannot be met by any union that confines its operations within one country alone'. They announced an agreement to seek a merger with the United Steel Workers of the US and Canada to form the first transatlantic union. 'Only a worldwide organising agenda has any long-term hope of levelling the playing field' (Simpson and Woodley 2007).

The high point of globalisation came in the 1990s, in the euphoria which followed the collapse of communism and 'the end of history'. This era of full-blooded, 'red in tooth and claw' globalisation may have already passed. The onward march of e-commerce and the idea that the world had entered a 'new economic paradigm' of endless economic growth was shattered by the dot-com crash in 2000 and the collapse of giant new-economy corporations such as Enron and WorldCom. Just as the economic confidence of the US was shaken, its sense of political and military invulnerability was shattered by the attacks of 11 September 2001.

Coupled with the US military response to 'the war on terror', there is a growing though implicit feeling that the war on terror will be lost unless the West wins the hearts and minds of the Third World. Hence the criticisms from both left and right of the aggressive neo-liberal policies of the IMF and the World Bank, and possibly a more caring approach to debt relief and aid.

At the same time there is a growing realisation that globalisation has not made the nation-state redundant. The role of the nation-state is to provide good governance. In an article previewing his new book, *State Building*, Francis Fukuyama of 'the end of history' quotes from the doyen of free-market economists, Milton Friedman, as saying that his advice to former communist countries 10 years ago had been to concentrate on privatisation. Now he feels that he was wrong. 'It turns out that the rule of law is probably more basic than privatisation' (Fukuyama 2004).

REFLECTIVE ACTIVITY 6.8

Why is Africa poor?

The United Nations Development Programme has two main approaches to the definition of national poverty. One approach calculates a Human Development Index for member states, based on an equation incorporating life expectancy, educational attainment and real income per head. The other categorises countries on the basis of their stage of economic and social development. The poorest of these are labelled as Least Developed Countries (or, popularly, the Fourth World). These countries are characterised by extreme poverty, civil war or ethnic clashes, political corruption, and government based on dictatorship, warlordism or kleptocracy ('rule by thieves'). On both measures, Africa, particularly, sub-Saharan Africa, does extremely badly (UNDP 2006). Of the bottom 30 countries on the Human Development Index, all except Yemen are in Africa. Of the 50 countries defined as least developed, 34 are in Africa.

Question

1   Why do you think that Africa has not shared in the growing prosperity of the rest of the world?

GLOBALISATION AND THE LABOUR MARKET

Does globalisation help or harm workers in developed countries? As always, the evidence is mixed. Legrain (2003) argued that it is very hard to separate out the impact of globalisation from the impact of higher technology. Manufacturing has been declining for many years in all developed countries, while at the same time manufacturing jobs have been outsourced to Third World countries. He suggests that most of the impact comes from technology rather than globalisation. He cites the example of Bethlehem Steel in the US, where the Sparrows Point plant in Maryland produces the same amount of steel as it did in the 1960s, but with 3,500 workers rather than 30,000 (Legrain 2003, p37). As he says, 'producing more with less is what economic growth is all about'.

Legrain makes an attempt to quantify the relative effects of globalisation and technology. Between 1990 and 2000, manufacturing's share of GDP fell by around 6 per cent, while the manufacturing trade deficit worsened by only 0.4 per cent of GDP (Legrain 2003, p40).

The impact on jobs has been disproportionately on unskilled workers. Third World countries have an abundance of unskilled workers, which suggests that it is jobs using unskilled workers which will be offshored from rich countries.

However, more recent work suggests that the impact of globalisation on rich-country workers may be greater than previously realised. Globalisation is becoming more complex. Increasingly parts of production processes are being offshored, rather than the whole process. This is known as 'high resolution globalisation', 'trade in tasks' (*Economist* 2007b) or vertical disintegration (*International Labour Review* 2006). A good example is the Barbie Doll. The raw material (plastic and hair) comes from Taiwan and Japan. Assembly takes place in the Philippines, Indonesia and China. Moulds come from the US, as does the last coat of paint. Marketing and R&D is centred in the US.

The rich world's comparative advantage in high-tech sectors is falling, as education levels in countries such as China and India are rising rapidly. China and India produce as many graduate scientists and engineers as the US, EU and Japan combined (*Economist* 2006a). Increasingly, higher-skilled jobs are being offshored – in software, medical diagnostics, finance and business consulting.

These findings are supported by a CIPD report on *Offshoring and the Role of HR* in January 2006 (CIPD 2006). A total of 589 organisations responded to a survey, covering 2.4 million employees. Of these, 14 per cent had offshored at least one activity in the past five years, 7 per cent are currently considering it and 4 per cent had decided against it. The most popular offshoring locations were India (53 per cent), followed by China (27 per cent) and Poland (18 per cent). A wide range of functions were offshored (Table 6.2).

Table 6.2 Offshored functions

Manufacturing and production	34 per cent of those who have offshored
IT support	24 per cent
IT development	22 per cent
Call centres/customer services	22 per cent
Financial, back office support	19 per cent
Product development	18 per cent
Accounts	16 per cent

Source: CIPD (2006)

Fifteen per cent have brought back activities that were previously outsourced. The most common motives for outsourcing were cost reduction (86 per cent), UK skills shortages (27 per cent), to improve processes (21 per cent), and involvement in a joint venture (21 per cent). The biggest disadvantages were seen as: managerial control is more difficult (48 per cent), associated job losses in the UK (44 per cent), language problems (30 per cent) and risk of disruption to supply (24 per cent).

Most interesting was the type of job lost (Table 6.3).

Table 6.3 Types of job lost to offshoring

Skilled	29 per cent
Semi-skilled	25 per cent
Managerial	19 per cent
Unskilled	15 per cent
Graduate	8 per cent

Source: CIPD (2006)

The report includes a case study of a telecommunications firm, which offshored 500 jobs to Delhi in 2004–05. It decided to employ these staff directly, rather than to outsource the operation, because it was felt that outsourcing might compromise quality of service and managerial control. Activities offshored included transactional processing for all operational areas, including order handling, part of engineering and sales support; processing of company payments and credit control; and IT support and development.

Motives for offshoring were to reduce costs; to take advantage of skilled Indian graduates; to exploit the differences in time zone; and to take advantage of less restrictive Indian employment law.

The company employed 4,100 staff across Europe, including 1,200 in the UK. Of these a total of 400 were made compulsorily redundant, with 100 of these redundancies in the UK (CIPD 2006, pp7–8).

A report by McKinsey in 2003 suggested that, financially, offshoring was a win–win situation. They claimed that every \$1 previously spent in the US and now offshored to India creates a benefit of \$1.47. The lion's share of this – \$1.14 – went to the US in the form of cheaper services and greater export of US goods to India, while 33 cents accrued to India as new wages, extra profit and extra tax revenue (Finch 2003).

However, Simon Evenett, professor of trade and development at St Gallen University in Switzerland, argues that the peak of manufacturing offshoring has passed. One reason for this is the increase in the price of oil in the last ten years or so. With oil at around \$100 a barrel, compared with \$25 in the mid-1990s, there is a strong incentive to shorten supply chains to minimise transport costs (Stewart 2013). Perhaps the trend in the future will be short-distance offshoring – the US to Mexico, or Germany to the Czech Republic.

The threat of globalisation seems to be increasingly to wages, rather than jobs. Real wages in the US, Germany and Japan are all falling. The share of wages in GDP is the lowest for three decades, while profits are at all-time highs. In the US, the share of profits in GDP rose from 7 per cent in 2001 to 13 per cent in 2006 (*Economist* 2006b).

Globalisation has boosted profits in several ways. Firms have reduced their costs by offshoring, while the bargaining power of workers in developed countries has been weakened as firms can always threaten to offshore. The global capital–labour ratio has massively shifted against workers. In the last 20 years, China, India and the former Soviet Union have effectively joined the world market economy, doubling the world supply of workers from 1.5 billion to 3 billion. Economic theory says that this would raise the return to capital and lower that to labour, which is exactly what has happened. At the same time, incomes have become more unequal. The top 1 per cent of workers in the US now receive 16 per cent of GDP, rather than 8 per cent in 1980.

The Case Study 6.7 examines some of the impacts of globalisation on the UK labour market.

CASE STUDY 6.7

THE OUTSOURCING OF CALL CENTRES

The call centre industry in the UK is large, employing 867,000 people, or 3 per cent of the workforce, in 2004 (Shah 2004). It is also a new industry, having grown from almost nothing over the past 15 years. As a result, there has been considerable concern about the steady movement of call centre jobs, particularly in the financial services industry, to India, particularly to Mumbai and Bangalore. Opponents of globalisation see this as an example of the detrimental effect of globalisation on UK employment, while supporters see it as a positive development, lowering costs for UK industry and so increasing national prosperity.

Both are right. The short-term effect is that the UK is losing jobs. Call centres in the UK were frequently set up in areas of high unemployment, and the loss of these jobs is disproportionately felt. On the other hand, if outsourcing increases the profits of UK companies, this should free up resources for future investment. A short-term loss must thus be set against a long-term gain.

The typical Indian call centre goes to great lengths to make their operators acceptable to UK consumers. The call centres operate on UK rather than

Indian time and operators are expected to keep themselves informed about the English weather and the latest plot twists in *EastEnders* (Warren 2007). However, there is some evidence that Indian call centres are less efficient than UK ones. One study claimed that UK operators answered 25 per cent more calls per hour, resolved 17 per cent more calls first time and stayed with their company three times as long, although this is offset by average salaries only 12 per cent of the UK level (Clennell 2004). This would suggest that UK companies which are more concerned with the quality of their customer service than with minimising their short-term costs should think very seriously before they outsource to India.

The long-run future of the call centre industry in the UK must lie with developing a more sophisticated knowledge-based, value-added service. Basic information-giving services can be better performed in India, or over the Internet. Already in 2004, according to the *Economist*, Indian call centre companies were starting to set up in the UK and US (*Economist* 2004).

GLOBALISATION AND THE RECESSION

Did globalisation cause the recession? Almost certainly not on its own, but it could be argued that elements of globalisation contributed to the recession. Probably the most important linkage is the way in which sub-prime loans in the US were securitised and parcelled up into collaterised debt obligations and then sold on as bonds to other financial institutions around the world. As noted in Chapter 4, by 2007 these were part of a syndicated debt iceberg worth $14 trillion, and the securities were so complex that no individual bank could adequately assess the individual risk which it was running – a risk compounded by the reckless way in which the lending agencies had given these bonds an

AAA rating. Only globalisation, and the complex computerised linkages which it had enabled between financial institutions worldwide, made this possible.

More generally, globalisation had encouraged an increasing emphasis throughout the Western world, and particularly in the US and UK, on the importance of finance. This encouraged a 'master of the universe' feeling among the banks, a feeling that they were untouchable and could do no wrong. This made the banks reckless and prepared to bend the rules, as discussed in Chapter 9 in relation to the manipulation of interest rates by Barclays Bank.

Going further back, it could be argued that growing income and wealth inequality in the US and UK, which has been attributed at least in part to globalisation, was itself a contributing factor to the sub-prime mortgage crisis in the US. Many of the so-called 'ninja' borrowers in the sub-prime market ('no income, no job, no assets') were in this position because their wages had been held down by globalisation (see the previous section in this chapter, *Globalisation and the Labour Market*).

More generally, the linkages created by globalisation mean that it is no longer possible for an individual country to insulate itself from the effects of the recession, as the Soviet Union and Nazi Germany could to a large extent in the 1930s. For several years China and India seemed to buck the trend, but eventually by 2012 even China became affected by the slowdown in demand for its exports. This then had a knock-on effect on those countries supplying China with raw materials, such as Brazil, Canada and Australia.

Will the recession slow the process of globalisation? Certainly the depression of the 1930s did slow globalisation. Most countries abandoned free trade, one of the major tenets of globalisation, and introduced protectionism, as well as competitive devaluations. Such an effect is less likely with this recession, as all major trading nations, including China, are members of the World Trade Organization and so tied by its anti-protectionism rules, which can be enforced by the WTO (Lin 2010). However, there are still worrying trends. The US in 2012, for example, claimed that the Chinese telecoms company Huawei was a threat to US security because of its alleged close links with the Chinese Communist Party and military – a claim indignantly denied by Huawei (Cellan-Jones 2012). In addition, some countries are taking action to manage the free movement of capital. Brazil, for example, has used taxes on foreign exchange to stem the appreciation of the real (Stewart 2013).

CASE STUDY 6.8

GLOBALISATION AND TAX AVOIDANCE

One unfortunate consequence of globalisation is that it facilitates tax avoidance (the perfectly legal exploitation of loopholes in the tax system, as distinct from the illegal tax evasion). Globalised companies have considerable freedom to manipulate their accounts in order to declare most of their profits in low-tax countries, thus minimising their tax bills.

This problem was investigated by the UK House of Commons Public Accounts Committee in October 2012. They summoned representatives of three American-owned globalised corporations (Starbucks, the coffee shop firm, Amazon, the online retailer, and Google, the Internet service provider). This case study will concentrate on Starbucks, which has always promoted itself as an ethical company.

The committee found that Starbucks had made a loss for 14 of the 15 years it has been trading in the UK. They found this 'difficult to believe' as the company had a 31 per cent share of the UK market and it had reported to its shareholders that the UK business was successful and making profits. They identified three ways in which profits were manipulated to reduce UK tax:

- Starbucks UK pays a licence fee of 4.7 per cent of turnover (recently reduced from 6 per cent) for intellectual property (use of the trademark, etc) to the European headquarters in the Netherlands. Starbucks admitted that they had a confidential but 'special' tax deal with the Dutch Government.
- The UK buys coffee from the Netherlands, including a mark-up, and the Dutch company then buys it from Switzerland, with a 20 per cent mark-up, increasing profit in the Netherlands and Switzerland, which has a 'very competitive' tax rate.
- There is an inter-company loan between Starbucks US and Starbucks UK, at an interest rate which the committee said was 'set at a higher rate than any similar loan we have seen' (Parliament Publications 2012).

Starbucks responded with a statement from its chairman and CEO, Howard Schultz, on 23 October. He pointed out that Starbucks UK had paid £160 million in National Insurance, VAT and business rate over the last three years. He also said that Starbucks always adheres to local tax rules. In the US, local accounting rules stipulated that taxable income in regional markets be calculated before accounting for the impact of inter-company licence and interest payments.

On this basis, the UK made an accounting profit. In the UK, however, tax law requires that taxable income is calculated after accounting for licence and interest payments. Hence, no taxable profit in the UK, and no tax. Schultz concluded 'we must do our best to strike a balance between profitability and social responsibility, and we will continue to strive to meet our own high ethical standards for how we... serve communities and operate in the countries where we do business' (Starbucks 2012a).

Margaret Hodge, the Labour chairman of the committee, was not impressed. The level of tax taken from multinational firms with large UK operations was 'outrageous and an insult to British businesses and individuals who pay their fair share' (BBC News 2012a).

The committee also pointed out that HM Revenue and Customs calculated the gap between tax actually collected and that which would be collected if all individuals and companies complied with both the letter and the spirit of the tax law. In 2010–11 this was £32.2 billion, barely down since 2004–05 (HMRC 2012). This represents half of the total UK education budget (Ashley 2012).

In response to the committee hearings, which were widely publicised, a boycott of Starbucks was organised through social media (the chief secretary to the Treasury, Danny Alexander, admitted that he was boycotting Starbucks) (Syal and Wintour 2012). This seems to have had an effect, as on 3 December 2012 Starbucks announced that although it planned to continue the licences payments, it would no longer use them to reduce its UK tax liability, and on 6 December announced that for the next two tax years it would pay £10 million a year to HRMC, whether or not it made a profit. This appears to be a reasonable, if not overgenerous, figure. Starbucks' main rival, Costa Coffee, is slightly bigger (40 per cent of the branded coffee shop market, as against Starbucks' 31 per cent) and paid corporation tax of £18 million in 2011–12 (Pratley 2012; Starbucks 2012b).

REFLECTIVE ACTIVITY 6.9

Globalisation and your organisation

What impact, if any, has globalisation had on your own organisation?

MANAGEMENT IN THE G20 – JAPAN, INDIA AND SOUTH AFRICA

This section examines HR issues in three major members of the G20 – Japan, India and South Africa. The Seminar Activity for this chapter examines the biggest and most dynamic of the G20 countries, China.

JAPAN

The best way to understand HR in Japan is through Japanese history. Until the mid-nineteenth century, Japan was a feudal society. Power was exercised through great land-owning families, the *daimyo* (equivalent to the barons in feudal England). They were answerable to (and frequently rebelled against) the hereditary military dictator, the *shogun*, who was himself answerable, at least on paper, to the figurehead emperor, who was seen as divine. Under the *daimyo* were the *samurai*, a military caste comparable to knights in medieval Europe, whose role was to serve their lord for life, sacrificing their own lives if required, and who in return received lifetime support from their lord. The whole system was based on mutual obligation. The duty of the samurai was reinforced by the concepts of *gambara* (will to endure) and *gaman* (stoical acceptance of hardship). Although the *samurai*'s role was originally purely military, by the nineteenth century they also undertook many administrative roles on behalf of their lord. The rest of the population, the merchants and peasants, were of little account, and the *samurai* had the right to kill a peasant without legal redress.

The feudal system was formally abolished after the Meiji Restoration in the 1860s, when the emperor seized back power from the *shogun* and embarked on a breakneck programme of modernisation, but the *samurai* system evolved seamlessly into the new Japan. Industrialisation was organised around huge industrial conglomerates, the *zaibatsu*, who in effect replaced the *daimyo*, while the samurai evolved into industrial managers. The *zaibatsu* were abolished by the Americans after 1945, but speedily re-emerged as *keiretsu*, who still dominate much of the Japanese economy – companies such as Mitsui and Mitsubishi.

Hangovers from the feudal system include:

- Lifetime employment – *nenkoseido*. Male employees and managers in large corporations, particularly the *keiretsu*, stay with the same company for life, with little recruitment above entry level and a promotion system based on seniority. Managers are predominantly generalists, who may well work in a number of specialisms during their career. There is little sense of a distinct HR progression.
- Loyalty to the company is paramount and there is almost total identification of the employee with the company. This extends to industrial relations, where unions are organised on an enterprise basis, with much movement of executives between the company and the union.
- The culture of organisations is based on the concept of *wa* (harmony). Conflict is to be avoided wherever possible. This extends to decision-making within the organisation. New proposals are circulated throughout the organisation on formal cards (*ringi*) and each department adds its comments to the *ringi*. The aim is to reach mutual

understanding (*nemawashi*). Decision-making is thus slow, but commitment to a decision, once taken, is strong.

- *Gambara* and *gamban* are still expected. Japanese managers work extremely long hours and a recognised illness in Japan is *karoshi* (death through overwork).
- There is an emphasis on perfection (reflecting Japanese institutions such as the tea ceremony and calligraphy), hence the Japanese obsession with quality.
- Those outside the *nenkoseido* system – workers in small companies, contract workers, women – have fewer rights and much inferior employment conditions.

The Japanese system has many strengths but also some weaknesses. Conformity is all and mavericks are not encouraged, as they threaten *wai*. A Japanese proverb says the protruding nail should be hammered down. It is also important to remember that the *nenkoseido* system only ever applied to a minority of workers. Even within the *keiretsu*, lifetime employment only applied to 'salarymen'.

The system has also come under increasing pressure since the onset of the long recession in 1990. For the first time, large companies such as Sony and Nissan have made large-scale redundancies among core workers, not just contract workers, and the *ringi* decision-making system has largely been abandoned as too slow. However, the underlying commitment to *wa* remains (Hales 2001).

INDIA

Three major influences have shaped the Indian approach to management – the legacy of the British, the legacy of Gandhi and the legacy of Hindu Vedic philosophy.

- The British left a tradition of bureaucracy (the 'permit raj'), which still permeates much of Indian management today.
- Gandhi left a preference for small-scale, village-based industry (symbolised by the spinning wheel), heavily protected by import tariffs and regulation. This is still seen as an ideal by many Indians, but in practice has been swept away by the economic reforms started by Manmohan Singh (see the Seminar Activity in Chapter 4).
- From the Hindu Vedic scriptures comes the concept of cosmic order, supported by common vision, universal brotherhood and equitable prosperity for all (Sharma and Talwar 2004). Business excellence can only be achieved through prosperity for all or by taking care of all stakeholders. The ultimate good is the good of society, not personal wealth or self-esteem. As one of the Vedic hymns puts it, 'One should sacrifice the individual for the sake of family interest, family for the sake of village, village for the sake of nation, and abandon everything for defending higher values of life' (Sharma and Talwar 2004). Modern Indian management gurus such as C. K. Prahalad and Rakesh Khurana stress capitalism's ethical and societal obligations (Crainer and Dearlove 2005).

The Vedic principles are clearly displayed in the philosophy of the leading Indian conglomerate Tata (although the Tata family are actually Parsees, not Hindus). The founder of the Tata group, Jamsetji Tata, said in 1868, 'in a free enterprise, the community is not just another stakeholder in business, but is in fact the very purpose of its existence' (Branzei and Nadkarni 2008).

SOUTH AFRICA

The African concept of *ubuntu* has striking similarities with the Japanese concept of *wa*. *Ubuntu* can be defined as humaneness – a spirit of caring and community, harmony and hospitality, respect and responsiveness (Mangaliso 2001).

Ubuntu stresses the collective – the family, the clan, the community – an exact parallel with the Indian Vedic approach. Kinship and teamwork are key to the concept. As in

China, age is equated with wisdom. *Ubuntu* permeates decision-making in South Africa. Just as with *nemawashi* in Japan, decision-making is a slow process, considering all points of view, and the aim is to reach consensus.

One practical application of *ubuntu* comes in reactions to recession. The *ubuntu* approach will be to share the burden in a fair way – leading to pay cuts across the board rather than lay-offs.

What do those explorations of management and HR practices in the non-Western world tell us? What is striking is the similarity of approach across Japan, India and South Africa. Each culture stresses harmony, consensus and community – a very different approach from the self-centred and profit-oriented approach of the West. There are clear parallels with the best practice of high-performance HRM (Marchington and Wilkinson 2008).

CASE STUDY 6.9

GLOBAL OR LOCAL HR?

In the September 2012 issue of *People Management*, Peter Reilly and Tony Williams examined the pros and cons of the 'one company' approach to HR in a globalised company (Reilly and Williams 2012).

They identify a number of advantages of the 'one company' centralised approach. These include:

- promotion of common values
- consistent treatment of staff
- export of good practice (including ethical issues such as child labour and regulation issues such as adherence to the requirements of the Sarbanes-Oxley Act)
- greater operational and cost control.

However, there are also downsides:

- stifling of innovation
- the centre gets out of touch
- ill-conceived policies are ignored or subverted and HR tends to get the blame – one example they quote is of a US–Sri Lankan joint venture where no employees were allowed to ride a motorcycle on company business as insurance was too expensive. This completely ignored the fact that many Sri Lankans can afford a motorbike, but very few can afford a car

- organisations see the value of diversity at home, but often ignore it overseas.

Their conclusion is that a compromise is usually best – the 'connected company' approach. This should be based on cost–benefit analysis. Where the costs of a one-company approach are high, but the benefits low, for example with local resourcing and employee relations, the local units should be given autonomy, but where the benefits outweigh the costs, for example with the HR information system, systems should be centralised. In the connected company, 'the goal of integration is retained... but within a model of devolved accountability to operating units to share/learn/reuse the common offerings in the light of their own particular needs' (Reilly and Williams 2012, p31). In addition, HR should always take into account cultural issues. As we saw in the previous section, the Eastern approach to business is based on consensus. Any attempt to impose Anglo-Saxon centralised command and control HR is unlikely to be successful (see also Reflective Activity 6.10).

REFLECTIVE ACTIVITY 6.10

Jaguar-Land Rover – a cultural football

Few companies have been through as many different international owners as Jaguar-Land Rover. Both Jaguar and Land Rover became part of British Leyland (BL) in 1968. In 1975 BL was nationalised and in 1988 it was sold to British Aerospace (BAe). In practice Jaguar and Land Rover, along with the rest of the group, was managed by Honda under a strategic alliance with BAe. In 1994, the whole group was sold to BMW, which itself sold out to Ford in 2000. Finally, in 2008, Ford sold Jaguar and Land Rover to Tata. Land Rover has thus successively been under British (both private and public), Japanese, German, American and Indian management.

The Dutch guru Geert Hofstede has identified what he calls his cultural dimensions, which he says accurately describe national characters. His dimensions are:

● *Power distance (PD)* – the extent to which societies accept that power is and should be distributed unequally. Organisationally, high power distance will lead to hierarchical organisations with large wage differentials.
● *Individualism (IDV)* – the degree to which individuals are integrated into groups. Collectivist societies with a low individualism score will have a high level of employment security and commitment to staff.
● *Masculinity/femininity (M/F)* – masculine societies are assertive and competitive, with high levels of organisational conflict.
● *Uncertainty avoidance (UA)* – the degree to which people feel comfortable in ambiguous situations. Low uncertainty avoidance is reflected in informal, unstructured organisations.
● *Long-term orientation (LTO)* – in organisations this will be reflected in short-term profit maximisation versus long-term growth.

Table 6.4 summarises those of Hofstede's findings which are relevant to Jaguar-Land Rover.

Table 6.4 Hofstede's cultural dimensions relevant to Jaguar-Land Rover

Country	PD	IDV	M/F	UA	LTO
UK	Low	High	Medium	Low	Low
Japan	Medium	Low	High	High	High
Germany	Low	Medium	Medium	Medium	Low
US	Low	High	Medium	Low	Low
India	High	Medium	Medium	Low	Medium

Source: Hofstede (2009)

To some extent, Table 6.4 is reflected in attitudes to quality at Jaguar-Land Rover. Under British management, quality was a low priority – most of the time the group was struggling for survival. Honda brought in a high priority for quality, with the emphasis placed on the 'soft' aspects – total quality management, *kaizen* (continuous improvement), quality circles, just in time – and a realisation that the pay-off from quality would be long term. BMW was also concerned with quality, with a shorter-term orientation and a more top–down approach, while Ford concentrated on 'hard' aspects of quality, such as Six Sigma. It is yet to be seen what Tata's approach will be, but evidence on Tata's management style suggests a high commitment to quality (see section on *India* above).

It is important to bear in mind that Hofstede's approach has been heavily criticised. One key criticism is that his basic research is very old, carried out between 1967 and 1973, and originally based solely on (mainly male) employees of IBM.

What other criticisms can you make of Hofstede's approach, (a) in general and (b) in relation to Jaguar-Land Rover? (You will find Marchington and Wilkinson (2008, pp29–31) useful.

SUMMARY

Both Europeanisation and globalisation are intensifying, and their impact on the UK's economy, society and organisations is increasing. This will affect all of us, as consumers, citizens, workers and professionals.

KEY LEARNING POINTS

- The European Union's key aims have always been to maintain peace in Europe (particularly between France and Germany) and to enhance prosperity.
- Although there is general agreement on these overriding aims, there are considerable differences of opinion about the future direction of the EU, epitomised by the single market, federalist and integrationist perspectives.
- The Commission is the executive of the EU, initiating and implementing policy; the Council of Ministers is the political decision-making body; the Parliament is mainly consultative; the European Court of Justice rules on the legal interpretation of the EU treaties and legislation.
- The EU expanded from 15 to 25 members in 2004, with the accession of mainly ex-communist countries from central Europe, and to 27 in 2007, with the accession of Bulgaria and Romania. This has necessitated the drafting of a new constitution, published in 2004, which was rejected by referenda in France and the Netherlands in 2005.
- The expansion in 2004 led to very large but initially unexpected immigration from the new members, particularly from Poland.
- The eurozone crisis is an almost certainly inevitable consequence of economic disparities between eurozone members.
- Since the mid-1940s, the world economic system has been regulated by three major international institutions: the IMF, the World Bank and GATT (now the World Trade Organization). All have been criticised by the left as imposing capitalist norms on the developing world.
- Multinational corporations tend to have polycentric employment patterns, while transnational corporations have geocentric employment patterns.
- Globalisation has been characterised as having three main elements: the expansion of markets, the transformation of politics and the emergence of new social and political movements.
- The theory of comparative advantage and international specialisation underpins the concept of globalisation. Globalisation has also become more feasible with modern developments in communications, particularly air transport and the Internet.
- Aisbett (2003) identified four main areas of concern over globalisation: an objection not to globalisation in principle but to the way in which it is skewed in favour of developed countries; loss of sovereignty to transnational corporations and to institutions such as the IMF and the WTO; neo-liberal or 'Washington Consensus' policies; and the rise of big corporations.
- Globalisation has almost certainly raised GDP in developing countries, while in developed countries it has held down inflation, but also real wages.
- Offshoring of jobs to developing countries increasingly affects skilled and professional jobs as well as the traditional call centre jobs.
- Globalisation may have contributed to the severity of the world recession from 2008 onwards.
- The HR systems in Japan, China, India and South Africa share a desire for harmony and a regard for stakeholders.

QUESTIONS

1   What are the key elements of the single market, federalist and integrationist approaches to the EU?

2   What are the main roles of the European Parliament?

3   What are the three criteria for accession to the EU?

4   Why was there such a high level of immigration from Poland to the UK after 2004?

5   What are the main roles of the IMF, the World Bank and the WTO?

6   What are the major differences between multinational and transnational corporations?

7   What do you understand by ethnocentric, polycentric and geocentric patterns of employment?

8   What were the main reasons for the collapse of the Doha Round?

9   Do you agree that transnational corporations have too much power?

10   In what ways does globalisation (a) help and (b) damage the Third World?

11   What do you understand by the expressions *wai* and *ubuntu*?

EXPLORE FURTHER

FURTHER READING

Books on the EU tend to be dry and fact-ridden, but two which are relatively readable are Neill Nugent (2006) *The Government and Politics of the European Union*, 6th edition, and Michelle Cini (ed.) (2007) *European Union Politics*.

Micklethwait and Wooldridge's *A Future Perfect: The challenge and hidden promise of globalization* (2000) is an easily readable (but positive) introduction to globalisation. More recent pro-globalisation books are Martin Wolf's *Why Globalization Works* (2005) and Philippe Legrain's *Open World: The truth about globalisation* (2003). Joseph Stiglitz's *Globalization and Its Discontents* (2003) is fiercely critical of the role of the IMF. In 'Is continued globalization of the world economy inevitable?' *The International Economy*, Summer 2004, Vol 18, No 3, 13 experts put forward their views on the future of globalisation.

For both the EU and globalisation, the way to keep up to date is read good-quality newspapers regularly. The same general advice applies as to Chapter 2 – make sure you get a balance of left- and right-wing views.

USEFUL WEBSITES

The BBC news website (www.bbc.co.uk) often has useful background information. For a generally anti-globalisation perspective, check out websites such as Oxfam (www.oxfam.org.uk) or ActionAid (www.actionaid.org.uk). The website of the thinktank Civitas (www.civitas.org.uk) has a useful series of factsheets on EU issues.

AUDIO AND VIDEO MATERIAL

The CIPD has two useful podcasts on globalisation – *Globalisation and HR* (podcast 13, November 2007), and *The Future of Global HR* (podcast 20, June 2008). Two videos from Oxford Martin (part of Oxford University) are valuable. One, by Professor Ian Goldin, *Globalisation for Development*, November 2012 (www.oxfordmartin.ox.ac.uk/videos/view/201), is a positive though critical view of globalisation, the other, by Pascal Lamy of the WTO, *Is Doha Dead?*, September 2012, is a short discussion of the future of the Doha Round (www.oxfordmartin.ox.ac.uk/videos/view/201). Finally, a *Wall Street Journal* video, *Europe at the Brink*, December 2011, gives an American perspective on the eurozone crisis (live.wsj.com/video/europe-at-the-brink---a-wsj-documentary).

SEMINAR ACTIVITY

HR IN CHINA

Management in China has been affected by two major factors – the influence of Confucianism and the influence of the Communist revolution.

Confucianism stresses harmony, respect, discipline and technical competence (Jacques 2009). This is reflected in a great respect for authority, particularly authority based on seniority and/or age. Chinese organisations are highly hierarchical, with considerable distance between managers and workers (no open-plan offices) and a high degree of formality (no first names, managers addressed by their name and job title – Engineer Wu, Accountant Liu, and so on) (Gamble 2003).

Chinese desire for harmony is very similar to the Japanese concept of *wai*, although the latter is derived from Buddhism rather than from Confucianism. A desire for harmony is also derived from the Daoist religion, widespread at the village level in China. The concept of yin and yang – balanced opposites – is a Daoist concept.

Also important is the concept of face. Managers will see any personal reprimand or expression of disapproval as a loss of face and a serious setback to their self-esteem, while a Western manager will treat a rebuke as just one of those things, quickly forgotten.

Shame is commonly used as a disciplinary device in Chinese companies – withholding favour, leading the subordinate to feel shame and lose face.

After the revolution, the Communist Party introduced the concept of the iron rice bowl (*tie fan wan*), whereby state-owned enterprises (SOEs), often owned by local authorities or the People's Liberation Army rather than directly by the state, were the mechanism through which welfare was delivered in China. They provided lifetime employment, housing, schooling, medical treatment and pensions, and literally protected their workers from cradle to grave. Since the reforms introduced by Deng Xiaoping 30 years ago, the iron rice bowl has slowly rusted away. Many SOEs have gone bust, while others have evolved into joint ventures with foreign companies or Chinese private enterprise companies like Galanz. The Chinese welfare state has virtually vanished and is now having to be slowly and expensively reintroduced. Urban workers with residence rights in cities now have access to basic state healthcare and pensions, but farmers and migrant workers do not.

Workers from the old SOEs have found it difficult to adjust to a more dynamic work environment, but there is an endless supply of new, young, usually female, workers from the provinces who have no preconceptions about work but who have been brought up to respect authority and to conform.

Another crucial factor in the development of attitudes in contemporary China is the Cultural Revolution, which raged throughout China from the mid-1960s to the accession of Deng Xiaoping as supreme leader in 1979.

The Cultural Revolution was a deliberate attempt by Mao Zedong to overthrow Confucian ideas of respect for authority. All sources of authority were attacked, leading to chaos throughout China. Those seen as opposed to permanent revolution were attacked verbally, and ritually humiliated, and frequently physically attacked as well. Deng Xiaoping was beaten up and exiled to run a small factory in the provinces, and his son was crippled for life. The Chinese people and their leaders now regard the Cultural Revolution period with horror, reinforcing the drive for stability and harmony. The Chinese leadership was also given a severe fright by the Tiananmen uprising in 1989, when China came within a whisker of suffering the same fate as the Communist regimes in Europe. The reaction of the leadership was to crack down on human rights, but at the same time to press ahead with economic reforms designed to increase the material prosperity of China and to be very flexible on employment rights.

When the author was in China in October 2012, he found people surprisingly prepared to talk about what they perceived as the shortcomings of the country. These included the ending of the iron rice bowl, the growing inequality in China, the rocketing cost of housing in the big cities and, above all, the endemic corruption. The Chinese Government is tacking all of these. Attempts to improve the welfare system were noted above, inequality is being tackled through a sharply progressive income tax system and by a rising minimum wage (noted below), the state is building 10 million low-cost housing units a year and strenuous efforts are being made to tackle corruption, with penalties including execution. However, as always in China, the good intentions of the central government are often thwarted by resistance from grass-roots officials (Hessler 2010).

All enterprises employing more than 25 workers in China are required to have a trade union committee, with local unions affiliated to the All China Federation of Trade Unions, with 170 million members, which reports to the Chinese Communist Party. The trade union leader in an organisation is usually the HR manager. The Chinese constitution does not guarantee a right to strike, but strikes are not prohibited and are common, especially in southern China. The 2007 Labour Contract Law requires employers to consult trade unions in the case of lay-offs and provides that workers who have served two consecutive fixed-term contracts of employment to move to an 'open-ended contract' with greater job security. China has a minimum wage, which increases by about 20 per cent a year. The Communist Party is happy to encourage higher wages, as it sees this as increasing domestic demand and also as promoting harmony. The trade union system also allows the party to remain in touch with grass-roots feelings (Emmott 2011).

The Chinese education system and the one-child policy have both had an impact on management in Chinese companies. Traditionally, Chinese education has been rigid and formalistic. Memory and rote learning has been encouraged and creativity discouraged. Anyone over about 30 was educated in this kind of system and these people form the middle ranks of Chinese companies. However, the Chinese Government has recognised that the economy needs to be more innovative and not just copy the West. The result is that creativity is now much more encouraged, at least in secondary and tertiary education.

There is also an official realisation of the importance of English, which is now the compulsory second language throughout the Chinese education system. Junior managers in their twenties have adequate English and are more flexible than their superiors. The one-child policy has ensured that junior managers are more confident and less respectful of authority than their seniors. As only children, they have been brought up as 'little emperors', used to getting their own way (Connor 2013). They want to be trusted to take decisions and they want a culture of honesty and openness (Connor 2010; Rush 2004; Meyer and Shen 2010).

There is a great shortage of good young managers in China and a ferocious war for talent. One company hired 50 graduates and after a year had held on to only one (Connor 2011). This has an impact on management development. In the West, if a firm doesn't develop its managers, they leave. In China, if it does develop its managers, they leave. It is significant that in China, most MBA students are top managers, rather than junior or middle managers.

The best HR leaders in China are developing the concept of the 'open family', which combines the values of openness (demanded by young managers) and family – the Confucian values of loyalty and service to the community (Connor 2010).

One factor unique to China (and to the overseas Chinese) is *guanxi*, or connections. This is a system of mutual obligation, whereby a favour made must be returned. This can override loyalty to one's employer and is second only in importance to loyalty to one's family. *Guanxi* can be used by management – doing favours for one's employees will create a reciprocal obligation – but on the other hand, it can be a danger to organisations. Vanhonacker quotes the example of a Chinese sales rep for a pharmaceutical company who sells drugs on the side from local companies that compete with his foreign employer, but with which he has a *guanxi* obligation. Selling competitors' products is a way to pay back favours, fortify *guanxi* and make money (Vanhonacker 2004).

The CIPD's Next Generation HR Asia project (Connor 2010, 2011) identified characteristics and strengths of 'next generation' HR leaders in China:

- a sense of purpose, which combines a set of values and a vision for the future
- humble authority, a recognition that they can best influence the business through others
- insight into the needs of the organisation, which extends beyond HR – good Chinese HR leaders are always business partners
- risk-taking – like everyone else in China, HR leaders are cautious but at the same time prepared to take risks
- fast implementation cycles – China is moving at a breakneck pace, and speed of implementation is often more important than excellence.

Question

1   What can the UK in general, and HR in the UK in particular, learn from China?

REFERENCES

ActionAid. (2006) *Confronting the contradictions: time for action on education.* London: ActionAid.

Aisbett, E. (2003) *Globalization, poverty and inequality: are the criticisms vague, vested or valid?* NBER Pre-conference on Globalization, Poverty and Inequality. October.

Akcapar, B. and Chaibi, D. (2006) Turkey EU accession: the long road from Ankara to Brussels. *Yale Journal of International Affairs.* Winter–Spring.

Ashley, J. (2012) Firms must pay their fair share of tax – this is war. *Guardian.* 3 December.

Barrell, R., Fitzgerald, J. and Riley, R. (2007) *EU enlargement and migration: assessing the macroeconomic impacts.* London: National Institute for Economic and Social Research.

Bartlett, C. and Ghoshal, S. (1991) *Managing across borders.* Boston, MA: Harvard Business School Press.

BBC News. (nd) Born abroad, immigration map of the UK. Available at: www.bbc.co.uk/news [Accessed 15 May 2013].

BBC News. (2005a) Available at: www.bbc.co.uk/news [Accessed 15 May 2013].

BBC News. (2005b) Q&A: Common Agricultural Policy. 2 February. Available at: www.bbc.co.uk/news [Accessed 15 May 2013].

BBC News. (2007) At-a-glance: EU treaty proposals. 23 June. Available at: www.bbc.co.uk/news [Accessed 15 May 2013].

BBC News. (2012) At-a-glance: census 2011 findings. 11 December. Available at: www.bbc.c.uk/news/uk-20677321 [Accessed 28 December 2012].

BBC News. (2012a) Starbucks 'planning changes to tax policy'. 3 December. Available at: www.bbc.co.uk/news/business-2058098 [Accessed 3 December 2012].

BBC News. (2012b) What could happen next if Greece leaves the eurozone? 18 June. Available at: www.bbc.co.uk/news/business-18074674 [Accessed 28 November 2012].

BBC News. (2012c) Eurozone crisis explained. 19 June. Available at: www.bbc.co.uk/news/business-16290598 [Accessed 28 November 2012].

BBC News. (2012d) Who's afraid of the euro crisis? 23 August. Available at: www.bbc.co.uk/news/business-18284747 [Accessed 28 November 2012].

BBC News. (2012e) EU summit: all but two leaders sign fiscal treaty. 2 March. Available at: www.bbc.co.uk/news/business-17230760 [Accessed 28 November 2012].

BBC News. (2012f) Q&A: EU fiscal treaty to control eurozone budgets. 2 March. Available at: www.bbc.co.uk/news/business-16057252 [Accessed 28 November 2012].

Boone, P. (2005) Effective intervention: making aid work. *CentrePiece.* Winter.

Branzei, O. and Nadkarni, A. (2008) The Tata way: evolving and executing sustainable business strategies. *Ivey Business Journal.* March–April.

Brockett, J. (2009) Working time rules are harming patients, say surgeons. *People Management*. 12 October.

Butler, S. (2012) Fresh, but not so easy. *Observer*. 9 December.

Cellan-Jones, R. (2012) Huawei hits back over US 'security threat' claim. BBC News. 4 December. Available at: www.bbc.co.uk/news/technology-2059477 [Accessed 6 December 2012].

Church, C. and Phinnemore, D. (2006) The rise and fall of the constitutional treaty. In M. Cini (ed.) *European Union politics*. 2nd edition. Oxford: Oxford University Press.

CIA. (2007) CIA World Factbook. Online version available at: www.cia.gov/library/publications/the-world-factbook/index.html [Accessed 18 April 2007].

CIPD. (2006) *Offshoring and the role of HR*. Survey report. London: Chartered Institute of Personnel and Development.

CIPD. (2009) *EU employment policy*. Worksheet. London: Chartered Institute of Personnel and Development.

CIPD. (2011) *Employment law: EU influence*. Factsheet. September. London: Chartered Institute of Personnel and Development.

Civitas. (2010) EU facts: the EU 2020 strategy. Available at: www.civitas.org.uk/eufacts/FSECON/EC12.htm [Accessed 28 December 2012].

Clark, R. (2005) *Contemporary strategy analysis*. 5th edition. Oxford: Blackwell.

Clarke, S. and Daley, C. (2010) The eurozone crisis. Civitas. Available at: www.civitas.org.uk/eufacts/ [Accessed 1 December 2012].

Clennell, A. (2004). Call centre switches jobs back from India to Britain. *Independent*. 23 January.

Cohen, R. and Kennedy, P. (2007) *Global sociology*. 2nd edition. Basingstoke: Palgrave Macmillan.

Connor, J. (2010) *The growth option: turbo-charging HR's impact in Asia*. Bridge/CIPD Next Generation HR Asia. London: Chartered Institute of Personnel and Development.

Connor, J. (2011) Eastern time. *People Management*. 21 January.

Connor, S. (2013) One child policy: China's army of little emperors. *Independent*. 10 January.

Crainer, S. and Dearlove, D. (2005) Indian think. *Business Strategy Review*. Winter.

Crane, A. and Matten, D. (2007) *Business ethics: managing corporate citizenship and sustainability in the age of globalization*. 2nd edition. Oxford: Oxford University Press.

Datamonitor. (2006) Tesco PLC company profile. May.

De Jonquieres, H. (2003) How enlightened international co-operation turned into a show case for indecision. *Financial Times*. 31 March.

Doward, J. (2009) Banana price war in supermarkets brings fear to the developing world. *Observer*. 11 October.

Doward, J. and McKenna, H. (2007) Immigration figures 'are false'. *Observer*. 29 April.

Draghi, M. (2012) Speech by Mario Draghi, President of the ECB. 26 July. Available at: www.ecb.int/press/key/date/2012/html/sp120726.eu.html [Accessed 4 February 2013].

Economist. (2003) The Doha squabble. *Economist (US)*. 29 March.

Economist. (2004) Growing up. *Economist*. 20 May.

Economist. (2006a) In the twilight of Doha. *Economist (US)*. 29 July.

Economist. (2006b) Trouble at till. *Economist (US)*. 4 November.

Economist. (2007) Ten years on: how Asia shrugged off its economic crisis. *Economist*. 4 July.

Economist. (2007a) Rebranding Thaksinomics. *Economist (US)*. 13 January.

Economist. (2007b) Home and abroad. *Economist (US)*. 10 February.

Elliott, L. (2004). What the WTO needs is a new Reformation. *Guardian*. 2 August.

Elliott, L. and Connolly, K. (2007) In 2005, G8 pledged $50bn for Africa. Now the reality. *Guardian*. 25 April.

Emmott, M. (2011) What's the future for employment relations in China? *Impact*. Vol 35. May.

Emmott, B., Crook, C. and Micklethwait, J. (2002) *Globalisation: making sense of an integrating world*. London: The Economist/Profile Books.

Finch, J. (2003) In India, it's service with a compulsory smile. *Guardian*. 17 November.

Fischler, F. and Lamy, P. (2003) Free farm trade means an unfair advantage. *Financial Times*. 1 April.

Fletcher, R. (2006) Thailand junta warns Tesco over expansion. *Daily Telegraph*. 28 September.

Ford, S. (2009) Working Time Directive tsar says the 48 hour week is good for nursing. *Nursing Times*. 2 June.

Fortune. (2006) Fortune Global 500. Available at: www.money.cnn.com/magazines/fortune/global 500 [Accessed 8 May 2007].

Fukuyama, F. (2004) Bring back the state. *Observer*. 4 July.

Gamble, J. (2003) Transferring human resource practices from the United Kingdom to China: the limits and potential for convergence. *International Journal of Human Resource Management*. Vol 14, No 3.

Ghemawat, P. (2003) The forgotten strategy. *Harvard Business Review*. Vol 81, No 11. November.

Gray, J. (1995) *Falsedawn*. London: Granta.

Hales, C. (2001) *Managing through organizations*. London: Thomson Learning.

Hall, A., Day, M. and Freeman, C. (2011) Germany braces itself for invasion of Polish workers as it follows EU immigration rules. *Daily Telegraph*. 1 May.

Hessler, P. (2010) *Country driving*. New York: Harper.

HM Revenue and Customs. (2012) Measuring tax gaps 2012; tax gap estimates for 2010–11.

Hofstede, G. (2009) Geert Hofstede Cultural Dimensions. Available at: www.geeet-hofstede.com/hofstede [Accessed 14 October 2009].

Hope, J. (2009) EU ban limiting doctors to 48 hour working week lifted over public health concerns. *Mail Online*. 16 October [Accessed 7 December 2009].

House, J. (2009) Calling time on doctors' working hours. *The Lancet*. 13 June.

House of Lords. (2008) *The economic impact of immigration: Vol I: Report (HL Paper 82-I)*. London: House of Lords Select Committee on Economic Affairs. April.

Iglicka, K. (2005) *The impact of the EU enlargement on migratory movements in Poland*. Warsaw: Centrum Stosunkow Miedzynarodowych (Center for International Relations). October. Available at: www.csm.org.pl [Accessed 30 May 2007].

Interbrand. (2006) Interbrandbest global brands 2006. Available at: www.interbrand.com [Accessed 18 June 2007].

International Economy. (2004) Is continued globalization of the world economy inevitable? *The International Economy*. Summer. Vol 18, No 3.

International Labour Review. (2006) The internationalization of employment: a challenge to fair globalisation? *International Labour Review*. Spring–Summer.

Jacobs, M. (2001) Bridging the global divide. *Observer*. 11 November.

Jacques, M. (2009) *When China rules the world*. London: Allen Lane.

James, W. and Sonny, A. (2006, 2012) *The Euro: Economic and Monetary Union*. Civitas. Last updated April 2012. Available at: www.civitas.org.uk/eufacts/FSECON/EC4.htm [Accessed 1 December 2012].

James, W., Butter, B. and Sonny, A. (2006, 2012) *Stability and Growth Pact*. Civitas. Last updated April 2012. Available at: www.civitas.org.uk/eufacts/FSECON/EC10.htm [Accessed 1 December 2012].

Jitpleecheep, S. (2001) Boots expansion is on hold in Thailand; to sell its wares in Tops supermarkets. *Bangkok Post*. 2 August.

Jitpleecheep, S. (2002a) Less is more for Boots in Asia. *Bangkok Post*. 8 December.

Jitpleecheep, S. (2002b) Boots slimming down. *Bangkok Post*. 6 March.

Jitpleecheep, S. (2002c) Superstore: saturation foreseen in big-store sector. *Bangkok Post*. 12 June.

Kirisci, K. (2007) Turkey in the EU: a win–win scenario. In M. Fraser (ed.) *European Union: the next fifty years*. London: FT Business.

Knight, L. (2012) Eurozone's long reform wishlist. BBC News. 26 June. Available at: www.bbc.co.uk/news/business-18560234 [Accessed 28 November 2012].

Legrain, P. (2003) *Open world: the truth about globalisation*. London: Abacus.

Lin, J. (2010) Globalization: after the recession. *The Times of India*. 6 January.

Lockwood, B. and Redoano, M. (2005) *The CSGR Globalisation Index: an introductory guide*. Centre for the Study of Globalisation and Regionalisation Working Paper 155/04. Warwick: CSGR.

Lucas, C. (2001) Doha spells disaster for development. *Observer*. 18 November.

Lungesen, D. (2004) Turkey's unrequited EU love. BBC News website. Available at: www.bbc.co.uk/news [Accessed 15 May 2013].

MacShane, D. (2006) Immigration: don't close our borders. *Economist (US)*. 30 October.

Madeley, J. (2001). No end to shackles. *Observer*. 21 January.

Mangaliso, M. (2001) Building competitive advantage from ubuntu: management lessons from South Africa. *Academy of Management Executive*. August.

Marchington, M. and Wilkinson, A. (2008) *Human resource management at work*. 4th edition. London: Chartered Institute of Personnel and Development.

Mason, P. (2012) Eurozone crisis: will the ECB's bond plan work? BBC News. 30 July. Available at: www.bbc.co.uk/news/business-19044341 [Accessed 28 November 2012].

Mathiason, N. (2003). Debt duties. *Observer*. 20 April.

McClanahan, P. (2012) Doha round trade talks explainer. *Guardian*. 3 September.

Meyer, E. and Shen, E.Y. (2010) China myths, China facts. *Harvard Business Review*. Vol 88, No 1/2. January/February.

Micklethwait, J. and Wooldridge, A. (2000) *A future perfect: the challenge and hidden promise of globalization*. London: Heinemann.

Migration Watch. (2007) Outline of the problem. 2 January. Available at: www.migrationwatch.org.uk [Accessed 27 May 2007].

Monbiot, G. (2007) If Britain wants to help Africa's poor, it must stop acting like an emperor. *Guardian*. 17 April.

Morris, H. and Willey, B. (1996) *The corporate environment*. London: Pitman.

NHS Employers. (2009) *Working Time Directive: frequently asked questions for Employer Implementation Teams*. September.

Nugent, N. (2006) *The government and politics of the European Union*. 6th edition. Basingstoke: Palgrave Macmillan.

Office for National Statistics. (2011) Polish people in the UK – half a million Polish residents. *Migration Statistics Quarterly Report.* August.

Ohmae, K. (1990) *The borderless world.* Glasgow: Collins.

Osborn, P. (2004) *Osborn's concise law dictionary.* London: Bloomsbury.

Parliament Publications. (2012) *Tax avoidance by multinational companies.* Public Accounts Committee. 3 December. Available at: www.publications.parliament.uk/pa/cm/201213/cmselect/cmpubacc/716/71605.htm [Accessed 3 December 2012].

Perlmutter, H.V. (1969) The tortuous evolution of the multinational corporation. *Columbia Journal of World Business.* Vol 4.

Peter, L. (2012) Q&A: Eurozone integration deal. 29 June. Available at: www.bbc.co.uk/news/business-18607756 [Accessed 28 November 2012].

Philips. (2007) Philips website. www.philips.com [Accessed 4 June 2007].

Philpott, J. (2007) Britain's eastern European migrant workforce. *Impact.* Issue 19. May.

Philpott, J. and Davies, G. (2006) No turning back? *People Management.* 14 September.

Pidd, H. (2011) Poland: immigration to UK is back for good life despite economic crisis. *Guardian.* 27 May.

Pidd, H. (2012) I stand in the school playground and all I hear is Polish. *Guardian.* 12 December.

Pratley, N. (2012) Row exposes timidity of the taxman. *Guardian.* 7 December.

Pucik, V. (2007) Reframing global mindset. In R. Schuler and S. Jackson (eds) *Strategic human resource management.* 2nd edition. Oxford: Blackwell.

Reilly, P. and Williams, T. (2012) One way to go? *People Management.* September.

Rollinson, D. (2008) *Organisational behaviour and analysis.* 4th edition. Harlow: Pearson.

Rosamund, B. (2005) Globalization, the ambivalence of European integration and the possibilities for a post-disciplinary EU studies. *Innovation: the European Journal of Social Science Research.*Vol 18, No 1.

Rush, S. (2004) Leading in China: a conversation with Elizabeth Weldon. *Leadership in Action.* Vol 24, No 2. May/June.

Ryle, S. (2002) Banana war leaves the Caribbean a casualty. *Observer.* 24 November.

Scholte, J.A. (2000) *Globalization: a critical introduction.* Basingstoke: Palgrave.

Segal-Horn, S. (2002) Global firms – heroes or villains? How and why companies globalise. *European Business Journal.* Vol 14, No 1.

Shah, S. (2004) India 'losing ground to UK in battle of the call centres'. *Independent.* 10 April.

Sharma, A.K. and Talwar, B. (2004) Business excellence enshrined in Vedic (Hindu) philosophy. *Singapore Management Review.* Vol 26, No 1.

Siemens. (2007) Siemens website. Available at: www.siemens.com [Accessed 4 June 2007].

Simpson, D. and Woodley, T. (2007) Organisation and solidarity across frontiers are the future. *Guardian.* 1 May.

Smith, H. (2012) Greeks take an axe to the forests to stave off a bitter winter. *Guardian.* 29 November.

Spencer, S., Ruhs, M., Anderson, B. and Rogaly, B. (2007) *Migrants' lives beyond the workplace: the experiences of Central and East Europeans in the UK.* London: Joseph Rowntree Foundation.

Starbucks. (2012a) Setting the record straight on Starbucks UK taxes and profitability. Blog posted by Howard Schultz. 23 October. Available at: starbucks.co.uk/blog/setting-the-record-straight-on-starbucks-uk-taxes-and-profitability [Accessed 3 December 2012].

Starbucks. (2012b) An open letter from Starbucks Coffee Company UK. Press advertisement. 7 December.

Stewart, H. (2013) WTO faces struggle to remain relevant as cult of globalisation fades. *Observer.* 13 January.

Stiglitz, J. (2003) *Globalization and its discontents.* London: Penguin.

Strupczweski, J. and Breidhardt, A. (2012) Eurozone, IMF secure deal on long-term Greek debt. *Reuters.* 26 November. Available at: www.reuters.com/article/2012/11/26/eurogroup-greece [Accessed 1 December 2012].

Swann, C. (2004). Sixty years on, and still contentious. *Financial Times.* 29 May.

Swyngedouw, E. (2004) Globalisation or glocalisation? Networks, territories and rescaling. *Cambridge Review of International Affairs.* Vol 17, No 1. April.

Syal, R. and Wintour, P. (2012) MPs go to war over tax as Starbucks smells the coffee. *Guardian.* 3 December.

Tesco Lotus. (2007) Tesco Lotus key facts. February. Available at: www.tescolotus.net/company/keyfacts.asp [Accessed 27 April 2007].

Thurow, L. (1999). *Creating wealth.* London: Nicholas Brealey.

Tisdall, S. (2007) Confident Turkey looks east, not west. *Guardian.* 26 March.

Transparency International. (2006) Corruption Perceptions Index. Available at: www.transparency.org/policy_research

Travis, A. (2010) David Cameron's empty immigration promise. *Guardian.* 11 January.

Tremlett, G. (2012) Bailout forces Bankia and other failed Spanish banks to make big cuts. *Guardian.* 29 November.

UNCTAD. (2001) *Transnational corporations and foreign affiliates.* Geneva: UNCTAD.

UN Development Program. (2006) *Human development report.* New York: UNDP.

Vanhonacker, W. (2004) When good guanxi turns bad. *Harvard Business Review.* Vol 82, No 4.

Venables, T. (2005) Multinationals: heroes or villains of the global economy? *CentrePiece*. Spring.

Walker, A. (2012a) Q&A: European Stability Mechanism. BBC News. 8 October. Available at: www.bbc.co.uk/news/business-19870747 [Accessed 28 November 2012].

Walker, A. (2012b) Eurozone: a very overcast outlook. BBC News. 15 November. www.bbc.co.uk/news/business-20344506 [Accessed 28 November 2012].

Warren, E. (2007) Stars of India. *People Management*. 22 February.

Watt, N. (2009) Tory leader ditches referendum and backs away from EU 'bust-up'. *Guardian*. 5 November.

Watt, N. (2013) Cameron to pledge in–out vote on EU. *Guardian*. 23 January.

Williams, F. (2001) Global foreign investment flows 'set to fall to 40%'. *Financial Times*. 19 September.

Wolf, M. (2005) *Why globalization works*. New Haven, CT: Yale Nota Bene.

Woods, N. (2000) *The political economy of globalisation*. Basingstoke: Macmillan.

Woods, N. (2007) *Power shift: do we need better global economic institutions?* London: Institute of Public Policy Research. January.

Demographic and Social Trends

DEMOGRAPHY

INTRODUCTION

Demography looks at populations – their sizes, characteristics and the way they change. It sounds like a dry and academic subject, but that is far from the truth. Population changes throughout the ages have been one of the major determining factors in economic development, political activity and social change. A growth in population can lead to a number of consequences. It can lead to wars, such as when the Roman Empire constantly fought with the barbarians in the search to extend its boundaries to secure more extensive food supplies for its growing population, or the sweeping hordes out of Mongolia and the Far East a few centuries later. It can also lead to extensive economic growth. It was only possible for the industrial revolution to get under way in the UK factories in the late eighteenth century with the growing supply of surplus labour from the countryside, following the enclosure movement and technological agricultural developments. Nor would the vast choice of international food and restaurants we enjoy today have happened without the post-war migratory patterns, first from the new Commonwealth countries, followed by young entrepreneurs from all around the world.

Rapid movements in demography have occurred in recent years. Throughout history, the human race has been young, but now that is changing. In the next 50 years, both birth rates and death rates will continue to decline so fast that populations will age dramatically. For the first time in history, there will be more elderly people than young people, with the average age rising from 24 in 1950 to 29 in 2010 and projected to rise to 39 in 2050. In a growing number of countries, the populations will actually start to decline. It is, indeed, likely that the world population itself will peak around the middle of the century (Wallace 2001; United Nations 2011).

These changes will change economies and working habits, revolutionise pensions and healthcare provision and even alter some of the markets for goods and services.

POPULATION GROWTH

In the year 1000, world population has been estimated to be at around 300 million. It grew slowly over the next 750 years to 728 million in 1750. Over the next 250 years, there has been a continuing spectacular growth, with a doubling of population to 1,500 million by 1900 and a further doubling to 3 billion by 1960. It has taken only 40 years for the population to double again to 6 billion.

The breakdown by continent of the growth from 1800 to 2010 is shown in Table 7.1.

Table 7.1 World population 1800 to 2010 (millions)

	1800	1850	1900	1950	1975	2000	2010
Asia	635	809	947	1,402	2,395	3,683	4,164
Africa	107	111	133	224	416	784	1,022
Europe	203	276	408	547	676	729	738
Latin America and Caribbean	24	38	74	166	322	519	590
North America	7	26	82	172	243	310	345
Oceania	2	2	6	13	21	30	36
World total	**972**	**1,262**	**1,650**	**2,524**	**4,073**	**6,055**	**6,895**

Source: United Nations (2011)

It can be seen that the growth has not been consistent across the world. Up until 1900, population increased rapidly in the developing world, but stayed relatively subdued in the poorer developing world. Since 1900, the bulk of the world population growth has been in the developing world, with an astonishing tripling of population in Africa and Latin America since 1950. This has been accompanied by a rapid slowing in growth in the developed world, especially in Europe, with some countries showing an absolute decline in recent years. Germany, for example, had a loss of 1.5 million between 1987 and 2011 (Vasager 2013).

In the ex-communist countries, the population has already fallen from 311 million in 1992 to 294 million in 2010, with sharp falls over this period in the Ukraine (from 51 million to 45 million – over 20 per cent) and Romania (from 23 million to 21 million). Further falls of over 10 per cent are expected by 2025 in Russia, Georgia, Belarus and Bulgaria (Lucas 2006; United Nations 2011).

In the UK, as shown in Table 7.2, the spurt in population took place in the nineteenth century and has slowed considerably since 1900. Scotland's population has actually remained static since 2001. However, for the UK as a whole, there have been tentative signs of a small reversal of this trend at the end of the 2000s.

The effects of the potato famine and lack of industrial development in Northern Ireland can be seen with an actual decline in population from 1851 to 1901 when vast numbers of young people left Ireland to go to the England mainland, America and the colonies. In more recent times, Ireland has reversed the generally European trend with a considerable growth in population, reflecting a more buoyant agricultural and industrial economy arising principally from joining Europe in 1973; greater economic opportunities have also halted mass migration abroad.

Table 7.2 UK population 1801 to 2011 (thousands)

	1801	1851	1901	1951	2001	2011
England	8,305	16,764	30,515	41,159	50,035	53,107
Wales	587	1,163	2,013	2,599	2,988	3,063
Scotland	1,608	2,889	4,472	5,096	5,258	5,255
Northern Ireland	*	1,443	1,237	1,371	1,701	1,811
Total	*	22,259	38,237	50,225	59,982	63,236

Source: National Statistical Office (2011)
* not available

DRIVERS OF POPULATION CHANGE

Taking the world as a whole, the only two factors controlling population change are the level of the *birth rate* and the level of the *death rate*. Within any particular country or region, another factor is important, namely the *migration in and out* of that country or region.

Birth rate

The *birth rate* is usually expressed in terms of the number of live births per 1,000 population. The fertility rate is the average number of births for each woman of child-bearing age. A rate of 2.1 is required to maintain the population over an extended period of time, excluding migration.

Table 7.3 Birth statistics – UK

	Actual births – annual average for decade (thousands)	Fertility rate
1900s	1,091	3.5
1930s	824	1.8
1950s	839	2.2
1960s	962	2.6
1970s	736	2.0
1980s	757	1.8
1990s	744	1.7
2000s	701	1.65
2010	808 (actual year)	1.99 (actual year)

Sources: Office of Population Censuses/Office for National Statistics (2012)

During the twentieth century, the fertility rate peaked at 2.95 in 1964, while the lowest year for births was 1977 (657,000).

The birth rate is determined by:

- the number of women in the population who are of child-bearing age, and
- the proportion of this group of women who actually have children – this is called the 'fertility rate'.

It is clear from Table 7.3 that there was a steady drop in the birth rate in the UK from 1900 to the early 2000s, with the exception of a baby boom in the 1960s (plus a similar shorter boom in the period 1946–49). The birth rate mirrored the fertility rate, although the latter has had greater variations.

Having said this, there has been a reverse in the decline of births in the UK during the early 2000s and a steadily rising fertility rate. This has been due to a number of factors:

- Up until 2008, there was continuing economic affluence, providing the sense of economic security allowing family units to trade off the risks of the potential loss of income. However, since 2008, this economic security has rapidly dispersed without any immediate decline in the fertility rate.
- The influence of government policies to encourage working women through a raft of measures including enhanced maternity pay and new rights to apply to work flexibly.
- The influence of an increased migrant population, especially from the Indian sub-continent, where larger families are the norm. By 2011, the number of live births had risen to 808,000, an increase of 100,000 over the average for the period 2000–09, with over 25 per cent of the babies born to mothers who came from outside the UK, compared with 12 per cent in 1990. The most common countries of origin of the mothers were Pakistan, Poland and India, whose fertility rate is around 2.5.

This trend has been in part responsible for a spurt in the UK population to over 63 million in 2010, an increase of over 500,000 per year over the previous five years. Another trend is that women are having children much later in life. The mean age of women having their first baby was 23.7 in 1970 but this had increased to 29.6 in 2010. An increasing number of women are childless. One in five women in their forties has no children compared with one in ten in the 1940s.

Table 7.4 compares the UK with other countries, showing that it is generally higher than the rest of Europe but lower than most developing countries.

Table 7.4 World fertility rates

	2010–11	Estimate 2050
UK	2.0	2.02
USA	2.1	2.09
Japan	1.4	1.82
Germany	1.4	1.87
Greece	1.4	1.88
China	1.6	1.77
Hong Kong	1.1	1.75
India	2.6	1.87
Pakistan	3.4	1.90
Brazil	1.8	1.66
Nigeria	5.5	3.41

	2010–11	Estimate 2050
Algeria	2.2	1.66
World	2.5	2.17

Source: United Nations (2012)

The suggested causes of the reduced fertility rate are as follows:

- Women are taking charge of their fertility. The widespread use of the contraceptive pill and other modern devices from the 1970s onwards allowed decisions to be taken on family planning, unheard of previously. Many women (and couples) have decided not to have families or to have just one child, often so that two careers can be pursued. This is connected with postponing starting a family until later. Having children usually brings a savage reduction in household income as one member, usually the mother, may stop working or go part-time.
- It is no longer necessary to have a large family as an insurance against obtaining care in older age. The extended family has generally declined in importance as the state has stepped in to provide or support services that have traditionally been carried out by family members.
- The cost of bringing up families has risen, especially in higher education, so the average expenditure on children has not fallen with the birth rate – it is simply a case of each child represents a larger financial investment, despite government financial incentives.
- In the wider world, children are no longer as useful as they once were. Fewer people live on farms where children can help out and child labour, although still an area of international concern, is far less prevalent and strong attempts have been made to eradicate this practice in recent years.
- About three-fourths of the African countries are presently participating in various family planning programmes. Most governments encourage private planned parenthood associations to carry out various phases of the programmes. Governments often integrate family planning in their maternal and child health services by emphasising birth spacing for health reasons.
- In addition to active family planning programmes, many African governments have taken legal measures to reduce fertility. For example, some countries have raised the legal age for marriage. Others have outlawed polygamy. Some countries also now limit child allowances for government officials to no more than three or four children and some limit the number of maternity leaves.

The effect of population changes on Japan is shown in Case Study 7.1.

CASE STUDY 7.1

JAPAN FACES CONTRACTION PAINS

Japan is getting old at an astonishing pace, a far cry from the position just after 1945. Then, the over-65s were around 5 per cent of the population, well below the figure for the other major economies. In 2007, the elderly accounted for 20 per cent of the population and average life spans have increased from 50 in 1947 to 82. By 2015, the proportion of the elderly will have risen to 25 per cent, thanks mainly to an unusually large post-war baby-boom generation who are now starting to retire at 60, the normal corporate retirement age.

The fertility rate fell below the 2.1 replacement level in 1970 and reached a low of 1.26 in 2005 before stabilising at 1.32 in 2007. In 2005, the actual population began to fall in absolute terms with very little migration allowed to balance the picture. From 127 million in 2007, it is estimated that the population will drop to 95 million by 2050, with the elderly accounting for 40 per cent of the total.

As the proportion of elderly citizens increases, so the number of young people declines. Around 16 million are currently in their twenties but, in the next ten years alone, this will drop to 13 million. Recent graduates are already reaping the benefit with more job offers than labour available, so pushing up the price of graduate jobs. However, the flip side is that today's young graduate must support an ever-larger proportion of retirees. By 2030, there will be two employees for each retiree; by 2050, the ratio will fall to 1.5 employees per retiree. Most commentators regard this as unworkable, as do most graduates, the majority of whom are not paying the fixed portion of their state pension scheme, which indicates that they expect the scheme to be closed before they retire.

The biggest falls in population are taking place in the countryside, where younger villagers have been migrating to the towns since the 1970s. The hugely inefficient agricultural sector has been subsidised equally hugely for 50 years, backed by massive tariffs to keep out foreign rice and other products. While the economy grew strongly, Japanese society went along with supporting traditional agricultural cultures and values, but the young voted with their feet and joined emerging, innovative industries and services. Now the over-65s make up 40 per cent of rural communities and 60 per cent of all farmers, so many communities have become unviable.

In response, one small isolated hamlet, down to nine villagers all over 60, has contracted with an industrial waste company to sell their valley and all its

farms so it will disappear under 150 feet of industrial ash. On a larger scale, Yubari, a former mining town on Hokkaido Island, has had a population fall from 100,000 to 13,000 since 1950 and has gone bankrupt through spending too much money trying to (unsuccessfully) promote the town's profile. Another town decided to actively shrink its physical environment, moving public institutions from the suburbs back into the centre of town and refusing permission for all additional dwellings outside a prescribed (and smaller) town boundary.

On the macroeconomic front, the Government has taken radical decisions over state pensions. Eligibility for the fixed part of the pension will rise from 60 to 65 in stages by 2014 and eligibility for the flexible (and larger) part will rise to 65 by 2026. Most commentators regard this as not fast enough. Businesses have a cultural problem with a higher retirement age. Pay is based very much on seniority so employees staying longer in the workplace would cost the organisation much more money. However, because older employees are respected, it would be extremely difficult to impose pay cuts when employees stay on to a later retirement age.

If the retirement age is delayed until 65 or 70, it would go some way to solving the decline of the supply of labour. Japan already has one of the highest proportions of the elderly still in the workforce. This is not because Japanese simply like to work or do not feel a useful part of society otherwise. For many it is that they have to work to survive. Most of these jobs are 'down-shifting' into menial work, such as repairs and night-watchman, with wages that are mediocre.

However, a bigger influence would be to increase the participation rate of women, which was 63 per cent in 2007, compared with 68 per cent in the UK or the USA. Cultural problems are even greater here, with male chauvinism dominating offices, a work culture of long hours and a shortage of childcare facilities. Japan still, apparently, does not have an expression for 'work–life balance'. Large numbers of women permanently drop out of the labour market when they have children. As the average Japanese father does not help in the home (partly due to the long-hours culture), this engenders anxiety from the wife about extending the family. By the time their children have grown up, they then have caring responsibilities for their ageing parents, often living with them.

In 2002, the Japanese Government announced that every Japanese woman who gives birth is to receive the equivalent of £1,700 plus up to £15,000 worth of help with childcare. The fact that this initiative is likely to cost around £5 billion indicates the degree of anxiety over the continuing decline in Japan's birth rate. So far, the effect seems to be marginal, even in the cities, as the attraction is limited of bringing up families in tiny Japanese apartments, where beds are folded up during the day and the father is not seen until late at night due to the long work-hours culture.

A rapidly ageing population, supported by fewer and fewer working people, could keep Japan in a state of semi-permanent recession. It is estimated that if current trends continue, young people in 2025 will have to pay around 25 per cent of their salary as a tax to simply keep pensions at their current level. It remains to be seen whether the financial inducements, the availability of 'baby shops' to help women with childcare and 'grandmother networks' to support young families will make any difference or whether women will continue to wait until their aspirations in the workplace have been better satisfied.

As a postscript, a scandal erupted in 2011 when it was discovered that 230,000 listed centenarians in Japan could not be found. Many had died unreported; a surprisingly large number of families had lost track of them under the strain of modern urban life despite the fact that records indicated they were being cared for by their relatives.

Sources: Norton (2002); *Economist* (2007); McNeill (2010)

Death rate

As measured by deaths per 1,000 population, the UK rate has fallen from 23 in 1851 to 11.5 in 2010. The advances of medicine, reduced infant mortality and generally improved health, clean water supply and sanitation facilities have allowed life expectancy to increase, as shown in Table 7.5. The gap between male and female life expectancy was six years in 1971 but has narrowed since then to four years.

Table 7.5 UK life expectancy

	Male	Female
1901	48	52
1950	66	72
1990	72	78

	Male	Female
2010	78	82

Source: National Audit Office (2010)

The UK life expectancy is around the European average, but some developed countries, such as Japan and Singapore, exceed our rates. So, as people live longer, the death rate falls. The actual number of deaths, however, has not fallen by the same proportion because the population has substantially increased over this period. In 1900, the number of UK deaths was 624,000 compared with 559,038 in 2010.

The picture is not rosy throughout the world. Although life expectancy in Europe averages 74 and in Asia it is 67, 28 per cent of all countries have a life expectancy of less than 60. The average for Africa is 50 and there are still sub-Saharan African countries where societies live with the appalling situation of life expectancy being less than 50, with the worst example – Sierra Leone – currently only 41 for women and as low as 39 for men. On top of poor health, there are numerous outbreaks of war and disease (especially HIV/AIDS and SARS), while poor living conditions are very common.

In developed countries, the main feature of a dropping death rate is the rapid ageing of the population with a rapid growth in the numbers over retirement age.

Migration

The third factor determining population levels is the number of people migrating into or out of a country. Clearly, if more people enter a country than leave it, the population will rise. International migration has always been substantial. Man's original ancestors migrated out of Africa to populate the world and most of North and South America, Oceania and parts of Southern Africa have been colonised by migrants who have replaced the small indigenous populations.

It has been estimated that about 191 million people live outside their country of birth or citizenship (UNFPA 2006). Political, social, economic and environmental upheavals have been the spur to large-scale movements. Religious dissension encouraged Puritan migration to America in the seventeenth and eighteenth centuries and persecution has forced Jewish populations to leave their homelands, be it Russia in the nineteenth century or Germany under the Nazis. Due to very poor economic and social prospects, the Irish migrated all over the world for 150 years, Chinese labour was used to build the American railroads and much of Dubai's current building boom is being built using Nepalese and Indian skilled craftsmen. Britain eagerly recruited in the West Indies and the Indian subcontinent in the early post-war years to staff the health service and public transport when local labour was in short supply. At the same time, there was a substantial outflow of skilled labour to take up new lives in Australia, Canada, New Zealand and South Africa, often under 'assisted passages' incentives.

On a world scale, certain migration paths are especially important, as Dicken (2003) explains:

> ... there are massive movements across the Mexico–United States border and from parts of Asia to the United States. Australia has become an important focus of migration from South East Asia... and from countries around the Mediterranean to Germany. (Dicken 2003, p521)

In general terms, the twentieth century has seen far more restrictions placed upon migrants by governments fearful of the economic and social consequences of mass immigration. Although immigration was never easy (both America and Australia veered towards operating a 'whites only' policy for decades), the latter half of the twentieth century has seen severe restrictions imposed by countries all over the world, exacerbated by fears of terrorism in the twenty-first century.

In the case of the UK, the Commonwealth Immigration Act in the mid-1950s imposed severe limitations on free entry for mostly ethnic would-be migrants and subsequent legislation tightened the regulations further. Commonwealth immigration dropped sharply from 150,000 per annum to less than 50,000 within a few years and has continued at roughly this rate until the 2000s.

Since the mid-1990s, the net inflow of migrants has escalated substantially, as shown in Table 7.6.

Table 7.6 UK net inflow of migrants (thousands)

1990	19
2001	190
2004	244
2006	200
2008	163
2011	220

Source: Migration Observatory, University of Oxford (2012)

For much of the 1980s and 1990s, there was a rough balance between emigration, mostly to the 'old' Commonwealth (Australia, Canada, etc) and America and immigration (mostly from the 'new' Commonwealth – Indian subcontinent and Caribbean). During the 2000s, however, there was a substantial rise in migrants from the European Union A8 accession countries, especially Poland, and an increase from the 'new' Commonwealth, with the numbers from Africa also rising. 2008 showed a sudden reverse of this situation, with a large number of migrants returning home, including an estimated 50,000 Polish workers, and applications for work permits from the A8 countries halved in the three months to December 2008 compared with 2007, a drop of 24,000 (*People Management* 2009). Additional barriers to immigration were introduced by the UK Government in 2006 with a revised points system reducing the number of potential applicants for work permits.

Case Study 7.2 illustrates the effect on the labour market of the rise in migration from Eastern Europe.

CASE STUDY 7.2

MIGRATION FROM EASTERN EUROPE AND ITS EFFECT ON THE LABOUR MARKET

This research paper examined the effects of the migration from the countries that acceded to the EU in 2004 and on whom no restrictions on movement and work were placed by the UK Government. These were Poland, the Czech Republic, Estonia, Hungary, Latvia, Lithuania, Slovakia and Slovenia, the so-called A8 countries.

Level of migration

Nearly 580,000 migrants from the A8 countries registered for work between 2004 and 2006 (Home Office 2007) and a further 100,000 have been estimated to be working on a self-employed basis. Poland is the main source, with 579,000 resident in the UK in 2011. And the effect on the internal Polish labour market has been so great that Poland has had to ease its own restrictions on entry of labour from the Ukraine, Belarus and Russia to fill skilled vacancies and gaps in the seasonal agricultural market (Polska 2006).

This is way in excess of the official UK government forecast figure in 2003 of around 10,000 per year. Expectations have been massively exceeded due to:

- A large number of migrants were already working unofficially in the UK and their registration allowed their work to be 'legal'.
- Most of the A8 countries have high unemployment figures (20 per cent in Poland, for example).
- Earnings in A8 countries are typically *six times lower* than in the UK.
- Working conditions, including health and safety provision, are often at a lower standard than in the UK.
- The arrival of cheap flights and coach travel has made the regular journeys cheaper and easier.
- The degree to which agency intervention would apply was greatly underestimated, especially in the building, agriculture and hospitality sectors.

On top of that, the freedom of entry from these countries has meant that an unspecified number have been able to settle permanently without restriction in most cases. Of that number, it is estimated that 380,000 have stayed on a permanent basis. However, this is only an estimate as there is no register of A8 migrants leaving the UK.

Nature of migrants, chosen work and pay levels

Most were young, with 80 per cent under 35, while 80 per cent had some form of qualification (mostly technical), although only 5 per cent have degrees. Only 6 per cent had dependants arriving with them. Around 70 per cent worked in low-paid, unqualified work,

such as process operation/packing and in warehousing (40 per cent), hospitality (18 per cent) and farming (4 per cent), while 6 per cent work as care assistants and sales assistants. The average pay was between £4.50 and £5.99 an hour.

Good for economy?

The Government has spelled out the apparent benefits of this unprecedented migration. They identify fewer jobs unfilled, less inflationary pressures (which could fuel higher pay increases) and faster economic growth. The Ernst &Young ITEM club estimated that the activities of the migrants reduced interest rates by 0.5 per cent and GDP was around 0.2 per cent higher (ITEM Club 2006). The Bank of England concluded that the level of unemployment that can be sustained without raising inflation has been lowered as migrants take the low-paid jobs that often remain vacant (Blanchflower et al 2007). Moreover, responses by employers rated migrants higher than conventional employees in terms of productivity, reliability, attendance and quality of work (CIPD/ KPMG 2005).

On the downside, however, there was some increased strain on the social infrastructure, notably housing, transport, hospitals and welfare. Overall, although the picture looked very positive, there was a contrary view from the House of Lords Economic Affairs Committee in 2008, which found no evidence of large-scale economic benefits and that immigration had a negative impact on the low-paid and training for young UK workers and contributed to high house prices.

Sources: Philpott (2007); McSmith (2007); Whitehead (2008); *People Management* (2013)

You should note that statistics for migrants are notoriously unreliable. Although records of those entering the UK are regarded as accurate, at least in terms of actual numbers, those leaving the UK, due to the less arduous emigration procedures, are not as accurate. Much of the estimates are made up of samples from the International Passenger Surveys and other surveys of migrants' intentions, which many commentators regard as suspect. Figures for illegal immigrants are completely unknown, with the UK Government refusing to even make an estimate. An example of the unreliability of the migration estimates arose when the Home Secretary, Jacqui Smith, had to apologise to Parliament in 2007 for underestimating by 300,000 the number of foreign workers entering the UK in the ten years up to 2007 (Stewart 2007).

Between 2001 and 2011, the number of UK residents who were born abroad had risen from 4.3 million to 7.5 million (13 per cent of the total population), with India (700,000), Poland (580,000) and Pakistan (480,000) being represented most heavily. The number of Poles has risen substantially from 60,000 in 2001, but those from the Republic of Ireland have dropped from 480,000 to 405,000. In London, those born abroad have risen to 40 per cent, an increase of over 1 million. However, many parts of Wales and the north of England have less than 3 per cent of the population in this category (Casciani 2012).

Comparing the statistics for those born abroad with Europe, the UK is twelfth overall but has the highest proportion of the larger countries (those with a population over 50 million).

On another front, there was a significant rise in asylum-seekers to the UK in the early 2000s, which peaked at 103,000 in 2002, but this figure rapidly fell to only 19,000 in 2011 (Home Office 2012). Government actions to speed up the system of dealing with applications has caused some reduction in applications but not eliminated the total. Only around 20 per cent of asylum-seekers have their application accepted but many are able to stay in the UK while their appeal is heard, which can take many months.

The reasons for the increasing numbers of migrants include:

- Britain's economic performance since the mid-1990s has been very positive, better than most of Europe, up until the onset of the recession in 2008. Even so, the job picture in the UK, especially in London, has been more resilient than in most European countries.
- There is a strong culture of entrepreneurship, with open opportunities for small businesses to flourish, perhaps more so than in other parts of Europe, although not so strong as in America.
- There are established ethnic communities from all parts of the world, allowing greater ease of transition and community support.
- The number of low-paid unskilled jobs available is very high, especially in the hospitality, caring and building industry. Some are in the black economy, encouraging asylum-seekers and illegal immigrants.
- In the education field, there has been a huge growth in undergraduate and postgraduate courses taken up by international students, who are able to help their financing through part-time work.

On coming to power in 2010, the Conservative-led coalition vowed to reduce annual net immigration to below 100,000 by 2015. Actions included tightening visa controls, making it difficult to get entry for study (although an exception was made in 2013 for Indian students), for work and to join relatives in the UK (*Economist* 2013a). Although net immigration fell by 25 per cent to 163,000 in 2012 (Bentham 2013), due to a sharp reduction in the number of students and a decline in the numbers entering from Eastern Europe, the impending freeing of entry restrictions for Romanians and Hungarians in 2014 may produce difficulties for the Government to reach its target, despite general public support for the policy.

Europe has been faced with a similar situation, although most countries show less hostility to migrants. While the UK's number of asylum-seekers represents 0.5 per cent of the population, Sweden's 333,000 represents nearly 4 per cent, while Austria's is 5 per cent. Asylum-seekers to France and Germany are currently running around half the UK rate.

ETHNICITY OF POPULATION

An inevitable development of the increase in migration has been a growth in the ethnic variation in most developed countries. In the UK, of 6.3 million who were born outside the UK, around 8 per cent of the population, some 5 million are from ethnic minorities, nearly double the figure in the 1970s (Ellis 2009). In the 2011 census, the number of respondents who defined themselves as 'White British' fell from 88 per cent in 2001 to 81 per cent. Ethnic populations have also become more widely spread. For example, in 2001, 80 per cent of African populations lived in London, but in 2011 this had declined to 58 per cent (*Economist* 2012a) The largest group are from the Indian subcontinent – around 55 per cent of the total, while West Indians make up a further 15 per cent (actually a declining proportion as many retire back to their countries of origin), with the remainder from Africa, Asia and the Middle East.

They have generally settled over the years in urban localities, with large congregations in inner east London boroughs and towns in the Midlands and the north of England. As a whole, they have a lower age profile with a much smaller percentage over 65, chiefly because migrants tend to be in lower age categories. Also, many migrants retire to their countries of origin.

Ethnicity of population is far greater in the United States, as shown in Case Study 7.3.

CASE STUDY 7.3

'LATINOS' ARE A MAJOR FORCE IN THE US ECONOMY

People of Hispanic origin (Latinos, as many prefer to be called') make up 12 per cent of the US workforce today, but this will become at least 25 per cent in 50 years' time due to their much larger families and current age profile. They originate from across Latin America, but predominantly Mexico, and their growth rate is 3 per cent per annum, compared with 0.8 per cent for the rest of America. As a group, they are a key catalyst for economic growth. In some of the larger cities, such as Los Angeles, they make up the majority of the under-18 age set. Their disposable income jumped 29 per cent from 2001 to 2004, double the pace of the rest of the population, and they have a growing influence on all consumer patterns, especially food, clothes and entertainment.

The Latino boom brings a welcome charge to the economy at a time when other countries' population growth has slowed to a crawl. Without a steady supply of new workers and consumers, a greying US might see a long-term slowdown along the lines of ageing Japan.

Yet this demographic change produces potential problems. One of the major issues relates to language. With a huge Spanish-speaking minority, there could be pressures for recognition of an official second language, much as French is in Canada today. This could harm assimilation and encourage a form of separatism in states such as California, just like it has been a major cause of conflict in Quebec.

Another issue is the perception that large numbers of poorly educated, non-English speakers undermine the US economy. Although the steady influx of low-skilled workers helps keep America's gardens tended and floors cleaned, those workers also exert downward pressure on wages, causing friction with other groups of workers in this sector.

A case in point is Harris County in Texas, which includes the city of Houston, where the population increased by 21 per cent during the 1990s. Forty-two per cent are of Hispanic origin and this ethnic group is responsible for 80 per cent of the growth. There are no zoning laws in the county, so developers can build wherever they think there is the demand. At the new 28,000-acre community of The Woodlands, a three-bedroom house costs around $130,000 (c£90,000) compared with an equivalent house in San Francisco costing $700,000. The area is surrounded by woodland and crime is very low.

Rapid growth in this form may eventually cause environmental problems, but it greatly slows the pace at which America ages.

Sources: *Business Week* (2004); *Economist* (2006)

Migration is a very emotive subject, bringing to the mix a number of political, economic, social and psychological issues. Broadly speaking, there are a set of reasons for encouraging migration and another set for discouraging it, as follows:

Encouraging migration

- We live in a global economy and we need to make the best use of all talents, from whatever the source.
- Migrants have energy and enthusiasm and a willingness to succeed. They have made a substantial effort to move from their home country and practice indicates that they are motivated to work hard.
- Most migrants are in the age group 18–40 and, in an ageing population, it is important to have a good source of younger labour.
- Migrants make up such a large proportion of the labour force, estimated at 7 per cent (Salt 2006), that the labour market would tighten dramatically if this source was reduced or eliminated. In fact, 15 per cent of firms employ 10 per cent or more migrants in their workforce (Smedley 2008).
- Migrants can fill the low-skill jobs that are currently difficult to fill – they prevent wage rates rising too high.
- It is not unusual for migrant entrepreneurs to offer ethnic goods and services which expand the marketplace to the benefit of the consumer. Thai food and ethnic textiles are obvious examples.
- It is arguable that it is more beneficial for the UK economy for migrants to carry out work in the UK rather than that work to be outsourced to a migrant's home country.
- Why should migrants be prevented from benefiting from the UK's successful economy? After all, for 200 years, the UK benefited from running the economies of its colonies, so it is time for those benefits to be shared.
- Remittances from migrants back to their home country have been substantial and help to alleviate poverty. For some African countries, such as Kenya, they account for bigger flows of capital than aid or foreign investment (*Economist* 2009b).

Discouraging migration

- The UK is very densely populated and an inflow of immigrants leads to pressure on housing and jobs.

- Where there is a large source of low-skilled labour, it discourages employers from becoming more productive by automating production or innovating the services provided.
- Too much migration encourages the black economy, which reduces tax revenue and is associated with crime.
- The process of policing and administrating prospective migrants is very expensive and difficult to carry out efficiently and fairly.
- Migrants can be socially marginalised, staying in their own communities, retaining their own cultures and religions and not integrating effectively. This can create social problems and difficulties with the next generation.
- Excessive migration can cause security problems, with international conspiracies leading to terrorist activity (Nichiporuk 2000).

OTHER DEMOGRAPHIC CHANGES

Working population

You will have seen in Chapter 3 the outline changes in the UK employment structure. Table 7.7 shows the comparative statistics for 2006 and 2012.

Table 7.7 UK labour market 2006 and 2012 (thousands)

	Male		Female		Total	
	2006	2012	2006	2012	2006	2012
Employed	12,800	12,953	12,480	12,785	25,280	25,738
Self-employed	2,780	2,966	1,020	1,314	3,800	4,280
Total labour market	15,580	15,919	13,500	14,099	29,080	30,018
Part-time	1,600	2,056	5,700	5,608	7,300	8,130
Temporary	700	671	800	762	1,500	1,433
Unemployed					1,400	2,530 (7.8 per cent)
Economically active					30,480 (79 per cent)	32,648 (78 per cent)
Economically inactive					8,120 (21 per cent)	9,439 (22 per cent)

Source: ONS (2012)

Compared with the early 1990s, there has been a growth of around 4.5 million in the total working population, made up of a natural growth in the population (including the rise in migrant workers) and an increase in the participation level. The rate of employment for women has risen much more steeply than for men, with the women's total rising by more than 2 million over the last ten years (see Chapter 3 for a discussion on *The feminisation of work*).

From 1992 to 2007, there was a steady reduction in *unemployment*, which halved over the period and led to a more confident labour market, so the number of temporary employees declined. However, the recession starting in 2008 substantially altered this picture, with a rise of 1 million in unemployed over the four-year period, although the rise halted by early 2012 and fell gently subsequently, into 2013.

Another factor which influenced the employment statistics was the number of adults claiming incapacity benefit (a proportion of which can be regarded as hidden unemployed), which rose to 2.6 million by 2008, an increase from 800,000 in 1983. In the following four years, both the Labour Government and the Coalition Government made strenuous efforts to tackle this high number with various reforms to the benefits system and it subsequently dropped to 2.4 million by 2012. Over 1.2 million of these claimants had been in receipt of the benefit for more than five years.

The number of people self-employed increased substantially in the 1980s under the Thatcher period, when entrepreneurial activity was strongly encouraged. However, it remained steady in the early 2000s but the onset of the recession had an effect of encouraging a proportion of those losing their job to go self-employed, so increasing their numbers by 400,000 by 2012, representing 27 per cent of the workforce.

The decline in the birth rate leading to an ageing population has already affected the size and nature of the potential working population, those within the age range 16 to 60 (female) or 65 (male). Table 7.8 shows this information starkly.

Table 7.8 UK working population – age distribution 1901 to 2026 (per cent)

	Under 16	16–24	25–44	45–64	Over 65
Males					
1901	34	20	28	15	4
1931	26	18	29	21	7
1961	25	14	27	25	9
1991	21	14	30	22	13
2001	21	11	31	23	13
2011	19	12	27	27	15
2026*	18	10	26	26	19
Females					
1901	31	20	28	15	6
1931	23	17	30	21	8
1961	22	13	25	26	14
1991	19	12	28	21	18
2001	20	10	29	23	18
2011	18	11	26	26	18
2026*	17	10	25	26	22

*forecast
Source: ONS (2011)

Table 7.8 shows that the younger male working population aged 16–44 has fallen from 48 per cent of the population in 1901 to 39 per cent in 2001 and is expected to decline further to 36 per cent by 2026, with a similar picture for women. The percentage in the age group 16–24 has actually halved. On the other hand, there has been a considerable growth in the older employee groups. In fact, the number of employees aged 50 and over has increased by 1.3 million (about 26 per cent) in the ten years up to 2004. Not all pensioners are an immediate drain on the economy as many choose to work after retirement age. There are around a million in this category, a figure that has risen by 34 per cent over the last ten years. However, they do face a degree of discrimination, as shown in Case Study 7.4.

CASE STUDY 7.4

AGE STEREOTYPES AND DISCRIMINATORY ATTITUDES TOWARDS OLDER WORKERS: AN EAST–WEST COMPARISON

This study compared age stereotypes among 567 respondents sampled in the UK and Hong Kong, and examined how these stereotypes were related to discriminatory attitudes at work. Compared with the Hong Kong sample, UK respondents saw older workers as more effective at work, but less adaptable to change. As expected, respondents' own age was predictive of positive age stereotypes, although for supervisors this relationship was moderated in the case of perceptions of work effectiveness. Stereotypical beliefs were found to significantly affect respondents' attitudes towards the training, promotion and retention of older workers, their willingness to work with older workers and their support for positive discrimination. Findings also suggest that anti-age discrimination policies in the respondent's organisation had a positive impact on beliefs about the adaptability of older workers and possibly also on attitudes towards providing them with training. Implications of the findings were discussed in light of the existing socio-political environment in the UK and Hong Kong.

Source: Chiu et al (2001)

Given that far more young people go on to further and higher education, with the government target of 50 per cent attending some form of higher education, this reduces the younger working population even further.

REFLECTIVE ACTIVITY 7.1

A development in the working population in recent years has been the growth of what is known as 'atypical employment', which is not full-time 9 to 5 employment. It covers part-time, shiftwork, teleworking and a host of variable working arrangements. What are the driving forces for this growth?

Participation rates

People used to work until they reached pensionable age (many, of course, did not last that long, worn out by heavy industrial work or poor diets). As late as 1975, 84 per cent of men aged 60–64 were 'economically active' in the UK, but this fell to 65 per cent by 1995. This was chiefly the result of the recession in the early 1990s, where many older men lost their jobs and found it difficult to obtain alternative employment. Many were disabled and obtained disability benefits which are higher than unemployment benefits. Organisations also encouraged older employees to take early retirement, sometimes providing generous redundancy payments or enhanced pensions.

By the early 2000s, this position was changing. Participation rates for men 50 to 64 rose from 65 per cent to 79.5 per cent from 1995 to 2005 (ONS 2007) and for those over retirement age it has risen from 7.5 per cent in 2000 to 12 per cent in 2012 (ONS 2012). This was partly to do with the prosperous economy where many part-time jobs are available, especially in the service sector, and partly to do with the decline in pension prospects arising from the two stock market crashes in 2003 and 2008, where the value of personal pensions declined by as much as 50 per cent. It is an unusual feature of the late 2000s recession that the number of post-retirement-age employees has continued to increase, both male and female. By 2012, there were 1.4 million pensioners in employment.

For women, there has been a substantial increase in the participation rate, rising from 63 per cent in 1979 to 75 per cent in 2009. Women have developed their careers, continued at work while raising a family or returned to work much more quickly than in previous decades. They have also taken up new careers and skills through obtaining qualifications, many through some form of government initiatives. Other support has come through the strengthening equal opportunity legislation, where the barriers to women's employment and development have been steadily removed.

The economically inactive can be regarded as a 'reserve army' that can be drawn on during periods of tight labour markets (Smallwood 2006). He explains that:

> There are huge economic benefits associated with a growing workforce, mirrored by the severe problems that arise when a country's population starts to decline. After all, gross domestic product growth over the longer term is the sum of the growth in the employed workforce and the rise in productivity of that workforce, so the faster the working population goes up, the faster the economy grows. Over the past decade, the growth in the working population has added well in excess of £50 billion to GDP, and swelled the treasury's coffers by nearly half that. (Smallwood 2006, p6)

The growth in European participation rates mirrors the UK situation, although the average rate is still lower at 78 per cent for men and 60 per cent for women in 2006. In France, for example, the male rate was 75 per cent and female 62 per cent, while the Italian rate for women was as low as 46 per cent in the same year.

REFLECTIVE ACTIVITY 7.2

Two organisations have just set up in an area of high unemployment and low participation, with the support of various government grants and loans. They are as follows:

Jones Supermarkets have set up a regional distribution centre to employ 450 staff in warehousing and logistics positions on 24/7 operations.

Williams Toys and Games have established a manufacturing and distribution centre to employ 200 staff. There is a seasonal element to the work so a number of staff will be working flexibly, including evening shifts and weekends for the busy autumn period. Most of the toys and games are imported finished or semi-finished, so the work is essentially unskilled and semi-skilled and involves a high element of packing and distribution.

Question

Given that setting up in the area will help reduce the unemployment rate, are there ways in which the organisations can help further improve the participation rate?

Sectoral employment

The number of people working in *manufacturing* has been declining since the 1950s, when it stood at over 6 million. Since 1993, however, there has been a particularly steep drop as work has migrated to the developing and emerging nations, especially China and India, so less than 3 million worked in manufacturing in the UK in 2012.

Table 7.9 Sectoral employment 2012 (thousands)

Selected sectors	2012	Change from 2011
Manufacturing	2,907	+59 (+2.1 per cent)
Construction	2,165	−24 (−1.1 per cent)
Public sector	6,798	−327 (−4.6 per cent)
Wholesale, retail	4,081	+60 (+1.5 per cent)
Financial services, information and communication	2,231	+82 (+3.6 per cent)
Hotels, catering	1,483	+36 (+2.5 per cent)
Education	3,055	−47 (−1.5 per cent)
Health	3,838	−59 (−1.5 per cent)

Source: ONS (2012)

Table 7.9 shows two further trends: first, a reflection in the changing pattern of consumer demand, where we spend much more money on consumer and leisure activities – holidays, eating out, shopping and at the hairdressers. (In fact, the highest rate of growth of any individual job from 1990 to 2005 was hairdressing.) Second, there was increased expenditure by the Labour Government on health and education, as promised in their election manifestos, which has led to an increase in jobs in both sectors and here the decline during the recession has been relatively slight.

But the biggest increase of all sectors is the category involving computer-related jobs. This will reinforce what you will read in Chapter 8 on technology, where IT developments (automation, communications) have replaced the need for skilled and unskilled labour in manufacturing. The major improvements in productivity have all taken place in this sector, so output has risen, prices have come down and overall industrial employment has diminished.

A further trend in this area is that a good proportion of jobs created from the time of the Labour Government in 1997 have been in the public sector, either directly or indirectly (Buchanan et al 2009), where 'para-state' jobs were included, which depended entirely on government funding. Of the 2.23 million jobs created, fewer than 1 million were true private sector jobs. All of the rise of employment in the West Midlands was in public sector jobs with no new private sector jobs generated overall. An interesting finding here was that the financial sector appeared to have made a negligible contribution to employment. The researchers concluded that the business model was undisclosed and unsustainable. Since 2010, the Coalition Government have reduced public sector employment with the policy of encouraging private enterprise to replace numbers employed, a policy which has had a modicum of success.

However, of the 524,000 jobs created in the private sector in the 12 months to June 2012, the great majority have been either part-time or temporary or through the increase in self-employment. The pay statistics have shown that such employment has not been well paid.

REFLECTIVE ACTIVITY 7.3

Consider the scenario where the main manufacturing employer in a country town, employing 1,500 staff, announces it is closing down.

Questions

1   What are the implications for the local economy?

2   What are the overall implications for the UK of the decline in manufacturing employment?

Changes in geographical population location

A final aspect of demography is the internal movement of population within countries. For over 200 years there has been a steady movement away from the land and into the cities around the world as agriculture has become mechanised and farms consolidated. In the last hundred years or so, this movement has extended in certain countries to widespread geographical patterns. In Italy, it has been a mass movement from the poor, rural south to the more prosperous urban north. In the UK, the movement is in the opposite direction with a general move from the industrial areas, especially in the north, to the more balanced economies of the south and east.

The population of the north-eastern counties of England actually dropped in the 1990s and population increases in Yorkshire and Lancashire were quite small. On the other hand, counties in the south-east, such as Cambridgeshire, increased by 10 per cent or more as an estimated 250,000 citizens moved from north to south (Brindle 1999).

TRENDS TO WATCH – AND THE FUTURE?

If the world's population continued to increase at its current rate, all estimates show such a growth to be completely unsustainable. Food and energy would run out, leading to the Malthusian nightmares of war, pestilence and disease, causing a decline in population to sustainable levels. Economists have been divided as to the scenario at 2050, with some estimates of population at 10 billion and still growing and others indicating a more conservative outcome. Happily, those with an optimistic viewpoint are becoming more plentiful. At a 2002 United Nations conference, the director of the population division, Joseph Chamie, confidently predicted a peak of 8 billion at 2040 followed by a falling world population at 2050 for the first time since the Black Death. Subsequent forecasts have been a little less optimistic, due to the surprising resurgence in fertility rates in some Western nations, but the consensus appears to identify around 2050 as the peak year of world population at around 9.2 billion.

The conference was called to discuss the implications of unexpectedly fast declines in fertility in dozens of countries, including some very large ones. Mexico, India and Brazil have all forecast a decline in their birth rate below replacement level within 20 years. The assumption that, as nations developed their economies, women settle down to 2.4 children, now appears erroneous. Women in developing countries appear to be to striving for the freedoms achieved in the developed countries where the decisions open to them include deciding not to have a family at all or just one child. Bangladeshi women today have 3.3 children while the Vietnamese have halved their fertility rate in ten years to 2.3, just above the replacement level (*Economist* 2009a). So far, fewer births will automatically result in eliminating population growth.

There is also a question mark over increasing life expectancy. It is still likely that we can all expect to live a little longer every decade, but AIDS has had a serious effect in sub-

Saharan Africa and is spreading its tentacles into other areas, with rapid growth in HIV in Eastern Europe, South America and the Far East. So the increase in life expectancy, although having in itself important consequences, will only marginally influence the long-term decline in population.

By 2013, most demographic studies concluded that world population would certainly peak around 2050 at about 9–10 billion and then begin a slow decline that, if extrapolated, would reduce to around 3 billion by 2300 (Hanlon 2013).

In the UK, the stabilisation of the fertility rate at around 1.9 will inevitably bring to an end the natural population growth, probably around 2035 or 2040, where it will peak at around 70 million, depending on migration assumptions, according to latest predictions. However, the Government Actuary's Department has reported that life expectancy is growing faster than previous predictions and should rise to 81 for men and 85 for women by 2030 (Doward 2003). If this occurs, the population will continue to grow for a little longer, although the average age of the population will rise.

However, there is no doubt that *the population will become older*. In 2030, 15 million will be over current pensionable age, compared with 11 million now. In 2007, the number of pensioners overtook the number of children. The average age is set to rise from 38.8 in 2000 to 42.6 in 2025.

To summarise, over the next 20 years, the world population will continue to grow rapidly, but this growth will then start to taper off and will probably reverse by the mid-century point. Populations in developed countries will become distinctly older and internationally diverse. An ageing world may bring a severe reduction in labour forces and greater pressure on the productive young. However, the number of older workers who will be in much greater health will increase substantially. Populations in developing countries will also age but from a very low base figure and will become internationally mobile.

IMPLICATIONS OF DEMOGRAPHIC PREDICTIONS

As indicated at the start of this chapter, demographic trends will have substantial implications across the world at local, national and international levels. We will examine these implications in outline for the following groups:

- implication for organisations, especially in the UK private sector
- implications for governments, especially the UK Government
- implications for international society.

IMPLICATIONS FOR ORGANISATIONS

A slowdown in population growth and an ageing population has effects both on the nature of the marketplace and on the sources of labour. Adaptations to their current business practices could take the following forms:

Sources of labour – with far fewer school-leavers and younger people generally, organisations will have to look elsewhere for labour, particularly if the economy reverts to growing steadily under the full employment conditions seen in the 16 years up to 2008. Alternative sources can involve moving away from the traditional full-time 9 to 5 job design and moving to a more flexible model where much greater use is made of part-time jobs, job-shares, flexible hours and working from home. These flexible modes can meet the working needs of those with caring responsibilities, principally (but not exclusively) women, and older people generally who are retired or semi-retired. Some retailers, such as B&Q and Tesco, have specifically targeted older potential staff, which has led not just to an easing of recruitment difficulties but to considerable customer satisfaction arising from the knowledge such staff bring to the job. As a spokesperson for Nationwide Building Society explained:

Many customers prefer dealing with more maturity and experience and older workers tend to be more loyal and committed. (*Economist* 2004)

Retailer ASDA offers a variety of flexible working practices, including 'Benidorm leave', where employees can take up to three months' unpaid leave in the winter to take an extended holiday. They also offer grandparents' leave and carers' leave together with a seasonal colleague's scheme which attracts older people to work ten weeks a year at the peak times. Store managers are encouraged to visit older people's clubs and these policies have resulted in the number of over-65 employees rising to 3,500 in 2006 (CIPD 2007).

Bridgend County Borough Council adopted, in the early 2000s, a number of policies centred on 'Age Positive' to combat a tight labour market and changing demography. These included allowing employees who work beyond retiring age to contribute to their pension, introducing a mentoring scheme that involves those coming up to retirement coaching younger employees in valuable skills and ignoring an employee's age when considering training and development opportunities (Persaud 2004).

A further example of a progressive approach to the employment of older employees is shown in Case Study 7.5.

CASE STUDY 7.5

ALLEVARD SPRINGS' APPROACH TO EMPLOYING OLDER WORKERS

Allevard Springs specialises in the design and manufacture of coil suspension precision springs for the automotive industry. At its factory in the Rhondda Valley, Glamorgan, staff turnover is very low, with 83 per cent of employees having worked in the plant for over five years.

Recruiting the right staff

The company has a positive view about employing older workers; there is no reference to age on application forms and recruitment decisions are based on a person's ability to carry out the job or task allocated to them and not on the basis of age.

Despite a high level of unemployment in the area, Perry Stephens, management services manager, says that:

> There is a shortage of skilled maintenance people, which older people play an important part in filling. For example, the company currently has five "super skilled" engineering technicians and two of them are

over 60 and one is over 50 years of age.

The company's view is that employers can benefit enormously from having older people in their workforce, bringing with them skills learned during their working life coupled with a willingness to continue to learn. Continues Perry: 'If somebody is capable of doing whatever job function is required, then age doesn't come into it.'

Keeping good staff

Perry says that although he is aware of the misconception that older people may take more time off work because of illness, this hasn't been his experience:

> I find that it's the exact opposite. There's quite a number of older people who haven't missed any time whatsoever, such as Paul, who's had one day off in over 20 years.

Perry also finds that older employees are just as happy as their other employees to work the usual shift patterns; 'We've got quite a few people in their late fifties still doing the regular shifts: 6.00–2.00; 2.00–10.00; 10.00–6.00.'

Each individual's training and development needs are informed by annual staff appraisals. Again, age is irrelevant in this process, as is seniority. All staff, whether on the shop floor or in senior management, receive their appraisal.

Flexible retirement

The company's retirement age is 65 but it is happy for employees to work beyond that. Jane is one employee who is interested in this possibility, after joining the organisation at the age of 60.

Jane was recruited on a temporary basis to help the purchase ledger clerk when the factory's accounts department found itself shorthanded. She had lots of previous experience and was able to use all of the necessary software program. When the accountant became aware of how skilled she was, she was asked to help with some other work.

Jane soon became a permanent employee and enjoys her role: 'Work keeps you active and keeps your mind alive, especially when you're learning new things. It also gives you a routine and you make friends too. It makes no difference whether you're young or older – working is a benefit to everybody.'

Other staff have retired and decided to return to the organisation – one for a further 15 months and another who is still enjoying work and plans to continue.

The business benefits for Allevard Springs of an age-diverse workforce include:

- low staff turnover – 83 per cent of employees have worked in the plant for over five years
- recruiting from wider talent pool and retaining experience helps to fill skills shortages
- wide age spectrum makes for a relaxed, friendly culture.

Source: DWP (2011)

It is unlikely that the offers of early retirement with enhanced pensions will be generous in the future. The UK Government has already moved away from funding such arrangements centrally, requiring each department or agency to bear the costs involved. This has already led to a substantial reduction in such offers and employees choosing early retirements currently have to fund this out of their own pension schemes, in most cases.

Given these factors, it is not surprising that a greater proportion of those over retirement age choose to continue to work, enhancing the participation rates of pensioners as detailed earlier. However, as in the example of Japanese older workers in Case Study 7.1, there is the danger of 'Balkanisation' of labour markets, where employees at both ends of the demographic market have poor job security, menial work and low pay (Roberts 2006).

Change in markets – as the patterns of population change, their consumer needs alter accordingly. With an ageing population, there will be a *decline* in demand for products for the young, such as baby foods and prams and, eventually, to products for teenagers and the age group 18–25. The brewing industry has seen a substantial decline in the demand for beer as the largest consumers have traditionally been those 18–25, a declining age group, although their drinking habits have also changed. Similarly, sales of teenage fashion goods – clothes, CDs, jewellery – have become sluggish in recent years. Although the per capita spending has increased as the general level of prosperity has risen, it does not make up for the reduced population in those age brackets.

On the other side, there are some sectors of industries which *gain* from an ageing population. The most dramatic is the travel and tourism industry as older people spend a higher proportion of their income on holidays than most other groups. For a number of cyclical reasons, they also have become a much wealthier segment of the community. Saga, floated on the stock market for close to £1 billion in 2004, is the clearest winner, providing a vast range of holidays – active and inactive – to a growing market, broadening their product range to insurance and other financial services.

On the financial front, it has been estimated that, worldwide, people over the age of 55 hold around 70 per cent of the planet's wealth and there is a huge market here for service providers involved in investments, pensions and general financial security, as shown in Case Study 7.6.

CASE STUDY 7.6

WEALTH ADVICE FOR THE ELDERLY IN THE US

Examples of some of the services provided especially for older US citizens include:

Reverse mortgages – in 2006, 76,000 US citizens took out mortgages where they receive a lump sum or a line of credit and do not pay any interest while the mortgage is running. All the fees and accumulated interest are paid off when the house is sold, usually (but not always) when the mortgagee dies. Currently, the federal government guarantees such mortgages, so that if a homeowner's debts are greater than the value of his home at the time of death, the estate will not have to make up the shortfall. This partly explains why the number of reverse mortgages taken out increased by 77 per cent over the total for 2005. However, fees can be very high for this financial instrument (as much as 10 per cent) and the mortgagees' heirs are not always happy by the way that the inheritance is eroded by high fees and interest payments.

Elder services group – a product marketed by Wells Fargo and other providers to the banks' ageing and generally prosperous clientele, the bank will handle investments, pay regular bills, process insurance claims, arrange and monitor healthcare (including the high costs associated with surgery and treatment in the US)

and provide regular reports on the client's financial situation. Some go further and give advice on funeral arrangements, nursing homes, organise taxi contracts when eyesight fails and even deal with regular logistics for pills and other pharmaceutical products.

Wealth management – an increasing number of providers are entering the market to handle investments for the elderly. Citigroup, for example, have built 17 regional 'planning centres' for its wealthy customers – mainly baby boomers on the edge of retirement with more than $5 million in assets to invest. They bring together tax and trust lawyers, specialists in insurance, philanthropy and experts in small business sales so all the options are covered. Wachovia have developed a financial programme that allows them to focus on customers with a minimum of $250,000.

Due to the complexity of this financial area and the declining faculties of some of the clients, the providers are increasingly attempting to avoid the 'hard-selling' approach. A number, including HSBC bank, are using older or even semi-retired employees to carry out the sales negotiations so, hopefully, the claims for mis-selling are reduced.

Source: *Economist* (2007)

REFLECTIVE ACTIVITY 7.4

Summarise the effects of an ageing population on the tourism, retailing and banking industries.

Housing presents an interesting reflection of demographic changes. Although the population is now growing only slowly, the price of houses has risen substantially due, mostly, to a somewhat unexpected higher demand. This has come about because, as the fertility rate drops and the population ages, there is no corresponding drop in the number of households. Whereas young children live with their parents, older people live mostly in their own housing unit. Many stay in their own homes looking after themselves to the end, or nearly to the end, of their lives, assisted by a benefits system that encourages such behaviour. Add to this the increase in divorce, which often creates additional demand for housing, and the rise in students living away from home, perhaps the rise in house prices is not so unexpected. A winner here has been the construction companies that provide retirement homes in the UK, such as McCarthy and Stone.

Other clear winners in the demographic stakes are those who market *products specifically for the elderly*. There will be growing markets for mobility products and those aimed at improving healthcare, from pharmaceutical products to private hospitals. These include:

● 'Nutraceuticals', including vitamins, nutrients, minerals and herbal extracts, a market estimated to be worth $8 billion in the USA alone. Nutritional scientists are working on a new array of food products that are scientifically designed to improve your health and longevity and which will have specific appeal to the middle-aged and elderly.
● There are more than 100 US bio-tech companies actively researching age-related disorders (Wallace 2001), such as the role of telomeres in cell ageing, which may keep skin young and elastic, and tissue engineering, which may offer the prospect of replacement parts for the body.
● Stannah lifts has become another household name, while magazines devoted to older readers (such as *Yours*) have substantially increased their circulations.

The same reasoning can be applied to the next age group down, call it 'middle-aged', where their demands for financial services (savings products, pensions) and some luxury products (Mercedes cars, boats and homes in the sun) have grown very strongly in recent years. Sales of prestige cars have held up very well in the UK since the recession started in 2008.

IMPLICATIONS FOR GOVERNMENTS, ESPECIALLY THE UK GOVERNMENT

For governments, the biggest potential difficulty arising from the ageing population is the increase in the *dependency ratio*. The dependency ratio calculation is the ratio of working-age population to the dependent population. The dependent population are children under 16 and older people over retirement age.

As the proportion of the population over retirement age increases, it puts a much greater strain on the working population, who need to fund the services for older people. As detailed above, there has been much greater reliance on the state for looking after older people. There is no doubt this strain will be with us soon, as shown in Figure 7.1.

Figure 7.1 UK dependency ratio – ratio of 16–64-year-olds to over-65s

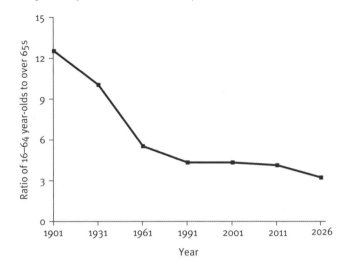

Figure 7.1 shows the startling change in dependency that has occurred already and will get worse in the future. Currently just over four employees provide earned income to support one pensioner. This will decline to just over three by 2026. The position is worse for other countries. For Germany, the ratio will be less than three by the same year and it will reduce to around two by 2040. By 2050, the Japanese ratio will have deteriorated to an astonishing 1.3. For the world as a whole, the current figure of nine is likely to reduce to four by 2050 (*Economist* 2009a).

The problem for governments is how to raise the increased revenue required from what could be a dwindling source of working population. It has been estimated that, in the UK, each pensioner costs the Government around £10,000 per year, net of any tax receipts, through the old age pension, a variety of benefits (housing, disability, etc) and the vast range of medical care (primary care, free prescriptions, hospital stays). Older people are much more prone to illness and therefore impose much greater costs on the health services. Sixty-five per cent of Department for Work and Pensions benefit expenditure goes to those over working age, equivalent to £100 billion in 2010–11, or one-seventh of public expenditure. Continuing to provide state benefits and pensions at today's average would mean additional spending of £10 billion a year for every additional 1 million people over working age (Parliamentary Business 2010).

It could be argued that some of the additional money required can be raised by savings on services to young people with reduced expenditure on maternity units and compulsory schooling, although any closure or reduction in services is met by solid resistance from the community. Because employees in their forties and fifties earn more than employees in their twenties, it is expected that increased tax revenue will go some way towards filling this gap.

The problem is acute in the fire service and the police force. Their pension fund allows retirement after 30 years' service on two-thirds of annual salary and many others retire early on health grounds. This has produced the situation where Merseyside Fire and Rescue Service has 1,678 working staff but is paying the pensions of 1,691 retired staff, and a similar situation exists in police forces in Lincolnshire, Northern Ireland and the City of London, among others. Efforts have been made to reduce the huge costs involved and police and fire crews who have joined the service since 2006 will have to work for 35 years (Watts 2008).

The *pension implications* are tough for the UK and America, but at least there is reasonable private pension provision that is located in properly funded systems. This, however, is the exception compared with the rest of the world. For most of Europe and other developed countries, the proportion of pensions paid by the state is very much higher and this is funded as transfer payments under a pay as you go (PAYG) basis, that is, directly out of taxation income, rather than from an actual fund of money that has been invested. A major cause of the Greek Government's financial crisis in 2010 was the overgenerous, unfunded state pensions.

Table 7.10 shows the implications for selected countries in terms of the huge government expenditure necessary to pay the pensions as a proportion of their GDP (gross domestic product).

Table 7.10 Public pension expenditure as a percentage of GDP

	1995	2020*	2040*
UK	4.5	5.2	7.1
USA	4.1	5.2	7.2
The Netherlands	6.0	8.4	12.1
France	10.6	11.6	14.3
Sweden	11.8	13.9	14.9
Spain	10.0	11.3	16.8
Germany	11.1	12.3	18.4
Italy	13.3	15.3	21.4

* estimate
Source: ECOFIN (2006)

There are already substantial problems in France, Germany and Italy over the high levels of public sector borrowing. The European Union has attempted with little success to fine these countries as part of the Stability Pact arrangements made at the time of the establishment of the euro to prevent governments incurring excessive expenditure to buy themselves out of financial difficulties. Many commercial organisations are moving production out of these countries to the UK, Eastern Europe and the developing world to avoid existing high taxation rates. So how such pension liabilities can be met is sorely testing the economic advisors and central banks in these countries. This problem has been exacerbated by the greatly increased level of government debt incurred to bail the banks out of the financial crisis which began in 2007 and the resultant recession.

REFLECTIVE ACTIVITY 7.5

Not all writers regard the pension liabilities as insurmountable or see the necessity of huge increases in taxation or reductions in benefit to solve the pensions problem. What do you consider to be the basis for their optimism?

A further problem arises from *irregular internal migration*. Those parts of the country that attract population are faced by considerable pressures on housing, transport and infrastructure services. For example, the housing shortages in London and the south-east of England have produced continuous shortages in essential public services, especially teachers and nurses, who cannot find affordable housing, especially in their early careers. Similar problems occur in the Milan and Turin areas of northern Italy. The governments are faced with planning dilemmas. If they allow housing on green belt land in and around London, it arouses massive opposition. If new roads are built to alleviate congestion, the traffic merely increases within a short time to clog up the system.

In some parts of the world, all of these difficulties gel into a bleak prognosis. In California, for example, the State Department of Finance has forecast a 75 per cent increase in population to 60 million by 2050, making it a 'country masquerading as a state' (Kyser 2007). This will lead to a water and power catastrophe, decaying infrastructure, education funding gaps and huge state debt.

Finally, there are problems associated with the *skills base*. Little has changed since Jackson (1998) explained that:

> One reason why the market has been unable to absorb the… unemployed has been the increasing demand for employees with appropriate skills and capabilities. Gaining entry to the labour market has become more difficult as manual occupations have declined and as employers have become more selective about recruits to jobs in the service and quaternary sectors. Britain needs a better trained workforce if it is to meet the challenge from its competitors in Europe and overseas and the current skills gap means that many find themselves excluded from the opportunities of employment. (Jackson 1998, p125)

Options for governments

The only two ways that governments can approach a solution to the financial problems brought on by longevity is to either raise taxes or reduce benefits. Some countries have already taken bold steps, such as New Zealand abolishing the universal right to an old age pension and the UK Government is raising the age when women can claim the pension to 65 in the period 2010–20, and the state pension to 67 for both men and women by 2028. It was originally planned for this to occur in 2046, but the clear financial requirement caused the Coalition Government to rapidly bring this forward and thereby save £60 billion. Other suggested benefit reductions are means-testing fuel allowances and reducing the age allowance in income tax.

However, bold steps in reducing benefits can be very damaging politically and are not taken lightly. Certainly people can be encouraged to increase their savings for the future by making a larger contribution to their pension schemes, which is done by most governments. In Japan, this has been very successful and the Japanese are the highest savers in the world. (Incidentally, this high saving and reduced consumption has contributed towards a prolonged recession in Japan through most of the 1990s and 2000s.)

Some commentators believe that is likely that when the full effects of the higher dependency ratio reach the population as a whole, society will be much more affluent and willing to pay the additional costs as part of the understanding that a measure of the decency of a society is how they look after vulnerable groups, such as the elderly. This will have the effect of placing a greater emphasis on community care for the elderly (Bartlett and Peel 2005).

An alternative approach is to attempt to reverse the demographic trends and to encourage bigger families. This can be done by providing greater financial incentives (tax reliefs and maternity/child benefits) and by encouraging organisations to be more family-friendly so that women are able to combine motherhood and a job more easily. The Chinese Government is moving away from the 'One Child Policy' instituted in 1979, as shown in Case Study 7.7.

CHINA AND THE ONE CHILD POLICY

By 2050, China will have more than 438 million people over 60, with 100 million aged over 80. There will be just 1.6 working-age adults to support every person over 60, compared with 7.7 in 1975. One of the unexpected outcomes of the One Child Policy has been to encourage Chinese families to be great savers. This is because the One Child Policy created a surplus of men and has driven up the cost of marriage, as more men compete with fewer women. To keep up, families with sons have been holding off spending to create wealth that boosts their son's marriage prospects. Economists have concluded that Chinese marriage-price inflation could account for as much as half of the increase in the country's household saving since 1990.

The spectre of an ageing population hangs heavy over Shanghai, where the proportion of working adults to retirees is low and threatens a major burden. Family planning authorities in the city are proactive in encouraging families with one child to have a second through extensive publicity and home visits, although financial incentives have not yet been introduced.

In 2013, the Chinese National Bureau of Statistics announced that the working-age population had shrunk by 3.45 million, chiefly as a result of the One Child Policy. Although there are signs that this policy may be loosened, the growing affluence and increased education is likely to balance the loosening effect and keep the fertility rate around 1.6. However, there are increasing signs that the reduction in the labour force is causing wages to rise and many goods to be less competitive, especially when compared with poorer Eastern economies, such as Vietnam. Academics argue whether the seemingly unending migration from the land to the cities is coming to a halt and that only further wage increases will encourage the flow to continue.

Sources: Coonan (2009); Dubner and Levitt (2009); *Economist* (2013b)

The problem is that such actions by governments, such as shown by Japan in Case Study 7.1, appear to have only a marginal effect on the indigenous population. Despite actions in similar forms by many governments in developed countries, it has done little to reverse the flagging fertility rate, with the exception of the UK and USA.

A drastic action could be to open the doors wider to migrants from developing countries. This makes a great deal of long-term economic sense but has a number of political obstacles to overcome in terms of the perceptions of migrants 'taking jobs' and the additional pressures on housing and transport.

One response to the overcrowding in some parts of a country has been to attempt to disperse government departments (as long ago as the early 1970s, the Department of National Savings was moved to Durham, for example) and to provide additional tax and benefit incentives to businesses to move to poorer regions, which is a major pillar in the European Union's economic policy.

The most drastic governmental action seen so far has been in Ulyanovsk, in Russia, where September 12 has been declared 'Conception Day' and couples that conceive under their 'Give Birth to a Patriot' programme can win cars, fridges or cash prizes (*Sunday Times* 2007).

Not everybody, however, insists that an ageing population is so great a problem. Mullan (2002) argues that demographic ageing has no determinate relationship to national economic activity and that modest levels of economic growth will be more than sufficient to create the wealth required to sustain the costs brought on by greater numbers of elderly dependants.

IMPLICATIONS FOR INTERNATIONAL SOCIETY

The global economy

The most worrying aspect of the current demographic changes is that the mature and ageing population appears to lead directly to reduced economic growth. Europe and Japan have seen the fastest decline in fertility rates and has also seen the slowest economic growth in the early twenty-first century. America, on the other hand, has had a milder strain and has managed to maintain a faster growth rate over the period. In the 'Tiger' economies – China, Korea, Taiwan – and on the Indian subcontinent, where fertility rates, although falling, still remain at or above replacement level, there is a much higher rate of economic growth.

The United Nations has projected that America, with its higher fertility rate and greater migration, will catch up Europe's population by 2040 (currently it is 100 million less) and exceed it by 40 million by 2050. The economic implications are far-reaching. The working population of Europe will start to decline in 2010 but, for America, the current steady growth in its workforce will even start to accelerate in 2025. This will result in the US economy growing twice as fast as that of Europe for the next 50 years. In 2000, America accounted for 23 per cent of global gross domestic product (GDP) compared with Europe's 18 per cent. By 2050, the United Nations estimates America's share will be 26 per cent while Europe's will have shrunk to only 10 per cent. By 2050, the American economy will be two and a half times as big as Europe's with all the additional political clout that this implies (United Nations 2011).

In reality, the only way this situation could be reversed would be by radically changing Europe's tight immigration controls, which is a very unlikely event, or if America's fertility rate dropped sharply, as it becomes a mature economy.

International migration of work

In the early 2000s, Barclays Bank and other financial institutions announced that they would be cutting their workforces and transferring chunks of their customer service and 'back-office' administration work to other countries, particularly India. The costs of carrying out this work in developing countries is just a fraction compared with UK costs and the workforces are young, educated, English-speaking and flexible in their approach to working hours and the nature of work. These decisions were made because the demographic changes, and the responses made by governments (India has invested heavily in English-speaking education), have made such countries good substitutes for UK labour.

This situation has been replicated around the globe. In America, work migration is an important political issue dividing the parties, while German unions have had to respond to threats to move industrial work in companies such as Volkswagen to Eastern Europe by agreeing to reduce hourly wages (see Case Study 7.8).

CASE STUDY 7.8

 EXAMPLES OF GERMAN JOBS EXODUS 2002–04

Lufthansa: European ticket sales based in Krakau, Poland. Aircraft engines serviced in Hungary, China and the Philippines.

Motorola: 600 engineering jobs moved to China. Repair work moved to Eastern Europe.

Deutsche Bank: Deutsche Software subsidiary moved to India with 4,000 jobs.

SAP, business software and systems: created 1,500 jobs in Bangalore, India and new 120-strong R&D centre in Shanghai.

Continental Tyres: three German factories closed – work transferred to three new factories in Romania, the Czech Republic and Slovakia.

Source: Woodhead (2004)

REFLECTIVE ACTIVITY 7.6

In 2003, the South African Government placed a prohibition on UK companies recruiting qualified nurses to work in the NHS, viewing the exodus of skilled workers such as nurses as a matter of long-term disaster for the country. Do you agree with this viewpoint? Discuss the issue from both viewpoints.

World's resources

In the twentieth century, the inventiveness, organisational powers and application of technology from farmers, merchants, entrepreneurs and companies of all sizes allowed the tripling world population to be adequately provided for in terms of food, water and power. Not completely, of course, with intermittent famines and a growing imbalance between rich and poor countries. However, it had been considered unlikely that such expansion of resources could continue at this breakneck pace for another 100 years. The availability of additional water resources in the current developing countries is likely to be the stumbling block to the easy accommodation of an additional 4 billion people who required a high lifestyle.

The forecasts of a levelling-out of the population by mid-century could be regarded, therefore, as good news for everybody. The strains on space and exploitation of a limited land mass, especially where global warming appears to be reducing capacity, may now be much lessened, although these pressures are brought about not just by numbers of population but by their overall demands. A richer, more consuming population still has the capacity to wreak enormous damage on our planet's infrastructure.

SOCIAL TRENDS

INTRODUCTION

This section analyses recent trends in society and social/family structure in the UK. It considers social mobility and inequality, and the continuing existence of poverty in the UK. This is followed by an examination of diversity in the UK, its desirability, associated difficulties and implications for management.

SOCIAL MOBILITY

Social mobility can be thought of in absolute and relative terms. The former refers to processes of adjustment in the income or occupational structure of the economy, indicating the number or proportion who move from one social class to another. The latter, sometimes called social fluidity, is associated with an individual's *opportunities* for progression within the social hierarchy. Social mobility can also be thought of as intra-generational (chances for social progression within an individual's own lifetime) and inter-generational (a comparison of achieved social position with that of one's parents) (Nunn et al 2007).

Other dimensions are the absence of poverty and access to decent standards of health and education. Quality of life varies with social class, ethnic group, gender and locality (Aldridge 2004).

Until the Second World War, there was considerable absolute social mobility in Britain, but downward mobility was nearly as common as upward. Since the Second World War, upward absolute social mobility has considerably outweighed downward, with the trend increasing – it is much higher for men born in 1950–59 (the latest available figures) than for men born in 1920–29 (the first group to have reached maturity after the Second World War). The main reason for this upward mobility is that there is 'more room at the top'. In 1900, the middle class made up 18 per cent of the population, while the working class made up 62 per cent. By 2010, the middle class was 46 per cent of the population and the working class 36 per cent.

The main interest in research in this area is that social mobility is generally associated with higher economic growth. So a country that successfully promotes social mobility is more likely to increase the general standard of living and opportunities for prosperity for all of its population (Nunn et al 2007).

While the picture on absolute social mobility looks positive, the picture is very different when one looks at relative mobility. Because the middle class is bigger, this means that children of middle-class parents have less risk of falling down into the working class, that is, downward social mobility has fallen. The result has been that the chances of a working-class child making it to the middle class have changed little – it is estimated that a working-class child is 15 times less likely to make it into the middle class than a middle-class child is to stay in the middle class.

Most worryingly, there is some evidence that social mobility, however it is measured, is slowing down. This is best shown by figures on income. Studies have been made of the correlation between fathers' earnings and offsprings' earnings. A correlation of zero would imply complete income mobility between generations, that is, that a father's income has no influence on his offspring's income, while a correlation of one would imply total immobility, that is, that an offspring's place in the income scale is exactly the same as his or her father's. For the UK correlations have been found of between 0.4 and 0.6 for sons' earnings, and between 0.45 and 0.7 for daughters. The higher the correlation, the less the income mobility and, by implication, the lower the level of social mobility.

Closer examination of the correlations shows two disturbing trends:

- Correlations are much higher in the UK than in countries such as Canada, Sweden or Finland.
- A comparison of those born in 1958 with those born in 1970 shows the correlations increasing – that is, social mobility in the UK is falling.

One study compared two sons both born in 1958 who left school in the 1970s. The parents of one earned twice as much as the parents of the other. By their early thirties, the son of the richer parents earned 17.5 per cent more than the poorer son. For two comparable boys born in 1970 who left school in the 1980s, the income gap had widened to 25 per cent (Blanden et al 2005).

In 2007, the educational charity the Sutton Trust researched the educational backgrounds of 500 leading figures in the law, politics, medicine, journalism and business. They found that over half had been educated in an independent school, although these only educate 7 per cent of the population, and that this figure had barely changed over the past 20 years. In addition, 47 per cent of the top 500 were Oxbridge educated (Sutton Trust 2007). A linked research report in 2010 found that social mobility had declined further, as shown in Case Study 7.9.

CASE STUDY 7.9

SOCIAL MOBILITY IN THE PROFESSIONS

This research report investigated the origins of those individuals entering into the top professions in the two British birth cohort studies. Sampling took place from two groups of 18,000 born in 1958 and 1970, identifying those who were working in the professions at age 33 and identifying their parents' income at birth.

Comparing the average family incomes in childhood of those working in the top professions indicates that those who go into professions come from families with incomes higher than average. More worryingly, this trend appears to have worsened for many of the professions considered for those born in 1970 compared with those born in 1958, with the gaps in family income between the top professions and the sample average increasing over time.

For example, those born in 1958 who went on to become doctors came from families with an income of 42 per cent greater than average, but this had increased to 63 per cent for those born in 1970. For accountants, the trend was even greater, with a figure rising from 1 per cent to 40 per cent between the two cohorts, while the figures for journalists/broadcasters rose from 5 per cent to 42 per cent. The only professions where this trend did not apply were teachers, academics and musicians.

The report investigated whether the ability (as measured by IQ) of those entering professions had risen over the period but found no significant difference.

Source: Macmillan (2010)

The factors that influence social mobility have been set out by Nunn et al (2007):

- *Social capital* – there is some evidence that traditional working-class social capital has declined, which may have weakened its assumed negative effects on social mobility, while other 'negative' forms of social capital have emerged, such as cultures of worklessness, anti-social behaviour and drug abuse. A lack of positive role models, peer pressure, poverty of ambition and risk aversion may serve as barriers to social mobility. By contrast middle-class families tend to have access to a wider range of social networks that are more advantageous from the point of view of enabling upward mobility and protecting against downward mobility.
- *Cultural capital* – can also help middle-class families to confer social advantages on their children, increasing their potential to move upwards and protecting them from downward movement in the social hierarchy.
- *Early years influences* – are seen as key to influencing later life chances. Convincing evidence shows that early experiences such as the quality of the home environment,

family structure, pre-school care and relationships with caring adults produce a pattern of development in later life that is hard to reverse, even through schooling.

- *Education* – appears to be one of the most important factors influencing social mobility. However, there is considerable evidence that the introduction and expansion of universal education systems in the UK and Western Europe have not led to increasing levels of relative social mobility. This is due to a range of factors, including the ability of middle-class families to take advantage of educational opportunities.
- *Employment and labour market experiences* – recent decades have seen the emergence of important labour market trends with implications for social mobility. First, substantial levels of worklessness and long-term economic inactivity have emerged in some areas and/or among specific population groups. Second, research has identified the emergence of a prominent 'low-pay – no-pay' cycle for some groups. There is also evidence that specific groups face particular disadvantages in the labour market and that women who take career breaks often have difficulty re-entering the labour market in the same position and, therefore, frequently experience downward social mobility after having children.
- *Health and well-being* – ill-health results from social and environmental factors identified with lower socio-economic status, and ill-health and caring responsibilities can lead to declining socio-economic status.
- *Area-based influences* – localised environmental problems appear to combine with socio-economic disadvantage to produce negative area-based influences on potential for social mobility. For example, inequalities in access to private transport combined with poorer quality provision in some important public services in deprived areas may mean that lower socio-economic classes are unable to exercise effective choices over access to these services.

In January 2009, the Government published a white paper on social mobility (*New Opportunities: Fair Chances for the Future*). This identified the crucial role of education as a driver of social mobility. Research has shown that children on free school meals (a useful proxy for poverty) have only half the average child's chance of getting five good GCSE passes (Toynbee 2009). This is crucial, as five good GCSEs is the entry requirement for A-levels, and 95 per cent of those with A-levels go on to higher education and the increased life chances that follow from this. The Government proposed paying bonuses of £10,000 to teachers working in the toughest schools, defined as the 500 'national challenge' schools where less than 30 per cent achieve five good GCSE passes including maths and English, and a high proportion are eligible for free school meals (Sparrow 2009). The Government also proposed to invest £57 million in an expanded nursery and childcare programme for 15 per cent of the most disadvantaged families.

The white paper also announced plans to set up a cross-party panel chaired by the former health secretary Alan Milburn, a leading Blairite, to identify ways to increase the number of people from low-income backgrounds entering professional jobs. Milburn's panel produced *Fair Success to the Professions* in July 2009 (Milburn 2009a). He pointed to an increased opportunity for social mobility if entry to the professions could be widened, as 90 per cent of the jobs likely to be created by 2020 would be professional and managerial. He updated the Sutton Trust figures in entry to the professions quoted above and found that, if anything, the independent school bias was increasing. Only 7 per cent of children attended private schools, but they made up 75 per cent of judges, 70 per cent of finance directors and a third of MPs. In nine out of 12 professions, including medicine and the law, the proportion coming from wealthy families was increasing (Jack 2009). Milburn also quoted evidence that of six (unnamed) European countries, the UK had the lowest rate of social mobility for men and the second lowest for women.

The report saw the key to social mobility as being in education. Private schools (and the best state schools) not only produced better-qualified children, but they also developed the soft skills of confidence, teamwork and interview skills through extra-curricular activities and mentoring. Later, privately educated children made full use of professional internship programmes, which were usually organised on the basis of 'who you know'. State school pupils had neither the aspirations, the skills nor the contacts to break into the charmed circle.

Milburn made a number of recommendations, including:

- university students to be recruited from wider social backgrounds
- no-fee degrees for students living at home
- professions to publish more details on the social background of their intakes
- better careers advice aimed at raising aspirations
- more extra-curricular activity for state school pupils (BBC 2009).

Milburn also stressed that it was not just the working class that was blocked from the professions. Writing in the *Observer*, he said, 'it will be more and more middle-class kids, not just working-class ones, who miss out,' and 'we need a new focus, unleashing aspirations, not just beating poverty' (Milburn 2009b). Milburn was subsequently appointed as chair of the Social Mobility Commission set up in 2011 to monitor social mobility and reduce child poverty.

In response to the first recommendation, the Government created the Office of Fair Access (OFFA) in 2012 with substantial budget to run access programmes and encourage universities to link in with education establishments at all levels, not just sixth forms. For example, Nottingham Trent University holds 'family fun evenings' for 10- and 11-year-olds from poorer areas and their parents to introduce them to higher education (Harrison 2012).

INEQUALITY

Inequality in society can be measured in a number of ways, but the easiest is distribution of wealth or income. Wealth is extremely unevenly distributed in the UK, although rather less unevenly than in the 1950s, and much less unevenly than in the 1920s, when the top 1 per cent owned over 60 per cent of marketable wealth (Abercrombie and Warde 2000). There is strong evidence that inequality in wealth fell over the period from 1954 to 1995. For example, the top 1 per cent of population owned 43 per cent of net wealth in 1954 but this had fallen to 19 per cent by 2005 (ONS 2006a). The main reason for this was the spread of home ownership, from 20 per cent just after the war to around 75 per cent by 1995. A detailed analysis comparing 1995 to 2005 is shown in Table 7.11.

Table 7.11 Distribution of wealth (UK) (per cent)

Population	1995 net wealth*		2005		per cent change
(deciles)	£'000	per cent of total	£'000	per cent of total	
Bottom 10 per cent	−4	−0.6	−6	−0.5	−40
20 per cent	−0.1	0	2	0.1	+2,000
30 per cent	2.8	0.3	27.2	1.6	+870
40 per cent	12.8	1.7	68.1	4.1	+430
50 per cent	30.2	4.5	101.1	6.1	+230
60 per cent	49.5	6.6	135.4	8.1	+170
70 per cent	70.5	9.9	174.4	10.5	+150

Population	1995 net wealth*		2005		per cent change
(deciles)	£'000	per cent of total	£'000	per cent of total	
80 per cent	98.2	12.5	224.3	13.4	+130
90 per cent	148.4	19.7	315.5	18.9	+110
Top 10 per cent	364.0	46.2	627.5	37.7	+70

*Adjusted for inflation
Source: Karagianaki (2011)

It is clear from Table 7.11 that wealth inequality has become more complicated over this period. The net wealth of the top 10 per cent has fallen from 46.2 per cent to 37.7 per cent while for the top 50 per cent wealth ownership has dropped from 98.6 per cent to 94.7 per cent as 90 per cent of the population has benefited from the general increase in wealth, which indicated an improvement in the distribution of wealth. The bottom 50 per cent are the main gainers in percentage terms. However, the bottom 10 per cent, often called the underclass, associated with worklessness and where the income, in a good many cases, is mainly from social benefits, still retain a net debt with little gain from the 10 years of general economic growth and prosperity.

The other caveat is that this evidence is based on declared UK wealth and incomes and does not include wealth and income put offshore or through a wide variety of tax avoidance schemes by the very rich, which distorts the earnings of the top 10 per cent.

An earlier report shows that, if we exclude the value of dwellings, wealth is more unevenly held. In 2002, the top 1 per cent held 35 per cent of all marketable wealth less value of dwellings, the top 5 per cent held 62 per cent, and the top 50 per cent held 98 per cent (ONS 2006b).

The same pattern emerges if one examines distribution of income, as shown in the Table 7.12.

Table 7.12 Distribution of income (UK) (before housing costs)

	1961	1979	1997	2007
Top 10 per cent	22.0	21.0	26.0	30.0
Top 20 per cent	37.0	35.0	41.0	42.1
Top 50 per cent	70.6	68.0	72.0	72.6
Bottom 10 per cent	4.2	4.2	2.1	1.5

Source: adapted from George and Wilding (1999) and Lansley (2009)

Key points from Table 7.12 are:

- Income inequality narrowed marginally between 1961 and 1979, but has widened substantially in the last 30 years.
- Margaret Thatcher's 'trickle-down' theory, that increasing the wealth and income of the rich would produce a trickle down of greater income and wealth lower down the scale, appears to be a myth if housing is excluded.
- Even when inequality was lessening, this did not benefit the bottom 10 per cent.

In the early years of the Labour Government, the share of the bottom 10 per cent improved slightly, largely as a result of Gordon Brown's use of tax credits targeted at the poorest, but inequality widened during the course of the 2000s. An increased emphasis on indirect rather than direct taxes, which started well before 1997, has tended to hit the bottom end of the distribution harder than the top. Since 1979, the proportion of income paid in tax by the lowest 20 per cent of taxpayers has risen from 31 per cent to 42 per cent, while the proportion paid by the highest fifth has fallen from 37 per cent to 34 per cent (Clark 2004). In fact, the poor pay a higher proportion of income in tax than the rich.

Inequality and the very wealthy

Inequality may well be still increasing if the focus is on the highest 1 per cent of earners. This group increased their share of national income by 3 per cent between 1997 and 2007, mostly due to the very large increase in boardroom pay and in the earnings of the very skilled in niche professions, such as banking, financial services, law, medical consultant and sport. In fact, the share of the top 0.1 per cent in 2007 was the same as it was in 1937 (Milne 2007).

This aspect of inequality has caused considerable social and political friction in recent years. Very great wealth has historically been created by talented individuals exploiting an exceptional invention, growing an industrial empire or by accumulating assets, especially land. However, from the mid-1980s onwards, a considerable number of large fortunes were won from the financial sector, especially forms of banking, such as hedge funds, equity funds and derivatives trading. These reached their peak in the years leading up to the financial crash of 2007–08, when many of the banking operations had to be bailed out by governments across the developed world. Although many of the bankers and traders lost their jobs, they kept all their winnings and were usually paid off in a handsome fashion, leading to the view that they won all ways round – when times were good, they received obscene pay, bonuses and profits; when times were bad, they received obscene compensation, paid for by the taxpayer. In addition, it was considered by many commentators that the work they did (especially speculating and selling complex financial instruments that the buyer did not understand) was, at best, of no social value and, at worst, fraudulent.

Gini coefficient

A method used by statisticians to measure inequality is the Gini coefficient. This expresses income distribution on a scale of 0 to 100, with 0 representing total equality. The higher the figure, the more uneven the distribution. The Gini coefficient figures have changed as shown in Table 7.13.

Table 7.13 UK Gini coefficient (before housing costs)

1961	1970	1979	1991	1997	2002	2008	2011
26	26	25	34	33	36	36	34

Source: George and Wilding (1999); Clark (2004); IFS (2009); Cribb et al (2012)

On the Gini figures, inequality was constant over the period 1961–79, widened greatly under the Thatcher Governments and widened a little more under New Labour. By 2011, somewhat surprisingly, there was a reduction back to the level of 1991. This has been due to the following causes:

- Earnings reduced across all component parts of the income distribution, with the pain being shared by all groups in the labour force, not just those becoming unemployed.
- The top earners suffered because of the increase in the top rate of tax from 40 per cent to 50 per cent (although this was reduced to 45 per cent in 2013).
- The Government continued to up rate benefits in line with inflation, leading to a higher increase in benefits than in earnings, a trend continued in April 2012 when benefits

were raised by 5.2 per cent while average earnings were less than 3 per cent. This had the effect of increasing the income of the poor and hence narrowed the wealth gap. (However, from 2013, the Chancellor changed course by pegging a number of benefits to 1 per cent for three years for those out of work to try to avoid the situation where those on benefits, mostly in the lower groupings, increased their earnings more than those at work.)

Inequality in the UK is higher than in the rest of the European Union. The figure for the EU (15 members) was 31 in 2011, with both France and Germany at around the 32 mark. Inequality is much less in Scandinavia, where it averaged 25. However, on a world scale, the UK does not fare so badly. The Gini coefficient in the US was 39, China at 41, Brazil at 51 and South Africa at 62 (*Economist* 2012b).

It could be said that this spread merely reflects that society's take on equality. In America and China, greater emphasis tends to be placed on equality of opportunity, with the general philosophy that those who succeed do so, generally, through their own effort by grasping opportunities that arise. However in China, the general dissatisfaction with the gap between the rich, often corrupt officials and the general population has led to a strong initiative to combat social inequality in 2013, including raising the minimum wage to 40 per cent of average urban wages, increasing taxes on the rich and raising expenditure on education, healthcare and public spending from 30 per cent of the total 2009 budget to 38 per cent by 2015 (*Economist* 2013c).

Europeans tend to be more egalitarian and wish to retain traditional cultures that have led to low income inequality. So they accept the state using a greater level of taxation.

High levels of inequality rarely lead to stable governments. Latin America, for example, has had the highest level of inequality in the twentieth century and also a history of unstable and impoverished states, although there are strong signs of a growing middle class, with the proportion of Latin Americans living in poverty dropping from 41 per cent in 2000 to 28 per cent in 2010 and two in five citizens upwardly mobile over that period (*Economist* 2012c).

However, the focus by many countries on redistribution of wealth by taxation and improving benefits has brought its own problems. High welfare-oriented economies reduce real poverty but also take away the self-help and entrepreneurial culture which may leave a sizeable underclass welfare-dependent at great expense to the community.

CHANGES IN FAMILY STRUCTURE

The move to smaller families and a higher participation rate for women has led to changes in the structure of families and the role of family members. Table 7.14 shows the change in family structures from 2001 to 2011.

Table 7.14 Changing family structures

	2001	2011
Married couples	72.4 per cent	67.2 per cent
Co-habiting couples	12.5 per cent	16.0 per cent
Same-sex couples/civil partnerships	0.3 per cent	0.7 per cent
Lone mother	12.7 per cent	14.2 per cent
Lone father	2.1 per cent	1.9 per cent
Total number of families	17 million	17.9 million

Source: ONS (2011)

Table 7.14 shows the continuing decline in the traditional married family. The number of co-habiting couples has risen by a third and the number of reported same-sex families has more than doubled, while lone mothers has risen to around one in seven of all families. Forty-seven per cent of all children were born out of wedlock in 2011, ten times the rate of 1911, where the figure was close to 4 per cent (Hall 2012).

The decline in the popularity of marriage is influenced by a number of factors, including the fact that women have become more independent. Women have equal rights and have proven over time that they have the potential and ability to support themselves and find that it may be easier to deal with temporary relationships or to leave unhappy marriages. They are also more work-focused, thus giving them less time to cope with their relationship. Working to support a family while trying to stabilise finances can influence the likelihood of a stressful marriage. Also, with both partners working (in most cases), there is less 'family time', which makes raising children difficult. This often happens in the stage where couples are raising young children.

The number of marriages has declined substantially over the last 40 years, as shown in Figure 7.2.

Figure 7.2 Marriages in the UK

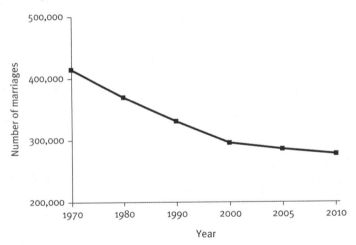

As a consequence of the decline in marriages, the number of UK divorces has fallen from 157,000 in 2001 to 131,682 in 2010.

Working women (especially those in full-time work) spend less time in domestic routines, which has led to a considerable growth in industries devoted to convenience foods, eating out and hired-in domestic help. Information from the Family Expenditure Survey shows that the proportion of income spent on eating out has increased by 50 per cent over the period 1980 to 2009.

The changes in the labour market have led to changes in the nature of society, as shown in an example from the 1980s in Case Study 7.10.

CHANGING SOCIETY IN SOUTH WALES

Doreen Massey carried out a survey of the implications of the massive closures of the steel and coal-mining industries in the early 1980s. She identified the difference between the former labour market, which was heavily male-dominated with a high proportion of manual and semi-skilled labour, and a new labour market that had grown up with economic restructuring. This was typified by new jobs in the electronics industries and high level of female employment. The previous labour market had created a patriarchal society that had remained relatively stable over many generations. The new market offered less stability and less security and led to changes in social patterns and family organisation.

Source: Massey (1984)

REFLECTIVE ACTIVITY 7.7

What actions can the Government take to mitigate the negative consequences of areas of declining manufacturing?

Other changes have involved the caring responsibilities for children becoming more shared between spouses, while there are many examples of active grandparents taking a substantial responsibility for day-to-day care of younger children.

On the other hand, there is the challenge of looking after older relatives, with around half living into their eighties and many into their nineties and beyond. In the past, many have lived in, making this an extended family, but, in Europe, this practice is declining, although it is still the norm in Japan. The need for a degree of personal privacy, the day-of-day medical and psychological challenges of coping with an elderly relative and the widespread growth in sheltered accommodation have been reasons for this trend.

Changes in family life are not just a UK phenomenon. In Europe, 37 per cent of births were out of wedlock in 2010 compared with only 17 per cent in 1990, with the figure for Scandinavian countries rising to over 50 per cent. The European marriage rate collapsed from 7.9 per 1,000 people in 1970 to 4.5 per 1,000 in 2010, while the divorce rate doubled between 1990 and 2008 from 1 per 1,000 people to 2 per 1,000 (Eurostat 2012).

POVERTY

Absolute poverty in the Ethiopian sense does not exist in the UK. A more useful definition is relative poverty, and this is inescapable in a society in which income is distributed unevenly. However, relative poverty can be defined in many different ways – assistance level, assistance level plus x per cent, half median earnings, 60 per cent of median earnings, before or after housing costs. The definition standardised throughout the EU is household income below 60 per cent of median income (after housing costs) – approximately £15,000 a year in 2011. On this definition, poverty rose steadily throughout the Thatcher and Major years, reaching a peak of 13.9 million people (nearly a quarter of the population) in 1997, falling since to 12.4 million in 2004 and then rising again to 14 million (16 per cent of the population) in 2011 (Clark 2004; Eurostat 2012). The UK was around the European mid-point of poverty levels in 2011, around the same level as

Germany, with the lowest being Iceland at 9 per cent and the highest Bulgaria at 22 per cent.

Poverty is particularly influenced by a number of factors:

- *Children* – not surprisingly, the percentage of households with children are around twice as likely to be under the poverty line as households without children. When New Labour came to power in 1997, one of its main objectives was to eliminate child poverty, which had grown from one in seven in 1979 to one in three in 1997. By 2003, they had reduced it to 2.6 million and this has further reduced to 2.3 million by 2011, over a million less than in 1998. One of the continuing difficulties has been the high level of poverty among lone-parent households. One in four of all children were in a lone-parent family and 72 per cent of this group were classed as in poverty. An example of research into child poverty is shown in Case Study 7.11.

- *Gender* – despite 30 years of equal pay legislation, average female hourly earnings are still only around 86 per cent of male earnings, and women on average work fewer hours than men. This particularly hits single-parent households headed by women (the vast majority).

- *Ethnicity* – whereas 20 per cent of white households are in poverty, this figure is much higher for ethnic households. For Bangladeshi households, 70 per cent are in poverty, and this compares with 50 per cent for black African households, 30 per cent for Indian and black Caribbean. However, after we take account of the fact that Indians on average have higher educational qualifications than whites, their 'like for like' earnings are lower. Reasons identified for this phenomenon include the high level of unemployment (25 per cent of Bangladeshi and black Africans), the high proportion of lone-parent families, the higher average number of children and work carried out in low-skilled and part-time work (Kenway and Palmer 2007).

CASE STUDY 7.11

👁 CHILD POVERTY

The London University's Institute of Education researchers carried out a study of 14,000 7-year-olds in 2008. They found that despite governments having spent billions to eliminate child poverty since 1999:

- Almost one-fifth of 7-year-olds live in severe poverty – homes where the total income, including benefits, is less than £254 a week (this is an average among those surveyed). The average income for families in the study was £563 a week, say researchers.

- Almost three-quarters of children whose parents are of Pakistani or Bangladeshi origin live in poverty – homes where the total income for a family with two children is under £330 a week. This is largely because of high unemployment rates for mothers and fathers, the researchers say.

- Just over half (51 per cent) of black 7-year-olds and just over a quarter of white 7-year-olds live in poverty, with three-fifths from these groups in single-parent families. Seven-year-olds are most likely to live in poverty in the north-east (40 per cent) and least likely in the south-west (22 per cent). The figure for London was 36 per cent. Just under 7 per cent of 7-year-olds living in poverty do not have two pairs of all-weather shoes, according to parents. Just under 50 per cent do not get pocket money.

- Just over half of mothers without any qualifications are in the poorest fifth, while 32 per cent of fathers without qualifications are in this group. More than half of the mothers and fathers with postgraduate qualifications are in the top income group.

- The mothers of the 7-year-olds were asked to place their children's behaviour in one of three categories: normal, borderline and/or serious behaviour problems. About 12 per cent of children in single-parent families and 15 per cent of children living with a step-parent were described as having serious behaviour difficulties. This is compared with 6 per cent for children living with both of their birth parents.

Source: Shepherd (2010)

Poverty matters because it affects future life chances. Infant mortality rates are twice as high for unskilled manual groups as they are for professionals. Life expectancy for male professionals in 2005 was 80, and for female professionals 85, while for unskilled manual groups the corresponding figures were 73 and 78 (Womack 2007). The lower your income, the more likely you are to be a victim of burglary.

The percentage of children aged between 5 and 15 experiencing mental disorders is between two and three times higher for those living in households with an income of less than £100 a week than they are for those in households earning over £700 a week. Most poor children fail. Their depressed parents are unable to give them aspirations (Toynbee 2009).

Poverty persists across the generations. Of people whose families were poor when they were in their teens in the 1970s, 19 per cent were poor in their early thirties, while where families were not poor in the 1970s, 10 per cent were poor as adults. Dividing 19 per cent by 10 per cent shows that the odds of being poor as an adult were doubled if one's parents were poor. For teenagers in the 1980s, the odds of being poor were quadrupled when parents were poor (Blanden and Gibbons 2006).

The rising number of single-parent families and the dependence of many such families on the benefit system, which is especially strong in the UK, presents a further financial challenge to governments as well as implications on housing provision and, in certain areas, an effect on crime.

How easy is it to move out of poverty? The answer seems to be not easy, but not impossible. Evidence from the British Household Panel Survey shows that just over half of the individuals who were in the bottom quintile (lowest 20 per cent) for income in 1991 were still there is 1996. In other words, half had escaped from dire poverty. Over a one-year timespan, 65 per cent stayed in the bottom quintile, and of those who escaped, most stayed in the bottom two quintiles (that is, the bottom 40 per cent) (Giddens 2006). McKnight (2000) found that the unemployed are most likely to gain employment in the lowest-paid sectors when they do find work, and that the lower paid are more likely to become unemployed than the higher paid.

Child poverty could be ended, but at a cost. It would involve a massive increase in child tax credits, estimated at £30 billion up to 2020. Barnard and Goulden (2006) point out that this only represents one year's economic growth. Money alone will not be enough. Considerable practical and emotional support in increasing the self-esteem of lone-parent families will also be needed, through the expansion of educational programmes such as Sure Start and employment programmes such as New Deal. Although Sure Start had an uncertain start providing limited overall benefits, by 2011, a research project found a good number of significant improvements arising out of the scheme, including more stimulating and less chaotic home environments (NESS 2010).

REFLECTIVE ACTIVITY 7.8

Poverty and inequality

In 2011 the average UK CEO earnings in the FTSE 100 companies was £4,771,000, taking into account bonuses and share options. The average UK wage was £25,790. This differential can be calculated at 185:1. In the USA, this differential is even higher, although it is much lower in most European countries.

Questions

1 Consider what the impact of these differentials is likely to be on the motivation of employees in the UK.

2 Should the Government take any action to reduce this differential?

3 Why should social inequality matter to employers? What can they do about it?

4 What action should the Government take, if any, to try to reduce social inequality?

CASE STUDY 7.12

DID POVERTY INCREASE UNDER NEW LABOUR?

One of the main aims of the Labour Government when they came to power in the UK in 1997 was to promote increased equality and thereby reduce poverty. The evidence on their achievements is mixed. As shown in Table 7.13, the Gini coefficient rose over the period 1997–2008, which means that income inequality increased. This would suggest that there has been an increase in relative poverty. However, the main reason for the rise in the Gini coefficient was the considerable increase in income at the very top of the income scale. This has the effect of pulling up average income, but not mean income (the income of the person in the middle of the income distribution). Mean income is considerably less than average income because of this skewed distribution of income. This would lessen relative poverty, except in the technical sense that 99 per cent of the population have got relatively poorer than the top 1 per cent.

Income after inflation has risen for every part of the population except for the bottom 3 per cent. As a result absolute poverty has increased for those at the very bottom of the income scale. However, the IFS points out that those with the lowest recorded incomes often have access to informal and unrecorded sources of income.

On child poverty, the record of Labour is positive, although it had not achieved its aim of halving child poverty by 2010. On the other hand, because resources have been directed towards families with children, there has been some increase in relative poverty among working-age adults without children.

As so often, the answer to the question must be – on the one hand, yes, but on the other hand, no. Unlike under Thatcher, Labour government fiscal policy has attempted to reduce poverty and inequality, but to some extent these efforts have been stymied by other social forces – the effects of globalisation, the acceleration of the bonus culture, and so on.

Source: IFS (2009)

REFLECTIVE ACTIVITY 7.9

Social class	Question
● 'there is no such thing as society' (Margaret Thatcher) ● 'the classless society' (John Major) ● 'we are all middle class now' (anon).	1 Explain each of these statements. Do you agree with any of them?

EQUAL OPPORTUNITIES AND DIVERSITY

The UK is a very diverse society: diverse in terms of race, sex, sexual orientation, religion, age, disability and life experience. Equality of opportunity is based on legislation and has as its main aim assimilation – that whatever a person's background, they should all have the opportunity to achieve the same outcomes. Diversity is much more about difference. The differences between the two are illustrated in Table 7.15.

Table 7.15 Comparing managing diversity with equal opportunity

Managing diversity	Equal opportunity
Is the concern of all employees, especially managers	Seen as an issue to do with human resource practitioners
Does not rely on positive action/affirmative action	Relies on positive action/affirmative action
Concentration on issues of movement within the organisation, the culture of the organisation and meeting business objectives	Less of an emphasis on culture change and meeting business objectives; premised more on moral and ethical objectives
Embraces a broad range of people – no one is excluded	Perceived as an issue for certain groups in the labour market such as women, ethnic minorities and people with disabilities
Ensures all employees maximise their potential and their contribution to the organisation	Concentration on issues of discrimination
Internally driven	Externally imposed
Aims for diversification	Aims for assimilation

In 2005 and 2006, the CIPD published three related Change Agenda documents on diversity, entitled *Managing Diversity, Measuring success* (CIPD 2006), *Managing Diversity: Learning by doing* (Taylor et al 2005) and *Managing Diversity: Linking theory and practice to business performance* (Mulholland et al 2005). These are invaluable in an understanding of diversity.

The CIPD defines diversity as 'valuing everyone as an individual – valuing people as employees, customers and clients' (CIPD 2008). Diversity is traditionally viewed as being concerned with categories of race, gender, ethnicity, age and disability, but true diversity is much wider than this. Anderson and Metcalfe (2003) identify three different types of workforce diversity:

● *social category diversity* – differences in demographic characteristics such as race and sex (the traditional definition)

- *informational diversity* – differences of knowledge, experience, functional background, etc
- *value diversity* – differences in personality and attitudes.

A need for diversity is being driven by economic and social change – a more culturally mixed society as a result of immigration, an ageing population, pressures of globalisation and the trend towards a 24/7 society. There are simply not enough white, English-born, young and middle-aged males to fill all the jobs. Managing diversity is seen as a much subtler process. Employees are not selected or promoted on the basis of ethnic or gender calculations but because of their individual and varied contribution that they can make to their job and the organisation.

There is clear evidence of a continuing inequality based on race and sex. The National Equality Panel (Hills 2010) found the following:

- White British pupils with GCSE results around or below the national median are less likely to go on to higher education than those from minority ethnic groups. Pakistani, black African and black Caribbean boys have results at the age of 16 well below the median in England.
- Compared with a white British Christian man with similar qualifications, age and occupation, Pakistani and Bangladeshi Muslim men and black African Christian men have an income that is 13–21 per cent lower. Nearly half of Bangladeshi and Pakistani households are in poverty.
- Girls have better educational outcomes than boys at school and are more likely to enter higher education and achieve good degrees, but women's median hourly pay is 21 per cent less than men's, although this difference has narrowed since the 1970s. In fact, median earnings differ by around 12 per cent for full-time earners but the big difference is in part-time rates, where women form the large majority and are crowded into low-pay sectors, such as catering, caring and retailing.

THE BUSINESS CASE FOR DIVERSITY

Although the equal opportunity (EO) legislation of the 1970s had an immediate impact in eliminating the worst excesses of sexist and racist behaviour, most organisations introduced EO policies and practices chiefly out of fear of the legal sanctions rather than seeing the long-term benefits that such action would bring.

However, by the 1990s it began to be realised that substantial *demographic changes* were occurring which would inevitably lead to skills shortages over the following years. The birth rate had fallen dramatically in the 1970s and there was little sign of recovery in the next 20 years, so it was known that the number of 16–25-year-olds would take a sharp fall. If the traditional sources of labour (young, white, qualified, full-time males) became much reduced, organisations realised that they would have to rethink their human resourcing policies and look for untapped sources of expertise. Job descriptions would need to become more flexible to accommodate part-time working; specifications would have to be altered to eliminate unnecessary requirements on height and lifting ability and broadened to envelop all sections of the community; working conditions and benefits would have to change to allow wheelchairs, language classes, career breaks and childcare facilities.

These changes in the work patterns were taken up by many employers, with females playing a larger part in business organisations. Interestingly enough, this played its part in the birth rate recovering somewhat in the 2000s, although it was also due partly to the increase in immigration to the UK of people of child-bearing age and to the generally prosperous period with low unemployment, which encouraged support for females to be able to retain their jobs and go back to work quickly, which became more the norm.

A second reason relates to the *changing nature of the workplace*. There was a sharp decline in industrial and manufacturing jobs in the 1980s and 1990s (over 2 million jobs were lost in this period) and this ran alongside a growth in the service sector. Whereas a large proportion of industrial jobs were held by men, the opposite was true for a majority of the service sector employment. One forecast is that 70 per cent of all new jobs to be created up to 2020 are expected to be taken by women. Companies in this sector have a positive incentive to encourage the best applicants by providing career opportunities and a supporting environment for all staff.

The growing emphasis on *customer relations* in a competitive economy is another reason for focusing on wider opportunities. Active diversity management can open up new opportunities and improve market share by broadening the customer base. This has been seen particularly in the financial sector, where banks and building societies are focusing on diversity issues in the way they target their products and services. They are becoming much more user-friendly to women, taking on board the increasing spending power of the female professionals and they are also addressing the needs of ethnic minority businesses.

Customers, in effect, were increasingly looking through the front door of the companies they buy from. If they did not like what they see in terms of equality or social responsibility, they would not go through the door.

The Halifax Bank recognised this opportunity by specifically targeting the Chinese community in Manchester, which was substantially unrepresented in the bank's employees. The business benefits of having a group of Mandarin or Cantonese speakers in the branches led to an immediate increase in mortgage business of around 40 per cent (Merrick 2001). JD Wetherspoon have deliberately spread their recruiting across all ages to reflect their customer base and now employs many staff over 70 and one over 90 (Syedain 2010). When HSBC recruited in the Birmingham area in the mid-2000s, 49 per cent of their intake were from ethnic minorities to match the local community (CIPD 2005).

Conveying an image as a *'good employer'* also has repercussions on equality issues. Companies seen to have high ethical stances, with such policies as 'dignity at work' which prevent harassment and bullying, become more attractive to both customers and potential employees. It improves the employer brand. On the other hand, those seen as dominated by a white, male culture may not appear to provide the environment required. Moreover, in the case of equal pay, there is no greater demotivating force in the workplace than a sense of injustice over pay by a large section of the workforce. Internal equity, including fair pay and treatment for men, women and minority groups, is a vital part of the perception of 'fairness'.

All these reasons have encouraged organisations to raise their profile on equality issues.

Jones (2006) has examined the business case in detail. She identifies a number of benefits:

- *Marketing* – sales tend to increase when staffing reflects the organisation's customer base – Lloyds TSB reported a 30 per cent increase in sales in branches where staffing was changed to reflect the ethnicity of customers.
- *HRI* – Rajan et al (2003) found that diversity led to higher staff motivation, higher retention and reduced recruitment costs. Diversity policies also made employees feel valued and respected, and this increased their sense of engagement.
- *Stakeholders* – diversity policies improve the organisation's image with its stakeholders.
- *Creativity and decision-making* – diverse organisations tend to be more creative. Diverse teams avoid the risk of group-think and tended to make better decisions. However, in some situations, homogeneous groups tended to perform better – where the main tasks were routine, and where the organisation was contracting rather than growing (Jones 2006; CIPD 2006).

REFLECTIVE ACTIVITY 7.10

Binna Kandola and the business case

The psychologist and diversity expert Binna Kandola has said that 'the search for the business case for diversity is an exercise in futility'. He argues that diversity is ultimately a moral issue and that what prevents diversity from moving forward is the bias and stereotyping that we all carry (Kandola 2009).

Do you agree?

If you are a CIPD member, you can read Kandola's articles on the *People Management* website.

MANAGING DIVERSITY

It is important to note that these benefits of diversity do not just happen. Diversity has to be managed effectively. Mulholland et al (2005) liken it to managing change. They quote the example of the turkey producer Bernard Matthews, who was suffering from a shortage of labour in rural Norfolk. This was tackled by bringing in immigrant labour from Portugal, which increased the proportion of Portuguese employees from 3 per cent to 30 per cent of the workforce. However, in order to make it work, Bernard Matthews developed local support networks, promoted local English language training and created partnerships with the Home Office, Norfolk Police and HSBC to facilitate integration of the new workforce.

Diversity strategies can operate at three different levels, and achievement of all three is necessary for an effective diversity policy (Jones 2006):

- *Representational diversity* – ensuring that the workforce is more representative of the population as a whole. The key here is recruitment.
- *Inclusive processes* – underlying processes – retention, progression, development, etc, must support representational diversity. Bernard Matthews clearly did this in the example quoted above.
- *Inclusive culture* – provide people with a culture where they feel respected. The attitudes of top management are critical here.

DIVERSITY

CASE STUDY 7.13

The war against crime

The Metropolitan Police has set up a Cultural and Communities Resource Unit, headed by a (black) detective chief inspector, Keith Fraser. The unit maintains a database of the range of backgrounds, lifestyles and specialisms in the Met and the City of London Police. The unit has 800 people on its books and has located experts who have helped with 700 criminal enquiries all over the country.

Examples of the work of the unit include:

- The murder of an elderly Bengali woman, where white officers were getting no co-operation from the community. Bengali officers immediately got co-operation.
- A Chinese person had been missing in the north of England for two weeks. A Chinese policeman from London found him in a day and a half.

- Tamil officers are investigating violence between rival Tamil gangs.
- A voodoo expert helped interpret seemingly innocuous but actually sinister objects sent to a Bangladeshi man.

As Detective Chief Inspector Fraser says, 'the unit highlights the true meaning of diversity and the fantastic opportunities and benefits it gives policing' (Cowan 2004).

Shariah mortgages

Islamic finance is regulated by *shariah* law. One of the main principles of *shariah* law is a prohibition on usury, the payment of interest. This makes a conventional Western mortgage impossible under *shariah* law. The solution developed by Islamic banks is a version of sale and lease-back. The customer in effect sells their house to the bank, pays rent (not interest) on it, and then at a later stage buys the house back from the bank. Interestingly, exactly the same process had developed in late medieval England to get round Christian prohibitions of usury. Unfortunately,

under UK law this represented two property sales, each of which was liable to stamp duty. In the 2006 Budget, Gordon Brown recognised this, and abolished the requirement for double stamp duty (Parker 2005).

Pearson

The publisher Pearson, which owns the *Financial Times*, came top of a 2009 survey of FTSE 350 companies, which measured both the quality of equal opportunities and diversity policies and the proportion of women on the board. The chief executive and the chief finance officer are both female. In 2003, 9 per cent of its staff were from ethnic minorities, and by 2009 this figure had increased to 15 per cent. This follows on from a five-year plan launched in 2002 to communicate diversity awareness to employees. It holds annual outreach programmes for students which help produce candidates for its internship scheme. The *Financial Times* is part of a scheme in Tower Hamlets which acts as a matchmaker between firms and ethnic minority jobseekers (Sunderland 2009).

An example of two different approaches by London boroughs to deal with integration is shown in Case Study 7.14.

CASE STUDY 7.14

ETHNIC INTEGRATION IN THE LONDON BOROUGHS OF NEWHAM AND TOWER HAMLETS

Newham, which includes the Olympic Park, is officially Britain's least white borough, with only 16.7 per cent, and a quarter of households having somebody who speaks English as a first language. To improve the rate of integration, Newham Council have taken a number of initiatives. Some are unsurprising, such as providing very cheap English-language classes. Some are less expected; at age five, each school child is provided with a (Western) musical instrument, to learn

Western style of music, which they can keep if they finish their music course; ethnic-language newspapers have been removed from all the libraries; no grants are available for any ethnic-based activity, from faith or religion. The council encourages street activities, as long as everybody is invited and nobody is excluded.

Tower Hamlets, the next door borough, on the other hand, where the demographics are very similar, has a mayor whose ruling council is 100 per cent Bengali, although Bengalis only make up a third of the population. A considerable amount of funds go towards ethnic and faith-based activities, where lunch clubs and arts classes tend to be separate and segregated. Language teaching is subsidised for each ethnic group.

Source: Gilligan (2012)

WOMEN ON THE BOARD

In 2009, Co-operative Asset Management, a fund manager, carried out a survey of female representation on the boards of FTSE 350 companies, extensively reported in the *Observer*. They ranked companies on two measures:

- the sophistication of equal opportunities and diversity policies
- female representation on boards of directors.

Companies tended to score better on theory than on practice. Many had impressive-sounding policies, and 94 per cent said they had an equal opportunities policy, but then failed to have women on their boards. Typical was Barclays, which scored 7.8 out of 10 for its policies, but zero for its board, which contained no women. Royal Bank of Scotland was even less diverse, as its board was not only all men, but also predominantly Scottish. This may in part explain the banking crisis. A separate survey showed that 89 per cent of business executives thought that the banking culture encouraged excessive risk-raking, and 83 per cent thought that this was fuelled by male machismo. The only company with a perfect score for both policies and practice was Pearson (see Case Study 7.13).

Overall, women held only 34 executive board seats out of 970. Most female directors were non-executives, and 130 companies (nearly half of the 297 companies that responded) had no women on the board. Of a total of 2,472 directorships, women held just under 10 per cent.

Opinion is divided over whether diverse boards improve performance. One study suggests that women on the board do not improve financial performance, but could improve governance, while another study found that firms with more diverse boards had better financial performance. However, commonsense suggests that companies which do not have female directors are missing out on an important source of talent.

Suggestions to improve the gender balance include:

- Increase the availability of flexible working. At lower levels of management, where flexible working is generally available, the gender balance is relatively equal. However, higher up the organisation, flexible working is less likely to be available and this discriminates against women.
- Overcome a tendency for male bosses to recruit in their own image.
- Provide mentoring and networking opportunities for female executives.
- Use succession planning to identify and fast-track outstanding female candidates.
- Shareholder pressure – Co-operative Asset Management intends in future to consider diversity when it is assessing company governance.

Many of these ideas were taken up by the Davies Report (2011) commissioned by the Department for Business,

Innovation and Skills. The report found that women only made up 12.5 per cent of total FTSE 100 directors and Lord Davis recommended that they should be aiming for a minimum of 25 per cent female board member representation by 2015. As part of the report Lord Davies and his panel state that companies should fully disclose the number of women sitting on their boards and working in their organisations as a whole, to drive up the numbers of women with top jobs in business.

The Coalition Government, however, rejected the concept of quotas, saying that 'women want and expect to reach the top on merit, not because of political correctness', and the best help the Government could provide was by attempting to reduce the cost of childcare and increasing its availability by providing increased grants to childcare providers and allowing parents on low incomes to recover part of their childcare costs.

By 2012, figures showed that the percentage of women on FTSE 100 boards had risen to a record 17 per cent.

An attempt to introduce compulsory quotas of 40 per cent representation on boards by the European Union failed in 2011 when the proposal was rejected by member states.

Sources: Sunderland (2009); Davies (2011); Hookham and Pancevski (2012)

A fuller discussion of organisational strategy on flexible working is found in Chapter 10.

KEY LEARNING POINTS

- The major demographic trends across the world are a major decline in the birth rate, population ageing and increasing migration, both of people and jobs. These trends are strongest in the developed world, especially Europe.
- These trends are likely to continue to produce a reversal of world population expansion around 2050. Developed countries are likely to be faced by declining populations before that time unless they change policies and allow higher rates of migration.
- These demographic changes provide opportunities for organisations to move into new product and service areas. The reduction in the availability of younger labour means that organisations will need to reorganise work patterns to encourage greater participation from women, older people and other groups.
- Governments will increasingly be faced with the need for higher expenditure on pensions, benefits and health services as a result of demographic changes. At the same time, the higher dependency ratio is likely to necessitate higher levels of taxation to finance this expenditure. Initiatives to combat these difficulties can include encouraging larger families through incentives, reducing benefits and stimulating personal savings for pensions and health.
- It is likely that an ageing population will be a less productive one, providing challenges for the world economy and wealth creation. There has been a rapid transferring of jobs and services around the world as an outcome of globalisation.
- Throughout most of the twentieth century, social mobility in the UK was high, as the absolute size of the middle class rose considerably at the expense of the working class, but these trends have slowed in recent years.
- There are considerable inequalities in both income and wealth in the UK, and these inequalities have been widening in recent years.
- Inequality is closely related to relative poverty, which has persisted in the UK and which leads to an impairment of the life chances of the poor.

- Equal opportunities is about assimilation, while diversity is about celebrating difference.
- Diversity is of different types: social category diversity, informational diversity and value diversity: differences in personality and attitudes.
- In order to manage diversity, it is necessary to achieve representational diversity, inclusive processes and an inclusive culture. The attitudes of top management are critical.

QUESTIONS

1   What have been the main changes in sectoral employment in the UK since 1992?

2   Provide five reasons why migration can provide benefits for an economy and set out five problems that migration can bring.

3   How can the UK Government handle the current crisis in pension provision due to the ageing population? What options does it have?

4   How is the 'participation ratio' measured and what has caused the rate to rise in the UK since the late 1990s?

5   What are the implications for organisations in terms of changing markets arising from demographic changes?

6   How can demographic changes affect HR activities and policies?

7   What is the difference between absolute and relative social mobility?

8   What is the Gini coefficient and what does it tell us about inequality in the UK?

9   Identify three main differences between equal opportunities and diversity.

10 Why is representational diversity only one element of a successful diversity strategy?

EXPLORE FURTHER

FURTHER READING

The most readable and dynamic book source on demography remains Paul Wallace's *Agequake* (see *References*). A more statistical approach can be found in *Demography: Measuring and modeling population processes* by Preston, Heuveline and Guillot (2000) (Wiley), while regular reports on all areas of UK demography can be found on the ONS website. Wider perspectives are given in books by Poston and Bouvier (2010) *Population and Society* (Cambridge), May (2012) *World Population Policies* (Springer) and Le Bras (2008) *The Nature of Demography* (Princeton University Press).

Social class and social mobility are discussed in any good sociology textbook. Recent research includes the CIPD (2013) report *Improving social mobility: inside the HR profession and beyond*. Poverty and inequality are covered in Vic George and Paul Wilding, *British Society and Social Welfare: Towards a sustainable society*. Excellent overviews of the evidence on social trends are given in two papers by Stephen Aldridge, an economist in the Prime Minister's Strategy Unit (formerly the Performance and Innovation Unit), listed in the *References*. A series of CIPD Change Agendas published in 2005 are valuable for diversity. You should read the excellent CIPD factsheets relevant to this chapter, which are regularly updated, including subjects such as *The psychological contract*, *Work–life balance* and *Diversity*, together with the regular legal updating the CIPD website provides.

USEFUL WEBSITES

The Work Foundation (www.theworkfoundation.com) publishes several research reports on social topics. The journal *CentrePiece* (www.cep.lse.ac.uk/centrepiece), published by the Centre for Economic Performance at the London School of Economics, has useful articles with social themes.

SEMINAR ACTIVITY

SOCIAL MOBILITY, EDUCATION AND THE MERITOCRACY

After the Education Act of 1944 it was thought that the 11-plus examination, which determined whether children would go to a grammar school (and receive an education leading to middle-class occupations) or to a secondary modern school (leading to working-class occupations) would increase social mobility by selecting on the basis of intelligence rather than fathers' social class. By the 1970s, the theory behind this was discredited and a switch was made to comprehensive education, whereby all children, whatever their intelligence or social background, would go to the same school. This does not seem to have been effective in increasing social mobility.

1   Why do you think that changes in the education system seem to have failed to increase social mobility?

In 1958 the sociologist Michael Young published *The Rise of the Meritocracy*.

In this book he examined the likely consequences of a society in which success was based solely on merit (that is, on ability) rather than on social background and in which there was total social mobility – in other words, something very like the aspirations of the 1944 Education Act. However, Young saw considerable downsides to this.

2   What do you think these downsides could have been?

The slowdown in social mobility is of increasing concern to Labour politicians. Typical is a speech made by Alan Milburn to the Institute of Public Policy Research in November 2004 (Milburn 2004).

3   Why do you think that New Labour were concerned about a fall in social mobility?

REFERENCES

Abercrombie, N. and Warde, A. (2000) *Contemporary British society*. 3rd edition. Cambridge: Polity Press.

Aldridge, S. (2001) *Social mobility: a discussion paper*. London: Cabinet Office, Performance and Innovation Unit.

Aldridge, S. (2004) *Life chances and social mobility: an overview of the evidence*. London: Cabinet Office, Prime Minister's Strategy Unit.

Anderson, T. and Metcalfe, H. (2003) *Diversity: stacking up the evidence*. London: Chartered Institute of Personnel and Development.

Baird, R. (2001) Britain's immigrants overstep line as numbers surge to 135,000 a year. *Express*. 16 November.

Barnard, H. and Goulden, C. (2006) *What will it take to end child poverty? Firing on all cylinders*. York: Joseph Rowntree Foundation.

Bartlett, H. and Peel, N. (2005) Healthy ageing in the community. In G. Andrews and D. Phillips (eds) *Ageing and place*. London: Routledge.

BBC. (2009) Glass ceiling blocking top jobs. July. Available at: newsvote.bbc.co.uk/mpapps/pagetools/proint/news.bbc.co.uk/1/hi/edcuation/81600 [Accessed 26 October 2009].

Bentham, M. (2013) Boost for PM on migration as influx falls by one third. *Evening Standard*. 28 February. p4.

Blanchflower, D., Saleheen, J. and Shadforth, C. (2007) *The impact of the recent migration from Eastern Europe on the UK economy*. Bank of England Working Paper. London: Bank of England.

Blanden, J., Gregg, P. and Machin, S. (2005) Social mobility in Britain: low and falling. *CentrePiece*. Spring.

Blanden, J. and Gibbons, S. (2006) Cycles of disadvantage. *CentrePiece*. Summer.

Brindle, D. (1999) Northerners heed south's siren call. *Guardian*. 27 August. p3.

Buchanan, J., Froud, J., Johal, S., Leaver, A. and Williams, K. (2009) *Undisclosed and unsustainable: problems of the UK business model*. Working paper. Manchester: Manchester University Centre for Research on Socio-cultural Change.

Business Week. (2004) America's Bebe Boom. 15 March. pp50–2.

Carvel, J. (2003) Marriage and family divorced as 41% of children reared in alternative ways. *Guardian*. 8 May.

Carvel, J. (2007) The figure that shows it pays to be a man. *Guardian*. 5 September.

Casciani, D. (2012) Census shows rise in foreign-born. Available at: www.bbc.co.uk/news/uk-20681551

Chiu, W., Chan, A., Snape, E. and Redman, T. (2001) Age stereotypes and discriminatory attitudes towards older workers: an East–West comparison. *Human Relations*. Vol 54, No 5. pp629–61.

CIA. (2009) Available at: www.cia.gov/library/publications/theworld-factbook/fields/2172.html [Accessed 29 October 2009].

CIPD. (2003a) *Managing the psychological contract*. Factsheet. London: Chartered Institute of Personnel and Development.

CIPD. (2003b) *Work–life balance. Factsheet*. London: Chartered Institute of Personnel and Development.

CIPD. (2005) *Managing diversity: people make the difference at work – but everyone is different*. London: Chartered Institute of Personnel and Development.

CIPD. (2006) *Managing diversity, measuring success*. Change agenda. London: Chartered Institute of Personnel and Development.

CIPD. (2007) *Age and recruitment*. London: Chartered Institute of Personnel and Development.

CIPD. (2008) *Diversity: an overview*. Factsheet. London: Chartered Institute of Personnel and Development.

CIPD. (2009) *The internship charter*. London: Chartered Institute of Personnel and Development.

CIPD/KPMG. (2005) *Labour market outlook*. Summer/Autumn quarterly survey report. London: Chartered Institute of Personnel and Development.

Clark, D. (2004) Unto him that hath. *Guardian*. 6 August.

Coonan, C. (2009) China relaxes one-child rule to beat pension crisis. *Independent*. 25 July. p18.

Cowan, R. (2004) Met harnesses its diversity in the war against crime. *Guardian*. 2 December.

Cribb, J., Joyce, R. and Phillips, D. (2012) Living standards, poverty and inequality in the UK. London: IFS. Available at: www.ifs.org.uk/comms/commm124/pdf

Davies, M. (2011) *Independent review of women on boards*. London: Department for Business, Innovation and Skills.

Dicken, P. (2003) *Global shift*. London: Sage.

Dorling, D., Rigby, J., Wheeler, B., Ballas, D., Thomas, B., Fahmy, E., Gordon, D. and Lupton, R. (2007) *Poverty, wealth and place in Britain 1968 to 2005*. York: Policy Press for the Joseph Rowntree Foundation.

Doward, J. (2003) Future imperfect as longer lifespan looms. *Observer*. 28 December. p9.

Dubner, S. and Levitt, S. (2009) www.Freakonomics.blogs [Accessed 5 December 2009].

DWP. (2011) *Allevard Springs case study*. Available at: www.dwp.gov.uk/docs/case-study-allevard-springs.pdf

ECOFIN. (2006) *The impact of ageing on public expenditure: projections for the EU25 member states on pension, health care, long-term care, education and unemployment, 2004–2050*. Brussels: ECOFIN.

Economist. (2004) Return of the wrinklies. 17 January. p24.

Economist. (2006) Now we are 300,000,000. 14 October. pp57–8.

Economist. (2007) From cheque books to checking pulses. 14 April. p85.

Economist. (2009a) The people crunch. 17 January. pp56–7.

Economist. (2009b) Go forth and multiply a lot less. 31 October. pp35–8.

Economist. (2012a) The London effect. 15 December.p25.

Economist. (2012b) For richer, for poorer. 13 October. World Economy Report. pp3–10.

Economist. (2012c) The expanding middle. 10 November. p52.

Economist. (2013a) An unwelcoming nation. 2 February. p26.

Economist. (2013b) Peak toil. 26 January. p52.

Economist. (2013c) A house divided. 9 February. p57.

Ellis, A. (2009) UK resident population by country of birth. *Population Trends* 135. Spring. London: ONS.

Eurostat. (2012) Poverty and social exclusion in the European Union. Available at: epp.eurostat.ec.europa.eu/cache/ITY_PUBLIC/3-08022012-AP/EN/3-08022012-AP-EN.PDF

Furlong, A. and Cartmel, F. (2001) Capitalism without classes. In A. Giddens (ed.) *Sociology: introductory readings*. Revised ed. Cambridge: Polity.

George, V. and Wilding, P. (1999) *British society and social welfare: towards a sustainable society*. Basingstoke: Macmillan.

Giddens, A. (2006) *Sociology*. 5th edition. Cambridge: Polity.

Gilligan, A. (2012) If someone asks, I'm British, end of Story. *Daily Telegraph*. 15 December. p31.

Hall, J. (2012) Children born out of wedlock increases. Available at: www.telegraph.co.uk/news

Hanlon, M. (2013) Stretch out, the human crush is almost over. *Sunday Times*. News Review. 20 January. p4.

Harrison, A. (2012) Social mobility: universities need to do more says Alan Milburn. Available at: www.bbc.co.uk/news/education-19990126 [Accessed 22 October 2012].

Hills, J. (2010) *Report of the National Equality Panel*. London: Government Equality Office.

HMSO. (2009) *New opportunities: fair chances for the future*. White Paper. London: HMSO.

Home Office. (2007) Accession monitoring report. February.

Home Office. (2012) Asylum. Accessed at: www.homeoffice.gov.uk/publications/science-research-statistics/research-statistics/immigration-asylum-research/immigration-brief-q3-2011/asylum

Hookham, M. and Pancevski, B. (2012) Minister for women rejects quotas for female bosses. *Sunday Times*.11 November. p6.

IFS. (2009) Have the poor got poorer under Labour? *IFS Observations*. October. Institute for Fiscal Studies.

ISER. (2002) Class matters. *ISER Newsletter*. October. Institute for Social and Economic Research.

ITEM Club. (2006) *Spring forecast*. London: Ernst & Young.

Jack, I. (2009) Onwards and endlessly upwards. *Guardian*. 25 July.

Jackson, S. (1998) *Britain's population*. London: Routledge.

Jones, A. (2006) *Rising to the challenge of diversity*. London: Work Foundation.

Kandola, B. (2009) Under the skin. *People Management*. 30 July.

Karagianaki, E. (2011) *The impact of inheritance on the distribution of wealth: evidence from the UK*. Paper 148. LSE Centre for Analysis of Social Exclusion.

Kenway, P. and Palmer, G. (2007) *Poverty among ethnic groups*. York: Joseph Rowntree Foundation.

Kurtz, S. (2004) The end of marriage in Scandinavia. *Weekly Standard*. Vol 9. p20.

Kyser, J. (2007) 60 million Californians by mid-century. *Los Angeles Times*. July 10.

Labour Market Trends. (2009) December. London: Office of National Statistics.

Lansley, S. (2009) *Life in the middle*. London: Trades Union Congress.

Lucas, E. (2006) Red fades to grey. *Economist*. 27 May. p46.

Macmillan, L. (2010) *Social mobility in the professions*. Bristol: Centre for Market and Public Organisations.

Massey, D. (1984) *Spatial divisions of labour: social structures and the geography of production*. Basingstoke: Macmillan.

McKnight, A. (2000) *Earnings inequality and earnings mobility 1977–1996: the impact of mobility on long term inequality*. Employment Relations Research Series No 8. London: Department for Trade and Industry.

McNeill, D. (2010) Mystery of Japan's 230,000 missing centenarians. *Independent.* 9 September.

McSmith, A. (2007) Figures show number of eastern Europeans in Britain exaggerated. *Independent.* 20 January. p24.

Merrick, N. (2001) Minority interest. *People Management.* 8 November. pp52–3.

Migration Observatory, University of Oxford. (2012) *The impact of migration on UK population growth.* Oxford: Migration Observatory.

Milburn, A. (2004) *Inequality, mobility and opportunity: the politics of aspiration.* Speech to the Institute for Public Policy Research. 9 November.

Milburn, A. (2009a) *Fair success to the professions.* London: HMSO.

Milburn, A. (2009b) The UK is an unequal society in which class background too often determines life chances. *Observer.* 19 July.

Milne, S. (2007) You can't say it's a problem and then do nothing about it. *Guardian.* 16 August.

Mulholland, G., Özbilgin, M. and Worman, D. (2005) *Managing diversity: linking theory and practice to business performance.* London: Chartered Institute of Personnel and Development.

Mullan, P. (2002) *The imaginary time bomb.* London: Tauris.

National Audit Office. (2010) *Tackling inequalities in life expectation in areas of worst health and deprivation.* London: HMSO.

National Statistical Office. (2011) Accessed at: www.statistics.gov.uk

NESS. (2010) *The impact of Sure Start schemes on 5 year olds and their families.* London: National Evaluation of Sure Start Schemes. November.

Nichiporuk, B. (2000) *The security dynamics of demographic factors.* Westport, CT: Rand Publishing.

Norton, C. (2002) Japan bribes mothers in bid for baby boom. *Sunday Times.* 15 September.

Nunn, A., Johnson, S., Monro, S., Bickerstaffe, T. and Kelsey, S. (2007) *Factors influencing social mobility.* Report 450. London: Department for Work and Pensions.

ONS. (2000) *Social trends.* London: HMSO.

ONS. (2006a) Distribution of wealth in the UK. *Social Trends.* Table s. 26. London: ONS.

ONS. (2006b) *Labour market trends.* December. pp32–3.

ONS. (2007) *16% of UK population are over the age of 65.* Accessed at: www.statistics.gov.uk/cci/nugget.asp?ID=949

ONS. (2011) *Family data.* Accessed at: www.ons.gov.uk/ons/rel/wellbeing/measuring-national-well-being/households-and-families/art---households-and-families.html#tab-Families

ONS. (2012) *Population data*. Accessed at: www.ons.gov.uk/ons/taxonomy/index.html? nscl=Population

Orton, M. and Rowlingson, K. (2007) *Public attitudes to economic inequality*. York: Joseph Rowntree Foundation.

Parker, M. (2005) Global scramble to jump aboard the bandwagon. *The Times*. 26 April.

Parliamentary Business. (2010) *Briefing paper*. Accessed at: www.parliament.uk/business/ publications/research/key-issues-for-the-new-parliament/value-for-money-in-public- services/the-ageing-population/

Pearce, F. (2002) We need more babies. *Sunday Times*. 17 March.

People Management. (2009) A8 requests down. 12 March. p14.

People Management. (2013) They come over here, they take our jobs, that we probably didn't want anyway. January. pp18–19.

Persaud, J. (2004) Carry on working. *People Management*. 29 July. pp36–7.

Philpott, J. (2007) Britain's Eastern European migrant workforce. *Impact*. Vol 19. May. pp24–7.

Polska. (2006) *Economic ministry*. Poland. Available at: www.poland.gov.pl [Accessed 12 November 2006].

Rajan, A., Martin, B. and Latham, J. (2003) *Harnessing workforce diversity to raise the bottom line*. London: Resource Group Centre.

Roberts, I. (2006) Taking age out of the workforce. *Work, Employment and Society*. Vol 20, No 1. pp67–86.

Roberts, K. (2001) *Class in modern Britain*. Basingstoke: Palgrave.

Rousseau, D. (2004) Psychological contracts in the workplace: understanding the ties that motivate. *Academy of Management Executive*. Vol 18, No 1. February.

Royal Mail recruits excluded groups. (2004) *People Management*. 28 October.

Salt, J. (2006) *Current trends in internal migration in Europe*. London: Migrant Research Unit, University College London.

Shepherd, J. (2010) Child poverty study shows fifth of UK youngsters severely affected. *Guardian*. 15 October. p23.

Smallwood, C. (2003) People power rings changes. *Sunday Times*. 10 August.

Smallwood, C. (2006) 'Reserve army' can defuse demographic time bomb. *Sunday Times*. 20 August.

Smedley, T. (2008) And now for the good news. *People Management*. 6 March. pp25–30.

Social Trends. (2006) HMSO.

Sparrow, A. (2009) Gordon Brown launches package of measures to boost social mobility. *Guardian*. 13 January.

Stewart, E. (2007) Apology over wrong migration statistics from Home Secretary. *Guardian*. 30 October.

Sunday Times. (2007) Russians told: have a baby and win a fridge. 19 August. p23.

Sunderland, R. (2009) Women still face a steep climb to the top table. *Observer*. 23 August.

Sutton Trust. (2007) *The educational backgrounds of 500 leading figures*. London: The Sutton Trust.

Syedain, H. (2010) A new era for age. *People Management*. 14 January. pp19–22.

Taylor, W., Piasecka, A. and Worman, D. (2005) *Managing diversity: learning by doing*. London: Chartered Institute of Personnel and Development.

Toynbee, P. (2009) Harman's law is Labour's biggest idea for 11 years. *Guardian*. 13 January.

United Nations. (2005) *Report on world fertility rates at 2003*. New York: United Nations.

United Nations. (2006) *State of world population*. Accessed at: UNFPA.org/swp/2006

United Nations. (2011) *World population prospects*. New York: Department of Economics and Social Affairs. Accessed at: esa.un.org/unpd/wpp/Excel-Data/population.htm

United Nations. (2012) *World fertility rates*. New York: Department of Economics and Social Affairs. Accessed at: data.un.org/Data.aspx?d=PopDiv&f=variableID%3a54

Vasager, J. (2013) Census highlights a divided Germany. *Daily Telegraph*. 1 June. p21.

Wallace, P. (2001) *Agequake*. London: Nicholas Brealey.

Watts, R. (2008) Retired staff outstrip serving firemen. *Sunday Times*. 26 October. p12.

Whitehead, T. (2008) Benefits of migrant labour 'overstated'. *Daily Telegraph*. 1 April. p14.

Womack, S. (2007) How occupation affects life expectancy. *Daily Telegraph*. 25 October. p13.

Woodhead, M. (2004) Exodus heralds end of Schoder's IT dream. *Sunday Times*. 17 November.

Young, M. (1958) *The rise of the meritocracy*. Harmondsworth: Penguin.

Technology

INTRODUCTION

No one doubts that massive technological advances have changed the world, as set out in the causes of globalisation in Chapter 6. The developments in information and communication technologies, biotechnology, energy supply and transportation have altered the world beyond recognition over the last 50 years. To put it more accurately, technological change enables massive changes to take place – changes in organisation, communication, products, marketing and distribution together with associated ways of managing people. The uniqueness of technology is that, once it has been invented, it cannot be 'un-invented'. Other resources can be used up (oil), can suddenly disappear (chief executives) or be replaced (buildings), but the technological knowledge will always survive. In fact, once one organisation uses that technology and gains competitive advantage, it needs to be adopted in some form by all the competitors to ensure survival.

The speed of technological advance is increasing, prompting even speedier changes in society. In fact, writing about examples is quite difficult because, by the time this book is printed, most of the examples will be out of date and the most influential changes of the next ten years are only known about by small cliques of researchers in multinational research and development labs and their counterparts in leading universities.

WHAT'S HAPPENING IN TECHNOLOGY?

PATTERNS OF TECHNOLOGICAL DEVELOPMENT

The common differentiation between man and other animals is the ability to design and use tools, so primitive technologies have been utilised for many thousands of years.

However, the beginnings of the industrial revolution in the mid-seventeenth century saw the early stages of fundamental technological growth, where machines replaced hand operations.

Although technological invention appears to follow a continuous and unrelenting line, a pattern has been identified by, among others, Hall and Preston (1988). Named K-waves, after the Russian Kondratiev, who first developed the concept in the 1920s, a 50-year cycle for each wave has been identified, as shown in Table 8.1.

Table 8.1 Kondratiev's K-waves

K1	1770s to 1830s	Early mechanisation in textiles and water power with the construction of canals, which lead to the first large-scale factories and companies.
K2	1830s to 1880s	Invention of steam power used in railways and machines, which lead to vastly improved communications and location independent of water sources.
K3	1880s to 1930s	Inventions of electricity, steel, chemicals and synthetics creating new industries with reliable and powerful energy leading to very large-scale production and control (trusts and cartels) and opening up of transportation and communication through cars and aircraft. Technologies were integrated to create assembly line techniques.
K4	1930s to 1980s	Explosion of development of cars and aircraft together with petrochemicals and consumer durables. Controlled through integrated manufacturing processes and by multinational organisations.
K5	1980s to current	ICT developments producing ability to source and manufacture flexibly across the world, creating global brands, communicated by television, radio and Internet technologies. Robotics allows complex manufacturing and medical processes.

There can be much debate about the timing of these waves and the overlapping feature of new technologies, but an economic pattern emerges that shows four stages. First, the invention and diffusion of the technology produces prosperity, especially for the organisations leading the way. However, after a period, demand slackens or competitors catch up, leading to a recession, where new investment falls. After such a period, the third stage is that of outright depression, arising from reduced activity and restructuring with mass unemployment before the final stage, recovery, appears, when the economic conditions improve sufficiently for the next wave of technological development.

REFLECTIVE ACTIVITY 8.1

There is some evidence that the current technological cycle is swinging towards a down phase. Set out the reasons why this down phase might be occurring and also explain why the contrary may be true – that the current technological phase is gathering more steam.

TYPES OF TECHNOLOGICAL CHANGE

Freeman (1987) identified four different types of technological change:

1   *Incremental innovations* – these are small-scale changes made at a local level. For example, a quality circle might come up with a new way to calibrate existing equipment in a factory.

2   *Radical innovations* – they change the way things are done. For example, the development of semiconductors rather than valves in the 1960s changed the ways in which computers could operate.

3   *Changes of technology systems* – these often involve linking together two existing technological systems to form a new system. For example, multimedia entertainment systems bring together computer and TV technologies.

4   *Technology revolutions* – these occur about every 50 years or so and revolutionise our approach to technology. One was the development of the steam engine in the 1770s, another, the growth of the railways in the 1830s. The development of the computer in the 1940s and the creation of the worldwide web/Internet have been the latest two.

INFORMATION TECHNOLOGY

In all technological developments, it is in the field of information technology that the speed of development has been the greatest, as has the effect upon society. A stream of inventions has followed the arrival of the first commercial computer in the 1950s. In *hardware*, the integrated circuits have become increasingly powerful through the invention of optical chips and biochips paralleled by the improvements in data storage systems. The price of PCs continues to decline while ever more powerful laptops and tablets allow work to be carried out at any location and on the move. In *software*, the ability to network information so it is available to multiple organisational users; to operate real-time systems so leisure activities, such as flights or theatre tickets can be booked electronically; in banking, money markets around the world are linked with instant access to information and market changes; programs can control tools to perform any task previously carried out by hand, such as cut, weld or burn; controls can be programmed into complex machinery which determines the output and the quality of the process.

All these developments have led to the computer being at the heart of business and, increasingly, private lives. Production, sales, distribution, finance, human resources, are all aided by computer systems which increase the speed of operation, while providing reliable operations, communications and storage. Recent developments, badged as 'business intelligence' (BI), aim to transform large amounts of data, often scattered across the organisation, into the key information that drives informed decision-taking, and delivering it in an easily read form through the computer screen to anybody where and when they need to know. So essential is this intelligence that the estimated worldwide market for BI systems in 2011 was around £29 billion. Data, in the form of intellectual property, can even be fed into a 3D printer, costing as little as £10,000, which can then produce a finished good, such as a toy. This is done by spraying successive layers of materials, such as polycarbonate or clay, forming an output far quicker and cheaper than starting with a lump of material and machining away the unwanted parts, so that objects like toys can be made as a small unit without the huge overheads of assembly lines. One of the suppliers to GE jet engines prints metal parts with such printers (*Economist* 2012a).

COMMUNICATION TECHNOLOGIES

Supporting the development in information technologies have been two major technological developments in communication. First, satellite communication, starting in the mid-1960s, has increased exponentially so that there are now over 100 geo-stationary satellites in orbit facilitating cheap and instantaneous communication and data transmission.

Second, the invention and development of optical fibre technology has provided a competitor in huge capacity handling at great speed. FLAG Europe-Asia, for example, is a 27,000 km system servicing half the world at lower and lower costs. An example (*Economist* 2000) is that the cost of transmitting the *Encyclopaedia Britannica* electronically from New York to Los Angeles was $187 in 1970. By 2000, the entire contents of the Library of Congress could be sent the same distance for less than $40.

Both these developments have led to the creation of mass markets, allowing consumers to be aware of the goods and services on offer. Even if incomes are low, the spread of multinational advertising and brand creation produces images that people can aspire to so that they become future consumers. Television has had the most dramatic effect because it makes no demands on a standard of literacy, unlike the printed word. The technological development improvements since its invention in the 1930s, which have consistently reduced the price and increased the quality and reliability, have had two effects on the mass markets. The first effect is direct, in that most television channels are commercial, so the products and services are directly communicated to the consumer. The second effect is more elliptical in that television programmes show styles of life that create the aspirational effect. This was most pronounced in Eastern Europe under communism where the nightly broadcasting of Western shows indicated clearly how far behind the communist economic model was compared with the West and contributed to its eventual collapse.

The swiftness of communication improves the effectiveness of markets. Producers and consumers widely use mobile phones to aid their business choices. Jensen (2007) researched the rapid spread of mobile phones among the Kerala fishermen off the Indian coast and found that they were able to land their catch in the markets which provided the best return. This reduced the overall price for consumers, provided more consistency of supply and prevented the widespread wastage which occurred when fish could not be sold. So a much more efficient market prevailed.

The most important example of the integration of communication and information technologies is the smartphone, where the portable package, available at an increasingly affordable price, provides web information and the ability to communicate by phone, text and email. 4G technology, launched in the UK in 2012, provides broadband Internet access to devices such as mobile phones and tablets at fast speeds and can be used for rich media, such as streaming videos.

TRANSPORTATION TECHNOLOGIES

The 'shrinking world' is a simplistic but accurate description of the rapid technological change since the 1940s, heralded by the invention of the jet engine and its development into the *commercial jet liner*. The time difference in travel by air compared with boat and train has been so substantial that it has created two linked mass markets. First, for the traveller, whether business or pleasure, for whom the swiftness and pleasure of the journey is joined to the associated activities it allows. Second, for the tourist, where the travelling is a means to take holidays in other countries and where a vast supporting infrastructure has been built up – hotels, holiday complexes, leisure activities. The break-up of the nationalised, non-competing flag-carrying airways has allowed the creation of a flood of low-cost carriers, bringing regular travel to the mass market. When linked to the online flight and accommodation booking systems, consumers have the ability to create their own holiday package at highly competitive rates, which has seen the demise of 50 per cent of holiday tour companies.

Another less publicised but of considerable importance has been the development of *containerisation* for the movement of freight across land and sea. It is such a simple and obvious development that it tends to be overlooked but it only started in 1956 and, before that time, loading and unloading cargo could be a slow, hazardous and wasteful activity (Levinson 2006). It was also associated with strong union presence in the ports of most developed countries, threatening strike action against developments that may reduce labour costs or employment. By the 1980s, the union power had been broken in both America and the UK and, today, the container can be 'stuffed' on the factory site, loaded and unloaded quickly by crane and enjoy protection against weather and theft throughout its journeys. In the 1960s, freight costs averaged 30 per cent of total costs for imported goods; under containerisation, which has been reduced to 1 per cent, a massive cost saving.

THE INTERNET

There has been an astonishingly rapid development of Internet technology since its origins in the US Defense Department in the mid-1970s and its commercial usage since the mid-1990s. It now affects all aspects of work and leisure at a steadily reducing cost that now puts their utilisation within the grasp of most citizens in the developed world and many in the developing world. Society communicates through emails, while hard-copy communications (such as letters) are used only in specific situations. Some organisations, such as easyJet, have attempted to become completely paper-free by scanning all the incoming post and insisting on all correspondence, internal and external, being carried out through emails. The Internet provides a huge range of information that is relatively simple for anybody to access. It facilitates buying and selling transactions to take place at the workstation.

REFLECTIVE ACTIVITY 8.2

Not all organisations have been enthusiastic to implement online buying and selling. What holds them back from gaining advantages in this area?

A more recent arrival is 'the cloud'. The cloud is the concept that the electronic information the consumer wants is stored and processed on computers somewhere else (in the 'cloud') and delivered to the consumer when and how they need it. The Internet becomes the operating system; online software runs in the computer's browser to create the files that are needed and these files are stored in remote data centres. Films can be streamed from the cloud directly onto netbooks, books streamed onto e-readers, music onto iPods and other imaginative applications appear daily (see Case Study 8.1). Software for our own device will not need to be upgraded because the software we use will be tested and constantly 'sprinkled' into the cloud by operators. No longer will there be a need to back up data or fear of losing our laptop because no important data will be stored on the devices (Arlidge 2009).

As Nicolas Carr explained:

A hundred years ago, companies stopped generating their own power with steam engines and dynamos and plugged into the newly built electric grid. The cheap power pumped out by electric utilities didn't just change how businesses operate. It set off a chain reaction of economic and social transformations that brought the modern world into existence. Today, a similar revolution is under way. Hooked up to the Internet's global computing grid, massive information-processing plants have begun pumping data and software code into our homes and businesses. This time, it's computing that's turning into a utility. (Carr 2008, p12)

The difficulty faced by the communication industry is how to continue to obtain income from their services (books, newspapers, TV, music) now that they are not being sold in the traditional way. The transfer from individual consumer purchase to subscription services may not generate as much income.

The main concern for businesses and individuals is security. Signing up for cloud services inevitably means providing both personal information but also surrendering all our data to the cloud provider. A hacker can obtain access simply by knowing a password, rather than having to get access to a computer system. A fire at a data storage unit could destroy vast amounts of data.

More distant worries include the fact that the individual consumer's data can be mined to provide a purchasing profile which will be profitable for advertisers, who can target each consumer individually, and that one company will emerge as the giant of the industry and, in effect, own all the data – every email or document produced. Here, governments are currently discussing future regulatory environments to prevent monopolies emerging.

CASE STUDY 8.1

SHOPPING – SOFTWARE APPLICATIONS

One of the cloud-based applications offered in 2009 by Google was Shop savvy, where the phone's camera becomes a barcode scanner which allows you to scan the barcode of a product you want to buy in one shop and data will be directed to your phone giving you a list of shops (with their locations) where it can be bought cheaper.

Facial-recognition software is being trialled in shop windows to identify features of shoppers and immediately present advertisements of items in the shop that may be of interest. For example, the camera (hidden within a digital display) may identify a teenage girl and the display will then advertise a new perfume endorsed by a popular pop singer; or it may advertise a hair dye when it identifies a more mature shopper. When the system becomes more sophisticated it may be able to identify likely clothes for the shopper or even headache tablets for those looking 'peeky' or holiday offers for those looking sad.

Sources: Arlidge (2009); Keers (2011)

WEB 2.0 AND SOCIAL MEDIA

Coined by Tim O'Reilly in 2004, Web 2.0 is a term which refers to the sociable and interactive aspects of the web which allow a user to discuss and share ideas. It is generally deemed a 'people-centric web as it stimulates networking and collaboration, including blogging and social networking'. Social networking sites are unique not just in the way that they allow individuals to meet strangers, but also that they allow users to articulate and make visible their round of social networks – with a public display of their connections through their list of 'friends'.

Facebook, the most prominent social networking site, is second only to the Google web search engine in terms of Internet traffic, with an estimated number of users worldwide approaching 1 billion and 26 million UK users. Twitter, a microblogging site begun only in 2007, had between 250 and 500 million users worldwide in 2012 (Bennett 2012). LinkedIn, essentially the business end of social networking, had a world-wide membership approaching 200 million, of which 10 million lived in the UK in 2012.

Organisations have made increasing use of social media in the fields of recruitment, communication, engagement and discipline, as explained later in the chapter.

Company involvement in social media touches on a number of ethical issues. These are, first, the subjects which are discussed on social media by employees and, second, the balance between the wider rights of individuals and the more specific explicit and implicit expectations of behaviour at work which could be upheld through employment law (Broughton et al 2011). In the first case, Valentine et al (2010) have found that dismissing a blogging employee is more likely to be considered ethical if the subject of the blog is work-related than if it is non-work-related. However, a key factor to be considered in both kinds of blogging is the 'moral intensity' of the content. The concept of moral intensity covers a range of factors, including the potential consequences of the comments made, for example the likelihood of an employee's comments harming the company and the scale of any harm.

BIOTECHNOLOGY AND MEDICAL TECHNOLOGIES

Biotechnology is the process of altering life forms, essentially through genetic modification. Arising from the fundamental discovery of the structure of DNA in 1953 by Crick and Watson, modification of biological processes allows such interventions as the introduction of new genes into organisms, breeding organisms to form new variants or treating organisms with new compounds.

One example of biotechnology is in the creation of genetically modified organisms (GMOs). Here, plants, animals and micro-organisms (bacteria, viruses) have had their genetic characteristics modified artificially in order to give them new properties. This could include a plant's resistance to a disease or an insect, the improvement of a food's quality or nutritional value or a plant's tolerance of a herbicide.

The implications for food production and medical advance are astounding. The biotechnology industry has promised a vast increase in food production which would be sufficient to eradicate all forms of under-nourishment world-wide. In medicine, applications promise the eventual eradication of genetic diseases, such as cystic fibrosis, as well as better understanding and treatment in common diseases and conditions, such as cancer and Alzheimer's disease. Governments around the world have co-operated in the massive genome project to map all human genes, which was successfully completed in 2004.

However, the outcomes in recent years have proved problematical. In food production, there has been considerable opposition to the acceptance of GM foods in many countries, especially the UK, to the extent that all UK trials of GM cereals were halted in 2004 and only restarted a few years later on a very limited basis under very strict controls. Many trials, however, have had to be abandoned due to protesters damaging the crops.

There have also been very few signs of long-lasting medical developments. In cystic fibrosis, for example, the discovery of the errant gene in 1984 has not led to any improved treatment due to technical problems of gene therapy processes, and results in other treatments have been mixed, as shown in Case Study 8.2.

CASE STUDY 8.2

GENE THERAPY

In 1999, Jesse Gelsinger, a 19-year-old with a rare liver disorder, participated in a voluntary clinical trial using gene therapy at the University of Pennsylvania. He died of complication from an inflammatory response shortly after receiving a dose of experimental adenovirus vector, a new device to direct the new gene to the appropriate location. His death dealt a blow to the confidence of scientists and halted all gene therapy trials in the US for some years and then only restarted for those diseases where no known cure was available.

In 2008, gene therapy was used in America to restore vision in patients with a rare and usually incurable form of blindness affecting around 6,000 people in the USA. The patients had a rare inherited disorder called Leber's congenital amaurosis, which begins eroding eyesight at birth and leaves them blind by their mid-twenties. Four of the six patients treated had much-improved eyesight. It is hoped that gene therapy may work particularly well with eye disorders because the immune system, which can reject the virus carrying the genes, isn't as active in the eye. And because it's easy to test vision, doctors know quickly whether the therapy works.

Sources: Subramanian (2004); Szabo (2008)

ARTIFICIAL INTELLIGENCE (AI) AND ROBOTICS

Artificial intelligence is the science and engineering of making intelligent machines, especially intelligent computer programs. It is related to the similar task of using computers to understand human intelligence. AI is studied in overlapping fields of computer science, psychology, philosophy, neuroscience and engineering dealing with intelligent behaviour, learning and adaptation.

Research in AI is concerned with producing machines to automate tasks requiring intelligent behaviour. These are synthesised in what are called 'expert systems'. Examples include control, planning and scheduling, the ability to answer diagnostic and consumer questions, speech and facial recognition. A recent development has been the extension into computer vision, where tests have shown that computers can be trained to 'recognise' complex objects in photographs marginally better than humans can (*Economist* 2007).

As such, the study of AI has also become an engineering discipline, focused on providing solutions to real-life problems, knowledge-mining and software applications, together with games. However, the world had to wait until 1977 for IBM's Deep Blue to beat the world chess champion, Garry Kasparov. One of the biggest difficulties with AI is that of 'comprehension'. Many devices have been created that can do amazing things, but critics of AI claim that no actual comprehension by the AI machine has taken place.

From the early days of computers, attempts have been made to replicate human activity, with the first industrial robot used by General Motors in 1961. Robots are utilised in four main ways:

1   *In place of humans* – the most common use has been in manufacturing, where robots have replaced humans in jobs that are dirty, dangerous and difficult. They work faster, to more reliable degrees of quality and can operate around the clock. The introduction of paint-spraying in car factories by robots reduced the labour force by 85 per cent and improved the quality standards by 90 per cent. Net-a-Porter, the retailer, operates a robot-only fulfilment factory in London (*People Management* 2013). They are now

seen in all manufacturing and agricultural environments, as examples show in Case Study 8.3. Another example is unmanned surveillance planes, both in the military and increasingly in civil surveillance, such as used in unauthorised migration watch on extended borders between the USA and Mexico and Russia and its neighbours.

CASE STUDY 8.3

INDUSTRIAL ROBOTS ARE RESHAPING MANUFACTURING AND AGRICULTURE

It would be tough to find a company seemingly more evocative of twentieth-century, 'old economy' America than Allied-Locke Industries. The family-owned-and-run manufacturing firm is headquartered about 100 miles due west of Chicago in rural Dixon, Illinois. No one walking onto Allied-Locke's low-light, high-decibel factory floor is going to mistake the place for the clean room at a semiconductor manufacturing plant. Allied's operations appear about as unglamorous and low tech as one might expect at a maker of chains and sprockets – except, that is, for a smattering of robots.

Although the pervasive grease and grime make these computerised machines with their articulated arms look like they originally came with the place, the robots – all adorned with user-friendly female names like 'Heidi' – are relative newcomers at the 300-employee firm. In 2000, the company picked up four used robots (they formerly resided in a now shuttered Caterpillar plant) for around $40,000 each to assist in the heated hardening of pins that help form the links in its chains.

Those four robots – along with seven more purchased since then for various tasks such as welding and loading – have allowed Allied-Locke to get more production out of the same number of workers. And that has helped it avoid new hiring. That sort of situation represents the other face of the well-publicised issue of America's declining manufacturing employment. If American workers aren't losing jobs

making Nike sneakers to Vietnamese workers, they are losing out to machines as companies look to increase productivity.

As the saying goes in manufacturing, 'automate or evaporate'. And robots represent the cutting edge of automation technology in the United States. While Japan is often thought of as most adept at the use of robots, America is now a top market for them. In 2003, North American manufacturing companies shelled out $877 million for robots and the amount is rising by over 20 per cent per annum.

Materials handling has remained the largest application for robots, followed by spot welding. The automotive industry is still the biggest robot user, ordering nearly two-thirds of robots sold across America.

Lettuce is California's main vegetable crop, growing $1.6 billion worth in 2010, accounting for 70 per cent of all lettuce grown in America. Thinning the crop has been a very costly labour-intensive task but a robot called 'Lettuce Bot' has been introduced, pulled by a tractor at two miles per hour and at 98 per cent accuracy. It starts by taking a photo of the plants as it passes, which it compares to a database of more than a million different backdrops of soil and other plants to help it decide whether the plant is a weed or a young lettuce growing too close to another. If this is the case, a nozzle at the back of the machine squirts it with concentrated fertiliser, which is more deadly than a

> pesticide, but acts as a feed to the remaining plants.
>
> Similar machines are in the planning stage to plant tulips and other bulbs, harvest, trim and package mushrooms
>
> and to water and rotate heavy potted plants around nurseries.
>
> Source: Pethokoukis (2004); *Economist* (2012b)

2 *Doing jobs that humans find difficult* – robots can be miniaturised to work in very confined spaces where access for humans is difficult or impossible, such as drains. They have been designed to work in areas affected by earthquakes or tornados to help to identify the trapped and injured.

3 *To help humans perform better* – in the military, robots have been utilised for walking through minefields, deactivating unexploded bombs or clearing out hostile buildings.

Boston Dynamics have produced a legged robot which can travel at three miles per hour, climb steep terrains and carry up to 120lb in rough terrain impenetrable to wheeled or tracked vehicles. Robots designed to help soldiers on the battlefield have to be carried onto the battlefield by those soldiers. For that reason, robot builders try to design 'man-portable' designs. A man-portable robot can be carried by a single soldier, usually in a special backpack.

For civilians, robots are developing much more slowly in the field of household gadgets to cook, vacuum and clean buildings. Mitsubishi, for instance, have designed and marketed a one-metre tall humanoid Wakamaru robot, costing around £7,000, to act as a mechanical house-sitter and secretary. It can recognise up to 10 faces and understands 10,000 words and can be utilised to watch over homes while owners are away, alerting them to possible burglaries, record notes and appointments and remind their owners with well-timed announcements. It can even monitor the condition of a sick person.

The driverless car has come a stage further in recent years with a specially adapted Volkswagen Passat, costing £265,000, which is licensed in Berlin to drive itself from one specified address to another on public streets. It uses sophisticated GPS, two screen-mounted cameras, six lasers, a spinning Velodyne laser scanner on the roof and radar front and back. Also tested in Germany is a car controlled only by human thought, which works by isolating and identifying the electrical patterns that are given off when the 'driver' thinks about a given course of action, such as braking or turning a steering wheel (Conway 2011).

4 *Training for humans* – Case Study 8.4 demonstrates the benefits of using robots for simulation purposes.

CASE STUDY 8.4

MEDICAL SCHOOLS USE ROBOT BIRTH SIMULATOR FOR TRAINING

The American Institute of Medicine, an arm of the National Academy of Sciences, estimates that as many as 98,000 US patients die annually from preventable medical errors. By using a robot and analysing in detail what went wrong, these errors can be engineered out. Noelle is a lifelike, pregnant robot used in increasing numbers of medical schools and hospital maternity wards.

The full-sized, blonde, pale mannequin is in demand because medicine is rapidly abandoning centuries-old training methods that use patients as guinea pigs, turning instead to high-tech simulations. It's better to make a mistake on a $20,000 robot than a live patient. The robot mannequins range in price from $3,200 to $20,000, the most expensive being the closest to approximating a live birth. She can be programmed for a variety of complications, can labour for hours and produce a breach baby or unexpectedly give birth in a matter of minutes.

She ultimately delivers a plastic doll that can change colours, from a healthy pink glow to the deadly blue of oxygen deficiency. The baby mannequin is wired to flash vital signs when hooked up to monitors. The computerised mannequins emit realistic pulse rates and can urinate and breathe.

A training session would involve a set of doctors and nurses tending to Noelle, who would be hooked up to standard delivery monitoring machines. However, in the corner would be an engineer from the manufacturer using his laptop to inflict all sorts of complications through wireless signals to the robot, which would override any pre-programmed instructions. The medical team would learn through their role-plays how to deal with all types of emergencies and the harm they inflict in making wrong decisions.

Source: Elias (2006)

IMPACT ON BUSINESS STRATEGY, GOODS AND SERVICES

The impact of new technology can be seen in two main developments: in business strategies and the method of operation, on the one hand, and in new products and services, on the other.

EFFECTS ON BUSINESS STRATEGIES AND OPERATIONS

The biggest effect is for organisations to have the ability to be *flexible* and to be *eager to change*. New developments put old technologies out of business quickly. For example, in the 1990s, only luxury cars had air conditioning; in the twenty-first century, few cars, except those at the very cheapest end, will sell without it. Given the extended period of design and development, manufacturers need to build in the ability to alter the standard product quickly and effectively to within a very tight budget. In reality, the product must combine extreme reliability that new technology has brought with design obsolescence to ensure the customer continues to purchase a company's new products.

Schumpeter (1976) identified the potential risks of not reacting quickly enough to major technological inventions as 'creative destruction', which can completely destroy the organisation. As an example, the arrival of digital technology in the early 2000s completely undermined Kodak's film and photographic paper operations. Although generally recognised as slow to react, they eventually produced their own digital equipment and provided innovations, such as self-service kiosks and an online printing service.

Associated with this trend is the need to *mass-customise* your products, perhaps something of a contradiction. Mass production is needed to produce the cost saving, but varieties are required to meet all the customers' varied needs. A good example in services is Compass PLC, which delivers thousands of catering contracts across the world, every one different but with some essential common sourcing, marketing and administration systems. The system becomes more complex but IT systems allow control and monitoring of every detail. The customised feature has altered manufacturing approaches to assembly lines, many of which have been abandoned in favour of *cell production systems*, where groups of multi-skilled employees work in teams to meet the differing production contracts, taking responsibility for quality, waste reduction and innovation.

The vast improvements in efficiencies in production, brought about through robotics and other IT processes, and the ability to manufacture on a global basis has led to a growing *decline in manufacturing in developed countries* as the technology has been transferred to developing countries, together with using the sources of cheap capital and labour. Examples have been given in Chapter 7 of outsourcing manufacturing from Germany to Eastern Europe and from UK call centres to India.

Technology has offered two additional *marketing opportunities*. Better knowledge of an organisation's customers through manipulation of a vast amount of purchasing data allows much closer targeting of their requirements, a process that retailers such as Homebase and Tesco have developed through loyalty cards (see Case Study 8.5). This quantity of information is only available to large organisations, but the second opportunity, the web, can be used by any sized business. In fact, the web has allowed many niche organisations to market, sell and distribute their products and services at low costs, many without the overheads of retail premises. Web-based business activity has expanded exponentially since the mid-1990s, especially business to business where sourcing can be fixed through web-based tendering or even a quasi-auctioning system. Web-marketing opportunities are a bonus for small firms by allowing them to access huge markets for specialised products.

CASE STUDY 8.5 — TESCO'S CLUBCARD

In 1995, Tesco launched their Clubcard and, by 2009, it had 16 million members (50 per cent of households) providing complex information on each individual's shopping habits. Dunnhumby, its majority-owned marketing subsidiary, processes 100 baskets a second, equal to 6 million transactions per day. Each product has 45 pieces of data; it is judged, for example, whether it is cheap or expensive, brand or own-brand, ethnic or traditional, exotic or basic. Non-food purchases have their own sets of classification. By their purchases, consumers are filtered by demographic, socio-economic and lifestyle characteristics. It is possible to generate a map of how the individual thinks, works and shops. They can be classified across 10 categories – wealth, travel, promotions, green, time-poor, credit, living style, creature of habit, charities – and into sophisticated sub-groups, such as whether they are pet owners and whether they cook for themselves often or not at all.

A personality build-up can define a 'Mrs Pumpkin' who makes pennies work when she shops, mostly uses cash, has a steady repertoire of products but experiments with new ones, has increased her spending on eco-friendly items, is involved in charity-giving, is rarely away and likes using the promotions offered.

This information is integrated with information in the public domain from Electoral Rolls, Land Registry and the Office for National Statistics to generate a profile of the area.

This information helps Tesco to decide on major strategic moves, such as the launch of Express convenience stores and the 'Finest' range and also in micro-strategies such as which products should go on to the shelves at what times and what personal communications and offers should be made to customers. For example, if customers have stopped buying bread for a period, they must be buying it elsewhere, so special cut-price bread vouchers are sent to them to entice them back. It is invaluable in launching specialised Clubcard clubs, such as a wine club and a mother and toddler club, which provide more direct marketing opportunities.

This personal information is then sold on to major suppliers who can use it to research and develop their product range according to shoppers' taste and individual promotions. The information itself has been classed in such a way that it circumvents disclosure provisions in the Data Protection Act, so it is difficult for individuals to know what Tesco's personal information on them contains.

Sources: Tomlinson and Evans (2005); Davey (2009)

REFLECTIVE ACTIVITY 8.3

It is evident that some forms of technological development provide organisations with a competitive advantage. One example is the invention by St Helens glassmaker Pilkingtons of the float glass process in the 1950s. This brought huge competitive advantages in both the quality of the sheet glass and the productivity levels. Apple's marketing of iTunes, where it was impossible for songs bought to be played on competitor's equipment, allowed Apple to capture 80 per cent of the US and UK market in the first two years and gave them huge bargaining power with the major record companies.

Think of a further THREE examples of this process and explain why such an advantage was gained in this way.

SPECIFIC PRODUCTS

The implications arising from the recent rapid developments in information technology and communications for the marketplace are substantial. Here are just a few examples at the time of writing:

- Increasing offering by subscriptions of movies, music and television/radio programmes by operators such as Disney, Comcast and Rhapsody will mean that programming-on-demand will take the place of normal TV and radio schedules. It is likely that the BBC will eventually set up a subscription service for all its huge archive of programmes. This will allow the viewer to choose exactly which episodes of, say, *Hello, Hello* or a set of 1970s *Play for Today* they want to watch, when they want to watch them.
- Flat-screen, computerised smart TVs consistently drop in price and become essential furniture of the networked home, with 4G bandwidth to fill the high definition screens.
- Myriad websites compete with TV, music and video producers and distributors. Individuals can beam up their own productions onto the web and become their own publishers.

Although there is little disagreement that technology has increased living standards generally, recent criticisms extend to the disproportionate economic power that now accumulates around companies who 'own the fastest computers with the most access to everyone's information'. Lanier (2013) has explained that citizens donate extremely lucrative information – our interests, demographic predilections, buying habits, cyber-movements – in exchange for 'free' admission into social media networks. In the financial world, for example, digitisation has allowed banks to repackage the 'information' of a mortgage debt and sell it on as increasingly complex financial products, while excluding the indebted home-owner from a percentage of the profits. Lanier argues that the early Internet years have placed such stress on open access and knowledge-sharing that it has distracted people from demanding fairness and job security in an economy predicated on data flow. He has also identified the strain on middle-level jobs in many professions that are being destroyed, especially in the music, legal and communication industries. Even universities are at risk as they are 'Napsterised' by the free flow of online information.

Lanier's greatest worry is the huge increase in power in what he calls the 'Siren Servers' – Google, Apple, Amazon and a handful of other companies able to monopolise 'big data' and able to quickly buy out (and often stifle) creative new companies who may act as competitors. Without greater state intervention through higher regulation and taxation of their activities, the risk becomes greater of technology's job-creation going into reverse, leaving a huge and growing pool of unemployed labour.

EFFECTS ON LABOUR MARKETS AND HUMAN RESOURCES

Technology both eliminates jobs and creates them. The introduction of railways in the nineteenth century eliminated most jobs in the canal transport industry but created a substantial net increase in jobs in total – in the rail industry itself, in the suppliers to the industry and in the associated expansion of industry and commerce that fast rail transport provided.

The same is true in today's technological changes. The IT software industry has created a huge number of jobs around the world, while the outcomes of their labour have reduced jobs selectively in manufacturing, distribution and administration. As mentioned earlier, introducing robotics into paint-spraying operations in car production, for example, has reduced the labour requirements in this function by 85 per cent. On the other hand, this technological change, among others, has reduced the price of the finished car to the extent that it is affordable to a greater mass market and employees in car manufacturing around the world continue to show a small overall increase.

It is the nature of the labour force that has changed with technological innovation. A polarisation has occurred with an increased demand for highly trained professional and technical employees and, at the same time, a reduced demand for low-skilled assembly and production operatives on the other. An even bigger decline has occurred in the demand for semi-skilled employees or those with traditional apprentice-served skills, most of which have been replaced by automation. This is also reflected geographically, with most of the employees in Silicon Valley and other high-tech clusters in America and Japan in the high-skills category, while the actual production of semiconductors, printers and other hardware is being carried out in East Asian countries and Mexico with largely low-skilled employees.

The perceived need for a reservoir of highly skilled employees has been the driving force for advanced countries, including the UK, to lay greater stress on achieving an increased percentage of the population to be qualified through higher education (the current target is 50 per cent) or through an education programme of skills achievements. Doubts remain, however, as to the value to the student of many graduate courses that appear attractive and enjoyable, such as many media arts courses, but offer little hope of long-term careers.

INCREASE IN TEMPORARY LABOUR

Information technology can provide information in a more reliable form and at a much more rapid rate. This allows organisations to respond far quicker to variations in consumer demand which, in turn, requires the labour market to become far more flexible.

Employers have responded in their employment model by making much greater use of non-standard employment, such as part-time or temporary employees. Supermarkets, for example, use their sales data to forecast precisely the number of checkouts required every hour of the year and use part-time employees to resource the varying needs. The need for temporary staff for Christmas and holiday periods can also be precisely pinpointed through the accurate data provided. This allows them to reach their business target of queues no greater than one or two people.

Case Study 8.6 shows a micro example of this process.

CASE STUDY 8.6

LETTUCE LEAVES AND THE LABOUR MARKET

It has become clear in recent years that consumers are steadily reducing their purchases of whole lettuces and increasingly purchasing packages of prepared lettuce leaves in a variety of forms. For supermarkets, this has provided an excellent opportunity with Tesco PLC selling over £150 million-worth a year, with a very high mark-up (as applies to most ready-prepared foods). But such packs have a very short shelf life, despite the chemical methods applied during their preparation. In addition, the purchase of such packs (often on impulse) varies very much in line with the weather.

Supermarket responses to this scenario are to assemble incredibly accurate information on purchasing trends, adjust for forecast weather conditions and put in their orders with a very short delivery time – usually no more than a day in advance, sometimes shorter. The suppliers, who are dealing with large orders they cannot afford to lose, in turn need to adjust their labour requirements flexibly. Most cannot afford to operate a system of on-call labour so they turn to labour service providers. One pack-house, for example, contracted in 2004 for 2.7 million hours of temporary labour for lettuce and other convenience salad packs. The providers, now known as 'gangmasters', have large groups of itinerant labour, mostly from overseas, who they call on a daily basis to meet heavily fluctuating demand in preparing lettuce packs and other highly seasonal goods.

Estimates of the immigrants (legal and otherwise) engaged in such work vary greatly, but it continues to rise by every report. Provista, a major player, recruits regularly from Eastern Europe, which goes some way to explain the increase of 70,000 in reported work permits from that area since the accession of a group of such countries in 2004.

Source: *Economist* (2004)

The direct implications for human resource practitioners of new technologies can be seen in the fields of recruitment and selection, teleworking and call centres and in the way the human resource operation is structured.

TECHNOLOGY IN RECRUITMENT AND SELECTION

Recruitment has moved a long way in the last few years. Initially the changes reflected the need to attract talent from the Generation Y group, who were early adopters of new technology but, as the use of the Internet and 3G and later technologies become universal, companies cannot afford to depend only on the printed word for their recruitment activities. This applies especially where companies are looking to recruit from Generation Z (those born from 1990), who have never known life without the Internet. Web-based recruitment is attractive because the response can be far quicker (possible except when filling in online application forms) and it works out far cheaper, even when using generic websites. The advance of e-recruitment saved the NHS £100 million from 2005 to 2008 with 95 per cent of applications received online and 99 per cent of shortlisting carried out online (Chubb 2008).

Company websites

Practically every organisation includes a career opportunity and job vacancy section on their website, and the company website came top of the effectiveness rating in a 2010 CIPD survey at 63 per cent. Some are more sophisticated than others.

Whitbread developed a dedicated recruitment website in 2004 called www.run-a-restaurant.com. In its first four months, the site was searched 100,000 times, resulting in 1,300 applications, which allowed their brands Brewsters and Brewers Fayre to recruit more than 60 per cent of their candidates directly and boosted the nine-day retention figure from 90 per cent to 95 per cent. It saved them a considerable sum of money.

Procter & Gamble has extended their web-based recruitment to devise a virtual career fair (Stevens 2010a). This six-hour event saw 1,200 people visit the fair, to view corporate videos and presentations and network with existing employees.

Generic websites

Sometimes called online job boards, there are a large number of Internet recruitment companies which can be divided into those that covers all areas, such as Monster and total jobs, while some sites deal with only one sector, such as NHS Jobs. The CIPD reported that 33 per cent of employees rated them as effective (CIPD 2010). All newspapers and magazines, including the CIPD, have developed their own online sites to run alongside the printed version.

CV scanning

Software has been developed which can scan CVs to see how closely they match the job specification in terms of experience, skills, qualifications and competences required.

Phone/ iPhone application

Various systems have been devised to attract applicants through their mobile phones. Adidas have developed an iPhone application specifically to drive graduates to its recruitment site, which yielded 4,500 applications in the first year (Evans 2011). A second example LV=, an insurance and pensions company which utilises interactive media, is shown in Case Study 8.7.

CASE STUDY 8.7

👁 LV= RECRUITS VIA INTERACTIVE MEDIA

Bournemouth-based LV= has introduced a scheme based on a series of posters, each of which features a real staff member. Interested jobseekers are invited to take a photo of the poster using their mobile phone and send it to a quoted number. Image recognition software will process the request and the person will then receive a pre-recorded phone call from the employee in the poster, in which they talk about their experiences in the company. This unusual approach is to pass the message that the organisation is highly creative and that insurance is not a stuffy or dull career and to confirm that the people in the poster are real employees.

Source: Brockett (2010)

Social networking

Many employers are now using social media to directly recruit. The main serious site is LinkedIn, and 14 per cent of employers rated them as effective in the 2010 CIPD survey. Most individuals who have such a site will ensure they are updated with a full review of their skills and experience, which can be easily viewed by employers. Global engineering company CH2M HILL has used the website to recruit 10 per cent of their hires in 2010 and typically use the platform as a sourcing stream for highly skilled roles commanding salaries of £50,000-plus. LinkedIn has recently announced the launch of a 'recruiter tool' for employers, which includes an engine for users to refer contact for a job and a function for recruiters and managers to exchange and give feedback on candidate profiles (Stevens 2011). Another example is KPMG, which uses social networking sites to tell students about campus events and setting up online communities for interns. It also communicates through the platform of Second Life (Chynoweth 2007).

A more unlikely user is CERN, the world's largest particle physics laboratory in Switzerland, as detailed in Case Study 8.8.

CASE STUDY 8.8

CERN – SOCIAL MEDIA CAN TRANSFORM THE QUALITY OF RECRUITMENT

CERN recruits professionals in a wide diversity of fields, not just in physics and engineering, so it advertises all job vacancies on Twitter, LinkedIn and Facebook. It goes further than this, however, because the intention is to interact with the potential audience such as candidates and with those who may know others who could wish to apply. For example, they use Facebook to host a weekly question-and-answer session led by one of the CERN recruiters, while LinkedIn provides a

forum for more specialised discussions. Since starting to use social media, CERN has seen the number of applications soar from 7,000 in 2008 to 24,000 in 2011, a far greater increase than can be explained by the recession. The range of communication media helps to clarify the requirement that appointments can only be made from one of the 20 states that fund the organisation.

Source: Cook (2012)

Automated telephone screening

Telephone screening is another new development. Here, an applicant calls a freephone number, day or night, and keys in their unique personal identification number, which automatically sets up a file for them on the company's HR system. During the interview, typically lasting 15 minutes, the candidate answers multiple-choice questions using their telephone keypad. The computer scores and weights their answers and automatically sends them an application form or schedules a face-to-face interview if they are successful. The system then sends the HR manager an interview schedule.

Initial testing

Large, well-known employers are often faced by a huge response for specific positions, especially in a graduate intake. Many have developed forms of online initial testing to reduce the number of applications to numbers they can handle without having to deal with each individually. Examples of this are John Lewis's Initial Situational Judgement test, detailed in Case Study 8.9, and L'Oreal's virtual business game, outlined in Case Study 8.10.

CASE STUDY 8.9

JOHN LEWIS INITIAL SITUATIONAL JUDGEMENT TEST

John Lewis received 3,500 applicants for its retail management graduate scheme in 2010 and, given the general economic situation, more were expected in subsequent years. Dealing with this in-house proved an impossible drain on HR resources and it was calculated that to manually screen each application would cost £6.00 each, so outsourcing was an expensive option.

The company therefore devised an online test which presented 20 scenarios all based around situations that a branch manager might typically face, each with four possible solutions. Applicants were required to rate each solution on a five-point scale ranging from 'counterproductive' to 'very

effective'. The answers are then automatically scored and those with the best scores progress to the next stage of the recruitment process.

To ensure an accurate assessment, a sample group of branch managers completed the test and their responses were analysed and used as a basis for the scoring system. A further benefit of the scheme is that it gives the applicant a semblance of a 'job preview' – an opportunity to understand the nature of the likely problems/issues that are faced in retail management.

The cost of this test was £4.50, so a saving of 25 per cent was made through devising this test.

Source: IDS (2011)

CASE STUDY 8.10

L'OREAL'S VIRTUAL BUSINESS GAME

L'Oreal introduced their online virtual business game 'Reveal' in 2010 as part of their graduate recruitment programme. Players move through the Reveal platform as avatar characters working on virtual projects and solving business tasks across various departments, including finance, sales, marketing and the supply chain. Participants are then assessed against what the company considers to be the best solutions for the problems posed. It is available in 10 languages as part of the firm's global graduate recruitment strategy. The game can be played

anywhere and people receive very in-depth feedback as they go through the exercises and tasks.

The best players who achieve great results are invited for interview. It is a way of bypassing the more formal part of the recruitment procedure as the company has a strong indication of the candidate's strengths. It is seen as a way of attracting candidates to the organisation and gives something back to them.

Source: Stevens (2010b)

Developments in this area are so fast that other devices will, no doubt, have been put in place by the time you are reading this section, so you will need to keep up with your contemporary reading in this subject.

Difficulties in using technology in recruitment

Not all professionals are wholeheartedly behind these new recruitment techniques, believing that ethical and practical issues remain unanswered. These include:

- Online applications make unreasonable demands on the time of the applicants, especially graduates who will need to make multiple applications to get their first job. Often the candidate only hears that the position has been filled when the extended form has been completed.
- The applicants may not always want to be judged quite so quickly and mechanically. Unless they have bought in to the computer processes (and IT staff probably have), they may prefer to apply to organisations with a more human face.
- Research by Microsoft (2010) has found that 40 per cent of their sample of 1,000 employers have chosen not to hire a candidate as a result of a negative online profile. Over 60 per cent of employers found no moral hazard in searching the web as part of a final check before offering a position.
- Online psychometric tests that are part of the application process are used to screen out 90 per cent of the candidates, which 'smacks of organisational expediency', according to Dulewicz (2004).
- Organisations are aware that some candidates get friends to complete the form for them or try under several names for practice (Harry Potter is very common). Organisations that set tests and business games online run the risk of a team of friends (and maybe their accountant parents) working together to produce a high-level solution which will allow them all to progress their application.
- The judgements made by telephone may enter into the realms of discrimination, in terms of age particularly, and will encourage a form of stereotyping when the specification cannot be overridden, as it can if handled by humans.
- Applicants may not be prepared for telephone interviews with instant forced choice judgements to be made which cannot be reversed, unlike in an interview situation where, if a question is not understood, it can be repeated or explained in another way. Ernst &Young decided to drop their phone interviews in 2008 after just one year's operation as too many applicants were passing this stage and little was gained while applicants and the organisation lost the face-to-face experience that built relationships (CIPD 2010).
- Sites do not keep their promises. A study by the consultancy The Driver Is (Welch 2003) found that only nine out of 33 companies who allowed jobseekers to register for emails alerting them when new jobs were posted had actually sent out alerts within three months of the candidate registering.
- A CIPD 2010 survey showed that only 3 per cent of respondents rated social networking sites as the most effective way of recruiting.

Some organisations have attempted to overcome some of the above difficulties. Marks & Spencer has eliminated competency-based tests because they take up too much time and clear with candidates first whether they are prepared to work shifts, weekends, be mobile and are eligible to work in the UK. Only then do they utilise online tests in numeracy, verbal reasoning and a 'talent screener', which judges their motivation. Successful candidates then move to the final stage, which is an assessment centre. The organisation believes that the online process has improved the success rate overall from 27 per cent to 37 per cent.

A further example of automated short-listing is the use of equipment to *electronically read CVs* using OCR (optical character recognition) software. The system's artificial intelligence reads the texts and, by using search criteria such as qualifications, job titles and companies where the applicant has worked, will produce a ranking list of applicants against the mandatory and optional aspects of the person specification.

This system is quicker and more consistent than if it were carried out manually but will only be as efficient as the search engine and will certainly miss many potential candidates, let alone the difficulty the technology faces in trying to understand poor handwriting.

REFLECTIVE ACTIVITY 8.4

What are the advantages and disadvantages to employers and employees of online recruitment?

TELEWORKING

The development of the world-wide web and associated technological innovations has facilitated the process of working at a distance to the employee or main contractor. The process allows a variety of models, ranging from the ability to work one or two days at home with a laptop to being a fully fledged teleworker hundreds of miles away where physical contact with the office site is restricted to an annual conference visit. As phones merge with computers, video calls will become far more common, with far-flung teams working on shared documents in virtual meetings.

Advantages of teleworking

- Productivity gains – employees working from home are often more productive. They get away from the frequent interruptions and distractions that pepper the working day. It is also in their interests to show they are more productive so the teleworking arrangement can continue.
- Employees can work out a work–life balance much more easily with more time spent at home. Caring responsibilities can be balanced with work to be completed, as long as the will and the self-discipline are present.
- Time-saving – for mobile teleworkers, the ability to complete tasks at remote locations, rather than returning to a central office, saves considerable time and expense. Time is saved on regular commuting to work.
- Reduced accommodation costs – most organisations sell teleworking to their boards through setting out the huge savings in accommodation costs, especially where these are in central city locations.

Difficulties that could arise

- Teleworking can be difficult to manage without the daily face-to-face contact. Managers often want quick answers to questions or a special task performed quickly. This is far more difficult with remote workers. Supervisors and managers need specialised training to manage the remote worker. Contact has to be regular but not too intrusive.
- Performance management systems need to be carefully devised. It has to be much more based on outputs and outcomes rather than traditional measures such as attendance. Regular meetings need to be held to discuss the employees' performance.
- Employees may not have the work distractions but they may have the home ones instead – children, other family members, friends, callers, etc, can all disrupt a steady work flow. Relationships with family members can suffer if the borders between work and home are not drawn tightly to everybody's satisfaction.
- Health and safety in the home needs to be carefully monitored.
- Dealing with confidential documents in the home setting has to be addressed.
- Some teleworkers feel too remote from the workplace. They miss the comradeship of the office and lose out on the regular gossip and social activities. There is also a general

concern that teleworkers lose training and promotion opportunities because of their low visibility.

An example of the benefits of teleworking is shown in Case Study 8.11.

TELEWORKING AT BAXTER INTERNATIONAL

CASE STUDY 8.11

Baxter International is a leading US manufacturer and supplier of technology relating to the blood and circulatory systems, employing over 40,000 worldwide. In the late 1990s, as part of their close technological relationships with Nortel Networks, they implemented Nortel's HomeOffice 2 system, which connects remote workers to the corporate phone system and intranet as if they were still in the office. This system matched their need for increased flexibility due to the following:

- The global and distributed nature of the business meant staff had to go to the office regularly in the early hours for audio conferences.
- Many of their offices, including the UK base at Compton in Berkshire, were in rural settings, leading to substantial driving involved for staff to get to and from work.
- The life-critical nature of the business meant that some staff need to available all hours to the hospitals and to be able to direct the action required through the organisation's system. This had previously meant 24-hour rotas in the workplace, which was unpopular.
- Similarly, call centre staff at their dialysis equipment supplying subsidiary cover the period from 8.00am to 10.00pm with every patient having a named agent. Working early and late was, again, not very popular.

Introduced in 1999, the scheme has become so popular that around 20 per cent of non-manufacturing staff now work from home, working out with their manager how often and when they come into the office. Worldwide, over 3,500 employees use the teleworking system.

The set-up cost per employee was around £3,000, including the Nortel system installation, a fax, copier, printer and scanner, a desk and ergonomic chair, fire extinguisher and a smoke detector. There are also ongoing costs as the company paid for ISDN costs and personal calls. Most employees concerned had already been issued with laptops.

The organisation has gradually changed its culture in response to its distributed system of operation. Performance management is now almost totally related to outputs. Managers with homeworkers have needed to be trained in target-setting, measurement and relationships with their staff, for example.

A number of additional benefits have arisen since the scheme began. Retention of existing employees has improved but so has the ability to trawl through a relatively small pool of crucial specialists who no longer will necessarily have to relocate to the company's main centres. This ability to avoid family disruption can be crucial in the decision as to whether to accept a job opportunity, as well as saving a large amount of relocation costs.

In addition, the proportion of staff returning from maternity leave has risen as many have joined the teleworking loop and take part in audio-conferencing to keep themselves up to date.

Overall, the scheme has been seen as very successful indeed, not just for the speed of take-up by staff but by the hard-nosed measures of increases in productivity – estimated at around 30 per cent on average. Alongside this has been the substantial saving in office space.

Source: *Flexible Working* (2000)

REFLECTIVE ACTIVITY 8.5

Research has shown that teleworkers often suffer from social isolation. Can you suggest ways that these effects can be mitigated?

CALL CENTRES

The invention and development of the automated call distribution (ACD) system, which both released the need for a switchboard operator and also provided detailed call information, has promoted the introduction of a growing number of call centres. In 2007, it was estimated that over 600,000 employees were UK call centre employees, a number that is increasing despite the dispersal of many such jobs to the Indian subcontinent, where labour rates are cheaper (Peacock 2007).

Operators work with the required database to answer customer queries or process sales and service agreements, and most build in an interactive instruction guide for the employee to follow, which reduces the time and cost for training. The technology also allows management to monitor calls to identify process glitches, training needs and earnings through any incentive scheme. Call centres can take a distributed form, allowing calls to be channelled to teleworkers at distant locations, with the technology allowing access to all necessary data.

The implications for human resource practitioners are quite complex here, where there has been much debate about the high staff sickness and turnover, quality of job design and the ethical nature of the job requirements.

REFLECTIVE ACTIVITY 8.6

Call centres have some of the highest staff turnover rates (average over 40 per cent) and absenteeism rates (over 6 per cent) in any UK employment sector. Can you suggest why this has happened and what should be done about it?

EFFECT ON THE STRUCTURE OF HUMAN RESOURCE OPERATIONS

Sparrow et al (2004) and Reddington et al (2005) have set out some of the opportunities that technology has provided in facilitating new and developing human resource systems:

● *Shared services* – the system adopted by many large organisations, such as Standard Chartered Bank, Whitbread and HSBC, to extract the routine HR processes from operating units and place them in a central service, not necessarily anywhere near a head office. Activities include payroll, record-keeping (attendance, starters and leavers, pensions), the operation of recruitment, job advertising and short-listing together with advice on company HR systems and employment law. Technology allows the access to the databank of information held at the centre that can be drawn upon by local managers and video-conferencing arrangements for wider discussion of action on, say, a difficult disciplinary situation. Many shared services have access to a network of experts for areas such as reward and benefits or selection testing.

- The savings that are made by using this system involve the cutting back of duplication of HR support at each operating unit (averaging 20–40 per cent), moving the work to low-cost locations, savings on purchasing of technology and services at one point rather than many and a near certainty that consistent decisions will be made, avoiding litigation in discrimination and other legal areas (Reilly 2000).

- *E-enablement of HR processes* – the ability to get HR information to and from, and support on to, line managers' desks without a formal HR intervention allows far more time for the HR department to focus on more strategic areas. The early stages of development here of access to policy documents and routine statistical processes has moved on to empowering line managers to take greater control of their HR responsibilities. They can access external information on pay and benefits, authorise pay increases, select the appropriate standardised terms and conditions to go in an offer letter, process key data on an individual's performance management and manage their staff and training budgets. Norwich Union (Parry et al 2007) had four key drivers when they introduced an HRIS self-service functionality in 2006:

    - *enabling line management* – encouraging managers to take more responsibility for managing their people through being able to access and maintain records
    - *improving and simplifying core processes* – providing real-time updates on core data, removing duplication and increasing online processing, increasing standardisation and economies of scale in administration
    - *adding value through HR expertise* – allowing HR resource to move from transactional to performance-enhancing activity, facilitating the introduction of new HR activities online, such as competencies and flexible benefits, encouraging individuals to take increased ownership of their own details and career management
    - *e-enablement of HR* – mirroring business practice.

- *Outsourcing of HR and shared services provision* – service centres and e-empowerment can be organised in-house or may be outsourced to firms that have the technological expertise to offer such services at low cost. For example, Arinso Corp have contracted with Shell to produce a shared services system utilised by over 100,000 employees across 45 countries (Glover 2004). HR departments may therefore be reduced in capacity, with interesting implications for career planning. The normal stepped climb up the organisation may instead become leaps between service providers and organisations, not unlike the current career path of senior management.

An example of shared services is shown in Case Study 8.12.

CASE STUDY 8.12

SHARED SERVICES ARE SUCCESSFUL IN SAVING MONEY AND MAINTAINING SERVICES

A Local Government Association (LGA) report in 2012 examined five shared services projects covering a range of co-operative arrangements between authorities, fire and rescue services and local NHS trusts. The report shed light on how efficiencies were being made by councils sharing back-office functions, including HR, IT and legal services. Savings are achieved through consolidating organisation structures, integrating information technology, reducing accommodation and improving procurement. The five projects had saved a total of £30 million between them.

It found that there was typically a two-year 'payback period' before the set-up and integration costs were cancelled out and savings kicked in. Initial savings came from reducing headcount and duplication of staff, in staff changes. Afterwards, further savings came from improved use of IT, reduced need for assets such as office space, and cultural change leading to better processes, the report said. Few problems were reported by the participants.

Although the savings were not sufficient to make up the 28 per cent cut in the money councils receive from central government, measures such as the shared service arrangements currently in operation at more than 200 local authorities have helped to dampen the impact.

Local authorities had been much more successful in sharing services than central government departments have, despite being hit by greater proportional spending cuts, said the LGA. While shared services have traditionally focused on back-office functions, many local authorities are now looking at which front-line services can also be shared.

Source: LGA (2012)

USING SOCIAL NETWORKING SITES IN HUMAN RESOURCES

There are a number of ways that the popularity of social networking sites can be utilised to improve human resources:

- In recruitment, as set out earlier in the chapter, organisations have transferred much of their recruitment profile on to an adapted social networking site (such as Facebook), which then enhances the brand to a younger audience.
- For induction and general employee communication, organisations such as Beds and Bars (see Case Study 8.13) have created a form of internal social networking. Many organisations strongly encourage their managers to take part in social networking activities. In MITIE, all top managers are required to open Twitter and Facebook accounts as the HR director considered that, if managers do not know how to use social media, they will not know how to engage with their employees and supply chain partners. Initially there were mixed results but others used the sites creatively, such as the pest-control division which tweeted about Archie, their mouse-detection dog (Syedain 2012).
- To encourage greater diversity, organisations have set up networks specifically for minority and gender groups which provide help and encouragement to members of those groups, raise awareness of the challenges faced by a particular group, help line managers to support them better and act as a forum for consultation with the business on policies and procedures.
- For knowledge management, organisations, such as InterContinental Hotels Group, have used social networking technology to allow employees throughout the world to connect with each other to share learning and develop skills. This process is estimated to cost only 5 per cent of the cost of a leadership workshop.

BEDS AND BARS EMPLOYEE CONSOLE

Beds and Bars operates a large number of hostels, pubs and bars across Europe and its workforce is primarily young. 'One of the key challenges we face in the youth travel industry is communication with our employees,' says Duane Vanner, People Manager, UK. 'Using a medium they are familiar with, can understand and respond to is essential when it comes to efficient and cost-effective on-the-job training.'

In early 2008, it was decided to create an interactive HRM tool based on social networking technology. Staff now log into the console as part of their introduction to the company and staff members are given a profile which they can update online. Through the console, employees can instantly communicate with each other across Europe, access custom-made training videos, apply for places on a variety of training courses and access internal job listings. The development challenges faced included the heavy security required for the site and ensuring it was fully functional across all platforms, including mobile phones. Vanner says that project's goals – to increase employee involvement in company learning activities, provide accurate and accessible up-to-date training and increase product knowledge and awareness – have all been met.

Source: *People Management* (2009)

A number of employment issues have arisen, however, regarding social networking.

The consensus among HR professionals and employment lawyers is that it is possible for employers to *discipline* those who make comments using social media sites. This is particularly the case where employee comments can be clearly considered defamatory and for criticising their organisation on their personal networking site, taking into account the fact that, in terms of the personal and temporary nature of such communications, this is far from uncommon. On occasions, it can be close to the boundaries of libel or deformation. In October 2008, 13 Virgin Atlantic crew members were dismissed following their participation in a discussion on Facebook during which it was alleged they brought the company into disrepute and insulted passengers. They had apparently criticised their company's health and safety standards and also called their passengers 'chavs'.

A more marginal case occurred in 2011, when an employee of BG plc was disciplined for uploading his CV onto his LinkedIn profile and registering an interest in 'career opportunities' because the company claimed that information on his CV was confidential and for breaching its conflicts-of-interest policy. The employee resigned, claiming constructive dismissal, and the two parties reached a confidential agreement so the issue of whether the employer was justified in its actions (especially complaining about the job-hunting aspects) was never known (Hodgkiss 2012).

On the other hand, however, a number of high-profile cases of employees being fired for usage of social media have resulted in the dismissals being overturned (Schoneboom 2011). One example was Joe Gordon, a Waterstone's employee who was dismissed in 2005 because of including some criticisms of his company in his satirical blog. He was offered reinstatement following a successful tribunal claim. Following such cases, many writers on employment law have argued that it is crucial for employers to have some kind of social media policy in place to determine what is acceptable and what is not. Such a policy would be intended to discourage employees from making certain kinds of adverse comments using social media and, in the event that employers find evidence of objectionable comments written by an employee, would make it easier from a legal point of view to take action against that employee (Broughton et al 2011).

Second, employees may engage in criticising other members of staff, including both colleagues and their own managers. This, in its extreme forms, can be regarded as cyber-bullying and the question arises as to whether the company should step in to stop extended and painful personal campaigns, under its duty of care responsibilities. If the organisation does not take appropriate disciplinary action against the posting of such information, it could be held vicariously liable for those comments and in breach of its duty of care owed to the employee about whom information was posted.

Third is the issue of whether employers should investigate potential employees' social networking sites to obtain a more detailed personal profile, including such areas as their drinking habits. However, there are potential dangers here for the employer, apart from the obvious risk of information from this source being unreliable. There is also the potential for a discrimination claim. An unsuccessful job applicant could bring such a claim if they feel that they were not successful in their job application because of a discriminatory perception of them by the prospective employer. For example, if a job candidate has a social networking profile that reveals their age, religious belief or sexual orientation and is invited to an interview and discovers that their profile was viewed by the prospective employer but they were not subsequently appointed (and they believed that they were the best candidate for the job), there is a chance that they may consider bringing a claim for discrimination.

Fourth, employees can spend a considerable time in the workplace on their social networking sites, generally referred to as 'cyberslacking'. In one study, employees admitted to at least one hour per week using the Internet and email for non-work-related purposes, of which Facebook and Twitter were two of the most used sites (Foster 2010). Some employers have decided to block such sites, including Portsmouth City Council in 2009, but other organisations have taken the view that this is draconian and that employees should be trusted in this area, as they are generally trusted with private phone calls and occasional personal web searches during working hours. Other organisations have become specific, including one which specifies allowing 'up to five brief emails a day' and another limiting employees to 'no more than 30 minutes a day use during break times'. In Foster's research, the views of employees are similarly broad. In response to the statement, 'I should be allowed unlimited access to email and Internet for personal use without restriction at work,' there was an almost symmetrical response from strongly agree through to strongly disagree.

An example of an integrated approach to using technology in developing the HR function is shown in Case Study 8.14.

CASE STUDY 8.14

IMPACT ON THE CHANGING ROLE OF HUMAN RESOURCES IN NORTEL

The company

Nortel is a recognised leader in delivering communications capabilities that enhance the human experience, ignite and power global commerce, and secure the world's most critical information. The company's next-generation technologies, for both service providers and enterprises, span access and core networks, support multimedia and business-critical applications and help eliminate today's barriers to efficiency, speed and performance by simplifying networks and connecting people with information.

HR structure

Nortel has over 30,000 employees worldwide servicing customers in over 150 countries and about 6,500 employees in Europe. The HR structure is based on the Ulrich (1998) model with HR shared service centres in four global locations, six HR delivery teams, four core HR strategy groups and a number of HR business partners supporting different parts of the business. Due to the volatile nature of the markets for their main products, the businesses have been reorganised on a number of occasions – from centralisation to decentralisation and from a hands-off approach to a more management-controlled style. Underlying Nortel's ability to make these changes has been the significant investment in IT infrastructure and particularly HR information systems.

Changing the system

In 2005, an HR Evolution project was launched which included the deployment of the SAP employee and manager self-service modules in 2006. Traditionally, HR has had the responsibility for people transactions and processes, but by empowering the managers in HR functions through the self-service tools, HR has been able to focus on delivering added value to the business in other areas such as strategy and process design.

Nortel's HR Shared Service Centre (SSC) became responsible for ensuring that the HR transactional services were delivered consistently across the company and for ensuring that any change request approved by the line manager is within company policy and guidelines, a job previously carried out by HR managers wearing their 'policeman' hat.

In effect, the new system has empowered the line manager to take decisions as if they themselves owned the business. No longer are they involved in a multi-layer, paper-based bureaucratic decision-making process – they are held accountable for the people changes they make that impact on their budget. Much more training has taken place to ensure that line managers are aware of HR policy and practice and the legislative context. It was well understood that, previously, there were too many HR staff touching every part of the transactional work. Under the new system, managers are expected to grasp the people action initiative and take responsibility for developing their own people skills, as well as those of their staff. One of the key skills is in clear objective-setting and communication of expectations, open discussion of issues that affect performance and honest feedback. No longer can they say, 'This is not in my hands, go and see HR.'

When it comes to obtaining advice and information, in the majority of cases line managers can find what they want on the intranet in areas such as recruitment, reward, termination, discipline and benefits. Where they need more help, managers or employees call the SSC and trained team members will guide them on policy interpretation or action required when unusual events have occurred. Where answers are not forthcoming from this source, the question is referred to members of the HR Delivery Teams where a specialist in, say, compensation delivery will provide the definitive answer. Their main role, however, is for process design, improvement and delivery where they work very closely with the SSC. As the processes evolve and new approaches and systems are defined, the delivery team will work out how best to translate the changes into workable end-to-end processes from the line managers, through the systems and on to the SSCs.

The technology is further utilised by constantly reviewing the SSC user metrics to identify the regular problems. The skills required to interpret the metrics and then translate them into process improvement activities are a new experience to the more 'traditional' HR professional.

The final part of the HR structure is the Core HR Strategy Group, which deals with employee relations, compensation and benefits, talent strategy and diversity. Here the designs for future people strategy are formulated, using data from all other HR groups, together with benchmarking and competitive intelligence exercises.

Technology is at the heart of all these changes. By automating as many

processes as possible and devolving others to management through the use of manager self-service, HR has been able to reduce significantly the amount of time spent on routine administration tasks, which thereby facilitates other non-administrative tasks, such as learning, recruitment and strategic analysis. This should allow HR professionals to manage the HR function in a strategic manner and to become the real partners in the business.

Note: Despite these innovations, Nortel went into administration in 2009 and bankruptcy proceedings were in progress in 2013.

Source: Parry et al (2007)

KNOWLEDGE MANAGEMENT

So great is the speed of technological innovation and so dominant are the changes that it brings in the form of new products, services or the way we live and work, that commentators have expressed the view that we now live in the 'knowledge economy'. Furthermore:

> A firms competitive advantage depends more than anything on its knowledge, or, to be slightly more specific, on what it knows, how it uses what it knows and how fast it can know something new. (Prusack 1997, pix)

Having the knowledge can be regarded as even more important than possessing the other means of production – land, buildings, labour and capital – because all the other sources are readily available in an advanced global society, while the right leading-edge knowledge is distinctly hard to obtain. Linked to this thinking is the concept of 'intellectual capital', which can be bought (and, if appropriate, stored securely) either through purchasing patents or intellectual property rights or through employing the highly skilled/intelligent employees/consultants who possess that capital (Stewart 2001).

This capital is not necessarily discoveries and processes that can be patented. Society is developing in such a way that services are becoming the dominant commodity over manufacturing. This means that skilled services in areas such as advertising, design, leisure and even sport can command very high fees – just look at the prices paid for the world's top 100 footballers, film stars or music performers. So wealth created in the economy is increasingly perceived as derived from knowledge and intangible assets (Storey and Quintas 2001).

REFLECTIVE ACTIVITY 8.7

Knowledge value

Do you see knowledge as a source of competitive advantage in the marketplace? If so, how?

Because it is such an important asset, organisations are starting to assess their own collection of knowledge bases and ensure they are available for use. This is not just about sorting patents but analysing the knowledge gained through the experiences of their skilled staff. In HSBC, for example, a senior manager has been appointed to identify banking expertise among staff and ensure this knowledge is not lost when they retire or leave the organisation and to organise ways that critical knowledge can be shared across the organisation. Part of the role is to develop 'tacit knowledge', such as the intuitive approaches to problem-solving in a particular work context or vague ideas about a new product or service, into 'explicit knowledge' that can be written down and communicated (Stredwick and Ellis 2005).

Consideration must also be given to the development of what Hansen et al (1999) refer to as *codification* strategies, where knowledge is codified and stored in databases where it can be readily accessed and used by employees, and *personalisation* strategies, where knowledge is closely tied to the person who developed it and is shared mainly through direct person-to-person contacts. How to ensure the balance between these two approaches is crucial to the success of knowledge management. For example, if greater emphasis is given to personalisation, there needs to be formal encouragement of a highly developed process of social networking to allow informal opportunities to arise for knowledge-sharing outside of standard meetings. Many knowledge-based companies organise social events, even organise company holiday weekends, for this purpose.

In the human resources field, how knowledge workers are recruited, trained and motivated has come under much scrutiny in recent years. As a group, research has shown that they can be distinguished by their demand for greater autonomy in their work, by their intrinsic motivation and greater sense of task satisfaction and by their emphasis on career-progressing projects rather than immediate financial gratification (Scarborough and Carter 2007). The implication is that recruitment pays as much attention to skills and potential as to actual knowledge and that the performance management process is crucial to retention success.

TECHNOLOGY – THE DARKER SIDE

Although technological developments generally lead to improvements in standards of living, not all are seen as universally benign. For every five citizens that welcome new products, job opportunities, improved quality and variety of services, better healthcare and ease of transportation, a sixth will see a darker side with bleaker effects. For example, the migration online of book and record sales and the invention of the e-reader have devastated the number of book and record shops on the high street.

Examining three of the short case studies illustrated in this chapter shows further illustrations of the darker side of technology:

- *Gene therapy (see page 362)*–in itself, this is a dispiriting case of unfulfilled expectations but there are further difficulties in this area. One of the success stories has been the development of devices to allow accurate screening for genetic disorders. This can be carried out at any age and even for unborn babies. The main benefit is that such disorders can be treated at an early stage so that the prognosis improves. However, this presents a number of problems. First of all, insurance companies (and employers who provide and pay for life insurance of their employees) are very interested in carrying out such tests before accepting insurance risk. For those citizens with no disorders and long life expectancy, life insurance costs would be cheap but pensions expensive. For those with a disorder, the opposite would apply, with life assurance virtually impossible to obtain. There is considerable debate currently as to whether such tests should be compulsory, the outcome of which would leave vulnerable citizens uninsurable and regarded as second-class. Alternatively, governments can attempt to force insurance companies to ignore the results of such tests and not apply prohibitive insurance costs. A second problem is the dilemma faced by the parents where pre-natal tests show up genetic disorders. It provides the opportunity for the birth to be aborted and some of the life-long pain averted, but such an irreversible decision is a very hard one to take and most parents (except those who already have one disabled child) choose to avoid taking such tests.

- *Lettuce leaves (see page 369)* – there are a number of ethical and regulatory issues surrounding this case. First, it is becoming very difficult to challenge the power of the largest supermarkets in demanding such tight schedules on suppliers and, subsequently, their employees. In America, Walmart, with over 25 per cent of the huge US market, virtually writes the rules with suppliers being unable to match their negotiating power. The situation in the UK is somewhat better, with a competing group of supermarkets matched against, in certain product areas, a similar group of large producers, but the growing dominance of Tesco is creating some worries for regulators. This issue is discussed further in Chapter 5 on regulation. The second issue is whether it is ethical for so much migratory labour, living in poor conditions, to provide fresh food for the community in the twenty-first century. It is hoped that they are protected in the UK by the National Minimum Wage, but many will slip through the net and the rules concerning deductions for accommodation are very complex with such situations being rarely investigated. Added to this are some safety issues, which were shown graphically by the death of 20 illegal Chinese immigrants working as cockle-pickers in Morecambe Bay in 2003. Consumers may demand fresh produce at affordable prices, but these may come at indefensible cost.

- *Shared services (see page 376)* – there are experiences of 'one product fits all' which may not apply in fast-moving, customer-oriented businesses. The quality of the service provided by unqualified staff can be questionable with a background in call centre work rather than human resources. Many opportunities for seriously effective HR interventions and innovations can occur through regular discussions about routine issues, often in informal settings, which are far less likely to happen under formalised shared services environments. Moreover, services that are shared across countries run the risk of cultural confusion.

THE DARKER SIDE OF EMPLOYMENT

Alongside the potential problems faced by employees in call centres, teleworking and social networking sites, there has been much research into the inherent problems that new technology brings to the workplace, demonstrating its dialectical nature, where advances in one direction produce problems of their own (Martin 2005). These can take various forms, such as:

- *De-skilling of manual work* – especially in industries such as house-building where pre-fabrication, using computer-controlled design and machine tools, has replaced many traditional skills. A major consequence in the UK has been the near collapse of trade training by large house-builders which, in turn, has led to severe shortages of servicing and maintenance trades, such as plumbers and electricians, where the market is dominated by small organisations. Even software work has been substantially automated and routinised.

- Call-centres have been roundly criticised as the new 'industrial sweatshops' with automatons working in psychic prisons on prepared scripts to finely tuned bonus schemes, leading to poor employee morale and depressive illnesses (see Case Study 8.15).

- Internet misuse can take a number of forms. One that has proved costly is the spreading of false information via the Internet. Employers can be held vicariously liable for their employees' activities when using the Internet and are responsible if staff send email messages that breach confidentiality or are defamatory. In the case of *Western Provident v Norwich Union*, Norwich Union was forced to shell out £450,000 in damages and costs for slander and libel after Western Provident discovered damaging and untrue rumours circulating on Norwich Union's internal email system. They were about Western Provident being in financial difficulties and being investigated by the Department for Trade and Industry (Hall 2004).

- The *intrusion of surveillance* technology has presented dilemmas for employers who have the responsibility and opportunity to monitor employees to ensure no laws are being broken (such as downloading of pornography) but appreciate employees' fears and resentment at such a process taking place. Monitoring attendance (through card-swiping security systems) and performance (such as call centre systems detailed earlier) have become cheap and accurate but present challenges to employment cultures where employees' trust and independence of action are highly valued. Surveillance may focus employees' attention on organisational and strategic targets but also have the tendency to discourage innovation (Taylor 2004).

- Research has indicated that it is possible to identify important personality traits by analysing as few as 50 "tweets" and thereby accurately channel advertisements to individuals (*Economist* 2013).

- A special *problem of e-business employment* is the lack of contact with the customer and a poor level of social interaction. This has led to higher levels of staff turnover than in conventional businesses (PricewaterhouseCoopers 2000). There has also been some sense of alienation related to virtual meetings, where the growth of video-conferencing has been surprising slow, although most evidence would support the view that the correct usage of mobile phones and emails has generally enhanced employees' social contact.

- Some commentators picture ICT in a tyrannical frame in the sense that it provides *more intensive work* through the huge amount of data it provides and the options available and it also *demands longer hours* at the work face through its additional ability to provide 24/7 coverage (Green 2002). However, not all research supports this view. In a CIPD-financed project, Nathan et al (2003) provided little evidence that ICT directly impacted on increased working hours. Employees were using more technology and they were working longer hours, but the causal relationship was not proven.

- Concerns have been expressed over the huge decline in newspaper advertising income as readers and advertisers turn to the Internet. This means that the disappearance of the independent free press becomes more likely, with the implication of fewer independent investigations in a democratic society. In America, income dropped from $63 billion in 2000 to $19 billion in 2012. Most newspapers are searching for a new online model with full or partial pay walls but few are generating sufficient income. At the same time, the power of online advertisers to observe and follow individual buying habits has led to invasive micro-targeted advertisements popping up regularly and strongly reinforcing such habits. Their success has meant that the migration of advertising to the web has accelerated swiftly (Sullivan 2012).

- Although many of the accident-driven jobs in traditional industries have been eliminated by automation, new health problems have emerged, both physical (repetitive strain injury, eyesight deterioration) and psychological (stress-related illnesses).
- Research has given an indication that technology can encourage work presenteeism (Churchard 2012). The availability of information throughout the day and night has increased the difficulty for employees to 'switch off', and the need to be up and running encourages coming in to work despite being ill or, at least, checking emails and other information when ill at home.

CASE STUDY 8.15

SUICIDES AT FRANCE TELECOM

Over an 18-month period during 2008–09, 24 employees at France Telecom committed suicide following the implementation of a wide-ranging restructuring plan called 'Time to Move'. A sociologist, Monique Crinon, who interviewed a cross-section of staff, identified feelings of being undervalued and low self-esteem running through the company from top to bottom. One senior worker in her fifties was demoted to work in a call centre and reported that she had stepped back in time to an era where mainly young women staff were terrorised and controlled. Employees had to make several sales an hour from dictated scripts, had to ask permission to leave for toilet breaks and had to file a written explanation for going one minute over a lunch break. The teams were repeatedly broken up with staff being moved to other centres at two days' notice, leaving workers feeling isolated and feeling like failures in a bonus-driven system. In a similar case, a 51-year-old employee was moved from a back-office job to a call centre and eventually committed suicide by throwing himself off a motorway bridge in September 2009.

Less than a week later, the company suspended the restructuring and Louis-Pierre Wenes, deputy chief executive and the architect of the restructuring, resigned.

Sources: Chrisafis (2009); Investortoday.co.uk (2009)

In labour market terms, a divide has developed between two major segments of employment – the knowledge-intensive organisations and the knowledge-routinised ones, called the 'hour-glass' model by Coyle and Quah (2004). Knowledge-intensive jobs use advanced and complex ICT skills and require high human capital levels. Employees work long and often unsociable hours but their jobs are often (but not always) associated with high pay, extensive training, career development and high personal and job satisfaction. Knowledge-routinised jobs, on the other hand, are lowly paid, require much lower levels of human capital and the routine ICT work provides much less personal satisfaction.

TRENDS TO WATCH – WHAT OF THE FUTURE?

'THE HORSE IS HERE TO STAY!'

Forecasting the effects of new technology is very tricky and many serious and well-respected forecasters have got their forecasts very wrong. In an excellent article by Smith (2004), which details truly awful forecasts, he quotes pioneers in the IT industry from whom we would have expected a clearer vision. For example, IBM forecast in 1952 that their worldwide sales of mainframe computers would be 52 and, 30 years later, had raised it to 200,000, roughly what they now ship a week. Even Bill Gates made gaffes, such as stating in 1981 that '640K should be enough for anybody'. Going further back, the president of Michigan Savings Bank advised people in 1901 against investing in the Ford Motor Company, quoting the statement at the top of this section.

There was a better performance by Kahn in his 1967 book *The Year 2000*, where he predicted computers, mobile phones, video recorders and satellite dishes. But he, like many forecasters since, seriously misjudged the effect of technology on working lives. Almost everybody has forecast that we would all be working far fewer hours (30 a week at most, according to Kahn), have much more holiday and retire very early. This was because technology would take away jobs, which it clearly does. What almost all futurologists failed to grasp is that, while some jobs disappear, more arise in their place. Production jobs have disappeared either through automation and robotics or to developing countries with cheaper wages. In their place have arisen industries that provide services – either business services, such as IT, financial services and all manner of consultancies, or those that provide personal services, such as leisure, health and beauty and personal finances. At the same time, services that used to operate for the few, such as hotels, eating out, travel and tourism, are now used by everybody in increasing numbers.

What is just as significant is that such new and developing industries are generally very labour intensive (automated hairdressing is still not with us), so technology has released employees from the grind of heavy production but provided instead the more sociable but equally routine (and absolutely vital) activities involved in such activities as 'housekeeping' in hotels and 'care working' in hospitals and old people's homes. This explains why the average working week has decreased only marginally in the last 25 years and why unemployment in flexible societies, such as the UK and America, remains very low.

KEY LEARNING POINTS

- Technological development can occur through incremental innovation, radical innovation, change in technological systems or technological revolution.
- 'Business intelligence' is a key concept where the aim is to transform large amounts of data, often scattered across the organisation, into the key information that drives informed decision-taking, and to deliver it in an easily read form through the computer screen to anybody where and when they need to know.
- Technological developments provide the capacity for organisations to be *flexible* and to be *eager to change*, in fields such as product design, advertising and marketing (especially on the web), customer relations and quality development.
- Technology has had a profound effect upon labour markets through facilitating novel flexible working practices, such as annualised hours, complex shift systems and multi-skilling, together with the development of sophisticated recruitment and selection processes.
- Human resource systems have been affected by the technological changes that allow systems of shared services, outsourcing and e-enablement of HR processes, especially recruitment and selection.
- Social media usage has increased substantially and many businesses encourage and integrate social networking processes into their core activities.
- It has been recognised in recent years that knowledge management is a vital process to ensure that organisations can collect, store and distribute key areas of knowledge that help create competitive advantage.
- Technological progress produces its own ethical dilemmas in areas such as gene therapy, consumer choice and outsourcing.

QUESTIONS

1 In what ways does technology offer improved marketing opportunities?

2 Name five difficulties associated with the employment of teleworkers.

3 Provide four examples of how technology helps HR administration and management become more efficient.

4 What is the difference, according to Freeman, between a radical and an incremental innovation?

5 Give three examples of developments in communication technologies and their effect on markets.

6 Provide four examples of how technology can provide difficulties in the employment setting, as well as benefits.

7 What are the four main cycles of K-waves?

8 Give four examples of the use of technology in the recruitment and selection process.

9 What is the connection between technology and flexibility requirements?

10 What are 'shared services' in the HR setting, how are they facilitated by technology and what savings are made?

EXPLORE FURTHER

The best source of contemporary technology and its effects is the weekly *Economist*, which has a dedicated section on this subject. Two useful learned journals in this area are *New Technology, Work and Employment* (Blackwell Publishing) and *Work, Employment and Society* (Sage), which often deal with the effects of technology on working practices and human resources. Recent articles in the former include:

Wheatley, D. (2012) Good to be home: time-use and satisfaction levels among home-based teleworkers. *New Technology, Work and Employment*. Vol 27, No 3. November. pp222–41.

Barnes, S. (2012) The differential impact of ICT on employees. *New Technology, Work and Employment*. Vol 27, No 2. June. pp120–32.

And in the latter:

Russell, B. (2012) Professional call centres, professional workers and the paradox of the algorithm: the case of tele-nursing. *Work, Employment and Society*. Vol 26, No 2. pp195–210.

Other valuable sources include:

Halil, W. (2008) *Technology's promise: expert knowledge on the transformation of business and society*. Basingstoke: Palgrave Macmillan.

Schmidt, S. (2008) *The coming of convergence*. Amherst, NY: Prometheus Books.

SEMINAR ACTIVITY

Consider the operation of HR systems in Case Study 8.11 (Teleworking at Baxter International) and identify where difficulties could arise, for both line managers and HR staff.

Identify the likely overall impact of such a structure on:

- employee engagement
- communication systems
- skills of HR staff
- careers for HR staff.

REFERENCES

Arkin, A. (2002) The package to India. *People Management*. 24 January. pp34–6.

Arlidge, J. (2009) Are our heads in the cloud? *Sunday Times*. Magazine. 9 August. pp42–5.

Bennett, S. (2012) *Twitter on track for 500 million total users by end of 2012*. Media Bistro. Accessed at: www.mediabistro.com/alltwitter/twitter-active-total-users_b17655

Brockett, J. (2010) LV= recruits via interactive media. *People Management*. 17 June. p14.

Broughton, A., Higgins, T., Hicks, B. and Cox, A. (2011) *Workplaces and social networking*. London: ACAS.

Business Week. (2004) Wireless. 21 June. pp62–5.

Carr, N. (2008) *The big switch – rewiring the world from Edison to Google*. New York: Norton.

Chrisafis, A. (2009) Stress and worker suicides mean the future's not bright at Orange. *Guardian*. 19 September. p9.

Chubb, L. (2008) Outsourcing recruitment would free up HR to focus on other priorities. *People Management*. 29 May. p9.

Churchard, C. (2012) Technology encourages work presenteeism. *People Management*. 1 February. Accessed at: www.peoplemanagement.co.uk/pm/articles/2012/02/technology-encourages-work-presenteeism-claims-research.htm

Chynoweth, C. (2007) War games. *People Management*. 3 October. p13.

CIPD. (2010) *Resourcing and talent planning*. Survey report. London: Chartered Institute of Personnel and Development.

Conway, G. (2011) No hands, no feet; I'm think-driving now. *Sunday Times*. In-Gear.3 April. pp4–5.

Cook, A. (2012) Social media can transform the quality of recruitment. *People Management*. October. p49.

Coyle, D. and Quah, D. (2004) *Getting the measure of the new economy*. London: The Work Foundation.

Davey, J. (2009) Every little bit of data helps Tesco rule detail. *Sunday Times*. Business. 4 October. p7.

Dicken, P. (2003) *Global shift*. 4th edition. London: Sage.

Dulewicz, V. (2004) Give full details. *People Management*. 26 February. p23.

Economist. (2000) Communication advances. 23 September. p24.

Economist. (2004) Salad days. 6 November. pp38–9.

Economist. (2007) Easy on the eyes. 7 April. pp85–6.

Economist. (2012a) The new maker rules. 24 November. p79.

Economist. (2012b) March of the Lettuce Bot. 1 December. Technology. p5.

Economist. (2013) No hiding place. 25 May. p86.

Elias, P. (2006) *Robot birth simulator used in med schools*. Associated Press. Accessed at: www.livescience.com/topics/robots

Evans, J. (2011) Wider appeal. *People Management*. May. pp47–50.

Flexible Working. (2000) Case: *teleworking* at Baxter International. October. pp11–14.

Foster, S. (2010) *In light of the increasingly integral role of the internet in the workplace, how do HR professionals best approach the monitoring and policing of its usage?* Unpublished master's dissertation. University of Bedfordshire.

Freeman, C. (1987) *Technology policy and economic performance: lessons from Japan*. London: Pinter Publishers.

Glover, C. (2004) Tomorrow's world. *People Management*. 26 February. pp40–41.

Green, F. (2002) *Why has work effort become more intense? Conjectures and evidence about effort-based technical change and other stories*. University of Kent Discussion Papers in Economics. July.

Hall, L. (2004) Where to draw the line. *Personnel Today*. 1 June.

Hall, P. and Preston, P. (1988) *The carrier wave: new information technology and the geography of innovation*. London: Unwin Hyman.

Hansen, N., Nohria, N. and Tierney, T. (1999) What's your strategy for managing knowledge? *Harvard Business Review*. March–April. pp106–16.

Hodgkiss, K. (2012) CV posting on LinkedIn. *People Management*. February. p20.

IDS. (2011) *Recruitment John Lewis Partnership*. IDS Study 941. May. pp27–8.

Investortoday. (2009) Boss at suicide firm France Telecom asks to go. 5 October. Accessed at: www.investortoday.co.uk

Jensen, R. (2007) The digital provide: information technology, market performance and welfare in the south Indian fisheries sector. *Quarterly Journal of Economics*. August.

Kahn, H. (1967) *The year 2000*. Basingstoke: Macmillan.

Keers, S. (2011) The ads that see you coming. *Sunday Times*. In-gear. 3 April. pp24–5.

Lanier, J. (2013) *Who owns the future?* London: Allen Lane.

Levinson, M. (2006) *The box: how the shipping container made the world smaller and the world economy bigger*. Princeton, NJ: Princeton University.

LGA. (2012) *The services shared: costs spared*. London: Local Government Association.

Martin, G. (2005) *Technology and people management*. London: Chartered Institute of Personnel and Development.

Microsoft. (2010) HR managers snoop online. *People Management*. 11 February. p15.

Nathan, M., Carpenter, G. and Roberts, S. (2003) *Getting by, not getting on, technology in UK workplaces*. London: The Work Foundation.

People Management. (2009) Beds and Bars employee console. 24 September. p26.

People Management. (2013) No sick pay, no back chat. June. pp16-17.

Parry, E., Tyson, S., Selbie, D. and Leighton, R. (2007) *HR and technology: impact and advantages*. London: Chartered Institute of Personnel and Development.

Peacock, L. (2007) Location beats pay as a top factor in attracting people to work in UK call centres. *Personnel Today*. 14 May.

Pethokoukis, J. (2004) Meet your new co-worker. *Money and Business*. 3 July.

PricewaterhouseCoopers. (2000) *HR in e-commerce survey*. London: PricewaterhouseCoopers.

Prusack, L. (1997) *Knowledge in organisations*. London: Butterworth-Heinemann.

Reddington, M., Williamson, M. and Withers, M. (2005) *Transforming HR: Creating value through people*. London: Elsevier.

Reilly, P. (2000) *HR shared services and the realignment of HR*. Institute of Employment Studies Report 368. Brighton: IES.

Scarborough, H. and Carter, C. (2007) *Investigating knowledge management*. London: Chartered Institute of Personnel and Development.

Schoneboom, A. (2011) Sleeping giants? Fired work bloggers and labour organisation. *New Technology, Work and Employment*. Vol 26, No 1.

Schumpeter, J. (1976) *Capitalism, socialism and democracy*. London: Routledge.

Smith, D. (2004) Prophet warning. *People Management*. 23 December. pp24–9.

Sparrow, P., Brewster, C. and Harris, H. (2004) *Globalizing human resource management*. London: Routledge.

Stevens, M. (2010a) Proctor and Gamble goes virtual to lure graduates. *People Management*. 22 April. p9.

Stevens, M. (2010b) L'Oreal's recruitment gets a virtual makeover. *People Management*. 3 June. p10.

Stevens, M. (2011) Social media. *People Management*. July. pp10–11.

Stewart, T. (2001) *The wealth of knowledge: intellectual capital in the 21st century organisation*. London: Nicholas Brearley.

Storey, J. and Quintas, P. (2001) Knowledge management and HRM. In J. Storey (ed.) *Human Resource Management: A critical text*. London: Thomson Learning.

Stredwick, J. and Ellis, S. (2005) *Flexible working practices*. London: Chartered Institute of Personnel and Development.

Subramanian, S. (2004) *Biotechnology and society*. Available at: www.chennaionline.com [Accessed 24 November].

Sullivan, A. (2012) Small and smart, the saplings that will rise after the press forest fire. *Sunday Times*. 16 December. p24.

Syedain, H. (2012) On my agenda. *People Management*. June. p39.

Szabo, L. (2008) Gene therapy takes a step forward. *USA Today*. Accessed at: usatoday30.usatoday.com/tech/science/2008-04-28-gene-therapy_N.htm

Taylor, R. (2004) *Skills and innovation in modern Britain*. ESRC Future of Work Programme Seminar Series. Swindon: Economic and Social Research Council.

Tomlinson, H. and Evans, R. (2009) Tesco stocks up on inside knowledge of shoppers' lives. *Guardian*. 20 September. p12.

Ulrich, D. (1998) *Human resource champions*. Boston, MA: Harvard Business School Press.

Valentine, S., Fleischmann, G., Sprague, R. and Godkin, L. (2010) Exploring the ethicality of firing employees who blog. *Human Resource Management*. Vol 49, No 1. pp87–108.

Welch, J. (2003). In the hiring line. *People Management*. 26 June. pp30–31.

CHAPTER 9

Ethics, Social Responsibility and Sustainability

LEARNING OUTCOMES

By the end of this chapter, readers should be able to understand, explain and critically evaluate:

- different approaches to ethics and ethical principles
- the problems involved in resolving ethical dilemmas
- whistleblowing
- the nature of professional ethics
- how far business ethics exist as something separate from general ethics
- values and codes of business ethics
- approaches to corporate governance
- the principles of risk management
- the principles and issues underlying corporate social responsibility
- the principles and issues underlying sustainable development
- the role of HR in sustaining corporate social responsibility and sustainability
- the role of the Government in corporate social responsibility and sustainability
- corporate social responsibility and profit.

INTRODUCTION

This chapter examines the nature of ethics and different approaches which can be taken to ethical problems. It discusses professional and business ethics, values and codes of ethics. The second half of the chapter analyses corporate governance, corporate social responsibility (CSR) and sustainability, the role of businesses, HR and the Government in promoting CSR, and the extent of compatibility between CSR and profit.

ETHICS

The theory of ethics can be extremely complex and in order to be of use in a day-to-day work situation, it must be made practical. Here we immediately run up against a problem. To philosophers, ethics is about the theory of right and wrong, not about the practical application of those principles. This is the area of morals. Ethics involves the values that a person seeks to express in a certain situation, morals the way he or she sets out to achieve this (Billington 2003).

A wider definition of ethics is given by Connock and Johns (1995). This includes three elements:

- fairness
- deciding what is right and wrong
- the practices and rules which underpin responsible conduct between individuals and groups.

Billington lists five distinctive features of ethics (Billington 2003, pp20–5):

1   Nobody can avoid ethical decisions. We all make ethical decisions every day.

2   Other people are always involved in ethical decisions. There is no such thing as private morality.

3   Ethical decisions matter – they affect the lives of others.

4   Although ethics is about right and wrong, there are no definitive answers. The philosopher can put forward principles which should guide decisions, but the ultimate decision is always down to the individual.

5   Ethics is always about choice – a decision where the individual has no choice cannot be unethical.

REFLECTIVE ACTIVITY 9.1

Ethical choice

Can you think of any situations where an individual has no choice about what action they should take – in a work environment, or any other situation?

ETHICAL PRINCIPLES

Billington identifies three different approaches to ethics:

- *Absolutism* – ethics are underpinned by absolute values, which apply in all societies and to all situations – the Ten Commandments. The problem here is that an absolutist might make decisions which could be seen as morally repugnant. For example, a pacifist who believes literally in the absolutist statement 'thou shalt not kill' would logically have found himself refusing to fight the evil of Nazism.
- *Relativism* – ethics depend on the situation and on the cultural mores prevalent at a particular time or place. Thus, for example, racism in Victorian England, or child labour in present-day Pakistan, must be seen as reflecting the mores of those societies – the 'when in Rome' principle. This approach has been criticised on two grounds – that it freezes the status quo and is therefore inherently conservative, and that in practice every major religion (Buddhism, Christianity, Confucianism, Hinduism, Judaism, Islam and Sikhism) subscribe to the absolutist golden rule (see Table 9.1) (Snell 1999).
- *Utilitarianism* – as Jeremy Bentham put it in the early nineteenth century, 'the good of the greatest number is the criterion of right or wrong' (Billington 2003, pp35–40, 119). This begs the question of what does 'good' mean?

Archie Carroll widened out these principles into 11 ethical guidelines (Carroll 1990) (see Table 9.1).

Table 9.1 Carroll's ethical guidelines

Name of principle	Description
Categorical imperative	You should not adopt principles of action unless they can be adopted by everyone else.
Conventionalist ethic	Individuals should act to further their self-interest as long as they do not violate the law.
Golden rule	Do unto others as you would have them do to you.
Hedonistic ethic	If it feels good, do it.
Disclosure rule	You should only take an action or decision if you are comfortable with it after asking yourself whether you would mind if all your associates, friends and family were aware of it.
Intuition ethic	You do what your 'gut feeling' tells you is right.
Means–end rule	You should act if the end justifies the means.
Might-equals-right ethic	You should take whatever advantage you are powerful enough to take.
Organisation ethic	Be loyal to your organisation.
Professional ethic	Do only that which can be justified to your professional peers.
Utilitarian principles	The greatest good of the greatest number.

Source: adapted from Carroll (1990)

The three most popular among managers were the golden rule, the disclosure rule and the intuition ethic.

Cavanagh et al (1981) identified three basic ethical philosophies:

- utilitarianism – the greatest good of the greatest number
- individual rights
- social justice – that is, collective rights.

Forsyth (1980) argued that ethical decision ideologies are based on two dimensions – idealism, the degree to which an individual believes that ethical behaviour always results in good outcomes, and relativism, the degree to which an individual believes that moral rules are situational. He constructed a two-by-two matrix based on these two dimensions (Figure 9.1).

Figure 9.1 Forsyth's ethical dimensions

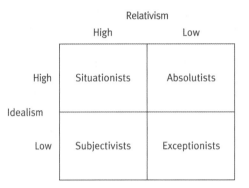

Source: based on Forsyth (1980)

- Situationists prefer to analyse each situation and to decide on appropriate moral behaviour based on this analysis.
- Subjectivists base their moral judgements on individual rather than universal principles.
- Absolutists believe in strict, universal moral codes.
- Exceptionists believe in universal moral rules as guides but are open to practical exceptions.

REFLECTIVE ACTIVITY 9.2

Examining bodies and ethics

Edexcel is one of four major examination boards in England, Wales and Northern Ireland. It awards 1.5 million qualifications a year, which include GCSEs, A-levels, BTEC qualifications, NVQs and GNVQs. Its annual turnover is £112 million. The other major examination boards are AQA (turnover £128 million) and OCR (turnover £77 million), and WJEC, which mainly operates in Wales.

Edexcel was formed in 1996 as a result of a government-inspired merger between BTEC, a quango (quasi-autonomous non-governmental organisation) which specialised in vocational qualifications, and the University of London Examinations and Assessment Council, owned by London University, which specialised in GCSE and A-level qualifications. At this stage Edexcel had charitable status.

Edexcel and the other exam boards are answerable in England to Ofqual, the regulator for the industry, and ultimately to the Department for Education, while WJEC is answerable to Ofqual and the Welsh Government.

Running an examination board is a high-risk activity. GCSE and A-level results are issued in a blaze of publicity each summer and any mistakes made by the exam boards are picked up by the media in a blaze of adverse publicity. Exam boards always seem to get the blame, even for things which are not their own fault.

In 2003, Edexcel was taken over by the media giant Pearson, a FTSE 100 company with wide interests, including the *Financial Times*, and the publisher Pearson Education. Pearson already had interests in examination systems overseas and saw it as its aim to 'globalise the marking process'. It is investing heavily in order to computerise the examination system, including online testing and marking.

Ken Boston, the chairman of the Qualifications and Curriculum Authority, said at the time of the takeover, 'I see no reason why we should blanch at private sector companies.' However, other commentators were less complacent. Martin Ward, deputy general secretary of the

Secondary Heads Association, said, 'the entry of a commercial organisation... has the potential for less accountability,' while Ted Wragg, emeritus professor of education at Exeter University, said, 'I feel alarmed about the future... People want to feel that an examination board is focused on standards, not profit.'

In 2011 a scandal blew up when the *Daily Telegraph* secretly filmed a WJEC seminar for teachers, who had paid £200 a head to attend, where the attenders were told which questions pupils could expect in the forthcoming exams. The *Telegraph* also quoted a named examiner at a seminar telling teachers that a compulsory question in the examination 'goes in cycles'. He gave the subjects for the forthcoming exam, saying, 'we're cheating, we're telling you the cycle'. When told that this information was not in the course specification, the examiner was alleged to have said, 'no, because we're not allowed to tell you'. An Edexcel examiner was alleged to have told a seminar that its examinations were easy. This was denied by Edexcel, who said that 'we do not actively market our exams as easier'.

The secretary of state, Michael Gove, called for an urgent investigation by Ofqual, and also raised the issue of whether there should be a single examining body. He said, 'The chief risk of market failure with qualifications is in regard to standards – the so-called "race to the bottom".' Chris McGovern, chairman of the

Campaign for Real Education, said, 'you wouldn't dream of having, say, different boards offering driving licences'.

Questions

1   Do you think that the public service role of Edexcel is incompatible with its private ownership?

2   What information do you think it is ethical for examining bodies to give to schools about examinations? How should this information be communicated?

3   What does Gove mean by the 'race to the bottom' and how would a single examining body alleviate this? Are there arguments in favour of having multiple examining bodies?

4   In August 2012, Pearson, the owner of Edexcel, announced that it was setting up its own university, Pearson College, to award business studies degrees, which would be validated by two colleges of the University of London. Does this create a conflict of interest given its ownership of Edexcel? How about the CIPD and other professional bodies, which run their own national examinations, but also validate courses offered by universities which lead to membership?

Sources: Lewis (2002); Curtis (2004); BBC (2011)

CASE STUDY 9.1

THE ETHICS OF MPS' EXPENSES

The MPs' expenses scandal made headlines for weeks in the summer of 2009. The *Daily Telegraph* had obtained tip-offs from a whistleblower, which it drip-fed into the public arena. The result was to finish many political careers and to throw the whole parliamentary system into disrepute.

Examples included Sir Peter Viggers' infamous duck island, Douglas Hogg's moat, Jacqui Smith's husband's 'adult' videos, Gordon Brown's cleaning bill and Cheryl Gillan's dog food.

Six different ethical categories can be identified:

1   *The silly but petty* – the dog food and the adult films.

2   *The silly but outrageous* – the duck island and the moat.

3   *The retrospectively punished* – MPs were allowed to claim cleaning expenses, with their reasonableness assessed by the Parliamentary Fees Office. However, when Sir Thomas Legg, the Commons auditor, reported in

October 2009, he retrospectively imposed a limit of £2,000 a year on cleaning, with the result that the Prime Minister, Gordon Brown, was required to repay over £10,000.

4   *Playing the system* – in one case an MP repaid a relatively small mortgage on his London home and took out an extremely large mortgage on his constituency home. The mortgage interest on this was claimed as an expense.

5   *Tax avoidance* – the widespread practice of 'flipping' mortgages. Inland Revenue rules permit the proceeds of selling a designated first house to be free of capital gains tax, but the sale of a second house is liable to CGT. In one case, an MP designated her constituency home as her main residence for one month, so avoiding CGT.

6   *Fraud* – in one case (an MEP rather than an MP), the person involved claimed a secretarial allowance of £3,000 a month, but paid his assistant only £500. The result in this case was a prison sentence.

I feel that the ethical implications in these cases are different. In the first case, no real ethical principles are involved, although they could fall foul of the disclosure rule. The amount spent on dog food was petty and Jacqui Smith claiming for the adult films was clearly a mistake. In the second case, the MPs involved should have thought of the disclosure rule. The sums of money involved in each case (over £1,000) were excessive and the MPs involved should have considered what public opinion would feel if these were made public.

The third case, retrospective punishment, raises more ethical issues for Sir Thomas Legg than for the MPs concerned. Retrospective punishment is generally viewed with disfavour by the UK legal system. As commentators pointed out at the time, £2,000 a year

does not cover much cleaning in London if you pay the London living wage, National Insurance, holiday pay and so on.

The fourth case, playing the system, is, I feel, unethical, although it is not in any way illegal, and some would see it as acceptable. I think it falls foul of the golden rule, the disclosure rule and the professional ethics rule. The fifth case, tax avoidance, again is not illegal, but would generally be seen as unethical, and again is covered by the golden, disclosure and professional ethics rules. The final case is clearly unethical as well as criminal.

Two problems with the expenses system were:

- An unclear distinction between expenses and allowances – in some cases MPs received allowances, for example for communications, which implies a right to claim up to the full amount of the allowance, while other spendings were designated as expenses, where the right is only to be reimbursed for actual spending. This distinction was not always clearly made in the press.
- The system of allowing MPs to take out mortgages on designated second homes and allowing mortgage interest on these second homes as an expense – this was justified on the grounds that most MPs needed a base in London as well as their constituency home. This not only permitted flipping, but also meant that even where there was no sharp practice, the MP would almost certainly make a capital gain (whether taxed or not) at public expense. It also raised the issues of cleaning and gardening, neither of which would have applied if an MP had been renting a serviced flat.

Eventually in November 2009 Sir Christopher Kelly, the chairman of the Committee on Standards in Public Life, produced a blueprint for a reformed system.

- MPs within commuting distance of London would no longer be able to claim for a second home. If they have to work late in Westminster, they could claim for an overnight hotel stay, capped at £125.
- Other MPs could claim for a second home, but must rent not buy, with rent capped at £1,250 a month.
- No more claims for cleaning, gardening or furnishing.
- Any capital gain on a state-funded mortgage should be 'surrendered to the taxpayer'.

- No communications allowance.
- A ban on MPs employing relatives, to be phased in over five years.

The issue of MPs' expenses is still a live one, as evidenced by the resignation from Parliament in November 2012 of ex-minister Denis MacShane.

Sources: Watt et al (2009); Watt and Stratton (2009); Stratton (2009); Summers (2009)

ETHICAL DILEMMAS

Managers face ethical dilemmas at work every day of their working lives. Some typical ones are examined in Reflective Activity 9.3. On the basis of interviews with managers in Hong Kong, Snell identified a number of typical sources of dilemmas (Table 9.2).

Table 9.2 Sources of dilemmas

Sources of dilemma	per cent incidence
Subordinates' perceived deceit, incompetence or disobedience	18
Policy, or request by superior, that is mistaken	25
Policy, or request by superior, that is ethically suspicious, exploitative or unfair	13
Improper, suspicious or unfair request from client, supplier or colleague	6
Conflicting instructions, decisions or directives from above	9
Caught in the middle of a direct conflict between other parties	5
Direct dispute with another party	6
Aware of another's misconduct, neglect or unfairness, but not directly responsible	8
Other	10

Source: Snell (1999, p347)

Snell's interviews also suggested four possible responses arising from requests by a superior to do something they knew to be wrong (Snell 1999, p348):

- 'little potato' obedience (quiet, fearful, humble, deferential conformity)
- token obedience (following orders half-heartedly and semi-incompetently)
- undercover disobedience (only pretending to obey, and keeping disobedience hidden)
- open disobedience (conscientious objection).

Carroll's ethical guidelines can be used as a template for resolving ethical dilemmas.

- Stage 1 – rank each of Carroll's guidelines (Table 9.1) from 11 (most important to you) to 1 (least important to you).
- Stage 2 – consider your ethical dilemma against each of the guidelines. If you can justify the action under a criterion, put + in the next column; if you cannot justify action, put –.
- Stage 3 – score each criterion by taking its ranking and putting + or – in front of it.
- Stage 4 – add up the scores. If the figure is positive, for you the action is ethically justified; if negative, it is unjustified.
- Stage 5 – if the overall score comes to 0, change the rank for your most important criterion to 12 and redo the sums.

Remember that this method can only tell you whether or not a particular action is ethically justifiable, not exactly what you should do about it.

An example of the scoring is in Table 9.3.

Table 9.3 Ethical scoring

	Rank	+/–	Score
You should not adopt principles of action unless they can be adopted by everyone else.	9	–	–9
Individuals should act to further their self-interest as long as they do not violate the law.	5	+	+5
Do unto others as you would have them do to you.	11	–	–11
If it feels good, do it.	2	–	–2
You should only take an action or decision if you are comfortable with it after asking yourself whether you would mind if all your associates, friends and family were aware of it.	10	–	–10
You do what your 'gut feeling' tells you is right.	6	–	–6
You should act if the end justifies the means.	1	+	+1
You should take whatever advantage you are powerful enough to take.	3	+	+3
Be loyal to your organisation.	4	+	+4
Do only that which can be justified to your professional peers.	8	–	–8
The greatest good of the greatest number.	7	+	+7
Overall score			–26

In the case of Table 9.3, the conclusion is quite clear: according to your values, you find this course of action ethically unacceptable and should not do it.

REFLECTIVE ACTIVITY 9.3

Ethical dilemmas

1   You are a personnel manager for a medium-sized company and you are faced with what you see as a series of ethical dilemmas. Consider how you would approach each scenario, and what ethical principles you would apply.

Scenario 1 – it is the custom in your industry for customers to be lavishly entertained. Your company gives each customer's sales manager a bottle of very good-quality malt whisky on his or her birthday, his or her partner's birthday, and at Christmas. Your purchasing manager expects similar perks from his suppliers.

Scenario 2 – your organisation is undertaking a number of redundancies. You decide who is to be made redundant. The production manager asks you to add a particular worker to the list. This worker does not meet any of your criteria for redundancy, but he is well known for not getting on with the production manager. You point out that if you sack this worker without justification, he will take you to an employment tribunal and will win a claim of unfair dismissal. The production manager's response is, 'Fine. It'll be worth it to get rid of him.'

Scenario 3 – you are responsible for training, and you have used an old friend of yours to run a recent training programme. Your friend met all your criteria and had adequate if not glowing references. However, the feedback from the programme is strongly negative. You are about to repeat the programme and your friend has asked you if they will be given a repeat contract.

How far do you think Snell's identified responses to ethical dilemmas are likely to be universally valid and how far do you think they reflect the culture of Hong Kong?

2 You are export sales manager for a large company. You have been approached by an intermediary, who has asked for a large commission to obtain his influence to secure a large overseas deal. Such bribes are a long-established part of doing business with that country. Using the Carroll template, decide whether you should pay the commission.

WHISTLEBLOWING

Whistleblowing describes a situation where an individual is so concerned about the behaviour of an organisation or of individuals within it that he or she feels constrained to raise this with a third party, who may be inside the organisation, but is normally outside.

De George (1999) argued that six conditions must apply before whistleblowing can be morally justified:

1 A product or policy of the organisation needs to have the potential to harm members of society.

2 The employee should report all the facts to their immediate supervisor.

3 If the immediate supervisor does not act effectively, the concerned employee should take the matter higher in the company, exhausting all internal channels.

4 The employee should hold documentary evidence to support their charges.

5 The employee must believe that whistleblowing will lead to a change in the product or policy (that is, don't sacrifice yourself pointlessly).

6 The employee must be acting in good faith without malice or vindictiveness.

THE PUBLIC INTEREST DISCLOSURE ACT 1998

The Public Interest Disclosure Act (PIDA) gives some protection to whistleblowers, although it does not give a right to whistleblow, as strict criteria are laid down which must be met. The Act also places the burden of proof on the complainant.

The disclosure must relate to a specified set of malpractices:

- a criminal offence
- failure to comply with a legal obligation
- a miscarriage of justice
- danger to health and safety
- damage to the environment

- deliberate concealment of any of the above.

Internal procedures can only be sidestepped (De George's steps 2 and 3) if:

- The employee reasonably believes they would be penalised by the employer for making the disclosure.
- The employee is concerned that evidence would be concealed or destroyed.
- The employee has previously disclosed essentially the same information to the employer.

If the whistleblowing case falls within the definitions of the PIDA, the employee will be entitled to compensation if he or she has been victimised or dismissed as a result of the whistleblowing act (Fisher and Lovell 2006).

PROFESSIONAL ETHICS

If you are thinking of words to describe a professional, you probably come up with words such as:

- qualified
- objective
- impartial
- honest
- competent
- accountable.

These words all imply ethical principles, and one main role of a profession is to set and maintain ethical standards for its members. Rosemary Harrison (2002, p139) stresses two aspects:

- qualified advice
- standing by the integrity of that advice.

This implies two ethical responsibilities:

- to the organisation for which one works (organisational ethics)
- to impartial integrity (an absolutist ethic, which lies at the heart of professional ethics).

Most professions lay down ethical standards for their members to follow through a code of ethics, and the Chartered Institute of Personnel and Development (CIPD) is no exception. Its *Code of Professional Conduct and Disciplinary Procedures* (2003) can be downloaded from www.cipd.co.uk.
   Lawton (1998, p88) suggests ten functions for a code of professional ethics:

1   to promote ethical, and deter unethical, behaviour

2   to provide a set of standards against which to judge behaviour

3   to act as guidance to decision-making

4   to establish rights and responsibilities

5   a statement indicating what the profession stands for

6   to create a contract between professionals and clients

7   to act as a statement of professional development

8   to legitimise professional norms and justification for sanctions

9   to enhance the status of the profession

10 a statement of professional conduct.

CASE STUDY 9.2

THE DISCIPLINARY POWERS OF THE CIPD

In an article in *Personnel Today* in October 2001, Paul Kearns argued that the CIPD should be prepared to 'strike off' negligent, incompetent or dishonest members, in the same way that the General Medical Council strikes off doctors or the Law Society solicitors. He argued that this was essential for the CIPD to have credibility as a profession, particularly given its new chartered status. The implication was that such a striking off should be public and that a person who had been struck off should be prevented from practising the profession.

In response, the Secretary of the CIPD, Kristina Ingate, made three points. First, a comparison with professions such as medicine or the law is not appropriate. Personnel is not a statutory closed shop, unlike medicine or law, and CIPD membership is not a requirement to work in the personnel field. Second, the CIPD has a disciplinary procedure and, as a last resort, members in breach of its Code of Professional Conduct can be expelled from the Institute, although admittedly this is likely to be for misconduct rather than for incompetence. However, she urges caution. By its very nature personnel is about human relationships, frequently in stressful situations. As a result, a complaint about a personnel practitioner will frequently either be totally unwarranted, or in reality a complaint against the policies or practices of the employer, rather than the individual practitioner. Third, CIPD members have high standards of both conduct and competence, and members are expected to keep their competence up to date through continuing professional development.

BUSINESS ETHICS

We have now moved some distance from our original concern with individual ethics. As we have seen, professions can impose ethics on their members. We now go one step further and consider whether there is, or should be, a distinct field of study called business ethics – in other words, does a business, organisation or public body have any ethical responsibilities over and above the ethical responsibilities of the individuals who work for it?

Peter Drucker argues that ethics is by its very nature a code of individual behaviour. As a result, a business has no ethical responsibilities separate from those of every individual. An act which is not immoral or illegal if done by an individual cannot be immoral or illegal if done by a business. For example, if an individual pays money to an extortioner under threat of physical or material harm, that individual has in no way acted immorally or illegally. However, he quotes the case of the Lockheed aircraft company, which gave in to a Japanese airline which extorted money as a prerequisite for purchasing its L-1011 airliner, and was heavily criticised for doing so. He says, 'There was very little difference between Lockheed's paying the Japanese and the pedestrian in Central Park handing over his wallet to a mugger' (Drucker 1990, p236).

It seems to me that Drucker's example is a poor one. The mugger can do the pedestrian a great deal of physical harm if he does not hand over his wallet. On the other hand, the airline could not positively harm Lockheed by not buying its plane. I would regard the Lockheed case not as extortion by the airline, but as bribery by Lockheed, and a clear case of breach of business ethics.

In contrast, Michael Hoffman argues that companies can be held morally responsible (Hoffman 1990, p250). Companies can be morally good or bad according to the consequences of their actions. They espouse values, and individuals coming into the corporation are subject to those values. These values are maintained and reinforced by the culture of the organisation. As a result, it is quite legitimate to talk of business ethics as separate from individual ethics.

REFLECTIVE ACTIVITY 9.4

The child labour dilemma

You are personnel manager for a UK clothing retailer. In addition to your personnel duties, you are also the company's ethics officer, responsible for implementing the code of ethics. One of your successful clothing lines are t-shirts which are assembled in Pakistan and imported into the UK.

Opening your emails today, you find a report from one of your buyers of his recent visit to Pakistan. He reports that in a plant in Lahore, he has seen girls who look no older than 10, sweeping the floor between the rows of sewing machines the other women work on. Your code of ethics does not specifically mention child labour, but it does contain a clause about treating all workers, both directly employed and employed by suppliers, with dignity and respect.

Your first action is to email Mansur Khan, your agent in Lahore, and to ask him to investigate. He reports back that working conditions aren't bad. The girls concerned are aged from 11 upwards and are the daughters of female production workers. He also says that child labour below the age of 14 is illegal in Pakistan, but there is widespread evasion of the law, which is not generally enforced.

Your first reaction is to tell your purchasing department to insist that the supplier stops employing the children or your contract with them will be cancelled. However, a friend then brings to your attention the view of the International Confederation of Free Trade Unions (ICFTU), which has called for clauses on labour standards to be incorporated into World Trade Organization (WTO) agreements, despite claims by developing countries that they could be used to prevent Third World goods competing against Western products.

The ICFTU is concerned by employers that pay low wages, use child labour, ignore health and safety standards and deny staff union representation. Some argue that free trade is exacerbating exploitation by allowing companies to relocate to wherever production costs are lowest, regardless of local employment standards. But NGOs and developing countries argue that if Third World countries are to compete in the global economy, they cannot afford to pay the same levels as Western employers because their productivity levels are much lower. Developing countries should not be denied the competitive advantage they gain from cheaper wages (see Hussain-Khaliq 2004, which draws an interesting distinction between child labour and child work).

You are now thoroughly confused. Do you have the right to impose Western moral principles on the factory in Lahore, if there is a risk that as a result the girls and their mothers will lose their jobs?

You decide that the best way forward is to use Archie Carroll's ethical principles.

Using in turn the golden rule, the disclosure rule, the intuition ethic and the utilitarian principle, think about what your response to this problem would be.

VALUES

Values underpin ethics and the values of an organisation underpin its business ethics. Organisational values answer the question 'what do we stand for?' – what are the key principles that matter to us? This is the second of three questions which organisations must ask themselves as they evolve their mission statement (see BITC 2000):

- What are we here to do? (purpose)
- What do we stand for? (values)
- What would we like to see ourselves become? (vision)

Values, as long as they are shared, help to bring together the people in an organisation and get them working for a common aim (purpose and vision). Successful companies place a high emphasis on values and share three characteristics (Deal and Kennedy 1990, p108):

- They stand for something.
- Management fine-tunes their values to conform to the environment of the organisation.
- The values are known and shared by everyone in the organisation, and are also known, understood and supported by key stakeholders.

A value-driven company is likely to be more consistent in its decision-making, to be single-minded, and not deflected from its long-term vision by short-term expediency. Its staff are also likely to be more committed and motivated, as long as they have ownership of the values. However, values can be counterproductive if top management behaviour is not consistent with their stated values. For example, one of the long-standing values of Marks & Spencer was support of suppliers, and the company lost a great deal of public sympathy when it axed long-standing suppliers in the UK in order to buy more cheaply abroad.

CODES OF ETHICS

One definition of a code of ethics is 'a written, distinct, formal document, which consists of moral standards which help guide employee or corporate behaviour' (Schwartz 2001, p27).
   Codes can be of three different types (Brinkmann and Ims 2003, p266):

- *educational* – aimed at increasing moral awareness and behaviour within the organisation
- *regulatory* – detailed rules for behaviour, which recognise moral conflicts and help with resolving them
- *aspirational* – laying down general values and communicating ideals to individuals within the organisation.

Poor codes of ethics tend to be inward-looking, to ignore external stakeholders and they tend to be regulatory and over-detailed. Many companies do not make their codes of ethics available to external stakeholders and some do not even make them easily available to their own staff (which would seem to make them totally counterproductive).
   Good codes of ethics recognise the importance of relationships with all major stakeholders, both internal and external, and involve stakeholders in their preparation. They are also clearly communicated to all stakeholders and training is provided to stakeholders in order to ensure that they are understood and effective.
   Even a good code of ethics is no guarantee of ethical behaviour. The existence of codes of ethics did not prevent the scandalous collapse of Enron and WorldCom in the US, or the deliberate over-statement of oil reserves by Shell. Just as with values, top management must live the code of ethics at all times. If they do not, all respect for the organisation is likely to collapse.

Finally, an American survey in 1987 measured opinions on codes of ethics among American businesspeople. Respondents were asked to comment on a number of statements, with responses coded from 1 (strongly agree) to 4 (strongly disagree) (Table 9.4).

Table 9.4 Opinions on codes of ethics

	Mean response
Professionals consider codes as a useful aid when they want to refuse an unethical request impersonally.	1.8
Codes raise the ethical level of the industry.	2.1
A code helps managers in defining clearly the limits of acceptable conduct.	1.9
In cases of severe competition, a code reduces the use of sharp practices.	2.7
People violate codes whenever they think they can avoid detection.	2.5
Codes are easy to enforce.	3.3
Codes protect inefficient firms and retard the dynamic growth of the industry.	3.3

REFLECTIVE ACTIVITY 9.5

Multigenome and its code of ethics

Multigenome is a US-based multinational research company. Its code of ethics is reproduced below.

Critically evaluate this code of ethics.

'Because we are separated – by many miles, by diversity of cultures and languages – we need a clear understanding of the basic principles by which we will operate our company. These are:

- that the company is made up of individuals – each of whom has different capabilities and potentials – all of which are necessary to the success of the company
- that we acknowledge that individuality by treating each other with dignity and respect
- that we will recognise and reward the contributions and accomplishments of each individual
- that we will continually plan for the future so that we can control our destiny instead of letting events overtake us

- that we maintain our policy of providing work for all individuals, no matter what the prevailing business conditions may be
- that we make all decisions in the light of what is right for the good of the whole company, rather than what is expedient
- that our customers are the only reason for the existence of the company.
- that we must use the highest ethics to guide our business dealings to ensure that we are always proud to be a part of Multigenome
- that we will discharge the responsibilities of corporate and individual citizenship to earn and maintain the respect of the community
- as individuals and as a corporate body we must endeavour to uphold these standards so that we may be respected as persons and as an organisation.'

CORPORATE GOVERNANCE

Corporate governance is concerned with:

- In whose interests should an organisation be run?
- How should these purposes be determined?

The two key issues in corporate governance are conflict of interest and accountability. Conflict of interest comes back to the agency issue discussed above. Managers are the agents of shareholders, but because of their control over key resources, particularly information, their power is greater than that of shareholders. How should this power be managed, and how should managers be held accountable to shareholders (and other stakeholders)?

CASE STUDY 9.3

CORPORATE GOVERNANCE IN THE VENETIAN REPUBLIC

The Venetian Republic dominated the Mediterranean for a thousand years, from its founding in the ninth century as a group of poor fishing villages to its abolition by Napoleon in the early 1800s. Much of its success was due to its elaborate system of corporate governance.

The head of the Venetian Republic was the Doge, who was elected for life. However, his power was strictly limited. Each Doge on election signed a contract (*promissione*), which set out and limited his powers and against which his performance was monitored each year. Over the centuries, these *promissioni* were progressively tightened. Weak or ineffective Doges were retired and really bad ones ran the risk of assassination. Even after his death, the Doge was still subject to independent review. If he was found to have been a bad or ineffective ruler, his family could be fined.

Each Doge was assisted by four Ducal Counsellors, who were independently appointed by the State, not by the Doge himself. Their term of office was short (two or three years), which meant that they could not become too powerful. There were also a whole series of other state committees, which ensured that leadership experience was widely diffused, providing a wide pool of potential Doges or Ducal Counsellors.

Source: McKee (2003)

Company law in the UK and US (the Anglo-Saxon model) supports the shareholder approach – companies must be run in the interests of their shareholders – although UK corporations do have legal responsibilities to other stakeholders. Other countries take a different approach to corporate governance. In Germany, companies have two-tier boards, a supervisory board and a management board (the Rhine model). The management board runs the company on a day-to-day basis, but is answerable to the supervisory board, which has shareholder, employee and third-party representatives on it and which represents the interests of stakeholders (Farnham 1999, pp300–1).

Big business in Japan is organised through large integrated corporations called *keiretsu* (Mitsui, Mitsubishi, etc). These are both vertical, where manufacturers, suppliers and sub-contractors are members of the same *keiretsu*, and horizontal, where the *keiretsu* companies operate in different markets. Mitsubishi, for example, is involved in gas, chemicals, plastics, steel, aluminium, cement, butter, brewing and paper (Charkham 1994, p77).

Customers and suppliers are thus frequently within the same *keiretsu*, and relationships with them are thus much closer than in the West (as a corollary, customers and suppliers outside the *keiretsu* might find themselves much more harshly treated, leading the system open to charges of cronyism). Japanese society is also heavily based on the concepts of family, consensus and *wai* (harmony). This leads naturally to a heavy reliance on the stakeholder approach. The hierarchy of interests tends to be customers first, employees second, managers third and shareholders last. The assumption was that managers and employees 'eat their rice out of the same pot', that is, that differentials should be narrow. The controversy over excessive 'fat cat' rewards to top management which is so prevalent in the UK would have been impossible in Japan. However, because the stakeholder approach is supported by culture rather than law, it is vulnerable to changes in that culture and has been shaken by the long recession in Japan over the last two decades.

In 1990, foreign institutional investors held 5 per cent of shares in Japanese companies. By 2006, this had increased to 26 per cent. These foreign investors want results now, not at some vague time in the future. Dore (2006) examined Japan's two most recent recoveries from recession, in 1986–90 and 2001–05. In the earlier period, wages rose by 19 per cent, salaries and bonuses of directors by 22 per cent, and dividends by only 2 per cent. In the later period, the balance was totally different. Wages were down by 6 per cent, directors' reward up by 97 per cent and dividends by 175 per cent.

Each system has its strengths and weaknesses, as summarised in Table 9.5.

Table 9.5 Corporate governance systems

	Strengths	Weaknesses
Anglo-Saxon model	Dynamic and innovative Fluid capital investment	Volatile and unstable Short-termism Weak governance
Rhine model	Long-term strategy Stable capital investment	Lack of flexibility Conservatism
Japanese model	Very long-term strategy Stable capital investment	Financial speculation Crony governance Weak accountability

Source: adapted from Johnson et al (2011, p174)

The conflict of interest and accountability questions are also tackled in different ways. In the US, the approach is one of compliance, where corporate governance regulations are laid down by law and must be followed. Typical is the Sarbanes-Oxley Act of 2002, which followed the scandals in Enron and WorldCom. This states that all companies listed in the US must introduce codes of conduct, ethics policies and whistleblower hotlines. This also applies to foreign companies seeking a listing on the New York Stock Exchange. However, the key weakness of the compliance approach is that it does not internalise corporate governance in the culture of the corporation. As with other law, determined managers will find ways to obeying its letter, but thwarting its spirit. Enron had a code of ethics and on paper abided by all legal requirements (Crane and Matten 2007).

The UK approach is to use voluntary codes of practice, but to force firms to issue explanations if they choose not to abide by them. The key to the UK approach is separation of powers. In 1992 the Cadbury Report called for separation of the roles of chairman and CEO in listed companies. The CEO represented the executive managers, while the chairman acted in the interests of shareholders. The supermarket chain Morrison's had a combined chairman and CEO (Sir Ken Morrison, the founder), until it took over Safeway in 2003, but its explanation, that in effect it was a family business, was accepted by the Stock Exchange. Cadbury also called for the increased use of non-executive directors (NEDs) on boards, who again would represent the interests of shareholders. This was strengthened by the Higgs Report in 2003, which called for NEDs to be a majority on boards and for them to be independently appointed to avoid charges of cronyism if they were selected through the 'old boy network' from among friends of the chairman or CEO (Fisher and Lovell 2006). Again the example of Enron illustrates the risk of cronyism. The vast majority of its directors were non-executive.

CASE STUDY 9.4

BARCLAYS BANK, LIBOR AND WILFUL BLINDNESS

Barclays Bank is one of the leading UK banks. During the banking crisis of 2008, it narrowly avoided being forced into a UK government rescue programme like Halifax Bank of Scotland and the Royal Bank of Scotland. However, evidence was produced in 2012 which suggested that Barclay's independent survival had been based on misleading, and possibly fraudulent, information.

The key to this is the obscure but very important interest rate, LIBOR (London Inter-Bank Offered Rate). This is the rate of interest at which banks are prepared to lend money to each other and it is set by the British Bankers Association based on information supplied by the banks. It is important in two main ways.

Many other interest rates, including some mortgage rates, are based on LIBOR. If LIBOR rises, millions of borrowers will have to pay a higher rate of interest.

If the interest rate figures submitted by an individual bank are above those submitted by other banks, this is interpreted by the financial markets as a sign of weakness and vulnerability at that bank.

In June 2012, the UK and US financial regulation authorities imposed a fine of £290 million on Barclays for manipulation of LIBOR. This was based on two separate series of incidents. Between 2005 and 2008, Barclays filed artificially high interest rate figures, in an attempt to force up LIBOR and boost its own profits. This was clearly fraudulent. In 2008–09, Barclays did the opposite, submitting artificially low figures to try to hide the extent to which it was under financial stress. This was successful and Barclays avoided a UK government financial rescue. Barclays later claimed that the 2008–09 policy was based on a 'nod and a wink' from the Bank of England, strenuously denied by the latter.

The head of Barclays Capital, the financial trading arm of the bank responsible for the LIBOR submissions, was the American banker Bob Diamond, who in January 2011 became the CEO of the Barclays Group. When the fine on Barclays was announced, there was considerable pressure on Diamond to resign, but instead the sacrificial lamb was the chairman, Marcus Agius, who offered his resignation, although he later agreed to stay on in the short term. Diamond initially refused to resign, saying that he had no idea that his traders were fiddling LIBOR, and only did so when put under intense pressure from Parliament, the Bank of England and the Financial Services Authority (FSA).

Gradually it became clear that LIBOR was not an isolated problem for Barclays. The FSA accused Barclays of having a 'gaming' culture, continually pushing at the boundaries of the regulatory rules, while the governor of the Bank of England said Barclays had been 'sailing too close to the wind across a wide number of areas'. The

FSA apparently expressed concern when Diamond was appointed as chief executive and also about the bank's culture under Diamond.

What went wrong? First, it is important to note that Barclays is not an isolated case. Many other banks are under investigation for LIBOR-related offences, while both HSBC and Standard Chartered were heavily fined by the US authorities for regulatory offences in August 2012. Part of the problem was clearly caused by the 'cowboy' approach of Diamond, and in denying that he knew anything about the LIBOR fixing, Diamond was either a fool (if he didn't know, he should have done), or a villain (he knew, but pretended he didn't, and did nothing about it – interestingly, Rupert Murdoch claimed similar ignorance about phone-hacking – classic examples of wilful blindness), but the real problem is the culture of the banking industry, particularly in financial trading.

Peter Cummings, the banker whose corporate loans division left HBOS close to collapse, was fined £500,000 in September 2012 and banned for life from the City. The FSA criticised his failure to 'exercise due skill, care and diligence by pursuing an aggressive expansion strategy within the corporate division, without suitable controls in place to manage the associated risks' between January 2006 and March 2008. It also said he failed to 'take reasonable care to ensure that the corporate division adequately and prudently managed high value transactions which showed signs of stress' in the run-up to the financial crisis (*Independent* 2012).

The esoteric nature of the business encourages a cultish sense of loyalty to the team and a concurrent feeling of contempt towards the rest of the world. Clients are 'punters', there to be manipulated. Rules are to be bent and those who observe them are 'suckers'

or 'wimps'. In such a culture, it is very difficult to be a whistleblower.

Anand, Ashforth and Joshi introduce the concept of a 'social cocoon' (Anand et al 2004). This is a micro culture created within a group where the norms may be very different from those valued by society or even the wider organisation (for example a bank dealing room). Membership in such a group is highly prized and employees are more likely to accept and adopt the norms of the group. Newcomers are socialised into the norms of the group by veteran members. Parallels can be drawn with the 'canteen culture' of the police and with the culture of street gangs.

Investment banking is notorious for its huge (some would say obscene) bonuses and at the same time for its insecurity. The weakest performers are regularly culled and when a new team leader is appointed, he or she is likely to bring in their own team. Bankers find it very difficult to move to another industry, as their skills are highly specialised. Again, ultra-short-termism is encouraged and whistleblowing discouraged (Luyendijk 2012). Parallels can be drawn with Premier League footballers.

In addition, banking has a cosy relationship with both politicians and regulators. Tony Blair is paid £2.5 million a year by J P Morgan, while half of the Conservative Party's funding comes from the finance industry. In 2008, there was a perception that banks were too big to fail, and they have received £12 trillion from the UK taxpayer (Chakraborrty 2012). When Paul Tucker was promoted to number two at the Bank of England, Bob Diamond emailed, 'Well done, man. I am really, really proud of you.' Tucker replied, 'You've been an absolute brick' (*Guardian* 2012).

What can be done? One solution is to break the bonus culture – clearly an HR issue. Another is to separate investment (wholesale) from high street (retail) banking, so if an investment bank fails, it would not be at risk of dragging down a high street bank with it. This was done in the US through the Glass-Steagall Act, not repealed until 1999, while something similar has been proposed by the Vickers Report (the Independent Commission on Banking) in 2011. This proposed ring-fencing wholesale from retail banking. This was accepted by the Government, but will not be implemented until 2019 (Treanor 2012; Zingales 2012). A third solution is to discourage some of the most esoteric and socially useless derivatives trading through some kind of transactions or Tobin tax (see Reflective Activity 9.7). The bottom line is that trust must be restored to banking.

In August 2012 Barclays appointed its head of retail banking, Antony Jenkins, as CEO to succeed Bob Diamond. In a series of symbolic moves, he accepted a remuneration package half that paid to Diamond, said that 'many things will have to change at Barclays, including compensation, across the group', and announced that in future the bank's target would be a return on capital of 11.5 per cent, rather than 13 per cent, implying much lower risk (Kollewe 2012).

CORPORATE SOCIAL RESPONSIBILITY

Corporate social responsibility (CSR) is the way in which an organisation expresses its values in behaviour towards stakeholders. The European Commission defines it as 'a concept whereby companies decide voluntarily to contribute to a better society and a cleaner environment' (European Commission 2001), while the DTI defines it as an organisation which recognises that its activities have a wider impact on society, takes account of the economic, social, environmental and human rights impacts of its activities and works in partnership with other groups and organisations (DTI 2002).

Archie Carroll puts forward a four-part model of CSR (Carroll 1991):

1   economic responsibilities – required by society

2   legal responsibilities – required by society

3   ethical responsibilities – expected by society

4   philanthropic responsibilities – desired by society.

Several key points come out of these definitions:

- CSR is voluntary. Mere compliance with legal requirements is not CSR. An organisation's CSR behaviour must go beyond the law.
- CSR is active. It involves behaviour, not just good intentions.
- CSR involves environmental as well as social responsibilities.
- CSR is often carried out in partnership with others.
- Although the EC only mentions companies, CSR extends to all organisations, public and private, profit-making and not-for-profit.

CSR can take a number of forms. These include:

- community involvement, frequently in partnership with other organisations – this can include sponsorship of worthy bodies, or direct involvement of the organisation's employees in community activities
- socially responsible investment, which can include ethical banking, and refusal by pension funds to invest in companies making, for example, armaments or cigarettes

- corporate governance, concerned with the behaviour of a company towards its shareholders, and including elements such as the appointment and responsibilities of non-executive directors
- fair trade – buying goods produced by suppliers who are, for example, organic, or non-employers of children, or not based in human rights-abusing countries such as Burma
- sustainability – acting in such a way as to assist the long-term survival of the planet.

Several of these are illustrated in case studies below, derived from winners of Business in the Community's *Awards for Excellence 2004* (www.bitc.org.uk/our-resources/case-studies).

CASE STUDY 9.5

THE CO-OPERATIVE BANK

The Co-op Bank launched its Ethical Policy in 1992, after consultation with customers. It launched its Partnership Approach in 1997, identifying seven groups of stakeholders, or Partners, and pledging to deliver value to them in a socially responsible and ecologically sustainable manner. It published its first triple bottom line (profit, society, environment) independently verified *Partnership Report* in 1998. The 2002 *Partnership Report* sets out 77 targets, in each case with the name of the individual in the organisation who is charged with its achievement.

It is the UK's biggest provider of financial services to the credit union movement, which tackles financial exclusion. Its community investment, at 2.7 per cent of pre-tax profits, is among the best in the UK. Its campaigns mobilise its customers to protest on international human rights issues, for example against the illicit trade in conflict diamonds – a source of finance which has fuelled civil wars and human rights abuses in Africa – and against the use of cluster bombs.

CSR has been criticised as often being little more than a PR stunt, designed to boost sales rather than to benefit society. This is particularly true of community involvement activities. This has been called 'cause-related marketing'. For example, Vodafone sponsors the England cricket team, but in return gets endless exposure of its logo on players' shirts during test matches. Tesco runs its Computers for Schools project, which supplies computers to schools, but only after customers have collected vouchers to verify their spend in Tesco stores (for a spirited condemnation of cause-related marketing, see Monbiot 2001).

Brammer, Millington and Pavelin (2006) analyse to what extent philanthropy is strategic. They define strategic philanthropy as the practice of giving corporate resources to address non-business community issues that also benefit the firm's strategic position and, ultimately, its bottom line (it is probably significant that one criterion for listing on the FTSE4Good stock market index is charitable giving of at least £50,000 a year). Strategic philanthropy can be seen as one end of a continuum, with altruistic philanthropy at the other. I think one criterion for altruistic philanthropy would be that the giving is to an unpopular cause (funding counselling for convicted paedophiles, for example). This is rare. Even the Co-op Bank, which together with the Body Shop is probably seen as one of the most ethical businesses in the UK, campaigns on issues generally seen as morally right, for example against trade in conflict diamonds or the use of cluster bombs.

Early in 1999, Industrial Relations Services carried out a survey of ethics in the workplace (IRS 1999). The survey asked why organisations were involved in community activities. Respondents could choose as many of the six responses as they wanted. The results were:

1   enhancement of corporate image (82 per cent)

2   moral obligation (62 per cent)

3   employee satisfaction (59 per cent)

4   develop staff potential (51 per cent)

5   promote the business (46 per cent)

6   improve profitability (15 per cent).

Short-term profits (number 6) were mentioned by only a small minority of respondents, while long-term profitability (numbers 1 and 5), employees (numbers 3 and 4) and moral obligation (number 2) were seen as much more important. Perhaps community involvement is a rare example of a true win–win situation (see also Kelly 1999).

REFLECTIVE ACTIVITY 9.6

Is your own organisation involved in the community?

Find out what community activities (if any) your own organisation is involved in. If possible, also try to find out why the organisation chose these particular activities. Was the primary motive short-term profits, long-term profits, employee benefit or moral obligation (or a mixture of several of these)?

CASE STUDY 9.6

FAIRTRADE

Fairtrade is one of the retail successes of the 2000s. Sales of Fairtrade coffee grew from £15.5 million in 2000 to £65.8 million in 2006, when it commanded 18 per cent of the UK roast and ground coffee market. Similar rates of growth have been seen for tea, chocolate and cocoa, and bananas.

Fairtrade is a product labelling scheme which acts as an independent guarantee that disadvantaged producers in the Third World are getting a better deal. Its standards are set by an international certification body, Fair Trading Labelling Organisations International, and administered at a country level by national Fairtrade organisations. In the UK the administering body is the Fairtrade Foundation, a charity set up by Cafod, Oxfam, Christian Aid,

Traidcraft Exchange and the World Development Movement.

The majority of coffee and cocoa is grown by small farmers, organised into co-operatives, while bananas and tea are usually produced on plantations. In the former case, it is the co-operative which is given Fairtrade certification, in the latter, it is the plantation, which guarantees minimum health and safety and environmental standards, and that no child or forced labour will be used.

In return, producers are guaranteed a price which is sufficient to cover sustainable production, plus a premium which is invested in community development. For example, the minimum price paid for Fairtrade cocoa is $1,600 a ton, plus $150 per ton premium, as long as the world (New York) price is below $1,600. If the New

York price rises above $1,600 a ton, the Fairtrade price will be the New York price plus $150 premium. This means that producers are guaranteed a stable price and they are insulated from market fluctuations, which in the case of primary products can be violent.

An example quoted on the Fairtrade website is the Juliana-Jaramillo group of banana farmers in the Dominican Republic. Until 1962, the Granada Food Company ran vast plantation estates in the area, providing housing, water supply and schools. In 1962, they pulled out of the area and the infrastructure collapsed. Granada even took the zinc roofs off the estate houses. The Government divided 15 per cent of the estates among local farmers, giving each worker about 15 hectares each.

In 2000, Fairtrade introduced the local farmers to a UK-based company, Mack Multiples, and they worked together to improve the quality of their fruit and to develop sales to Sainsbury's. A local farmer, Alfredo Martinez, says that he is now guaranteed a minimum price, receives money weekly and is making twice what he was before Fairtrade. Environmental standards have been improved and education and health standards have been restored.

However, not everyone is so impressed with the Fairtrade achievement. First, Fairtrade is not necessarily the same as ethical sourcing. For example, Marks & Spencer sells Fairtrade cotton clothing. This guarantees that the raw cotton was produced ethically, but not necessarily that the whole of the supply chain was ethical. In any case, Fairtrade cotton only makes up about 1 per cent of that purchased by M&S each year.

Second, there is a feeling that Fairtrade is being exploited by large retailers. They see the Fairtrade label as a way to segment socially aware consumers, who are willing to pay a premium price for Fairtrade products. The result is that the main beneficiaries are the supermarket groups, rather than the Fairtrade producers.

Third, major producers are also jumping on the Fairtrade bandwagon. The best known is Nestlé, whose Partner's Blend coffee has Fairtrade certification. This is seen as unacceptable by some ethical campaigners, who point to the long-standing claims that Nestlé unethically promotes its powdered milk compounds in Third World countries.

Fourth, Fairtrade has been criticised by some economists, particularly Americans, because it is seen as biased towards co-operatives and because it guarantees a minimum price. The rival US-backed scheme, Rainforest Alliance, does not guarantee a price and has been described as 'Fairtradelite' by its critics. This became a bone of contention in the attempted takeover of Cadbury by the US food conglomerate Kraft in 2009. Cadbury has obtained Fairtrade certification for its Dairy Milk chocolate, while Kraft has Rainforest Alliance certification for its Kenco coffee. Kraft argued that it opposes Fairtrade because it provides a subsidy that distorts the workings of the open market.

Finally, building on Kraft's point, some economists claim that Fairtrade, by guaranteeing a price above the world price, is in effect encouraging overproduction. Fairtrade counters by saying that for all commodities, Fairtrade is only a small percentage of world output and that the Fairtrade price gives farmers surplus income which encourages them to diversify.

On balance, like me, you may well think that Fairtade benefits the Third World and should be encouraged, but as with most things, the situation is not as simple as it appears at first sight.

Sources: Fairtrade website; Crane and Matten (2007); Murray (2006);

Economist (2006); Prosser (2007); Bowers (2009)

SUSTAINABILITY

Sustainability is about our responsibility to the ultimate stakeholder: our own future and the future of the planet. We are using up the resources of the earth and degrading the planet at an increasing rate, and this can only be at the expense of future generations. Sustainable development is 'development that meets the needs of the present without compromising the ability of future generations to meet their own needs' (Fisher and Lovell 2006, p21). This definition stresses that sustainability must be based on needs, not on wants. DesJardins (2007) quotes the formula I = PAT. Environmental impact (I), is the product of population (P), consumption per head or affluence (A), and technology (T). A sustainable society will limit its population growth, avoid excessive consumerism and promote technology which reduces resource use. 'To operate sustainably, an organisation must... [be] supportive of the survival of the physical environment and also the communities and economies in which it operates' (*Accountability Primer: Sustainability* n.d.).

DesJardins quotes the example of Gold n'Plump Poultry in Minnesota, which processes 4 million pounds of chicken a week. Its waste water treatment plant produces large amounts of solid waste. Each week it sends 100,000 lbs of solid waste to Mississippi Topsoils, where it is combined with residential waste and sawdust to produce saleable compost. An opposite example is the UK's trade in gingerbread. Every year the UK imports 465 tonnes of gingerbread, while at the same time exporting 460 tonnes. This results in excessive use of resources in transportation and increases the UK's carbon footprint, for no obvious benefit (Simms 2009).

At the macro level, we have the problem of global warming and the associated climate change, the result of the excess of greenhouse gases, particularly carbon dioxide, in the atmosphere, caused at least in part by our excessive burning of fossil fuel. This can only be tackled at global level (global social responsibility). The Kyoto Treaty in 1999 committed industrialised countries to large reductions in carbon emissions, but this effort was frustrated by the refusal of the Bush Administration to ratify the treaty. The UK is fully committed to the Kyoto principles and has introduced a Climate Change Levy on polluting industries.

At a micro level, sustainability concerns us all, organisations and individuals alike. At an individual level, it is as basic as composting our garden waste rather than sending it to landfill sites and turning off our television sets at night rather than leaving them on standby. At an organisational level, it can be about energy conservation and also about the kind of activities highlighted in the Case Study 9.7 and Reflective Activity 9.7.

CASE STUDY 9.7

PLASTIC BAGS – AN UNSUSTAINABLE OPTION?

Seventeen billion plastic carrier bags are used in the UK every year, 14 billion of which are given away by supermarkets. Only one in 200 of these are recycled. The rest go into landfill, weighing 100,000 tonnes, where they take up to 1,000 years to decompose. The vast majority of bags are made from oil derivatives. Most are non-degradable, a few are degradable – they break down when exposed to sunlight (but not in landfill) and a very few are biodegradable, made of corn starch, and do break down in landfill.

Several countries have taken action to control their use of plastic bags. In 2002, Bangladesh banned them outright, as they were causing flooding by blocking storm drainage channels during the monsoon. They are also banned in South Africa, and San Francisco is the first US city to impose a ban. Taiwan has banned plastic plates, cups and cutlery as well as plastic bags, leading to a 25 per cent cut in its landfill.

Ireland took a different route, introducing a tax of 15 cents (about 10p) a bag in 2002. This cut plastic bag usage by at least 90 per cent, although some small bags are exempt. Usage has slowly crept up again since 2002, leading to an increase in tax to 22 cents in July 2007.

In the UK there are no official restrictions on the use of plastic bags, although the Scottish Parliament considered and rejected a tax of 10p a bag in 2006, and a MORI poll suggested that throughout the UK 63 per cent would support a 10p tax. London is considering a ban, while the former prime minister, Gordon Brown, has said that he would like to see a total ban on single-use plastic bags. However, as at January 2013, the Coalition Government had still not taken a decision (Hickman 2013).

The small town of Modbury in Devon became the first town in Europe to ban plastic bags in April 2007. None of the town's 43 traders, including the Co-op supermarket, issues plastic bags.

Individual stores have taken unilateral action. IKEA charges 10p a bag and has seen plastic bag use fall by 97 per cent. The discount stores Aldi and Lidl have always charged for bags.

Tesco, the heaviest bag user of all, with 4 billion bags issued each year, costing it £40 million at 1p per bag, introduced a scheme in 2006 whereby customers received one 'green' Clubcard point, worth 1p, for each bag which they reused, whether or not the reused bag originally came from Tesco. This is intended to cut Tesco's usage by 25 per cent, or 1 billion bags a year. Each bag saved saves Tesco 1p, so the only net cost to Tesco is when it pays out for other stores' bags. Tesco has also made all its bags degradable (but not biodegradable).

Tesco's move has been welcomed by the Government, but criticised by Friends of the Earth as 'a very small step' and a 'greenwash', as it does nothing to cut the excessive amounts of food packaging used by Tesco and all other supermarkets, and because Tesco has chosen not to go biodegradable.

However, the plastic bag industry is fighting back. Barry Turner, the chairman of the UK Carrier Bag Consortium, claims that although plastic bags are made from oil, they use by-products such as naphtha, ethylene and propylene, which would otherwise have to be flared off. He also criticises the use of paper bags rather than plastic. Paper bags weigh more than plastic, are four times as expensive to produce and, most seriously, whereas plastic bags in landfill remain inert, paper bags decompose to release the greenhouse gases methane and CO_2.

Although the obvious response to Turner's claims is 'he would say that, wouldn't he', the situation is clearly more complex than at first sight. Perhaps the ideal solution is that advocated by Sainsbury's – the more

extensive use of 'bags for life', more heavy duty bags which sell for 10p, can be reused many times, and which the store guarantees to replace free when they wear out, whereupon Sainsbury's send the worn out bag for recycling.

Sources: Turner (2006); Finch and Allen (2006); Butler (2006); *Economist* (2007); Barkham (2007); Aldred (2007); Wintour (2007); Hickman (2009)

REFLECTIVE ACTIVITY 9.7

Tobin tax and global warming

What is a Tobin tax?

It is a transaction tax, originally proposed by the US economist James Tobin in the 1970s. It would impose a small levy on all financial transactions throughout the world. Tobin originally proposed a 1 per cent tax, but what is now being suggested is much smaller – 0.05 per cent or even 0.005 per cent.

How much money would it raise?

The sums involved are enormous. The volume of financial transactions in the global economy is estimated to be nearly 75 times as big as global GDP, most of it in speculation on the derivatives markets, which are seen as of dubious real value. Adair Turner, chairman of the Financial Services Authority, described some City activities as 'socially useless'. A 0.005 per cent levy on foreign exchange trades alone would raise $30 billion, while a study by the Austrian Government suggested that a 0.05 per cent levy on UK financial trades would raise $100 billion a year (and $420 billion worldwide), even if it led to a two-thirds fall in transactions.

Who would pay for the tax?

Like all output taxes, the cost would be shared between buyers and sellers – the financial speculators and the banks.

Who is in favour?

France and Germany have been in favour for some time, and Gordon Brown announced his conversion in November 2009. At present, the US and the IMF are opposed, although some economists close to the Obama administration are thought to be in favour.

What has this got to do with global warming?

In order to combat global warming, all economies must invest huge sums in greener energy technologies. The West can afford this, but the developing world, and India and China, cannot. Coal is the primary energy source in both India and China. A clean coal-fired power station is 50 per cent more efficient (that is, less polluting) than the average plant in India and China. Implementing clean coal technology would cost India up to $8 billion a year. Gordon Brown has proposed that only half of the proceeds from a Tobin tax should be spent at home. The other half would finance economic development and climate change reduction in the developing world.

Question

1   What do you think would be the practical obstacles to the implementation of a Tobin tax?

Sources: Elliott (2009); Mathiason and Treanor (2009)

SUSTAINABLE AND UNSUSTAINABLE DEVELOPMENT

CASE STUDY 9.8

Sustainable development: the king's sufficiency economy in Thailand

In the period between 1986 and 1997, the Thai economy grew at a rate of 9 per cent a year, the fastest in the world at that time. However, although material prosperity increased, this came at a high cost. Farming changed from self-sufficiency to a much higher-risk monoculture. Social problems and inequality increased, as did the overexploitation of Thailand's natural resources. All this worried the King of Thailand, a trained scientist who had been influenced by the conservationist ideas of Schumacher as expressed in his book *Small is Beautiful*.

When the Thai economy crashed in 1997, the first of the Asian Tigers to fail, it became clear that those organisations which survived the crash were those that were low risk, which had relied on their own resources rather than borrowing and those which had worked together in social communities.

This led the King, who is revered in Thailand even by his political opponents, to implement his ideas of the King's Sufficiency Economy, which became part of official national policy in the Thai National Economic and Development Plans in 1997. However, Thai governments in the late 1990s and early 2000s also followed a policy of easy access to external capital, the opposite of a sufficiency economy. It was not until the tenth National Plan, in 2007, that the King's ideas were fully implemented.

The Sufficiency Economy is summarised in the official version of 1999:

'Sufficiency Economy is the Philosophy that addresses the way of living and practice of the public in general from the family unit and the community to the national level, in development and management of the country towards the middle path [a key tenet of Buddhism], especially in developing the economy to keep up with the world in an era of globalisation. The word "Sufficiency" means moderation and reasonableness including the need to have self-immunity to be ready against any internal and external shocks ... All members of the nation ... need to develop their commitment to the importance of knowledge, ethical, integrity and honesty to conduct their lives with perseverance, toleration, wisdom and knowledge, and precaution so the country has the strength and balance to respond to rapid and widespread changes materialistically, socially, environmentally, and culturally from the outside world' (quoted in Puntasen 2008, p48).

By doing this, the society develops the attributes of a stable system. To quote Puntasen, 'We have "interest of life" rather than "self-interest" ... we are interested in the idea of "no-self", which leads to compassion and co-operation, rather than competition.'

Could the concept of the King's Sufficiency Economy be applied in the West? Probably not on any large scale, as it runs so counter to the dominant paradigms of Western capitalism, but it may well be applicable at an individual level. All organisations could also benefit from a less cavalier attitude to borrowing and risk.

Unsustainable development: prawn farming in Bangladesh

Prawn (or shrimp) farming in 2004 was worth $6.9 billion at the farm gate, and $50–60 billion at retail prices. In 2001, the UK imported prawns worth £353 million. The leading producers are Thailand, China, Indonesia, India,

Vietnam, Ecuador, the Philippines, Bangladesh, Mexico and Brazil. It is estimated that 600,000 people in Bangladesh are dependent on prawn farming, and export of prawns is Bangladesh's second largest source of foreign exchange.

Small-scale prawn farming in Bangladesh makes a valuable contribution to the rural economy. Sixty per cent of the agricultural land of Bangladesh is flooded for up to six months of the year. It makes good economic sense to farm prawns during the flood period, and rice once the floods have receded (Bhalla 2011). However, increasingly prawn farming is being carried out in large, permanent extensive farms. Here, there is a heavy environmental cost.

Most large prawn farms are built in coastal areas where mangrove forests thrive. Mangroves are among the most productive ecosystems on the planet and support a great variety of marine life. Mangroves, through their roots, help stabilise a coastline and capture sediments; their removal has led to a marked increase of erosion and less protection against floods. But mangroves across the globe are being cleared to make way for intensive prawn farms. Nearly 40 per cent of world mangrove loss has been attributed to shrimp farming. In Bangladesh, mangrove swamps are common land, and thus vulnerable to land grabs by the rich, and the expulsion of small farmers who, as squatters, have few legal rights. Ash quotes a case where sea defences were deliberately breached in order to flood common land with salt water and ensure that the land was only fit for prawn farming (Ash 2005).

Prolonged use of a prawn pond can lead to an incremental build-up of sludge at the pond's bottom from waste products and excrement. Flushing a pond never completely removes this sludge and, eventually, the pond is abandoned, leaving behind a wasteland, with the soil made unusable for any other purposes due to the high levels of salinity, acidity and toxic chemicals. A typical pond in an extensive farm can be used only a few years. An Indian study estimated the time to rehabilitate such lands as about 30 years. A Thai study estimated 60 per cent of the shrimp farming area in Thailand was abandoned in the years 1989–96. Not only is the availability of useable farming land reduced, but increased levels of salinity can contaminate freshwater sources (Lawrence 2003; Lawson 2003).

CASE STUDY 9.9

COSTA RICA – A MODEL OF SUSTAINABLE DEVELOPMENT

Costa Rica is a small, seemingly unremarkable country in Central America. However, it is remarkable as the only country in the world to abolish its army, in 1949, following a short but bloody civil war. It decided to divert the money saved not to tax cuts, but to increased spending on education and health – as was said at the time, 'the army would be replaced by an army of teachers' (Ministerio de Cultura, Juventud y Deportes 2004). The country had already set up a socialised national health service in 1941 (well before the UK). The results have been spectacular. Public education to high school level is free and universal, and the literacy rate is 95 per cent. Infant mortality rates and life expectancy are higher than in the US (Seager 2009). The political system is stable and democratic, and the country has the lowest level of corruption in Latin America (except

Chile) (Transparency International 2012).

Costa Rica also realised that its main national asset is its beautiful and varied countryside and its diverse and exotic wildlife, making it ideal for eco-tourism. Twenty-five per cent of its land area is in national parks and other protected areas, the highest in the world, and it is the only country in the world to have totally abolished hunting.

The New Economics Foundation's Happy Planet Index combines measures of a country's environmental footprint with the happiness of its citizens. On this measure in 2009 and 2012 Costa Rica is the best in the world (the UK is 74th, the US 114th) (Seager 2009). It is the only country in the world to meet all five of the UN Development Programme's criteria to measure environmental sustainability (UNDP 2011).

Sources: as cited, plus the author's own experiences in Costa Rica, February 2013.

RISK MANAGEMENT

An important element of sustainability is risk management. Risk management is not necessarily about avoiding risk – it is about assessing risk and ensuring that it is consistent with the strategy of the organisation, whether it is risk-averse or risk-seeking. On the whole, an organisation seeking sustainability will tend to be relatively risk-averse.

Risk management is about answering several questions:

- What risks are we facing?
- What are the underlying causes of those risks?
- What is the likelihood of the risky event occurring?
- What is the outcome if the risky event does occur? Risk is measured by likelihood times outcome.
- What can be done about the risk? Possibilities include avoidance, reduction, retention or transfer (see below).
- What decision is taken about the risk?
- How can decisions be tracked, monitored and reviewed?

It is important to note that in identifying a risk, we must identify its causes rather than its symptoms. A technique for doing this is an Ishikawa, fishbone or cause–effect diagram (named after its inventor, Kaoru Ishikawa, a Japanese quality expert). This is frequently done in a group as a brainstorming exercise. An effect is identified and then possible causes for this effect are brainstormed. These are then grouped into major categories and the problem is further brainstormed to identify sub-causes, plotted as sub-bones on the skeleton diagram (Figure 9.2). Categories commonly used for problems with a large HR element are the four Ps – Place, Procedure, People, Policies.

Figure 9.2 An Ishikawa diagram

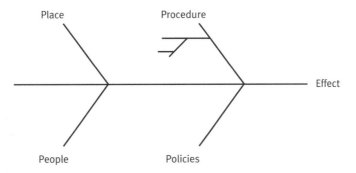

Quantitatively, two risks (likelihood x outcome) might appear identical, but one may have a high likelihood (say 50 per cent) and a low financial cost (say £10,000), and the other a low likelihood (say 0.1 per cent) and a high financial cost (say £5 million). Each would represent a risk of £5,000, but how they are treated is likely to be very different. In the first case, the risk may be ignored (that is, retained within the organisation), while in the second case, it is likely that the risk will be transferred (through insurance).

The possible strategies for dealing with risk include:

- *Avoidance* – here a risky activity is not performed at all. For example, after the terrorist attacks in London in July 2005, many Americans avoided all travel to the UK. In a business context, avoiding risk usually means also giving up the opportunity of profit, so except in extreme cases it is unlikely to be a viable strategy.
- *Reduction* – this involves the use of methods which reduce the severity of the loss or the likelihood of it occurring. An example here is the prohibition on the use of hand-held mobile phones while driving.
- *Retention* – here the risk is accepted when it occurs. This will frequently be done where the risk is small, or where a very large organisation finds it cheaper to self-insure rather than pay insurance premiums to another organisation.
- *Transfer* – here the risk is transferred to someone else, usually through an insurance contract, but also sometimes through outsourcing. This is commonly used for risks which have a low likelihood of occurrence, but which would be catastrophic if they did happen – for example, the second scenario discussed above, where the likelihood of occurrence was very low (0.1 per cent), but the outcome very high (a loss of £5 million). Here the risk is only £5,000, but the organisation might be prepared to pay a higher insurance premium than this (say £10,000) to eliminate the risk.

Once a decision has been taken about how to manage a particular risk, this decision then has to be monitored and periodically reviewed, as the risk parameters may change over time.

THE RNLI

Sustainability is not just about efficient use of resources. At an organisational level, it is about managing the organisation in such a way as to maintain its long-term viability. Among many other things, this involves:

- taking a long-term rather than a short-term perspective
- prudent risk management
- developing and maintaining a culture that creates a shared sense of purpose and a shared value system which supports sustainability.

We can see the opposite of each of these in the way that many financial institutions were managed in the run-up to the credit crunch in 2007–09:

- almost total emphasis on short-term profit maximisation
- a willingness to take high financial risks, with little evidence of any risk management

- a bonus system based on huge rewards for short-term success and a willingness to poach whole investment teams from each other.

An example of the opposite approach is the Royal National Lifeboat Institution (RNLI), one of Britain's oldest (founded in 1824) and most successful charities.

The RNLI has:

- a long-term planning horizon, which includes a 20-year strategic plan
- long-term financial planning, which recognises the risk that social and environmental changes may adversely affect the RNLI's income in the future
- a very strong sense of purpose that underpins the RNLI's core mission – 'the charity that saves lives at sea'.

Source: CIPD (2009)

CORPORATE SOCIAL RESPONSIBILITY, SUSTAINABILITY AND HR

Carroll identifies four philosophies of organisational responsiveness to CSR (Carroll 1979):

1 *Reaction* – the company denies all responsibility for social issues, claiming that they are the responsibility of government (the Friedman approach).

2 *Defence* – the company accepts responsibility but fights it, doing the least that seems to be required (the tobacco industry?).

3 *Accommodation* – the company accepts responsibility and does what is expected of it (most major companies in the UK).

4 *Proaction* – the company does more than is expected (Body Shop, the Co-op Bank).

Who should be responsible for directing an organisation's policy on ethics and corporate social responsibility? There are three leading contenders, each reflecting a particular perception of ethics and CSR:

- *marketing/PR* – if CSR is primarily seen as a marketing tool and the key relationship being that with customers (defence)
- *the company secretary* – if CSR is primarily seen as a matter of regulation and the key relationship being the corporate governance one with shareholders (accommodation)
- *HR* – if CSR is primarily seen as a cultural issue and about human behaviour and the key relationship being that with all stakeholders (proaction).

The theory on ethics and CSR would strongly suggest that the policy can only be meaningful if it permeates all the activities of the organisation and if everyone in the organisation truly internalises the policy, rather than merely paying lip-service to it. This would suggest that HR should be the lead department. However, of even greater importance is that, whichever department is in day-to-day charge, top management, in the form of the CEO, should at all times behave ethically themselves. Just as quality has total quality management, ethics/CSR requires total ethical management.

So what in detail should be the role of HR in ethics/CSR?

- *Helping to identify the values of the organisation* – HR should have experience with values, and is well placed to canvass opinions on values across a wide range of stakeholders. Here HR has a clear strategic contribution to make.
- *Drawing up a code of ethics* – HR should be used to drafting policies, many of which themselves have a clear ethical content.
- *Behaving ethically in its own relationships with a key stakeholder, the organisation's own staff* – here the concept of the 'psychological contract' is important (CIPD 2003, pp18–19). This defines the implicit deal between employer and employees, as distinct from the formal deal contained in the contract of employment. It is an understanding about what each side can expect from the other. This has two implications for HR in the context of ethics/CSR: the psychological contract should itself be an ethical one, and the concept of the psychological contract can be extended to relationships with other stakeholders.
- *Managing the culture of the organisation* – a culture which fully supports ethics does not just happen; it has to be nurtured, maintained and communicated.
- *Development* – if staff in an organisation are presented with a CSR policy and a code of ethics, it will mean nothing to them until they are thoroughly trained in what they mean and how they should be implemented. This presents HR with a crucial development role, at all levels of the organisation. Some help here is likely to come from the launch of the DTI's online CSR Academy in July 2004 (see *Personnel Today* 2004).
- *Maintaining the 'employer brand'* – increasingly companies want brand values to be reflected in everything that the organisation does. An ethical brand value has clear marketing advantages and recruitment/retention advantages (see CIPD 2003, p23).

There is some evidence in a recent CIPD survey that HR has a smaller role than it thinks in CSR. Eighty-six per cent of HR professionals agree that there is a vital role for HR in embedding corporate responsibility, but only 56 per cent of non-HR managers agree with this (Gifford 2012). Clearly HR must not only champion CSR, but also be seen to do so.

HR should also have a leading role in promoting and maintaining sustainability. It could take part in setting up an environmental policy, and in the development, training and communication that supports such a policy.

The policy could include:

- *Energy minimisation* – turning off lights and computers overnight and at weekends, lowering central heating temperatures to 19°C, use of video-conferencing rather than energy-hungry face-to-face meetings.
- *Transport policy* – choosing less polluting company cars, subsidised parking for staff who car-share, public transport loans or subsidies, loaning bicycles to staff, etc. Boots has reduced staff car journeys by 20 per cent through its green transport plan.
- *Flexible working and homeworking* – flexible working can enable staff to avoid rush-hour congestion, so saving on energy, and also makes bicycle usage more attractive (Davies and Smith 2007).

The TUC has promoted a Green Workplaces Project, which helps to ensure trade union support for sustainability initiatives. A joint union–management environment group at Scottish Power found that a call centre site had 200 old-fashioned VDU screens, with high energy usage. Half of these were currently left on at night and at weekends. Switching to low-energy screens and PCs, and development of a 'switch it off' culture could help to save a third of the site's emissions of CO_2. Actual savings in 2006–07 were 5 per cent (TUC 2007).

In January 2010, just before his death, the management guru C.K. Prahalad published an article in the *Harvard Business Review* entitled 'The Responsible Manager', which set out his views on the manager's social responsibilities. To summarise, these were:

- Understand the importance of nonconformity.
- Display a commitment to learning and developing yourself.
- Develop the ability to put personal performance in perspective.
- Be ready to invest in developing other people.
- Learn to relate to those who are less fortunate.
- Be concerned about due process.
- Realise the importance of loyalty to organisation, profession, community, society and, above all, family.
- Assume responsibility for outcomes as well as processes.
- Remember that you are part of a very privileged few.
- Expect to be judged by what you do and how well you do it – not by what you say you want to do.
- Be concerned about the problems of the poor and the disabled, accept human weaknesses, laugh at yourself – and avoid the temptation to play God. Leadership is about developing modesty, humility and humanity (Prahalad 2010).

Not bad precepts for the person, the manager and the organisation!

REFLECTIVE ACTIVITY 9.8

Institutional racism

In 1999 the Macpherson Report on the murder of Stephen Lawrence identified the principle of institutional racism. The report defined this as 'the collective failure of an organisation to provide an appropriate and professional service to people because of their colour, culture or ethnic origin. It can be seen or detected in processes, attitudes and behaviour which amount to discrimination through unwitting prejudice, ignorance, thoughtlessness and racial stereotyping which disadvantages minority ethnic people' (Home Office 1999). Macpherson argued that because of its ingrained culture (the so-called 'canteen culture'), the Metropolitan Police was institutionally racist. This does not mean that every Met officer is racist, nor that there is a deliberate policy of racism in the organisation, but that the organisation is unthinkingly racist in its attitudes and behaviour.

After the publication of the report, the Met pledged itself to eliminating institutional racism, as did other police forces.

Question

1   What actions could the police take to eliminate institutional racism?

CORPORATE SOCIAL RESPONSIBILITY AND THE GOVERNMENT

The Government has two main roles in CSR. First, the Government is itself a major employer and a major purchaser and supplier of services. In this role, it can and should behave ethically, just like any other organisation.

However, the Government also has a role in the promotion of CSR (Cowe 2004). In March 2000, the first minister for corporate social responsibility was appointed, within the Department for Trade and Industry.

The main interest of the Government has been in securing greater transparency. The Pensions Act of 2000 requires pension fund trustees to make a statement of investment principles, disclosing their policy on social, environmental and ethical issues. Its Company Law Review led to the introduction in 2005 of a requirement on all public companies to include an Operating and Financial Review in their annual report to shareholders. In addition, the Government set up a CSR Academy in 2004.

However, locating the responsibility for CSR within the DTI has inevitably led to an emphasis on the corporate governance aspects of CSR. Other departments clearly also have an involvement in CSR – the Department for Work and Pensions in pensions, the Department for International Development in trade and aid aspects of CSR, and the Environment Department in issues of pollution, sustainability and climate change. The involvement of the Government is likely to increase.

It could be argued that governments should go further and follow a policy of governmental social responsibility. In Chapter 4 we looked at the difference between gross domestic product and standard of living. We could go further and distinguish standard of living and quality of life. The latter is dependent on factors such as easy access to high-quality public services, a low level of crime, a sense of community (as argued by Putnam 2000), and a high degree of equality (as argued by Wilkinson and Pickett 2009)(see also Fox 2012). The New Economics Foundation's 'measure of domestic progress' (MDP) model subtracts social and environmental costs and resource depletion from GDP. By the new measure, the UK economy peaked in 1976. The divergence of the two measures has been especially stark in the past 30 years, with an 80 per cent increase in GDP but a sharp fall in MDP – fuelled by rising social inequalities in the Thatcherite 1980s – which the Labour Government failed to curb (Herbert 2004).

One government which takes its social responsibilities seriously is that of the small and remote Himalayan kingdom of Bhutan, as examined in Reflective Activity 9.9.

REFLECTIVE ACTIVITY 9.9

Gross National Happiness

Bhutan is a small, poor Buddhist kingdom in the Himalayas, between India and China. In 1972 its then king, Jigme Singye Wangchuck, proposed the concept of *Dzongkha*, or Gross National Happiness.

His argument was based on the perceived difficulties with the universally used concept of gross domestic product, a measure of the annual output of a country. This included output which did not add to well-being, such as defence, police and pollution clean-up, while it did not include other measures which did add to well-being, such as volunteer work and unpaid domestic work. It also did not take account of income distribution. Thus, GDP was not a good indicator of standard of living, even if the latter was defined as purely economic.

In addition, some forms of economic development are uneconomic if measured on a cost–benefit basis, particularly as in many cases the benefits are private, accruing to individuals or corporations, while the costs are public, borne by the community as a whole.

The concept of Gross National Happiness signalled commitment to building an economy based on Bhutan's culture and its Buddhist spiritual values. It held that material and spiritual development occur side by side and reinforce each other. Four principles underpinned the concept:

● promotion of sustainable development

- preservation and promotion of cultural values
- conservation of the natural environment
- establishment of good governance.

These were then operationalised into eight measures:

- physical, mental and spiritual health
- time balance
- social and community vitality
- cultural vitality
- education
- living standards
- good governance
- ecological vitality.

In 2007 Bhutan ranked eighth out of 178 countries in subjective well-being and was the only country in the top 20 to have a very low GDP (Nelson 2011).

Questions

1   What are the difficulties in calculating Gross National Happiness?

2   Is Gross National Happiness a concept that is only relevant to a country such as Bhutan, which is small, isolated, little involved in world trade, and with a high degree of reverence for its king and his ideas?

THE BOTTOM LINE

Do corporate social responsibility and ethical behaviour increase a company's profits? A series of studies suggests that they do.

First, corporate social responsibility seems to benefit an organisation's reputation. In 2002, Business in the Community carried out a survey on what the public thought of corporate responsibility (BITC 2002). Business leaders in general are not trusted. Only 25 per cent of respondents trusted them to tell the truth – only ahead of politicians and journalists, and well below doctors and teachers. This suggests that business has a lot of ground to make up. The public wants business to be responsible. Only 2 per cent think that companies should maximise their profits, regardless of society or the environment. Eight times as many thought companies should make a major contribution to society, regardless of cost.

Responsible behaviour also affects people's purchases. Eighty-six per cent in 2002 thought it very or fairly important that the organisation shows a high degree of social responsibility, up from 68 per cent in 1997. One in six people have actively boycotted a product on ethical grounds in previous years.

Is this evidence conclusive? No. It is suggestive, but little more. If you were interviewed by Business in the Community, you might have a shrewd idea of the kind of answers which the interviewer would like! It is also unfortunately true that there is often a gap between what people say they do and what they actually do.

The second piece of evidence is a report written by the management consultants Arthur D Little in 2003, again for Business in the Community (BITC 2003). This identifies a number of benefits from CSR:

- It offers a means by which companies can build the trust of their stakeholders. This is supported by the American strategy guru Michael Porter, who is reported as saying that how a company is perceived by its stakeholders is becoming a source of competitive advantage (Golzen 2001).
- CSR offers more effective management of risk. CSR encourages firms to understand and empathise with society and the environment, and this makes it more likely that they will be proactive about social and environmental risk.
- CSR helps to attract and retain a talented and diverse workforce.
- CSR stimulates learning and innovation within organisations.
- CSR facilitates access to capital. Over half of analysts and two-thirds of investors believe that a company that emphasises CSR is attractive to investors.

- CSR improves competitiveness, market positioning and profitability. The report quotes from Collins and Porras' *Built to Last*, a pioneering study in the 1990s, which compared successful companies which had been in business for at least 50 years with a control group who had been less successful. They found that a key characteristic of the successful 'visionary' companies was that they had a core purpose beyond making money (Collins and Porras 2000).

Is the Arthur D Little evidence conclusive? It is certainly very strong. Although some of the findings are based on opinion, others are based on hard evidence of changes in behaviour.

The third study was carried out by the Institute of Business Ethics in 2003. This examined a sample of FTSE 350 companies which were perceived as being ethical (they had had a code of ethics in operation for at least five years, they scored highly on *Management Today*'s annual league table of 'most admired companies', and they were rated highly by the specialist ratings agency SERM on their 'socio-ethical risk management'). These ethical companies were compared with a control sample.

The ethical companies were found to score more highly on three measures of financial performance – market value added, economic value added and price/earning ratio. On a fourth measure, return on capital employed, they did less well until the stock market collapse of 2000, but have performed better since then, suggesting that their profits are more stable (Caulkin 2003; Maitland 2003).

Is this evidence conclusive? Again, it is very strong, but unfortunately it is not conclusive. There is clearly a strong correlation between ethical behaviour and profits, but this does not prove that the ethical behaviour causes the profits. The link may be the other way round – profitable companies may be more likely to be ethical – or both may be the result of some unknown third factor.

A more theoretical approach was taken by Reitz, Wall and Love (1998). They concentrated on the relatively narrow area of business negotiation and argued that taking an unethical stance in negotiation has four major costs:

- *Rigidity* – unethical negotiators will tend to stick to the patterns of negotiation which have paid off in the past. They will thus trap themselves in a rigid bargaining position which can be matched and exploited by their opponents.
- *Damaged relationships* – if a bargaining partner feels that he has been manipulated through underhand tactics, he is likely to feel embittered and to seek revenge.
- *Sullied reputation* – success in business frequently depends on reputation. If you get a reputation for cheating or other unethical behaviour, this will harm your future business prospects.
- *Lost opportunities* – negotiation is about finding a win–win situation, whereby both sides gain. A reputation for sharp dealing may lead potential partners to avoid making concessions to you for fear that you will not make concessions back.

Their conclusion is that ethical negotiation is not only morally desirable, it is also good business.

REFLECTIVE ACTIVITY 9.10

CSR and profits – the contrary view

A strong case against CSR has been made by David Henderson (2001). He makes the following points:

1   CSR involves organisations in higher costs and, in so far as it means that they may forgo some activities seen as non-responsible, lower revenue. The result will be lower profits (although he admits that in

some cases, this could be offset by gains as a result of enhanced reputation). This argument is supported by evidence that in 2003, the Dutch insurance company Aetna spent 20 million euros in order to comply with the US Sarbanes-Oxley regulations, introduced after the Enron scandal (Targett 2004).

2   Some of the leading CSR companies have gone through spectacular collapses in profits. He cites the US jeans manufacturer Levi Strauss, but the same point could be made about the Body Shop and Ben & Jerry's ice cream.

3   The CSR agenda is frequently set not by 'society' but by non-governmental organisations (NGOs) such as Greenpeace, which he sees as anti-capitalist pressure groups and as unrepresentative of society as a whole.

Critically evaluate these arguments.

SUMMARY

This chapter has analysed the nature of personal and professional ethics, whether or not it is possible to see business ethics as a distinct ethical area, the principles and application of stakeholder theory, the use of values and codes of ethics, the nature and importance of corporate social responsibility, and the nature and importance of sustainability in an era of climate change. The roles of both HR and the Government are stressed.

KEY LEARNING POINTS

- Three main approaches can be taken to ethics and these lead to a larger number of ethical guidelines. The most commonly used of these are the golden rule, the disclosure rule and the intuition ethic.
- All managers face ethical dilemmas on a daily basis in their work.
- Professionals have an ethical responsibility both to their organisation and to impartial professional integrity.
- There is a considerable argument over whether a separate business ethic exists.
- Stakeholder theory holds that organisations have responsibilities to a wide range of stakeholders.
- Values underpin ethics and an organisation's values underpin its business ethics.
- Codes of ethics, unless they are internalised in the organisation's culture, do not guarantee ethical behaviour.
- Corporate governance is concerned with issues of conflict of interest and accountability.
- Corporate social responsibility is the way in which an organisation expresses its values through its behaviour towards stakeholders.
- Sustainability or sustainable development is concerned with safeguarding the environment for future generations.
- Risk management is an important element of a sustainability strategy.
- HR has a key role to play in promoting CSR and sustainability.
- The Government has an important role in promoting CSR and sustainability.
- Although the evidence is not totally conclusive, it appears extremely likely that there is a positive correlation between CSR and profit.

QUESTIONS

1   Distinguish between the absolutist, relativist and utilitarian approaches to ethics.

2   Describe the golden rule, the disclosure rule and the intuition ethic.

3   According to De George, what conditions must apply before whistleblowing is morally justified?

4   Does an organisation have any ethical responsibilities over and above those of the individuals within it?

5   Define purpose, values and vision.

6   How useful are codes of ethics?

7   Define corporate governance.

8   What are the key features of corporate social responsibility?

9   Define sustainable development.

10 In the context of risk management, what do you understand by risk avoidance, risk reduction, risk retention and risk transfer?

11 What is the role of HR in supporting CSR and sustainable development?

12 What elements could be included in an environmental policy?

EXPLORE FURTHER

FURTHER READING

Stephen Connock and Ted Johns' *Ethical Leadership*, published by the CIPD in 1995, is a useful summary of ethical issues from an HR standpoint.
The CIPD has published a useful factsheet on *Corporate Responsibility* (revised in December 2011). It also published in February 2012 a collection of thought pieces, *Responsible and Sustainable Business: HR leading the way*.
Excellent books on ethics are Colin Fisher and Alan Lovell's *Business Ethics and Values*, 2nd edition, 2006, although this is rather heavy going, and Andrew Crane and Dirk Matten's *Business Ethics*, 2nd edition, 2007.
A 2011 *Harvard Business Review* article by Beard and Hornick (It's hard to be good, Vol 89, No 11, November 2011) profiles five 'good' companies.

USEFUL WEBSITES

A useful website is Business in the Community (www.bitc.org.uk), which contains a number of useful reports and case studies on ethics and CSR.

AUDIO AND VIDEO MATERIAL

The CIPD has a podcast entitled *Corporate Responsibility and HR*, published in April 2012. There are two *Harvard Business Review* videos on YouTube (www.youtube.com/user/HarvardBusiness): *Build a Strategy for Sustainability* and *A Brief History of Doing Well by Doing Good*. There is also a video entitled *Business Ethics*, designed for use with US high school students, which discusses a number of ethical dilemmas (www.youtube.com/watch?v=SDPsSyoZNIw).

RESPONSIBLE TOURISM

In 1999, Richards and Gladwin put forward their definition of a socially sustainable enterprise (Richards and Gladwin 1999):

'The characteristics of a socially sustainable enterprise are that it would:

1   return to communities where it operates – selling as much as it gains from them

2   meaningfully include stakeholders impacted by its activities in associated planning and decision-making processes

3   ensure no reduction in, and actively promote, the observance of political and civil rights in the domains where it operates

4   widely spread economic opportunities and help to reduce or eliminate unjustified inequalities

5   directly or indirectly ensure no net loss of human capital within its workforces and operating communities

6   cause no net loss of direct and indirect productive employment

7   adequately satisfy the vital needs of its employees and operating communities

8   work to ensure the fulfilment of the basic needs of humanity prior to serving luxury wants.'

Explore Worldwide is a UK tour company, specialising in small group exploratory holidays. Its brochure stresses its commitment to sustainability:

'Respecting our planet

Our commitment to responsible tourism

Explore's dedication to Responsible Tourism is the driving force behind our Environmental Policy. Far from being an abstract ideal for us, Responsible Tourism shapes all our major decisions – from the concept that "Small Groups Leave Fewer Footprints" to the choice of local agents and suppliers.

Here are our guidelines in a nutshell:

● By operating in small groups, we minimise the impact on the local culture and resources, whilst blending in more easily.

● We issue our travellers with clear guidelines on responsible tourism. These cover a variety of issues from littler and waste disposal in remote areas, to begging and artefacts. We encourage customers to buy local crafts and support local skills, but never to buy products that exploit wildlife or harm the habitat.

● We use locally owned suppliers wherever viable to provide and run services. This ensures that the local economy benefits directly. We also expect local suppliers to meet our standards, with particular consideration for the environment.

● When recruiting Tour Leaders, we assess their environmental credentials and then train them to our own standards. They are also required to complete a Responsible Tourism Audit on each tour.

● Throughout a tour, the Leader will encourage the education of our customers on the social workings of a region. And part of their role is to make sure that the local communities benefit from our visit, ensuring that we will always be welcome.

Explore's passion for travel goes beyond the yearning for discovery. Ours is a reasoned, tried and tested approach to the enjoyment of a truly amazing planet.'

Source: Explore Worldwide (2004)

Critically evaluate Explore's Responsible Tourism policy against Richards and Gladwin's principles.

Mark Ellingham, the founder of the *Rough Guide* series, has recently declared that 'binge flying' constitutes a threat to the global environment. 'If the travel industry [ignores] the effect that carbon emissions from flying are having on climate change, we are putting ourselves in a very similar position to the tobacco industry.'

Source: Hastings (2007)

Is overseas tourism unsustainable?

REFERENCES

Accountability Primer: Sustainability. (nd) www.accountability.org.uk

Aldred, J. (2007) Q&A: Plastic bags. *Guardian*. 13 November.

Anand, V., Ashforth, B. and Joshi, M. (2004) Business as usual: the acceptance and perpetuation of corruption in organizations. *Academy of Management Executive*. Vol 18, No 2. May.

Argenti, J. (1993) *Your organisation, what is it for? Challenging traditional organizational aims*. Maidenhead: McGraw-Hill.

Ash, L. (2005) Prawns: Bangladesh's mixed blessing. BBC. 17 February.

Barkham, P. (2007) World asks town that banned the plastic bag: how can we do it too? *Guardian*. 12 May.

BBC. (2011) Government calls for 'fundamental reform' of exam system. 8 December.

Beard, A. and Hornick, R. (2011) It's hard to be good. *Harvard Business Review*. Vol 89, No 11. November.

Bhalla, A. (2011) Prawns bring profits for Bangladeshi farmers. AlertNet/Reuters. 15 December. www.reuters.com/article/2011/12/14/prawns-net-profit-for-flood-hit-banglade-idINDEE7BD05720111214 [Accessed 16 August 2012].

Billington, R. (2003) *Living philosophy: an introduction to moral thought*. 3rd edition. London: Routledge.

BITC. (2000) *Putting your heart into it: purpose and values*. Report of the Business Impact Task Force 2000. Business in the Community. www.bitc.org.uk.

BITC. (2002) *The public's views of corporate responsibility*. Available at: www.bitc.org.uk [Accessed 27 September 2004]. London: Business in the Community.

BITC. (2003) *The business case for corporate responsibility*. London: Business in the Community.

Bowers, S. (2009) Kraft chews on a sweeter deal for Cadbury. *Observer*. 8 November.

Brammer, S.J., Millington, A. and Pavelin, S. (2006) Is philanthropy strategic? *Business Ethics: A European Review*. Vol 15, No 3.

Brinkmann, J. and Ims, K. (2003) Good intentions aside: drafting a functionalist look at codes of ethics. *Business Ethics: A European Review.* Vol 12, No 3.

Butler, S. (2006) Would you like a bag with that, Madam? *The Times.* 7 October.

Carroll, A.B. (1979) A three dimensional model of corporate social performance. *Academy of Management Review.*Vol 4.

Carroll, A.B. (1990) Principles of business ethics: their role in decision making and an initial consensus. *Management Review.* Vol 28, No 8.

Carroll, A.B. (1991) The pyramid of corporate social responsibility: towards the moral management of organizational stakeholders. *Business Horizons.* July–August.

Caulkin, S. (2003) Ethics and profits do mix. *Observer.* 20 April.

Cavanagh, G., Moberg, D. and Velasquez, M. (1981) The ethics of organizational politics. *Academy of Management Review.* Vol 3.

Chakraborrty, A. (2012) You've been bankered. *Guardian.* 3 July.

Charkham, J. (1994) *Keeping good company: a study of corporate governance in five countries.* Oxford: Oxford University Press.

CIPD. (2003) *Code of professional conduct and disciplinary procedures.* London: Chartered Institute of Personnel and Development.

CIPD. (2009) *Shared purpose and sustainable organisational performance.* Research insight. London: Chartered Institute of Personnel and Development.

CIPD. (2011) *Corporate responsibility.* London: Chartered Institute of Personnel and Development.

CIPD. (2012) *Responsible and sustainable business: HR leading the way.* London: Chartered Institute of Personnel and Development.

Collins, C. and Porras, J. (2000) *Built to last: successful habits of visionary companies.* 3rd edition. London: Random House.

Connock, S. and Johns, T. (1995) *Ethical leadership.* London: Chartered Institute of Personnel and Development.

Cowe, R. (2004) Commanding heights. *Guardian.* 8 November.

Crane, A. and Matten, D. (2007) *Business ethics: managing corporate citizenship and sustainability in the age of globalisation.* 2nd edition. Oxford: Oxford University Press.

Curtis, P. (2004) Market graders. *Guardian.* 17 August.

Davies, G. and Smith, H. (2007) Natural resources. *People Management.* 8 March.

Deal, T. and Kennedy, A. (1990) Values; the core of the culture. In A. Campbell and K. Tawadey (eds) *Mission and business philosophy.* Oxford: Butterworth-Heinemann.

De George, R.T. (1999) *Business ethics.* 5th edition. New Jersey: Prentice Hall.

DesJardins, J. (2007) *Business, ethics and the environment.* New Jersey: Pearson/Prentice Hall.

Dore, R. (2006) Japan's shareholder revolution. *CentrePiece.* Winter 2006/07.

Drucker, P. (1990) What is 'business ethics'? In A. Campbell and K. Tawady (eds) *Mission and business philosophy.* Oxford: Butterworth-Heinemann.

DTI. (2002) *Business and society: corporate social responsibility.* London: Department for Trade and Industry.

Economist. (2006) Voting with your trolley. 9 December.

Economist. (2007) Plastics of evil. *Economist (US).* 31 March.

Elliott, L. (2009) Brown is right: rich western banks must pay for developing nations to go green. *Guardian.* 9 November.

European Commission. (2001) Promoting a European framework for corporate social responsibility.

Explore Worldwide. (2004) 2004–2005 brochure. Available at: www.explore.co.uk [Accessed 24 September 2004].

Farnham, D. (1999) *Managing in a business context.* London: Chartered Institute of Personnel and Development.

Farnham, D. (2010) *Human resource management in context.* London: Chartered Institute of Personnel and Development.

Finch, J. (2012) Barclays: six things we learned. *Guardian.* 5 July.

Finch, J. and Allen, K. (2006) Tesco offers carrot to reduce use of plastic carrier bags. *Guardian.* 5 August.

Fisher, C. and Lovell, A. (2006) *Business ethics and values: individual, corporate and international perspectives.* 2nd edition. Harlow: FT/Prentice Hall.

Forsyth, D.R. (1980) A taxonomy of ethical ideologies. *Journal of Personality and Social Psychology.* Vol 39, No 1. July.

Fox, J. (2012) The economics of well-being. *Harvard Business Review.* Vol 90, No 1/2. January/February.

Friedman, M. (1962) *Capitalism and freedom.* Chicago: Chicago University Press.

Friedman, M. (1970) The social responsibility of business is to increase its profits. *New York Times Magazine.* 13 September.

Gifford J. (2012) HR's role in corporate responsibility: still not convinced? *Impact.* Vol 41. December.

Golzen, G. (2001) What's the big idea? *Global HR.* September.

Guardian. (2012) Leading article: Libor scandal: gunfight on Threadneedle Street. *Guardian.* 18 July.

Harrison, R. (2002) *Learning and development*. 3rd edition. London: Chartered Institute of Personnel and Development.

Hastings, M. (2007) Binge flying is just the beginning. The only way to stop this is a severe tax. *Guardian*. 7 May.

Heffernan, M. (2012) *Wilfulblindness*. London: Simon & Schuster.

Henderson, D. (2001) *Misguided virtue: false notions of corporate social responsibility*. The Institute of Economic Affairs. www.iea.org.uk

Herbert, I. (2004) When national happiness peaked. *Independent*. 17 March.

Hickman, L. (2009) Do we really need to ban the bag? *Guardian*. 11 August.

Hickman, L. (2013) Why is then government dithering over a plastic bag charge in England? *Guardian*. 24 January.

Hoffman, M. (1990) What is necessary for corporate moral excellence? In A. Campbell and K. Tawady (eds) *Mission and business philosophy*. Oxford: Butterworth-Heinemann.

Home Office. (1999) *The Stephen Lawrence Inquiry: report of an inquiry by Sir William Macpherson of Cluny*. London: The Stationery Office.

Hussain-Khaliq, S. (2004) Eliminating child labour from the Sialkot soccer ball industry: two industry-led approaches. *Journal of Corporate Citizenship*. No 13. Spring.

Independent. (2012) Banker who broke HBOS is fined £500,000. *Independent*. 13 September.

Industrial Relations Services. (1999) IRS Employment Trends 675. March.

Johnson, G., Whittington, R. and Scholes, K. (2011) *Exploring strategy*. 9th edition. Hemel Hempstead: FT/Prentice Hall.

Kearns, P. and Ingate, K. (2001) Should the CIPD strike off poor practitioners? *Personnel Today*. 23 October.

Kelly, E. (1999) Corporate citizenship costs more than cash. *Professional Manager*. January.

Kollewe, J. (2012) Scandal-hit Barclays turns to safe pair of hands. *Guardian*. 31 August.

Lawrence, F. (2003) Is it OK to eat tiger prawns? *Guardian*. 19 June.

Lawson, A. (2003) Bangladesh prawn farmers hit back. BBC. 20 May.

Lawton, A. (1998) *Ethical management for the public services*. Buckingham: Open University Press.

Lewis, J. (2002) Testing time. *Personnel Today*. 9 April.

Luyendijk, J. (2012) Banking: high risk culture. *Guardian*. 29 June.

Mahony, C. (2007) Under new ownership. *People Management*. 12 July.

Maitland, A. (2003) Profits from the righteous path. *Financial Times*. 3 April.

Mathiason, N. and Treanor, J. (2009) Brown in secret push to sell 'Tobin tax' to City. *Guardian*. 10 November.

McKee, G. (2003) Managing human nature: leadership lessons from Venice. *Leader to Leader*. April.

Ministerio de Cultura, Juventud y Deportes. (2004) Abolicion del Ejercito en Costa Rica. San Jose, Costa Rica.

Monbiot, G. (2001) Superstores brand us to ensure we belong to them. *Guardian*. 31 July.

Murray, S. (2006) Fair trade products: confusions reigns over labelling. *Financial Times*. 12 June.

Nelson, D. (2011) Bhutan's Gross National Happiness index. *Daily Telegraph*. 2 March.

Personnel Today. (2004) CSR help is at hand. *Personnel Today*. 27 July.

Prahalad, C.K. (2010) The responsible manager. *Harvard Business Review*. Vol 88, No 1/2. January/February.

Prosser, D. (2007) Fairtrade is booming – but is it still a fair deal? *Independent*. 24 February.

Puntasen, A. (2008) Sharing wisdom from the East: lessons from the King's Sufficiency Economy in Thailand. *Interconnections*. No 2.

Putnam, R. (2000) *Bowling alone*. New York: Simon & Schuster.

Reitz, J., Wall, J. and Love, M.S. (1998) Ethics in negotiation: oil and water or good lubrication? *Business Horizons*. May–June.

Richards, D. and Gladwin, T. (1999) Sustainability metrics for the business enterprise. *Environmental Quality Management*. Spring.

Schwartz, M.S. (2001) A code of ethics for corporate codes of ethics. *Journal of Business Ethics*. Vol 41.

Seager, A. (2009) Costa Rica is world's greenest, happiest country. *Guardian*. 4 July.

Simms, A. (2009) Questions for a new world. *Guardian*. 17 November.

Snell, R. (1999) Managing ethically. In L. Fulop and S. Linstead (eds) *Management: a critical text*. Basingstoke: Macmillan.

Stratton, A. (2009) MPs' expenses: Christopher Kelly outlines reforms. Guardian. guardian.co.uk. 4 November [Accessed 11 November 2009].

Summers, D. (2009) British ex-MEP Tom Wise faces jail after £36,000 expenses scam. Guardian. guardian.co.uk. 5 November [Accessed 11 November 2009].

Targett, S. (2004) Is good governance good value? *Financial Times*. 17 April.

Transparency International. (2012) Corruption Perception Index 2012. www.transparency.org/cpi2012/results [Accessed 23 February 2012].

Treanor, J. (2012) Vickers criticises government for watering down reform proposals. *Guardian*. 15 June.

Treanor, J. et al (2012) Chief banking regulator; 'Barclays had culture of gaming – and of gaming us'. *Guardian*. 17 July.

TUC. (2007) *Green Workplaces Project 2006–7: Objectives and outcomes report*. London: Trades Union Congress.

Turner, B. (2006) Plastic bags are much the lesser evil. *The Grocer*. 11 February.

UN Development Programme. (2011) *Human Development Report*. New York: UNDP.

Watt, N., Taylor, M., McVeigh, K., Topping, A., Siddique, H. and Sturcke, J. (2009) MPs' expenses: what the latest information reveals about key figures. Guardian. guardian.co.uk. 18 June. [Accessed 11 November 2009].

Watt, N. and Stratton, A. (2009) Anger and anarchy among MPs at extent of Legg's demands. Guardian. guardian.co.uk. 14 October. [Accessed 11 November 2009].

Wilkinson, R. and Pickett, K. (2009) *The spirit level*. Harmondsworth: Penguin.

Williams, R. (2001) Under pressure, under pressure, under pressure. *Business Review*. September.

Wintour, P. (2007) Brown sets tough targets for reducing carbon. *Guardian*. 20 November.

Zingales, L. (2012) Why I was won over by Glass-Steagall. *Financial Times*. 10 June.

Strategic Management

INTRODUCTION

This chapter will analyse the nature of strategic management and identify different models of strategy. It will analyse the stages of strategic decision-making – analysis, choice and implementation. The last part of the chapter will concentrate on the nature and practice of change management.

WHAT IS STRATEGIC MANAGEMENT?

The origins of strategy are military and concern the art of war. A *strategos* was a general in command of a Greek army. Quinn (1980) identifies three elements of strategy:

- *Goals or objectives* – what is to be achieved and when it is to be achieved. Major goals which affect an organisation's overall direction are strategic goals.
- *Policies or guidelines* which set out the limits within which action should occur – major policies are strategic policies.

- *Programmes* lay down the sequence of actions necessary to achieve objectives – they set out how objectives will be achieved within the limits set by policies.

In other words:

- Where do we want to get?
- What actions should we take to get there?
- How can we carry out these actions?

The essence of a strategy is to build a position so strong that the organisation will achieve its objectives no matter what unforeseeable forces attack it (that is, how can we win whatever the enemy does?). Effective strategies should:

- contain clear and decisive objectives – sub-goals may change in the heat of battle but the overriding objective provides continuity over time
- maintain the initiative
- concentrate power at the right time and place
- have built-in flexibility so that one can use minimum resources to keep opponents at a disadvantage
- have committed and co-ordinated leadership
- involve correct timing and surprise
- make resources secure and prevent surprises from opponents.

Strategic decisions have a number of characteristics:

- They are concerned with the scope of an organisation's activities – the boundaries which an organisation sets to its activities.
- They are concerned with matching the activities of an organisation to its environment.
- They are concerned with matching the activities of an organisation to its resource capability.
- They often have resource implications for an organisation – if current resources do not permit a particular strategy, can the necessary resources be acquired?
- They affect operational decisions – a whole series of implementing sub-decisions must flow from the making of a strategic decision.
- They are affected by the values and expectations of those who have power in and around the organisation – its stakeholders.
- They affect the long-term direction of an organisation (Johnson et al 2011).

Strategy can be seen at several levels:

- *corporate level* – concerned with the overall scope of the operation, its financial performance and the allocation of resources to different operations
- *competitive or business unit level* – how to compete within a particular market at the level of a strategic business unit (SBU)
- *operational level* – how the different functions of the organisation contribute to the overall strategy. This level is often seen as tactical rather than in any real sense strategic, but it can equally be seen as the implementation stage of strategy.

Strategic management is about doing the right things. It is:

- ambiguous
- complex
- non-routine
- organisation-wide
- fundamental
- involving significant change
- environment- or expectations-driven.

Operational or tactical management is about doing things right. It is:

- routinised
- operationally specific
- involving small-scale change
- resource-driven.

MODELS OF STRATEGY

CORPORATE PLANNING

This was a product of the 1950s and 1960s, a period with a largely placid environment. Detailed corporate plans covering the whole organisation were drawn up by a central planning team and then agreed by top management. The details of the plan were extremely complex, as were the models used, but the planning process itself was relatively simple because the corporate future was expected to be a continuation of the past. The role of line management was to implement the plan. The main exponent of corporate planning was Igor Ansoff. There are clear parallels with the system of central planning as used to run the Soviet Union.

The strength of the corporate planning approach is its rigour and the vital information which is collected in the course of drawing up the plan. However, it has a number of weaknesses. It is inflexible – the plan is too vast and complex to cope with rapid change in the environment. However, some of the best corporate planners – those at Shell – coped with this by developing a range of scenarios about the future environment. One of these forecast exactly the huge rise in oil prices which happened in 1973, with the result that Shell could react very quickly to the new situation.

Centralised corporate planning is also demotivating. Nobody owns the plan except for the planners – the line managers who have to implement it have no commitment to it. At worst, corporate planning was an academic exercise and the plan was put away in a drawer and quietly forgotten.

Classical corporate planning in the Ansoff sense has probably gone forever. The external environment is now too turbulent for the luxury of a comprehensive plan, while the rigid top–down hierarchical approach to management is also a thing of the past. Classical strategic management has had to adapt to a new world and has become the rational approach. Some elements of classical planning do survive, including the need for a rigorous analysis of the external environment and of internal capabilities. Strategic management is still about doing the right things and, as we will see later, still goes through the stages of analysis, choice and implementation. These three stages form the core of all the major textbooks on strategic management, particularly of Johnson and Scholes' *Exploring Corporate Strategy*, originally published in 1983, and now in its ninth edition, renamed *Exploring Strategy* (Johnson et al 2011), having sold millions of copies and contributed to the education of generations of management students.

The rational planning school defines an objective in advance, describes where we are now and uses a prescriptive approach in which 'the three core areas – strategic analysis, strategic development and strategy implementation – are linked together sequentially'. In addition, Chandler, who famously argued that organisational structure follows strategy, supposes that strategy is determined centrally and, then, implemented structurally.

EMERGENT STRATEGIC MANAGEMENT

The emergent approach to strategy formulation has been characterised by trial, experimentation and discussion – that is, by a series of experimental approaches rather than a final objective. Emergent strategy is undertaken by an organisation that analyses its environment constantly and implements its strategy simultaneously. Emergent strategy, with its acknowledgement that uncertainty is here to stay, has the potential to address the current challenges of organisations and the corporations charged with their management (Carr et al 2004).

This model emphasises adaptability in the face of a turbulent environment. There is no rigid long-term plan, although there are long-term visions and values. Strategy becomes bottom–up, as line managers react to or anticipate changes in the environment. The organisation has to be very responsive to changes in the environment, which requires managers at all levels constantly to monitor the environment. The organisation becomes a learning organisation in the fullest sense of the term, as it is constantly scanning and learning from its environment. Strategy ceases to be a purely linear process and now emerges through a process of experimentation and trial and error.

Leading exponents of the emergent strategic management concept are:

Tom Peters – *In Search of Excellence* in 1982 (Peters and Waterman 1982) stressed the importance of a number of attributes for excellence, which emphasised values, simplicity, quick reactions and understanding the customer:

- stick to the knitting
- close to the customer
- productivity through people
- autonomy and entrepreneurship
- hands-on, value-driven
- bias for action
- simple form, lean staff
- simultaneous loose–tight properties.

He followed this up with *Thriving on Chaos* in 1985 (Peters 1985), where he argued that the organisation should cope with chaos by becoming chaotic itself – being in a continual state of flux.

Michael Porter – Porter approached strategic management as an economist. He stressed the importance of the competitive position of an industry (the Five Forces) (1980), the nature of generic strategies and the importance of the organisation's value chain in identifying its competitive advantage (1985).

Ralph Stacey – in *The Chaos Frontier* (1991) and *Strategic Management and Organisational Dynamics* (1993), he developed the application of chaos theory to strategic management. The environment facing organisations is one of chaos – multiple and ultimately unpredictable reactions follow from a single event. The further the forecaster looks into the future, the more outcomes become possible. As a result the organisation must be highly responsive and reactive. The role of top management is to develop and support creativity and innovation.

Gary Hamel and C.K. Prahalad – in *Competing for the Future* (1994), they stressed that the key role of management is to manage the organisation in such a way that it is flexible and able to respond to a changed environment. This means identifying and developing the core competencies of the organisation. We will return to this later. Hamel later developed the ten principles of revolutionary strategy (Hamel 1996):

1 *Strategic planning isn't strategic* – it assumed that the future will be more or less the same as the present.

2 *Strategy-making must be subversive* – strategy is about breaking rules and assumptions.

3 *The bottleneck is at the top of the bottle* – top managers are most resistant to change.

4 Revolutionaries exist in every company.

5   *Change is not the problem, engagement is* – senior managers fail to give people responsibility for managing change.

6   *Strategy-making must be democratic* – senior managers must recognise that creativity is spread throughout an organisation.

7   *Anyone can be a strategy activist* – senior managers must see activists as positive, not as anarchists.

8   *Perspective is worth 50 IQ points* – organisations have to use all their knowledge to identify unconventional ideas.

9   *Top–down and bottom–up are not the alternatives* – both are necessary.

10 *You can't see the end from the beginning* – strategy can often throw up surprises.

The key is that organisations must be run as a hotbed of innovation. Of a thousand unconventional ideas, probably only ten have the power to transform a business, and there is no way to identify these ten in advance. The role of leadership is to enable this experimentation to happen. One way to do this is to define the values of the organisation within which experimentation can take place. Hamel quotes the example of Virgin, which has more than 150 different businesses, but all are united by the proposition that the brands will imply customer value, fun and funkiness. The result is willingness to think outside the box. He contrasts this with Coca-Cola, which has been notoriously slow to innovate. Hamel describes a meeting with its chairman, Roberto Goizueta. Hamel asked him what his dream was for Coca-Cola, and Goizueta said, 'That anywhere in the world, if somebody turns on a tap, out comes Coca-Cola.' No outside the box (or outside the tap!) thinking here.

Second, Hamel identifies the true innovators as being heretics, lovers of novelty and deeply empathetic with customers, and he stresses that all these things can be taught. This teaching is the role of top management.

For more on Hamel's ideas, see Bernhut (2001).

Chan Kim and Renee Mauborgne – Kim and Mauborgne have developed the concept of Blue Ocean thinking. A Blue Ocean is a strategic area where competition is minimised and therefore full of opportunity. This contrasts with Red Oceans, which are overcrowded, rivalry is intense and competition is bloody. Blue Ocean strategy is all about finding strategic gaps, finding or creating market spaces which are not currently served. This might involve developing a totally new product or service, or, more likely, developing a new element to an existing product or service (Kim and Mauborgne 2004).

James Quinn – in *Strategies for Change: Logical Incrementalism* (1980), Quinn developed the concept of logical incrementalism, that strategy does not consist of a big bang, but rather of a series of small steps (incrementalism). Johnson et al (2011, pp405–6) identify four main elements of the Quinn model:

- *Environmental uncertainty* – constant environmental scanning is needed.
- *General goals* – over-precise objectives might stifle innovation.
- *Experimentation* – best bottom–up.
- *Co-ordinating emergent strategies* – this is the role of the leadership – facilitation rather than direction.

A parallel is the way in which Texas software company Trilogy manages its 'fast cycle' development and consulting work. Rather than step sequentially through phases of planning, design and operation (as in an industrial process), Trilogy loops rapidly through each of these activities again and again, each time generating a prototype – a product, however rough, that can be experienced directly and to which makers and customers can react (Austin and Devin 2004).

The main danger with the incremental approach is strategic drift. By definition, incremental change is small change rather than transformational change. There is a tendency to experiment, but only within a very narrow range of possibilities. Organisations become victims of their past successes, but fail to pick up that they are drifting away from their environment, which is changing more rapidly than they are. Eventually, the only choices are transformational change or death.

HENRY MINTZBERG AND STRATEGIC MANAGEMENT

One of the most trenchant critics of corporate planning has been the Canadian guru Henry Mintzberg. His writings include *The Rise and Fall of Strategic Planning* (1994). He argues that old-style corporate planning was all about left-brain activity – numbers, linearity, analysis. Strategic management is right-brain – ideas, patterns, relationships, intuition. He talks of crafting strategy, rather than planning strategy.

Mintzberg is famous for his *Five Ps of Strategy*:

- Strategy as a **plan** for action – here the strategy is made in advance of the actions to which they apply and it is applied consciously and purposefully. However, as we will see later, outcomes may not be as expected.
- Strategy as a **ploy** – a manoeuvre to outwit opponents.
- Strategy as a **pattern** – a pattern of behaviour becomes a strategy. If a particular course of action tends to lead to favourable results, a strategy emerges. The strategy is the result of events, rather than the cause of them. A variation on this he calls the umbrella strategy, where top management lays down broad principles and line managers have autonomy to act within these principles. Here strategy is both planned and emergent.
- Strategy as **position** – strategy here is about finding a niche in the market, a position which balances the pressures of the environment and the competition.
- Strategy as **perspective** – here the strategy reflects how the organisation views the world and its place in it. A classic example is Hewlett-Packard's 'H-P way', where the whole approach of the organisation is based on engineering excellence and innovation. The important thing here is consistency in behaviour.

Planned strategies often require modification as they are implemented, as environmental or organisational factors change. It is very rare that a long-term strategic plan can be implemented over a period of years without modification. The intended strategy may not be realised in practice and, even if it is, it may not achieve the desired results.

Mintzberg stresses that there is not an either-or choice between rational and emergent approaches to strategy. They are opposite ends of a continuum. Depending on the nature of the environment, either may be appropriate. Harrington et al (2004) argue that the more dynamic the environment facing an organisation, the more appropriate an emergent approach will be, and vice versa.

WHITTINGTON, PROCESSES AND OUTCOMES

Whittington (2001) stresses that we must go beyond the deliberate corporate strategy–emergent strategy dichotomy. These are different processes, and we should also consider different outcomes, either pluralist or revenue-maximising. If we plot outcomes against processes, we get a two-by two matrix, as in Figure 10.1.

Figure 10.1 Whittington, processes and outcomes

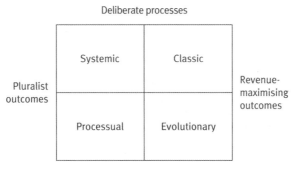

Source: based on Whittington (2001)

Whittington's matrix gives four possible combinations:

● Classic (deliberate process, revenue-maximising outcome) – this is the model of top–down corporate planning.
● Systemic (deliberate process, pluralist outcome) – the planning process is rational, but it also takes account of social, political and human factors.
● Evolutionary (emergent process, revenue-maximising outcome) – this stresses flexibility in the pursuit of a single goal.
● Processual (emergent process, pluralist outcome) – strategy emerges through experimental bargaining about both processes and goals.

THE ELEMENTS OF STRATEGIC MANAGEMENT

The analysis so far may seem extremely complex, but the important thing to remember is that the essence of strategic management is very simple. It consists of getting answers to four questions:

1 Where are we?

2 Where do we want to get?

3 How can we get there?

4 What do we have to do to get there?

From this we can derive the three elements of strategic management:

● *Strategic analysis* – tackles the first two questions – what is our current position and where to do we want to go?
● *Strategic choice* – the third question – how can we get there, that is, what strategy should we choose?
● *Strategic implementation* – what do we have to do to implement our chosen strategy?

STRATEGIC ANALYSIS

Strategic analysis is concerned with the strategic position of the organisation. What are the key characteristics of the organisation, what changes are going on in the environment and how will these affect the organisation and its activities? The aim is to form a view of the key influences on the present and future well-being of the organisation:

- expectations of stakeholders, the culture of the organisation and, most important, the organisation's vision and values
- the environment, as identified through a STEEPLE analysis – the main problem is to distil out of the complexity the key environmental impacts for the purposes of strategic choice
- resources – strategic capability is about identifying strengths and weaknesses by considering the key resource areas of the business such as physical plant, management, finance, products, etc.

Classical corporate planning saw environmental analysis as the key element in strategic analysis, while emergent strategic management sees culture and values as most crucial.

Gap analysis

The extent to which there is a mismatch (a gap) between current strategy and the future environment is a measure of the strategic problem facing the organisation. As Figure 10.2 shows, over time the current strategy is likely to get more out of line with the environment and a planning gap will grow.

Figure 10.2 Gap analysis

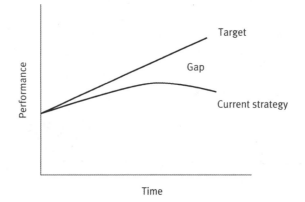

The organisation needs to choose a new strategy which will ensure that this gap is filled.

STRATEGIC CHOICE

Strategic choice involves three steps:

1   *Generation of strategic options* – three levels of analysis are involved here – what fundamental or generic strategy should be followed; within this generic strategy, what strategic directions are needed; and then what methods of strategic direction are most appropriate?

2   *Evaluation of strategic options* – this involves testing options for suitability (do they fit the generic strategy and will they provide the desired results?); feasibility (are resources available or obtainable?); and acceptability (do they fit the values of the stakeholders?).

3   *Selection of strategy* – either logically, using some kind of weighting criteria, or politically.

STRATEGIC IMPLEMENTATION

Strategic implementation involves resource planning, organisational structure, systems, change management techniques, etc.

STRATEGIC ANALYSIS

VISION, MISSION, VALUES AND OBJECTIVES

Vision, mission, values and objectives are closely linked and often confused. However, they are clearly distinguished by Peter Senge in *The Fifth Discipline* (1990):

- Vision is the *what* – the picture of the future we want to create, or the desired future state of the organisation (where do we want to get?).
- Mission is the *why* – the overriding purpose of the organisation, its scope and boundaries (what business are we in, why do we exist?).
- Values are the *how* – the underlying beliefs and ethical stance which drives how the business behaves (how are we going to behave while we are getting there?).
- Objectives operationalise all the other three – a precise statement of where we want to be and when, which turns the vision, mission and values into concrete quantifiable terms. It is frequently said that objectives should be SMART:

  - **S**tretching
  - **M**easurable
  - **A**chievable
  - **R**elevant
  - **T**ime limited

CASE STUDY 10.1

CADBURY AND A FAILURE OF VALUES

The chocolate manufacturer Cadbury was founded in Birmingham in 1824 by John Cadbury, a local Quaker. Like other nineteenth-century Quakers, Cadbury was a committed social reformer. He founded the Animals' Friend Society, which later became the RSPCA. The company remained true to its Quaker principles and was a shining example of corporate social responsibility long before the term was invented. It took a leading role in promoting education in Birmingham, built the Bournville model village for its workers, was the first company in the country to introduce a half day on Saturday and launched a pension fund as early as 1906 (Cadbury 2007).

The emphasis on Quaker values continued well into the twentieth century, as long as the company was directly controlled by the Cadbury family. It was a member of the family, Adrian Cadbury, who produced one of the first reports on corporate governance in the early 1990s.

It is clear from the Cadbury website that the company is still very proud of its Quaker heritage, and so it came as a great shock when the company was fined £1 million for a breach of safety regulations which led to a salmonella outbreak. What was worse was that the outbreak was a direct result of the company's own policy. In 2003, it had changed its policy on salmonella contamination from a 'zero tolerance' policy, where product was destroyed automatically if any trace of salmonella was detected on test, to a policy allowing a 'tolerable level' of salmonella. This was despite scientific

---

opinion that no level of salmonella could be regarded as safe.

In January and February 2006 there were 36 positive tests for salmonella, but the company did nothing until it was linked to an outbreak of salmonella poisoning in June 2006, in which at least 42 people were infected (Williams 2007). It then recalled all the products concerned. It is estimated that the recall and the resultant bad publicity cost the company £40 million (Tait and Wiggins 2007).

In the company's trial under food hygiene regulations, it was claimed by the prosecution that the change in policy was a deliberate and cynical act of cost-cutting. The judge said the company had fallen 'seriously short' of its obligations, but accepted the company's defence that although it was negligent, it was not deliberately aiming to cut costs. Simon Baldry, the former managing director of Cadbury Trebor Bassett, was one of the casualties of a management shake-up which followed the product withdrawal (Elliott 2007).

Contrast this with the approach of the US pharmaceutical company Johnson & Johnson, which had as one of its leading products Tylenol, heavily sold as a painkiller, particularly for children. In 1982 someone replaced Tylenol capsules on sale in Chicago with cyanide capsules and seven people died. The reaction of Johnson & Johnson's leadership was to go back to *Our Credo*, its expression of its values first written in 1943:

> We believe our first responsibility is to the doctors,

nurses, and patients, to mothers and fathers and all others who use our products and services. In meeting their needs everything we do must be of high quality... (Johnson & Johnson website)

All stocks were destroyed and the product was immediately withdrawn across the US, counselling and financial assistance were given to the victims' families, and after six months the product was re-launched with new triple-safety tamper-resistant packaging.

What this case shows is that the higher an organisation's standards and values, the more serious are any shortcomings in failing to meet those standards. Johnson & Johnson 'walked the talk' where its stated values were concerned; Cadbury did not.

However, it seems that Johnson & Johnson is losing its ethical edge. It has experienced a number of recent scandals in the US. Erik Gordon of the University of Michigan blamed these failings on the current CEO, Bill Weldon, and his 'relentless focus on the bottom line'. Gordon says, 'The major function of the credo is like... wrapping yourself in the American flag. It is to distract people from what is going on' (Knowledge@Wharton 2012).

What these cases show is that the higher an organisation's standards and values, the more serious are any shortcomings in failing to meet those standards.

The mission and objectives of the organisation are constrained by four main factors (Johnson et al 2011):

- *Corporate governance* – external constraints on the organisation, set by company law; reports of investigations such as the Cadbury Report on non-executive directors or the Greenbury Report on directors' pay; regulatory bodies such as the Financial Services

Authority; and targets and controls imposed by the Government on public bodies (for example, Best Value for local authorities).

- *Stakeholders* – stakeholders can influence the organisation's strategic direction through their power and/or their interest.
- *Business ethics* – ethics can impact on an organisation at three levels: general ethical policy; how the organisation interprets its corporate social responsibility when it formulates its strategy; and the ethical behaviour of individuals within the organisation. Clearly ethics is all about values, particularly the values of top management.
- *Culture* – culture in organisations operates at three levels:
  - values, often written down as part of the mission statement, but often vague, like 'service to the community'
  - more specific beliefs, often expressed as policies
  - taken-for-granted assumptions – the organisational paradigm – the 'way things are done here'. At grass-roots level, these may often be in conflict with the values and beliefs officially expressed at a higher level. For example, the police force in the UK is totally committed to eradicating 'institutional racism', but at the level of 'canteen culture' there are still racist PCs.

THE MISSION STATEMENT

This is the most generalised statement of organisational purpose. It sets the direction of the organisation and provides a benchmark against which policies can be evaluated.

An effective mission statement should achieve the following:

1 It should be visionary and long term. It is meant to inspire and drive the organisation.

2 It should clarify the main intentions and aspirations of the organisation and the reasons why the organisation exists.

3 It should describe the organisation's main activities and the position it wishes to attain in its industry.

4 It should contain a statement of the key values of the organisation in relation to its stakeholders.

5 It should be taken seriously within the organisation.

6 It should be a focus for activity, which can serve as a continual guide, rather than a closed aim which can be fully achieved.

However, there are two great dangers with mission statements. The first is a risk that they can appear grandiose, or even ridiculous. Too many overblown mission statements have tended in the past to lead to the whole concept being treated with ridicule. Typical is the *Dilbert* website (www.dilbert.com), which contains a mission statement generator, which will produce randomly generated mission statements.

The other danger is that the mission statement may become set in concrete. The external environment may change in a way that renders the mission statement obsolete, and a hindrance rather than a help to strategy formulation.

REFLECTIVE ACTIVITY 10.1

The WEA (Northern Ireland)

The Workers Educational Association (WEA) in
Northern Ireland publishes
its mission statement and WEA values
on its website (www.wea-ni.com), as follows:

The WEA mission statement

We will make learning accessible to all men and
women, especially those removed from the
educational experience. As well as offering
opportunities to individuals we will assist those
who wish to work collectively for the benefit of
their communities and for the good of society
as a whole.

The value base of the WEA

The WEA has been a catalyst for social change
since it began in Belfast in 1910. The following
values underpin our commitment to social
change:

Social inclusion – we make special efforts to
reach those most removed from the learning
experience.

Voluntarism – we provide opportunities for
people to volunteer to work both individually
and collectively for the betterment of our
society.

Active citizenship – we equip people to play a
full role in the social, economic, cultural and
political life of our society.

Building alliances – we work closely with others
to improve opportunities for learning.

Sharing experience – we share good practice to
promote mutual learning.

Equality – we promote equality of opportunity
through learning.

Evaluate the WEA mission statement against
the six characteristics of an effective mission
statement listed above.

RESOURCE ANALYSIS

Resource analysis is internal to the organisation. It is concerned with the strengths and
weaknesses parts of SWOT analysis, and measures the efficiency and effectiveness of an
organisation's resources and their degree of fit with the external opportunities and threats
also identified through SWOT. Ideally strengths should support opportunities and be able
to counteract threats. Resources should be seen in the widest sense, to include the
organisation's competitive position, as identified through techniques such as Five Forces
and portfolio analysis. However, SWOT analysis has severe limitations. The most
important of these is that it is subjective – different analysts will identify totally different
strengths and weaknesses. Stevenson (1989) found no consensus among the managers in
the companies he studied on the strengths and weaknesses of their companies. Higher-
level managers tended to be more optimistic about the balance of strengths and
weaknesses than lower-level managers.

Prahalad and Hamel (1990) identify the concept of the core competences of the
organisation – those factors which give the organisation its key competitive advantages.
Unlike resources, which are tangible, tradable and easily replicable, competences are based
on the accumulated knowledge and skills of the organisation, are unique to it and difficult
to copy. They are based on people rather than things. Examples are the way in which Dell
Computer builds all computers individually to order, or the reputation of the Body Shop
as an ethical crusader. Other analysis has suggested that the crucial competence needed by
all organisations is the ability to be nimble, flexible and responsive to rapid and
unpredictable changes in the external environment. The core competence model is very
closely connected with the resource-based model of strategic HR.

Core competences can be based on:

- *Cost-efficiency* – many advantages based on cost-efficiency are not really core competencies, as they can relatively easily be copied by other organisations. One which may lead to a core competence is cost-efficiency based on experience – the more experience an organisation has, the lower its costs tend to be.
- *Value added* – is the organisation more effective than the competition? In the early stages of the quality movement in the 1970s and 1980s, quality could be a core competence. Now it is a given – it is expected of all organisations and it does not in itself give a competitive advantage. Value added is more likely to be experienced by the customer through service than through the product itself – Dell does not necessarily sell a better computer, but it gives the customer a flexible computer configured to his or her requirements.
- *Managing linkages*, between different stages of production, or through alliances with other organisations – for example, the low-cost airlines like easyJet and Ryanair pioneered the use of Internet-based ticket booking systems and paperless tickets, giving them both a cost and an effectiveness advantage, as well as allowing a very flexible pricing system. They also offer web links to suppliers of hotels and car hire.
- *Robustness* – how easy is it to ensure that the competences are difficult to copy?

Johnson et al (2011) have developed the VRIN model as a way of assessing the strength of core competences

- **V** – value – core competences are of value when they provide potential competitive advantage at a cost that allows an organisation to achieve acceptable level of return. The key components here are taking advantage of opportunities and neutralising threats; value to customers, providing potential competitive advantage and cost.
- **R** – rarity – rare competences are those possessed uniquely by one or a few organisations. However, rarity may not last.
- **I** – inimitability – those competences that competitors find difficult to imitate or obtain. This is based on superior performance and linked capabilities (see above).
- **N** – non-substitutability – to what extent can competitors substitute other core competences for ours?

Teece (2007) has introduced the concept of dynamic capabilities – an organisation's ability to renew and recreate its strategic capabilities to meet the needs of changing environments. He suggests there are three types of dynamic capabilities: those concerned with sensing opportunities and threats, those concerned with seizing opportunities and those concerned with reconfiguring the capabilities of the organisation. There are clear parallels here with Hamel's concept of permanent revolution.

If it can develop a number of core competences, an organisation can greatly strengthen its strategic position. However, there is the danger that over time the core competences may no longer match the external environment. If computing becomes based on mobile phones rather than PCs and laptops, Dell's core competence may prove to be a weakness rather than a strength.

REFLECTIVE ACTIVITY 10.2

Harry Potter and the Portents of Doom

Bloomsbury Publishing was founded in 1986 by Nigel Newton, still the company's chairman. His mission was to publish books of the highest quality and to bring quality to the mass market (Bloomsbury 2007a). The company initially grew slowly and by the early 1990s its turnover was barely £10 million. It then went public in

1994, raising £5.5 million, followed by a rights issue in 1998 which raised another £6.1 million.

By then Bloombury's fortunes had been transformed when it accepted a children's book from an unknown author, J.K. Rowling. This was published as *Harry Potter and the Philosopher's Stone* in 1997, and the rest is history. Bloomsbury owns the English language rights to *Harry Potter* throughout the world except the US (where the rights are owned by Scholastic). Worldwide sales of the first six *Harry Potter* books totalled 325 million (Jordan 2007).

As the sales of *Harry Potter* soared, so did Bloomsbury's fortunes. Turnover rose from £20 million in 1999 to £109 million in 2005, while profit rose from £2.6 million in 1999 to £20.1 million in 2005 (Bloomsbury 2007b). However, events were then to show how dependent the company was on *Harry Potter*. The sixth book, *Harry Potter and the Half-Blood Prince*, was published in July 2005, and no Potter title appeared in 2006.

The result was that both sales and profits collapsed in 2006. 2006 turnover was £74 million, lower than 2003, while profits slumped to £5.2 million, the lowest figure since 2000. All the fall was due to a fall in turnover in the children's division (basically *Harry Potter*) (Shelley 2007).

Fortunately for Bloomsbury, the last book in the series was still in the pipeline, *Harry Potter and the Deathly Hallows*, published in July 2007. In the first 24 hours 2.6 million copies were sold in the UK, plus another 400,000 English-language copies in Germany (Bloomsbury 2007c).

Clearly the success of the seventh and final title will generate healthy profits for Bloomsbury in 2007, but this boost is likely to be short-lived because of the peculiar nature of the *Potter* market.

The major supermarkets all see *Harry Potter* as an ideal vehicle for a short-term price war. In a sense the fact that retailers make no money out of the book does not matter to Bloomsbury, because they get their £9.89 a copy anyway. But in another sense it does matter. The typical pattern with a bestselling book is that it is initially published in hardback at a high price, with only moderate but very profitable sales. Then a year later, a paperback edition appears, at a lower price, but with greater volume. The publisher has two bites at the apple. This does not happen with *Harry Potter*. Because of the discounting and hype, people who might have waited for the paperback buy the hardback instead. As a result sales of *Harry Potter* are minimal after the year in which the title is published.

Bloomsbury is a classic example of an organisation whose success is resource-driven. Its key asset is the intellectual property embedded in the *Harry Potter* titles. Like a pharmaceutical company with a blockbuster drug, it must ensure that a stream of new products is developed to replace the blockbuster. If this is not done, profits collapse.

Question

1   How can Bloomsbury escape from The Portents of Doom and ensure its long-term future?

STRATEGIC CHOICE

GENERIC STRATEGIES

The concept of generic strategy was introduced by Michael Porter (1985). He identified possible strategies as being:

- *Cost leadership* – an organisation will succeed if it can achieve lower costs than its competitors, but sell its products at or near the industry average price.
- *Differentiation* – an organisation will succeed if it can produce a differentiated product which commands a premium price, but at the same time keep its costs to the industry average.
- *Focus* – an organisation will succeed if it concentrates on a niche market, in which it can achieve either cost focus or differentiation focus.

Porter argued that, depending on the circumstances, any of the three generic strategies could be viable, but that a mixed or hybrid strategy, combining two of the generic strategies, was highly unlikely to be viable.

Porter's model is now a quarter of a century old, and it was developed a long time before the rise of the Internet and e-commerce. However, a study by Kim, Nam and Stimpert (2004) found that at least in the case of B2C (business to consumer) e-commerce, Porter's model still held, with one important exception.

The characteristics of B2C seem to make cost leadership an attractive strategy. E-commerce has very low entry barriers, strategic initiatives and pricing are transparent and can easily be copied by competitors, and there are increasing returns to scale. It therefore makes sense to opt for low prices in order to build up market share quickly. However, although cost leadership was a good entry strategy, it was less effective in the medium term. Because of the ease of market entry, it was all too easy to get into a cost-cutting and ultimately unprofitable price war.

Differentiation was also an effective strategy. Although price was the most important factor for low-value items, for higher-value ones like computers, furniture and cars, brand was more important, and so was the level of service. A superior level of service was some protection against the entry of low-cost competitors. Amazon was successful because of its enormous stock list, quick delivery and added-value services such as personalised recommendations. Focus was also effective. A niche market was a cheap way to enter and an easy way to develop and deliver value to the customer.

In their empirical research, Kim et al made two interesting findings. One was that despite Porter, the most effective strategy was a hybrid cost leadership–differentiation one, such as that pursued by Amazon. The second was that hybrid 'clicks and mortar' companies, with both a high street and an Internet presence, were more effective than 'pure play' e-commerce companies. Clicks and mortar companies often had an established brand reputation and also could offer additional services, such as the ability to return goods bought online to a local store.

The next case studies illustrate the application of two of Porter's generic strategies

CASE STUDY 10.2

RYANAIR – A SUCCESSFUL FOCUSED COST LEADER

In 1991, Ryanair was a small, unsuccessful Irish airline, when its newly appointed CEO, Michael O'Leary, went to America to meet Herbert Kelleher, Southwest Airlines' founder. The low-cost carrier had transformed the economics of air travel in the US. From Kelleher, O'Leary learned the importance of cost control, through the use of one type of plane, point-to-point flights only and elimination of all frills (*Business Week* 2006).

Since then, Ryanair has pushed the Southwest business model even further and has become the biggest and most profitable low-cost airline in Europe. Its success is based on three pillars – cut costs to the minimum ('nail down

costs'), 'give nothing, sell everything' and efficiency.

Cost-cutting

- Ryanair flies only one type of plane – the Boeing 737-800. This enables economies of scale in pilot training and maintenance.
- Ryanair's seat density on the 737 is 189, 15 per cent more than other airlines.
- Ryanair places its orders for aircraft in a counter-cyclical fashion, taking advantage of weak demand to wring better prices out of Boeing. For example, it placed a very big order in the immediate aftermath of 9/11. In 2007, it was rumoured by the

Financial Times to be selling some of its planes second hand for more than it had paid for them (Done 2007).

- The company's planes are stripped of all non-essentials – seats do not recline, there are no window blinds and no seat-back pockets. This shaves several hundred thousand dollars off the cost of each plane.
- Like other low-cost airlines, Ryanair does not use travel agents, thus saving up to 15 per cent commission, but it has gone further than its rivals in promoting booking over the Internet, which minimises handling costs. By 2007, 98 per cent of bookings were made over the Internet.
- Ryanair does not use air bridges at airports – passengers must walk to the plane. This saves on airport charges.
- Ryanair is notorious for using secondary, but very cheap, airports. These are often some way from the city which they nominally serve. Copenhagen-Malmo is actually in Sweden, not Denmark, and Frankfurt-Hahn is 140 km from Frankfurt. As easyJet repeatedly points out, this means that Ryanair's low fares are deceptive, as further transport costs are needed to reach the final destination. The secondary airports used are desperate for Ryanair's business and are prepared to offer extremely good terms.
- Advertising on planes is widespread, as well as liveries which attack other airlines.
- Extensive use is made of Eastern European (particularly Polish) cabin crew.
- Aircrew are worked hard. Ryanair pilots fly 887 hours a year, close to the legal maximum of 900. easyJet pilots fly 780 hours a year (Felsted 2003).

As a result of its rigorous cost-cutting programme, Ryanair's costs are two-thirds of those of easyJet, 60 per cent of

UK holiday charter airlines and half that of full service carriers (Thompson 2005).

Charges

- Ryanair is notorious for charging its staff for perks normally seen as free: crew must pay for their own uniforms, they must pay for water drunk on flights and they are banned from recharging their mobiles on company power sockets.
- Like other low-cost airlines, passengers are charged for refreshments on flights.
- Ryanair was the first airline to introduce a charge for baggage. This has the effect of raising revenue and also of cutting the number of bags carried, so lowering baggage-handling costs by an estimated £20 million a year (*Air Transport World* 2006a). By 2009 the charge was £15 per bag per way.
- In September 2007 it introduced a charge for checking in at the airport, which could only be avoided by checking in online (Milmo 2007). By 2009, it was also charging for checking in online. It also charges £5 per person per flight for payment using a credit or debit card.
- In 2002, Ryanair was heavily criticised when it refused to provide wheelchairs for disabled passengers at Stansted. A court ruling in 2004 judged that the responsibility for disabled passengers was shared between the airport and the airline. Ryanair's response was to place a 33p surcharge on all its ticket prices, which raised far more revenue for Ryanair than the costs which it was claimed to cover (Starmer-Smith 2006).

In 2009, easyJet made £511 million from baggage fees, insurance, early boarding and credit card fees – a fifth of its total revenue. Both the total and the proportion will be at least comparable for Ryanair (Milmo 2009).

Ryanair has made few friends. On the other hand, millions of travellers like its low fares. The airline is also unquestionably good at what it does.

Efficiency

As Ryanair gleefully points out on its website, the airline is extremely efficient. It claims:

- the best on-time record in Europe (91 per cent on-time arrivals in 2003, compared with 83 per cent for British Airways and 82 per cent for easyJet)
- the lowest level of cancellations
- fewest lost bags – 0.6 bags per 1,000 passengers in 2003, compared with BA's 14.2 (Ryanair 2003).

Results

Ryanair's model seems to be successful. In 2005, it had the fourth highest operating profit in Europe (behind BA, Air France-KLM and Lufthansa), and the twelfth highest in the world, the eleventh highest net profit in the world, and the fifteenth highest number of passengers carried (*Air Transport World* 2006b). In August 2005, for the first time it carried more passengers than the entire worldwide BA network (Ryanair 2007).

Conclusion

Ryanair seems to have got the focused cost leadership business model cracked. However, there are three potential clouds on the horizon:

- In 2007, Ryanair operated 136 planes. However, it also had orders which would take its fleet size to 262 (Done 2007). Given Ryanair's flight pattern, it requires 250,000 passengers a year (per plane) to operate a plane profitably. To fill all the planes on order, Ryanair would have to nearly double its present number of about 45 million passengers a year. Can the company's growth rate be maintained indefinitely?
- The full-service carriers are fighting back. They have cut their fares, increased their online bookings and heavily marketed their own selling features – meals, free drinks, seat allocations, more convenient airports.
- There are ominous signs that O'Leary is being distracted from the business model. In 2006, he tried to take over the Irish state carrier Aer Lingus when it was privatised, with the intention of operating it as a going concern, including its long-haul flights.

CASE STUDY 10.3

NORTHERN ROCK: A FAILED FOCUSED DIFFERENTIATOR

Over a weekend in the middle of September 2007, the UK experienced the first serious run on a bank for a century. Hundreds of people queued for hours outside the branches of Northern Rock, desperate to withdraw their savings before the bank collapsed. How had a previously well-respected bank come to such a pass?

Northern Rock was a typical building society – taking in deposits from its members and lending these out as

mortgages. It was safe, solid and respectable. Its share of the national mortgage market was 2 per cent. It was also very popular in the north-east because it had been very sympathetic to miners in mortgage arrears during the mining strike of the early 1980s.

In 1997, it demutualised, forming Northern Rock plc, and its status changed from a building society to a bank. As a public company its priorities changed. Rather than providing a service for its members, its priority was now to make profits for its shareholders. Within months, it showed a new face when it was criticised by the Office of Fair Trading of being 'cavalier' for unilaterally changing the terms offered to its depositors (Hughes and Tighe 2007).

Unlike some of the other demutualised ex-building societies, Northern Rock did not attempt to develop general banking services, but continued to specialise in mortgages. However, it was faced with problems in expanding in this area. First, it only had 79 branches, mainly concentrated in the relatively impoverished north-east. This limited its ability to raise funds from depositors (known as retail funds). By comparison, the leading building society, Nationwide, had over 700 branches, and the big high street banks had thousands.

Northern Rock tackled this problem by raising funds through the interbank market, from other financial institutions (known as wholesale funds). As a building society, it would have been limited by law from raising more than 50 per cent of its funds from the wholesale market, but no such restrictions applied to banks (BBC2 2007). At its peak in the early autumn of 2007, Northern Rock raised more than three-quarters of its funds from the wholesale market, on terms ranging from overnight to three months.

Wholesale borrowing is generally regarded as more risky and volatile than retail borrowing. Although retail depositors can in theory withdraw many of their funds on demand, in practice they are highly unlikely to do so. On the other hand, other banks will move their money elsewhere if they think they can get a better return. Northern Rock's reliance on wholesale funds was described by one experienced banker as akin to overtaking a queue of traffic on the outside of a bend – 'everyone knows it

works (for a time), but only fools or the inexperienced would attempt it' (Croggon 2007).

Even when Northern Rock obtained more funds, it still had to persuade people to take out more of its mortgages. It did this through aggressive lending policies. It became known as the bank which would lend even if you had a patchy credit record. It was also prepared to lend more than other banks or building societies. In 2002, it introduced its Together loan, which allowed a borrower to borrow up to 125 per cent of a property's valuation, or six times' annual income. As other lenders were not prepared to lend more than four times' income, borrowers flocked to Northern Rock.

Massive expansion continued throughout the first half of 2007, at a time when increasing warnings were being issued of the frothy state of the UK housing market and of a worrying level of consumer debt. In the first half of 2007, Northern Rock took a 25 per cent share of the new mortgage market, making it the biggest mortgage provider (Collinson and Seager 2007).

With hindsight, it was clear that Northern Rock was over-trading and taking unacceptable risks. In June 2007 it was forced to issue a profits warning and its shares started to fall. Its strategy was described by Professor Willem Buiter, one of the founder members of the Bank of England's Monetary Policy Committee, as 'an extremely aggressive and high-risk strategy' (Duncan and Webster 2007).

Northern Rock might still have got away with it had it not been caught up in the backlash from a separate but related financial crisis, the sub-prime crisis in the US. Here, US financial institutions had pursued a Northern Rock-style strategy of aggressive lending to poor credit risks (the sub-prime market), eventually leading to a collapse of the US housing market in the summer of

2007. One consequence of this was a freezing-up of the interbank lending market in the UK, as well as the US. This meant that Northern Rock, which continually needed to roll over its wholesale borrowing, faced a liquidity crisis.

The crisis for Northern Rock came to a head on Thursday, 13 September, when the bank applied to the Bank of England for emergency assistance (known as 'lender of last resort'). On Friday, 14 September, the Bank of England agreed to lend virtually unlimited funds to Northern Rock, but at a penal rate of interest, believed to be 7 per cent.

This should have been the end of the crisis, but Northern Rock retail depositors interpreted this as a sign that the bank was about to fail, and a run on the bank's cash started and quickly accelerated. Bank deposits are guaranteed, but only up to a maximum of £35,000, and only up to 90 per cent. On Friday and Saturday, a sum estimated to be between £2 billion and £3 billion was withdrawn from Northern Rock branches. Eventually, to stop the run, the Chancellor, Alistair Darling, announced on Monday, 16 September, that the Government would guarantee all deposits in Northern Rock, without limit. The immediate crisis was over, but the troubles of Northern Rock then became part of the general financial crisis of 2008–10. Northern Rock was nationalised and the deposit guarantee was raised to 100 per cent of £50,000.

This case illustrates several important points. One is that Northern Rock's strategy differentiated it from the rest of the mortgage industry, but only at the price of unacceptably high risk. Second, the case demonstrates the nature of moral hazard. The Bank of England was reluctant to intervene at an earlier stage in the crisis because of the risk of moral hazard – that in effect a rescue would reward Northern Rock for its reckless behaviour and might encourage other institutions to be reckless in the future. Eventually, the Bank of England had no choice and was forced to intervene to safeguard the stability of the whole banking system, as there was a risk that the panic might spread to other institutions. The bailout safeguarded not only Northern Rock's depositors, who were innocent victims, but also the bank's management and shareholders, who should have known better (Davies 2007).

Porter's generic strategy concept has been further developed by Bowman and Faulkner (1996), who propose the strategy clock, based on a combination of price and perceived added value. They identified eight possible strategies:

- *low price/low added value* – not likely to be feasible in the long term unless the organisation operates in a protected niche
- *low price/standard added value* – equates to Porter's cost leadership
- *low price/high added value (hybrid)* – the strategy pursued by Japanese companies in the 1970s and 1980s, when they were gaining a foothold in European markets
- *standard price/high added value (differentiation)* – this would be a sensible strategy as a progression from the hybrid strategy
- *high price/high added value (focused differentiation)* – likely to be a niche strategy, similar to Porter's differentiation focus
- *high price/standard added value* – not a long-term viable strategy; why should customers pay more if they are not gaining added value?
- *high price/low added value* – only feasible for a monopoly in a market which is not contestable

- *standard price/low added value* – not viable in the long term; what is in it for the customer?

SELECTION OF STRATEGIES

This is concerned not with what strategies should be chosen, but how they should be chosen. Johnson et al (2011) propose four models:

FORMAL EVALUATION

Here the choice is based solely on analytical techniques. The decision process is impersonal and rational, and appears to be objective. This avoids the risk of taking decisions solely on gut feeling, but it should be remembered that a lot of the analytical techniques are themselves in practice subjective.

ENFORCED CHOICE

Here choice is imposed on the organisation from outside. This may be because of the dominant influence of an external stakeholder – for example, a supplier to Marks & Spencer has very little control over its own strategy. However, in the long term, even a firm in this situation does have some strategic choice – to widen its customer base, for example.

LEARNING FROM EXPERIENCE

The emphasis here is on incremental change on a pilot basis with operating units, and then the application of the experience learned from this throughout the organisation. This method is increasingly used by government, which trials new policy initiatives through a pilot study before going for a national launch, and by many manufacturers, who test-market new products before attempting a national launch. It is similar to Quinn's concept of logical incrementalism, which we discussed earlier. The advantage is that it pushes responsibility for strategic development down the organisation, but there is the possible disadvantage that there is never a fundamental strategic rethink – the organisation can suffer from strategic drift.

COMMAND

Here the dominant stakeholder (who may be the CEO, the biggest shareholder, or a government department) selects the strategic direction and imposes it on the organisation. This has been the experience of the National Health Service, which has had fundamental strategic change imposed on it by successive governments at regular intervals.

EVALUATION OF STRATEGIES

Possible strategies should be evaluated on three levels: suitability, acceptability and feasibility.

Suitability

Is this a strategy which will produce a sound fit between the organisation and its environment?

- Will it exploit opportunities in the environment and avoid or neutralise threats?
- Will it capitalise on the organisation's strengths and core competences and avoid or neutralise weaknesses?

Various analytical techniques can be used to help answer these questions:

Life cycle analysis – the consultants Arthur D Little have identified the life cycle/ portfolio matrix (see Johnson et al 2011). Here the strategies which should be adopted depend on the stage of the product/industry life cycle (embryonic, growing, mature or ageing), and the competitive position of the organisation (dominant, strong, favourable, tenable or weak). For example, the prescribed strategies for a strong firm in a growing industry are: fast grow, catch up, attain cost leadership or differentiation; while for a weak firm in an embryonic industry they are: find niche, catch up or grow with industry. The model is open to criticism, as the definitions used are subjective (what is a favourable position in one environment may be a weak one in another), and because, like all models, it ignores all variables except those actually built into the model (stage of maturity and competitive position). For example, it ignores speed of technological development.

Portfolio analysis – we discussed the Boston Matrix in Chapter 3. Briefly, this categorised product lines on a matrix of market share and market growth rate, as:

- *Cash cows* – low market growth, high market share
- *Stars* – high market growth, high market share
- *Question marks* – high market growth, low market share
- *Dogs* – low market growth, low market share.

Here the preferred strategic options would be to attempt to balance the portfolio between stars and cash cows. Stars are profitable, but they do not generate much cash, while cash cows may be less profitable but are highly cash-generative. Hence use cash cows to finance stars. As with the life cycle model, this is superficially attractive, but again it ignores other variables.

Value chain analysis – value chain analysis is yet another model developed by Michael Porter. He says that the activities of an organisation should be seen as a sequence of primary events:

- inbound logistics, deliveries, storage, etc
- operations
- outbound logistics (warehousing, wholesalers, deliveries, etc)
- marketing and sales
- service

while underpinning all of these were support activities:

- the firm's infrastructure
- human resource management
- technology
- procurement (purchasing, raising capital, recruitment).

All of these serve to add value for the organisation and form the value chain. The greater the synergies between the various elements, the greater the added value. Conversely, the whole value chain is only as strong as its weakest link. The aim of strategy should therefore be to strengthen the value chain as a whole, by building on existing strengths or correcting weaknesses.

For example, the primary part of the chain might be strong, but the organisation might have problems caused by high turnover of staff. The strategic choice here would be to concentrate on improving staff turnover using HR techniques. Alternatively, the product might be strong, but its reputation is let down by poor after-sales service. After digging deeper, it might be discovered that the IT systems supporting service are inadequate.

The strength of the value chain technique is that it forces an analysis of how the organisation actually functions and it avoids over-concentration on some of the more obvious strategic possibilities, such as merger or takeover. The weakness is that it is exclusively inward-looking. It should be combined with a rigorous analysis of fit with the environment.

Acceptability

Strategies have to be acceptable to internal and external stakeholders. This can be assessed in three ways: return, risk and stakeholder reaction.

Return can be assessed using a range of standard accounting techniques, including profitability analysis (discounted cash flow, etc), shareholder value analysis (looking at the overall increase in value for the shareholder, using techniques such as economic value added), or cost–benefit analysis (looking at non-financial as well as financial factors).

Risk can be assessed using techniques, including:

- *Break-even analysis* – if the break-even point for the new strategy is a very high percentage of capacity, the project is highly risky.
- *Ratio analysis* – if the new strategy will result in very low levels of liquidity, as measured by standard ratios, it is high risk.
- *Sensitivity analysis* – how sensitive is the profit of the project to a shortfall in any of the key financial variables?

Stakeholder reactions can be assessed using techniques such as stakeholder modelling. Stakeholders may well have strong views on risk and these should be taken into account.

CASE STUDY 10.4

STAKEHOLDER ACCEPTABILITY

An acceptable strategy – Ben & Jerry's and Unilever

Ben & Jerry's ice cream was one of the leading lights of the ethical business movement. It was not only concerned to trade ethically; it also wanted to change the world. It donated heavily to radical causes and was deeply involved in the anti-globalisation movement. These values were fully supported by its staff and customers, both key stakeholders.

In April 2000, Ben & Jerry's was taken over by the strait-laced Anglo-Dutch conglomerate Unilever, a classic representative of the globalisation that Ben & Jerry's had opposed. Although it had a good ethical reputation, Unilever was in no sense radical. Ben Cohen, the joint founder of Ben & Jerry's, forecast that the takeover would lead to the destruction of the company.

However, when Unilever appointed a 25-year Unilever man, Yves Couette, to run Ben & Jerry's, he was given the licence to be a 'grain of sand in the eye'

of Unilever. He abandoned his suit and tie and followed a deliberate policy of empowerment and delegation. Tough profit targets were set, but Couette pointed out to staff that this would mean that more money would be donated to charity through the Ben & Jerry Foundation, which would continue to have a free hand to support any charity or movement which it chose.

An unacceptable strategy – Marconi

Throughout the 1980s and 1990s, GEC was seen as a safe, rather stolid company, dominated by the safety-first philosophy of its long-time chairman, Arnold (Lord) Weinstock. The company prospered in household electrical goods and defence electronics and built up a bank balance of several billion pounds. It appealed to risk-averse shareholders.

In the late 1990s, new management, headed by George Simpson, decided on a radical new strategy. The defence electronics business was sold to British

Aerospace, most of the domestic electric businesses (Hotpoint, etc) were sold, and the company, now renamed Marconi, began a dash for growth in the exciting new world of Internet electronics. The rationale was that Marconi would benefit from the dot-com boom which was raging at the time.

Unfortunately, the purchases were made right at the peak of the dot-com bubble, and when the bubble burst, many of the new acquisitions were effectively worthless. Marconi's share price plummeted, and when the company eventually went through a financial restructuring, shareholders effectively lost all their money.

Like all shareholders, the Marconi shareholders should have realised that any share investment is by its very nature risky, but they could legitimately argue that they had originally bought their shares in GEC precisely because it was seen as a low-risk company (Birkinshaw 2004).

Feasibility

Strategies have to be feasible in terms of resource availability. Techniques to measure this include:

- *Funds flow analysis* – what is the implication for future cash flows? If sufficient cash is not currently available, can it be acquired on reasonable terms?
- *Break-even analysis* – what is the break-even point given the present cost structure? If the break-even point is too high, can the cost structure be improved?
- *Resource deployment analysis* – what are the key resources and competences required for each strategy? Does the organisation already possess them? If not, can it reasonably acquire them?

STRATEGIC OPTION SCREENING

Several methods can be used to screen options to see whether they meet criteria on suitability, acceptability and feasibility. These include:

Ranking

Here options are assessed against key factors in the environment, resources and stakeholder expectations, and a score (or ranking) established for each option. To take a very simple example, assume that a company has two strategic options, A and B, and two success criteria, profitability and stakeholder acceptability. It has established that it regards profitability as more important and has given this a weighting of 70. Stakeholder acceptability has a weighting of 30 (producing a total weighting of 100).

Strategy A scores 50 out of 70 for profitability, but only 10 out of 30 for stakeholder acceptability. Strategy B scores less well on profitability, scoring 30 out of 70, but it scores 20 out of 30 for stakeholder acceptability.

This gives a total score for strategy A of 60/100 (50 + 10), and a total score for strategy B of 50/100 (30 + 20). Strategy A is thus the preferred option.

Decision trees

Here options are progressively eliminated by testing them against various criteria. For example, a company has two decision criteria, high growth (most important) and low cost (less important). It is considering four strategies:

- Strategy W – high growth, high cost
- Strategy X – high growth, low cost

- Strategy Y – low growth, low cost
- Strategy Z – low growth, high cost.

The first decision step would eliminate strategies Y and Z, because they are low growth, leaving W and X. The next decision step would eliminate W, leaving X as the preferred strategy.

Scenario planning

Here the options are evaluated against various scenarios for the future. For example, if the organisation thinks that the most likely future for UK exchange rate is stability, this would favour a policy of manufacturing in the UK. If the most likely scenario is seen as a rising pound, this would favour manufacturing overseas.

REFLECTIVE ACTIVITY 10.3

Strategic evaluation

A risk-averse firm with a strong current financial position, but little access to long-term capital, has decided that it must adopt a policy of unrelated diversification in order to reduce its dependence on a declining industry. It has evaluated a number of areas for diversification and decided on the appropriate industry to enter. It is now considering the best way to enter the new market.

Its options are:

A – Develop and manufacture a new product.

B – Manufacture an existing product under licence.

C – Set up a joint venture with a firm that already has expertise in this field.

D – Buy out a firm already in the industry.

E – Market under their brand name an existing Taiwanese product not currently imported into the UK.

They have established the following criteria and weighted them as follows:

		Weighting
A	Low risk	40
B	Speedy entry into the market	20
C	Low capital cost	20
D	Profitability	15
E	Short payback period	5

Questions

1   Discuss the advantages and disadvantages of each method of entry.

2   Using your own judgement, assign scores to each strategy and rank them.

STRATEGIC IMPLEMENTATION

The final stage in the strategy process is implementation – having decided on the chosen strategy, how is it put into practice? Frequently this will be the most difficult phase of the whole process. It involves a key competency of all managers – the ability to manage change.

INCREMENTAL AND TRANSFORMATIONAL CHANGE

Most of the writers on strategic implementation distinguish between incremental and transformational change, although their terminology varies. Johnson et al (2011) see strategic change on a two-by-two matrix, type of change and extent of change. A small change is incremental, a large change transformational. Each is of two types, dependent on whether the change is proactive or reactive. Proactive incremental change is tuning, reactive incremental change adaptation, while transformational change is divided into planed and forced change.

Walton (1999) defines transformational change as change which results in entirely new behaviour on the part of organisational members. He sees transformational change as in its very nature strategic. However, drawing on the work of Quinn on logical incrementalism, he sees incremental change as a possible route to strategic change. He also identifies transitional change, the process of carrying out change.

Porter (1999) concentrates on the outcome rather than the process. Changes such as the introduction of re-engineering or total quality management are transformational, but they are not strategic. He sees them as improving operational effectiveness rather than changing the strategic position of the organisation. They are about doing better the same things as the competition are doing. Operational effectiveness is about running the same race faster; strategy is about running a different race.

MODELS OF CHANGE

The classic model of change was identified by Lewin in the 1950s and developed by Schein in the 1980s (Armstrong 1999; Walton 1999). They identified three stages in change management:

- *Unfreezing* – creating a readiness for change, through creation of a sense of anxiety about the present situation. The sequence here is to enable those involved to be convinced of the need for change.
- *Movement* – taking action that will encourage the desired new behaviour patterns. This involves doing things differently, based on access to new information, and identifying with new role models.
- *Refreezing* – embedding the new ways of working into the organisation.

Lewin also developed the concept of force field analysis – analysing the restraining and driving forces within the organisation which oppose or support the proposed change and then taking steps to encourage the driving forces and decrease the restraining forces.

Beer took a different approach. He argued that the approach which tries to change attitudes in order to change behaviour is flawed. He argued that change should be approached in an opposite way – put people in new roles which require new behaviours and this will change their attitudes. This is similar to the theory of cognitive dissonance, which we discussed in Chapter 9 in relation to ethics. Beer proposed a six-stage model of change (CIPD 2004):

- Mobilise commitment to change through joint analysis of problems.
- Develop a shared vision.
- Foster consensus and commitment to the shared vision.
- Spread the word about the change.
- Institutionalise the change through formal policies.
- Monitor and adjust as needed.

The Lewin and Beer models both come out of relatively placid environments. They have been criticised for their assumption that it is possible to plan an orderly transition from one static state to another static state (Burnes 2004). In a more dynamic and chaotic environment like that experienced at present, a more continuous and open-ended change process is more appropriate. They also assume that a 'one size fits all' model of change is appropriate, whereas a more modern perspective would be to take a contingency approach and to argue that each organisation has a unique relationship with its environment. Its approach to change should reflect this.

The emergent approach to change as put forward by Burnes and Shaw (CIPD 2004) stresses that change is not linear – it is not a movement from state A to state B – it is continuous and messy. Just like its environment, an organisation is in a continuous state of flux, and the forces for change emerge as the organisation engages with its environment. Change in this model is bottom–up rather than top–down, and it emerges through experimentation. What is important is to ensure that the organisation is responsive to change, and the best way of doing this is to ensure that the organisation is a learning organisation.

McCann (2004) relates change directly to the changing nature of the environment. In a placid environment, change is likely to be episodic, that is, low level and easily managed. Here the objective is to control change. Organisations cope with this by building some slack into their systems, which can act as a buffer in periods of change. As the environment grew more turbulent, change became continuous. Here the objective is to embrace change, by building agility into the organisation and removing barriers to change. Finally, in a very turbulent environment, shocks such as 9/11, the credit crunch or the swine flu pandemic will lead to disruptive change. To cope with this the organisation must prepare for change, by planning for contingencies and assuring a capacity for recovery and renewal.

OPEN SYSTEMS

The open systems school is primarily interested in seeing organisations in their entirety and therefore takes a holistic view rather than a particular perspective. This is reflected in its approach to change. Burke (1980) suggested this is informed by three factors:

- Sub-systems are interdependent. Therefore account must be taken of the dependence of other parts of the organisation.
- Training, as a mechanism for change, is unlikely to succeed on its own. This is because it concentrates on the individual and not on the organisational level. Burke argues that 'there is scant evidence that attempting to change the individual will in turn change the organisation'.
- For success, organisations need to tap into and direct the energy and talent of their workforce. This involves the removal of barriers and the promotion of positive reinforcement. Given that change is likely to require altering such things as norms, reward systems and work structures, the approach must therefore be at an organisational level, rather than an individual or group perspective.

Open systems approaches have attracted much research and interest but some shortcomings have been identified. Butler (1985) argued that social systems are so complex that sorting out all the cause and effect relationships may be impossible, while Beach (1980) argued that open systems theory runs the risk of being abstract rather than operationally useful.

MANAGING CHANGE

Kotter (1995) proposes an eight-step plan for transformation:

1   Establishing a sense of urgency – realising that change is needed.

2   Forming a powerful guiding coalition – a powerful and influential group of change leaders is needed.

3   Creating a vision – what will things be like after the change is achieved?

4   Communicating the vision.

5   Empowering others to act on the vision.

6   Planning for and creating short-term wins – a long change process that appears to be getting nowhere can be demotivating. Building in some short-term wins can improve morale.

7   Consolidating improvements and producing still more change.

8   Institutionalising new approaches – similar to Lewin's refreezing process.

Bridges and Mitchell (2000) identify three stages in a change programme:

1   *Saying goodbye* – letting go of the way that things used to be.

2   *Shifting into neutral* – the in-between stage when nothing seems to be happening, but everyone is in a stressful state of limbo. In the case of a major merger, this phase might take two years.

3   *Moving forward* – when people have to behave in a new way.

They describe seven steps in managing transition:

1   Describe the change and why it must happen – in one minute or less.

2   Make sure that the details of the change are planned carefully and that someone is responsible for each detail.

3   Understand who is going to have to let go of what.

4   Make sure that people are helped to let go of the past.

5   Help people through the neutral zone with communication, stressing the '4 Ps':

- the purpose – why we have to do this
- the picture – what it will look and feel like when we get there
- the plan – how we will get there
- the part – what each person needs to do.

6   Create temporary solutions to the temporary problems found in the neutral zone.

7   Help people launch the new beginning.

👁 **MOSES IN THE WILDERNESS**

CASE STUDY 10.5

Bridges and Mitchell discuss the change management techniques used by Moses on his way to the Promised Land.

Magnify the plagues – Moses had to convince a key stakeholder (Pharaoh) that change was needed – that he had to let the Jews go. He did this through creating problems for Pharaoh – the seven plagues. The worse the current situation seems, the greater the impetus for change.

Mark the ending – after the Jews crossed the Red Sea, there was (literally) no going back.

Deal with the 'murmuring' – don't be surprised when people lose confidence in the neutral zone. Moses faced lots of whingeing. He dealt with it by talking to people about their concerns.

Build up change champions – Moses and his lieutenant Joshua appointed a new cadre of judges to champion the change.

Capitalise on creative opportunities – it was in the Wilderness, not in the Promised Land, that the Ten Commandments were handed down.

Resist the urge to rush ahead – not much seems to be happening in the neutral zone, but it is where the true

> transformation takes place. Moses was in the Wilderness for 40 years!
>
> *Different stages need different leadership styles* – Moses was an ideal leader for the neutral zone, but the Promised Land required a new type of leadership, provided by the conqueror of Jericho, Joshua.

RESISTANCE TO CHANGE

Pugh (1978) sees organisational change as a paradox. Situations and problems which cry out most strongly for change are the very ones which resist change most stubbornly. Individuals perceive change as a threat and react like rabbits caught in the headlights of a car – they go rigid.

Resistance to change can be better understood if you view organisations as a coalition of interest groups in tension. The organisation is a particular balance of forces which has been hammered out over time. Any change which threatens the current balance will encounter resistance. Combine this with psychological resistance from rigid people under threat and it is easy to see how managing change is difficult. Organisations are ultra-stable – they run like mad to stay in the same place.

As a consequence, real organisational change often:

- comes about much too late
- is a response to a threat posed by situations of considerable failure
- happens with insufficient thought and little consideration of alternatives
- is in order to live to fight another day.

At a more immediate level, change is most likely to be acceptable by individuals or departments who are basically successful in their tasks but who are currently experiencing difficulties. They will have the two basic ingredients of *confidence in their ability* and *motivation to change*. The next most likely to change are the successful. They will have the confidence but might not have the motivation. The least likely to understand and accept change are the unsuccessful.

An effective manager:

- anticipates the need for change
- diagnoses the nature of the change that is required and carefully considers alternatives
- manages the change process over a period of time so that it is effective and accepted.

Pugh has six rules for managing change effectively:

1   Work hard at establishing the need for change.

2   Don't only think about the change, think through it. This means thinking about the effects the change will have on individuals in terms of their jobs, status, prestige and so on.

3   Initiate change through informal discussions to get feedback and participation.

4   Positively encourage those concerned to give their objections.

5   Be prepared to change yourself.

6   Monitor the change and reinforce it.

Resistance to change can be of two types:

1   resistance to the content of change – that is, opposition to the specific nature of the change

2   tesistance to the process of change – that is, opposition to how to the change is introduced.

Each might be a perfectly rational response to change, however inconvenient to management.

Armstrong (1999) identifies eight reasons why individuals might resist change:

1 the shock of the new – people tend to be conservative and they do not want to move too far from their comfort zones. To this I would add regret for the passing of the old

2 economic fears – threats to wages or job security

3 inconvenience

4 uncertainty

5 symbolic fears – the loss of a symbol, like a car parking space, may suggest that bigger and more threatening changes are on the way

6 threats to interpersonal relationships

7 threat to status or skill – a change may be seen as deskilling

8 competence fears – concern about the ability to cope or acquire new skills.

On the other hand, Woodward and Hendry (2004), in a survey of financial service organisations in the City of London, found that while change put pressure on employees, a majority saw change as a part of organisational life and felt positive about it.

THE ROLE OF HR IN CHANGE MANAGEMENT

The crucial role of HR in change management can be clearly identified using Beer's model of change. HR intervention is crucial at each stage of the model, as follows:

1 *Mobilise commitment to change through joint analysis of problems* – HR should play a leading role in benchmarking and other environment-scanning techniques and so help to spot the need for change. HR staff are likely to be the organisers of the teams and workshops who are involved in problem identification and analysis. Underpinning this should be a learning organisation, in which HR should be a prime driver.

2 *Develop a shared vision* – this involves an understanding of the culture of the organisation and the ability to support and direct the visions which underpin the culture.

3 *Foster consensus and commitment to the shared vision* – it is essential that those affected by the change should feel that they have ownership of it. Developing and supporting ownership is a key HR skill, as is the fostering and supporting of change champions.

4 *Spread the word about the change* – here, as noted by McCarthy (2004), communication is key. McCarthy stresses that this should involve communication *with*, rather than communication *at*, those involved. He suggests the concept of 'conversation' as being appropriate here.

5 *Institutionalise the change through formal policies* – this may well include the development of new HR policies on recruitment, reward and development. It is crucial that the reward system supports the new ways of doing things, for example.

6 *Monitor and adjust as needed* – HR policy will need to be proactive after the change process is apparently completed. Development policies should be responsive to the need for any new competencies which become apparent.

Armstrong (1999) identifies a number of 'guidelines for change management', in most of which the role of HR is key. These include:

- commitment and visionary leadership from the top
- understanding the culture
- development of temperament and leadership skills at all levels which support change
- an environment conducive to change – a learning organisation
- full participation of those involved, so that they can own the change
- the reward system should recognise success in achieving change
- a willingness to learn from failure – a support culture rather than a blame culture
- support for change agents
- protection of those adversely affected by change.

Ridgeway and Wallace (1994) discuss the role of HR in managing a common strategic change – a takeover. Here matching the culture of the predator and the target are key. They quote from Furnham and Gunter (1993) on how such a match should be identified. It would involve:

- identifying the culture of the acquiring company
- deciding on any changes needed to ensure that culture supports the proposed strategy
- identifying potential acquisitions and their cultures
- isolating likely changes to those cultures
- designing a format for assessing other cultures
- establishing criteria by which to identify suitable acquisitions.

Crucial here is establishing how the senior management of the target company will fit with the acquirer's culture, and what senior staff gaps will be exposed.

The HR department of the acquiring company will also be responsible for ensuring that the procedures and systems of the two companies are compatible, or can be made compatible, including any industrial relations implications. During the takeover process, the HR department also needs to manage communication. This will involve close liaison with PR, as employees of the target company will get a lot of their information about the takeover via the media.

REFLECTIVE ACTIVITY 10.4

Pearmount College

Pearmount College is a medium-sized further education (FE) college in the town of Hetherleigh (population 75,000). In many ways it is a typical FE college. In its Ofsted inspections, most aspects are rated as satisfactory (grade 3, the middle of the five grades available). A third of its courses are rated as above average, a third as below average. However, Pearmount is not typical in that it is a tertiary college. Unlike most FE colleges, it is responsible for all post-16 education in Hetherleigh. This gives the college a particular social responsibility. As the only post-16 provider, it cannot be selective in its recruitment policy. It is expected to provide educational opportunities for all of the post-16 population in the town.

There are four main types of post-16 providers, all of which compete to score highly in government league tables. These are school sixth forms, which are often selective; sixth form colleges, which are almost always selective; tertiary colleges, which are normally non-selective; and ordinary FE colleges, which tend to offer mainly vocational courses rather than A-levels. The main league table competition is between sixth forms, sixth form colleges and tertiary colleges, and concentrates on A-level results. Sixth form colleges tend to score more highly than school sixth forms and tertiary colleges. A recent Ofsted inspection of Pearmount noted that its A-level results were at the FE college average, but below the average for sixth form colleges. It also criticised teaching as unimaginative, although it said that some vocational provision was excellent.

Post-16 education is funded by the Learning and Skills Council, under government guidance. Government funding policy is to concentrate on three main target areas – full-time 16–19 education, adult basic literacy and numeracy skills, and adult level 2 qualifications (broadly GCSE grade A–C level). FE and tertiary colleges have responded to this by withdrawing from adult education, unless it fits into the funding priorities, or is fully funded by employers. Pearmount is typical in this. Over the last decade it has withdrawn from many advanced vocational and professional part-time programmes and concentrated much more on full-time 16–19 programmes. The other continuing pressure from the LSC is to drive up the quality of further education provision, with the threat of withdrawing funding from courses within the priority areas which are deemed to be of low quality.

Jim Merryweather was appointed as the new principal of Pearmount College in September 2006, following the retirement of his predecessor, who had taken an active role in the town. Within a month of taking up his post, he produced a new teaching and learning strategy for the college. This stressed individual daily targets for students, with daily assessment and measurement of achievement; all assignment work to be completed in college; and fortnightly reports to parents on progress and attendance. His aim was to make the college one of the best sixth forms in the country.

Although there was some concern that the new strategy seemed to focus solely on full-time 16–19 students, it was broadly welcomed by teaching staff and rapid progress was made in its implementation.

However, Jim also faced the problem that many of his staff were ageing, while others, who mainly taught vocational programmes for adults, were seeing much of their workload disappearing. Clearly the college staffing needed to be restructured. One way to do this could have been an early retirement

programme, but what often happens in these programmes is that the people opting to take early retirement are the very people who you do not want to lose. Another option could have been a programme of retraining and redeployment.

Jim's solution was to propose a radical restructuring, which was announced just before the Easter holidays in April 2007. A new staffing structure was proposed, with more higher-paid posts, but also some low-level posts with a salary ceiling well below that previously available to lecturers. All members of staff were expected to re-apply for posts under the new structure, with the clear expectation that some would be unsuccessful.

In addition, holidays were reduced and the normal working week was increased to 37 hours, all of which could in theory be spent teaching. The working week was also extended to five and a half days, and staff could be requested to work on Saturdays. Staff would no longer be entitled to overtime or time off in lieu.

The reaction of staff was one of horror, particularly as the new posts were advertised internally immediately, although the proposals came under the 90-day consultation period for major redundancies. Teaching staff held a number of one-day strikes, were fully supported by their union and the students' union, and also attracted a lot of support within the town.

By the end of the summer term in 2007, half the teaching staff had been made redundant, had found new posts or had taken early retirement. There was severe concern that college staffing would be inadequate to meet demand in 2007–08, and also that the adverse publicity would dissuade many potential students from attending the college.

Questions

1 Critically evaluate Jim's strategy for implementing change at Pearmount College.

2 What techniques do you think can be used to overcome resistance to change?

STRATEGIC LEADERSHIP

WHAT DO STRATEGIC LEADERS DO?

In this section we examine the practical things which strategic leaders do to contribute to the success of the chosen strategy(ies) of the organisation.

WHAT BUSINESS ARE WE IN?

One of the first tasks of a leader is to define what business we are in. Defining a business too narrowly could lead to stagnation, while defining it too widely may lead to imprecision and drift.

In 2001, Hornby, the model railway company, was in trouble. Shareholders wanted to sell the company, but nobody wanted to buy it. The company was seen as staid and old-fashioned. Seventy per cent of its sales were to adult hobbyists, and 30 per cent to children, and marketing was heavily based on nostalgia for a vanished world of stream railways. After the failure of the attempt to sell the company, new management was brought in, and Frank Martin became chief executive. He was horrified to find that the old management had just turned down the licence to make a Hogwarts Express set to tie in with Harry Potter and he quickly reversed the decision (Teather 2007).

What business is Hornby in? The old management felt that it was a hobby business and should not be interested in products, like Hogwarts, aimed at children. Martin took the view that this was short-sighted. The hobbyist market was ageing, and unless a new segment of customers was attracted, the business would eventually die. Under his leadership, licensing of media tie-in properties has become an integral part of the business. This seems to have been the right strategic decision, as the share price is now eight times higher than when he first joined the business.

DEVELOPING VISION AND SHAPING VALUES

The strategic leader determines or is associated with an overall vision that motivates others, helps create the shared beliefs within which people can work together more effectively and shapes more detailed strategy developed by others in an organisation.

The Unilever chief executive Paul Polman epitomises value-driven leadership. He stresses how Unilever tries to gain the trust of its customers with respect to sustainability, and notes the importance of having personal values aligned with those of one's employer. He has driven Unilever's 'sustainable living plan', launched in 2010. This has three objectives, to be achieved by 2020: to cut the environmental impact of Unilever's products in half, to source sustainably all its agricultural supplies and to improve the health and well-being of a billion people worldwide (Bird 2010; Saunders 2011).

ENCOURAGING LEARNING

The learning organisation is an organisation that is capable of continual regeneration from the variety of knowledge, experience and skills that encourages questioning and challenge. Watkins and Marsick (1993) identify seven dimensions of the learning organisation:

- Create continuous learning opportunities.
- Promote dialogue and enquiry.
- Promote collaboration and team learning.
- Empower people towards a collective vision.
- Establish systems to capture and share learning.
- Connect the organisation to its environment.

- Provide strategic leadership for learning.

The aim of top management should be to facilitate rather than direct strategy development by building pluralistic organisations, where knowledge is readily shared and experimentation is the norm.

RESOLVING DILEMMAS

Chief executives most often work in a pressure-cooker atmosphere where two kinds of tension are present. The first kind is the natural tension that exists among top teams, in which talented, driven people who have to work together are also competing with one another for results, power and stature. The other kind is performance tension: the stress caused by three pairs of important objectives that, in many companies, come into conflict on a daily basis. These are profitability versus growth, the short term versus the long term, and the success of the organisation as a whole versus that of its individual parts. The most successful chief executives are the ones who get these tensions right (Favaro and Joni 2010).

MANAGING POLITICAL PROCESSES

Strategies develop as the outcome of bargaining and negotiation among powerful interest groups. Top management must understand the configuration of power within the organisation. Control over the allocation of resources is a useful asset for overcoming possible resistance. Another ploy is to build alliances with sympathisers and marginalisation of those resistant to change. However, powerful groups in the organisation may regard this as a threat to their own power.

STAKEHOLDER RELATIONSHIPS

The previous section has dealt with the management of internal stakeholder groups. However, possibly an even more important task of the CEO is to manage relationships with external stakeholders. In many cases this may involve educating key stakeholders on the need for change. Paul Polman of Unilever provides a good example of this. He is convinced that the pursuit of short-term maximisation of shareholder value has led to widespread addiction to artificial highs and ultimately to the financial crash of 2008–09.

He says, 'To drag the world back to sanity, we need to know why we are here. The answer is for consumers, not shareholders. If we are in synch with consumer needs and the environment in which we operate, and take responsibility for society as well as for our employees, then the shareholder will also be rewarded.' In line with his commitment to long-termism, Polman has abandoned earnings forecasts and quarterly financial reports to the City. When this was announced, the share price dropped 10 per cent. Although painful in the short term, in the long term this moved the Unilever shareholder base nearer to Polman's ideal, as it will have been those shareholders who sought short-term maximisation who sold out (Saunders 2011).

LEADING STRATEGIC CHANGE

Leadership is the process of influencing an organisation in its efforts towards achieving an aim or goal. This involves envisioning future strategy, aligning the organisation to deliver that strategy and embodying change.

NINE ROLES OF STRATEGIC LEADERSHIP

In 2003, Loren Appelbaum and Matthew Paese identified nine roles of strategic leadership (Appelbaum and Paese 2003).

1   *Navigator* – analyses large amounts of sometimes conflicting information. They understand why things happen and which factors really matter in the overall scheme of things.

2   *Strategist* – focuses on creating a plan for the future. Strategists make decisions that drive the organisation towards its goals.

3   *Entrepreneur* – always alert for creative and novel ideas. Able to develop ideas that have never been thought of.

4   *Mobiliser* – gains support and resources they need to accomplish goals.

5   *Talent advocate* – ensures the organisation has people with potential to meet present and future organisational needs.

6   *Captivator* – build upon an established foundation of trust to instil people with feelings of excitement and belonging.

7   *Global thinker* – understand and accept international cultural differences, and behave in a way that accommodates people's varying perspectives.

8   *Change driver* – focuses on continuous improvement. Identifies ideas for change and becomes the force driving the change home.

9   *Enterprise guardian* – makes decisions that are good for the shareholder, even if the decisions cause pain to individuals or the organisation.

There is no one best style of strategic leadership. Successful strategic leaders adjust their style to the context they face – situational leadership.

THEORY E AND THEORY O

Beer and Nohria (2000) distinguish between Theory E and Theory O as approaches to managing change.

Theory E is top–down, pursues economic value, and emphasises structures and systems and financial incentives. It can be characterised as a 'hard' approach to change. There are clear parallels to the traditional approach to strategic planning.

Theory O is bottom–up as well as top–down, based on developing organisational capability, culture change, participation and experiment. It is a 'soft' approach and has parallels with emergent planning.

However, Beer and Nohria also stress that combinations are possible:

● Start with Theory E and move on to Theory O – that is, a hard approach to shock the organisation into facing up to change and then a soft approach to actually getting the change through.
● Use both approaches simultaneously.
● Combine direction from the top with participation from below.
● Use incentives to reinforce rather than to drive change.

STYLES OF CHANGE LEADERSHIP

Johnson et al (2011, pp473–5) identify a number of styles of change leadership within the generic approaches:

● *Education* – persuading others of the need for and means of strategic change. This approach is long term, but ultimately involves a willingness to change throughout the organisation.
● *Collaboration* – the involvement of those affected by strategic change in setting the change agenda. However, a negotiated agenda for change may be a compromise that satisfies nobody. If it does not satisfy key stakeholders, it may not work.

- *Participation* – the strategic leader retains co-ordination of and authority over processes of change but delegation of elements of the change process. This can help to build commitment, but runs the risk that employees may see it as manipulation.

The first three styles here are all examples of Theory O.

- *Direction* – the use of personal managerial authority to establish a clear strategy and how change will occur. Change is sold to subordinates who must implement it. This can provide fast change, but there is a risk of either passive or even active resistance.
- *Coercion* – the imposition of change or the using of edicts about change. This may be necessary in a crisis, but is very unlikely to be effective at other times.

These last two styles are examples of Theory E.

Style of leadership is partly a function of the personality of the leader, but great leaders can adapt their style to different contexts (situational leadership):

- Time and scope – education or collaboration is suitable for incremental change, while control or directive approaches may be more suitable for transformational change.
- Capability and readiness for change.
- Power – a hierarchical organisation will tend to favour a directive style, while a networked or learning organisation will favour collaboration and participation.

They stress that the styles are not mutually exclusive. Styles can and often should change sequentially, while different styles may simultaneously be suitable for different stakeholders.

REFLECTIVE ACTIVITY 10.5

BP and the Gulf of Mexico disaster

In the spring of 2010, a BP deep water oil rig in the Gulf of Mexico exploded, killing 11 people and injuring a further 17. This was bad enough, but the disaster then continued for a further six months, leaking 5 million barrels of crude oil into the Gulf, polluting beaches and destroying the local inshore fishing industry.

Dealing with the disaster was the responsibility of BP's CEO, Tony Hayward, a trained geologist. His immediate handling of the disaster was seen as very complacent. He played down the scale of the disaster at all opportunities. The *Observer* (Wachman 2010) accused him of 'aloofness, wry smiles and stiff upper lip'. He was reported as saying that the amount of oil which had leaked was 'relatively tiny' compared with the 'very big ocean', while he also said during one tour of the Gulf, 'I want my life back.' He was also seen on a yacht at Cowes in July, not perhaps the most tactful way to take no doubt much-needed relaxation (Webb 2010). In October he resigned as BP CEO and was

replaced by an American from Mississippi, Bob Dudley.

Reflecting back on the crisis later, Hayward said, 'If I had a degree in acting from RADA rather than a degree in geology I may have done better.' He admitted that BP had virtually no contingency plans to deal with the crisis, because there had never been a serious deep water accident before. 'The equipment to contain and disperse on the seabed... had never been designed or built. It simply did not exist' (Macalister 2010). BP was forced to make up its response as it went along, making it look 'fumbling and incompetent'.

Clearly Hayward was at fault for attempting to justify himself too much. The only sensible response in such a situation is to apologise immediately, profusely and frequently. However, there were some mitigating factors:

- BP was not the only company at fault. Halliburton, the US contractor infamous for its close association with ex-Vice President Dick Cheney, botched the cementing job on sealing off the well, while the rig operator

Transocean had switched off fire alarms on the rig because of false alarms. The US oil regulator, MMS, also appeared to have been lax.

- The US media, and even to some extent President Obama, was determined to vilify BP. The company was always described as 'British Petroleum', to emphasise its foreignness, although it had changed its name to BP many years earlier. Half of BP's business and 40 per cent of its shareholders are in the US. If anything, it is a US company which happens to be headquartered in London.

- Evidence has emerged that perhaps Hayward was right when he played down the extent of the disaster. In June, the Americans suggested that the slick might even reach Europe (Clark 2010), but by August, only a quarter of the leaked oil had not been dispersed, and by October, 93 per cent of the Gulf fisheries were reopened.

Critically examine the leadership style of Tony Hayward, and the management culture of BP.

Ridgeway and Wallace (1994) identify a number of competencies required for effective change leadership. These are:

- *intellectual skills* – intellectually curious and able to handle ambiguity
- *influencing skills* – assertive, proactive and energetic
- *counselling and people skills* – sensitive, flexible and adaptable, with a high tolerance of pressure.

While this list is solid, I think that it misses the true essence of change leadership. A good change leader must above all be driven by a vision of the future, and be able to inspire others with that vision. This involves a high sense of values, exceptional communication abilities, a sense of inspiration and the ability to empower others with the vision. All of these qualities are illustrated in Case Study 10.6.

CASE STUDY 10.6

NELSON MANDELA

Nelson Mandela is almost universally recognised as the last, and one of the greatest, inspirational leaders of the twentieth century. His career illustrates the characteristics of a brilliant change leader.

Mandela was born in 1918, a member of a chiefly clan in the Xhosa tribe. He trained as a lawyer and was drawn at an early age into the struggle against white domination through his membership of the African National Congress. The political struggle intensified in the 1950s after the election of the white supremacist National Party government and the establishment of the apartheid system of racial segregation in South Africa.

In the early 1960s, Mandela was on trial for his life. His statement from the dock in his trial put forward his vision: 'I have fought against white domination. I have fought against black domination. I have cherished the ideal of a democratic and free society in which all persons live together in harmony and with equal opportunities. It is an ideal which I hope to live for and to achieve. But, if needs be, it is an ideal for which I am prepared to die.'

Mandela was sentenced to life imprisonment on Robben Island, where he was to remain for 27 years. For much of this he was under a hard labour regime. A telling incident from his imprisonment throws more light on his vision. A particularly tough prison governor imposed a brutal regime on the prisoners, but when he was transferred, he wished Mandela and the other ANC leaders the best for the future. To Mandela, this illustrated the possibility of redemption. The man was brutal not because he had a brutal nature, but because he was conditioned by a brutal system. Like the Catholic Church, Mandela distinguished between the sin and the sinner. From this came his concept of redemption and reconciliation, which was to be a driving force of his presidency.

By the mid-1980s, another key player had entered the scene – F.W. De Klerk, the new National Party leader. De Klerk recognised that the apartheid system must go and that a settlement must be negotiated with the ANC. In Bridge's terms, this marked the end of the old system and a move into the neutral transition zone. After lengthy negotiations, Mandela was released from prison in 1990. A new constitution was negotiated, leading to democratic elections in 1994 and the election of Mandela as the first democratic president of South Africa.

Mandela now faced his most severe test as a leader – how to hold the new South Africa together and forge a new multiracial democratic state. He faced threats on all sides. A right-wing Afrikaner element was threatening civil war and there was also an undeclared civil war between the ANC and the Zulu Inkatha Freedom Party. The Zulus were the largest tribe in South Africa and resented the power held by the Xhosa Mandela.

Mandela's approach was to use symbolic acts of reconciliation. He visited the widow of the architect of apartheid, Hendrik Verwoerd. He also presented the Rugby World Cup to the victorious South African team wearing a South African rugby shirt. Rugby is an Afrikaner sport in South Africa, with almost totally white support. This action helped to reconcile the Afrikaner community to the new South Africa. He also pursued reconciliation with the Zulus. The Inkatha Freedom Party leader, Mangosuthu Buthelezi, was made minister for home affairs, and number three in the government, after Mandela and the vice-president Thabo Mbeki.

Mandela also used the idea of redemption through the Truth and Reconciliation Commission, which he launched with Archbishop Desmond Tutu. The idea here was that perpetrators of political crime could confess their involvement and receive public absolution. Mandela insisted that this should apply as much to members of the ANC as to the agents of the apartheid regime.

Mandela's last great act of leadership was to recognise that by the end of his term as president in 1999, the transition phase had ended and that South Africa was into the new beginning. Even his greatest admirers would not call Mandela a great administrator and he recognised that a new type of more structured leadership was now needed. He therefore retired, leaving the way for Thabo Mbeki, a less charismatic but more structured politician, to succeed him.

When the sculptor Rodin was asked how he would sculpt an elephant, his reply was that he would start with a very large block of stone and then remove everything which was not elephant. Mandela had a similar vision. Everything which was not part of his vision of a democratic, multicultural South Africa was irrelevant, including bitterness, revenge and recriminations.

SUMMARY

This chapter has discussed the nature of strategy and its transition from a corporate planning to a strategic management perspective, with a greater emphasis on contingency, experimentation and learning. We have identified the crucial role of change management and of the change leader in ensuring that strategy is implemented as planned.

KEY LEARNING POINTS

- Quinn identifies three elements of strategy – goals, policies and programmes.
- Strategy can be analysed at several levels – corporate, business unit and operational.
- Approaches to strategy are connected with the nature of the environment. In the 1950s and 1960s, a placid environment encouraged the rational, logical corporate planning approach, while a more turbulent environment since the 1970s encouraged the more contingent, experimental strategic management approach.
- The leading exponent of the corporate planning approach was Igor Ansoff, while the leading exponents of the strategic management approach are Tom Peters, Michael Porter, Ralph Stacey, Gary Hamel and C.K. Prahalad, James Quinn and Henry Mintzberg.
- It is important to distinguish between intended strategy and realised strategy.
- Strategic analysis is concerned with the strategic position of the organisation. What are the key characteristics of the organisation, what changes are going on in the environment and how will these affect the organisation and its activities? This involves an analysis of the expectations of stakeholders; the culture of the organisation; the organisation's vision and values; the environment, as identified through a STEEPLE analysis; and the key resource areas of the business.
- The extent to which there is a mismatch (a gap) between current strategy and the future environment is a measure of the strategic problem facing the organisation.
- Vision, mission, values and objectives are closely linked, and often confused.
- The mission and objectives of the organisation are constrained by corporate governance, stakeholders, business ethics and culture.
- The mission statement provides a benchmark against which policies can be evaluated.
- Resource analysis is internal to the organisation. It is concerned with the strengths and weaknesses parts of SWOT analysis, and measures the efficiency and effectiveness of an organisation's resources.
- Prahalad and Hamel identify the concept of the core competences of the organisation – those factors which give the organisation its key competitive advantages.
- The concept of generic strategy was introduced by Michael Porter and developed by Cliff Bowman.
- Possible strategies should be evaluated on three levels: suitability, acceptability and feasibility.
- Transformational change is change which results in entirely new behaviour on the part of organisational members and is in its very nature strategic.
- Bridges and Mitchell identify three stages in a change programme: saying goodbye, shifting into neutral and moving forward.
- Resistance to change can be rational and must be managed. This is one of the key functions of HR in change management.
- The critical role of a change leader is to be inspirational and visionary.

QUESTIONS

1   Explain what Quinn means by his three elements of strategy.

2   Why is the corporate planning approach inappropriate for a turbulent environment?

3   What is the role of gap analysis in strategic planning?

4   What are the differences between vision, mission, values and objectives?

5   What do you understand by the expression 'core competence'?

6   Explain the concept of generic strategy as developed by Michael Porter.

7   How can a proposed strategy be evaluated?

8   What are Pugh's six rules for managing change?

9   Why might individuals resist change?

10 What are the six stages in Beer's change model?

11 What are the key requirements for transformational leadership?

EXPLORE FURTHER

FURTHER READING

The leading UK text on strategic management is Gerry Johnson and Kevan Scholes, *Exploring Corporate Strategy*. A new edition (the ninth) was published in 2011 (with Richard Whittington). Other valuable strategic management texts are John Thompson with Frank Martin, *Strategic Management: Awareness and change*, 5th edition, 2005, Robert Clark, *Contemporary Strategy Analysis*, 5th edition, 2005, and Bernard Burnes, *Managing Change: A strategic approach to organisational dynamics*, 4th edition, 2004. *Academy of Management Executive* May 2002 (Vol 16, No 2) devotes virtually the whole issue to a discussion of Michael Porter's *Competitive Strategy*.

USEFUL WEBSITES

QuickMBA (www.quickmba.com/strategy/generic.shtml) has some useful articles on strategic issues, including one on Porter's generic strategies, which discusses fits between generic strategies and Porter's Five Forces. Knowledge@Wharton (www.knowledge.wharton.upenn.edu/category.cfm?cid=7), published by the Wharton Business School at the University of Pennsylvania, has useful strategic case study articles.

AUDIO AND VIDEO MATERIAL

The CIPD has produced a number of useful podcasts: podcast 56 (July 2011), *The importance of creating and sustaining a sense of shared purpose within organisations*; Podcast 32 (July 2009), *Building leadership capability for change: an interview with Gary Hamel*; and a double podcast, 31 parts 1 and 2, *Making change happen*. YouTube has a video, *Michael Porter on Competitiveness* (youtube.com/watch?v=y51_cnpP99U).

THE UK BEER INDUSTRY

Introduction

The UK beer industry forms a fascinating case study. The structure of the industry is unlike that of the rest of British industry. Until the late 1990s, it was also very insular, with little contact with either European or world trends in the beer industry. In the last 15 years it has changed from almost exclusively UK ownership to a situation where most of the industry is owned by European or American companies. It is also an industry which has experienced enormous changes in its structure and product range over the last 40 years and which was thrown into turmoil by government-inspired change since 1989.

In the rest of Europe (with the exception of the Republic of Ireland and Belgium), beer means lager – a pasteurised product which is light in texture and colour and drunk cold. In the UK, lager has a large and growing share of the market, but beer in the UK also means ale and stout.

The beer industry in the UK was unusual before 1989 in being heavily vertically integrated. Some brewers controlled their own sources of raw materials, including malt and hops, and in some cases water, but much more important was forward integration. Much beer is draught beer, sold through pubs and clubs, known as the on-trade. The remainder is sold in bottle or can through off-licences and increasingly supermarkets, known as the off-trade. The off-trade, particularly beer sold through supermarkets, has considerably increased its share of the market in recent years.

Of approximately 78,000 public houses in the UK in 1989, 46,000 were owned by brewers, including 34,000 owned by the Big Six companies. These were known as tied houses, because they were tied to the brewer, and obliged to sell its products, which may include spirits, wines and soft drinks as well as beer.

About 70 per cent of tied houses were tenanted, with the other 30 per cent being managed by employees of the brewery. Tenants pay rent and take a margin on all goods and services sold. Traditionally, rents were pegged below market levels, but in return the tenant was obliged to buy his beer from the brewer at a price set by him.

Other public houses were free houses, which were owner-occupied and normally could buy their beer from wherever they chose. However, in some cases a loan tie system operated. Here the brewer made a low interest loan to the publican, who in turn was obliged to sell the brewer's products.

The industry has been marked by a very considerable number of mergers, which reduced the number of companies from around 350 in 1950 to 64 in 1989. The structure of the industry was firmly established by the mid-1960s, when the Big Six brewers (Bass, Allied, Whitbread, Watney, Scottish &Newcastle and Courage) controlled 67 per cent of production. By 1989 that had increased to 75 per cent. In addition, as noted above, they owned nearly half the public houses.

Trends in the industry

Beer production in the UK peaked in the late 1970s and has declined gently thereafter. Consumption has followed the same pattern. Beer consumption per head peaked in 1979 and by 2007 had fallen by over 20 per cent. Over the same period, wine consumption has risen by two and a half times. In 1979 beer represented 60 per cent of alcohol drunk, while by 2007 this had fallen to

40 per cent (Institute of Alcohol Studies 2010).

Both imports and exports are historically of minor importance in the industry, mainly due to the cost of transporting a product which is mainly water. Beer which appears to be foreign is usually brewed in the UK under licence. However, in recent years the most rapidly growing segment of the market has been premium lager, much of which is imported from Europe.

The product mix decisively shifted in the period from 1960 to 1990. In 1960, 99 per cent of all beer consumed was ale, while by 1990 lager had overtaken ale and made up 51 per cent of all sales. This had risen to 74 per cent in 2010. Standard lager has a 40 per cent share and premium lager 34 per cent. The main forces behind this seem to have been that the British acquired a taste for lager on European holidays; lager was seen as a young person's drink and also as a drink that was acceptable to both sexes; its taste and quality were totally predictable and national brands of lager were heavily promoted by the brewers.

Another long-term trend in the market has been the success of real ale. By the early 1970s, although most beer sold was still ale, it was overwhelmingly a pasteurised 'dead' product. Real ale, or cask-conditioned ale, is by contrast a 'live' product, with the result that although its quality is much higher, it is more difficult to serve and does not keep as long as pasteurised beer. In the early 1970s, it appeared that real ale was likely to disappear from the market. It was then rescued by the activities of the Campaign for Real Ale (CAMRA), a classic example of an interest pressure group. Thanks to CAMRA's efforts, real ale revived and thrived. It is relatively easy to set up a real micro-brewery. Many free houses have done this and you can more or less do it in your garden shed. Micro-

breweries also have favourable tax treatment.

The Big Six brewers consolidated their dominant market position during the 1970s and 1980s through takeovers. They were also themselves in some cases the victims of takeovers. Watney was taken over by Grand Metropolitan, at the time predominantly a hotels group, but later a component of the wine and spirits conglomerate Diageo, while Courage passed to the Australian brewer Fosters. The third member of the Big Six to be involved in a merger was Allied, which merged with the food group J Lyons to form Allied Lyons.

The overall structure of the industry was analysed by the Monopolies and Mergers Commission in 1989. They identified over 200 brewing companies, classified as:

- Six national brewers (Allied, Bass, Courage, Grand Met, S & N and Whitbread). They had 75 per cent of UK beer production.
- Eleven regional brewers, such as Greene King and Wolverhampton and Dudley. They had 11 per cent of beer production.
- Forty-one local brewers, such as Adnams. They had 6 per cent of beer production.
- Three brewers without tied estate (Carlsberg, Guinness and Northern Clubs Federation). They had 8 per cent of beer production.
- 160 other brewers, mainly very small and local, with less than 1 per cent of beer production.

One key trend of the 1980s and 1990s was the growing internationalisation and homogenisation of the drinks industry. Throughout Europe, including the UK, the trend was towards lighter drinks, including lager rather than ale, light spirits like Malibu and Baileys rather than traditional spirits like gin or rum, wine, fruit juices, mineral water and colas.

Pubs became less of a male, beer-drinking stronghold. More pub drinking was done by women, who were more likely to drink lighter, less alcoholic drinks, and pubs became more of a family place to eat as well as to drink, although to some extent this trend was inhibited in the UK by the restrictive licensing laws. These in theory prohibited children under the age of 14 from entering bars. Increasingly the traditional pub was replaced by theme pubs (Irish-style bars, etc) and pub-restaurants.

An impact of the recessions at the beginning of the 1980s and 1990s was to encourage a trend towards drinking at home, rather than in pubs. This was assisted by a trend towards canned lagers rather than bottled beers, increasingly sold through supermarkets, usually at a price considerably below that charged in pubs.

The on-trade was also hit by demographic trends. The key pub drinking segment is the 18–25 age group, but from a peak of 23 per cent of the adult population in the early 1980s, this age group fell to a trough of 14 per cent in 1995.

In 1987, the Office of Fair Trading referred the brewing industry to the Monopolies and Mergers Commission (MMC) for investigation as a potential complex monopoly. This was legally possible although the biggest firm in the industry, Bass, only had a 22 per cent share of the market, below the single-firm monopoly threshold of 25 per cent. Of particular concern was the way in which the price of beer was rising more rapidly than the general rate of inflation and the potentially anti-competitive effects of the tied house system. The MMC carried out a painstaking investigation of the industry and reported in 1989.

The MMC found that a complex monopoly did indeed exist and that it acted against the public interest in three main ways:

- Prices had been rising too rapidly.
- Consumer choice was restricted because one brewer usually did not allow another brewer's beer to be sold in his pubs.
- The tenant's bargaining position was critically weaker than the landlord's (the brewer).

The MMC's particular concern was with the Big Six national brewers and their recommendations were mainly aimed at this group. After negotiation these recommendations became the Beer Orders.

The Beer Orders specified that:

- No brewer should own more than 2,000 pubs, plus 50 per cent of the excess number owned over 2,000. This meant that the Big Six brewers had to dispose of 11,000 pubs. None of the regional brewers owned more than 2,000 pubs.
- Tenants of pubs owned by brewers with more than 2,000 pubs (but not managers) to be allowed to stock a 'guest' beer (a beer brewed by a third party).
- The loan tie to be abolished.

The clear intention was that competition in the industry should be considerably increased, by limiting the impact of the tied house system and by opening up opportunities for smaller brewers to get a foothold in the tied houses through the guest beer concept. The hope was that many, if not most, of the pubs sold by the Big Six would be sold to their tenants and become free houses. Events were to show, however, that the brewers were ingenious in circumventing the spirit of the Beer Orders, while obeying its letter.

Trends in the industry since 1989

Production and consumption in the UK has continued to decline since 1989. In the 1990s, overall sales fell by 9 per cent. Two major factors influencing the level of sales are the weather, with hot summers boosting sales, and major sporting events, particularly the football World Cup. Within this overall declining market, the trend towards lager has continued, with the biggest growth coming in imported premium continental lager.

The trend towards a growth in the off-trade at the expense of the on-trade (pubs and clubs) has continued. The off-trade grew from 20 per cent in 1989 to around a third in 2000, 40 per cent by 2006 and 49 per cent in 2010. Supermarkets account for 28 per cent of business. This trend has been assisted by technological developments, which have enabled canned beer to be served with a head similar to that of draught beer – the so-called 'widget', a miniature nitrogen gas cartridge built into the can. The purchasing power of the big supermarkets is as significant in beer as in other grocery products. It was reported in the summer of 1993 that Tesco was able to import Stella Artois lager from Belgium at a price which undercut Whitbread, then the UK distributor, by 25 per cent. The supermarkets also followed an aggressive pricing policy on beer, which saw its store price halve between 1998 and 2002. This policy was financed by a cut in the price which was paid to the brewers, described by Scottish &Newcastle as 'a blood bath'.

A further trend has come about as a result of the introduction of the European Single Market in January 1993. UK residents can now import alcoholic drinks from EU countries without limit, as long as the article has paid duty in an EU country and it is to be consumed by the importer him or herself. Importing for resale is a criminal offence, but very difficult to prove.

Licensing laws are being liberalised. Already all-day opening is possible, between the hours of 11am and 11pm. A children's certificate scheme, allowing under-14s to be admitted, came into force in January 1995. The Licensing Act of 2003 allows pubs to alter their opening hours to suit local demand. This may mean that some pubs will choose to operate on a 24-hour basis.

The reaction of the brewing industry to the Beer Orders and other changes in the environment has been a massive restructuring. This started in October 1990 with a merger of the brewing interests of Courage and Grand Metropolitan. Under the deal, Courage acquired Grand Met's breweries, which it had originally obtained when it took over Watney, and Grand Met ceased brewing entirely. In return Courage and Grand Met set up a joint company called Inntrepreneur, managed by Grand Met, which took over nearly all of Courage's pubs and many of Grand Met's. This was the first appearance of the phenomenon which was to dominate the industry, the giant pubco, a company which ran pubs but did not brew.

In January 1993 came the launch of Carslberg-Tetley, a joint venture of Allied Lyons, the European seventh biggest brewer, and the Danish company Carlsberg, the European number three. Carlsberg already brewed lager in the UK, and because it had no tied estate, had built up its strength in the off-trade. Allied was strong on the on-trade, but weak on the off-trade. The deal was investigated and cleared by the MMC. Allied Lyons then merged with the wine and spirits company Domecq, and became Allied Domecq. The new company took the strategic decision to pull out of brewing. In 1996, Bass tried to acquire Allied's interest in Carlsberg-Tetley, but was blocked by the MMC. Carlsberg then bought out the Allied interest, but maintained the Carlsberg-Tetley name. Its Tetley Bitter is the best-selling cask ale in the UK.

Bass, the market leader, pursued a consolidation strategy, rationalising its production by closing three of its twelve breweries. The company sold 2,700 pubs to comply with the Beer Orders, many of them to new pubcos who agreed to take their beer from Bass. Whitbread, the long-standing number three in the industry, steadily lost ground, and fell to number five. In 1995, Scottish & Newcastle acquired Courage, immediately taking it to number one in the market.

By the late 1990s, the Big Six had shrunk to four – Bass, S & N, Carlsberg-Tetley and Whitbread. They were soon to shrink further when in quick succession the Belgian brewer Interbrew, maker of Stella Artois, acquired the brewing interests of first Whitbread and then Bass.

In addition, S & N moved into a leading position in Europe with the acquisition of Brasseries Kronenbourg, the number one beer brand in France, from the French food conglomerate Danone. Interbrew was then forced to sell off many of the brewing interests which it had acquired from Bass. These were purchased by the American number two, Molson Coors, while Interbrew retained ownership of the Bass brand. The American number one, and the biggest brewer in the world, Anheuser-Busch, brewed a small amount of Budweiser in the UK, but was not a leading player in the UK market. The series of mergers resulted in a market dominated by Scottish & Newcastle, InBev and Molson Coors. S & N had a UK market share of 27 per cent in 2006, Molson Coors 20 per cent, and InBev (formed by the merger of Interbrew and the Brazilian company AmBev in 2004)

19 per cent (*Economist* 2004). Bass renamed itself Six Continents, and later demerged into two companies, Intercontinental Hotels, which concentrated on hotels, and Mitchells and Butlers, a pubco (Kew and Stredwick 2008).

In 2008, Scottish & Newcastle was acquired jointly by Heineken and Carlsberg. Heineken took S & N UK, while Carlsberg took most of the interests outside the UK, including Kronenbourg. By 2010, market shares in the UK were: Heineken 30.0 per cent, Molson-Coors 21.9 per cent, Anheuser-Busch InBev (the result of a merger in 2008) 19.8 per cent, and others 28.2 per cent. The global market was not quite so concentrated, with the leading three players (Anheuser-Busch InBev, SAB Miller and Heineken) having a 41.1 per cent market share (Datamonitor 2011a, 2011b). The world growth areas are seen as Africa and Asia, especially China. AB InBev expects to generate 6 per cent of its profits from China by 2021 (currently 1 per cent), while SAB Miller expects to up profits there from 2 per cent to 19 per cent (Neville 2012).

Adnams plc

Adnams is a medium-sized real ale brewery based at Southwold in Suffolk. As well as brewing, it also has a pub estate, runs hotels and cook shops, imports and distributes wine, and operates a distillery.

Suffolk is a stronghold of real ale. The largest regional brewer, Greene King, is based in Bury St Edmunds, while the local brewer Mauldon is based in Sudbury. Adnams stresses its East Anglian roots. It is the largest employer in Southwold. Casks of Adnams ale used to be delivered to the pubs of Southwold by horse and dray until September 2006, when the distribution centre was moved to a new location two miles outside the town. Adnams' most recent advertising campaign has the slogan: 'Beer from the Coast'.

The Sole Bay Brewery in Southwold was purchased in 1872 by George and Ernest Adnams. The company was incorporated in 1890 and has remained independent since then. The Adnams family was joined in 1902 by Pierse Loftus and his brother Jack, and Adnams still has members of each family on the board, with Jonathan Adnams as chairman and Simon Loftus as a non-executive director.

The company has a complicated corporate structure, which means that control is held by the Adnams and Loftus families through A (voting) shares, although these represent a small percentage of the total share capital. This arrangement runs counter to the best principles of corporate government and has been criticised by one major holder of B (non-voting) shares. To compensate B shareholders, they receive a higher level of dividend than the A shares.

In his Chairman's Statement in 2011, Jonathan Adnams was critical of the Government's escalator beer duty, increasing by more than inflation each year. He also criticised the tax subsidies given to micro-breweries, worth on average £200,000 a year, and not available to Adnams (Adnams 2011a).

Adnams' profits peaked before the recession in 2007 at £4.2 million; they then slumped to £1.5 million in 2008 and had recovered to £3.3 million in 2011. The biggest driver of beer business success in 2011 was the market for drinking at home. Having had a tough 2010, this business made a major move forward in 2011. Over 20 per cent of beer is now sold in bottles, cans and mini-casks.

Adnams opened a distillery in Southwold towards the end of 2010. It had a very promising first year of operation. As a new business, the volumes sold have inevitably been small, but they exceeded expectations. The company already sells vodka, gin and liqueurs, and expects to sell its first whisky in 2013, after maturing it in wood for the required three years.

Adnams has long held to a values-led approach. To quote from the Adnams Values Statement (2011b):

- 'We're committed to managing the environmental impact of our operations, treating our employees well and having fun while we're at it.
- At Adnams we want to make sure that our impact on society is a positive one, expressing the company's values in ways which combine social and business benefits with long-term sustainable success. We work for the long term, looking beyond immediate success to a sustainable future.
- We deal with people openly and honestly, building strong, supportive relationships.
- We expect commitment to these values, and aim to translate them into everyday realities.
- We value our place in the community, and work to enhance the quality of local life.
- We take pride in all that we do, aiming to be a beacon to inspire others.'

Another aspect of the values approach is staff remuneration. 'We make no claims to be high payers, but we do seek to provide a good range of benefits and we have stood clear of the gross pay inequality that has been seen in some other places. The ratio of our highest salary to our average salary is a relatively modest 8.8 times' (Adnams 2011a).

Adnams' strategy is a differentiation one, based on:

- A strong identification with East Anglia in general, and Southwold in particular – as Southwold is an up market seaside resort, this reinforces other elements of the strategy.

- Concentration on the premium sector of the real ale market – the company produces a limited range of beers, supplemented by special brews, which are either seasonal or commemorate particular events.
- Increasing emphasis on the off-trade, beer sold to drink at home – premium real ale (unlike standard lager) is not subject to heavy price cuts in supermarkets.
- Brand extension – with the brand being stretched to include pubs and hotels, wine merchanting, upmarket cook shops, and now spirits.
- Sustainability – Adnams launched a carbon-neutral beer in 2008 – its Adnams East Green product is produced for Tesco supermarkets. Adnams also opened a new energy-efficient brewery in 2008 – the

company opened a new brewery in Southwold in 2008, which it described as the first brewery in the UK to include a full energy recovery plant. It also switched to lightweight bottles in 2007 (Datamonitor 2009).

Questions

1   Analyse key drivers of change in the UK beer industry since the 1980s and identify opportunities and threats facing the industry in 2012.

2   Critically evaluate, using appropriate techniques, the following elements of Adnams' strategy:

- local identification
- the distillery
- sustainability.

REFERENCES

Adnams. (2011a) *Annual report 2011*. www.adnams.co.uk [Accessed 20 August 2012].

Adnams. (2011b) *Values statement*. www.adnams.co.uk [Accessed 20 August 2012].

Air Transport World. (2006a) Ryanair: ryanair.com. July.

Air Transport World. (2006b) The world's top 25 airlines. July.

Ansoff, H.I. (1965) *Corporate strategy*. Harmondsworth: Penguin.

Appelbaum, L. and Paese, M. (2003) What senior leaders do: the nine roles of strategic leadership. *Development Dimensions International.* (www.ddiworld.com/products-solutions/listing/strategic-leadership-experience/white-papers-monographs) [Accessed 18 July 2012].

Armstrong, M. (1999) *Managing activities*. London: Institute of Personnel and Development.

Austin, R. and Devin, L. (2004) Successful innovation through artful process. *Leader to Leader*. Spring.

Barney, J. (1991) Firm resources and sustained competitive advantage. *Journal of Management*. Vol 17, No 1.

Battersby, J. (1999) Nelson Mandela's moral legacy. *Christian Science Monitor*. 10 May.

BBC2. (2007) *Working Lunch*. 19 September.

Beach, S. (1980) *Personnel*. London: Macmillan.

Beer, M. and Nohria, N. (2000) Cracking the code of change. *Harvard Business Review*. May–June. Vol 78, No 3.

Bernhut, S. (2001) Leading the revolution: Gary Hamel. *Ivey Business Journal*. July.

Bird, A. (2010) Leading through values: An interview with Paul Polman of Unilever. *McKinsey Quarterly*. No 1.

Birkinshaw, J. (2004) The destruction of Marconi. *Business Strategy Review*. Spring. Vol 15, No 1.

Bloomsbury. (2007a) *Summary of corporate milestones*. www.bloomsbury-ir.co.uk

Bloomsbury. (2007b) *Financial results*. www.bloomsbury-ir.co.uk

Bloomsbury. (2007c) *Press release – record breaking first 24 hours of Harry Potter and the Deathly Hallows*. 23 July. www.bloomsbury-ir.co.uk

Boroughs, D. (1999) Proving that one man can make a difference. *US News and World Report*. 24 May.

Bowman, C. and Faulkner, D. (1996) *Competitive and corporate strategy*. Homewood, IL.: Irwin.

Bridges, W. (1995) Breaking with the past. *Human Resources*. September–October.

Bridges, W. and Mitchell, S. (2000) Leading transition: a new model for change. *Leader to Leader*. Vol 16. Spring.

Burke, W. (1980) *Organisation development*. Toronto: Little Brown.

Burnes, B. (2004) *Managing change: a strategic approach to organisational dynamics*. 4th edition. London: Pitman.

Business Week. (2006) Walmart with wings. 27 November.

Butler, V. (1985) *Organisation and management*. London: Prentice Hall.

Cadbury website. (2007) www.cadbury.co.uk [Accessed 18 June 2007].

Carr, A., Durant, R. and Downs, A. (2004) Emergent strategy development, abduction, and pragmatism: new lessons for corporations. *Human Systems Management*. Vol 23. March.

CIPD. (2004) *Change management*. Factsheet. London: Chartered Institute of Personnel and Development.

Clark, A. (2010) BP's behaviour was shameful. But it wasn't the only one to blame for the Gulf disaster. *Observer*. 31 October.

Collinson, P. and Seager, A. (2007) Northern Rock crisis: call to City grandees that threw lifeline to drowning bank. *Guardian*. 15 September.

Crainer, S. and Dearlove, D. (2003) Windfall economics. *Business Strategy Review*. Vol 14, No 4. Winter.

Croggon, P. (2007) Letter to the editor. *The Times*. 17 September.

Datamonitor. (2009) *Adnams case study: overcoming the poor performance of the recessionary UK beer market*. London: Datamonitor.

Datamonitor (2011a) *The UK beer industry*. London: Datamonitor.

Datamonitor (2011b) *The global beer industry*. London: Datamonitor.

Davies, G. (2007) The roots of moral hazard. *Guardian*. 15 September.

Done, K. (2007) Ryanair orders 27 Boeing jets. *Financial Times*. 31 May.

Duncan, G. and Webster, P. (2007) MPC founding member comes out swinging against Bank's bailout decision. *The Times*. 15 September.

Economist. (2004) An awful lot of brewing in Brazil. 6 March.

Edwards, C. (2004) Five-star strategy. *People Management*. 8 April.

Elliott, V. (2007) Cadbury fined £1m for selling contaminated chocolate bars. *The Times*. 17 July.

Favaro, K. and Joni, S. (2010) Getting tensions right: How CEOs can turn conflict, dissent, and disagreement into a powerful tool for driving performance. *Strategy + Business*. Autumn. No 60.

Felsted, A. (2003) The Dublin-based airline has become a leading force in European aviation. *Financial Times*. 4 November.

Furnham, A. and Gunter, B. (1993) *Corporate assessment*. London: Routledge.

Hamel, G. (1996) Strategy as revolution. *Harvard Business Review*. July–August.

Hamel, G. and Prahalad, C.K. (1994) *Competing for the future*. Boston, MA: Harvard Business School Press.

Harrington, R., Lemak, D., Reed, R. and Kendall, K. (2004) A question of fit: the links between environment, strategy formulation and performance. *Journal of Business Management*. Vol 10, No 1. Spring.

Hughes, C. and Tighe, C. (2007) Impregnable self-belief takes a battering. *Financial Times*. 15 September.

Institute of Alcohol Studies. (2010) *Alcohol consumption in the UK*. IAS Factsheet. www.ias.org.uk/resources/factsheets/consumption-uk.pdf [Accessed 20 August 2012].

Johnson, G., Whittington, R. and Scholes, K. (2011) *Exploring strategy*. 9th edition. Harlow: Pearson.

Johnson & Johnson website. (nd) www.jnj.com/connect/about-jnj/jnj-credo [Accessed 25 February 2011].

Jordan, D. (2007) Time comes for Harry to fly to the rescue. *The Times*. 4 April.

Kew, J. and Stredwick, J. (2008) *Business environment*. 2nd edition. London: Chartered Institute of Personnel and Development.

Kim, C. and Mauborgne, R. (2004) Blue ocean strategy. *Harvard Business Review.* Vol 82, No 10. October.

Kim, K., Nam, D. and Stimpert, J. (2004) Testing the applicability of Porter's generic strategies in the digital age: a study of Korean cyber malls. *Journal of Business Strategies.* Vol 21, No 1.

Knowledge@Wharton. (2012) Patients versus profits at Johnson & Johnson: has the company lost its way? 15 February. www.knowledge@wharton.upenn.edu/article.cfm?articleid=2943 [Accessed 28 August 2012].

Kotter, J. (1995) Leading change – why transformation efforts fail. *Harvard Business Review.* March–April.

Lewin, K. (1943) Defining the 'field at a given time'. *Psychological Review.* Vol 50.

Lord, R. (1990) A measure of corporate success. *The Times.* 30 July.

Macalister, T. (2010) BP thought Gulf oil spill 'simply could not happen', says ex-boss. *Guardian.* 11 November.

McCann, J. (2004) Organizational effectiveness: changing concepts for changing environments. *Human Resource Planning.* Vol 27, No 1.

McCarthy, B. (2004) How to manage organisational change. *People Management.* 9 December.

Milmo, D. (2007) Ryanair introduces £4 check-in fee as latest surcharge to slash costs. *Guardian.* 25 August.

Milmo, D. (2009) EasyJet warns of tough winter ahead after profits decline by £80m. *Guardian.* 18 November.

Mintzberg, H. (1994) *The rise and fall of strategic planning.* Hemel Hempstead: Prentice Hall.

Mintzberg, H. (1998) Five Ps for strategy. In H. Mintzberg, J.B. Quinn and S. Ghoshal (eds) *The strategy process.* Revised European edition. Hemel Hempstead: Prentice Hall.

Mintzberg, H. and Waters, J. (1985) Of strategies deliberate and emergent. *Strategic Management Journal.* Vol 6.

Moore, K. (2011) Porter or Mintzberg: whose view of strategy is the most relevant today? *Forbes.* 28 March.

Neville, S. (2012) Bitter battle as brewers jostle for their place at the bars of Asia and Africa. *Guardian.* 4 September.

Peters, T. (1985) *Thriving on chaos.* New York: Macmillan.

Peters, T. and Waterman, R. (1982) *In search of excellence.* New York: Harper & Row.

Porter, M. (1980) *Competitive strategy: techniques for analysing industries and competition.* New York: The Free Press.

Porter, M. (1985) *Competitive advantage: creating and sustaining superior performance.* New York: The Free Press.

Porter, M. (1999) *On competition.* New York: The Free Press.

Prahalad, C.K. and Hamel, G. (1990) The core competence of the corporation. *Harvard Business Review.* May–June.

Pugh, D.S. (1978) Understanding and managing organisational change. *London Business School Journal.* Vol 3, No 2.

Quinn, J. (1980) *Strategies for change: logical incrementalism.* Homewood, IL.: Irwin.

Ridgeway, C. and Wallace, B. (1994) *Empowering change: the role of people management.* London: Institute of Personnel and Development.

Ryanair. (2003) *Economy and mobility: the Ryanair business model.* www.ryanair.com

Ryanair. (2007) www.ryanair.com/site/EN/about [Accessed 18 July 2007].

Saunders, A. (2011) The MT interview: Paul Polman. *Management Today.* March.

Senge, P. (1990) *The fifth discipline.* London: Century Business.

Shelley, T. (2007) Bloomsbury looks for magic after Potter. *Financial Times.* 4 April.

Stacey, R. (1991) *The chaos frontier: creative strategic control for business.* Oxford: Butterworth-Heinemann.

Stacey, R. (1993) *Strategic management and organisational dynamics.* Harlow: Pearson Education.

Starmer-Smith, C. (2006) Disabled groups attack 33p Ryanair levy. *Daily Telegraph.* 13 May.

Stevenson, H.H. (1989) Defining corporate strengths and weaknesses. In C. Bowman and D. Asch (eds) *Readings in strategic management.* Basingstoke: Macmillan.

Tait, N. and Wiggins, J. (2007) Cadbury in record £1m fine for unsafe chocolate. *Financial Times.* 17 July.

Teather, D. (2007) Model executive puts Hornby back on track. *Guardian.* 21 December.

Teece, D. (2007) Explicating dynamic capabilities: the nature and microfoundations of (sustainable) enterprise performance. *Sustainable Management Journal.* Vol 28. August.

Thompson, M. (2005) *Strategic management: awareness and change.* 5th edition. London: Thomson.

Tomlinson, H. (2001) Stop me and buy a Ben & Jerry's. *Independent on Sunday.* 9 December.

US Department of Commerce website. (nd) www.ouedu/deptcomm/dodjcc [Accessed 25 February 2011].

Wachman, R. (2010) When disaster strikes our corporate giants, sorry does seem to be the hardest word. *Observer.* 26 December.

Walton, J. (1999) *Strategic human resource development.* London: FT/Prentice Hall.

Watkins, K.E. and Marsick, V.J. (1993) *Sculpting the learning organisation: lessons in the art and science of systemic change.* San Francisco: Jossey-Bass.

Webb, T. (2010) 'I needed RADA degree in acting,' says ex-BP chief. *Guardian.* 9 November.

Whittington, R. (2001) *What is strategy – and does it matter?* 2nd edition. London: Thomson.

Williams, R. (2007) Cadbury fined £1m for salmonella offences. *Guardian.* 17 July.

Wood, W. and Finch, J. (2009) Borders failed as Friends moved on. *Guardian.* 27 November.

Woodward, S. and Hendry, C. (2004) Leading and coping with change. *Journal of Change Management.* Vol 4, No 2. June.

Workers' Educational Association (WEA) in Northern Ireland. (nd) *Mission statement and WEA values.* (www.wea-ni.com)

Wray, R. (2006) Bloomsbury's profits drop without Potter's magic this year. *Guardian.* 12 December.

CHAPTER 11

HR, Strategy and Performance

CAN HR INFLUENCE EVENTS?

Although there may be considerable doubt concerning the actual role HR should perform and how it should be done, human resource professionals established a place at the senior management table by the early 1990s through their ability to identify and solve practical problems in fields such as recruitment, employee relations and training. HR professionals and researchers then turned their attention to interpreting and reinforcing the maxim that *'people make the difference'*.

Researchers have attempted to identify whether adopting HR practices can make an observable difference in practice to organisational performance in measurable terms. If it can be proven that the adoption of human resource systems, policies and procedures, this will reinforce the claim that HR has to have a seat on the top table and a co-responsibility for strategic initiatives. This has often been referred to as *'opening the black box'*.

OPENING THE 'BLACK BOX'

In attempting to examine the impact of HR practices on organisational performance, a number of researchers have discovered some impressive and direct impacts and influences. This is referred to by Ramsey et al (2000) as 'the 'high road' approach to management, in which organisations choose to compete primarily on quality and rely especially on human resource development and employee contributions to succeed in this.

Much of this research has been carried out in the US, with the best-known being Mark Huselid (1995). He carried out in-depth surveys in top companies, matching the nature of the HR practices against performance measures, such as growth, productivity and profits. Using market value as the key indicator, he found that organisations with significantly above-average scores on using HR practices provided an extra market value per employee of between $10,000 and $40,000. He also found that the introduction of such practices led to an immediate impact (Guest 1998).

In the UK, a CIPD-financed project by the University of Sheffield's Institute of Work Psychology (West and Patterson 1998) concluded that HR practices are not only critical to business performance, but also have a greater importance than an emphasis on quality, technology and R&D in terms of influence on bottom-line profits. For example, effective HR practices were found to account for 19 per cent of the variation in profitability and 18 per cent in productivity, while R&D accounted for only 8 per cent. This led them to conclude that the most important area managers should emphasise is the management of people.

Some of these findings have arisen from broad surveys across sectors and others from selected industries. Thompson (2000), for example, investigated 400 UK aerospace companies and concluded that high-performing organisations, as measured by value added per employee, tend to use a wider range of innovative HR practices covering a higher proportion of employees. The greatest differentials between higher- and lower-performing organisations (as measured by value added per employee) was in the use of two-way communication systems, broader job gradings and employees being responsible for their own quality.

A more detailed survey of such studies can be found in Marchington and Wilkinson (2008).

THE ROLE OF HR IN RAISING PERFORMANCE

It therefore appears evident from research detailed above that human resources can make a sizeable contribution towards raising organisational performance. There are two major viewpoints as to how this can be done:

- First, a number of projects have been set up to examine what makes up a truly exceptional collection of HR practices, often called *'bundles'*, that raises performance in the organisation.
- Second, there has been a considerable debate, one that is still very much alive, as to whether such a collection of practices (called *'best practices'*) will work in every situation, or whether the context and nature of the organisation puts different demands upon the practices to be operated (called *'best fit'*). A third model is the resource-based model, which has close links to the core competence model.

BEST PRACTICE APPROACH – 'BUNDLES' OF HR PRACTICES

At the same time that researchers were attempting to prove conclusively that successful and effective HR practices improved the bottom-line performance, it became clear that a differentiation needed to be made between such practices: in effect, that some worked better than others and, more critically, that although individual practices may be relatively unsuccessful, when brought together in a 'bundle' their combined outcome was much greater than their individual contribution. A number of writers have formulated these bundles into what they call a system of 'high performance' or 'high commitment', indicating that using the full set will inevitably lead to improved organisational performance. It is emphasised by all the researchers that these bundles have to be coherent and integrated to have their full effect.

The *level of commitment* shown by employees is seen as key to high performance. Without such a commitment, employees will not be prepared to develop their skills and competencies, take on board the enhanced responsibilities for quality, work organisation and problem-solving and 'go the extra mile' to come up with improvements and innovations or improve the customer's experience. That is why a number of researchers use the level of commitment as a key reflection of organisational success from a people management viewpoint.

For Purcell et al (2003), a committed employee will use discretionary behaviour in that the employee can give co-operation, effort and initiative because they want to, arising out of the fact that they like their job and feel motivated by the systems in place, especially the HR ones.

Researchers have found that a high level of commitment comes about from the implementation of the following HR practices:

EMPLOYEE INVOLVEMENT

The thinking here is that it is impossible to gain the employees' trust if they do not both have the essential business information available to management and that they have at least the opportunity to be consulted on important issues that may affect their jobs and the way they are carried out. This passes the message that employees are treated as mature, intelligent beings, not just 'hands' or 'labour' who leave their brains in their lockers. The process of involvement can include briefing groups, staff surveys, focus groups or more sophisticated systems such as quality circles or recognition schemes. It can also extend to financial involvement through employee share-ownership. Marchington (2001) points out from his research that these practices are very popular with employees (80–85 per cent of employees involved in such practices want them to continue), although he adds the disillusioning caveat that some employees enjoy working with them because it is 'better than working' or 'gives me a half hour off work'.

EMPLOYEE VOICE

Millward et al (2000), by using the data from the 1998 Workplace Employee Relations Survey (WERS), have shown the close association between positive responses in attitude surveys and direct voice arrangement. A 'voice' for the employees does not have to be through a formal trade union and it is certainly not just ensuring there is a formal grievance procedure. The importance of this practice is that the employer recognises the importance of employee group viewpoints and suggestions and that the employee does not feel isolated so important issues can be raised in a formal (or informal) setting without the employees themselves having to, in effect, raise their heads above the parapet.

There has been a greater emphasis in recent years on the concept of *employee engagement*, which combines the better features of involvement and employee voice (see Seminar Activity at the end of this chapter).

HARMONISATION OF TERMS AND CONDITIONS

'Everybody works for the same team' is a common form of encouragement from senior management but falls on deaf ears if there is a clear manifestation of differing benefits at varying levels in the organisation. When Japanese companies began setting up satellite operations in the UK in the late 1970s and early 1980s, one of the surprises to commentators was the degree of egalitarian symbols on display.

In Nissan in Sunderland, for example, there was one canteen serving everybody and it was frequented by all staff including senior management; everybody was on the same level of holiday entitlement and wore the same overalls. Employees respected the equality and it fed the belief in the 'one company' ethos, leading in turn to effective teamworking at all levels (Wickens 1987).

EMPLOYMENT SECURITY

The 'jobs for life' culture evident some 30 to 40 years ago no longer exists. Rather, it never really existed in the first place, except in pockets of the public services, such as prisons and the post office. Employees may have had a clear, well-trodden career pathway set out, but the precise directions, both geographically and occupationally, may have worked out very differently from expectations and preferences. In the last 20 years, the global and business environmental changes have caused such changes in employment that the pathway has become one made up of crazy paving and employees have to lay it themselves!

So how can any business promise employment security? The theorists indicate that the security is of a different dimension. There may be short-term guarantees of employment, such as 12 months or of the life of a large-scale contract or, more usually, it is the cultural imperative of the organisation that redundancies will only take place as a very last resort. Internal transfers, skills retraining, short-time working will all be alternatives to try to extend the employee's contract as long as possible to get over difficult times. It is, in effect, the opposite of the tough employer's 'high and fire' short-term employment policy. It keeps to the HRM thinking that the employee is a critical asset, not a cost to be reduced.

Alongside these practices to encourage commitment, there are a group of practices that integrate with the organisation's business strategy:

SOPHISTICATED RECRUITMENT AND SELECTION

Sophistication is essentially the combination of recognising the importance of bringing into the organisation the right people with the right skills and personality (having a strategic approach to human resource planning) and carrying out careful and detailed recruitment and selection procedures. These procedures especially refer to using psychological tests and structured interviews that match people effectively to the organisational culture, to the job and the team requirements.

EXTENSIVE TRAINING AND DEVELOPMENT

It is clearly not enough to select the right people. In a swiftly changing world, employees need to constantly learn new jobs, which involves developing their skills and knowledge. They must also be prepared for enlargement of their jobs and to be ready for promotion opportunities. The emphasis switches in a subtle way from the organisation organising training courses to the organisation encouraging employees (individually or in groups) to undertake learning experiences, which can take many forms. The 'ideal' form of this item in the bundle is of employees undertaking self-directed life-long learning within the framework of a 'learning organisation'.

SELF-MANAGED TEAMS

The practice of allowing teams to have greater control over their work is a relatively recent one, although theorists, such as Mayo and his colleagues at the Hawthorne production plant in America in the 1930s, have been advocating it throughout the twentieth century. It is linked closely to involvement and, in a fully fledged system, team members are involved in decisions concerning work rotas, breaks, changes in production processes, leave and sickness arrangements. Moreover, they are encouraged to think about and promote local improvements on an individual and team basis. It involves reducing the power and day-to-day authority of local management, but, at the same time, retains their accountability. The research has shown that, when it works well, it is closely associated with high productivity and overall performance.

EXTENSIVE SYSTEMS OF FLEXIBILITY

If constant and rapid change is the norm, successful organisations need a workforce that is flexible enough to respond quickly to the required changes. They need to be multi-skilled, willing to work hours that suit the customer and willing to switch jobs and locations when necessary. The organisation also needs to have in place facilities to increase and reduce the employee numbers when required through systems of annualised hours or use of temporary and short-term contracts or by outsourcing work.

PERFORMANCE PAY

The emphasis on high-performance outcomes inevitably has meant that pay systems are geared to reflect the level of performance. Employees' pay at all levels is contingent; in other words, it has an element that varies depending on the success of the outcomes. Examples of these systems can include bonus schemes for production employees and call centre staff, incentive systems for sales and service staff and executive bonuses for directors. Commitment should be encouraged by aligning the pay of employees with organisational performance.

Given that a bundle of HR practices leads to improved performance, it follows that using this bundle is the best thing to do. In theory, it becomes a set of 'best practices' which can be universally applied.

The CIPD Shaping the Future project (Evans 2008) identified a number of enablers and barriers to high performance. Enablers included:

- shared purpose
- clear strategy
- strong leadership
- performance management that is lean and mean but not destructively so.

Barriers included:

- lack of clarity in performance management
- middle managers, who may not be good leaders.

HR could be either an enabler, if it took up the opportunity to make a strategic contribution, or a barrier, if it is isolated from the rest of the business.

REFLECTIVE ACTIVITY 11.1

NHS workers and best practice HR

Recent research in the NHS asked 200 workers at a range of levels to indicate how they saw HR practices fitting together. Three sets of practices were generally seen as combined together. These were:

1   Professional development, through appraisal, training and career development.

2   Employee contribution, through communication, teamworking and employee involvement and participation.

3   The employee deal, through recruitment, pay, non-monetary rewards, work–life balance and employment security.

Question

1   Do you agree with these combinations of HR practices? Would you put other combinations together?

Source: adapted from Marchington and Wilkinson (2008)

When reading the previous section it may have occurred that there does not appear to be much consensus as to what HR practices make up the full set. Each item of research comes up with a different set of best practices, some of which overlap with other research, but each has a special leaning. Angela Baron of the CIPD suggests that high performance does little more than describe an approach to managing organisations that aims to stimulate discretionary effort and utilise skills. As she says, is this any different from good HR? She also doubts how widespread the approach actually is. A 2008 survey by the UK Commission on Employment and Skills found that just under a third of UK organisations take a high-performance approach, but as she says, this may be because they were not sure what the term meant but thought it sounded like a good thing (Baron 2011). On the other hand, a report quoted in *People Management* in June 2012 suggests half of staff are not aware of their organisation's HR polices (*People Management* 2012).

In America, Bosalie and Dietz (2003) have reviewed ten years of research in this area and have found little that recommends a common approach, with the practices reported more extensively being training and development, participation and empowerment, performance pay and information-sharing through involvement.

On the other hand, a 2012 study by the Boston Consulting Group and the World Federation of People Management Associations (Strack et al 2012) found that companies highly skilled in core HR practices experienced up to 3.5 times the revenue growth and up to 2.1 times the profit margin compared with less skilled companies. In particular, high-performance companies:

● build stronger leaders
● do more to attract, develop and retain talented people
● treat and track performance with transparency.

However, a closer reading of the report shows that BCG were examining each best practice in isolation; they were not evaluating a package of best practices.

There is also doubt about the universality of the best practice approach – will it lead to better performance in all organisations, regardless of the environment in which they operate? Purcell has stated that this claim leads us 'down a utopian cul-de-sac' (Purcell 1999, p36).

Marchington and Grugulis (2000) suggest that best practice (high-commitment HR) is more likely when:

● employers are able to take a long-term perspective
● labour costs are a low proportion of total costs
● knowledge workers can be rewarded for using their discretion
● firms and workers are in a strong market position.

This package would seem to fit perfectly with a high-tech Silicon Valley company such as Hewlett-Packard in the 1990s, but the struggles that H-P has had in the 2000s suggest that even here the link may be transitory.

 REFLECTIVE ACTIVITY 11.2

Nike and best practice

In the late 2000s the sportswear company Nike developed an HR training programme to strengthen HR in its contract manufacturers. Eight factories in Vietnam and eight in southern China were involved in 2008–09.

Each factory completed an employee satisfaction survey to better understand the top issues facing workers and to measure trust and respect in the factory. Factories brought their survey results to the HR training sessions so that they could apply the insights of their workers to the creation of action plans and HR best practice.

Training modules included hiring practices, worker training and development, worker empowerment and retention, worker–management communication, compensation, performance management and building a strong HR function. The factories also established a learning community to promote ongoing learning and sharing of practices.

Following the training, the factories implemented their specific action plans. One set goals for reducing the number of workers reporting dissatisfaction with the behaviour and attitude of their direct supervisor from 15 per cent to 5 per cent. Another set goals to increase the technical skill levels of the workers.

Comments on the programme included:

'The HRM workshop was able to highlight the importance of having a strong HR system.'

'If HR is strong, we use effective processes to recruit the right people and develop them with a foreseeable career path.'

'The HR tools we received are helping us follow our projects closely.'

'HRM created a community where each factory set out the boundary of its own experience and knowledge. In return, each factory received many good practices.' (Nike 2010)

Question

1 To what extent do you think that this case study provides evidence to support the best practice model?

CASE STUDY 11.1

L'OREAL AND THE TALENT ADVANTAGE

L'Oreal is the world leader in beauty products. The linchpin of its growth strategy is building 'talent advantage' – a strategic approach to developing its talent portfolio and allocating resources:

- incentivising leaders to identify and develop talent in their teams
- motivating talent to move to strategic high-growth areas by linking career development opportunities to those areas

- appointing talent managers in crucial markets to reinforce local recruitment and promote the employer brand
- establishing talent incubators to feed the talent pipeline
- enhancing career visibility and leadership expectations by establishing clear, uniform definitions of talent and performance standards.

BEST FIT APPROACH

Because the extensive research reveals such a varied set of bundles and performances, considerable doubt has been shed on whether the application of the set of bundles or best practices will lead inevitably to improved performance. Many writers, therefore, have taken an alternative view that there is no 'holy grail' of practices which will magically improve organisational performance. What works well in one organisation may fail dismally in another, where the context may be totally different. In a private sector organisation (a manufacturing company, for example), you may well expect performance pay to be widespread and to form the bulwark of performance management and motivation systems; however, in the voluntary sector (a hospice charity, for example), it is highly unlikely that any of the staff would work under a performance pay scheme. The context, the vision, the values – they are so different.

Huselid himself comes down firmly on the side of a range of possible bundles, based on the reasoning that sustained competitive advantage depends partly on being able to develop arrangements that are hard to imitate (the resource-based concept). If the 'holy grail' was quite distinctive, every organisation would immediately adopt it and the competitive advantage would be lost.

Thompson (2000), similarly, is reticent in recommending wholesale adoption of the innovative HR practices associated with high-performing aerospace companies: 'That is probably too simplistic a message' (p19). Marchington and Grugulis (2000) adopt the same viewpoint: 'Best practice, it seems, is problematic… there are times when they appear to be contradictory messages' (p1121).

How do you know which HR practices an organisation should adopt? Only by a combination of knowing and understanding the true nature and strengths of the organisation, so you can eliminate those practices that have little chance of success, and then by experiment.

In the knowledge-intensive firms, the best fit of practices has been found to be the kind that develops intellectual and social capital needed in order to acquire business and manager customer relationships. Here, the crucial aspect is the development of knowledge-sharing processes, not just the knowledge and skills of the workforce (Swart et al 2003).

Purcell's (1999) distinct preference for 'best fit' has led him to urge a much greater emphasis on sharing employee knowledge throughout the organisation. If organisations have unique circumstances that require unique sets of HRM practices, it is vital that the knowledge and understanding of both circumstances and practices are held in common by all employees. With Peter Boxall, he argued that best practice HR is much more likely where the production system is capital-intensive or high-tech. Firms characterised by intense, cost-based competition, such as supermarkets, typically adopt a low-skill model of HR (Boxall and Purcell 2008). An example of a highly successful company whose HR practices could not be further from the best practice model is Ryanair, which was extensively discussed in Chapter 10.

Although there appears to be extensive evidence of HR practices adding to organisational improvement, there are a number of critics who doubt the close association. The greatest is Legge (2001), whose scepticism has been consistent and vociferous for many years. She points out the vagueness of definition of the 'best practice', such as performance pay, and the appropriateness of the measures used for organisational success. She also doubts whether the use of the practices actually influences the performance (the lack of causality).

There have also been studies that demonstrate that HRM practices can lead to a deterioration in working life. Danford et al (2004) researched the high-performance HR practices introduced in an aerospace company but found some major negative impacts on the employees, such as substantial downsizing, a superficial implementation of empowerment and a lack of trust between the parties.

Best fit HR has also been linked to the life cycle model. For example, an organisation in the start-up stage will concentrate in its recruitment on obtaining the best workers to fill gaps, in the growth stage it is more concerned with succession issues, in maturity in maintaining its workforce, and in decline in managing downsizing (Farnham 2010; Kochan and Barocci 1985).

Just as with the best practice model, best fit has been heavily criticised:

- Just as with best practice, it is heavily prescriptive. It assumes that a particular set of HR practices will be suitable for an organisation with a particular strategic configuration, or a particular stage in the life cycle.
- It is oversimplified. Organisations are unlikely to be solely prospectors (that is, in the start-up stage), or solely defenders (that is, in the maturity stage). For different products

or services, they could be either. It is also often difficult to identify exactly where an organisation is on its life cycle. It will tend to lurch from one stage to another, and perhaps even back again (Boxall and Purcell 2008).

- It is static. As organisations change their strategy in response to changes in the external environment, are they going to change their HR policies as well?
- Some organisations have no strategy beyond day-to-day survival. What are their best fit policies?

Can the best practice and best fit models be reconciled? One way of doing so is that put forward by Boxall and Purcell (2008). They argue that the surface level of HR – that which determines day-to-day action – is likely to be based on best fit, while the underlying level, reflecting values and principles, could well be based on best practice principles. A parallel can be drawn with the absolutist and relativist models of ethics discussed in Chapter 9.

COMPETITIVE STRATEGY AND HR PRACTICES – PORTER, SCHULER AND JACKSON

Michael Porter argued in *Competitive Advantage: Creating and sustaining superior performance* (1985) that firms need to choose between three fundamental approaches to gaining competitive advantage:

- cost reduction
- quality enhancement
- innovation.

The HR implications of these strategies were examined by Schuler and Jackson (1987). Firms pursuing a cost reduction strategy concentrate on tight controls, minimisation of overheads and economies of scale. The emphasis is on quantity rather than quality. They will pursue cost reduction through increased use of part-time and temporary employees, outsourcing (including offshoring to low-wage countries), low wages (at or close to minimum wage levels), minimal levels of training and development, explicit job descriptions that allow little room for ambiguity, narrowly defined career paths, and short-term, results-oriented performance appraisals. There is usually little employee involvement and unions are likely to be discouraged. An extreme example of a cost reduction strategy is that pursued by some gangmasters, who sometimes employ illegal immigrant labour at below minimum wage levels, and with little or no consideration for health and safety. After the Morecambe Bay tragedy in 2004, when 23 illegal Chinese immigrant cockle-pickers were drowned, the Gangmasters Licensing Authority was set up to regulate employment in agriculture, fishing (including cockle-picking) and food processing, but in 2009 Oxfam reported that gangmasters had subsequently moved into the less regulated construction, hospitality and care sectors, where there were still reports of workers being paid as little as £50 for a 49-hour week (Oxfam 2009).

Firms pursuing a quality-enhancement strategy are likely to be much more attractive to work for. Their employment practices are very close to the high-commitment HR model, emphasising sophisticated methods of recruitment and selection, and extensive and long-term training and development. There will be high levels of employee involvement and empowerment, and there is likely to be a high degree of job security. Pay is competitive and there is likely to be a concern for work–life balance. Unions are common and there is likely to be a partnership approach to industrial relations. HR has a key role in supporting the organisation's culture. Quality-enhancing firms are also likely to be concerned with the HR practices at their suppliers. It is vital to the success of the quality enhancement strategy that suppliers buy into it. A classic example is the Japanese-owned segment of the car industry.

With an innovation strategy, people are managed in order to work *differently* (unlike either the cost reduction strategy, where they are encouraged to work *harder*, or the quality strategy, where they are encouraged to work *smarter*). The emphasis is on informality, flexibility and problem-solving. The HR implications are:

- an emphasis on creativity
- long-term focus
- high level of co-operative, interdependent behaviour
- moderate degree of concern for both quality and quantity
- a high degree of risk-taking
- personal and self-development, rather than employer-directed T&D
- a high degree of ambiguity and unpredictability
- an emphasis on individuality, with little demand for unions
- an emphasis on profit-sharing, rather than high wages.

A classic example of long-term successful implementation of an innovation strategy is the American company 3M, which is discussed in Case Study 11.2.

CASE STUDY 11.2

INNOVATION AT 3M

One of the most innovative companies over the past 80 years has been 3M – an abrasives manufacturer that broke its own mould by inventing masking tape in 1925, and which has carried on producing highly innovative new products ever since, from the audio tape to Post-It sticky notes. Its latest new idea is Post-It Picture Paper, which marries the Post-It technology to photographic paper, allowing users to print out pictures from their computer straight on to Post-Its.

How does 3M do it? The secret is bottom–up innovation. Someone in the labs, or manufacturing or marketing comes up with a new idea. When he has convinced his supervisor that he's on to something interesting, he will be set up with a small budget and told to get on with it. Harry Heltzer, who developed the idea that became Scotchlite, for adhesive reflective road marking, and later reflective signs, eventually went on to become president of 3M (Grant 2008).

To facilitate the innovation process, 3M has had a long-running policy which permits all research or marketing employees to spend up to 15 per cent of their (and the company's) time on their own projects. In addition, the company operates two career ladders, which make it possible for a technical person to move as high as vice-president without having to take on a managerial role. The result: for years 3M was number one on Boston Consulting Group's Most Innovative Companies list, and it was praised in Jim Collins' and Jerry Porras' best-seller *Built to Last* in 1994.

Larry Wendling, 3M's vice-president of corporate research, identified 'The Seven Habits of Highly Successful Corporations':

1. From the chief executive down, the company must be committed to innovation.

2. The corporate culture must be actively maintained.

3. Innovation is impossible without a broad base of technology – 3M is a leader in 42 different technologies.

4. Networking, both formal and informal – the scientists themselves run an annual symposium for all 9,700 R&D personnel, where ideas and ongoing projects are shared.

5. Set individual expectations and reward employees for outstanding work. Hundreds of employees –

selected by their peers – are honoured for scientific achievement every year.

6 Quantify efforts – 3M carefully tracks its spending to see whether its R&D money is spent wisely.

7 Research must be tied to the customer (Arndt 2006).

However, in the late 1990s the dream started to go sour. At a company which has prided itself on earning one-third of its revenue from products invented in the previous five years, the proportion had fallen to a quarter, and by the late 1990s, the company's share price was stagnating.

In 2000, 3M appointed James McNerney as its new CEO. McNerney was the first outsider ever to head the 100-year-old company. He came from General Electric, where he had been a disciple of the legendary Jack Welch. His mission – to bring discipline to 3M. He sacked 8,000 workers (11 per cent of the total) and imported GE's Six Sigma programme, a world-renowned statistical quality control technique. The basis of Six Sigma was to reduce variability, and so lower cost. The two main Six Sigma tools were DMAIC (define, measure, analyse, improve, control), and, more critical for 3M, Design for Six Sigma (DFSS), which

aimed to systemise the new product development process. DFSS stressed constant review and quick results. The result was that incremental improvement took precedence over blue-sky research. Traditionally, 3M had allowed researchers years to tinker with new ideas. The consensus within the company was that a new product like Post-It would have been impossible under a Six Sigma regime.

The results of the McNerney regime were predictable. The share price shot up and so did short-term profits, but innovation stagnated. From number 1 on the Most Innovative Company list in 2004, 3M fell to second in 2005, third in 2006 and seventh in 2007.

In 2005, McNerney left to head Boeing and was succeeded by George Buckley, a scientist who quietly proceeded to reverse many of his predecessor's reforms. He said, 'Perhaps one of the mistakes we made as a company – it's one of the dangers of Six Sigma – is that when you value sameness more than you value creativity, I think you potentially undermine the heart and soul of a company like 3M' (Hindo 2007). He has exempted the research scientists from DFSS and increased the R&D budget by 20 per cent. As one 3M executive said, 'We feel we can dream again.'

MILES AND SNOW AND EMPLOYMENT SYSTEMS

Miles and Snow (1978) suggest four main ways in which organisations can cope with and manage their environments. These involve an interaction between the organisation's strategy, its culture and its environment. They can be:

1 *Defenders* – they operate in generally placid environments. They do not actively search for new opportunities, but concentrate on maximising the efficiency of their existing operations. They are very vulnerable to a sudden shift in their environment.

2 *Prospectors* – they are attracted to turbulent environments. They are constantly experimenting with novel responses to the environment. They thrive on change and uncertainty, but pay little attention to efficiency. They are decentralised and promote creativity and innovation. They are thus vulnerable if the environment settles down.

3 *Analysers* – they are successful poachers. They watch competitors for new ideas and adopt the successful ones. Their approach to the environment is therefore second

hand and they let the prospectors make the mistakes. A classic example of the analyser strategy is the video-recorder war. Sony pioneered the industry with the Betamax format, but was eventually defeated by Matsushita and its VHS format. They are seeking at the same time to maintain their shares in existing markets and to exploit new opportunities. They can be seen as a hybrid between defenders and prospectors. One variant of the model distinguishes analysers with or without innovation.

4   *Reactors* – they make adjustments to their strategy when forced to do so by environmental pressures. Unlike the defenders, they are prepared to change, but they are even more market followers than the analysers. They are not prepared for change and do little planning. Miles and Snow see this strategy (or lack of it) as basically a failure mode.

Organisations must recognise that a strategy which suited them very well in the past may no longer be appropriate if the nature of the environment which faces them has changed. For example, big national airlines, which were highly bureaucratic and cost-efficient, were highly successful in the tightly regulated environments of the 1960s and 1970s, but were hard hit by more agile budget airlines (Southwest in the US, Ryanair and easyJet in the UK) as the airline market was deregulated and became more turbulent.

In appropriate types of environment, each of the defender, prospector and analyser strategies can be successful, but the reactor strategy is unlikely to be successful in the long term.

Many later scholars have tested the validity of Miles and Snow's model and generally have confirmed their findings. For example:

- Shortell and Zajac (1990) found that defenders are the first type of organisation to adopt new production technologies; analysers the first to adopt new management systems; and prospectors the first to develop new products.
- Gimenez (1999) found that among Brazilian small and medium enterprises, reactors were the least successful in terms of increasing their turnovers.
- Peng, Tan and Tong (2004) found that in China, state-owned firms followed defender strategies, privately owned firms prospector strategies and foreign-owned forms analyser strategies.

Delery and Doty (1996) extended Miles and Snow's analysis and looked at the degree of fit between the organisational models and HR systems. They concentrated on the defender and prospector models (they see the analyser model as a middle-of-the-road system, with elements of both defender and prospector).

They argued that the defender organisation concentrated on efficiency, on producing existing products in a better way, rather than developing new ones, and that this could be best supported by what they described as an internal employment system, which stressed:

- internal career opportunities and recruitment, with well-defined career ladders
- extensive formal training, with a high level of socialisation within the organisation
- behaviour-based appraisal, largely used for developmental purposes
- transparent pay structures based on hierarchy and seniority; little profit-sharing
- employment security
- a high degree of employee participation, with unions likely to be recognised
- highly defined jobs
- a well-established HR function, with considerable influence.

The prospector organisation constantly searches for new products and markets. The emphasis is on being new rather than being efficient. This is best supported by what they call a market-type employment system, which stressed:

- hiring from outside rather than developing insiders, with little use of career ladders

- little formal training, and only based on short-term needs
- results-based appraisals, with little tolerance for failure
- incentive-based pay systems
- very little employment security
- little employment voice, with unions tolerated at best
- loose and flexible job definitions
- limited role for HR.

A defender organisation is thus likely to attract someone looking for a long-term career, but not for excitement, while working for a prospector organisation is likely to be a lot more stimulating, but much more short term (see also Marchington and Wilkinson 2008, pp152–3).

Delery and Doly attempted to test their hypotheses empirically through an analysis of the US banking industry, but their findings were not particularly strong. They only examined one role within the banks, that of loan officer. They obtained questionnaire results from 216 banks, but only a minority of these fitted either the market or the internal employment models. Two-thirds were middle of the road in their employment policies. They found that banks that implemented a prospector strategy 'reaped higher return from more results-oriented appraisals and lower levels of employee participation than did banks that relied on a defender strategy' (p826). However, although the theory suggested that internal career paths were more consistent with a defender strategy, their empirical research found the opposite. In general, they found that in the banking industry, 'the closer a bank's employment system resembled the market-type system, the higher its performance' (p827).

REFLECTIVE ACTIVITY 11.3

The Miles and Snow model

'The Miles and Snow model is essentially only relevant to the private sector.'

1   Do you agree?

2   Which, if any, of Miles and Snow's categories best fits your own organisation?

Burton et al (2004) examine the degree of fit between Miles and Snow's categories and a firm's organisational climate – its degree of trust, morale, conflict, reward fairness, leader credibility, resistance to change and scapegoating. They distinguish four types of climate:

- the group climate
- the developmental climate
- the rational goal climate
- the internal process climate.

The group climate is concentrated on internal focus with high trust and morale. The developmental climate is more externally oriented, also with high trust and morale – and low resistance to change. The rational goal climate is externally oriented to succeed, but with lower trust and morale, and low resistance to change. And, the internal process climate is more mechanical with a high resistance to change.

An internal process climate and a group climate, both being focused inwardly, are not very adaptive to the needs of a prospector or analyser-with-innovation strategy. In contrast, the developmental climate is too experimental for the efficiency focus of the defender strategy.

The internal process climate is rules-oriented and inwardly focused, well suited for a defender strategy where the focus on process is important, but such a climate does not change or adapt quickly and is not necessarily aligned with the organisation's strategy. It makes for a particularly severe misfit with innovative strategies and for prospectors.

REFLECTIVE ACTIVITY 11.4

Mechanistic and organic organisations

Mary Jo Hatch (1997) distinguishes between mechanistic and organic organisations. Mechanistic organisations specialise in routine activities with strictly demarcated lines of authority and responsibility. Tasks are highly specialised. Organic organisations have less specialisation. They are less formalised and hierarchical than mechanistic organisations, and use lateral communication.

Question

1   What parallels can you see between the analyses of Hatch and Miles and Snow?

THE RESOURCE-BASED VIEW

The resource-based view of HR has much in common with Prahalad and Hamel's (1990) core competence theory. Prahalad and Hamel argue that core competences are those factors which give an organisation its competitive advantage. As discussed in Chapter 10, the effectiveness of core competences can be assessed through the VRIN model:

- V – value
- R – rarity
- I – inimitability
- N – non-substitutability.

The resource-based view (RBV) of HR applies the core competence model to people factors within the organisation. How many times have you heard the phrase 'people are our greatest asset'? RBV is linked to the human capital approach, where people are seen as an asset to the organisation.

When we look at the relationship between strategy and HR it is clear that while best fit is an outside-in model, where the mix of HR practices is influenced by the external environment, mediated through the chosen strategy, RBV is inside–out. The external environment is seen as too volatile and unpredictable on which to base a viable strategy, so the strategy is chosen to fit with the organisation's (HR) core competences.

There is some debate about whether the RBV should be concerned just with managers and others with decision-making ability in the organisation, or whether it should be concerned with all employees. Marchington and Wilkinson (2008) stress the latter. Another debate is about whether the RBV relates to people, HR practices and processes, or both. Boxall (1998) distinguishes between 'human capital advantage', based on employee skill, and 'organisational process advantage' such as learning and co-operation and the HR policies which support them. Together these form 'human resource advantage' – employing better people *and* using better HR processes.

The final report of the CIPD's Shaping the Future project (Miller 2011) identified eight themes important for sustainable organisational performance:

- alignment – the fit between the values, behaviours and objectives of stakeholders, and the organisation's purpose
- shared purpose – within the organisation
- leadership

- locus of engagement
- assessment and evaluation
- balancing long- and short-term horizons
- agility
- capability-building.

From this the report drew ten insights for HR leaders:

1 The organisational change response needs to be truly agile and enduring, not a knee-jerk reaction.

2 It's a fine balance between alignment and flexibility. Avoid over-alignment.

3 Shared purpose can only be achieved by finding the human connection beyond profit or short-term efficiency.

4 Collaborative leadership brings sustainability.

5 Middle management have a valuable transforming and translating role, but are often bypassed.

6 An over-focus on today's needs is talent tunnel vision.

7 Truly understanding employees' locus of engagement can avoid the risk of over-attachment and underperformance.

8 Perceptions of unfairness undermine employee engagement.

9 Process-heavy organisations are often insight-light.

10 Leaders don't always know best about the long-term vision.

CASE STUDY 11.3

NHS DUMFRIES AND GALLOWAY: DYNAMIC DELIVERY IN DIFFICULT TIMES

NHS Dumfries and Galloway serves 149,000 people in southern Scotland and employs 5,000 people. In the late 2000s it launched its Delivery Dynamic Improvement (DDI) programme. The aim of the programme was to equip managers and clinical leaders with the knowledge and skills to enable them to build shared responsibility for dynamic continuous improvement in services provided to patients, as proposed in the Darzi Report (see Reflective Activity 11.5).

Issues identified included:

- *Organisational purpose* – most employees engaged with the core purpose of improving healthcare in the region and tackling health inequalities.
- *Cross-functional working* – DDI encouraged cross-functional working, knowledge-sharing,

ownership and innovation across teams and professional boundaries. This was seen as a key enabler of sustainable performance.

- *Employees* – they were high quality, committed and passionate about patient care.
- *Communication* – generally positive, possible to feed views upwards.
- *Career progression and talent development* – viewed as potential enabler of performance.

The trust identified enablers to performance:

- a sense of purpose that allows staff to engage with the community through a person-centred approach
- improvements in cross-functional working and communication

- knowledge-sharing.

Threats to performance were:

- *Internal* – disconnected middle management. A feeling that 'this is how we've always done things', and that we're pretty good already.
- *External* – the Coalition Government's deficit reduction programme, which aims to reduce the trust's costs by 4 per cent through robust vacancy management, review of fixed-term contracts, etc. Pressure on public sector pay and pensions (Miller 2011).

It could be argued that this case illustrates either best practice or resource-based HR. In the last resort, it does not matter which it is. If it works, the label is irrelevant. As the Chinese leader Deng Xiaoping said, 'It doesn't matter whether a cat is black or white so long as it catches mice.'

Like the best practice and best fit models, RBV can be criticised. First, where did the key resource or the core competence come from in the first place? It is very unlikely that it merged fully formed; it is much more likely that it evolved over time and that it did so through interaction with the environment. Business cannot be purely inside–out, totally ignoring the environment. The environment is there, it matters and it imposes constraints.

Second, key resources are not for ever. As we saw with the EVR model in Chapter 1, resources and the environment can get out of alignment over time, as the environment changes. In the early 1990s, British Airways pursued a policy of building on the strengths of its staff through empowerment. The then group managing director, Bob Ayling, was quoted in 1993 as saying: 'I would like to create an environment where there is genuine communication of information, discussion of ideas and acceptance of decisions taken. What I am aiming to create is a company where the management are responsive to an intelligent workforce' (Harrison 1993). However, by the late 1990s, and increasingly since, with the rise of Virgin Atlantic and the budget airlines Ryanair and easyJet, BA has been forced into successive rounds of cost-cutting, and the empowerment environment has been replaced by one of mutual suspicion. At the other end of the airline industry, Ryanair has been hugely successful through a programme of ruthless cost-cutting and a willingness to ignore anyone who gets in their way. For staff this has meant a determined anti-union policy (unlike BA, which has strong unions). However, Ryanair is ultimately dependent on discretionary spending. Even at very low fares, no-one has to take a Ryanair flight, and as the recession drags on, Ryanair's environment is turning more and more hostile.

In the last resort, it could be argued that the only key resource that really matters is that of extreme flexibility in the face of a potentially chaotic environment, and to achieve this flexibility the organisation must be a learning organisation.

REFLECTIVE ACTIVITY 11.5

The Darzi Report – High Quality Care for All

In 2007, the incoming Prime Minister, Gordon Brown, appointed the eminent surgeon Lord Darzi as a junior health minister. This was part of a general move to bring non-politicians into government, known colloquially as the GOATS – government of all the talents. Darzi's brief was to lead the NHS Next Stage Review, to develop a vision of the NHS fit for the twenty-first century. Darzi's report, *High Quality Care for All*, was published in June 2008 (Department of Health 2008).

The central theme of *High Quality Care for All* was putting the patient first. This involved:

- *Better access to primary care* – the report recommended 152 new GP-led health centres (polyclinics), open 12 hours a day, seven days a week, providing a range of services under one roof, including many previously only available in hospitals, such as blood tests, x-rays and ultrasounds. This proposal was controversial because it was felt that patients would lose contact with an individual GP and might have to travel further to a GP, but the advantages of local access to specialist services was thought to outweigh this. By the summer of 2009, 50 polyclinics were open. Other recommendations included 100 new GP practices in under-doctored areas, of which 65 were open in 2009, and extended opening hours at GPs. By 2009, three-quarters of GP practices were open either in the evening or early morning and/or at weekends, ahead of the target of 50 per cent.
- *Faster access to drugs and treatment* – more resources were put into the National Institute for Health and Clinical Excellence (NICE), enabling it to assess new drugs more quickly. New out-of-hours services, run by nurses, were also set up, and measures were taken to ensure that where people wished to die at home, they were given support to enable this.
- *Empowering patients* – personal health budgets are being developed, giving patients with chronic conditions more say in their treatment. Over 9 million people now have an individual health plan. To improve patient privacy, mixed-sex wards were to be phased out by 2010.
- *Making the NHS safer* – investment has been made to combat hospital-transmitted infections. Rates of both *C. difficile* and MRSA infections have fallen by more than target. From April 2009, all elective admissions are screened for MRSA.
- *Preventing ill-health* – one long-running criticism of the NHS is that it is really a National Illness Service, treating illness rather than preventing it. Measures are being taken to identify those at risk of heart disease and to prevent obesity, and NHS health checks are to be offered to everyone aged 40 to 74.
- *Improving quality* – NICE will publish quality standards setting out what quality care will look like in various specialties, and every NHS organisation will be required to publish annual Quality Accounts. The Care Quality Commission was set up in April 2009, with tough enforcement powers to ensure high-quality care.

Like many other organisations, the NHS is having difficulty in internalising the drive to higher quality. NHS trusts initially self-assess for quality through a tick-box exercise, which is usually accepted by the CQC. Basildon and Thurrock University Hospitals Foundation NHS Trust received a 'good' performance rating, and 13 marks out of 14 on 'safety and cleanliness' in 2009 on the basis of its self-assessment. However, when the CQC examined death rates for the trust, it found them a third higher than expected – 350 excess deaths a year. It then carried out two on-site inspections and found blood-splattered floors and equipment, and mould growing in medical machines (Bowcott 2009; Asthana and Campbell 2009).

Darzi recognised that although the initiative to improve quality must come from the centre, actually internalising a quality culture can only be done locally. Clinicians should be empowered to lead change locally, being given ownership of budgets and accountability for the quality of their services and freedom to set their own clinical priorities within national targets. This would encourage creativity and innovation. Progress in quality should be recognised through accreditation schemes.

Darzi recognised that his vision had a 10–15-year timespan, and some progress has been made in the first year. The director of policy at the NHS Confederation, Nigel Edwards, thinks he can see changes already taking place 'at the coalface'– 'people are talking about the quality agenda' – but Chris Ham, professor of health policy and management at Birmingham University, fears that the recession will lead to financial belt-tightening in the NHS, and a possible resurgence of command and control rather than empowering leadership (Carlisle

2009). Time will tell. The NHS adopted its Constitution in 2010, but it is not at all clear what effect the Coalition Government's NHS reform programme will have on the further implementation of Darzi.

1   How attractive do you think that the Darzi programme is to stakeholders in the NHS?

2   In the light of the information in this Reflective Activity and in Case Study 11.3, do you think that the Darzi programme is an example of best practice or best fit?

We have now gone full circle. We stand by the model put forward in Chapter 1, that there is a two-way relationship between HR and the environment, and we feel that the best fit model is the most appropriate way to understand this relationship.

KEY LEARNING POINTS

- There are three major models of strategic HR – the best practice, best fit and resource-based models.
- Links can be identified between Porter's generic strategies and HR strategy and practice.
- Miles and Snow have identified four different ways in which organisations react to their environments, and these can be shown to have connections to HR practice.

QUESTIONS

1   What HR practices are normally identified as part of a high-performance workplace?

2   In what situations is the best fit model more appropriate than the best practice model?

3   What are the links between the core competence and the resource-based view of HR?

FURTHER READING

The Final Report of the CIPD project on Shaping the Future, Jill Miller, *Sustainable Organisation Performance: What really makes the difference* (2011) is useful. John Walton's *Strategic Human Resource Development* (1999) is useful for the HR contribution to strategic management, while Mick Marchington and Adrian Wilkinson's *Human Resource Management at Work* (2008) and David Farnham's *Human Resource Management in Context: Strategy, insights and solutions* (2010) are excellent on the best practice, best fit and resource-based models of HR.

USEFUL WEBSITES

Ivythesis has a useful article on best practice versus best fit approaches to strategic HRM, which draws heavily on the work of Armstrong and includes a case study on Intel in Ireland (ivythesis.typepad.com/term_paper_topics/2010/11/best-practice-vs-best-fit-approach-to-strategic-human-resource-management.html).

AUDIO AND VIDEO MATERIAL

The CIPD has produced a useful podcast: podcast 30 (April 2009), *Building sustainable high performance*.

MODELS OF HR

The three major models of HR – best practice, best fit and resource-based – have been extensively discussed in this chapter. Using the material here, in Chapter 3 and 4 of Marchington and Wilkinson's *Human Resource Management at Work*, and in the following case studies, critically examine the three models.

Case Study 1 – Japanese multinationals in the UK

Doreinger, Lorenz and Terkla (2003) discussed the extent to which Japanese high-performance work practices were used in Japanese-owned manufacturing plants in the UK, the US and France. In this case study we will look mainly at the evidence for the UK.

The authors investigated the extent to which Japanese manufacturing transplants used four practices which they saw as typical of high-performance work systems – job rotation, quality circles, self-managing teams and employee responsibility for quality

control. They found that 66 per cent of plants surveyed in the UK used at least one of these practices, but only 2 per cent used all four. By far the most common practice used in the UK was employee responsibility for quality control, used by 60 per cent of respondents. None of the other three practices was used by more than 20 per cent. Results were comparable in France, but the US made more use of quality circles and self-managed teams.

The typical pattern for a Japanese transplant is that senior management will be Japanese, with long experience of operating high-performance work systems in Japan. However, HR will usually be the responsibility of Western managers, hired because of their familiarity with local industrial relations practices. Their role is to design hybrid HR systems that adapt Japanese practices to local conditions.

High adopters of Japanese practices (using three or more of the techniques) have made a significant move towards partnership arrangements, with employee involvement in decision-making, high investment in training, opportunities for the career advancement of shop floor workers and long-term employment guarantees.

The central obstacles to the greater adoption of high-performance practices were lack of skills and training, and status. Employees with formal technical qualifications were reluctant to work directly alongside production workers in the same team.

A producer of photocopiers and fax machines had used Japanese supervisors and team leaders as teachers and technical troubleshooters. When they were replaced by British supervisors, the company found that the new supervisors lacked the knowledge to teach and troubleshoot across the whole range of assembly jobs. Operators had little problem-solving experience or ability, and the new supervisors did not have the skills to train them. The result was that operators lacked the ability to take an effective part in quality circles and continuous improvement (*kaizen*), and these initiatives failed.

Case Study 2 – The Bosman case and the football transfer system

Before 1995, a professional footballer could only move to another club with the agreement of his current club, even if his contract with the current club had ended. The buying club had to purchase the player from his current club, through the payment of a transfer fee, unless a free transfer was agreed. The latter was only common in the case of a player nearing the end of his career. The current club could prevent a transfer, even if the player was out of contract.

Jean-Marc Bosman, a Belgian footballer with RFC Liège, wanted to be transferred to the French club Dunkerque. Liège refused without the payment of a transfer fee, which Dunkerque was unwilling to pay. Bosman claimed that as an EU citizen, he had the right of freedom of movement within the EU and that the existing transfer system prevented him from exercising this right.

The European Court of Justice found in his favour in 1995. As a result, transfer fees for out-of-contract players were illegal where a player was moving between one EU country and another. In effect, an out-of-contract player would always move on a free transfer.

The implications of the case for the structure of the football industry have been far-reaching:

- Small clubs have been hard hit. Previously, they recruited young talent, with the hope that the player would develop and could then be transferred to a bigger club for a large profit. After Bosman, they could only benefit from player development if they signed the young player on a long contract. This was very high risk, because if the player did not develop as hoped, they would be stuck with paying his wages until the end of the contract.
- To protect their investments in star players, bigger clubs also signed them on longer contracts. This meant that if a club were relegated, they would be forced to continue to pay star wages which they could no longer afford in a lower division. When Leeds were relegated from the Premier League, they were forced to sell their star players such as Jonathan Woodgate at cut-price rates, just to get their salaries off the payroll.
- Player power was vastly increased. Star players either had the security of a long contract, or they could hold out for much higher wages when negotiating the renewal of a contract. Alternatively, when their contract ended, they could move elsewhere and demand a high signing-on fee

(often running into the millions) from their new club.

Sources: Pearson (nd); Fordyce (2005)

Case Study 3 – Engaging for success

In the summer of 2009, David MacLeod and Nita Clarke produced a report for the Department for Business, Innovation and Skills on employee engagement (MacLeod and Clarke 2009). Their brief was 'to take an in-depth look at employee engagement [one of the key components of the high-performance workplace], and to report on its potential benefits for companies, organisations and individual employees' (p3).

Employee engagement proved elusive to define. The report found more than 50 definitions, including the useful 'you know it when you see it'. Eventually, building on the work of David Guest, the report defined employee engagement as 'a workplace approach designed to ensure that employees are committed to their organisation's goals and values, motivated to contribute to organisational success, and at the same time to enhance their own sense of well-being. Engaged organisations have strong and authentic values, with clear evidence of trust and fairness based on mutual respect, where two-way promises and commitments – between employers and staff – are understood, and are fulfilled' (p9).

The report found a strong correlation between high levels of employee engagement and measures of performance:

- Highly engaged organisations averaged 18 per cent higher productivity and 12 per cent higher profitability than those with low engagement.
- Fifty-nine per cent of engaged employees say that their job brings out their most creative ideas compared with 3 per cent of disengaged employees.
- Engaged employees take an average of 2.69 sick days a year, the disengaged 6.19 days.
- Engaged employees are 87 per cent less likely to leave the organisation than the disengaged.
- Seventy-eight per cent of engaged employees would recommend their company's products or services, as against 13 per cent of the disengaged.

The flipside is that disengagement costs money. While 30 per cent of workers were engaged, 20 per cent were disengaged, and there is some evidence that this figure may be rising (p15). Between 1992 and 2001, the proportion saying they had a great deal of discretion over how to do their job fell from 57 per cent to 43 per cent. Forty-two per cent would refuse to recommend their organisation as an employer to family or friends. Gallup suggested that in 2008 the cost of disengagement to the UK economy was between £59.4 and £64.7 billion (p17).

The report quotes many case studies. One concerns the construction equipment company JCB, which was hard hit by the recession in the construction industry in 2008. In October 2008 it proposed a shorter working week to the union, GMB, in order to avoid over 300 redundancies. Running up to the ballot, JCB held face-to-face sessions with employees to explain the background to the business situation and the steps that were being taken in response to it. As a result, employees understood the rationale behind the company's proposals and decisions. The union ballot voted two to one in favour of the shorter working week, although this meant a pay cut.

REFERENCES

Arndt, M. (2006) 3M's Seven Pillars of innovation. *BusinessWeek*. 10 May.

Asthana, A. and Campbell, D. (2009) The worst NHS wards… where safety is a lottery. *Observer*. 29 November.

Baron, A. (2011) *Is there such a thing as high performance working?* Reward blog. London: Chartered Institute of Personnel and Development.

Bosalie, P. and Dietz, G. (2003) *Commonalities and contradictions in research on HRM and performance*. Academy of Management Conference. August.

Bowcott, O. (2009) Hospital condemned over cleanliness gave itself top marks. *Guardian*. 28 November.

Boxall, P. (1998) Achieving competitive advantage through human resource strategy: towards a theory of industry dynamics. *Human Resource Management Review*. Vol 8, No 8.

Boxall, P. and Purcell, J. (2000) Strategic human resources management: where have we come from and where are we going? *International Journal of Management Reviews*. Vol 2, No 2.

Boxall, P. and Purcell, J. (2008) *Strategy and human resource management*. 2nd edition. Basingstoke: Palgrave Macmillan.

Burton, R.M. and Obel, B. (1998) *Strategic organizational diagnosis and design: developing theory for application*. Boston, MA: Kluwer.

Burton, R.M., Lauridsen, J. and Obel, B. (2004) The impact of organisational climate and strategic fit on firm performance. *Human Resource Management*. Vol 43, No 1.

Carlisle, D. (2009) One year on: Darzi's long and winding road. *Health Service Journal*. 25 June.

Danford, A., Richardson, M., Stewart, P., Tailby, S. and Upchurch, M. (2004) High performance work systems and workplace partnership: a case of aerospace workers. *New Technology, Work and Employment*. Vol 19, No 1.

Delery, J. and Doty, H. (1996) Modes of theorizing in strategic human resource management: tests of universalistic contingency, and configurational performance predictions. *Academy of Management Journal*. Vol 39, No 4.

Department of Health. (2008) *High quality care for all*. The Darzi Report. London: Department of Health.

Doeringer, P., Lorenz, E. and Terkla, D. (2003) The adoption and diffusion of high performance management lessons from Japanese multinationals in the West. *Cambridge Journal of Economics*. Vol 27.

Evans, C. (2008) *Enablers and barriers to high performance working: insights from the first Shaping the Future café event*. London: Chartered Institute of Personnel and Development.

Farnham, D. (2010) *Human resource management in context: strategy, insights and solutions.* London: Chartered Institute of Personnel and Development.

Fordyce, T. (2005) 10 years since Bosman. BBC Sport. news.bbc.co.uk/sport1/hi/football [Accessed 14 October 2009].

Gimenez, F. (1999) Miles and Snow's strategy model in the context of small firms. www.baer.uca.edu/research/icbs/1999

Grant, R. (2008) *Contemporary strategy analysis.* 6th ed. Oxford: Blackwell.

Guest, D. (1998) Combine harvest. *People Management.* 29 October.

Harrison, M. (1993) Getting a grip on the flying shop. *Independent.* 22 November.

Hatch, M.J. (1997) *Organization theory: modern symbolic and postmodern perspectives.* Oxford: Oxford University Press.

Hindo, B. (2007) At 3M, a struggle between efficiency and creativity. *BusinessWeek.* 11 June.

Huselid, M. (1995) The impact of human resource management practices on turnover, productivity and corporate financial performance. *Academy of Management Journal.* Vol 38.

Kochan, T. and Barocci, T. (1985) *Human resource management and industrial relations.* Boston, MA: Little Brown.

Legge, K.(2001) Silver bullet or spent round? Assessing the meaning of the 'high commitment management/performance relationship'. In J. Storey (ed.) *Human resource management: a critical text.* London: Thomson Learning.

MacLeod, D. and Clarke, N. (2009) *Engaging for success, enhancing performance through employee engagement.* London: Department for Business, Innovation and Skills.

Marchington, M. (2001) Employee involvement at work. In J. Storey (ed.) *Human resource management: a critical text.* London: Thomson Learning.

Marchington, M. and Grugulis, I. (2000) 'Best practice' human resource management: perfect opportunity or dangerous illusion. *International Journal of Human Resource Management.* Vol 11, No 6.

Marchington, M. and Wilkinson, A. (2008) *Human resource management at work.* 4th edition. London: Chartered Institute of Personnel and Development.

Miles, R.E. and Snow, C.C. (1978) *Organizational strategy, structure and process.* Maidenhead: McGraw-Hill.

Miller, J. (2011) *Sustainable organisation performance: what really makes the difference. Shaping the Future, final report.* London: Chartered Institute of Personnel and Development.

Millward, N., Bryson, A. and Forth, J. (2000) *All change at work: British industrial relations, 1980 to 1998 as portrayed by the Workplace Industrial Relations Survey Series.* London: Routledge.

Nike. (2010) Case study: HRM in practice FY08/09. www.nikebiz.com/crreport/content/workers-and-factories/3-12-0-case-study-hrm-in-practice.php [Accessed 5 September 2012].

Oxfam. (2009) *Turning the tide: how best to protect workers employed by gangmasters, five years after Morecambe Bay.* Oxford: Oxfam.

Pearson, G. (nd) University of Liverpool FIH Factsheet: the Bosman case, EU law and the transfer system. www.liv.ac.uk/footballindustry/bosman.html [Accessed 14 October 2009].

Peng, M.W., Tan, J. and Tong, T.W. (2004) Ownership types and strategic groups in emerging economies. *Journal of Management Studies.* Vol 41, No 7. November.

People Management. (2012) Half of staff not aware of HR policies, figures show. *People Management.* 8 June.

Porter, M. (1985) *Competitive advantage: creating and sustaining superior performance.* New York: The Free Press.

Prahalad, C.K. and Hamel, G. (1990) The core competence of the corporation. *Harvard Business Review.* May–June.

Purcell, J. (1999) Best practice and best fit: chimera or cul-de-sac? *Human Resource Management Journal.* Vol 9, No 3.

Purcell, J. (2005) *Business strategies and HRM: uneasy bedfellows or strategic partners?* University of Bath Working Paper 16. www.bath.ac.uk/management/reaearch/pdf/2005-16.pdf [Accessed 26 August 2012].

Purcell, J., Kinnie, N. and Hutchinson, S. (2003) Open minded. *People Management.* 15 May.

Ramsey, H., Scholaris, D. and Harley, B. (2000) Employees and high performance work systems: testing inside the Black Box. *British Journal of Industrial Relations.* Vol 38, No 4.

Schuler, R. and Jackson, S. (1987) Linking competitive strategies with human resource management practices. *Academy of Management Executive.* Vol 1, No 3.

Shortell, S.M. and Zajac, E. (1990) Perceptual and archival measures of Miles and Snow's strategic types: the role of strategic orientation. *Academy of Management Journal.* Vol 33, No 4. December.

Strack, R., Caye, J-M., von der Linden, C., Quiros, H.Y. and Haen, P. (2012). *From capability to profitability: realizing the value of people management.* Boston, MA: Boston Consulting Group/World Federation of People Management Associations.

Swart, J., Kinnie, N. and Purcell, J. (2003) *People and performance in knowledge-intensive firms.* London: Chartered Institute of Personnel and Development.

Thompson, M. (2000) *The competitive challenge: final report: the bottom line benefits of strategic human resource management.* London: Society of British Aerospace Companies.

Walton, J. (1999) *Strategic human resource development.* London: FT/Prentice Hall.

West, M. and Patterson, M. (1998) Profitable personnel. *People Management*. 8 January. pp28–31.

Wickens, P. (1987) *The road to Nissan: flexibility, quality, teamwork*. Basingstoke: Macmillan.

Wood, P. (1995) The four pillars of human resource management: are they connected? *Human Resource Management Journal*. Vol 5, No 5.

Index